Lunar Shad

The Predictive Power
of Moon Phases & Eclipses

By Dietrech Pessin

Lunar Shadows, First US Edition, © Copyright 1997,
First Edition published in Russia © Copyright 1998
Lunar Shadows III: The Predictive Power of Moon Phases & Eclipses
© 2009 Igloo Press / ISBN: 0-9787608-1-6

Published by Igloo Press
Tucson, Arizona
www.igloopress.net

Dedication

I dedicate this book – to my son Micah, and Martin G. White.

In memory of
Bonnie Wilson 1931-2007
The Bountiful Astrologer of Mesa, AZ.

&

Anne N. Vick of Mesa AZ
June 5, 1924 - December 12, 2008

With Gratitude

When writing this book I came to realize I was co-creating with a near entity that had taken on a life of its own, Lunar Shadows. The many stories that passed over my desk from the players in life and love, taught me what I am continually learning my craft. I'm reminded of the value in paying attention, and remain intrigued by the incredible window of astrology.

My appreciation is extended to my clients who've kept my career budding, and to the constant flow of motivated students, to the ever precious encouragement of my peers, and to my loyal radio listeners and website visitors.

I'm pleased to acknowledge my website team Lisa and Jan Paul Von Wendt at Uni-comp from Natick, Massachusetts, for their endless generosity and tech labors. Thank you for the efforts of brilliant astrologers, Anne Vick and Nelda Tanner. Also thanks to my editor and graphic designer at Igloo Press: Scott Stanley, Debra White-Stanley, and Mary Bodine.

A special thanks to those that bring me support, warmth and constant encouragement; Naomi Bauer, Kim Burgess, Richard Close, Kathi D'Agostino, Patricia Iyer, Martha Harrington, Kathleen Krivak, Sally Pelliccia, and Lisa Ruffino. I remain ever grateful for the knowledge passed onto me from the greater universal source.

Foreword

Dietrech Pessin is one of those astrologers that comes along once in a lifetime – or perhaps more in keeping with this book, once in a blue moon. Very rarely do we have the opportunity to learn from someone who has pioneered a field of astrology and presented work that we can all put to practical use in our own astrological endeavors, whether we see clients, ponder mundane matters, or write forecasts. I think so highly of Dietrech's work that in mid-2005 I got in touch and invited her to England to teach for my school, the London School of Astrology.

For some time, students had heard me teach many of the techniques found in these pages but I felt it was time they learned it directly from the authority herself. So a trip was planned for October/November 2005, and this revised and expanded edition scheduled to coincide with the tour. As an astrologer who writes, consults and teaches, I spend much time getting to the 'heart of the chart' – focusing on essential components and major themes of the horoscope. It is ironic to note that despite an influx of new significators said to improve chart delineation, computer programs offering countless additional features, and the search to 'prove' astrology, the most important advances in recent years have been based upon the age-old cycles of the Earth, Sun and Moon – work pioneered by Dietrech in this book.

Dietrech first wrote about the Lunar Gestation Cycle when Jupiter traveled from the final degrees of Libra into the sign of Scorpio. A full Jupiter cycle later sees this exceptional contribution to astrological literature republished, revised and replete with twelve further years of observation and practical application. Perhaps part of the book's charm – and that of its author – is that in true Libra-Scorpio style, it has been able to convincingly persuade astrologers to delve deeper and explore further the profound meanings of the Solar and Lunar cycles. Lunar Shadows III joins the list of a mere handful of books that really change the ways in which astrologers develop and practice their craft.

Frank C. Clifford
Astrologer
London, England

Author **Dietrech J. Pessin** works as a full-time consulting and teaching astrologer with an international clientele. She began studying astrology in 1974 with Oscar Weber in Quincy, MA. A longtime resident of New England, she has enjoyed teaching astrology since 1985. Dietrech Pessin worked as a 900-Line Astrologer for five years from 1991-1996, and describes the experience as her "emergency room internship of astrology." While working for the 900-Line company, she also wrote copy for Astroscope, the monthly supermarket check-out-line astrology booklet. She has been featured in Boston newspaper reports, appeared on Boston's TV News, and has been a guest on several major radio stations.

Her weekly astrological report is heard live on WZBC FM Radio, Boston, MA. Ms. Pessin has lectured internationally on her eclipse research and related book, Lunar Shadows. The Russian Edition of the original Lunar Shadows has experienced national success as a leading astrology book. Ms. Pessin has also held the post of Research Director of NCGR (National Council for Geocosmic Research) in Boston, Massachusetts.

Astrolabe, the publisher of the popular astrology program Solar Fire, first added Dietrech Pessin's Moon Family work to their software program with their 2000 edition. Dietrech Pessin has lectured widely in both the US and Europe. With a well organized, practical, and unique approach to astrology, she continues to share her method during lectures, extended workshops, and private consultation. She may be reached through her publisher or by email at: dietrechpessin@lunar-shadows.com. You may also see her writing by visiting the Lunar Shadows web site at www.Lunar-shadows.com

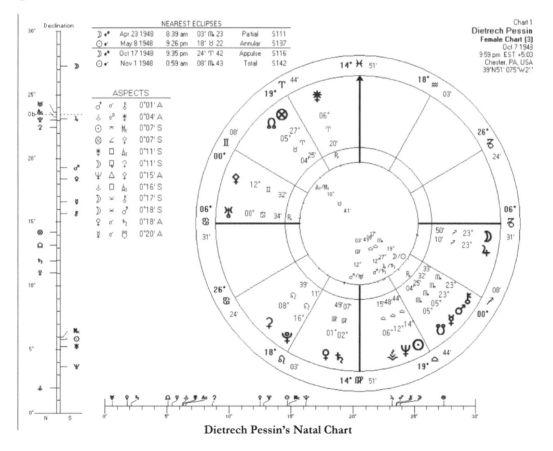

Dietrech Pessin's Natal Chart

Introduction

After years of data collection and study, I discovered a linkage between Moon phases occurring at nine-month intervals over a two-and-a-quarter-year period. The discovery clearly revealed a pattern to the events in our lives. Each of the four quarters of the Moon, including the New Moon, First Quarter Moon, Full Moon and Last Quarter Moon, occur near the same sign and degree of the zodiac on a nine-month cycle. I call this linkage the Lunar Gestation Cycle. Having identified the Lunar Gestation Cycle, I labeled each related group a Moon family. What I learned from interviewing clients and students was that not only was there a chronological significance to the dates in a Moon family, but also a powerful connection with the details of personal storylines. An extended scenario often perfectly matched the dates in a Moon family. A closer look revealed that some Moon Families had a greater and often longer impact if a family contained a Solar and or Lunar Eclipse.

I first became fascinated with the impact of eclipses after attending a lecture by Priscilla Costello in 1985. I later found eclipses rich with material for current trends in any chart, natal, progressed or transit. I recognized that eclipses spoke very directly to my clients' pressing issues. I could easily see that eclipses left a vivid imprint on their lives and offered endless possibilities for research. When my research expanded to encompass Moon Families containing eclipses, my predictive work changed dramatically. I was now able to more accurately forecast up-and-coming events, even after compiling layers of transit and progression data. My primary question to the client became "When did it begin? What is the date of the onset of your issue?" Having determined that date, I was able to locate the relative Moon phase, determine the Moon family and then pinpoint with remarkable accuracy when the matter would resurface at its next stage of development. From there I was able to identify and describe the full cycle of the matter by including all the dates of the Moon Family. My clientele multiplied threefold.

The Lunar Gestation Cycle is the first Moon cycle noted to roughly parallel the nine-month human gestation cycle. This cycle groups the four subsequent Moon Phases, New, First Quarter, Full and Last Quarter as a family of Moons all related by the same zodiacal degree. One full cycle is completed in approximately the same amount of time it takes Saturn to travel through a sign. Its application coincides with the progressing scenarios in our lives, neatly matching to the dates of the cycle in nine-month intervals. The Lunar Gestation Cycle acts as a trigger or timer for its family member, the eclipse. The need for prediction is nearly eliminated, as we learn how events are packaged. We'll explore in this book how events have their own timetables that easily arrange with the Lunar Gestation Cycle.

What Is In This Book

You will find the foundation for the book in Chapter One, Moon phases and the Lunar Gestation cycle. The tools given there offer a traceable link to eclipses, which expands our current understanding of common Moon phases. The chapters that follow lead you through a treatment of Moon signs and what to expect at the various phases. The seventh chapter of the book is filled with "Astrological Tools" that will introduce the language of astrology to the beginner. If astrology is a new subject for you, read chapter seven first to become acquainted with astrological terms. This may assist you in absorbing the main text. There are four categories describing the planets and asteroids, and useful tools for delineating aspects in a chart. Readers familiar with the language of astrology will find chapter seven filled with helpful tips for quick reference and teaching.

There is a generous appendix containing four large data resource tables:

Table I.   Solar and Lunar Eclipses in Chronological Order 200 Years
Table II. Solar and Lunar Eclipse in zodiacal Order and in Metonic Cycle Groups 200 years
Table III. Moon Families 1927-2050
Table IV. Traditional Monthly Moon Phases 1990 - 2050

All charts in this book are constructed using tropical Placidus houses, the True Node, the four major asteroids (Ceres, Pallas, Juno and Vesta), plus Chiron. The major aspects used between two points are: conjunction 0°, sextile 60°, square 90°, trine 120° and the opposition 180°. Included are the minor aspects: semi-sextile 30°, semi-square 45°, sesqui-quadrate 135° and quincunx 150°; plus the essential parallels and contra-parallels of declination. Because I use the Sun/Moon midpoint and the Ascendant/Midheaven (ASC/MC) midpoints consistently, these are inserted in many of the charts.

How to Find a Moon Family with Solar Fire Astrological Software.

If you use Solar Fire software, you will find my Moon Family and eclipse work available in Solar Fire to calculate specific Moon families. You will also find this information in the appendix of this book. This feature is found in Solar Fire 4 or later.

Cast a chart for any point in time of your interest. With the chart highlighted,
Go to the |Chart| option on the tool bar.
See the drop down list and select |Lunar Phase|.
Find options:
|Phase Family (New)|
|**Phase Family (in progression).**|

The option that produces the best results is by selection
|**Phase Family (in progression).**|

This selection allows you to find the related Moon family for that very date. For example, with a chart for December 1, 2008 highlighted (before you go into the Lunar Phases menu) the program finds all four members of the related Moon Family that began with the New Moon in March 2008.

Otherwise when selecting Phase Family (New) the program creates a Moon Family of four Moon phases for the next New Moon that occurs on December 27, 2008.

Developing a Relationship with Symbolism

You wouldn't be reading this book if you were not attracted to symbolism. Astrology is the art of symbolic interpretations from the pictures in the sky. We cast a chart of symbols or glyphs by placing a picture of the heavens (the horoscope) at a specific moment for the purpose of translating the meaning of the symbols into common language. We use keywords from a list of planets, signs, aspects, layering their meanings in order to form a phase for a better understanding. As we develop we layer keywords for houses, midpoints and various updating techniques such as transits and progressions.

In the study of astrology, aspects are calculated by measuring the distance between two planetary bodies or two points in the heavens. Each aspect has its own harmonic vibration. You'll find a full treatment of aspects in chapter seven on Astrological Tools. Although this book was written in a style not to exclude a non-astrologer, I would suggest that if you're new to astrology you begin by reading the Astrological Tools section in chapter seven. This will give you a foundation to apply the concepts of this book to understanding the patterns of your life's storyline. It is helpful to refer to these symbols for the charts that appear in this book

The use of the nine-month cycle is applicable to any event at any point in time, with or without the use of an entire Moon Family. To answer the question surrounding any issue, note how events from nine months ago might apply to your current situation. Did you have a dream about something nine months ago that you are involved with today? Maybe it was then you took a workshop and became inspired to become involved in a new project; or you could have started a new job and now find the honeymoon has worn off. Perhaps you were involved in an accident, met someone new, got married or maybe you began planning a long trip. Whatever your issue you can be assured it will continue to develop and grow and pattern itself into the fabric of your life over time.

Our affairs appear to incubate over this Lunar Gestation Cycle, over which time we have an opportunity to interact with others, develop our interest, change our direction, or bring elements to a completion. I have read in older astrological literature, "*the timing of events always waits for the Moon.*" This work addresses that issue and unlocks what I imagine to be a lost key to some of the "timing" questions related to the events in our lives seeded by eclipses. Astrologers and novices alike will likely benefit from the versatility of my Moon Phases method. In astrology practice, projecting the timing of events is key to working with people who want answers to the question of "when." Many of us have included eclipses in our chart studies for years. Connections made to a Moon Family allow us to connect the dots in understanding the cycles of our lives. Understanding Moon Families expanded my practice and gave me a deeper understanding of the complexity of my clients' lives in both long and short term. Using this method you can discover how astrology works as a practical tool for your personal and business decisions as well as understanding the regularity of the patterns in your life. Each astrologer has a style that speaks to them.

By studying the cycles of the Moon and planets the patterns of your life become apparent. The patterns that planetary cycles and eclipses create appear for me like mirrors in time. These mirrors hold themselves against history and the patterns of our lives. I enjoy seeing how they lend perspective to both the cyclical and the spontaneous.

You'll discover after doing your own research that nothing I say is to be considered a hard-and-fast rule. I have learned 98% of my astrology from hands-on experience. My background has given me a respect for the weight of both detailed research and the telling anecdote. Because of this, I would like to invite readers to share with me their ideas and stories. I love learning new things. Please feel free to share your wisdom, experience, and opinions by emailing me at dietrechpessin@lunar-shadows.com or by visiting my website to view my workshop and speaking schedule at www.lunar-shadows.com.

Enjoy the Phases of Your Life,

Dietrech Pessin
Astrologer

LUNAR SHADOWS III

Table of Contents

Chapter 1

Lunar Cycles

Insight into Personal Narratives
using the Lunar Gestation Cycle

Each of the major events in our lives is seeded at a New Moon and developed into maturity with a hidden cycle of the Moon called the "Lunar Gestation Cycle." This powerful nine-month cycle reveals a phenomenon of timing that presents the seasons of your narrative in the clear framework of a "Moon Family" composed of four lunar phases, what I've termed the Lunar Gestation Cycles.

You will discover how each of the major events in your life has four primary stages that mark the evolution of your stories over each two-and-a-quarter year period. Once you understand the agenda of each of those four stages, you can follow the development of that event's particular storyline into the future. To do this you are going to use information found in two related Moon phase tables, Traditional Monthly Moon Phases and Moon Families (included here in the book) that correspond to the dates of these major events.

The use of the nine-month cycle is applicable to any event at any point in time, with or without the use of an entire Moon Family. When contemplating a question surrounding any issue, note how events from nine months ago might apply to your current situation.

The Lunar Gestation Cycle was vividly displayed in the story that began with the United States 2000 presidential election. The Gore v. Bush election in 2000 captivated the attention of voters when the outcome became too close to call. As you'll probably recall, that election was decided on December 12, 2000 by the U.S. Supreme Court in favor of George W. Bush. Nine months later the world stood still on September 11, 2001, the day the US suffered terrorist attacks in three states that destroyed the World Trade Center, damaged the Pentagon, and crashed a plane into a Pennsylvania field. Nine months later, the President became deeply engaged in selling the invasion of Iraq to Congress. It took another Lunar Gestation Cycle to pass, but eighteen months after September 11, 2001 the U.S. invaded Iraq on March 19, 2003. Then nine months later, US troops capture Saddam Hussein on December 13, 2003.

By this time we realize that the subjects of our lives are not a string of isolated or random events. They intricately connect to a bigger picture. How we make these connections often describes this bigger picture. And the bigger picture has cycles (some long, some short) that are woven into the events of your life every time you reflect on your past and plan for your future. We already know this intuitively. But when an event at one time reminds us of a similar event at another, we're often not conscious of the longer-term connections made over time.

Often just the knowledge of the four dates in a Moon Family will trigger a journey through your memory, leading you to a deeper insight as to how your own stories unfold within nine-month intervals. In addition, you will develop a remarkable relationship with the many stories in your life as you map their developing stages.

One Man's Moon Family Story
Here's a client— we'll call him Mr. Martin— whose story fits perfectly into the Lunar Gestation Cycle concept. He came for a consultation the same day he called, September 28, 1994. Mr. Martin was completely distraught about a dreadful custody battle for his two children. With no success, he had spent his savings on a lawyer to win him visitation rights. He wanted to know if he would ever be able to see his children again. I looked at my list of Moon phases and collected all four Moon Family members related to the Last Quarter Moon taking place that day (the appointment day). I gave my client that list of Moon Family dates and asked him if they were related to his story. The dates were June 30, 1992; March 31, 1993; December 28, 1993 and lastly, the current date, September 28, 1994.

In surprise, he exclaimed, "Oh yeah, on June 30th in '92, my wife's father died and she took the kids to his funeral in New Jersey. We were living in New Bedford, MA at the time. She never came back. On March 31, 1993, I found out where she was living and drove to New Jersey to see my kids. When I knocked on the door, she screamed and called the cops. She had me arrested for trying to kidnap my children and for unpaid child support. I never entered the house but now had a serious legal matter to deal with. Later, using her mother as a liaison, I was able to get my wife to agree to let me see my kids when I paid the child support. On December 28, 1993, I paid her the back support with money from the sale of my house. After taking the money, she told me she did not have to let me see the kids and to get lost. The only receipt for the $17,000 I gave her was my word against hers. After years of attempts to settle this legally, I find my lawyer remains ineffective and seems to be doing nothing to help me. I am now at my wits' end and out of money and still can't see my kids."

How to Find the Dates Related to the Story
The dates in Mr. Martin's story were unusually close to exact; the dates of your story may not fit as exact to the theory. However, many of the stories that I hear are actually this close or within a day or so. A two-week range from the Lunar Gestation Cycle date is also commonly reported. You may find a tight parallel of your stories to Moon Families. Later we will explore additional clues about this story, but now I want to show you how I found the dates that so perfectly fit his storyline. They are found in a table of Moon phases that covered a *period of two and a quarter years*. I titled the table Traditional Moon Phases, because they fall in the natural chronological order common to each month. We all know the natural order of the Moon phases: New Moon, First Quarter Moon, Full Moon and Last Quarter Moon. Looking at the table in the Appendix, view any row from left to right to find four phases within a month.

There is a different group of phases in the same order, from New through Last Quarter, but separated at nine-month intervals. This is key to unlocking a forever useful and predictable timetable. By collecting all four phases, a group is formed which I call a *family of Moon phases*. The dates of the

New Moon	First Quarter Moon	Full Moon	Last Quarter Moon
06/30/92 08°♋57'	07/7/92 15°♎14'	07/14/92 22°♑34'	07/22/92 00°♉19'
07/29/92 06°♌54'	08/5/92 13°♏16'	08/13/92 20°♒55'	08/21/92 28°♉35'
08/28/92 05°♍03'	09/3/92 11°♐40'	09/12/92 19°♓34'	09/19/92 27°♊07'
09/26/92 03°♎35'	10/3/92 10°♑37'	10/11/92 18°♈40'	10/19/92 26°♋02'
10/25/92 02°♏41'	11/2/92 10°♒12'	11/9/92 18°♉14'	11/17/92 25°♌23'
11/24/92 02°♐21'	12/2/92 10°♓20'	**12/9/92 18°♊10'**	12/16/92 25°♍06'
12/24/92 02°♑28'	12/31/92 10♈44	01/08/93 18♋15	01/14/93 25♎01
01/22/93 02♒46	01/30/93 11♉08	02/06/93 18♌13	02/13/93 24♏55
02/21/93 02♓55	03/01/93 11♊05	03/08/93 17♍50	03/14/93 24♐36
03/23/93 02♈40	03/30/93 10♋28	04/06/93 16♎59	04/13/93 23♑53
04/21/93 01♉52	04/29/93 09♌12	05/05/93 15♏38	05/13/93 22♒45
05/21/93 00♊31	05/28/93 07♍25	**06/04/93 13♐55**	06/12/93 21♓16
06/19/93 28♊46	06/26/93 05♎19	07/03/93 12♑02	07/11/93 19♈37
07/19/93 26♋48	07/25/93 03♏10	08/02/93 10♒12	08/10/93 18♉00
08/17/93 24♌53	08/24/93 01♐15	08/31/93 08♓41	09/09/93 16♊35
09/15/93 23♍53	09/22/93 29♐48	09/30/93 07♈37	10/08/93 15♋32
10/15/93 22♎08	10/22/93 28♑58	10/30/93 07♉06	11/07/93 14♌52
11/13/93 21♏32	11/20/93 28♒47	**11/29/93 07♊03**	12/06/93 14♍33
12/13/93 21♐23	12/30/93 29♓04	12/28/93 07♋15	01/04/94 14♎25
01/11/94 21♑31	1/19/94 29♈33	01/27/94 07♌23	02/03/94 14♏16
02/10/94 21♒38	02/18/94 29♉51	02/28/94 07♍13	03/04/94 13♐53
03/12/94 21♓29	03/20/94 29♊40	03/27/94 06♎33	04/02/94 13♑08
04/10/94 20♈53	04/18/94 28♋49	04/25/94 05♏22	05/02/94 11♒57
05/10/94 19♉48	05/18/94 27♌21	**05/24/94 03♐43**	05/31/94 10♓27
06/09/94 18♊17	06/16/94 25♍26	06/23/94 01♑47	06/30/94 08♈46
07/08/94 16♋29	07/16/94 23♎18	07/22/94 29♑47	07/30/94 07♉07
08/07/94 14♌38	08/14/94 21♏14	08/21/94 28♒00	08/29/94 05♊42
09/05/94 12♍58	09/12/94 19♐29	09/19/94 26♓39	09/27/94 04♋39

Moon Family are what I gave to my client. In the example, the bolded cells show the eclipses and will be addressed extensively later. The marked cells show the Family connections.

The nine-month Lunar Gestation Cycle connects four related Moon phases in their natural sequence that forms a Moon Family. The Moon phases separated at the nine-month intervals are all in the same zodiac sign and are close in degree. Think of the degree and sign as the Moon Family's address. You will be able to do a Moon Family search with this address.

The Logic Behind Finding the Moon Family on a List of Traditional Moon Phases
It's easy. From the table in the Appendix collect a Moon phase from each column and look down the list

by nine months to match the sign. Beginning at column no.1 under New Moon see the date 06/30/92 and zodiacal location reads 08°♋57 Cancer´. Look directly to your right in the next column with the heading First Quarter Moon and scan down to the fi rst place you see the same sign. This sign & 3will be nine lines down at the date 03/30/93 and zodiacal position for the First Quarter Moon at 10°♋28 Cancer. In the third column see a list of Full Moons. Repeat the procedure, looking down 18 lines to the date 12/28/93 with the zodiacal location for the Full Moon at 07°♋15 Cancer. Following the same procedure, 27 lines down and under the Last Quarter Moons is the date 09/27/94 and its location at 04°♋39 Cancer. All four Moon phases occur nine months apart, related by sign, and are close to the same degree, so I named the Lunar Gestation Cycle for its nine-month mimicking of the human gestation cycle.

The Lunar Gestation Cycle and the Human Gestation Cycle

The Lunar Gestation cycle correlates with calculations for the time period from conception to delivery that averages 40 weeks. The 40 weeks is more accurately 38 weeks of the actual gestation period. A doctor uses the first day of the last menstrual period that occurs approximately two weeks before ovulation, but conception actually occurs during ovulation, allowing the fetus to spend approximately 38 weeks in the womb. For our purposes, convert the 38 weeks into 266 days and divide by the 29 days in a lunar month. The result is 9.1724 months, very close to the period of one Lunar Gestation Cycle of 266-270 days.

Moon Families Leading to a New Generation

Let's return to Mr. Martin now. His story followed the dates of one Moon Family beginning June 30, 1992. I will show you how it further connected to another Moon Family beyond our appointment. His saga began with a New-Moon Solar Eclipse (a super Moon phase we will explore later). At the time of our consultation, two-and- a-quarter years had passed, taking him through all four stages of major life change that were ignited at that June 1992 Solar Eclipse. My meeting with him in September 1994 was at the Last Quarter Moon belonging to the same family of the '92 Solar Eclipse. I found a new Moon Family, a sort of a "new generation" that repeated a new set of Moon phases at approximately the same zodiac degree on June 28, 1995. This new generation would begin — yep, you guessed it— nine months later, and breathe new life into his story.

As it turned out, Mr. Martin won visitation rights and brought his kids home to Massachusetts from New Jersey within two weeks of June 28, 1995, the first date in the new generation Moon Family, a New Moon that occurred at 6° of Cancer. That summer, Mr. Martin's story developed into his new life as a divorced dad with all the challenges of co-parenting.

Not all Moon Families repeat after the Last Quarter Moon. Next generation Moon Families cluster around Solar and Lunar Eclipses. A deeper explanation of this is found in the later chapter on Lunar Phases under Metonic Cycle. (See page 71.)

Up to this point, the Moon Family is the most important fact. It not only lays out a timetable to frame the story for deeper discussion, but it also remains useful as a tool for projecting into the future when the next major event will occur without making specific predictions.

Every story has a Moon Family and a timetable. The astrologer does not need to be a fortune teller spouting out predictions. The most important factor is not "what is going to happen" but "when." By answering *when,* the available tools such as progressions, primary transiting aspects, solar returns etc. all assist in filling in and rounding out the picture.

The Evolution of a Story and its Timing.
Each phase has its own platform for action with clues clearly pointing to the next type of activity that surfaces at the following Moon phase in a Moon Family (or a new generation). It then reactivates the ongoing saga. Each Moon phase draws matters into the next stage of a grander plan.

The Agenda of Each Moon Phase
1. **New Moon** - begins with the seeding of something new.
2. **First Quarter Moon** – reveals emerging issues that require action.
3. **Full Moon** – marks a culmination and a full exposure of plans or issues.
4. **Last Quarter Moon** – brings closure, reviews, rewards, and payments given or received.

In this way, more extensive astrological techniques such as transiting aspects, progressions and solar returns are not required to extract the key elements to the core issue. The Moon Family acts as a guide to naturally evolving events. In using this method, astrologers might consider themselves free from predicting *what will happen* in a story. In this case, a more important question is *when* the story will be reactivated. You can confidently inform the client, "The next stage in your story occurs on the following date…..." Later, we'll examine how the unique qualities of a Moon Family shed light on a story's outcome in advance.

The Formation of Moon Phases and Some Primitive Astronomy
The familiar 29-day lunar month, also called the synodic cycle, contains the four phases of the Moon we see each month on calendars. This "set" of Moon phases, beginning at the New Moon, relate chronologically as they mature to the next phase within this synodic cycle. Within this monthly cycle, the Sun is advancing approximately one degree each day. Let's look at what happens to create the four Moon phases in the monthly synodic cycle.

From an elementary perspective, we all know the Moon completes one cycle along the path around our globe's celestial belt, extending 8° on either side of the *ecliptic* containing the twelve constellations bearing the names of the zodiac signs. So the Moon travels through all the signs of the Zodiac once each month. Each sign is approximately 30° wide. The Sun and planets all appear to travel this path at various rates. Roughly one revolution of the Sun on this path will take a year (365.25 days) and the planets Mercury and Venus less than a year, Mars two years, Jupiter 12 years, Saturn 29 years, Uranus 84 years, Neptune 164 years, Pluto 248 years.

Of course, we realize that the earth and planets travel around the Sun and it is only an optical illusion that the planets and Sun revolve around the earth. Remember that our zodiac is also the view from earth's perspective and we see only our solar system. It may seem strange that the principals of astrology were founded on optical illusions, but the mathematicians of this ancient study calculated planet positions more accurately than today's computer-generated programs. One very important illusion holds an enormous weight in the study of astrology: that the Moon appears equal in size to the Sun. We know it's due to the Moon's size and distance from earth, but when reading any chart the Moon holds equal significance to the Sun. The Sun rules the day sky and the Moon rules the night sky.

The Synodic Cycle and the Lunar Gestation Cycle
You already realize a synodic cycle is renewed at the next New Moon in approximately 29 days, but bear with me. During each 29-day synodic cycle, the Sun and Moon are New at zero degrees of separation and then they begin to separate at different rates. The Sun will advance about one degree each day and the Moon will advance about one degree every two hours. After approximately seven days, the Sun has advanced approximately 7-8° beyond the point where the New Moon occurred, and the Moon has advanced 90° and forms its first hard angle to the Sun. It is at the "hard angles" where the phases are created and a First-Quarter Moon occurs. Follow another 7-8° in the Sun's route and about a week later the Moon creates the next major angle at 180°, and the Moon will be completely full. After another week, the final aspect in this synodic cycle occurs between the Sun and the Moon at the Last Quarter Moon. The Moon will have traveled 270° beyond the Sun's new position. The Sun is now approximately 28° from the New Moon at the beginning of the synodic cycle. Because these four phases all occur within one synodic cycle, it may appear that they are related to one another. In one sense you are right, because they are the four quarters in one lunar cycle. However, they are more unrelated than related. Notice in the small table the Moon occurs at each phase in four (out of twelve) different zodiac signs and therefore at four different locations along the 360° zodiac wheel at the celestial equator. The degree and sign in traditional Moon phases are the position of the Moon at each Moon phase.

Another way to look at the Moon phases is to locate the Moon's position in relationship

Traditional Moon Phases			
New Moon	First Quarter Moon	Full Moon	Last Quarter Moon
3/20/04 00°Aries 39′	03/28/04 08°Cancer 38′	04/5/04 16°Libra 00′	04/12/04 22°Capricorn

to the Sun in a chart. The chart on the next page shows only the Sun and Moon of all four Moon phases found in one synodic month that are listed in the accompanying table. Note the Sun advances by about 6-8° at the following phase. The Moon will be in a different sign at each phase.

These four charts represent the four phases of the Moon that complete a full synodic cycle in one month. Notice the Moon is in four different signs at each phase while the Sun stays in Aries. With my knowledge of the Lunar Gestation Cycle, I look at these four charts and see four phases, each belonging to four different Moon Families.

A note about the Sun and the planets: they too each have similar phases to the Sun. Cast a chart beginning with the Sun's conjunction to a planet, then chart when the Sun will square, oppose and finally square to the planet before renewing the conjunction.

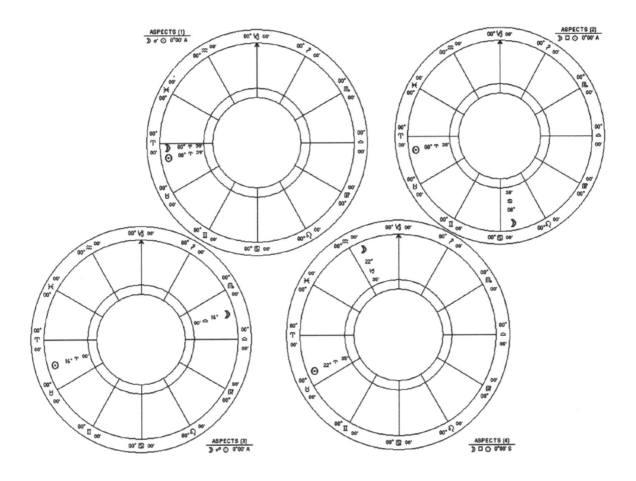

As we leaned with Mr. Martin's story, it takes much longer than a month for most events to experience a full cycle. For a seed to sprout it may take much longer than just one week, which is the average period of time between a New Moon and a First Quarter Moon. For that sprout to come to full bloom it could take as much as six weeks. The same principles apply to the phases of the Moon: just as a plant reveals its life in stages, all New Moons develop their stages much like human embryos with the Lunar Gestation Cycle.

So now when we talk about a *Moon Family*, we're not referring to a Moon cycle in the synodic month but *a group of four sequential Moon phases* all *near the same zodiacal address*: each phase occurs very close to the same degree and same sign of the zodiac, but each is *separated by nine-month intervals*. The nine-month Lunar Gestation Cycle will develop your story to the next logical stage with an *action agenda* typical of each type of phase. *A complete Moon Family cycle takes 2 ¼ years to show all four Moon phases.*

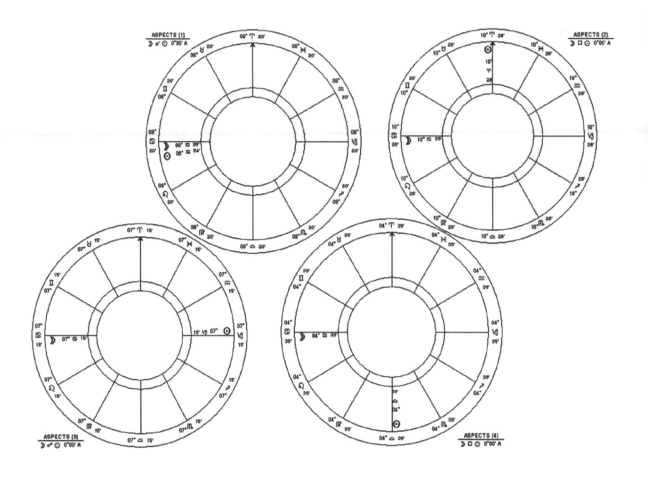

The next four charts show the Moon at the First House position in each Moon phase chart, to demonstrate that the Moon holds the space for a Moon Family. Notice how the Sun occurs in a different sign at each of the consecutive phases in the Moon Family. Each phase of the related Family members occurs nine months apart and near the same degree of the zodiac of the New Moon in the first phase.

Some Moon Families Have Hot Addresses
All Moon Families begin with a New Moon at the head of their family. By constructing the charts for all four family members, you can create a Moon phase family album for further study. Eclipses are easy to spot in the Moon Family Tables in the appendix, in bold type. Some family albums are more distinguished than others because they contain a "super New Moon" or a "super Full Moon" called a Lunar Eclipse. Some Moon Families have both a Solar and Lunar Eclipse. The four example charts above began with a Solar Eclipse at the New Moon phase. Let's find out why only some New Moons are eclipses.

What is an Eclipse?

Eclipse (e¹-kl¹ps") *n.* **1.a.**
The partial or complete obscuring, relative to a designated observer, of one celestial body by another. **b.** The period of time during which such an obscuration occurs. **2.** A temporary or permanent dimming or cutting off of light. - *From the* American Heritage Dictionary

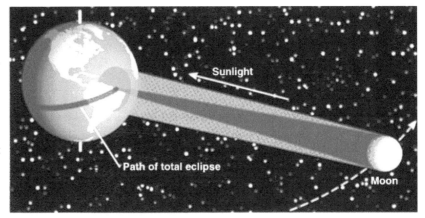

At least a twice a year, there can be a Solar Eclipse at a New Moon or a Lunar Eclipse at a Full Moon. It all has to do with the arrangement of the Sun, Moon and earth at the time of obscurity. An oversimplification of a Solar Eclipse is the Sun and Moon become conjunct in two directions instead of the usual singular alignment at the *celestial equator*. The second quasi-conjunction aligns the Sun and Moon in the perpendicular direction called parallel in declination. Both alignments only happen when a New or Full Moon occurs at the intersection points of both circles called the nodes of the Moon.

(If ever you get the chance to attend a lecture on Great Circles by Gary Christen, don't miss it!) Let's start with a definition of a conjunction. The Heritage Dictionary defines a conjunction as *"a position of two celestial bodies on the celestial sphere when they have the same celestial longitude."* Translation: two bodies joined at the same zodiacal point.

In order to understand the role eclipses play in astrology there are a number of terms either in or related to the above definition of an eclipse that we should clarify.

Ecliptic

The American Heritage Dictionary defines e·clip·tic as follows (¹-kl¹p"t¹k) *n.* **1.** The intersection plane of the earth's orbit with the celestial sphere, along which the sun appears to move as viewed from the earth. **2.** A great circle inscribed on a terrestrial globe inclined at an approximate angle of 23°27' to the equator and representing the apparent motion of the sun in relation to the earth during a year.

The Sun appears to travel along the ecliptic, a great circle at a 23°27' tilt. Twice a year the Sun reaches the maximum 23°27' distance from

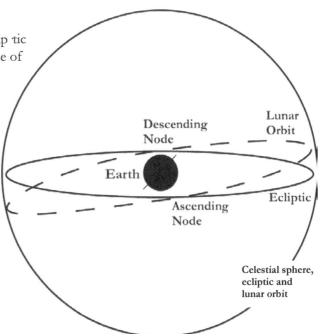

the celestial equator at summer and winter solstices. The Moon travels along its own path or lunar orbit that is inclined approximately 5.15°. Their paths will cross at two points – the nodes of the Moon. The ascending node is where the Moon crosses when traveling north and the descending node when the Moon travels south. When the Sun and Moon conjoin at a node, there will be an eclipse.

Declination, Parallel and Contraparallel

The 23°27' tilt is very important when studying eclipses and all other matters related to declination measured from the celestial equator.

Declination is the measurement of two bodies at equal distance, that are both above or below the celestial equator. When an alignment occurs in declination, both bodies are either north or south to the celestial equator. This is called parallel. When this occurs and both the Sun and Moon are conjunct at the New Moon, then a Solar Eclipse will occur.

When two bodies are at opposite points of declination – for instance, one planet north and the other matching the degree but south – this is called contraparallel. A contra-parallel occurs between the Sun and Moon during a Lunar Eclipse, when they are in opposition to one another at the Full Moon.

The north degree in declination is above the celestial equator and its symbol is plus (+). The south position is symbolized with a minus (-).

Sun + Moon Conjunctions Align with Parallels Only Near the Lunar Node

The term node is derived from the Latin word for "knot." The knot perfectly describes the lunar nodes that are invisible intersection points where the Moon travels from north to south in declination. The nodes intersect the plane of the earth's orbit around the Sun along the celestial equator, with the plane of a great cycle of the Moon forming a triple alignment of the Sun, Moon and Earth. The triple alignment at a New Moon forms a "super conjunction" of both parallel in declination and another conjunction at a node of the Moon. If you are in the area of visibility, your view will be a straight shot to the Moon over the Sun at a Solar Eclipse. If at a Full Moon Eclipse, the earth would be perfectly situated between the Sun and the Moon. It is the earth's shadow that passes over the Moon. The nodes of the Moon are powerful portholes that are a major topic.

> **What do the ancient Celtic remains of Ireland tell us about lunar cycles?**
> *Some time after 6,000 years ago, there arose a remarkable community of people on this island. As if from nowhere, these astute, organized, intelligent and capable people claimed their stake on this country and began constructing permanent, indelible monuments which were to stand the test of eons of time. They were the megalithic builders.*
>
> *Their constructions are Ireland's best known, most explored, and possibly least understood monuments. The most famous of these, Newgrange, is a magnet for tourists, who flock to the Boyne Valley*

every year in huge numbers. In 1999, there were 297,000 visitors to Newgrange, and numbers have been rising steadily. The nearby megalithic passage mound at Knowth has recently opened to tourists also, and the third major Brugh na Boinne site, Dowth, is also open to the public. What is it that attracts people to these sites? What do they come to see? What are they told about these remarkable monuments?

Above the roofbox of Newgrange, there are a series of eight markings, which the authors have suggested could represent the eight years of the Venus cycle. This eight-year cycle of Venus ties in very closely with the metonic cycle of the moon, and may have been recorded elsewhere at Brugh na Boinne, as we will see later.

Speculation aside, it is clear that more research needs to be done on this aspect of the astronomy of Newgrange. The Irish name for Newgrange is Brugh na Boinne. The word Boinne, from which the River Boyne is derived, means "White Cow," and the ancient goddess Boann may have been associated with the Moon. Indeed, some researchers have pointed out that the period of gestation of a cow is equivalent to nine and a half synodic lunar months. The word Brugh is interesting too. Traditionally it has been interpreted by academics as meaning "mansion" or "house," but there is a word Brú which I have found to mean "womb" (MacCionnaith Foclóir, 1938). Could the real meaning of Newgrange be "The womb of the Moon"? The symbolism and interplay between the various elements involved leads to further speculation about the whole purpose of the site. We can imagine a full Moon rising over the hill of Red Mountain, shining across the valley and the Boyne River, which has the same meaning as the Milky Way in the sky, and may in fact have been seen as its earthly reflection. The Irish for Milky Way is "Bealach, or bothar, an Bó Finne" - the way or the road of the white cow. Perhaps the quartz façade on the front of Newgrange is supposed to be another representation of the Milky Way.

Source: http://www.mythicalireland.com/astronomy/ancientastronomers.html

It is my observation that the Nodes of the Moon acts as the Earth's toggle switch. Earthshaking events can occur whenever they are activated by transit to a natal or progressed planet or a significant transiting planet to the natal Nodes. Such a scenario was in place in 2005 during Hurricane Katrina (see chart on the next page). The transiting South Node of the Moon at 14° Libra sent a riveting shock to the United States' Saturn, as seen in its chart. We also see the deep devastating effects of a stationary transiting Pluto, standing still at 21° Sagittarius, in opposition to the U.S. Mars that sits on President Bush's North Node thus Pluto bearing pressure on Bush's South Node. At the same time the transiting Nodes formed a square to the U.S.'s Cancer Sun and G. W. Bush's Cancer Sun.

The Nodes of the Moon are hotspots where all the action takes place. They hold the key to the complex 18.6 year cycle, the long path of the Moon's orbit. The 19-year repeat of a New Moon at the Nodes is called the Metonic cycle. We will discuss this cycle at length. *One nodal cycle is approx. 6800 days or 18.5997 years.*

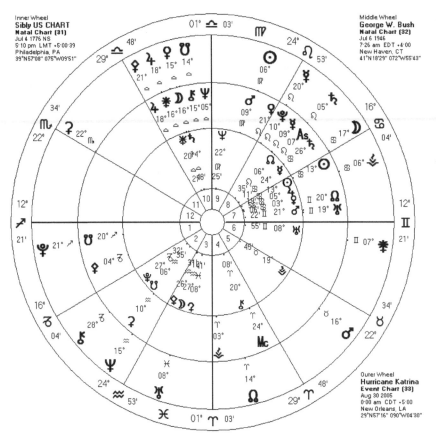

Inner Wheel
Sibly US CHART
Natal Chart [31]
Jul 4 1776 NS
5:10 pm LMT +5:00:39
Philadelphia, PA
39°N57'08" 075°W09'51"

Middle Wheel
George W. Bush
Natal Chart [32]
Jul 6 1946
7:26 am EDT +4:00
New Haven, CT
41°N18'29" 072°W55'43"

Outer Wheel
Hurricane Katrina
Event Chart [33]
Aug 30 2005
0:00 am CDT +5:00
New Orleans, LA
29°N57'16" 090°W04'30"

Research of the nodal cycle links it to climate clocks, long-term herring cycles and tidal cycles. I am sure the research would prove interesting with other animal and plant cycles. Currently we are experiencing extremes in weather patterns, part of which are forecasted by the Moon traveling at extreme north and south declinations that occur in 19 year cycles. This fascinating phenomenon is a familiar topic in extreme north and south skies. In Knowth, Ireland there exists a tradition of celebrations honoring the appearance of the Moon once every 19 years. When the Moon reaches the extreme north declination once in 19 years (as seen in this attending graph), it appears as a rare visitor to the villagers of Knowth. To the rest of the world, this phenomenon

also accompanies severe weather patterns and high tides. The Moon's extreme declination occurred in December 2004 when the tsunami in the Indian Ocean washed away so many lives. The same extreme declination of the Moon was present with Hurricane Katrina on August 30, 2005 that broke the levees and flooded New Orleans. Let's take a look at the Moon at its greatest declinations with a graphic perspective.

The Moon's orbit is located most of the time in the northerly or southerly portions of the sky at a 5.2° incline from the celestial equator. (p.18 *The Secret Language of the Stars and Planets*) During a lunar cycle, the Moon appears to lie on the ecliptic twice a month at one of two points; the ascending or descending node and the Moon slips from the north to south declination. These points travel backwards through the signs from Aries back to Pisces then Aquarius, etc. They move at the rate of about 20° a year or 18-20 months for each sign returning in approximately 18.6 years.

When the Sun travels close to a Node, it too appears to lie on the ecliptic; when the Moon joins the Sun (at a New Moon) there will be a Solar Eclipse. When the Sun is at a Node and the Moon is opposite the Sun and at the other node, there will be a Lunar Eclipse. When a planet reaches the same zodiacal point as a Node and is joined by the Moon there will be an *occultation*.

You can tell by looking at a natal chart if a person was born near an eclipse. If the Sun is conjunct a

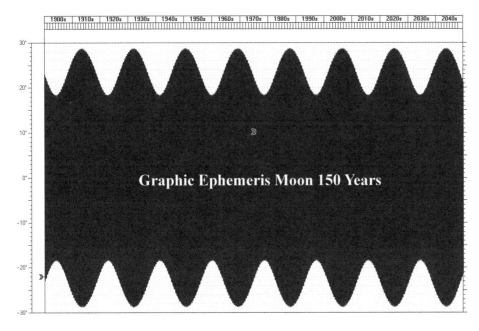

Graphic Ephemeris Moon 150 Years

node, the person is likely to have been born within two weeks of a Solar or Lunar Eclipse.

Metaphorically, I think of the nodes as intersections along two highways in the sky. The highway of the Moon's path around the Earth crosses the highway of the apparent path (celestial equator) of the sun around the Earth. The celestial equator holds the quality of both the ASC-DSC and the orbit of the Moon acts as a MC-IC. Combine the two planes at one point called the "knot" or the node, and they hold the quality of the ASC/MC midpoint (the point I refer to as "toggle switch" of the horoscope). This is the answer to why, when activated, they bring attention to both polarities; one is the individual/partner and the other, their home/career. The nodes are the toggle switch to the greater cycles in one's life. Along the 18.6 year nodal cycle there is a repeat of the phases of the Moon beginning with the repeat of an eclipse near the same degree every 19 years. Halfway through the cycle at 9.3 years, the cycle flips and the Moon phases appear at mirror reflective degrees on the opposite side of the zodiac. This is because the Moon's cycle of extreme southerly or northerly rising points appears to rise.

When studying a chart, a planet conjunct or square a node plays a prominent role in the life of the individual.

I think of these relationships as the Ascendant (north node)-Descendant (south node) for our solar system. We know them as intersection points where eclipses take place when a New or Full Moon is conjunct the nodes, within 18° for a Solar Eclipse and 12° for a Lunar Eclipse respectively. The intersection point causes this overly wide-orb-zone. This width allows greater opportunities for massive amounts of energy to enter our cosmic porthole. My personal belief is that the nodes are the doors where our souls enter this world. We come in with a group that chooses to work together for this lifetime with our special team.

When the Sun is within orb of the intersection point it is Sol's biannual time of the year. The Sun's arrival at a node broadens our Earth's view into the universe. Have you noticed when there are meteor showers within weeks of any eclipse, the showers are more spectacular? It happens when the meteors coincide with the eclipse season. The Sun's close proximity to the nodes seems to bring the universe closer to Earth with the opening of a wide-angle lens.

I received some help from the very talented and brilliant Robin Heath when I was last invited to lecture in England. He is author of several books, including *The Key to Stonehenge*. We shared a mutual admiration of one another's work, our understanding of astrology, and eclipses. I was genuinely pleased in the interest he took in the patterns I discovered as a sub-cycle within the Metonic cycle, that is, the *Moon Families* which are the foundation for this book.

Robin describes eclipses as:

> *"The plane of the Earth's orbit around the Sun is not aligned to that of the Moon's orbit around the Earth. Each month, the Moon therefore rises above the ecliptic for half the month then descends beneath it for the remainder of the month. The points at which the Moon intersects the plane of the Earth's orbit are called lunar nodes and the Moon's rising above the ecliptic defines the North Node whilst the South Node defines the point at which the Moon is found below the ecliptic.*
>
> *For an eclipse to occur there must be a Full or New Moon near to one of the Nodes. Because the Sun is necessary within the eclipse, this means that twice each year there is an eclipse season of about 34 days when both Solar and Lunar Eclipses will occur, although not always visible from a given location on the Earth.*
>
> *The lunar nodes travel backwards around the zodiac at a rate of about 20 degrees per year. This means that the Sun conjuncts a given node in a year minus this period - every 346.6 days - a period known as the eclipse Year. Thus, eclipse 'seasons' occur every 173.3 days - half of this period – and eclipses gradually rotate backwards around the calendar taking 18.62 years (the nodal period of revolution) to complete their round."*

Eclipses are classified as either **total or partial.** Twelve New Moons occur a year. To quote Mr. Heath, *"more precisely, New Moons occur 12.368 times a year. Sidereal lunar months (lunar orbits) occur exactly that plus unity, 13.368 times a year."* When a New Moon or Full Moon occurs within the orb limits of the nodal axis, either a total or partial eclipse occurs. If the orb is no greater than ±11° 15', the New Moon conjunction to the nodal axis will align in a total Solar Eclipse formation. On the other hand, a New Moon conjunction to the nodal axis at a maximum limit of ±18° will align in a partial Solar Eclipse formation.

A Lunar Eclipse occurs at least twice a year when there is an alignment of the Sun in opposition to the Moon at a Full Moon at the Nodes in line with Earth. This forms a "super opposition," a Lunar Eclipse. The accompanying picture is a rough drawing that depicts the alignment of the Earth, Sun, Moon and the Nodes of the Moon on the celestial ecliptic at the time of a Lunar Eclipse. The Moon is not always found at the south node position. This picture therefore depicts a south node Lunar Eclipse. A Lunar Eclipse with the Moon at the north node would be a north node Lunar Eclipse and would occur six months later.

The cycle of a New Moon that occurs at either the north or south node is much greater than the renewal of the 28-day synodic cycle, as a New Moon will renew at 19-year intervals as part of the Me-

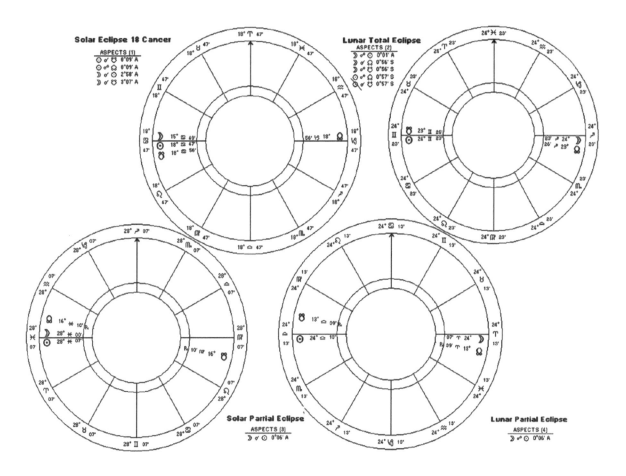

tonic cycle that repeats between 57-59 years.

Frequency of Eclipses in a Year

If you listen to the meteorologist reports they would have you believe we will not see another eclipse for some obscure length of time. It might be true that an eclipse may not be visible in your area, or a certain type of eclipse may not repeat for a number of years. Actually, eclipses are not rare events at all. Eighty percent of the 20th century experienced at least two Solar Eclipses each year. Three Solar Eclipses occurred 15 out of 100 years. But interestingly, *four* Solar Eclipses occurred in the years 1917, 1946, 1964 and 1982. The super active years of 1805 and 1935 had *five* Solar Eclipses in addition to two Lunar Eclipses.

In the 21st century the more active years are 2011, 2029, 2047, 2065, and 2094, each having four Solar Eclipses. Years with three Solar Eclipses are found in 2018, 2019, 2036, 2038, 2054, 2057, 2058, 2083 2084, 2087 and 2098. Of course the remaining years will have at least two. No year was found to have five Solar Eclipses in the 21st Century.

The Symbolic Meaning of a Solar Eclipse

Astrological delineation becomes an art when a seasoned practitioner reads a chart. Such a seasoned practitioner holds a keen knack for layering symbolic and technical information. He or she cultivates the tone of planets by considering sign placement, dignities, aspects to one another and primary angles as well as the planets' cycles. The astrologer will note the strength of sign and substance of house and planet distribution and even planet declinations, midpoints and hidden aspects. This list of tasks may be blended with yet another stack of data which may include historical relevance and whatever strong experience the astrologer relates to the information. The horoscope is eventually brought to a conclusion or a projection of various possibilities after only moments of contemplation. Whew!

With the latest computer-generated divination, the blending technique tackles at best a couple of layers of information at a time. To simmer the entire collection of data to the point of a creating a statement is truly an art. Reading the chart of an eclipse is not that different from reading the chart of an individual. It has a personality with strengths and weaknesses and has key points that will act as triggers. To begin framing a grasp of the symbolic meaning of an eclipse, you must first collect the astrological details that will lead to a better understanding of the eclipse chart.

The significant astrological details of an eclipse are:
* whether it is a Solar or Lunar Eclipse
* the sign symbolism of the eclipse
* the exact degree of the eclipse
* the degree of a planetary station and the Planet
* any planet in hard aspect to the eclipse degree or the nodal axis
* the tightest aspects between planets in the eclipse chart
* the geographical location of the eclipse path
* the first planet to cross the eclipse point and when
* the date the node will or did reach the eclipse point

The last item is a hot astrological date. You should cast a chart for the moment the node reaches the eclipse point as supplementary data to the eclipse chart (see later chapters on eclipses).

The tables of eclipses in the Appendix show a list of Solar and Lunar Eclipses at the respective north or south Node of the Moon, which holds its own symbolism. A reference for eclipses with the exact time and duration is found in an ephemeris or an astronomical table of eclipse phenomena or on many astrological software programs. There are many sites on the internet discussing the finer astronomical details of any eclipse. For such data such as duration, path of the shadow and full definition of the type of each eclipse, I found a long list of such sites by typing in "eclipses" on the Google search engine.

Using the symbol of renewal at a New Moon, this phase relates to an event the way an acorn relates to an oak. Once planted into the ground, it has the capacity to grow into a tree of significant size. A New Moon graduates to eclipse status within 18° of the nodes of the Moon.

The effect of this super New Moon (or Lunar Eclipse at a super Full Moon), when aligned with the nodes and the Earth, is magnified to heightened level. Historically and personally speaking, events coupled to the time of an eclipse are significant. Look into the night sky days before any New Moon or Solar Eclipse. Watch the Moon diminish to a mere sliver, and then totally disappear. This period of the month is called "the dark of the Moon." During the dark of the Moon there is, visually, no Moon. Like ancient astronomers/astrologers, who connected astronomical observation to human and geological events, you might pay specific attention to the weather, location of earthquakes and other geological events in relation to an eclipse. Continue your study and pay attention to the topics sweeping through political circles. Listen for themes in the stories of your neighbors, friends and family.

A brief list of what the Moon in astrological terms represents:
* Daily routine
* Home
* Attitude, emotional response and moods
* People who are: woman, mother, wife, infant, or close female

Let's take a walk through the development of the symbolic notions that formed the list above. Select something from the list such as "daily routine."

No Moon in the night sky = no light:
* Maximum darkness
* Activity conducted in the dark
* Hidden forces at work
* More will be revealed
* Matters develop over time

Conclusion: Because the Moon is hidden, one is to assume this mysterious time is filled with unseen influences that are yet to be developed. Without the light of the Moon, its hidden symbolism may suggest it as a time of "wait and see." You may find it to be a time more practically spent observing, dreaming and taking in experience rather than any outward action. Initiate from the level of intention rather than through clear and public action. *The notion of new beginnings makes this a receiving and collecting time.* Think of the conjunction as a closed door of a house. The door and the hinges are tightly fit, keeping the interior from plain view. All you see is a door. This door is your starting place. You don't know what your next action may be until the door opens enough for you to catch a peek into the house. What you find may be friendly or not.

As with the Sun and Moon at the New Moon, more will be revealed when the actual light of the Moon begins to develop and you have some "light on the matter." When the Moon separates from the Sun and grows larger in the sky, it brings greater clarity for action. At the full Moon, the pair will be at their greatest separation and the light of the Moon at its fullest. At that time, the symbolic full development of matters is brought into the light.

Before science proved otherwise, the size of the Sun and Moon appeared fairly equal. The Sun ruled the day and the Moon ruled the night in ancient astrology studies. The Moon's bright disk against a black mysterious sky may explain why much of the symbolic treatment of the Moon in mythology gives the Moon precedence over the Sun. The Moon was known as the "Mother of the Universe" by the Egyptian priests. Ancient Upper Egypt was called the "Land of the Moon" and the Babylonians held the Moon in greater regard than the Sun. The Sun in mythology has gained both god and goddess status.

A Solar Eclipse creates a charge that can be felt in our personal affairs for years. This can be a time when we promote enterprise and other self-interest. A Solar Eclipse will push matters to the forefront for immediate attention. The time around a Solar Eclipse is an extremely busy time filled with stress and demands. It can be viewed as a progressive brainstorming process that develops over a period. Again the invisible Moon at the time of a Solar Eclipse makes this an unpredictable time, leaving a period of unknowns to be revealed later. This is a time to proceed with caution when engaging in new projects.

Many of us may notice dramatic changes near eclipse dates. For instance, a dowser notes at the time of an eclipse that the energy grid lines along the path of an eclipse are dramatically wider. Extreme weather, major disasters, and other dramatic events occur immediately around an eclipse. Here are a few examples of news headlines near Solar Eclipse dates.

* The Solar Eclipse of January 15, 1991 at 25° Capricorn is the date of the Gulf War with U.S.-led forces. The Solar Eclipse on January 25, 1990 at 6° Aquarius occurred near the date when accused drug lord, General Manuel Noriega, surrendered. The eclipse on March 18, 1988 at 28° Pisces brought indictments to Lieutenant Colonel Oliver North and Vice Admiral John Poindexter for their roles in the Iran/contra affair.

* A Solar Eclipse on November 12, 1985 at 20° Scorpio accompanied the eruption of the Nevado del Ruiz volcano in Columbia which set off an avalanche of mud that killed 25,000 people. Another example of geological disaster occurred with the Solar Eclipse of August 11, 1999 at 18° Leo containing a grand fixed cross. Turkey suffered several quakes killing thousands of people. An earthquake with the magnitude 7.7 killed 2,000 in Taiwan. In the same short span of time, Earth movements were detected in many other areas around the world.

* The world mourned during the eclipse of September 1, 1997 at 9° Virgo with the death of Princess Diana that had occurred the day before. More grief was expressed with the passing of Mother Theresa a week after Diana's death.

* One of the most spectacular examples of the impact of a Solar Eclipse in regard to the life of a public figure was the Solar Eclipse at 28° Leo. Its conjunction to the regal fixed star, Regulus, caught the world's attention on August 22, 1998. The eclipse occurred within three days (three degrees) of the U. S. president Bill Clinton's birthday (thus Sun). The effects of that eclipse brought Clinton before

the grand jury amidst probably the most humiliating sex scandal to reach a global audience, with the independent council's highly publicized "Starr Report" (I can't help but note the symbolic connection of "Star" to that of the eclipse's alignment with Regulus.) The Starr report, published and distributed throughout the world, violated the privacy of everyone involved. Clinton was the first president to face charges while holding the office of President of the United States.

In a similar respect, increased pressure is noticed in all our personal affairs near eclipse dates and for some the changes are dramatic during an eclipse season. Look for new developments, new ideas and new people to remain in your life for years when they come to you during an eclipse season.

By investigating a table of eclipse dates, found in the appendix, you may notice that many of these dates are within two weeks of some of the biggest events in your life. These dates may occur close to the time when you first left home, when you began your first major job, when you bought or sold a house, when you were married or divorced, when you had an operation or serious accident or when you opened your own business.

You will find some of the eclipse dates to be close to the greater events in your life. Others are ignited when the eclipse degree is triggered by another type of astrological event. Some triggers are transiting events and others are progressed events. We will discuss Eclipse Triggers in their own chapter. We will also learn that eclipses do not occur at random positions along the zodiac belt but are each part of greater cycles, the 1300+year Saros cycle and the 19-year Metonic cycle. The Metonic cycle will be discussed in its own chapter and will have a table in the Appendix.

The Symbolic Meaning of a Lunar Eclipse
Nature's Circuit Breaker

The Lunar Eclipse is a very special event. The interference from the Earth, blocking the stream of light from the Sun to the Moon, makes this a remarkable time unlike any other Full Moon event during the year. The Earth acts as nature's circuit breaker, bringing an overflow of energy back down to Earth.

This notion becomes all too clear at the presence of a cataclysmic event, often a reaction to the magnetic shift during a Lunar Eclipse. We can understand this energy using the image of a quiet peaceful town engaged in routine activities when disrupted by a tornado, activated volcano or hurricane.

The symbolism of the interference is that of an unexpected complication resulting from the emergence of another body (as represented by the Earth) intercepting the continuous flow of events intended by the originator. The interception produces an altered version of conditions, manipulated by things or those outside the realm of its origin. Circumstances "beyond your wildest dreams" come to mind although many times the events around a Lunar Eclipse can go unnoticed. It may seem common to have breakdowns and disruptions that lead you to a turning point.

The impact of a Lunar Eclipse can disrupt our personal lives by turning them upside down and inside out with events like births, deaths marriage and divorce. Investigations by outsiders may tear lives apart. The Earth's interception can act as a busy body in the form of a government body or an overseeing body of some type such as licensing boards or examination boards. This could represent actions taken by the interceptor to bring matters back to the norm, as when a criminal is removed from the general population, brought to trial and incarcerated. The indications here invite the public to endorse and witness a change to restore safety and stability. These major changes in an individual's life might be moving from single status to married, or the reverse, married to divorced. In these cases a third party is required to be present, to negotiate or witness the event. Most people have a wedding of some sort, and if divorcing, will be in a courtroom or a lawyer's office with others.

You may experience the impact of a Lunar Eclipse as a time of more emotional pressure and a sense of endings or urgency. Often there is a need to surrender or "let go," a principal associated with Pluto's symbolism. There are things you have never thought of that take on a momentum beyond your control.

Symbolically, the Lunar Eclipse may mark the *end of a particular phase* in your life. Due to intense focus on the Moon's "super opposition" to the Sun, the bi-annual events are the most public times of the year. The symbolism of the sign Aries/Libra comes to mind during any Full Moon, as the seventh house qualities represent the full view of the public eye. Since a Lunar Eclipse is such a major event, it brings matters hidden for months or years out into the open, often for your entire little world to see. This is the added dimension of the nodes. The nodes are the intersection point of two great circles; one running around the Earth from the path of the Sun, the other running over the Earth from the path of the long cycle of the Moon. This is a time when "all the cards are on the table" and information is shared even with those you did not intend. Therefore a Cancer/Capricorn quality enters into the mix with a super Full Moon and you, the significant other, the public at large and your family can become involved in an event that emerges around a Lunar Eclipse.

This often makes this time particularly stressful for personal relationships. The issues of personal relationships have a natural tendency to sort themselves out during a Lunar Eclipse season, often bringing old matters to a head. You may experience ending a period of independence with marriage or regaining your independence through divorce. It may simply mean you are managing your relationships in a totally different way.

Anything having to do with other people, or players involved in your activities, will take priority during the Lunar Eclipse season. You may be able to locate people and things that have been lost or hard to find. Legal matters and open conflicts are prominent at the time of a Lunar Eclipse as they are common to Libra symbolism as well. Lunar Eclipses bring long-term projects and goals to fruition. This is a time filled with the pressure of deadlines. In addition, it marks a time for major renovations or reorganizations.

The news around the time of a Lunar Eclipse is a perfect source to study the nature of Lunar Eclipses. While waiting at an airport the day before the Lunar Eclipse on April 2, 1996, I caught a newscaster literally announcing the "marriage" between two telephone companies. CNN news reported "There are wedding bells for Southwestern Bell and Pacific Western Bell." This news flash was very appropriate to the Lunar Eclipse symbolism, especially the 14° Libra 31 zodiacal position of the eclipse. One month prior, a royal decision to divorce was announced when Princess Diana agreed to Prince Charles' request for divorce. The divorce decree was finalized August 28, 1996.

Five days before the Lunar Eclipse on February 20, 1989 at 1° Virgo 59', the Soviet Union completed its troop withdrawal from Afghanistan. The Soviet Union invaded Afghanistan in 1979 with both Solar and Lunar Eclipses occurring in Virgo and Pisces. After ten years of wasted effort, and the loss of hundreds of thousands of lives, the U.S., Saudi Arabia and Pakistan joined efforts to train anti-Soviet forces, forcing the Soviets out of Afghanistan. As a result of this training the internal power struggle to control the country began, and from this the Taliban rode to power.

Another example of the results of the impact of Lunar Eclipses coincided with the February 9, 1990 Lunar Eclipse with the long-awaited release from prison in South Africa of Black Nationalist leader, Nelson Mandela. His release date was actually February 11, 1990.

Following the Lunar Eclipse on August 6, 1990, newspaper headlines announced on August 7th that President George Bush, Sr. was sending US troops to Saudi Arabia, in the face of a possible invasion by Iraq. Five months would pass before the U.S. actually engaged in the Gulf War, but it was at the time of the August '90 Lunar Eclipse that it became clear to the world that trouble was evident.

During the week of the Lunar Eclipse on November 29, 1993, Time Magazine's cover story read, "CASTRO'S CUBA - THE END OF A DREAM."

The Unabomber, Ted Kaczynski, was caught at the Lunar Eclipse on April 4, 1996 after an eighteen-year career of bombing in America.

One astrological opinion claims that the symbolic impact of a Solar Eclipse is greater than that of a Lunar Eclipse. This may be true, but you may feel differently if you are on the receiving end of a Lunar Eclipse and your life has dramatically changed by its impact. Check your personal history with both Solar and Lunar Eclipse dates to chronicle your life events. For most of us, our Lunar Eclipse events list may be as long as our Solar Eclipses events.

What If Your Story Begins Close to an Eclipse?
If the date for the beginning of your story falls within a week of a Solar or Lunar Eclipse, choose the eclipse for your Moon phase. If a Solar or Lunar Eclipse is involved in your story, it may create a marked change in your life. Many events that occur within the eclipse season, which is a 38-day period around a Solar Eclipse, are considered eclipse events. Choosing a Moon Family related to your topic allows you to zero in on the timing of the various stages of your story. We'll look at the variations between some Moon Families in the Moon Phase Family Album.

The Moon Phase Family Album

A Moon Phase Family album is simply the four charts of any Moon Family. By locating the variations between Moon families, you find symbolic information regarding the strength of the phases and the importance of the events that cluster around eclipses. In the Appendix each set of tables have the eclipses marked with bold text. Eclipses also have their own tables.

Some variations of Moon Families show phases that contain:
* A Solar Eclipse
* Both a Solar and Lunar Eclipse.
* A New Moon Family with a Lunar Eclipse
* A very ordinary Moon Family with no eclipses
* A Moon Family with a Last Quarter Moon related to the Solar Eclipse in nine months

Solar and Lunar Eclipses elevate the impact of all the Moon phases in their Moon Family. If your story belongs to a Moon Family containing an eclipse, look for the eclipses in the table in the appendix labeled Metonic Cycle. Sometimes it's the first or the last of the 57-59 year Metonic cycle and that is another clue for your story. Any eclipse will indicate:
* A recurring theme repeated from 19 years ago that will repeat 19 years in the future
* Added longevity regarding the events surrounding eclipses
* A deeper impact on to your personal life
* Deeper ties and lasting bonds with the people surrounding the events
* A change in the way you continue on in a given direction

In one way or another, the Moon phase that is closest to the initiation point of your story can be followed back to a Solar or Lunar Eclipse. It is the stories that begin close to an eclipse that are highly interesting. Some Family albums seem very strange.

Here is a unique Moon Family that begins with a Solar Eclipse at 0°32'Gemini on 5/21/93.

This Moon Family has the most powerful family album of all Moon Families because it contains both Solar and Lunar Eclipses, which is not always the case. There is something else unique about this Moon Family album: the family members are not all in the same sign, but they are still part of the same family. It is obvious with the narrow orb between phases that they are related. The other identifying factor shows their sequential phases separated by nine-month intervals, connecting them to one Moon Family. This overlapping of signs occurs because the eclipse is located at the zero degree. Let's take a closer look at this powerful family.

Super Moon Family with Both a Solar and Lunar Eclipse													
Solar Eclipse				First Quarter Moon				Full Moon Lunar Eclipse				Last Quarter Moon	
May 21 1993	00°	♊	31'	Feb 18 1994	29°	♉	51'	Nov 18 1994	25°	♉	42'	Aug 17 1995	24° ♉ 43'

The Lunar Eclipse in a Solar Eclipse Moon Family

All Eclipses belong to a Moon Family because they are Moon phases— extraordinary Moon phases but still Moon phases. Some Lunar Eclipses belong to the same Moon family that began with a Solar Eclipse.

Each Lunar Eclipse comes equipped with its unique set of lessons and awarenesses based on a list of variables.

Polarities are the theme in a Lunar Eclipse because of the obvious Sun Moon opposition at the polar opposite nodes of the Moon. Themes can be noticed that are particular to sign and polarity, such as:
*   The individuality/partnership theme of Libra/Aries or the acquisition/sharing theme of Taurus/Scorpio and travel/learning theme with the Gemini/Sagittarius polarity.
*   As with pairs of Solar Eclipses, it is important to study the pairs of Lunar Eclipses occurring at opposite points of the zodiac and that are six months apart. These points of the zodiac appear as cosmic bookends containing an elongated focus of a particular theme.
*   Planetary aspects of the eclipse chart give a Lunar Eclipse individuality. Aspects that hold the strongest impact in a Lunar Eclipse chart are conjunctions and oppositions and squares. Especially note the planets in opposition as they match the harmonic of the Sun/Moon opposition of the Lunar Eclipse. They carry the same energy and draw added polarities into the arena of action. Parallels and contra-parallels are powerfully dynamic aspects in any eclipse chart as they are the vital component that allows the eclipse event to occur. Without the Sun/Moon parallel at a Solar Eclipse and the contra-parallel at the Lunar Eclipse, the shadow cast on the Earth during an eclipse would not occur.
*   Keep in mind the nature of root member in the Lunar Eclipse Moon Family. Is it a New Moon or Solar Eclipse?

A Lunar Eclipse in a Solar Eclipse Moon Family carries a bigger punch and is more likely to ignite greater events over the 18-month period it takes to produce the Lunar Eclipse. We get the powerful beginning at the Solar Eclipse and a powerful ending or exposure at the Lunar Eclipse. Such a Super Moon Family set the political stage for one of the major shifts in power in American government in forty years.

The story began during a Solar Eclipse season of May 21, 1993 when a big news story in the Clinton administration fed future events with major consequences. Hillary Rodham Clinton was the focus of attention. She took a highly visible role in the administration and many were threatened by the power she had been given. They balked that she was not elected and should not have such a dynamic role setting policy. The Republican party was livid about her power and proceeded to send her back to writing children's books and cookbooks, the intended role for all good first wives. Following the Eleanor Roosevelt model, Ms. Rodham Clinton was ambitious and had her own agenda, eventually earning a seat in the Senate in the 2000 election. A few years later, First Lady Laura Bush was encouraged to have a stronger voice and more prominent role.

Astrologically there were several interesting notes about this eclipse. For one, the Solar Eclipse at 0° Gemini 32' produced a Lunar Eclipse as a family member but in a different sign, Taurus. Often found when an eclipse occurs at 0° or 29° of a sign, the Moon phases may fall into the neighboring sign and still remain within orb of the Solar Eclipse. This eclipse at 0° Gemini bore these characteristics in its Moon Family.

This added dimension of any eclipse family makes an interesting study presented at all four Moon phases. The Solar Eclipse at zero degrees symbolizes a special point will be made. Gemini (the sign of stories with many sides to be told) at the zero degree indicates it will be a big story with ears, arms and legs. All of which fits perfectly with the "Travelgate Scandal." Gemini rules both travel and scandal, and set the stage within hours of the May 21st eclipse when Hillary Rodham Clinton became the object of Travelgate. Seven employees were dismissed on May 19 from the White House travel office, of which five were reinstated by May 25th. Allegations emerged suggesting that President Clinton's family and friends had a vested interest in White House business. "Travelgate" was one of the topics targeted by the forty million-dollar investigation by the White House Independent Council, Ken Starr, who made many expensive investigations of the Clintons.

A Solar Eclipse at 21°Scorpio 32' on 11/13/93 has a First Quarter Moon near-

Solar Eclipse Family, No Lunar Eclipse												
Solar Eclipse				**First Quarter Moon**				**Full Moon**				**Last Quarter Moon**
Nov 13 1993	21°	♏	32'	Aug 14 1994	21°	♏	14'	May 14 1995	23°	♏	35'	Feb 12 1996	22°	♏	55'

est that degree at 21° Scorpio 14 and nine months later on 8/14/94. The Full Moon related to this family occurs nine months later on 5/14/95 at 23° Scorpio 35, followed up by its Last Quarter Moon nine months later on 2/12/96 at 22° Scorpio 55. In this example, the Full Moon does not occur close enough to the nodal axis to create a Lunar Eclipse.

An Ordinary New Moon Family With a Future Lineage to a Lunar Eclipse

There are Lunar Eclips-es that are not related to Solar Eclipses, as in the above example with a non-eclipse New Moon that occurred on

Ordinary New Moon with a Future Lineage to Lunar Eclipse												
New Moon				**First Quarter Moon**			**Lunar Eclipse**				**Last Quarter Moon**	
Sep 3 2005	11°	♍	21'	Jun 3 2006	13°	♍	13'	**Mar 3 2007**	**13°**	♍	**00'**	Dec 1 2007	08°	♍	56'

9/3/2005 at 11°Virgo 21'. Its First Quarter Moon appears on 6/3/2006 at 13°Virgo 00'. Because the Full Moon of this family occurred within the limits of the Nodal axis, this Moon Family gave birth to a Lunar Eclipse on 3/3/2007 at 13° Virgo 13' with its Last Quarter Moon occurring at 8° Virgo 56' on 12/1/2007, making this Moon Family very special.

Ordinary Moon Family Connects to a Lunar Eclipse in the Future

A Moon Family with no obvious unique characteristics could in fact be located at a special zodiacal ad-dress. The New Moon Family of September 15, 1993 at 23° Virgo is an example of this because The New Moon occurs at a Lunar Eclipse degree at some time either in the future or past. Its last quarter phase on December 15, 1995, occurred two and a quarter years before the

A Moon Family with No Eclipses is Connected to a Lunar Eclipse in the Future											
New Moon			First Quarter Moon			Full Moon			Last Quarter Moon		
Sep 15 1993	23°	♍	16'	Jun 16 1994	25°	♍	26'	Mar 16 1995	25°	♍	59'	Dec 15 1995	22°	♍	45'

Lunar Eclipse at 22° Virgo on March 13, 1998. This could prove to be an important Moon Family in current affairs, since the events surrounding the dates of any of the Moon Family members on September 16, 1993 could be connected to the major ending cycle that presents itself at the Lunar Eclipse on March 13, 1998.

A Hot Moon Family With a Last Quarter Phase Connected to the Solar Eclipse in Nine Months

Likewise, there is a Solar Eclipse connection at its Last Quarter phase in another Moon Family's. A very powerful New Moon on March 20, 2004 at 0°Aries 39' is unique just because it occurs at zero Aries. That is the degree that

Hot Moon Family With Last Quarter Phase Connected to Solar Eclipse in Nine Months											
New Moon			First Quarter Moon			Full Moon			Last Quarter Moon		
Mar 20 2004	00°	♈	39'	Dec 18 2004	27°	♓	07'	Sep 17 2005	25°	♓	16'	Jun 18 2006	27°	♓	12'
Solar Eclipse			First Quarter Moon			Full Moon			Last Quarter Moon		
Mar 19 2007	28°	♓	07'	Dec 17 2007	25°	♓	05'	Sep 15 2008	22°	♓	54'	Jun 15 2009	24°	♓	56'

reaches the world axis; powerful events occurred in the month of this family's Full Moon phase, September 17, 2005. The world watched as the United States underwent the relocation of homeless citizens and the bungled rescue and cleanup after Hurricane Katrina in New Orleans. This family's Last Quarter Phase on June 18, 2006 at 27° Pisces 12 is related to the a Solar Eclipse nine months later on March 19, 2007 at 28° Pisces 07'. The related events to all of these Moon phases will produce dramatic stories.

As you might imagine, a first or last quarter Moon related to a Solar or Lunar Eclipse could produce events of greater significance than some other quarter Moons. Note whether a first or last quarter Moon might be a member of an eclipse Family.

The Power Point New Moon - Not a Family Member at All

There are New Moons and Full Moons that occur about 90° and around 90 days prior to a Solar or Lunar Eclipse that are matched by a similar degree but in a different sign and the same modality (cardinal, fixed and mutable). They are not connected to the eclipse by the Lunar Gestation Cycle but act as a trigger to set the stage for the events that will cluster at the eclipse. We will take another look at Power Point New Moons later.

Greater insights can be formed by studying the charts of all the members in the Family Album. Look at each of the charts in the Family Album separately by noting the aspects; then, see what the other planets are promising. You may find a way to sift through and sense the outcome of any given eclipse by reading the other charts in the family. Using the family album as a reflective tool allows a deeper understanding of the events in the future. In the Family of Moons, look for the quiet development of matters and follow them through into their resolution phase. We can look at Mr. Martin's story again for more clues.

The Many Clues of One Moon Phase

We have not looked at Mr. Martin's chart, yet we can find many new leads. Let's start with his phone call to me at the Last Quarter Moon on September 28, 1994 at 4° Cancer. I use the time when a client first contacts me for indicators about their needs. Before I cast the phone call chart, I begin with the Moon phase to begin listing clues.

The study of astrology is like a detective story; by reading the signs and symbols, you are able to collect clues in layers. The more I learn about astrology the more I learn to stick to the basics. Follow the leads and eventually you will draw conclusions.

A Quick Guide of Moon Phase Agendas

Each phase of the Moon has its own agenda with a personality colored by its sign. One phase pushes events along to the next phase. Another way to look at this is that one thing leads to another, and before you know it there are signals gathered from the amount of light at each stage.

The New Moon has no light and we are all in the dark and more will be revealed.
The First Quarter Moon is building light, called waxing so you are beginning to see.
The Full Moon, the brightest phase has the maximum awareness; all the cards are on the table.
The Last Quarter is a waning light; your issues are winding down. You need to grab what you can and get ready for the next dark period when the Moon is New again.

The client's call for his appointment led me to believe several things inherently common to *Last Quarter Moon phases:*

*   He had a very pressing matter; the First and Last Quarter Moons are crisis-oriented.
*   He had a full experience with his topic and was not in the dark as with a New Moon.
*   He had completed a series of steps over time and wanted to close the matter.
*   He was seeking a reward for his efforts.
*   He needed to clean up the past concerning these matters.
*   He wanted to retain what was salvageable and to seed the future.
*   He was fully aware, experienced and ready to move on to the next stage for a new beginning.

I further concluded from this last stage of a Moon Family the following:

*   Because a Solar Eclipse occurred at the head of this Moon Family, matters were profound and enduring and connected to a 19-year cycle.
*   Seasoned issues on the table accumulated over a period of at least two-and-a-quarter years.
*   The Lunar Gestation Cycle connects a second Moon Family (a next generation) in nine months that extends the matter into the future.

There are more clues in the signs and the degrees of the Moon phase that help you to understand the nature of the issues even before you begin any discussion. Each sign of the zodiac has a rulership or a domain over a long list of common topics. Signs are broken down into categories of elements (fire, earth, air and water), and modalities (cardinal, fixed and mutable).

There are clues related to zodiac sign and modality— each zodiac sign is grouped into one of three categories (Cardinal, Fixed and Mutable). The mode signifies the functionality of the sign. The modality of this Cancer Moon sign is Cardinal and signifies:

* The issues are highly creative and cut into new ground.
* The matters are action oriented and have strong seasons of change.
* The matters affect the four cornerstones of ones life: the self, the partner, the family and the career.
* Matters could be brought into a public domain.

The last clue is the Moon's zodiac sign. In this example it was a Cancer Last Quarter Moon. Cancer rules matters involving the following:

* Mothers
* Babies
* The family unit
* Land and real estate
* Strong emotions
* Boundary issues

Did you notice all of these clues were in Mr. Martin's story? You can see that my thinking was deductive, not a psychic trick. All the information was there. The use of the Moon tables and knowledge of basic astrological symbolism can give you a head start into the study of natural cycles.

A seasoned astrologer has the symbolism committed to memory. If you are new to the symbolism of astrology, go to the chapter called Astrological Tools for a quick guide to stay connected to the material. Like any new language, it is best learned when you have a personal interest. Take a short list of keywords for each point or planet to stay close to the basics and build your list when you become familiar with basic natures.

Getting Started
1. Begin by locating the Moon phase closest to the date when your story began in the Table of Traditional Moon Phases in the Appendix. The closest date should fall within 3.5 to 4 days of your event or story, large or small. (See Appendix LXI)
2. You can find a symbol key in the introduction and at the end of the book to identify the sign of Moon phase. (See pg 176)
3. Use the keywords from the Astrological Tools chapter to understand the nature of the sign when your Moon phase began. (See pg 174)

Locate the Dates for Your Story with a Moon Family
1. Go to the Moon Family Tables (See Appendix XXVII)
2. Find your Moon phase under the column of New Moon, First Quarter Moon, Full Moon or Last Quarter Moon.

3. Follow your Moon phase to the beginning of the row and jot down all of the family members in your Moon Family.
4. Find the date and phase when your story began in the Moon Family
5. Read from the chapter on Moon phases, about the Moon phase when your story began. If your story began with a New Moon read about all four phases to grasp an understanding of the various stages of development.
6. If your Moon Family shows a date in the future, you can project your story into the future and read the following next stages.

Personalizing the Moon Phase Tables
You may want to locate the Traditional Phases of the Moon in the Appendix to follow along in the next section.

Each of the Phases of the Moon has its own drama to unfold. Reading the chart of any eclipse or Moon Phase shows information about the potential influence it has on our lives. Find important dates in your life and match them to the nearest Moon Phase from the tables in Chapter 7, Astrological Tools. Keep a record of the Moon Phase and its date for future reference.

Zoom in on important dates in your recent history and tag the events with the nearest Moon Phase. For example: Let's imagine you met a new love on October 7, 1996. You could see there was a Solar Eclipse that occurred on October 12, 1996, just five days after you met. Choose the October 12, 1996 Solar Eclipse that you found under the New Moon column to tag your event. Since the eclipse is a greater astronomical event than a Quarter Moon, it has a more dominant influence. We will continue to locate dates for the important events in our lives. When the event in question occurred midway between a regular New Moon and a First Quarter Moon, then tag your event to the First Quarter Moon. Likewise, if the event in question occurred midway between a Full Moon and a Last Quarter Moon, assign the event to the Last Quarter Moon.

You've now located the Moon phase closest to your issues. It's the Last Quarter Moon on 7/26/97. With that in mind, go to the Moon Family Tables in the Appendix on page XXVII. Begin your search by looking under Last Quarter Moons.

Your Moon Phase is under the Last Quarter Moon column second from the bottom.

Moon Families															
New Moon				**First Quarter Moon**				**Full Moon**				**Last Quarter Moon**			
Jul 10 2002	18°	♋	00'	Apr 9 2003	19°	♋	42'	Jan 7 2004	16°	♋	40'	Oct 6 2004	13°	♋	30'
Aug 8 2002	16°	♌	04'	May 9 2003	18°	♌	27'	Feb 6 2004	16°	♌	54'	Nov 5 2004	13°	♌	09'
Sep 6 2002	14°	♍	20'	Jun 7 2003	16°	♍	41'	Mar 6 2004	16°	♍	43'	Dec 4 2004	13°	♍	14'
Oct 6 2002	13°	♎	02'	Jul 6 2003	14°	♎	36'	Apr 5 2004	16°	♎	00'	Jan 3 2005	13°	♎	27'
Nov 4 2002	12°	♏	15'	Aug 5 2003	12°	♏	29'	**May 4 2004**	**14°**	♏	**42'**	Feb 2 2005	13°	♏	33'
Dec 4 2002	**11°**	♐	**58'**	Sep 3 2003	10°	♐	36'	Jun 3 2004	12°	♐	56'	Mar 3 2005	13°	♐	14'
Jan 2 2003	12°	♑	01'	Oct 2 2003	09°	♑	11'	Jul 2 2004	10°	♑	54'	Apr 1 2005	12°	♑	23'
Feb 1 2003	12°	♒	09'	Nov 1 2003	08°	♒	20'	Jul 31 2004	08°	♒	51'	May 1 2005	10°	♒	59'
Mar 2 2003	12°	♓	06'	Nov 30 2003	08°	♓	05'	Aug 29 2004	07°	♓	03'	May 30 2005	09°	♓	10'
Apr 1 2003	11°	♈	39'	Dec 30 2003	08°	♈	17'	Sep 28 2004	05°	♈	45'	Jun 28 2005	07°	♈	08'
May 1 2003	10°	♉	43'	Jan 29 2004	08°	♉	40'	**Oct 28 2004**	**05°**	♉	**02'**	Jul 27 2005	05°	♉	10'
May 31 2003	**09°**	♊	**20'**	Feb 27 2004	08°	♊	53'	Nov 26 2004	04°	♊	55'	Aug 26 2005	03°	♊	29'

That entire row contains all four Lunar Gestation Cycles in the Moon Family. This Moon Family album has a Solar Eclipse at the New Moon so it's probably an event of lasting significance in some way. It's in the sign of Taurus indicating a matter of money, family tradition, possessions or earnings.

Looking at the table in the Appendix find an event in your life and practice finding both the Traditional Moon Phase and then follow it over to the Moon Family Table to spot the Moon Phase influencing your present issues in life. When did this process begin? Where are you in that cycle now? When will it be completed? Does it continue into a next generation Moon Family? Does it pick up again near a Lunar Eclipse 9.5 years after a Solar Eclipse? Random predictions are no longer necessary, because each life event has its own time-table.

For example: if you received an insurance settlement on July 23, 2005, that date fell between the Full Moon and the Last Quarter Moon of that week, so you should tag the event to the Last Quarter Moon. An insurance settlement would match the symbolism of the Last Quarter Moon. The symbolism of the Last Quarter Moon brings the reward for your efforts and often the check is in the mail at that phase. Look at the accompanying short table of Traditional Moon Phases for this example.

Tagging Your Event to a Moon Phase														
Traditional Moon Phases														
New Moon				First Quarter Moon				Full Moon				Last Quarter Moon		
Jul 6 2005	14°	♋	31'	Jul 14 2005	22°	♎	16'	Jul 21 2005	28°	♑	47'	Jul 27 2005	05°	♉	10'
								July 23, 2005 falls between these two phases.						

You can apply these same principles to the date of your birth. However, the tables for the Moon phases do not go back more than a decade or so. You can find your pre-natal Moon Family one of two ways. You may purchase a book called an ephemeris, which lists planet positions throughout the 20th century, available in bookstores that carry astrology books. Try Amazon.com for Neil Michelson's *Concise Ephemeris*, which contains Moon phases. You can find the Solar and Lunar Eclipses before your birth in almost any ephemeris. In the Appendix of this book you will find tables for Moon Families from 1991-2028 after the tables of Traditional Moon Phases. There are also tables of Solar and Lunar Eclipses in chronological order from 1950-2075. Then there are tables of Solar Eclipses in groups of the 19 year Metonic cycles.

About Moon Family Tables

The Moon Family table design in the appendix is used for many forms of study and research. The Moon Family members are listed under their appropriate columns of New Moons, First Quarter Moons, Full Moons, and Last Quarter Moons but are separated by the nine-month Lunar Gestation Cycle.

For locating Moon Families related to important dates in your life, match the date of the event and see the related Moon Family members on the same row. Their dates are separated by nine-month intervals. For example: let's imagine today is July 26, 1997 and you see on your calendar there is a Last Quarter

Moon. As we learned earlier, the seed belonging to this Last Quarter Phase was planted 2¼ years ago at a New Moon. Now you want to find the related Moon Family members. Look under the column of Last Quarter Moons and find a related date, July 26, 1997. There is a Last Quarter Moon listed at 3° Taurus 47'. Other Moon Family members are found on the same row.

The Moon Family Tables can be used in conjunction with the Traditional Moon Phase Tables. First, find the Traditional Moon Phase Tables found in the appendix on page LXI. Zoom in on the week when a topic first surfaced in your life and tag the Traditional Moon Phase that is closest to the matter. Do you remember in the section, "How To Use The Moon Phase Tables", we met a new love on October 7, 1996. In that example, we used the Solar Eclipse that occurred on October 12, 1996 to tag the event. Go to the Moon Family Table and find October 12, 1996 under the New Moon column. Look for the remaining Moon Family members on the same row.

The dates will be relevant to the progression of the relationship in nine-month intervals. It may go something like this: Nine months after the initial October 1996 meeting, you may discuss the appropriate next step in your relationship within two weeks of July 12, 1997 at the First Quarter Moon. A wedding may take place near the Full Moon of April 11, 1998, and you may buy a house or conceive a child within 2 weeks of the Last Quarter Moon of January 9, 1999. In the past, you may have suffered anxiety about a relationship. You may have felt it was moving too slowly. This anxiety may have caused you to push the relationship beyond its natural time schedule and inadvertently damage the process. With help from the Moon Families Tables, you may develop the patience needed to allow for the natural development of the relationship instead of worrying about the next step. You will find all things have their own time schedule at nine-month intervals.

Use the tables to research the development of any event in your life. Look for resurfacing themes, or a continuing saga, associated with the dates of all four Moon Family members. Many notice the timing can be two weeks off from the dates of Moon Family members.

Example: A man was interviewed for work at a new company near the New Moon at 24° Scorpio on November 17, 1990, and he began working six weeks later. On August 17, 1991, there was a First Quarter Moon at 23° Scorpio, the man received great reviews and was offered more responsibility. A large monthly writing assignment was added to his other duties with a small increase in pay. Since this was the man's first writing assignment, he agreed to the below-average compensation.

The day of the Full Moon at 26° Scorpio on May 16, 1992 (conjunct his natal Mars), the man had emergency surgery, and the deadlines for the writing assignments became a problem. By February 13, 1993, a Last Quarter Moon occurred at 24° Scorpio 55; now the work was an enormous job for too little pay. The man asked for a raise in pay, but his request was refused. On the second anniversary of the man's original contact with the company, there was a Solar Eclipse at 21° Scorpio on November 13, 1993; the man gave the company his resignation. He resumed working for them again nine months later when a First Quarter Moon occurred at 21° Scorpio on August 14, 1994. The company closed, three months later, again near the anniversary date.

You can see how, at the return of Moon Phases at the same degree and sign, the cycles begin again regarding the same issues. Plus, the anniversary date of a New Moon or eclipse often revives the issues. Hunt down events in your journal, or track your actions through notes in your checkbook or appointment calendars; have fun predicting when they will resurface.

Chapter 2

Moon Phase Agendas

The Moon phases in the natural order show a clear agenda from start to finish. Not even a flower's full cycle is completed within one lunar cycle. But let's imagine you planted a seed. We'll use this metaphor to describe the individual energies at each phase.

Imagine you push a seed into the soil during a New Moon. Even though the Moon is absent in the sky when the Moon is new, there is plenty going on during this dark period. You can relate this invisible activity to a time of renewal and conception, when an incredible amount of energy is being released at this seed stage. Your generic seed has the capacity to produce a pansy or a poplar tree.

A feeling of hope and encouragement is associated with this time. As the gardener watches for some sign of life, he can feel this highly potent stage is operating quietly in the dark. So much mystery surrounds a New Moon when the only thing you know at this stage is that (something) a seed has been planted. The seed may not mature at all, but he still must wait. If he digs into the soil to see if anything is going on he can disrupt and destroy natures' process. There is not much for you to do at this stage but wait and see. You will be given more information at the next stage.

At the first quarter the new seedling is visible when it breaks the ground and springs into action. At this *time of action*, there is a demand for attention and you can be involved in the seedling's agenda as its caregiver. You need to nurture it with the proper amount of sunshine and water, and watch for when it outgrows the infant quarters of its seedpod and reaches out with roots to mark its hold for the future. If the seedling is a weed, you can easily remove it at this time or continue to nurture the new plant to its full bloom stage at the Full Moon.

At this time, there is a full awareness of the total plant. Is it a first-prize winner, or could it simply have wonderful possibilities? This is the second chance to ditch it in the weed pile, if necessary. Any problems or special needs associated with the plant are clearly visible now, as well as the need for any adjustments in nurturing. At this time, all of the flower's charms are out in the open, clearly visible for everyone to see. It is a time to enjoy the beauty produced by the joint efforts between the natural potential of the seed and your ability to successfully raise it. Your response may be to go public with your flower and enter it into a flower show or add it to a bridal bouquet.

This flower was worthy of collection, so the next action stage is at the Last Quarter Moon stage when you can invest in its future. By allowing the plant to wither and go into a rest stage, you can collect its precious seeds as your reward to show the plant in the future.

Although this is a retirement stage of sorts, it is really a stage of action. With age comes experience; there is a need to plan for the next cycle. At this time, one is gathering, reviewing the conditions of the seeds, sorting and storing them for the future. Make sure the seed bin is free of pests and remove all poorly-developed seeds, so you don't carelessly bring them into the next cycle. You can think of this as the performance review. Mix the new seeds with the prize seeds from past cycles.

We can use the metaphor of the flower as a guide to what to expect when you find the Moon phase related to your story. By knowing there is an agenda you can expect to know certain things at the appropriate level development. What stage is your story's agenda?

1. **New Moon** -Your awareness is on new events and you have the knowledge that this is a "wait and see" period.
2. **First Quarter** - A readiness that encourages the development of new endeavors, or a response with action when called upon.
3. **Full Moon** - Engage, reciprocate. Display, commit and enjoy.
4. **Last Quarter** - Receive and pay. An action of closure or review. A time to revisit and reap the rewards of your efforts.

Much like when using horary rules, the clue to the *phase agenda* is applied to the first contact from the individual or some other event that is "the first."

* The first contact of a message left on your voice mail
* The first mail received regarding an issue
* When meeting someone for the first time
* When you first felt sick
* First sex with a partner
* First time an idea surfaced
* First visit from an important player in your scenario

Whatever it is, I want to know when it first happened. I will note your first call. I will record the beginning of any topic you give me.

The New Moon
At the time of a conjunction, the Sun and the Moon have just met. This is a brand-new encounter in a new sign and at a new degree. At this point they act in tandem, seeing matters from the same perspective without objectivity or obvious differences. The pair are at the beginning of their relationship. The rest of the solar system adds to the chemistry of this special event. The relationships that the other planets have with one another and to the Sun and Moon contribute to the agenda seeded at this time.

What Is The Meaning Of A New Moon?
With their darkened and invisible sides at work, New Moons have a hidden or subconscious influence. New Moons bring new ideas, fresh starts, new developments, new beginnings and new people into one's

life. Often the meanings of all these new beginnings are not clear until the First Quarter Moon at the same degree and sign, approximately nine months later. This does not mean that it will take nine months to get a new idea off the ground, but it may mean that the next greatest event that results from the new idea may take nine months to materialize. It may be like working on an old car and gathering all its needed parts; some parts need to be ordered, some may not do the job the first time. During this time you are able to turn the ignition and actually hear the engine run, but you won't take it on the road until the nine-month mark. More will be revealed over time. There's probably more work to be done, but at least you can see some results. Thinking of the New Moon as the seed stage allows you to plant ideas. But first observe what comes to you. The conjunction of the New Moon has a spark that can be loosely related to the firing-up found in the natural zodiac's Aries energy.

What Is A Client Asking At A New Moon?

Clients seeking advice at a New Moon are, to some degree, "clueless" and confused. They are looking for clarity and direction. They will express frustration and impatience. Just as there can be a density in the air, these clients can be difficult to reach, but very open to seed planting. A positive influence toward bringing their creative principles into action would help them to find what they want. After all, you can only light a path; they have to do the walking. I resist directing anyone to do anything. I find out what they want and offer them good dates to put their plans into action. The astrologer is also in the dark at the New Moon period. I use various techniques to attempt to extract additional meaning from the client's chart when they contact me or come for an appointment at a New Moon. Without going into explanation of technique, below is a list of some things I might do for deeper study:

* From the option titled "Harmonics" in *Solar Fire,* I cast a Sun/Moon arc transformation chart.
* Cast the ninth harmonic chart, as it represents the person's greatest joy.
* Cast a chart for the prenatal New Moon.
* Study their Sun/Moon midpoint.
* Investigate the progressed chart with both solar arc angles and the Daily Mean Quotidian Angles (Q2)
* Use the sign symbolism of the New Moon as a clue.
* Study the chart of the New Moon for any repeat of natal angles. Does the client show many oppositions?
* What, if any, are the oppositions in the New Moon chart? Do the same for other aspects.
* What transiting charts are on the angles of the natal chart.
* Study closely all conjunctions in the natal chart.
* With Solar Fire 6 Deluxe version, cast the valuable Age Harmonic +1 and note all exact aspects; follow with list from dynamic reports for a period of time to search for all hard aspects with exact dates.

Due to the myopic perspective of the New Moon's conjunction, there is usually a lack of foresight. Look back over the past nine months. The level of experience and preparation for this New Moon might have been revealed nine months ago when a Last Quarter Moon occurred at this same degree. The client may have finished something up. Ask them if they've keep any part of that activity for the future. The New Moon could involve the things saved.

Very often, New Moon clients will want to start something new. Many people want to open a new business or get married on a New Moon, and I always advise against this. It is not a good time, because there is not enough light. They lack the all of the pertinent facts. More time is needed for matters to develop and to gather additional information because there is a lack of preparation at this point. Even if a great deal of preparation has already been done, if the start date comes under the New Moon then it is quite probable something has been overlooked and needs to be rechecked.

The New Moon conjunct a planet is very powerful. Find out what is developing by noting the planet, sign, and house where it occurs. The client may not always recognize the new beginnings, since they are still undercover. Yet, a sense of anticipation and desire for change in the area contacted by the New Moon will be apparent. A New Moon conjunct a planet can signify that the person has control over the developing matters related to that planet. Give the client a list of keywords to meditate upon. Invite them to plant their intentions with positive thought, and ask the great universal support energy to help move it along.

For instance if a New Moon:
*   Is conjunct the natal Sun or Mars, this could mean they are looking for a new job. The client will be able to direct the job search and have control over that process.
*   Opposes their Mars, the client may have their eye on a job, but will find it is out of reach. This probably was not apparent when they applied for the job.
*   Squares the client's Mars, they could be entering into a renewed contract at their present job with reservations on both sides. Things are changing. It may even be that very shortly major shifts occur in the job structure. The client may actually be thinking seriously about changing jobs, but not taking aggressive action (although they're taking *some* action) at this time. Another possibility for the square is to read it as, "No, for now." There is great potential later, but it could take as much as two and a quarter years to produce serious results. If the offer seems fair, it could lead to something better down the road or the client may benefit by staying put for now.

I do not discourage anyone from doing what he or she really wants to do. Everyone has their own path and mission in life and it is not up to astrologers to change their course. If there is an apparent danger, explore how to reschedule activities around dangerous transits. For some people, the only time they travel is when there appears to be the most dangerous aspect. It may take that kind of tension to get that individual on a journey without experiencing danger. Sharing information regarding cycles and trends and explaining what they can expect assists the client in making his or her own decisions. For an astrologer to project fears, judgments, beliefs, and expectations onto a client is a disservice to both the client and the astrological profession.

To demonstrate the impact of a New Moon we will use the chart of a producer of major entertainment events for a case study. We will call her Producer. In this example, we are using a 21° Sagittarius New Moon shown as the outer wheel of the bi-wheel with the chart of the producer in the center. At the top of the chart page find a horizontal graph displaying the Producer's natal planets from 0° to 30°, called a 30° sort. The 30° sort allows us to quickly spot the producer's natal planets receiving the influence. Keep your eye

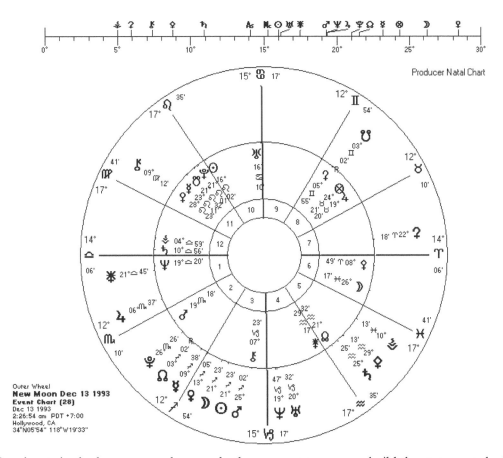

Biwheel of Producer, New Moon

Producer Natal Chart

Outer Wheel
New Moon Dec 13 1993
Event Chart (28)
Dec 13 1993
2:26:54 am PDT +7:00
Hollywood, CA
34°N05'54" 118°W19'33"

on the planets in the box as some leave and others may appear as we build the story over the life of the Moon family.

We can see the New Moon in the Producer's third house and by looking at the 30° sort find the planets listed at each degree where they occur in the chart but without signs. By focusing only on the planets at a specific degree, you are able to assimilate the information to form an impression of how the person receives the transiting event. In this case we look to the degree where the New Moon occurred, 21°. Collect all the planets and points listed at or near 21° from the 30° sort, and place them in a box to form a picture. Planets found in a 4° orb around the 21° can be included in the list. Therefore any planet 4° before or after 21° is collected.

New Moon
21° ♐ 23'
✳ ♂ ♃ ♆ ♇ ☊ ☿

Use an orb no greater than 3° to collect planets from the grid.
We will use the box of planets to gain an impression of the impact from the New Moon. The goal is to make a statement by stringing together planet keywords to form a sentence. For this exercise, we are not using sign keywords. Read through the mean-

ing of the planets in chapter 7 to get an idea for keywords. Select one word for each planet and create a sentence. Here is a very brief list of planet keywords.

Shuffle the words for a more coherent idea. Blend their meanings into a single phrase. The house where the New Moon occurs should be taken into consideration and added to the data you collect. Later, assess the energy differences of particular aspects as a separate process. But first, focus on the collected essence of the combined energies of the planets.

This group of planets appears too large to form a concept, but when it is broken down, it becomes manageable.
* Connections to (North Node X) = people
* with money in powerful positions (Pluto w)
* who offer partnership (Juno })
* to expand (Jupiter R)
* your imaginative (Neptune U)
* ideas (Mercury O)
* projects and jobs(Mars Q).

Here is what happened at the time of this New Moon. The client received a promise (New Moon) from her new (New Moon) financial backer (Pluto) to fund the writers (Mercury) and create a business plan (Mars, Jupiter) for her current creative project (Mars, Juno, Neptune).

The New Moon creates a tight trine to her natal conjunction of Pluto, South Node, and Mercury. At first glance, the trine to the Leo planets does not seem to present any problems to the producer's chart. But, any time Pluto is in the picture, I ask, what is this really going to cost the client? Anytime Neptune is involved I ask what is it you are ignoring that could dissolve the life out of this matter. She was also undergoing an

Ruling Planet		Planet Keyword
Mars	♂	action/force/man/projects/jobs
Venus	♀	beauty/money/woman/counselor/love
Mercury	☿	thought/document/child/messenger/ analyze/organize/worker
Moon	☽	emotions/baby/mother/private side/cycles/routine
Sun	☉	vitality/creator/leader/your presence
Pluto	♇ ancient-ruler ♂	transformation/power/lender/controller/oppressive/obsessive/heavy matters/insurance/death/reproduction
Jupiter	♃	broader perspective/expansion/professor/mentor /clergy /freedom/open spaces/the way out
Saturn	♄	father/structure/CEO/commitment
Uranus	♅, ancient-ruler ♄	awaken/invention/citizen/rebellion
Neptune	♆, ancient-ruler ♃	divine inspiration/imagination/isolation/vague/ illusive/deception/musician/alcholic/spiritual activities
North Node		self &relationships/connections & significant unions/health/wellbeing of your body
South Node		attracting others/matter re:significant other
Chiron		old wound/healer/practitioner/teacher/ knowledge/mercy/lessons
Ceres		abandomment/serious matters/food/basic needs/children/care given and received/under the care of/cereal/food issues/supplies/refridgerator contents
Pallas		experts/counselors/wisdom/repeated patterns/nature of relationships/ excellence/profound events
Vesta		investments/realestate/housing/domes/ protection/sacred space
Juno		marriage/partnership/contracts/to decorate/honor/superficial matters/appearances/victim advocate
Ascendant		yourself/personality/body/the window of your world
Midheaven		father/dept head/boss/other authorities figures/public matter effecting you, your world

important life change indicated by transiting Neptune square Neptune. This square often accompanies an illusive period, making it difficult to obtain commitments.

The stand-alone chart of the New Moon is a very heavy chart. It contains one of the most difficult aspects of that year, the square between Saturn and Pluto. Mars plays into the energy since it sextiles Saturn and is semi-sextile Pluto. These aspects suggest that events that begin at this time are designed (Mars) to change (Pluto) the structure (Saturn) of life. The Mars component also suggests battles and high levels of competitive struggles. Mars forms a sextile to Saturn indicating an opportunity to be taken seriously.

Noting the impact of the transiting Saturn square Pluto, we find that the deepest changes in the producer's life are being directed at her Moon at 26° Pisces 16' and her Venus at 28° Leo 23, to which transiting Mars at 25° Sagittarius 2 creates a tight square to her Moon, along with an exact trine from transiting Pluto. With Pluto square her natal Venus and opposed by transiting Saturn, this creates a very difficult T-square. (Even trine aspects from oppressive Pluto can be problems).

The name of her project is the Women's Project. The Moon/Venus symbolism couldn't scream any louder than that! Transiting Saturn blocks progress and causes worry and concern since it sits in direct opposition to her Mercury, creating a semi-sextile behind her Moon which shows hidden blocks to her sixth house of projects.

At this time, the client reported enormous encouragement from the backer and they engaged in a contract to develop ideas even though the New Moon warned of unseen potential for trouble. We will look at this chart again in nine months, at the First Quarter Moon of this New Moon Family, to see what developed.

Things to Do on a New Moon.
The question of how to time events in order to gain the best results shows that any action taken on a New Moon can be very risky. Because of the darkness and unseen potential of a New Moon, one should wait for more information before taking action or making major decisions. A First Quarter Moon is better informed, but it is not until the Full Moon that all the cards are on the table concerning the matter.

One can, however, be adventurous in a creative way. Go somewhere you have never gone before, take a workshop on a brand-new topic. Engage in something particularly inspirational: read a new book, sign up for a new type of class, write down all the new people you meet unexpectedly. If you are an artist of any sort, start a new project and watch it develop with a life of its own. Write a new poem, compose a song, create a new color palette or a new studio arrangement. Work in a different light setting or at a different time of day. Record your dreams and thoughts. Go outside your normal routine for inspiration. Take a sentimental journey to use old memories for soulful new works. Brainstorm with others in your field.

For businesses, observe cycles and do some research at this time. Set up test projects but have no expectations and observe their development. Create a think tank. Consider hiring an advisor or business coach for inspiration and guidance. Network. But keep in mind that starting actual new projects could cause a lot of unforeseen grief. Hiring new people on a New Moon could also bring problems later.

Beware of accepting promises at this time, since enthusiasm is abundant but follow-through is limited. Make no final choices or commitments.

For personal and spiritual growth, plant a couple of actual seeds and plant the intention of your own wishes along with them. Nurture the seeds and watch them grow. Make a wish list and look back on it in nine months. Record all your dreams for a few days, before and after a New Moon, and reflect on them nine months later. It is a great time for yoga and meditation, journal-writing, personal inventories, and imagery work.

Avoid jumping into new relationships when meeting new people at a New Moon. An element of mystery surrounds this time period and you will find out more about the person later. I find relationships that begin with meeting someone at a New Moon indicate that one or both parties are not ready. They don't know themselves well enough and this is often not a good match. This is not to say that all new encounters on a New Moon will end in disappointment. I certainly have seen the reverse. But the New Moon chart must be just right for all parties concerned.

Regarding family matters, go with the flow and do not initiate anything new. In reference to daycare, catering and care giving, any changes at this time may be premature and warrant adjustment later. New developments that arise will need your action when there is more light from the Moon, which could be as soon as in a few days.
This time is best used for dreaming up new ideas and going with the flow, to be led into the perfect situations for you. Create a new look. Save your doodle pad for it could illustrate blueprints for the future. Remember to record your dreams. Keep dates on dream journals and watch how dreams materialize in nine months.

First Quarter Moon
The First Quarter Moon is a "turning point." The Sun and Moon have grown beyond a place of oneness and into separate sets of experience. There are differences at the point of the first square, and this can be a time of clash and stress. Breaking through the ground the way a seedling must is no small feat because it must fight its way through the soil to reach the light of the Sun. This is an ambitious time. This is the first square represented by the Cancer portion of the zodiac. Cancer is ruled by the Moon and matters of a cyclical nature and is associated with the recurring cycles of the Moon.

What is the Meaning of a First Quarter Moon?
At a First Quarter Moon, there is a great burst of energy and growth. It is an active and courageous time with sharp and strong challenges. There is a lot of forward motion and drive toward progress.

Often problems are present. The crisis that occurs at this time is likely to be a credit for the future, as even a painful experience can send you into a positive leap forward. Conflict between males and females are one of the traits of Moon square Sun. Most often, events happen right on the day of Quarter Moons.

The kinds of events that have a real First Quarter Moon quality go beyond the seed stage and on to the next level of activity. This is where one becomes actively involved with matters that had their beginnings nine months ago.

There could be an air of ambition and enthusiasm in whatever you are doing. You are becoming enlightened and moving at an energetic, forward pace. It is a time of coming around the corner but not a time to cut corners. A particularly strong sense of purpose is evident with a First Quarter Moon that is related to a Solar Eclipse nine months prior. Things "take off." Ideas that were only dreams back at the Solar Eclipse (or New Moon) are now developing a life of their own and pressing you to make them a reality. The light of the First Quarter Moon is still growing and suggests there are potentials that need more research and direction is still a question.

What is a Client Asking at a First Quarter Moon?

This is a crisis Moon. At First Quarter Moons, people are often stressed. When a client calls at a First Quarter Moon, they can be anxious and looking for more specific direction. The events that surface at the First Quarter Moon might have been initiated nine months ago. So cast the chart for the New Moon that occurred near the same degree. People find themselves actively involved in the process that had begun at the New Moon nine months ago. They have some idea what matters are developing but still they do not have enough information to make definite plans. They often are at a stage where they want to get something off the ground but they are not sure how to go about it. They want to know if their ideas will work, if a particular person has potential to build a relationship with them or they may simply want to know when things are going to start clicking in their lives. If they started a new business nine months ago, they are telling you about their difficulties. The problems are beginning to surface and they are wondering whether they should hang in or drop it. They may feel pressured to search for a new job, since problems at work are common at these times. Let's check in with the producer we met at the New Moon. This is the same chart but cast with the First Quarter Moon on September 12, 1994, a Moon Family member of the New Moon on December 13, 1993.

First Quarter Moon
12-Sep-94
☉♅⚵♂♃♆♇☊

This First Quarter Moon places the transiting Sun in her twelfth house of hidden matters, things behind the scenes. Keep in mind that this Moon Family originated with the New Moon at 21° Sagittarius 23'. Also watch the aspects from the transiting Sun in each Moon Phase. The position of the Sun will tell you who has control over the situation. This First Quarter Moon at 19° Sagittarius 28 creates a new picture by collecting the natal planets within a 4° orb, as before with the New Moon example. Note that the Sun and Uranus have been added to the group.

Whenever there is a change in planets in the picture, look for a change in the players of the drama that

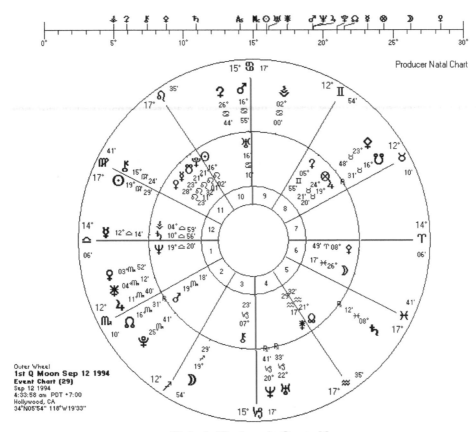

the individual is experiencing. Matters will take interesting turns related to that drama. If a natal planet drops out and does not return, someone important may leave the situation. If planets are added, new developments and new people are added to the scenario.

On the very day of the First Quarter Moon, the producer received her first check. The check was dreadfully delayed and far short of the money promised. The small check was a shock to the producer. She had used her own money to pay for expenses based on the promises given. The addition of Uranus to the picture describes the shock and reversals, as the Sun illuminates the matter but it also rules her ego and creative processes. The illumination revealed unpleasant, though much needed, information. She now had to consider legal action to get the funds that had been promised. At the time she received the check, she had terrible problems with the writers who worked in her office at her home. They were fighting among themselves and not producing the work they were hired to do. Mercury leaving the picture of planets in the box, showed a need to change writers. Everything about the project was upside down.

Once again, look at the Moon Phase chart as a standalone to see what planets are in conflict. Mercury squares Mars in three days, an aspect of verbal and written disagreements. This aspect involves the client's Midheaven, Ascendant, and natal Uranus. The Mars aspect triggered sudden abrupt changes involving her personally, because it was a time of attack and battle. The trine from transiting Mars to her natal Mars in her second house, sextile her natal Jupiter in the eighth house, is probably what brought any money at all. The fact that her money planets are tied into Neptune can remain a problem when dealing with promises from others.

Transiting Saturn at 8° Pisces 11 is semi-square to Uranus at 22° Capricorn 32. This is another aspect of conflict as the two energies usually try to defeat one another. Saturn wants structure and stability; Uranus wants to shake things up to make room for change. Transiting Uranus is in the producer's fourth house of home and security and transiting Saturn is located in her fifth house of creative pursuits. Transit-

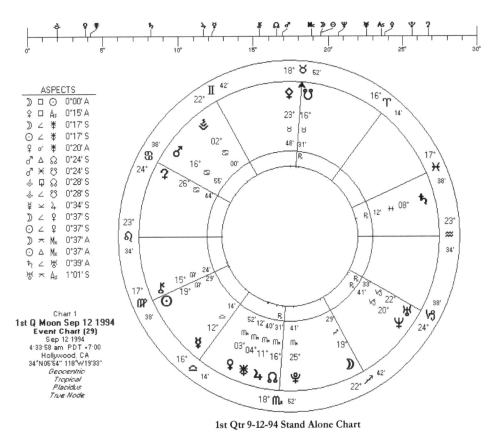

ASPECTS

☽	□	☉	0°00' A
♀	□	As	0°15' A
☽	∠	☿	0°17' S
☉	∠	☿	0°17' S
♀	∠	☿	0°20' A
♂	△	☊	0°24' S
♂	✶	☋	0°24' S
⚷	⊓	☊	0°28' S
⚷	∠	☋	0°28' S
☿	⚹	♃	0°34' S
☽	∠	♀	0°37' S
☉	∠	♀	0°37' S
☽	⊼	Mc	0°37' A
☉	△	Mc	0°37' A
♄	∠	♅	0°39' A
♅	⊼	As	1°01' S

Chart 1
1st Q Moon Sep 12 1994
Event Chart (29)
Sep 12 1994
4:33:58 am PDT +7:00
Hollywood, CA
34°N05'54" 118°W19'33"
Geocentric
Tropical
Placidus
True Node

1st Qtr 9-12-94 Stand Alone Chart

ing Uranus quincunx, her Mercury not only caused all sorts of adjustments and left her with the problem of finding new writers, but she also relocated from the east coast to the west coast at that time. Major events to natal Mercury are often present at the time of relocations - influencing a change to one's neighborhood.

At a First Quarter Moon, it is important to keep an eye on the Sun's location since this is where the current control is located. With the Sun in the twelfth house, the indications might be she is losing control over the projects. The controlling factor is illusive. There are too many problems, hidden and otherwise. We will look at the situation again in nine more months at the Full Moon of the Moon Family.

Things To Do On The First Quarter Moon

This is a good time to work hard, not relax. This is not a contemplative time, but a hot action time and it is often filled with competition. Full speed ahead, with an eye open for possible obstacles is a good way to proceed. One must be careful not to invest more than your interest is worth since there is a tendency towards over-optimistic indulgence with this phase. Remember, you will be paying for any over-extensions you make now, at the Last Quarter Moon that occurs in a year and a half. You may be filing a petition or starting classes. If your work is in the arts, you may want to begin work on a new project by gathering the tools you will need. It could be a great time to start writing a book, begin a painting or search for locations for a poetry reading or art show. You may want to book musical appearances for a future date near the Full Moon.

For business matters, review contracts for short-term ventures and set up appointments. Visit potential purchase sites for land or housing. Make a preliminary offer. Invest with small amounts. Continue working on design changes and develop options to go along with the primary plans. Delay choices for decorating with colors or any final-touch decisions since your project is not fully developed. Advertising layouts should be delayed at least a couple of days to a week. Plan for expansion with a moderate purse, for there are many unseen expenses in nine months. Replenish supplies for offices and job locations, keeping in mind the temptation to overspend at this time.

If you are notified of a legal matter, it may or may not be related to an event nine months ago and you will be required to take some action. Keep your cool until you have all the facts. For personal and spiritual development, this may be a good time to continue personal research. Reach out to new people who share similar interests. Join group meetings to exchange like-minded principles. Make plans with new people to slowly get to know each other. All commitments are premature at this time.

The Full Moon
Since the time of the New Moon, the Moon has had many separate life experiences and new perspectives at a distance from the Sun. The Moon now is mature, developed, and it possesses the capacity to receive and reflect. Situated at 180° from the Sun, the Moon sits at its greatest distance in its cycle. This degree has an association with the sign of Libra and its ruler Venus. Therefore, there is a strong focus on public and social matters and relationships. An opposition is never experienced alone. If there is not a partner in your life, then a situation or person will oppose you or receive your opposition. The total image of the Full Moon makes it the ruler of the public eye, no matter in what sign it occurs. All Full Moons show the Moon at its maximum visibility. The Sun and Moon had their introduction at the New Moon and now with the full, committed, and present face of the Moon, they marry.

What is the Meaning of a Full Moon?
The Full Moon is a time of complete awareness, a time of total engagement or involvement with others. All the cards are on the table, and all of the facts are revealed. This is a time of full, head-on challenges. I like to do most of the things that I want to have a strong future between the First Quarter and Full Moon. Not at exactly the Full Moon or after.

A Full Moon is a time of realization and the fulfillment of one's efforts. It can be the end of an era or relationship as one knows it. Cycles break their stride and take on greater challenges. A faster pace or total breakdown is likely. One way or another, things will not remain the same. Something will end, be dropped or be finished. Deadlines are the order of the day. Major deadlines occur at Lunar Eclipses.

During a Full Moon there is restlessness and sleeplessness due to excess energy in the air. The tides are high. All creatures are refueling their needs as they feed by the light of the Moon. More people are out

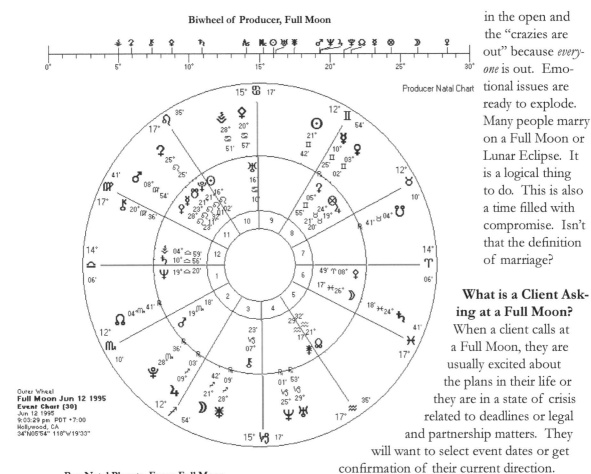

Biwheel of Producer, Full Moon

Producer Natal Chart

Outer Wheel
Full Moon Jun 12 1995
Event Chart (30)
Jun 12 1995
9:03:29 pm PDT +7:00
Hollywood, CA
34°N05'54" 118°W19'33"

Box Natal Planets, Focus Full Moon

New Moon	First Quarter Moon	Full Moon
13-Dec-93	12-Sep-94	12-Jun-95
21° ♐ 23'	19° ♐ 29'	21° ♐ 42'
⚷ ♂ ♃ ♇ ☊ ☿	☉ ⚷ ⚷ ♂ ♃ ♇ ☊	⚷ ♂ ♃ ♇ ☊ ☿

in the open and the "crazies are out" because *everyone* is out. Emotional issues are ready to explode. Many people marry on a Full Moon or Lunar Eclipse. It is a logical thing to do. This is also a time filled with compromise. Isn't that the definition of marriage?

What is a Client Asking at a Full Moon?
When a client calls at a Full Moon, they are usually excited about the plans in their life or they are in a state of crisis related to deadlines or legal and partnership matters. They will want to select event dates or get confirmation of their current direction. They have a plan of action and want to bring it out into the open. They could be planning a wedding or business opening. They may be having difficulties in their personal relationships or with business partners, often with legal consequences. They are fully aware that pressing matters at this time require fulfillment or closure. They are no longer confused and they want help making sound decisions and choices. They are looking for encouragement and validation.

Again, we see the over-worked, under-paid producer, now experiencing the Full Moon on June 12, 1995 at 21° Sagittarius 42; notice that transiting Saturn is conjunct her natal Moon. She finally gave up and let the bankrupt Women's Project end on the Full Moon. Another point to note is the Full Moon occurs at the exact degree as that of the New Moon a year and a half before. This intensifies the level of involvement and the profound response. The 21st degree exactly aspects the producer's nodes and Pluto. The effects of Pluto are a deeply gripping force that you'll do anything to release. It also indicates something must change. Pluto is a planet of change.

In the Full Moon chart, a square between Mars and Jupiter triggered the relationship of the producer's natal Mars opposition Jupiter and it brought a stroke of good luck. Uranus at the 29th degree of Capricorn, quincunx natal Venus, would also contribute to a sudden turn of events. The producer found a new financial backer who loved her new project and encouraged her to submit a full proposal. The producer also found reliable new writers and other key figures to make the new project a success.

At a Full Moon, it is important to keep an eye on the Sun's location as this is where the current control is located. When a Full Moon falls in a house, it obviously affects the opposite house because the Sun is in opposition to the Moon. *The area in your chart that indicates the point of control is where the transiting Sun is located.* Therefore, at the time of a Full Moon, find the Sun's position and this is where you find the most control.

For example, a Full Moon at 24° Pisces means the Moon is located at 24° Pisces. The Sun therefore is located at 24° Virgo. If the Full Moon point is conjunct one of your planets, then the matters pertaining to the planet are temporarily out of your reach, and the control goes to the significant other of whatever is your personal scenario. The Sun's position has the control. The oppositions place matters out of your reach and sometimes you are aware of who the individual is that gained while you lost. Let's imagine there was a Full Moon on your Mars and you applied for a job that was never really available. It had been promised to someone else before you applied. The application was part of a process that the employer needed to cover. You unknowingly applied for a job that was out of your reach. You later found out who got the job.

Things To Do On The Full Moon

This is one of my favorite times to take action because well-lighted, fully-developed information is available at the Full Moon. Openings of any sort have maximum exposure at this time and people are more social and open to interaction. They are feeding their needs by the light of the Moon.

For businesses, this is a time to merge, contract, commit, unite with partners and begin legal cases. It is time to announce any new business ventures or go public with matters that need to come out in the open. Any illegal activity is sure to be noticed at this time. The Full Moon is great for publicity and public contact and to announce candidacies.

If your work is in the arts, it is time to present your talents and invite important parties. Have a show.

This is a good time to practice personal and spiritual development, to have a wedding or any kind of merger. It is a time, as well, for separations and divorces. It is a time to throw a party. At Full Moons, everyone shows up. Meeting a new romantic partner at this time often will bring people out who have just suffered a separation. They are usually out in the open about their status. They are seeking closure and comfort. Sometimes they are ready to become involved.

I like to book medical appointments at a Full Moon because areas and disorders that are hard to diagnose are out in the open. Even though blood flows higher at a Full Moon, operations have great success because all necessary matters are visible and more easily attended to. Hunt for lost friends or family members. Seek and find what you are looking for.

The Last Quarter Moon

The Last Quarter Moon is a time of return and review. As in mythology, it is the time of the crone. You may find wisdom, experience and patience at the Last Quarter Moon. It is a time of reaping what you have sown in the past and of harvesting the fruit of your labors. The Last Quarter takes place at 270° past the New Moon. On the natural zodiac, this particular degree is occupied by Capricorn, ruled by Saturn, and therefore it has an association with like matters. The Capricorn association is related to aged and seasoned perspectives. Business, career, and parental matters are common with this Moon Phase. Check the Moon phase sign to get more clues.

What Is The Meaning Of A Last Quarter Moon?

Like the First Quarter Moon, this is another very busy time and a time of much work. Matters and people resurface from the past, demanding your attention. At this time, you are wrapping things up and getting ready to move on into the next New Moon Phase of your life. Therefore, it is a time of serious evaluation. What have you done over the past two and a quarter years since this Family's New Moon occurred? Has your investment paid off? It is time to take stock in the future without skipping over the responsibilities associated with this time. Debts will be called, and payoff and reviews from outside interests are waiting in line. If the last two and a quarter years have been well-tended, this can be a period of reward. Otherwise, watch out for people and things coming out of the woodwork, looking for you to pay up.

What is a Client Asking at a Last Quarter Moon?

Many questions at a Last Quarter Moon have to do with the past in some way. If someone from the past appears back in their lives, people may ask if this will be permanent. There are a lot of career questions. Some are anxious to see what is next in their lives now that they are at the top of their current goals. Many people will be experiencing reviews at work, while others are dealing with authority figures in some way. Many questions regarding the care of elderly parents will come up at this time. This is a time when the check is in the mail and the rewards have arrived.

We can see in the next chart that our producer is also at the Last Quarter Moon stage in the development of her drama.

Here at the Last Quarter Moon, the transiting Sun conjuncts her natal Moon. This conjunction from the Sun puts the concerns of the Moon and the sixth house issues in the control of the client. Finally, things are really going her way. The new project is well-supported, since she received a large check on the very day of the Last Quarter Moon. Her new writers are productive and creative. Transiting Saturn and Mars, also conjunct the natal sixth house Moon, can bring both security and progress to her project. Her backer is an older woman with her son as assistant and they are experienced in the entertainment business.

Since a conjunction from the transiting Sun puts matters in the hands of the client, a square will say, "No, for now." An opposition puts matters in the hands of the op-position. At a Last Quarter Moon, it is important to keep an eye on the Sun's location, since this is where the current control is located. Simply stated, the Sun rules.

A couple of inter-esting notes about the Sun opposed the producer's natal Moon at the First Quarter Moon when she could not get the funding she needed. At the final quarter phase of this Moon Family the Sun is con-junct her natal Moon. Her natal Moon in the sixth house, for this entrepreneur, indicates she lives and breaths her career. Her emotional body had been consumed with her work. When she finally got the support she required for her creative life, she met the love of her life and began her first long-term relationship in April 1996. An interesting point about the group of planets at the Last Quarter phase was that Juno dropped out and her Part of Fortune came in. The Part of Fortune is not only about mate-rial fortune but it's a kind of relationship indicator. The reasoning is that the Part of Fortune represents the arc opening between the Sun and Moon. With much research in this area I have found the Sun and Moon are the primary male and female indicators. Their arc is a powerful love finder I call the "Har-monic Chord."

Currently our producer is working on another global project and is seeking funding. Her Moon is the

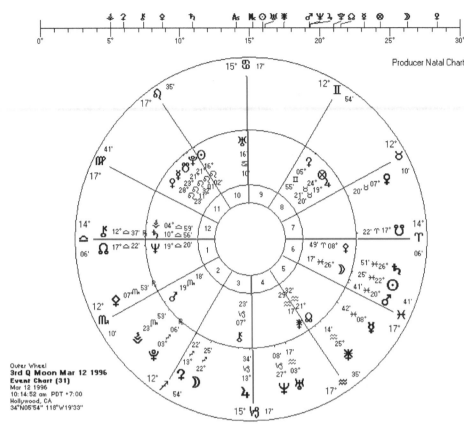

Producer Natal Chart

Outer Wheel
3rd Q Moon Mar 12 1996
Event Chart (31)
Mar 12 1996
10:14:52 am PDT +7:00
Hollywood, CA
34°N05'54" 118°W19'33"

Biwheel of Producer, Last Quarter

New Moon	First Quarter Moon	Full Moon	Last Quarter Moon
13-Dec-93	12-Sep-94	12-Jun-95	12-Mar-96
21° ♐ 23'	19° ♐ 29'	21° ♐ 42'	22° ♐ 25'
⚹♂♃♆♇☊☿	☉☿⚹♂♃♆♇☊	⚹♂♃♆♇☊☿	♂♃♆♇☊☿⊗

Box Planets Last Quarter

object of a high profile Full Moon on September 17, 2005 at 25° Pisces, when she will meet with a new backer for $15 million to fund her project. It looks encouraging.

Things to Do on the Last Quarter Moon?

At this time of collecting the seeds for the future, it is important to offer recognition where deserved. Award and acknowledge jobs well done. Write summaries of judgments for constructive purposes. Take inventory of both home and business. Make well-thought-out public announcements. Promote yourself based on past success. Make career moves. Buy property. Invest in things that have stood the test of time. Save money.

Approach highly-placed family members or business associates for funds. Have a family reunion. Contact old friends and family. Break out of old molds and review the past with a sense of humor. Nurture the old and secure the environment for the future. Clean up exposed details of your past. Anything left untended can come back to haunt you.

Call for money owed to you. Make arrangements to pay off creditors. Hold on to things with promise but dispose of things that hold no future potential. Eliminate waste and dead weight. Clean things up because appearances are important at this time.

Cooperate with authority but do forge ahead. Beware of promoting untested ideas. This can be a time of sudden death to business. Beware of putting your reputation on the line unless you are completely ready. All critical eyes are open now. Follow the rules for now. Bending system rules or laws can be very risky, but this may be an effective tactic given all the facts necessary to make a wise decision. Contact people to discuss possibilities for future projects.

The Museum Fund Manager

Here is another very interesting example of Last Quarter Moon activity. The following chart belongs to a fund manager of a museum who came for a consultation amidst a job crisis that could bear consequence to her career.

It was Sunday when the client called, panicked that her career as a fund manager was over. She became aware of an error that could cost not only her job, but the future of the museum. She was tortured with the possibilities of what the next day might bring. Her appointment was scheduled on the day of a Last Quarter Moon. We will rename her Cathy. Here is what happened.

Cathy became abruptly aware at 4:30 in the afternoon on April 17, 1998 that she had overlooked an overdraft in February that created a huge financial error. The museum was under reconstruction and Cathy had written, in error, a requisition that caused an overdraft of the museum's account. The bank mailed an overdraft notice in March '98 during Mercury retrograde but she also missed that. On April 17, two days before the Last Quarter Moon at 29° Capricorn, the bank sent a notice that it was calling for full payment of the loan of five million dollars. Cathy was in a panic. She did everything she could to explain in the half hour before the weekend began and now was suffering while she waited to hear whether the bank would forgive the error or not.

I pulled out my Moon Family Tables and located our then current date of April 19, 1998 and found it under the column of Last Quarter Moon along with the following Moon Family:

I asked Cathy if these dates meant anything to her regarding this situation. "Yes," she said. "All of the dates are directly related to the process of the reconstruction loan for the museum." On January 19, 1996, the museum signed a two million dollar loan for a term of ten years (Mercury was retrograde). On October 18, 1996, the loan was re-negotiated for five million dollars to be paid in fifteen years. On July 21, 1997, the construction begun and on April 17, 1998, the loan was called for a defaulted loan.

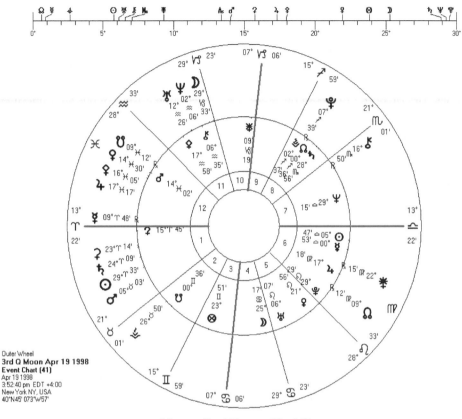

Outer Wheel
3rd Q Moon Apr 19 1998
Event Chart (41)
Apr 19 1998
3:52:40 pm EDT +4:00
New York NY, USA
40°N45' 073°W57'

Museum Fund Manager Natal Chart

New Moon	First Quarter Moon	Full Moon	Last Quarter Moon
1/20/1996	10/19/1996	7/20/1997	4/19/1998
29♑45	26♑38	27♑28	29♑33

Moon Family Fund Manager

With the help of a kind person, the mistake was forgiven. Her panicked call came in on a void of course Moon. That told me then that nothing would come of it. Another positive point was the Sun was in her first house at the Last Quarter Moon phase. This is the best place for matter to be under your own control. Three months later, Cathy's wedding took place in the beautiful setting of the museum. A month after the wedding, she took a new job that tripled her income which was threatening to her husband who earned considerably less. Three months after the wedding her father passed away. Four years after a July 11th wedding she divorced. Currently in 2005 she holds the best job in her career and she is thriving.

A Moon Family Drama

A very attractive 44-year-old married woman contracted chicken pox in October 1991. This was three months prior to a North Node Solar Eclipse at 13° Capricorn 51', on January 4, 1992. (The events within a period of three months prior to an eclipse are directly related to that eclipse. This is explained in the section "Power spots of the Year.") The events that occurred at this time were the seeds that caused dramatic change in the woman's life. The woman began receiving abusive remarks from her husband about her unattractive appearance due to the chicken pox. She pleaded with him to have patience for the disease to pass, but the remarks were becoming very damaging to her self-esteem and their relationship. He continued without mercy and it ended the marriage for her. On, Tuesday, January 4, 1992, the woman filed for divorce. She remained living in the same house with her husband for an additional nine months. She said she needed the time to arrange for a new life.

On October 3, 1992, there was a First Quarter Moon at 10° Capricorn 37' (within 5 degrees of the eclipse that occurred January 4, 1992), and the woman moved out on her own.

She had her first date as a separated woman nine months later at the Full Moon that occurred at 12° Capricorn 2' on July 3, 1993. The court date for the divorce was set nine months later, coinciding with the Last Quarter Moon at 13 Capricorn 8 on April 3, 1994.

The eclipse of January 4, 1992 at 13° Capricorn 51' took place in the woman's sixth house of health maintenance, conjunct her Venus within a 5 degree orb. Her Capricorn Venus depicts the age difference between her and her

Solar Eclipse	First Quarter Moon	Full Moon	Last Quarter Moon
1/4/1992	10/3/1992	7/3/1993	4/4/1994
13♑51	10♑37	12♑02	13♑08

Moon Family Drama

husband of twenty years. Venus is the ruler of Libra on her Nadir (fourth house cusp), which rules her home and Taurus is intercepted in her tenth house of career. Her entire life was altered by her decision to divorce since she then left her home and career in the south and relocated to Massachusetts.

The following chart of the Lady with the Chicken Pox shows her natal planets listed in a thirty degree sort in the strip at the top.

With regard to the Lady with the Chicken Pox, we are looking for aspects from the Solar Eclipse that occurred at 13° Capricorn 51'. By listing the planets in the thirty degree sort, the planets which are aspected by this Moon Phase are easily spotted and the natal planet groups become an important delineation tool. If we blend the energies of all the planets in the planet groups, we get a good sense of the issues occurring at the time of the 13° Capricorn eclipse and the events that followed it.

The convergence of the Moon, Pluto and Ceres in the same natal group picture brings to mind the myth of Pluto's abduction of Persephone (Ceres' daughter). In the myth, Ceres (the mother) and Persephone (her daughter) were a tightly-bonded pair. As a young woman, Persephone had never left her mother's side. One day while picking flowers in a field, Persephone was abducted by Pluto, the God of the

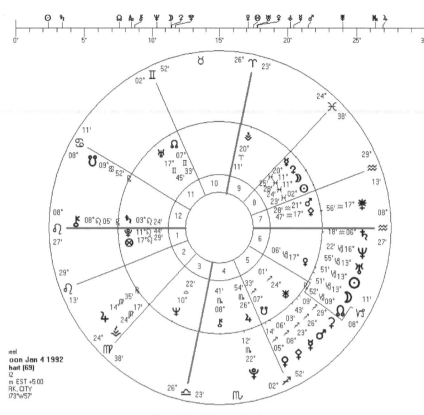

"Lady With Chicken Pox" Chart

Underworld. Pluto was older, remarkably over-powering and controlling. The separation from Persephone caused Ceres enormous grief. As the Goddess of Agriculture, her sorrow brought a withering end to the food and grain on Earth. Hence, the birth of Winter.

This client had been physically abused, betrayed and abandoned by many different characters in her life, which can be typical issues when difficult Pluto aspects are indicated. Her fear was that her husband loved her only when she was beautiful.

The above eclipse was the first phase of the process that was to change the way this woman took care of herself (Venus in Capricorn: practical love, reserved emotions). The eclipse to the woman's Ascendant and Venus brought about a desire to care for herself more lovingly and to have more loving relationships in her life.

The effect of the eclipse on the woman's Venus/Neptune/Uranus is perfectly described by the outbreak of chicken pox. The planetary combination of Venus/Neptune/Uranus is delineated as an illness (Neptune) with sudden ruptures (Uranus) of an aesthetic (Venus) nature. Chicken pox comes on suddenly and is a cosmetic disaster. Nine months later, the woman sought the services of a plastic surgeon to correct the deep scarring on her face (ASC, Venus, Uranus, Pluto) left by the chicken pox.

The decision to end the relationship was not isolated to that incident. There had been a series of abusive events over the years and she simply could not tolerate the pain any longer. This woman also suffered the loss of her mother through suicide. Her father was a prominent physician and was physically abusive to both her and her mother.

Woman With A Dream

A less complicated example of a Moon Family scenario involves a 45-year-old client who worked as a department head in an architectural firm and who had a dream on December 13, 1993.

On that date, there was a New Moon at 21° Sagittarius 23'. She dreamed she was a full-time student studying for her Masters in Management. This did not seem like a feasible notion at the time but she made note of her dream in her journal. She began tossing the idea around and imagining how her life would change with the management degree from

New Moon	First Quarter Moon	Full Moon	Last Quarter Moon
13-Dec-93	12-Sep-94	12-Jun-95	12-Mar-96
21° ♐ 23'	19° ♐29'	21° ♐ 42'	22° ♐ 25'

Moon Family Woman's Dream

her dream. Nine months later, there was a First Quarter Moon at 19° Sagittarius 29' on September 12, 1994. The woman took out a large loan and enrolled in a full-time Masters program for Management. Near the Full Moon of the same Moon Family on June 13, 1995 at 21° Sagittarius 42', she began searching for a topic for her thesis. The deadline for the thesis was on the heels of the Last Quarter Moon occurring on March 12, 1996 at 22° Sagittarius 25'.

Events of greater significance are more likely at these four major Moons. Note whether a First or Last Quarter Moon might be a member of an eclipse Family. Greater insights or acts of resolution are hidden in this Family Album. Look separately at each of the charts that are in the Family Album and with the aspects, see what the other planets are promising. You may find a way to sift through and sense the outcome of any given eclipse by reading the other charts in the family. Things may become clearer as you look for the quiet development of matters as seen in the Family of Moons and then follow them through into their resolution phase.

News Making Last Quarter Moons

An example of the importance of Quarter Moons brings to mind several Last Quarter Moon events. The terrorist attacks on September 11, 2001 occurred the day after a Last Quarter Moon. Hurricane Katrina picked up its winds to a category five status at the Last Quarter Moon on August 26, 2005. The hurricane caused the break of levees that flooded New Orleans. Pope John Paul II died on the day of a Last Quarter Moon, April 2, 2005.

By collecting the four family-members that form a Moon Family, we have a chance to see the importance of this reliable tool for personal journal work. The best part about it is that there is no need to make actual predictions. Simply identify the issue by date and locate the Family of Moons. As the Moon Phases aspect particular planets related to an issue, watch the drama unfold. The Moon Phase Family pattern will indicate the next date when these topics will resurface. This system is incredibly rich with implications and the possibilities for further research appear endless.

Using this technique of Moon Phase Families helps to develop a sense of timing as well as a grounded foundation and it has proved itself to be reliable in delineation, prediction, process identification and the timing of matters and events. Working with it, you will find it neatly complements transit, progressed and natal chart studies. Learning to work with astrology in this way – grasping the concept of the Moon's motion through cycles – gives a greater sense of appreciation that perhaps all the celestial bodies may be part of a living and breathing organism.

One of the keys to this work is to first understand the nature of each Moon Phase, its personality and the type of activity that each phase characterizes. It describes a progressive view of an issue in four major stages.

You will see how the newly-invisible planted seeds of a New Moon became visible and sprout into action when the First Quarter Moon enters the same degree and sign nine months later. The Full Moon then brings full development for all to see. The Last Quarter Moon assesses, reviews, and takes stock in preparation for the future. Each of the Phases is separated by a nine-month interval from the next.

Each lunation relates to a prior lunation at the same degree and sign. This pattern often relates to the underlying patterns in a life story. Or another way of putting it is that it offers another way to describe time. This brings to mind that there are no isolated incidents and that all things are part of a big picture. With this work, a piece of the puzzle can be found by tracing a Lunar phase back through to its origin.

These Moon Phase Families have a story of their own. The degree and sign of one Phase will be triggered to create a new chapter in an ongoing process in the next phase. This is the drama of the events which are part of our daily lives. Each event takes time to develop. For instance, a new idea is a seed planted at a New Moon or Solar Eclipse. The idea becomes tangible at the First Quarter Moon, and it will be obvious to the public at the Full Moon stage. When the Moon reaches the Last Quarter, the idea has been processed to near completion as it starts to reap the reward of its efforts or comes to a point of resolution.

You may not be an astrologer nor do you need to be one to understand and use the Lunar Gestation Cycle principals. Whether you are studying a chart or just recollecting your personal narrative, you are now equipped with a timing tool that reveals the age old adage "for everything there is a season." You will know when your story has ripened to the next major stage.

Past Present and Future Grid

Just as we collected the planets from the 30° sort to find which planets fell under the influence of the Moon phases for the Producer's chart, we will go another step to view a chart with the 30° sort in a grid of Past, Present and Future. The focus for this exercise is to pinpoint the developing impact of Eclipses and become sensitive to the shifting of focus in our storylines that occurs at the Pivoting Point New Moons three months before and after a Solar Eclipse. We will be using the *Traditional Moon Phases* tables for this exercise. By doing this we can develop a *natal forecast* of current Moon Phase trends with this Past Present and Future Grid.

Begin by drawing a grid of four columns as shown in the example on the next page.

1. Using the Traditional Moon Phases tables, collect for your grid a row of Moon phases containing a past solar eclipse that occurred approximately a year ago,
2. Followed by a recently past solar eclipse, full month of phases, that occurred approximately six months ago,
3. A New Moon month that occurs three months before the next solar eclipse which is the Pivoting Point New Moon.
4. Copy the row containing the nearest current solar eclipse with all the phases for that month,
5. Follow by the Pivoting Point New Moon three months in the future.
6. Copy the solar eclipse month three months after the Pivoting Point New Moon.

(*Note: the Pivoting Point New Moon month does not always occur three months after an eclipse as the nodes shift at a greater rate, giving the timing for the next Solar eclipse to occur in five months and not six months.*)

In the next step we learn how to create *natal planetary picture groups* by listing natal planets into the *30° Sort*. Priscilla Costello used the 30° planet sort in a lecture she gave in 1985 on eclipses at the Boston Chapter of NCGR. The 30° sort was the first tool that inspired me to organize astrological data and was a turning point in my astrology studies. I continue to use this sort with every chart consult. As extra study, I include the current planet stations and secondary progressions along with the natal planets. For now we will keep our sort simple. Here is how to create a 30° sort.

	Solar Ecl or New Moon			First Quarter Moon			Lunar Ecl or Full Moon			Last Quarter Moon		
A Year Ago Solar Eclipse Month	**Oct 13 2004**	**21°**	**♎**	**06'**	Oct 20 2004	27°	♑	51'	**Oct 28 2004**	**05°**	**♉**	**02'**	Nov 5 2004	13°	♌	09'
	Nov 12 2004	20°	♏	33'	Nov 19 2004	27°	≈	15'	Nov 26 2004	04°	II	55'	Dec 4 2004	13°	♍	14'
	Dec 11 2004	20°	♐	22'	Dec 18 2004	27°	♓	07'	Dec 26 2004	05°	♋	12'	Jan 3 2005	13°	♎	27'
hs Before Next Eclipse, Power Point New Moon	Jan 10 2005	20°	♑	21'	Jan 17 2005	27°	♈	16'	Jan 25 2005	05°	♌	34'	Feb 2 2005	13°	♏	33'
	Feb 8 2005	20°	≈	16'	Feb 15 2005	27°	♉	25'	Feb 24 2005	05°	♍	41'	Mar 3 2005	13°	♐	14'
	Mar 10 2005	19°	♓	54'	Mar 17 2005	27°	II	18'	Mar 25 2005	05°	♎	18'	Apr 1 2005	12°	♑	23'
Recently Past Solar Eclipse Month	**Apr 8 2005**	**19°**	**♈**	**06'**	Apr 16 2005	26°	♋	42'	**Apr 24 2005**	**04°**	**♏**	**20'**	May 1 2005	10°	≈	59'
	May 8 2005	17°	♉	52'	May 16 2005	25°	♌	36'	May 23 2005	02°	♐	47'	May 30 2005	09°	♓	10'
	Jun 6 2005	16°	II	16'	Jun 14 2005	24°	♍	04'	Jun 22 2005	00°	♑	51'	Jun 28 2005	07°	♈	08'
hs Before Next Eclipse, Power Point New Moon	Jul 6 2005	14°	♋	31'	Jul 14 2005	22°	♎	16'	Jul 21 2005	28°	♑	47'	Jul 27 2005	05°	♉	10'
	Aug 4 2005	12°	♌	48'	Aug 12 2005	20°	♏	28'	Aug 19 2005	26°	≈	50'	Aug 26 2005	03°	II	29'
	Sep 3 2005	11°	♍	21'	Sep 11 2005	18°	♐	50'	Sep 17 2005	25°	♓	16'	Sep 25 2005	02°	♋	18'
Nearest Solar Eclipse Month	**Oct 3 2005**	**10°**	**♎**	**19'**	Oct 10 2005	17°	♑	34'	**Oct 17 2005**	**24°**	**♈**	**13'**	Oct 24 2005	01°	♌	44'
	Nov 1 2005	09°	♏	43'	Nov 8 2005	16°	≈	46'	Nov 15 2005	23°	♉	46'	Nov 23 2005	01°	♍	43'
	Dec 1 2005	09°	♐	31'	Dec 8 2005	16°	♓	24'	Dec 15 2005	23°	II	48'	Dec 23 2005	02°	♎	05'
hs Before Next Eclipse, Power Point New Moon	Dec 30 2005	09°	♑	32'	Jan 6 2006	16°	♈	19'	Jan 14 2006	24°	♋	05'	Jan 22 2006	02°	♏	27'
	Jan 29 2006	09°	≈	32'	Feb 5 2006	16°	♉	19'	Feb 13 2006	24°	♌	20'	Feb 21 2006	02°	♐	31'
	Feb 27 2006	09°	♓	16'	Mar 6 2006	16°	II	07'	**Mar 14 2006**	**24°**	**♍**	**15'**	Mar 22 2006	02°	♑	01'
Next Future Solar Eclipse Month	**Mar 29 2006**	**08°**	**♈**	**35'**	Apr 5 2006	15°	♋	34'	Apr 13 2006	23°	♎	37'	Apr 20 2006	00°	≈	54'

Your Planetary Group Grid Will Look Like This

Personal Past, Present and Future Grid

Traditional Moon Phases Eclipses in Bold Print

	Solar Ecl or New Moon			First Quarter Moon			Lunar Ecl or Full Moon			Last Quarter Moon		
A Year Ago Solar Eclipse Month	**Oct 13 2004**	**21°**	**♎**	**06'**	Oct 20 2004	27°	♑	51'	**Oct 28 2004**	**05°**	**♉**	**02'**	Nov 5 2004	13°	♌	09'
Recently Past Solar Eclipse Month	**Apr 8 2005**	**19°**	**♈**	**06'**	Apr 16 2005	26°	♋	42'	**Apr 24 2005**	**04°**	**♏**	**20'**	May 1 2005	10°	≈	59'
Power Point New Moon	Jul 6 2005	14°	♋	31'	Jul 14 2005	22°	♎	16'	Jul 21 2005	28°	♑	47'	Jul 27 2005	05°	♉	10'
Nearest Solar Eclipse Month	**Oct 3 2005**	**10°**	**♎**	**19'**	Oct 10 2005	17°	♑	34'	**Oct 17 2005**	**24°**	**♈**	**13'**	Oct 24 2005	01°	♌	44'
Power Point New Moon	Dec 30 2005	09°	♑	32'	Jan 6 2006	16°	♈	19'	Jan 14 2006	24°	♋	05'	Jan 22 2006	02°	♏	27'
Next Future Solar Eclipse Month	**Mar 29 2006**	**08°**	**♈**	**35'**	Apr 5 2006	15°	♋	34'	Apr 13 2006	23°	♎	37'	Apr 20 2006	00°	≈	54'

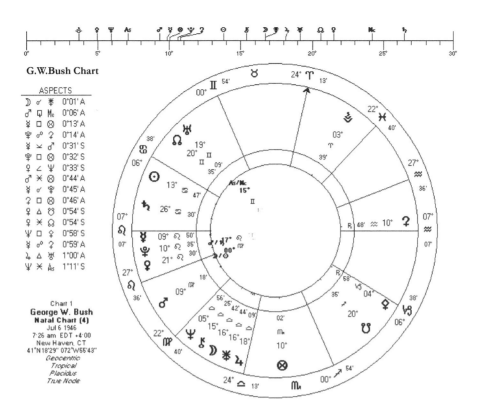

G.W.Bush Chart

ASPECTS

☽ ♂ ⚹	0°01' A	
♂ ⛢ M꜀	0°06' A	
⚷ □ ⊗	0°13' A	
♀ ☍ ♀	0°14' A	
⚷ ⚼ ♂	0°31' S	
♀ □ ⊗	0°32' S	
♀ ∠ ♆	0°33' S	
♂ ⚹ ⊗	0°44' S	
⚷ ♂ ♀	0°45' A	
♋ □ ⊗	0°46' A	
♀ △ ☊	0°54' S	
♀ ⚹ ☊	0°54' S	
♆ □ ♀	0°58' A	
⚷ ☍ ♀	0°59' A	
♃ △ ⛢	1°00' A	
♆ ⚹ As	1°11' S	

Chart 1
George W. Bush
Natal Chart (4)
Jul 6 1946
7:26 am EDT +4:00
New Haven, CT
41°N18'29" 072°W55'43"
Geocentric
Tropical
Placidus
True Node

Creating a Personal 30° Planet Sort for G.W. Bush

30° Sort	Planets & Points	
*30°& 0	Moon/Sun midpoint	
1		
2		
3		
4	⚶ ♀	Vesta, Pallas
5	♆	Neptune
6		
7	Asc	Ascendant
8		
9	♂ ☿	Mars, Mercury
10	⊗ ♇ ⚳	Part of F, Pluto, Ceres
11		
12		
13	☉	Sun
14		
15	⚷ , Asc/Mc midpoint	Chiron
16	☽ ⚵	Moon, Juno
17	Mars/Saturn Midpoint	
18	♃	Jupiter
19	⛢	Uranus
20	☊ ☋	Nodes
21	♀	Venus
22		
23		
24	Midheaven	Midheaven
25		
26	♄	Saturn
27		
28		
29		
**0 & 30		

*Use this line to insert all points at 30° - for the purpose of a solid visual grouping.

**Use this line to repeat planets and points at 0° - for the purpose of a solid visual grouping.

Your practice grid will be similar to this example. Collect your planets using a 3° orb.
(G.W. Bush chart used here.)

Personal Past, Present and Future Grid			
Traditional Moon Phases Eclipses in Bold Print			
Solar Ecl or New Moon	**First Quarter Moon**	**Lunar Ecl or Full Moon**	**Last Quarter Moon**
Oct 13 2004 21° ♎ 06'	Oct 20 2004 27° ♑ 51'	**Oct 28 2004 05° ♉ 02'**	Nov 5 2004 13° ♌ 09'
♃ ♅ ♀ ☊ Mc Cell 1	Mc ♄ ☽/☉ Cell 2	⚶ ♀ ♆,Asc Cell 3	☉ ⚷, Asc/Mc, ☽ ⚵ Cell 4
Apr 8 2005 19° ♈ 06'	Apr 16 2005 26° ♋ 42'	**Apr 24 2005 04° ♏ 20'**	May 1 2005 10° ♒ 59'
☽ ⚵ ♃ ♅ ♀ ☊ Cell 5	~~Mc ♄~~ ~~Cell 6~~	⚶ ♀ ♆ ,Asc Cell 7	Asc ♂ ☿ ⊗ ♇ ⚳ Cell 8
Jul 6 2005 14° ♋ 31'	Jul 14 2005 22° ♎ 16'	Jul 21 2005 28° ♑ 47'	Jul 27 2005 05° ♉ 10'
☉ ⚷, Asc/Mc, ☽ ⚵ Cell 9	♃ ♅ ♀ ☊ Mc ♄ Cell 10	♄ ☽/☉ Cell 11	⚶ ♀ ♆,Asc Cell 12
Oct 3 2005 10° ♎ 19'	Oct 10 2005 17° ♑ 34'	**Oct 17 2005 24° ♈ 13'**	Oct 24 2005 01° ♌ 44'
Asc ♂ ☿ ⊗ ♇ ⚳ Cell 13	⚷ Asc/Mc Cell 14	Mc, ♄ Cell 15	☽/☉ ⚶ ♀ Cell 16
Dec 30 2005 09° ♑ 32'	Jan 6 2006 16° ♈ 19'	Jan 14 2006 24° ♋ 05'	Jan 22 2006 02° ♏ 27'
♆ Asc ♂ ☿ ⊗ ♇ ⚳ Cell 17	☉ ⚷, Asc/Mc, ☽ ⚵ ♃ ♅ Cell 18	♀ Mc, ♄ Cell 19	☽/☉ ⚶ ♀ ♆ Cell 20
Mar 29 2006 08° ♈ 35'	Apr 5 2006 15° ♋ 34'	Apr 13 2006 23° ♎ 37'	Apr 20 2006 00° ♒ 54'
♆,Asc ♂ ☿ ⊗ ♇ ⚳ Cell 21	☉ ⚷, Asc/Mc, ☽ ⚵ ♃ Cell 22	☊ ♀ Mc, ♄ Cell 23	☽/☉ Cell 24

30° Sort	Planets & Points
30°& 0	☽/☉ midpoint
1	
2	
3	
4	⚶ ♀
5	♆
6	
7	Asc
8	
9	♂ ☿
10	⊗ ♇ ⚳
11	
12	
13	☉
14	
15	⚷, Asc/Mc midpoint
16	☽ ⚵
17	Mars/Saturn Midpoint
18	♃
19	♅
20	☊ ☋
21	♀
22	
23	
24	Midheaven
25	
26	♄
27	
28	
29	
0° & 30	

We will use the chart of the U.S. President George W. Bush and watch as his natal planetary groups advance through the grid from the New Moon phases through to the Last Quarter Moon phases. The current events in the US will be reflected in developing stages of the natal planetary groups. This may shed some light on the drastic conditions in this country and his administration.

Collect the planets at the degrees of each of the lunar phases and draw points under the corresponding box as we did with the producer.

Notes for the Cells in The Past, Present and Future Grid with G.W. Bush planets:
Cell 1- the MC overlaps between two different phases. This denotes strong attention brought to the career area for Bush. The October 13, 2004 solar eclipse remained as an influence during the 2004 U.S. Presidential election.

Cell 2- the MC overlap brings the Lunar Gestation Cycle New Moon from January 2004. The issues during that time would have been back on the table for Bush at this First Quarter Moon. The presence of the Moon/Sun midpoint indicates the man was taking the events very personally during the week of that Moon phase.

Cell 4 – This was the group that was under the influence of the Last Quarter Moon during the election. The Sun is his vital core, and with this president Chiron reminds me of the cowboy side of his personality. The ASC/MC midpoint shows how the surrounding events effect his entire life and all those close to him. The Moon and Juno shows his alignment with his chosen partners. This group moves under the New Moon phase (Cell 9) on his birthday.

Cell 9 – The July 6, 2005 New Moon occurred a day before the horrible London Transit Bombings where Bush was attending the Global Conference. The terrorists seemed to take advantage of Bush's presence and attention. This Moon phase created a shift in the energy from the April 8, 2005 eclipse when the world waited for Pope John Paul to pass and a new Pope was selected.

There is so much more to be said about this grid example that will have to wait, perhaps for a lecture.

Take special note when a planet drops off and others are added. Check the keyword list for the people represented by these planets. As the events in your life are reflected in stages that match the development of your natal planetary groups, you will be better prepared to step back for an objective look at the circumstances in your life and when the changes are expected.

Using the blank grids supplied in the book, add your planets for any time period of your own interest.

The planets are listed in the grid in the order they appear on 30° sort using an orb of 4°. When planets overlap into next phase, reduce the orb to 3°.

With these blank forms you can explore the activities and events in your life that correspond with natal planetary groups advancing through the grid. Have fun.

Barack Obama

Barack Hussein Obama was born August 4, 1961 at 7:24 PM (birth certificate) in Honolulu, Hawaii. A solar eclipse occurred one week after his birth, exactly conjuncting his descendant at 18°♌. His Leo Sun sits in the sixth house at 12°Leo32'. The solar eclipse at 9°♌ occurred just before the Democratic National Convention. A solar eclipse at 6°♒ occurred at Obama's inauguration. Barack Obama offers an excellent example of the ways in which eclipses mark key junctures in personal story lines.

6° Aquarius
Interestingly enough, the solar eclipse series of 6°♒ maps Obama's ascent to the White House in 2009. His story begins with very important prenatal events in the last metonic cycle near this 6th degree mark. Obama then comes into authorship of the events of his life as a new metonic cycle group rings in a promising future.

Personal Past, Present and Future Grid

Traditional Moon Phases Eclipses in Bold Print

	Solar Ecl or New Moon				First Quarter Moon				Lunar Ecl or Full Moon				Last Quarter Moon			
A Year Ago Solar Eclipse Month	**Oct 13 2004**	21°	♎	**06'**	Oct 20 2004	27°	♑	51'	**Oct 28 2004**	05°	♉	**02'**	Nov 5 2004	13°	♌	09'
Recently Past Solar Eclipse Month	**Apr 8 2005**	19°	♈	**06'**	Apr 16 2005	26°	♋	42'	**Apr 24 2005**	04°	♏	**20'**	May 1 2005	10°	♒	59'
Power Point New Moon	Jul 6 2005	14°	♋	31'	Jul 14 2005	22°	♎	16'	Jul 21 2005	28°	♑	47'	Jul 27 2005	05°	♉	10'
Nearest Solar Eclipse Month	**Oct 3 2005**	10°	♎	**19'**	Oct 10 2005	17°	♑	34'	**Oct 17 2005**	24°	♈	**13'**	Oct 24 2005	01°	♌	44'
Power Point New Moon	Dec 30 2005	09°	♑	32'	Jan 6 2006	16°	♈	19'	Jan 14 2006	24°	♋	05'	Jan 22 2006	02°	♏	27'
Next Future Solar Eclipse Month	**Mar 29 2006**	08°	♈	**35'**	Apr 5 2006	15°	♋	34'	Apr 13 2006	23°	♎	37'	Apr 20 2006	00°	♒	54'

Personal 30° Planet Sort

30° Sort	Planets & Points
30° & 0	
1	
2	
3	
4	
5	
6	
7	
8	
9	
10	
11	
12	
13	
14	
15	
16	
17	
18	
19	
20	
21	
22	
23	
24	
25	
26	
27	
28	
29	
0° & 30	

The following chronology for Barack Obama, dating back to 1963, maps key eclipse related events regarding the 6°♒ solar eclipse groups.

Solar eclipse 5°♒, 1963: Barack's mother Ann Dunham and father Bara7ck Obama, Sr. marry in Feb 1961, separate in **1963**, and divorce in 1964.

Solar eclipse 5°♒, 1982: Barack's father dies in a car crash nineteen years after the separation in **1982**. The solar eclipse at *5°♒* in 1982 was the last in that metonic cycle group. A new metonic cycle group began in 1990 at 6°♒.

Solar Eclipse 6°♒, 1990: The New York Times reported February 6, 1990, "The Harvard Law Review, generally considered the most prestigious in the country, elected the first black president in its 104-year history. The job is considered the highest student position at Harvard Law School".

Solar eclipse at 6°♒, 2009: Barack Obama is inaugurated President of the United States as the first African American to hold this office.

Solar Eclipses linked with the 19 year Metonic cycle and the related Lunar Eclipses		
Solar Eclipses	**Lunar Eclipses**	
	Jul 26 1915	02 ♒ 25
Jan 24 1925 04° ♒ 8	Jul 26 1934	02 ♒ 48
Jan 25 1944 04° ♒ 33	Jul 26 1953	03 ♒ 12
Jan 25 1963 04° ♒ 52	Jul 26 1972	03 ♒ 23
Jan 25 1982 04° ♒ 53	Jul 26 1991	03 ♒ 15

	Jul 27 1980	04 ♒ 52
Jan 26 1990 06° ♒ 35	Jul 28 1999	04 ♒ 58
Jan 26 2009 06° ♒ 30	Jul 27 2018	04 ♒ 44
Jan 26 2028 06° ♒ 11	Jul 27 2037	04 ♒ 29
Jan 26 2047 06° ♒ 0	Jul 26 2056	04 ♒ 30

A related lunar eclipse can be found nine and a half years after a solar eclipse near the same degree. This event is midway in the nineteen year metonic cycle. The complete table of metonic cycle groups of solar eclipses and their related lunar eclipses can be found in the appendix.

26° Aquarius

Obama's prenatal eclipse at 26°♒ occurred February 1961. His prenatal solar eclipse is the first of four in a nineteen year metonic cycle group near the same degree ending in 2018. A new metonic cycle group begins at the 29th degree of Aquarius eight years later in 2026. In the following table below you can see that a very important lunar eclipse occurred at 24°♒ in August 2008 when Barack was nominated as the candidate at the DNC (August 28, 2008).

Solar Eclipses linked with the 19 year Metonic cycle and the related Lunar Eclipses		
Solar Eclipses	**Lunar Eclipses**	
	Aug 17 1951	23 ≈ 25
Feb 15 1961 26° ≈ 26	Aug 17 1970	23 ≈ 49
Feb 16 1980 26° ≈ 50	Aug 17 1989	24 ≈ 12
Feb 16 1999 27° ≈ 8	Aug 16 2008	24 ≈ 21
Feb 15 2018 27° ≈ 7	Aug 17 2027	24 ≈ 11

	Aug 18 2016	25 ≈ 52
Feb 17 2026 28° ≈ 50	Aug 19 2035	25 ≈ 55
Feb 16 2045 28° ≈ 43	Aug 18 2054	25 ≈ 41
Feb 17 2064 28° ≈ 24	Aug 17 2073	25 ≈ 26
Feb 16 2083 28° ≈ 15	Aug 17 2092	25 ≈ 29

It is the 6° ≈ solar eclipse group linked by the nineteen year metonic cycle that took him to the White House, including solar eclipses at 6°≈ in 1990, 2009, 2028 and 2047.

Barack Obama's January 20, 2009 inauguration occurred six days before the solar eclipse at 6°≈30'. You can see in the Moon Family table that the eclipse degree was represented by a Full Moon at 8°≈50' on July 31, 2004; it occurred just three days after Obama gave his first public speech as the keynote speaker at the Democratic National Convention. That 2004 full Moon was a Moon family member headed by a New Moon on February 1, 2003 at 12°≈, near the time of Obama's announced run for the U.S. Senate. You can see that this New Moon in February 2003 was opposite Obama's 12° Leo Sun. His victory for that seat occurred near a last quarter Moon at 13° Leo in November 2004. That last quarter Moon in November '04 was not a Moon family member. However it acted as a trigger to the events seeded with the February 2003 New Moon.

Moon Families related to 2009 Obama Inauguration

New Moon	First Quarter Moon	Full Moon	Last Quarter Moon
Obama announced his run for US Senate. Feb-1-2003. 12° ≈ 9	1-Nov-2003 08° ≈ 19	Obama Speech at Democratic National Convention 31-Jul-2004 08° ≈ 50	1-May-2005 10° ≈ 58
			Won US Senate seat 5-Nov-2004 13° ♌ 9
This New Moon family begins three years before the 2009 eclipse. 29-Jan-2006 09° ≈ 32	It became known that Obama was considering a run for the presidency in Oct 2006. He announced his decision three months later. 29- Oct-2006 06° ≈ 19	30-Jul-2007 06° ≈ 31	After losing key states in the primaries, Hilary Clinton is pressured to drop out of race for presidency. 28-Apr-2008 08° ≈ 39
Obama Inauguration Solar Eclipse 26-Jan-2009 06° ≈ 29	26-Oct-2009 02° ≈ 44	26-Jul-2010 02° ≈ 59	25-Apr-2011 04° ≈ 34
23-Jan-2012 02° ≈ 41	22-Oct-2012 29° ♑ 8	22-Jul-2013 00° ≈ 5 22-	22 Apr-2014 02° ≈ 6
Perhaps Obama Leaves office 28-Jan-2017 08° ≈ 15	27-Oct-2017 04° ≈ 41	Lunar Eclipse 04° ≈ 44 27-Jul-2018	26-Apr-2019 06° ≈ 23

With these degree points in mind, you can now look for the approach of important events as they relate to the above calendar in the life of Barack Obama, his presidency, and the United States.

Chapter 3

The Moon Moods for Eclipses and Moon Phases

The Moon rules the unconscious mind and mundane behaviors. The Moon's sign placement influences our feelings and instinctive, routine behaviors, creating a collective mood. These moods are most heavily detected at the Moon phases. As we learned earlier, an eclipse is also a phase of the Moon. At this time, I will refer to eclipses as Moon phases.

To learn the impact of a Moon phase on your chart, begin with the sign meanings. A phase's mood or activities related to mode and sign is always extremely relevant. I find the more basic and literal the interpretations, the more accurate you can be when forecasting trends for yourself and clients. When examining any transiting Moon phase, keep in mind the initiating New Moon (which at times I refer to as the "Mother Moon") of the Lunar Gestation Cycle. If a Moon phase occurs closely in aspect to natal planets, its impact will not go unnoticed.

The following sign placement descriptions are intended to describe the collective tone or mood of an eclipse and the transiting Moon phases. *They are not intended for natal interpretation.* It's the writers intention that the energy of a transiting Moon phase or eclipse should be read as a separate entity.

Action Times
Moon phases in Cardinal Signs (♈, ♋, ♎, ♑) are action Moons. Activity is initiated, and there is a considerable amount of hope and motion in the air. Plans are being fired into action and ideas move quickly off the drawing board into action. These are enterprising, fast-moving times and they will push those who drag their heels.

With Moon phases in Aries and Libra, the focus is on relationship versus individuality. Business mergers, marriages, and divorces are high on the agenda. For those who are slow to make long-term commitments, the Aries/Libra Moon phase will help you along. On the other hand, it could facilitate the end of a hopeless relationship or filing for divorce. Legal matters are also high on the list, especially with Moon phases in Libra.

When the Moon phases are in Cancer and Capricorn, the topics are family versus career. Parents and authority figures are most frequently talked about. Family gatherings of significant size can occur with Moon phases in Cancer or Capricorn. Real estate matters and moving and changing jobs are also hot topics with Moon phases in Cancer and Capricorn. Matters of caretaking and nurturing, both of one's aging parents or one's children, are often the focus. Confidence levels of the individual are spoken of more at Cancer/Capricorn Moon Phases.

Reading the drama of any Moon phase as a standalone chart shows information regarding the potential influence on our lives.

Fixed Times

With the Moon phases in Fixed Signs (♉, ♌, ♏, ♒) the tone is too complex to be easily answered or solved. It is time to take care of business. Heavy life issues, major core process and survival skills are high on the agenda during these times. Stubborn problems are prevalent. Moon phases in fixed signs can be the most serious of all the Moon phases.

When the Moon phases are in Taurus and Scorpio, the topic is usually money. Taurus rules money and Scorpio rules other peoples' money, making money the number one topic when the Moon Phases are in these signs. Matters around tradition and property disputes are evident, as are often found with estate settlements. Topics include mortgages, investments, bounced checks and the opening and closing of accounts of all sorts. The subjects of pregnancy, birth, death, great gains or losses also come with the Moon phases in Taurus and Scorpio.

Even with the Moon in Leo and Aquarius, there are deliberate intentions concerning creative pursuits, entertainment, romance and vacations. Children are a top priority. You are more likely to have parties instead of just talking about them. These can also be serious business signs. Leo Moons are times of delegated authority and money matters. Speculation and money from parents and real estate are activated with Leo Moon phases. With the Aquarius Moon phases, partners or banks are engaged in speculation, along with concerns of money matters from business operations. This could also be a time for a greater focus on group activities. Aquarius Moons want to implement and innovate, to modernize and renovate. Individual needs are secondary to the good of all.

Changeable Times

Moon Phases in Mutable Signs (♊, ♐, ♍, ♓) are changeable times. Mutable signs all have something to do with information and its development. Gemini is the sign for the collection of information; Virgo is the sign for the organization of information; Sagittarius is the sign for the distribution of information and Pisces is the sign of the assimilation of information.

The motion associated with mutable signs brings musical chairs to mind. People are either not where you expect them to be or they seem to be everywhere at once. The need for chatter makes people more communicative but the information exchanged should be checked for accuracy since there is a lot of storytelling with mutable phases. With Moon phases in mutable signs, information is in various stages of development, from thinking, writing, and discussing, to calling and decision making. People are more mobile and flexible and they tend to visit others more freely. It is a social time.

Gemini and Sagittarius are Moon phases of the greatest amount of travel energy. Travel agents are busier than usual. You may find that people who never venture out will take short trips during these Moon phases. Vehicles could be a topic, not only as a means of transportation, but also in terms of buying vehicles. It is a time for learning something new and expanding one's awareness or just exchanging stories. The use of computers to access the "information highway" is an example of the expansion of mutable energy.

During Virgo Moon phases, the focus is on a specific task or on people at work. People become more detail-oriented and conscious of schedules. Household routines become the focus. Health maintenance and appointments at the doctor's office are more likely.

Pisces Moon phases are active with services for others involving sacrifices of some sort. The topics may be focused on addictions and struggles with indulgences. There are often strange news events, such as the group suicide of the "Heavens Gate Society" which occurred at the Pisces eclipse on March 1997. The mass suicide led by Jim Jones in 1978 also occurred with an eclipse in Pisces.

Transiting *(Non-Natal)* Moon Moods Through the Signs

This section is not designed for interpretation or natal birth charts, but rather the interpretation of patterned events in moon phase.

With a **Moon Phase in Aries,** there is a desire for change and progress, as well as a drive for a sense of purpose. An Aries Moon can create a faster-paced collective mood, hotter tempers, higher levels of confidence and a tendency to act first and think later. People tease more and tend to be noisy. Once begun, projects are soon dropped. People are less intimate in personal relationships but more likely to be sexual. "The new thing" is the order of the day, with innovative ideas arising at accelerated rates. A quick return for your efforts is the more common objective, with a lack of patience. There can be a fearlessness that allows you to charge full speed ahead without looking both ways. There are far more fires and big bangs of all sorts with this Phase. Over-enthusiasm, the salesman's hard sell and aggressiveness can irritate others.

When the **Moon is in Taurus,** there tends to be a focus on finances, and often money comes through on these days. This is the Moon of tradition, concerned with matters of the family and gatherings. "Food First" for Taurus Moons. Bonding is more apparent with loved ones. There are urges for gardening indoors or out, or just for getting more grounded. You may be carting about people or supplies. (Before automated vehicles, the bull pulled carts of supplies and people.) Taurus Moons can be lazier and more indulgent than usual. This can be a slow-moving time with no rushing about or high blood pressure.

A **Gemini Moon** brings a considerable amount of communication, more talking, more letters and calls, as well as more running around and short trips. Travel agents are busier when the Moon is in travel signs. You may find yourself trying to juggle several matters at once. Above all, information and decisions are the flavor. Don't believe everything you hear with the Moon in Gemini. Whether the information is true or false is to be determined by all other factors. People tend to act scattered and "spaced out" with split concentration during this Moon.

When the **Moon is in Cancer,** the nesting desire is greater. The "baby" side of people surfaces and emotions are highly visible. People stick to their clans and cliques and are less likely to socialize with outsiders, remaining more comfortable with close family members. Matters of saving and providing for necessities are concerns. Food preparation and shared meals are more important. Matters of real estate and patriotism are Cancer-related. Issues involving dependency or defensiveness are likely to arise with the Moon here. Very often people are "crabby." What people need for survival also takes precedence. Headlines are more dramatic than usual.

Leo Moons can be very serious when dealing with some core matters in life. Children for instance, are a subject that needs to be taken very seriously. With the **Moon in Leo,** people may want to find a party, they may want to play instead of work or there may be a more playful attitude at work. Children may be in the limelight, and love and romance in the air. A desire to take charge and direct action is common with a Leo Moon. People tend to be more demanding and they tend to be bossier. Leo is a magnetic sign, pulling your attention to all the little stages of life. The desire to present your creative work and seek applause is evident. The "show off" is characteristic of the Leo Moon.

A **Virgo Moon** puts the focus on everyday operations as well as on food, maintenance, health matters and health care providers. A desire to clean house and to organize is strong with this Moon. More attention is paid to mundane and routine tasks. It is a good time for cooperation with others. Believe it or not, sexual intrigue is used as a bartering or manipulative tool when the Moon is in Virgo. However, powers of discrimination are higher. The exaggerated discrimination of the Virgo Moon can be perceived as judgmental and picky.

When the **Moon is in Libra,** people want to cooperate or establish partnership in their activities, hashing out agreements, tending to legal matters and balancing the scales in all areas. People are more open to social activity. Matters of marriage or the marriage of ideas could very well surface. There can be indecisiveness which stands in the way of progress; however, the right decision is likely to follow. Watch for business mergers. Often, the ultimate goal of "peace at all costs" takes precedence. It is a time when people give in because they are tired of fighting.

Scorpio Moons tend to direct emotions inward. People may react to psychological slights, real or imagined. "Payback" or "getting even" can be a mode of behavior. Threats are a tactic of reaching one's objective with Moon phases in Scorpio. Often there are issues regarding other people's money or loans. Scorpio is a money sign, so there may be checks in the mail. Sexuality is on the surface. A Scorpio Moon is a powerhouse of resources. This serious Moon surprisingly has a very funny sense of humor and considers sarcasm an art form. There may be more power struggles and control freaks running loose. Watch out for the inevitable scorpion sting. Brooding and ugly behavior is a common mood with a focus on family disputes. Scorpio Moons are passionate with the object of their attention and, at times, driven to obsessive behavior. If they cannot engage the object of their desire, a period of frustration and boredom may set in because Scorpio seeks to maintain a high level of intensity. During the time when the Moon travels through the sign of Scorpio, you may become aware of information regarding pregnancies, births, deaths, estates, insurance and accounting matters. As a rule, this Moon is very good for conducting business with loans, mortgages and estates. This is not a Moon for lightweights. Know your opponent and be extremely well-prepared. If you take on a major challenge, hide any sign of weakness. A good sparring partner is sometimes what the big guy is looking for. Retail business often fairs very well during Scorpio Moons.

A **Sagittarius Moon** often brings a desire to run free, far from responsibility. Discussions can get quite philosophical and or political. Cultural events such as concerts and plays are the order of the day. People and letters from foreign places may arrive. News or progress related to advertising and publishing is likely. Religion is in the news. Attitudes are more optimistic. The "flow" is more likely to be in your favor. Directions and directives often change midstream, possibly because the grass is always greener on the other side.

Hard-working **Capricorn Moons** are dead serious about their work. The "rules" command the day. Progress and status are important. Important people that "count" are around, as well as people you can count on. Your physical appearance, political correctness, and presentation of your work are out in the open for the scrutiny of anyone in a position to make judgments. Caring about what other people *think* is often most important. The tone might be something like, "It is not as important to be happy as it is to be correct and successful." Make sure all your ducks are in a row. As a result, the pressure is great to be successful. Criticism runs high during Capricorn Moons and if you have not invited criticism as a constructive asset you could receive a blow to your confidence. This can be a time of when people are more sensitive or very "thin skinned." Capricorn can often expose matters of low self-esteem and gloomy feelings. There tends to be an emotional coldness during this time. Fathers, bosses, and authority figures are the main characters at the time of the Capricorn Moon. Architecture, big business, corporate structures and government offices are the focus.

With an **Aquarius Moon,** the unusual, brand new, and bizarre are the order of the day. It is usually a social Moon. And Aquarius rules anything alien or alienating. In Star Trek, First Officer Riker said to Captain Picard of the Star Ship Enterprise, "The unexpected *is* our normal routine." There is an expectation for everything to change, and, for some, it feels like impending doom. However, Aquarius is a fixed sign, indicating that things may not really have changed; just one's viewpoint. This in itself can be significant. The Aquarius Moon offers the possibility of a new view. Aquarius rules mirrors and tape recorders, where reflection and repetitiveness are modes of behavior. Incessant talkers are reported, debating any passing point.

A **Pisces Moon** can inspire, sympathize, or empathize. It may seek an escape, sometimes with mind-altering substances. It can be a time that seems to offer divine intervention. Strong feelings of faith combined with a need to make a spiritual connection. During this Moon, people can be overly sensitive and may feel victimized. In a water sign this moon is apt to bring water to the surface in the form of tears. On a mundane level, there may be all sorts of sneaky behavior behind the scenes. Clandestine affairs love a Pisces Moon. Intuition runs high, so trust your gut feelings. Create something poetic or stroke the day with shades of inspiration. Help someone; service and sacrifice are Pisces' middle names. Watch out for a period of self-pity.

Chapter 4

Eclipses in Concept and in History

"The sun shall be turned into darkness and the Moon into blood, before the coming of the great and awesome day of the lord." **Acts 2:20**

Some historians believe the Babylonians discovered Lunar Eclipses a few hundred years before being able to accurately predict the timing of an eclipse in the fourth century B.C. With the use of this long range prediction cycle, called the *Saros cycle*, historians are able to calculate the date and location of past eclipses and compare the information with ancient records to *fix a date* to the chronology of historical events. Documents containing accounts of eclipses became valuable markers to frame a passage in time as the ancient references rarely noted exact dates.

Historians found ancient China to have the earliest record of a Solar Eclipse. That date was fixed and given as October 22, 2134 B.C, give or take two hundred years. The story recorded in the ancient Chinese document *Shu Ching* is retold in Bryan Brewer's book *ECLIPSE, the Sun and Moon did not meet harmoniously.* He describes the woe of two royal astronomers when they failed to predict an eclipse. The common belief in China was that an eclipse was caused by an invisible dragon devouring the Sun. When warned of the up-and-coming event, archers were able to chase away the dragon by shooting arrows into the heavens at the horrific sight. Their efforts were rewarded by the return of the Sun when the eclipse ended. Unfortunately, the pair of astronomers were beheaded for their oversight. The lack of warning, I imagine, caused a lack of preparation needed to stockpile the number of arrows it must have taken to complete the task of disabling the devouring dragon.

Numerous accounts are made in history connecting the occurrence of earthquakes with eclipses. In his writing of the Peloponnesian War, Thucydides, the Greek historian, remarks that earthquakes occurred more frequently when there was an eclipse of the Sun.

Not all cultures portend an eclipse to predict disastrous events. The Eskimos and Tlingits of Arctic America currently believe an eclipse to be a divine providence. In Tahiti, an eclipse is associated with the marriage of the Sun and Moon and their disappearance is a symbol of their lovemaking.

During one's lifetime, there may be several opportunities to view an eclipse of either the Sun or the Moon. Both before and after the ability to predict an eclipse was developed, these spectacular shows instilled fear and inspired the prophecy of upcoming spiritual events. Imagine not knowing what was happening while watching the sun become a black disk, as the Moon crossed over its face leaving only a bright fringe of light. Surely this must have appeared to be the end of the sun, man's life-giving source.

The sky was a vast source of messengers. The constellations, the stars, the Sun, Moon and even the clouds were considered representative of people.

On occasion the Moon at a Lunar Eclipse can appear "blood red" as the shadow of the earth is cast over the face of the Moon and darkens it. A prophecy in the Bible reads: *"The sun shall be turned into darkness and the Moon into blood, before the coming of the great and awesome day of the lord" (Acts 2:20).*

Even though the Chinese and Babylonians had earlier knowledge of eclipse cycles, the Greek astrologer Meton was the first to write about a cycle of eclipses in his book entitled *Enneadecaterides*. Various cycles of the return of the Moon were used to define calendars. A synodic month is the time from one lunation to the next equaling 29 days, 12 hours, 44 minutes and 2.8 seconds. A Lunar return is the time it takes the Moon to return to a specific point each month.

In his book *Interpreting the Eclipses*, Carl Jansky writes that since 747 B.C. there have been reliable records of eclipses, many of which can be found in the British Museum (p. 1979). Documents have been found with details of eclipses that occurred during the reign of kings, along with lists of royal lineage. The Chaldeans made the most important discovery of the Saros cycles, which became the first accurate tool for predicting eclipses years or centuries in the future. Saros means "repetition" in Babylonia's ancient tongue. Historical records show that eclipses have often coincided with great geological changes such as earthquakes, floods and fires, along with governmental upheavals including military advances and toppled regimes. The actual eclipse path, which is the shadow cast on the earth from the Moon passing over the Sun during a Solar Eclipse, is known to attract more activity then other points on the globe during a particular eclipse season. In our personal lives, an eclipse can leave us in the wake of welcome or unwelcome news.

At least twice a year, we have the opportunity to observe the impact of an eclipse, and to note the direct astrological and geological effects left in the path of these powerful events. If you enjoy puzzles, patterns and cycles, the study of eclipses is likely to trigger a lifelong interest as the avenues of research are endless. At minimum, eclipses deliver fresh astrological information each time they occur. Current economic, political, geographical, regional and ecological trends during eclipse seasons show references to historic cycles and patterns that make for interesting studies. This study opens the door to both subjective and objective astrological research as you trace topics through the window of the Solar and Lunar Eclipses of the past, present and future.

Eclipse Cycles and Their Patterns
Solar Eclipses are found in very long cycles of 15,000 years to shorter cycles of 1,300 and very brief cycles of 57 - 76 years. Each cycle has its specific characteristics and timing.

Saros Cycle

One eclipse cycle is the Saros Cycle named after a Greek lexicographer named Suidas. The word "saros" means to be repeated. The Saros Series is a broad cycle of eclipse groups or families that extends over a period of approximately 1300 years. Each Saros Series is labeled with a number, 1 North through 19 North, and the opposite set is labeled 1 South through 19 South, for their respective North and South Pole origins.

A Saros Cycle begins as a tiny partial eclipse at the North or South Pole. Said another way, a Saros Cycle begins as a New Moon 15° to 18° from the Nodes of the Moon, qualifying as a partial eclipse at the North or South pole.

This initiating partial eclipse chart can be used to delineate the essence of an entire series of eclipses within the approximate 1300-year lifespan of that Saros Series. The series of eclipses spiral toward the earth's equator, dotting the globe with eclipses every 18 years and 9 to 11 days. Each eclipse will advance about 120° across the earth and a bit south (or north depending on its originating pole) and approximately one degree closer to the Nodal Axis. Subsequent eclipses become more total as they approach the earth's equator. After passing the equator in its trek to the opposite pole, the remaining eclipses of the series pull away from the nodes of the Moon at the same rate as in the approach, resuming a partial eclipse status throughout the end of its cycle. There are as many as 71 to 73 Solar Eclipses in each Saros Series. The extra 9 to 11 days of the 18-year cycle accounts for the 10-degree separation between zodiacal positions of each Saros series member. Since the members of a Saros cycle do not occur at the same degree, they are not as easy to spot. A table of each series in the Saros Cycle is found with the birth chart of each Saros Series in the best source for further study of the Saros Cycle: The *Eagle and the Lark* by Bernadette Brady, published by Samuel Weiser Inc., York Beach, ME. Bernadette delineates each of the initial Solar Eclipses of the Saros series as a reference that can be used to study any current eclipse series member.

Metonic Cycle

Source: Web site of the Technology Museum of Thessaloniki http://www.tmth.edu

METON OF ATHENS (fl. 5th century BC)

MATHEMETICIAN, ASTRONOMER, ENGINEER

Life

Meton was the son of Pausanias and a native of Athens (like Demosthenes, he was from the Deme of Leuconoe, between present-day Stavros and Paiania). He studied engineering and geometry (reference in Phrynichus and Aristophanes) and astronomy (reference in Theophrastus) with Phaeinus of Athens, who made astronomical observations from his observatory on Lycabettus Hill (432 BC). He is cited by Theophrastus in his "On signs of weather" and also by Vitruvius. One of the craters on the Moon has been named "Meton" in his honour. None of his written work has survived.

Work

Meton is known for the 19-year "Metonic Cycle" which he introduced into the ancient Athenian

The Metonic Cycle finds the repeat of an eclipse pattern at nearly the same degree and repeats in sets. Robin Heath explains, "This cycle is different from the Saros cycle, thus the Sun has made a return, the Moon is in the same degree of the zodiac and thus holds to the same phase with the Sun."

Robin agrees this cycle serves as a fine tool for human lifetime astrology. The Metonic Cycle consists of sets of eclipses that repeat four or five times at 19-year intervals which allows the cycle to range 76-95 years.

Try this interesting personal study: locate your prenatal eclipse (or postnatal eclipse if it was very close to your birth) within a set of Metonic Cycles that repeat at the same degree for 76-95 years. Note how mature the cycle was at your birth. Did you enter this life at the beginning, middle or end of a set of Metonic Cycles? How might that relate to events in your life? Another idea for a study would be to locate the Metonic Cycle that affects each of your planets. Note when the cycle ends or a new one begins, and record your findings related to the events in your life. When studying the chart of the United States this might prove very interesting as the cycles would have varying impacts, especially at the shift of a new cycle.

A few examples of the Metonic Cycle show four separate eclipse groups at varying lengths. Complete tables of the Metonic Cycle are available on page XIX in the appendix.

The Eclipse Families are linked by the 19-year Metonic Cycle and range over a period of 76-95 years. That is a repeat of 19 yrs, four to five times. A trick for spotting them is to read the last number of the year. For instance, if the year is 2005, search backwards by 19 years and if the year ends in six, you have a member. Said another way, view an Eclipse Family group from the bottom line up to see the last digits of the dates incline.

While working as a 900-Line Astrologer in the early nineties, I studied the call records and found four peaks in a year when the volume of callers increased, as did the urgency of their calls. Many people called with similar tones in varying phrases such as: "I just received notice of …," "Today my husband told me…," "My son just lost his job…," and "My doctor said I need…." You get the idea. I recorded the four high stress points and found their commonality: they clustered around eclipse dates. They also reflected periods in which the Sun traveled approximately 90° beyond the eclipse point at the New Moon that fell between the north and south node solar eclipse degrees. In most years the eclipses fell

♈	♉	♊	♋	♌	♍	♎	♏	♐	♑	♒	♓
1				0	0	1	1			1	1
2				1	1	2	2	2	2	2	2
3	3			2	2	3	3	3	3	3	3
4	4	4			3	4	4	4	4	4	4
5	5	5				5	5	5	5	5	5
6	6	6	6				6	6			
		7	7								
		8	8	8							8
			9	9							
			10	10	10	10					
				11	11	11				11	11
12				12	12	12	12	12	12	12	12
13	13				13	13	13	13		13	13
	14	14				14	14	14	14	14	
15	15	15					15	15	15	15	15
16	16	16				16	16			16	
	17	17	17								
		18									
		19	19	19							
			20	20							
22			21	21	21	21	21	22	21	21	22
23				22	22	22	22	23	22	22	23
24	24	25			23	23	23	24	23	23	24
25	25	26			24	24	24	25	24	24	25
	26	27	27			25	25	26	25		26
	27	28	28				26			26	
		29	29				27				

♈	♉	♊	♋	♌	♍	♎	♏	♐	♑	♒	♓
	0	0	0	0	0	0	0	0	1	2	
			1	1				1	2		
							2	2	3		3
								3	4	4	4
											5
6	7	6	6	6	6	6	6			6	6
7	8	7		7	7	7					7
8	9	8	8	8	8	8	8				8
9	10	9	9	9	9	9	9	10		6	
10		10	10	10		10	10	11			
		11					11	12	12		
							12	13	13	13	
16	16		16	16	16			14	14		14
17	17	18	17	17	17	17			15	15	
18	18	19	18	18	18	18	19			16	
19	19		19	19	19	19	20	20		17	17
	20		20	20	20	20	21	21			18
21	21	21				21	22	22	22		19
								23	23	24	
			25					24	24	25	25
	26	26		26	27	27			25	26	26
27		27	27	27	28	28			26	27	27
28	28	28	28	28	29	29				28	28
29			29	29			29				29

Examples of Metonic Cycles

Three examples of a 76 year Metonic Cycle			
Mar 28 1968	08°	♈	19
Mar 29 1987	08°	♈	18
Mar 29 2006	08°	♈	35
Mar 29 2025	08°	♈	59

Sep 22 1968	29°	♍	30
Sep 23 1987	29°	♍	34
Sep 22 2006	29°	♍	20
Sep 21 2025	29°	♍	5

Nov 2 1910	08°	♏	47
Nov 1 1929	08°	♏	36
Nov 1 1948	08°	♏	44
Nov 2 1967	09°	♏	7

Find the complete data collection of Metonic cycles in the Appendix

Three examples of a 95 year Metonic Cycle			
May 21 1993	00°	♊	32
May 20 2012	00°	♊	21
May 21 2031	00°	♊	4
May 20 2050	00°	♊	2
May 20 2069	00°	♊	19

Jun 30 1935	08°	♋	5
Jun 30 1954	08°	♋	10
Jun 30 1973	08°	♋	32
Jun 30 1992	08°	♋	56
Jul 1 2011	09°	♋	12

Jul 11 1953	18°	♋	30
Jul 10 1972	18°	♋	37
Jul 11 1991	18°	♋	59
Jul 11 2010	19°	♋	24
Jul 11 2029	19°	♋	37

six months apart, but not always. Some years, because of the travel rate of the nodes of the Moon and the location of the New Moon degrees, a solar eclipse occurs five months after the previous eclipse. Keeping in mind the more equally-divided year when the solar eclipses occur six months apart, we will first view these stress points called "Power Points of the Year," and locate the angular New Moon three months between the eclipses.

As in the illustration on this page, you can adjust this eclipse map when the next Solar Eclipse occurs five months after the last eclipse. The Pivot Point new moons are still marked at the 90° or three month intervals. Most often people are focused on a dominant story or related theme for about six months.

The six-month influence of an eclipse began to make more sense as I listened to the shift in people's stories three months prior to an eclipse, winding down three months prior to the next one. The following diagram is an example of how the year appears, using the north node and south node eclipses with the New Moons at 90° angles as virtual corner markers for a year.

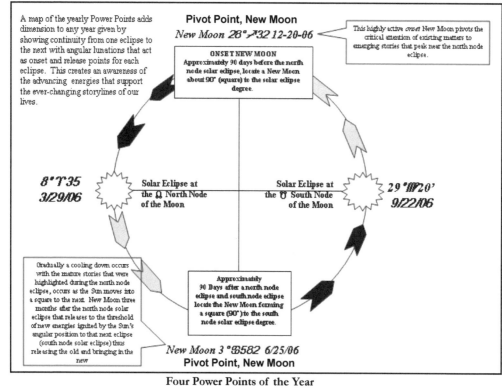

A map of the yearly Power Points adds dimension to any year given by showing continuity from one eclipse to the next with angular lunations that act as onset and release points for each eclipse. This creates an awareness of the advancing energies that support the ever-changing storylines of our lives.

Pivot Point, New Moon
New Moon 28° ♐ 32 12-20-06

ONSET NEW MOON
Approximately 90 days before the north node solar eclipse, locate a New Moon about 90° (square) to the solar eclipse degree.

This highly active *onset* New Moon pivots the critical attention of existing matters to emerging stories that peak near the north node eclipse.

8° ♈ 35
3/29/06

Solar Eclipse at the ☊ North Node of the Moon

Solar Eclipse at the ☋ South Node of the Moon

29° ♍ 20'
9/22/06

Gradually a cooling down occurs with the mature stories that were highlighted during the north node eclipse, occurs as the Sun moves into a square to the next. New Moon three months after the north node solar eclipse that releases to the threshold of new energies ignited by the Sun's angular position to that next eclipse (south node solar eclipse) thus releasing the old and bringing in the new

Approximately 90 Days after a north node eclipse and south node eclipse locate the New Moon forming a square (90°) to the south node solar eclipse degree.

New Moon 3 ° ♋ 582 6/25/06
Pivot Point, New Moon

Four Power Points of the Year

A simple example of this can be seen in the story of a client who struggled when she put her house on the market near the New Moon three months before the solar eclipse on April 8, 2005. Her broker was not showing the house, and my client was sure there was a conspiracy designed by her neighbor, a town official, to prevent her from selling this house. I assumed my client was suffering anxiety-induced paranoia, but as it turned out her fears proved to be correct. Her broker was tight with the neighbor and they feared my client would sell to someone they did not approve. Once clear about the broker and neighbor, she fired the broker and hired a new one three months later, at the time of the April 8, 2005 solar eclipse. A buyer finally put a deposit on the house six weeks after the April eclipse, and the bank closing occurred June 30, 2005. On July 5, 2005 (the day before a Pivoting Point New Moon), the client called in a relaxed state of mind, having settled into her new house with a new question. This time she wanted to know the best time to put her husband's office property on the market.

By digging into your history to test the four Power Points of a year, you will notice your storylines heat up and then cool down as new issues take precedence and the mature issues fade into the background three months before a solar eclipse. In addition, you will know when to expect matters to shift from the influences of one eclipse to the next.

These principals can be applied to news stories without the need of a chart. The symbols offered by eclipse signs clearly tell the nature of the matter. Now with two public trials of sex accusations against Michael Jackson, we reflect back to the first case, when his troubles began. There is no accurate source for Jackson's birth time, so there is no birth chart used or needed to make this point as we can observe in the dates of the developing story in Jackson's first public court case.

First, we will lay out the four Power Points in year that began with a north node solar eclipse in Scorpio, November 1993. The Scorpio symbolism leaves no mystery of the news related to a scandal regarding sexual deviance. Locating the Power Point New Moon prior to this eclipse was not a difficult task as the news broke with the accusation on August 17, 1993, the day of a Power Point New Moon. Let us look at the surrounding events, and their relationship to the four Power Points of that year.

* On August 17, 1993, the news story broke in which Michael Jackson was accused of sexually molesting a thirteen-year-old boy. This was the date of a Power Point New Moon at 24° Leo 53'.
* Three months passed. On November 13, 1993, the day of the eclipse, Pepsi (a primary source of income for Jackson) dropped Jackson's contract pending the outcome of the allegations. The solar eclipse occurred at 21° Scorpio 32'.
* News of an undisclosed out-of-court settlement surfaced in February 1994. The Power Point New Moon occurred on February 10, 1994 at 21° Aquarius 38'.
* The south node solar eclipse occurred May 10, 1994 at 19° Taurus 48'. News of Michael Jackson was entirely absent from the media. At that time, he secretly married Lisa Marie Presley. It was not till the next Power Point New Moon on August 7, 1994 at 14° Leo 38 that an announcement was made of the marriage.

The now infamous interview conducted by Martin Bashir with Michael Jackson was broadcast on February 6, 2003. The world watched Michael Jackson dangle his infant over a balcony, showing his fans his new son. Although the date of February 6, 2003 is not a Power Point New Moon, a First Quarter Moon was nearby at 20° Taurus 17' on February 9, 2003. The Sun of the First Quarter was at 20° Aquarius 17' — close to the anniversary date of the Power point New Moon on February 10, 1994, when Jackson settled the 1994 case.

Lunar Eclipses have Power Point Full Moons
Regardless of your pop culture status, by using the same principal, you can create a Lunar Eclipse Power Point map. As mentioned earlier, you can develop the eclipse cross by finding the correlating Full Moons that create 90° squares to the Lunar Eclipses.

The use of an actual chart is optional. It is the timing of the onset New Moon that is important here. Of course, there are other New Moons or Full Moons that contain strong transiting factors, like a powerful planetary station or a strong planetary configuration that will present great levels of drama. However, the yearly map provides a guide to the shifting energies that set the stage for the evolution events related to eclipses.

Special Eclipse Triggers
Imagine the eclipse degree as an address along the zodiac path. Throughout the 19-year cycle, this degree is re-visited by other notable events that reactivate the influence of an eclipse.

As we learned in Chapter One entitled "Lunar Cycles: Insight into Personal Narratives using the Lunar Gestation Cycle", any transiting Moon phase at the same degree as a solar or lunar eclipse can trigger the degree of an eclipse and awaken its influence, as well as all its drama. As we just learned, a Power Point New Moon square that same spot activates an eclipse within a 5 to 6 degree orb. Other transits will trigger an eclipse point into action too, such as the yearly return of the Sun and, at times, a monthly return of the Moon. A planetary station at an eclipse degree, occurring as much as two years prior to an eclipse, can trigger its energy and show the eclipse's earlier or later influence. I have found the strongest single event that ignites a solar or lunar eclipse is when the nodes of the Moon cross the degree of an eclipse. (We will go into this at length after we review the following points.)

The Planet First To Cross The Eclipse Point
Aside from the zodiacal sign of the eclipse, the planet first to cross the eclipse point can contribute to the dominant theme of an eclipse. Any later transiting planet passing over that point can trigger the energy of a past eclipse. Should a planet hover over the zodiacal point by a change in direction, the emphasis of that planet is stronger than the swifter transiting planet.

A Note about Eclipse Zodiacal Degrees and Secondary Progressed Planets and their Angles.
Keep a close watch on your secondary progressed planets and angles as they cross eclipse points, past and future. These events indicate some of the strongest personal events and changes of circumstances on a personal level. Along with the Solar Arc angles, I use the daily angles called the Mean Quotidian Q2 that are especially sensitive to eclipse degrees. This method of study is the focus for workshops and lectures.

Secondary progressions spring into action when an eclipse degree appears on an angle. The angle, ASC, DSC, MC and IC symbolism is activated as the progressed chart is awakened.

Some eclipses seem to have a tenacious hold on a time frame, shown by special events of transiting planets that coincide with the degree of an eclipse. These special events revive the eclipse or act as an early trigger. These triggers simply match the degree of the eclipse or create hard aspects to that point.

Most often a pair of planets captures our attention for a year or more. Such was the case of the Saturn-Pluto opposition that began their first of three oppositions: the first on August 5, 2001; the second on November 2, 2001; and the final opposition May 25, 2002. This aspect was considered a dominant transiting aspect. It became a focal point of every major event within that time period.

At the time of this writing, a parallel between Neptune and Pluto is a dominant transiting aspect. The symbolism of Neptune and Pluto can be described as deep transformation and change to land and resources as a result of water and oil. That symbolism was all-too-real on December 26, 2004, during the huge tsunami that devastated the Indian Ocean region. On August 30, 2005 the huge hurricane Katrina devastated New Orleans. The aspect recurs on January 28, 2006, and remains within orb of the parallel aspect through July 8, 2006.

When studying the eclipse season, the dominant transiting aspect adds another dimension to symbolism of an eclipse.

Here is an older example of a dominant transiting aspect. These configurations can hold the space for an eclipse degree throughout the year. This is common when the retrograde motion of planets creates multiple aspects, as with the Jupiter/Saturn square that occurred at 18° Sag/Pisces on November 11, 1995, which was also the point of the Saturn Direct Station on November 21, 1995. In this example, we located a Solar Eclipse at the same 18 degrees of Pisces on March 7, 1997. Another example was the prolonged Mars opposition to Saturn in Libra/Aries from January 9, 1997 until July 28, 1997. That opposition held the space for a set of Lunar Eclipses at 4° Aries/Libra, particularly active all year. The same 4° Libra Lunar Eclipses began getting attention from the 5° Libra Mercury Direct Station during the year before on October 14, 1995.

One vivid example of a planetary aspect that held the space for an eclipse was the Mars/Jupiter conjunction at 26° Aquarius on January 20, 1998.

This conjunction was applying its influence, though not quite exact, on January 17, 1998, the day that President Bill Clinton answered the deposition of the Paula Jones case, initiating the White House sex scandal of the relationship between Clinton and White House intern, Monica Lewinsky. There are many exciting points in this chart that are interesting to note as a stand-alone chart. For one, transiting Saturn at 14° Aries was opposite the Saturn in the US Chart.

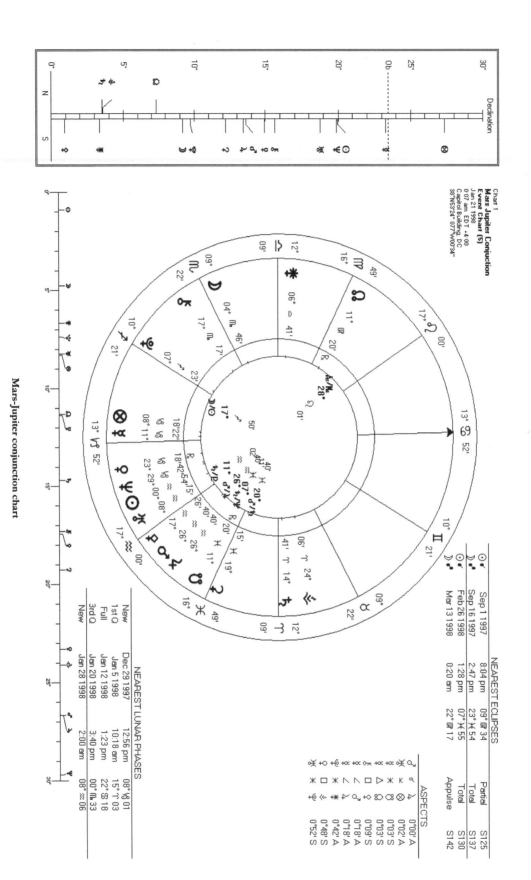

Mars-Jupiter conjunction chart

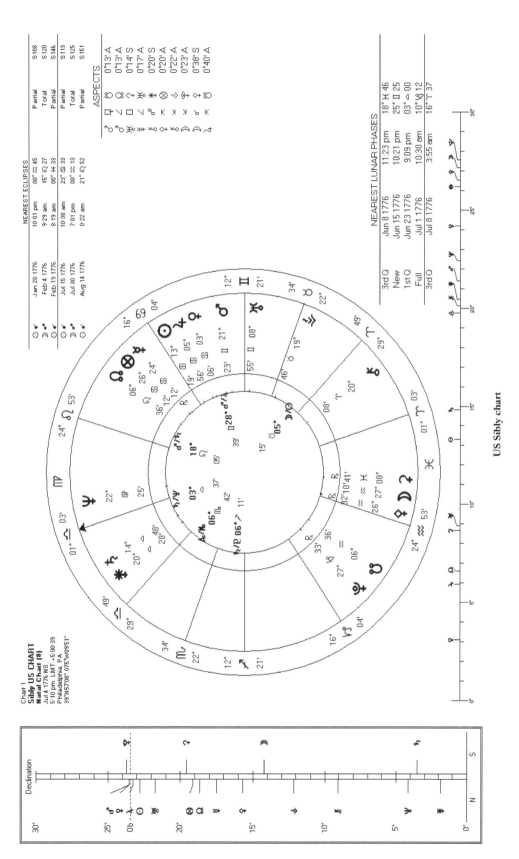

US Sibly chart

Chart 1
Sibly US CHART
Natal Chart (8)
Jul 4 1776 NS
5:10 pm LMT +5:00:39
Philadelphia, PA
39°N57'08" 075°W09'51"

NEAREST ECLIPSES

☉ ☌ ☽	Jan 20 1776	10:01 pm	00° ♒ 45	Partial
☽ ☌	Feb 4 1776	9:29 am	15° ♌ 27	Total
☉ ☌	Feb 19 1776	8:19 am	00° ♓ 33	Partial
☽ ☌	Jul 15 1776	10:38 am	23° ♋ 33	Partial
☽ ☌	Jul 30 1776	7:01 pm	08° ♒ 13	Total
☉ ☌	Aug 14 1776	0:22 am	21° ♌ 52	Partial

ASPECTS

♂ ⊡ ☿	0°13' A			S108
♃ ∠ ♅	0°13' A			S120
♅ ∠ ⊕	0°14' S			S146
♄ ∠ ♃	0°17' A			S113
♃ ☍ ⊗	0°20' S			S125
♃ ⚻ ⊗	0°20' A			S151
♀ ⚻ ⊗	0°22' A			
☽ ⚻ ♇	0°23' A			
♃ ⚺ ♇	0°38' S			
♃ ⚻ ☍	0°40' A			

NEAREST LUNAR PHASES

3rd Q	Jun 8 1776	11:23 pm	18° ♓ 46	
New	Jun 15 1776	10:21 pm	25° ♊ 25	
1st Q	Jun 23 1776	9:09 pm	03° ♎ 00	
Full	Jul 1 1776	10:30 am	10° ♑ 12	
3rd Q	Jul 8 1776	3:55 am	16° ♈ 37	

Declination

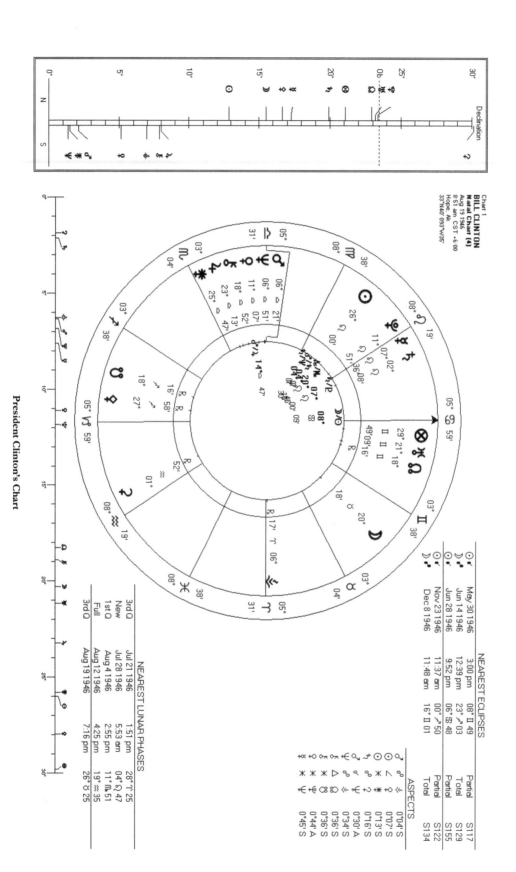

President Clinton's Chart

Eclipse and Mars - Jupiter Activity 12-92 through February 1999

Point 1	Point 2	Point 1	Point 2		Point 1	Point 2	A Few Notes Relating Events to Bill Clinton's Chart
Moon	Lunar Eclipse			Dec 9 1992	18°Ge10' D		conjunct Clintons North Node
Mars	Square	Jupiter		Jan 16 1993	14°Cn27' R	14°Li27' D	square/conjunct Clinton's Mars'Jupiter midpoint
Jupiter	Retrograde			Jan 28 1993	14°Li42' R		conjunct Clinton's Mars'Jupiter midpoint
Mars	Direct			Feb 15 1993	08°Cn41' D		conunct Clinton's Sun/Moon midpoint
Mars	Square	Jupiter		Mar 12 1993	12°Cn04' D	12°Li04' R	square/conjunct Clinton's Mars'Jupiter midpoint
Sun	Solar Eclipse			May 21 1993	00°Ge32' D		0° Gemini gives the world something to talk about
Jupiter	Direct			May 31 1993	04°Li45' D		Conjunct Clinton's Ascendant
Moon	Lunar Eclipse			Jun 4 1993	13°Sg55' D		Close to Clinton's nodes
Mars	Conjunct	Jupiter		Sep 6 1993	16°Li10' D	16°Li10' D	square/conjunct Clinton's Mars'Jupiter midpoint
Sun	Solar Eclipse			Nov 13 1993	21°Sc32' D		Square Clinton'sAsc/MC midpoint
Moon	Lunar Eclipse			Nov 29 1993	07°Ge03' D		Sextile Clinton's Mercury & Saturn/Pluto midpoint
Mars	Square	Jupiter		Feb 15 1994	14°Aq24' D	14°Sc24' D	Trine and semi-sextile Mars/Jupiter midpoint
Sun	Solar Eclipse			May 10 1994	19°Ta49' D		Conjunct Clinton's Moon
Moon	Lunar Eclipse			May 24 1994	03°Sg43' D		Trine Saturn and sextile Asc
Mars	Opposite	Jupiter		Jun 1 1994	06°Ta10' D	06°Sc10' R	Square Clinton's Mercury
Jupiter	Direct			Jul 1 1994	04°Sc46' D		Square Clinton's Saturn
Sun	Solar Eclipse			Nov 3 1994	10°Sc54' D		Square Clinton's Pluto
Moon	Lunar Eclipse			Nov 18 1994	25°Ta42' D		Square his Sun and conjunct his Moon
Mars	Retrograde			Jan 2 1995	02°Vi40' R		Conjunct Clinton's Saturn/Neptune (the weakest point in a chart) midpoint
Mars	Direct			Mar 24 1995	13°Le10' D		Conjunct Pluto
Jupiter	Retrograde			Apr 1 1995	15°Sg23' R		Conjunct Clinton's South Node
Moon	Lunar Eclipse			Apr 15 1995	25°Li04' D		Conjunct Clinton's Juno (marriage partner) It was 1995 when Monican arrived.
Sun	Solar Eclipse			Apr 29 1995	08°Ta56' D		Sextile Clinton's Sun/Mn midpoint, square Mercury & Saturn/Pluto midpoint
Mars	Square	Jupiter		Jun 13 1995	09°Vi01' D	09°Sg01' R	
Jupiter	Direct			Aug 2 1995	05°Sg32' D		Sextile Clinton's Mars-Neptune conjunciton
Moon	Lunar Eclipse			Oct 8 1995	14°Ar54' D		Opposite Clinton's Mars'Jupiter midpoint
Sun	Solar Eclipse			Oct 24 1995	00°Sc17' D		A sexy eclipse degree
Mars	Conjunct	Jupiter		Nov 15 1995	19°Sg10' D	19°Sg10' D	Square Clinton's nodes
Moon	Lunar Eclipse			Apr 3 1996	14°Li31' D		Conjunct Mars/Jupiter Midpoint & US Saturn
Mars	Square	Jupiter		Apr 15 1996	17°Ar06' D	17°Cp06' D	Square/opposite Clintons Mars/Jupiter midpoint
Sun	Solar Eclipse			Apr 17 1996	28°Ar11' D		Trine Clinton's Sun
Jupiter	Retrograde			May 4 1996	17°Cp39' R		Square Chiron
Mars	Opposite	Jupiter		Aug 7 1996	08°Cn54' D	08°Cp54' R	Conjunct-opposite Clinton's Sun/Moon midpoint
Jupiter	Direct			Sep 3 1996	07°Cp49' D		Conjunct Clinton's Sun/Moon midpoint
Moon	Lunar Eclipse			Sep 26 1996	04°Ar17' D		Opposed Clinton's Ascendant-Mars-Neptune
Sun	Solar Eclipse			Oct 12 1996	19°Li31' D		Conjunct Clinton's Chiron (another sexual indicator)

Eclipse and Mars - Jupiter Activity 12-92 through February 1999

Point 1		Point 2		Point 1	Point 2	A Few Notes Relating Events to Bill Clinton's Chart
Mars	Retrograde		Feb 5 1997	05°Li55' R		Conjunct Clinton's Ascendant-Mars-Neptune
Sun	Solar Eclipse		Mar 8 1997	18°Pi31' D		Square Clinton's nodes
Moon	Lunar Eclipse		Mar 24 1997	03°Li35' D		Conjunct Clinton's Ascendant-Mars-Neptune
Mars	Direct		Apr 27 1997	16°Vi44' D		Square Clinton's nodes
Jupiter	Retrograde		Jun 9 1997	21°Aq56' R		Opposite Clinton's Sun
Sun	Solar Eclipse		Sep 1 1997	09°Vi34' D		Opposite Clinton's Sun
Mars	Square	Jupiter	Sep 4 1997	13°Sc49' D	13°Aq49' R	
Moon	Lunar Eclipse		Sep 16 1997	23°Pi56' D		
Jupiter	Direct		Oct 8 1997	12°Aq06' D		Opposite Pluto
Mars	Conjunct	Jupiter	Jan 21 1998	26°Aq40' D	26°Aq40' D	These points oppose Clinton's Sun and are parallel on the same day.
Mars	Parallel	Jupiter	Jan 21 1998	-13°22'	-13°22'	The parallel enforces this to be a most powerful conjunction like a planetary eclipse.
Sun	Solar Eclipse		Feb 26 1998	07°Pi55' D		Opposite Pluto
Moon	Lunar Eclipse		Mar 13 1998	22°Vi23' D		
Mars	Square	Jupiter	Jul 2 1998	27°Ge41' D	27°Pi41' D	
Jupiter	Retrograde		Jul 17 1998	28°Pi04' R		
Moon	Lunar Eclipse		Aug 7 1998	15°Aq22' D		Monica Lewinsky was before the Grand Jury at this Lunar Eclipse
Sun	Solar Eclipse		Aug 21 1998	28°Le48' D		The solar eclipse conjunct Clinton's Sun.
Moon	Lunar Eclipse		Sep 6 1998	13°Pi40' D		
Mars	Opposite	Jupiter	Nov 6 1998	18°Vi14' D	18°Pi14' R	Square Clinton's nodes
Jupiter	Direct		Nov 13 1998	18°Pi10' D		Square Clinton's nodes
Moon	Lunar Eclipse		Jan 31 1999	11°Le20' D		Conjunct Pluto
Sun	Solar Eclipse		Feb 16 1999	27°Aq08' D		Opposed Clinton's Sun

Many powerful connections to the President's chart can be seen in Clinton's natal chart, best viewed as a stand-alone chart. Just a few:
* See the stunning Mars/Jupiter midpoint in Clinton's first house.
* Reference that to the U.S. Chart at the same point at 14° Libra, where you can find the US Saturn opposite the Saturn in the Mars/Jupiter chart.

Here are some simple keywords and phrases related to the Mars/Jupiter conjunction opposite President Clinton's 26° Leo Sun:
* Mars = battles
* Jupiter = legal
* Conjunction = the seed or initiation point
* Opposition = the opponent and the public view

Aquarius – the sign that opposes the center stage represented by Leo; is the view from the audience, the people.
* 26° Aquarius – opposes President Clinton's Leo Sun at 26° Leo (the executive, the star). - placing the conjunction in the 7th house from his Sun which indicates opposing energies involving a significant entity or person and can engage in battle.
* 26° Aquarius – opposes the Solar Eclipse point 28° Leo to follow in six months after the deposition.
* 26° Aquarius – conjuncts the U.S. Moon located at 27° Aquarius, seen in the chart cast for July 4,1776, 5:10 pm (known as the Sibley chart) is = the public and people of the country.

Six months later and two days before Clinton's birthday, a solar eclipse occurred on August 22, 1998 at 28° Leo 48, which opposed the January Mars/Jupiter conjunction. The Mars/Jupiter planet pair remained engaged with Clinton's chart throughout the largest drama in his life. Each time an aspect of some sort formed between Mars and Jupiter, the Clinton case showed a marked change in Clinton's favor. Even at the impeachment hearing, the midpoint of Mars/Jupiter crossed 0° Capricorn, a cardinal point called the world axis, at exactly December 15, 1998 at 4:20 PM EST. The impeachment trial ended on February 12, 1999, when the Senate acquitted Bill Clinton of perjury on a Friday afternoon. On this day the transiting Sun, at 23° Aquarius joined the Mars-Jupiter conjunction of '98.

Many interesting events between the Mars/Jupiter pair set the soap opera stage beginning with the Clinton Inauguration in January 1993 and beyond. Nearly every aspect and planetary station involving Mars and Jupiter involved Clinton's chart. Clinton's Mars/Jupiter midpoint is conjunct the U.S. Saturn. Many of the solar and lunar eclipses involve the following, just to note a few and some ideas of how I use them.

* Sun: attracts personal attention.
* Moon: home, wife, interaction with women.
* Sun/Moon midpoint: a marriage point and male-female integration point that is in the high profile position at his Midheaven.
* Ascendant: personal, involves the self and alters your image.

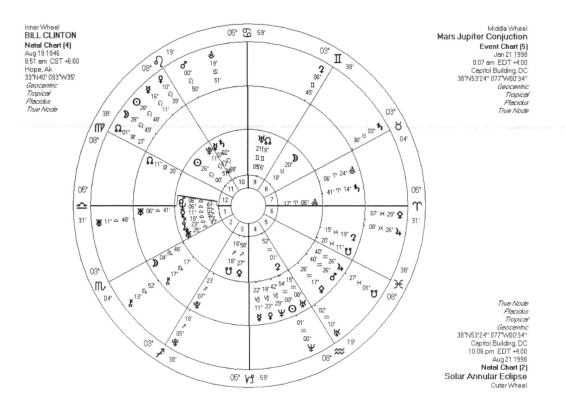

Inner Wheel
BILL CLINTON
Natal Chart (4)
Aug 19 1946
8:51 am CST +6:00
Hope, Ak
33°N40' 093°W35'
Geocentric
Tropical
Placidus
True Node

Middle Wheel
Mars Jupiter Conjunction
Event Chart (5)
Jan 21 1998
0:07 am EDT +4:00
Capitol Building, DC
38°N53'24" 077°W00'34"
Geocentric
Tropical
Placidus
True Node

True Node
Placidus
Tropical
Geocentric
38°N53'24" 077°W00'34"
Capitol Building, DC
10:06 pm EDT +4:00
Aug 21 1998
Natal Chart (2)
Solar Annular Eclipse
Outer Wheel

* Ascendant/MC midpoint: the toggle switch of your chart; when activated, affects every house in your chart.
* His nodes of the moon: the point where your personal actions and activities are joined with others, merged with the public forum (similar to the MC), and engaged with your private world (similar to the IC).
* His First House Mars/Jupiter Midpoint: where one engages in battle or business ventures. An exaggerated sex drive.
* Mercury: meetings, gossip.
* Saturn/Pluto midpoint: point where deep structural change occurs.

.

Transiting Nodes of the Moon Triggers Eclipses

The Moon and each planet have their own north and south nodes. The nodes of the Moon are the markers for the location of the eclipses. The nodes are the points at which eclipses take place. Nodes have a collective quality that relates to "Moon," as the Moon represents the people as well as a general mood, or what we are all doing now. Sign symbolism speaks its loudest at the Moon's nodes. When the Moon's nodes travel through a sign, and they do so in a retrograde direction, for 18 months, we all draw on the energy of that sign and get a strong dose of the symbolism, especially when an eclipse occurs.

We are aware that the nodes of the Moon are points where the Moon crosses from north to south along the celestial equator, thus the "north marker" or "south marker." When the Moon crosses one of its nodes, at minimum, emotions rise; and news events heat up often because people are in a reactionary mode of behavior. Human and animals are more sensitive. This point needs clarity because frequently we drop the Moon's reference to "the nodes" and consequently fragment the foundation of their symbolism. In astrology, symbolism is attached to everything that moves, circles, aligns, aspects and more. The nodes of the Moon have been an elusive subject in astrology for years. I began to get a grip on their symbolism when I first realized that they are intersection points. And of course, that means something. I think of an intersection of two roads crossing, with travelers from various directions that meet for a moment at one spot. Some people turn on to a new road. Others continue on their path.

Beyond this clarification, I experienced an epiphany about the nodes of the Moon when watching the most spectacular Leonid Meteor Showers in years, on November 18, 2002. The meteors are named Leonid, and they appear to shoot from the constellation of Leo. On that night, the meteors were rapidly streaking across the sky by hundreds an hour. The visual range in the sky was broader than other meteor showers, making this a truly special event. The Leonid Showers always occur in November but when I realized the Sun was approaching the transiting nodes of the Moon, it became clear to me why we had this wide-angle view of the showers. There would be a solar eclipse in sixteen days. The close proximity of the Sun to the Moon's nodes not only is the formula for an eclipse when the Moon reaches the Sun, but it widens our view of the heavens, bringing our visual range of the universe closer to earth.

This wide-angle symbolism applies to the interpretation of the nodes of the Moon. Therefore when there is activity around the Moon's nodes, expect exaggerated and magnified events, like the spectacular Leonid Showers of 2002. The symbolism of planets when crossing the Moon's nodes in any chart inflates and brings special attention to these planets. In a natal chart the individual may possess special talents or triggers related to the basic symbolism of the planet. Greatly consider the sign, as that is amplified as well. When the transiting Moon's nodes cross a sensitive point such as an eclipse degree, a past, present or future planet station degree, or even a Moon phase degree, events will become more pronounced, such as when a car accident becomes a 100-car pile-up, etc.

Expect your world to invite experiences through a wide opening. Imagine yourself opening a standard-size door to your home. Then imagine how, when the Moon's nodes cross a sensitive point, your door can widen to the size of the Mississippi River. Your experiences speed up and the numbers of opportunities or other events increase and begin to rapidly flow in.

The transiting nodal axis holds the most important focus. These nodes are extremely sensitive points in any chart. In my work, the nodes are given the closest attention in natal, progressed or transit charts. The nodes of the Moon are a focal point of study in transit and in horoscopes, providing important clues to personality sketches and health matters. They also offer clues to the coming or going of major personal relationships, and major life-changing events that often become public knowledge. This usually occurs when activated by an eclipse, which also indicates your natal nodes of the Moon have returned or oppose the natal position. The transiting nodes of the Moon trigger eclipses when they pass over the degree of a solar or lunar eclipse. The transiting Node of the Moon can be found passing over the degree of an eclipse as early as 7 to 8 months before or as late as 7 to 8 months after the actual date of an eclipse. I found it to be one of the strongest triggers of an eclipse. It can bring a preview or review of the influence of the eclipse.

The first and second week of December 1996 provided a vivid example of the transiting node in action. It crossed over the point of the preceding Lunar Eclipse of September 26, 1996 at 4° Aries 17' and it caused a lot of attention. A couple of my clients literally showed up at my door unannounced in a state of crisis. Many called regarding the same issues we had spoken of at the Lunar Eclipse in September.

Brief Examples:

* A man whose birthday is September 26th was in the process of dividing a business with his partner. The split was moving along amicably but slowly until December 17, 1996, when his partner had him arrested.

* A new family of three had just finished building their house in Maine. They were at a Christmas party on December 18, 1996. When they came home, they found their house had burned to the ground.

* Two partners had a major blow-up that precipitated the end of their business together on December 18, 1996.

The transiting nodes, also, prove to be very good timing tools. They are worth closer observation. More research is needed, because there is not an abundance of material written about them.

What an Eclipse Means to You,
Published by the Boston Chapter of the National Council of Geocosmic Research Fall Issue 2003.
Some Exciting Eclipse Triggers
The Transiting Node Triggers the Eclipse Point
by Dietrech J. Pessin

The transiting lunar nodes conjoin an eclipse point either before or after the eclipse actually occurs, creating a hot time period for newsmaking events. None of the following events occurred on eclipse dates but they all have one thing in common: their stories began within days of the lunar nodes crossing an eclipse point. (Both the true node and the mean node are considered.) For example:
* August 14, 2003: the largest electrical blackout in North American history
* March 20, 2003: the U.S. invaded Iraq
* October 7, 2001: the first strike of the War on Terrorism began with the bombing of Afghanistan
* September 11, 2001: the World Trade Center attack
* November 25, 1999: the rescue of the Cuban youngster, Elian Gonzalez, on Thanksgiving Day

These events scream for an astrological connection. If we look for the relationship between eclipse points and transiting nodes, the above events break down this way.

* The Iraq war began with the true node at 1°14' Sagittarius a full eight months before the November 23, 2003 Solar Eclipse at the same degree.
* The huge Eastern U.S. electricity blackout and the murder of pedophile priest John Geoghan in a Leominster, Massachusetts prison occurred in August 2003 when the transiting nodes crossed the November 19, 2002 Lunar Eclipse at 27°33' Taurus and the May 16, 2003 Lunar Eclipse at 24° 53' Scorpio
* A Solar Eclipse took place on December 25, 2000 at 4°14' Capricorn; the World Trade Center's twin towers were destroyed when the transiting node reached that degree eight and a half months later
* The official War on Terror began in Afghanistan on October 7, 2001 when the transiting node reached the June 21, 2001 Solar Eclipse point of 0°10' Cancer.
* The rescue of tiny Elian Gonzalez occurred seven months before the 8 Leo Solar Eclipse of July 31, 2000 with the transiting node conjunct that degree.

The eclipse table that follows is divided in the middle with Solar Eclipses on the left and Lunar Eclipses on the right. Each has three columns: the eclipse date, the eclipse position, and the date the lunar node transits the eclipse point.

Make a note of what your experiences were around November 8, 2003 - events like phone calls, new people, social settings, unexpressed desires, the voice in the head that starts as a whisper and keeps getting louder, etc. *These things may come right to the foreground* when the node reaches 16 Taurus on February 4, 2004. The 14 Scorpio Lunar Eclipse in May 2004 will also be triggered in February 2004. This is similar to the Lunar Eclipse triggered by the nodal transits last August 2003 which created a high level of activity.

For those of us not in the news, think back to March 2003 to connect the stories in your life to the time period of the Solar Eclipse of November 2003. You may have had very dramatic changes that occurred in March 2003 and you may be getting a handle on what turned your life upside down from back then. They don't have to be major events. Here are few examples;

* My current website was created in March 2003 and evolved to subscription status in November 2003.
* A friend discovered her son was ill in March 2003. The entire year was consumed with his treatments, all of which failed until the week before the November eclipse.
* A client had become aware of an infringement of his software product by a well-known company. He began legal proceedings at the time of the fall eclipse.

Solar Eclipses			|| Lunar Eclipses		
Eclipse Date	Eclipse Position	Node reaches eclipse point	|| Eclipse Date	Eclipse Position	Node reaches eclipse point
11-Aug-99	18Le21	1-May-99	|| 28-Jul-99	04Aq58	6-Dec-99
5-Feb-00	16Aq02	26-May-99	|| 21-Jan-00	00Le26	6-Apr-00
1-Jul-00	10Cn14	7-Apr-01	||		
31-Jul-00	08Le12	5-Nov-99	|| 16-Jul-00	24Cp19	18-Aug-00
25-Dec-00	04Sg14	2-Sep-01	|| 9-Jan-01	19Cn39	15-Oct-00
21-Jul-01	00Cn10	Oct 07 2001	|| 5-Jul-01	13Cp39	1-Mar-01
14-Dec-01	22Sg56	12-Mar-02	|| 30-Dec-01	08Cn48	22-Apr-01
10-Jun-02	19Ge54	10-Apr-02	|| 26-May-02	05Sg04	15-Feb-03
			|| 24-Jun-02	03Cp11	9-Sep-01
4-Dec-02	11Sg58	20-Sep-02	|| 20-Dec-02	27Ta33	20-Jul-03
31-May-03	09Ge20	20-Oct-02	|| 16-May-03	24Sc53	17-Aug-03
23-Nov-03	01Sg14	23-Mar-03	|| 9-Nov-03	16Ta13	4-Feb-04
19-Apr-04	29Ar49	26-Dec-04	|| 4-May-04	14Sc42	17-Feb-04
14-Oct-04	21Li06	9-Jun-05	|| 28-Oct-04	05Ta02	15-Aug-04
8-Apr-05	19Ar06	4-Jul-05	|| 24-Apr-05	04Sc20	19-Aug-04
3-Oct-05	10Li19	18-Dec-05	|| 17-Oct-05	24Ar13	21-Feb-05

There is probably a list of your own events that come to mind for this eclipse season and now you may realize that those events have been in progress since last March. You can now look forward to the next eclipse trigger that will further develop your fall 2003 eclipse stories, next August 2004 with a First Quarter Moon at 1° Sagittarius.

Moon phases at 45° angles from a Solar Eclipse as with the Full Moon that occurs six weeks prior to a Solar Eclipse and the Full Moon occurring six weeks following a Solar Eclipse will prove eventful. Additionally, it's important to remember that the phases of the Moon trigger eclipse points.

The Phases of the Moon Trigger Eclipse Points: A Powerful Grip On History
Published to Lunar-Shadows.com, March 2003, by Dietrech Pessin

Over the past two-and-a-quarter years, the United States has experienced some of the most stunning events in its recent history. This story begins with the presidential race in the fall of 2000, following a series of events that connect to the current Last Quarter Moon on March 24, 2003.
Setting the stage for the 2000 election, we look back to Christmas of 1992, when both periods had a common theme. There was a Solar Eclipse (also referred to as a New Moon) on Christmas Eve at 2° Capricorn, when George H. Bush was leaving office with the matter of Saddam Hussein unfinished and a major source of regret. The stage was set to replay this scenario the next time a Solar Eclipse would occur early in Capricorn on Christmas of 2000. Gore and Bush were locked in the biggest U.S. political drama in over one hundred years, awaiting a decision from the Supreme Court, as to who would be president.

The election of 2000 is reminiscent of another strange presidential election when a candidate lost the election after winning the popular vote in 1888. One source notes that President Benjamin Harrison gained his political progress from what was tagged as "Republican trickery and vote buying to defeat Cleveland." Grover Cleveland actually won the popular vote but lost the election when the Electoral College decided to close the election. The eclipse for that election occurred at 11' Capricorn. Four years later, Cleveland ran again and won the election.

The events of the Capricorn Solar Eclipse in December, 2000 are relatively typical in their timing, as the impact of an eclipse has a "hot zone," which generally occurs 11 to 18 days before and/or after the actual eclipse date and follows through into the future for at least two-and-a-quarter years. The two-and-a-quarter year timeframe is divided up into four nine-month periods. During this time, subsequent related Moon phases – the First Quarter Moon, the Full Moon and the Last Quarter Moon – are found to occur after a Solar Eclipse (New Moon). In the "Lunar Gestation Cycle," the subsequent Moon phases all contact the eclipse degree at these nine-month intervals. The Lunar Gestation Cycle follows the thread of a story as the related events, at each subsequent Moon phase, set the stage for the evolution of the original story. This example is noted when nine months after the December 12, 2000 decision to select Bush as president, this country suffered the devastating loss on September 11, 2001.

Close by was the First Quarter Moon at 1° Capricorn on September 24, 2001, which was related to the Solar Eclipse of December 2000. Following along the same thread is a Moon Family member, nine months later, in June 2002, which was a Full Moon, the Lunar Eclipse at 3° Capricorn. At that time there was a major military buildup and the campaign for war with Iraq became the primary focus of the Bush administration. Then, five days before the March 24, 2003 Last Quarter Moon at 4° Capricorn, we actively engaged in a war in Iraq.

The theme that follows through this Lunar Gestation Cycle may be relatively transparent. The timing may seem uncanny but perfectly logical when related to the pattern found within the Lunar Gestation Cycle, making the timing of these events as predictable as connecting-the-dots:

Cycle of Events in Lunar Gestation Cycle

Solar Eclipse
12/25/00 04°14′ Capricorn — President Bush was selected within days of the Christmas Eclipse of 2000 on December 12, 2000 at 9:54 pm, and the U.S. Supreme Court ruling allowed George Bush to become president.

First Quarter Moon
09/24/01 01°24′ Capricorn — Nine months later a First Quarter Moon at 1°24' Capricorn occurred in September 2001, just after the devastating World Trade Center attack.

Lunar Eclipse
06/24/02 03°12′ Capricorn — Nine months after that, in June2002, the president was desperately trying to sell his war campaign at the time of the Full Moon at 3°11' Capricorn. It was during this time when the now famous Downing Street Memo revealed the plan for war was prearranged.

Last Quarter Moon
03/25/03 04°00′ Capricorn — The president was finally successful nine months later and the war began - a total of two and a quarter years from the time of the December 2000 Solar Eclipse,. It was just days before the Last Quarter Moon at 4°00' Capricorn on March 24, 2003.

At the point during the Last Quarter Moon in March 2003, the *transiting south node triggered* the eclipse point at 1°14' Sagittarius, the exact point of the fall 2003 Solar Eclipse.

Note: Saddam Hussein was captured on December 13, 2003, three years after the Supreme Court ruling that led to the selection of George W. Bush for President.

Practice These Techniques with Your Charts.

Along with your natal chart apply these techniques to your progressed charts (secondary and solar arc progressions), and your solar return chart. Use Composite and Relationship charts or any event chart such as a wedding chart, house purchase chart, opening of business chart, etc.

* Look for dominant transiting aspects applying to your charts.
* Add the power-point New Moons and eclipse degrees into your chart.
* Cast an individual chart for the moment the node crosses the eclipse point and compare to your chart.
* Cast charts for all four phases in the Lunar Gestation Cycle to see which are activating your planets.

Have fun finding the significant clues for what an eclipse means to you.

Chapter 5
Solar Eclipses

The North Node Solar Eclipse

On occasion two Solar Eclipses will occur six months apart in close opposition to one another, one at the North Node of the Moon and the other at the south node of the Moon. For example the Solar Eclipse at 28° Leo in the summer of '98 followed by the Solar Eclipse at 27° Aquarius in the winter of '99. This pairing will signal a long, pointed focus of issues and a time of very long proceedings. A North Node Solar Eclipse is a New Moon at the North Node (N.N.) of the Moon. The North Node Solar Eclipse represents the beginning of major life issues, ones that are concerned with our identity, ego and physical body because of the reference to first house symbolism. This would include matters concerning personal freedom and space. This eclipse could present matters that require immediate attention. It initiates issues concerning the self that highlight a "me" principle. There is an individual quality to a N. N. Solar Eclipse that may have you deeply involved in matters that revolve around a single objective. At the time of a N. N. Solar Eclipse, you may be working alone or enthusiastically involved with a great new venture. This eclipse's orientation is enterprising and impacts by delivering the beginning of something new.

North Node Solar Eclipse Through The Signs And Houses

The following are brief ideas about the impact of the North Node Solar Eclipse through the signs:

Aries or First House: This eclipse can bring a focus on personal beginnings. There can be attention to your overall health, body building or cosmetic surgery. Independence may be the theme and sometimes relationships can be difficult to maintain at this time, with the increased potential for aggression, resentments and pioneering urges. This may be a learning period about your personality. You may feel identified with a mission or an important cause. You may grapple with gender issues or want a totally new outlook for your life.

Taurus or Second House: This may bring a major focus on money, matters of material possessions, acquisitions and evaluation of personal assets. If you are not concerned with material details, this eclipse may increase your involvement with management of money or stocks and bonds. If your spending habits have been an issue, this eclipse can bring about a change of habits. How you earn money may change. You may begin earning a living doing what you love. You may focus on your personal value system in an important way. You may actually feel more loved and appreciated. Your worth can increase both psychologically and on paper. You may become involved with gardening in a major way.

Gemini or Third House: Communication, short distance travel, transportation, siblings, and neighbor and neighborhoods are the dominant matters during a N. N. Solar Eclipse in Gemini or the third house. This could bring a period of increased short trips, visitors, visiting and errands. Your attention could be set on a sibling or neighbor. Mercury's influence on Gemini puts the focus of this eclipse on neighborhood. This could lead to a major relocation, such as moving across the country or moving "out on your own" for the first time. There is more paperwork than usual. You may feel compelled to write. You could be the subject of someone's article that may or may not lead to publication. Gemini eclipses have an abundance of nervous energy and will often produce anxiety. Your personal perspective may be heightened in regard to how you make decisions. You could receive an important message that proves to be a piece to a puzzle you have been looking for. One way or another, the importance of information and how you proceed with the facts can be the focus of this eclipse.

Cancer or Fourth House: With an eclipse in Cancer or the fourth house, matters of the home, real estate, nurturing, parents, and personal boundaries are the issue. You could make a major move, or buy or sell a house. Or you could even begin a career change due to the accent on the 4th and 10th House axis. The family as a clan and its history may move into the foreground. You could discover new family information or dig into your genealogy. You could embark on a journey of self-discovery into the roots of your being. You may establish, reestablish or break family bonds.

Leo or Fifth House: With an eclipse here, your time may be devoted to children. Your creative efforts could turn into something more important. Your love life could be highlighted, energizing the house that rules play. Taking vacations could be the theme in this time period. Money could be gained from real estate or parents. Creative enterprises of all kinds are emphasized. Matters of the heart become central. An eclipse in the fifth house activates gambling and speculation, or places these issues are expressed or addressed.

Virgo or Sixth House: The N. N. Solar Eclipse here will cause the greatest amount of change in the general routine maintenance of home, office and vehicles. There will be a focus on food, all aspects of health care maintenance, daily routines, schedules and habitual patterns. Jobs could change, or major shifts could happen in routine tasks, job routines, coworkers and unions. There can be a serious change in the way you get along with workers and employees. Food is always a concern of this house. Your diet or tastes may change drastically. Pets and their needs are important now. A burst of physical energy may assist in much attention being placed on home repairs. There is more patience for details in daily living. You may create more organized space in home and office, or you could begin a new type of service for others.

Libra or Seventh House: This is the house of partnerships. Marriage does not always occur, but often it does, especially if the ruler of the seventh house is favorably indicated. You may find there are shifts or struggles with your very closest friends. Or you may find a powerful tie with someone new. Your roommates may change or they could get married. This eclipse brings new energy into your social circle. Legal matters begin with an eclipse in Libra or in the seventh house.

Scorpio or Eighth House: If you have been waiting for estate settlements or money from legal matters, this eclipse can produce needed activity in these areas. Insurance matters are the concern of this house. You may also find a way to repair a poor credit line with this eclipse. Your partners may be settling their money debts and putting long overdue obligations to rest. Very often, the issues of this house are expressed psychologically. This could be a time of total transformation. Pregnancy, fertility and childbirth can be a focus. You could be experiencing feelings of abandonment or issues of being robbed emotionally. Changes in the ideas or behavior of your sexuality could occur with this eclipse. A major violation of your trust might be the issue with an eclipse in Scorpio or your eighth house. An obsessive relationship could begin with an eclipse in this house.

Sagittarius or Ninth House: This can mean a whole shift in your cultural orientation. You may become involved with people whose culture is foreign to you. One or more long journeys may occur. An eclipse in the ninth house broadens one's perspective. If you want something published, this is the time. Your sibling's mate could be the focus of an important change that you get drawn into. Politics could begin to play a role in your life. One of the most significant things that may happen is a marked increase in your need for space and freedom.

Capricorn or Tenth House: This is an eclipse that brings attention to your greatest goals. This is a time when you may work your hardest on a career objective. Or it could be a time when you are recognized for your accomplishments in your career, moving you ahead. There may be issues pertaining to the boss or the company where you work. If you are the boss, there still may be matters to deal with regarding authority figures or organization. Proper presentation and your outer image become incredibly important. If the ruler of this house receives difficult aspects, there could be an extended period of time without a job when you might be paralyzed with a fear of failure. You may find yourself at the head of your family in some way, perhaps making decisions for an elderly family member or becoming their primary caretaker. You may have your mind on a home of your own, but you'll still have to wait for a New Moon or an eclipse in your Fourth House.

Aquarius or Eleventh House: More often than not, people become involved in some sort of group at this time. You may be drawn to participate in community efforts. Stepchildren or the mate of your child can be the focus. A grown child may move into his or her own home or bring home a friend to stay for an extended period of time. Matters around the topic of alienation are likely; you may feel alien to your family, friends and coworkers or you may find that your "acting out" behavior alienates those around you.

Pisces or Twelfth House: Visits to the hospital could be on the agenda with this eclipse. Someone from the past may resurface and create a problem. I have seen people find their soul mate with an eclipse in their twelfth house. Relationships have a simpatico bonding style when begun under this eclipse. There are often issues around substance abuse. There could be a focus on poetry and dreams of visits to the Orient. This could be the start of a whole new mystical study. A study of your self and the inner relationship you have with yourself is a good way to use the energy of this eclipse. For those who suffer from long-term depression, an eclipse here may bring them out of isolation, through medication or other methods. This eclipse could provide much-needed downtime for doing work behind the scenes. This can be one of the more inspiring eclipse positions.

South Node Solar Eclipse

A South Node Solar Eclipse is a New Moon at the South Node of the Moon. At a South Node (S. N.) Solar Eclipse, the influence is still focused on beginnings but from a seventh house perspective. It initiates issues with relationships and engages a mate, partner, roommate or any other significant person in your affairs. The essence of this eclipse brings great importance to the new things you do with others, or things that are old and familiar. Its impact is likely to leave you with an entirely new perspective based on powerful interactions with others. Unlike the N. N. Solar Eclipse whose presentation is the "me" perspective, the S. N. Solar Eclipse has a "we" orientation. The impact of this eclipse stimulates a heightened level of the individual's awareness because external influences are projected onto you. The "ball" is in another person's "court." You are the receiver, not the server. You may find yourself responding to the demands of others and unable to find time for your own needs.

This eclipse invites you to become more social and integrated with society as a whole. There can be a "coming out" quality to the S. N. Solar Eclipse, related to the various house placements. This eclipse could be experienced as a clearing-away time, making way for the more positive events coming to you during the North Node eclipse six months later. This could also be a time of distancing and separation. You may also be involved in a clean-up process, or you could separate from situations that are no longer working in your life.

Matters needing compromise and debate are more likely to progress at a South Node eclipse. Health concerns are focused on the "significant other," although eclipses are famous for bringing any health matter to the surface. This may also be the case with an eclipse in aspect to the Sun, Moon, Nodes, Ascendant or Mars.

The South Node Solar Eclipse puts matters out of your reach or in someone else's "court." Investigate how the South Node Solar Eclipse aspects your significant other's chart, to indicate how your needs are being perceived. It will be their objective or perspective that puts the matter in your court. You don't have to be a partner to be a significant other. This can be a best friend, an opponent in a legal battle or the opposite party in any number of scenarios.

An example of this comes to mind with a woman who was the legal heir to an estate, expecting the matter to be settled in a matter of days. Then, a distant relative from the "old country" received word of "Uncle Harry's" passing and filed a claim to the estate. The "ball" was then out of the woman's "court" and under the control of others.

A South Node Solar Eclipse brings public exposure. Information tends to be uncovered and the facts come out into the open. If you are not ready to have your activities in public view, then don't talk about them. On the other hand, if you do want to get noticed, find a way to put your talents or ideas out in the open by advertising, writing a book, singing in public or branching out in your business. The high visibility quality with this eclipse could give needed publicity. People seem less focused on their personal problems at this time, and deal with life with a broader, more objective perspective. This is not a time of isolation, as people will find themselves pulled into the dramas of others. One's actions are related to the outer world or they become obvious to the outer world.

The following is a gruesome example of how a South Node Solar Eclipse brought a very isolated individual right out into the open.

On July 23, 1991, Jeffrey Dahmer's last victim escaped and ran stark naked through the streets of the city, screaming that Dahmer was trying to kill him. When police finally entered Dahmer's apartment, they were horrified to find the body parts of eleven men. A South Node Solar Eclipse on July 11, 1991 at 18° Cancer 59' fell in the killer's ninth house only four degrees from a conjunction to Dahmer's Midheaven at 23° Cancer 15'. The Midheaven is the most public point in your chart and it is a place of public recognition. It is often labeled the point of fame or failure. Dahmer's retrograde Saturn, located in the third house at 17° Capricorn 58, was opposed by the eclipse. Saturn is the planet of responsibility. The Solar Eclipse in opposition to Dahmer's Saturn placed the pressure outside Dahmer's control. A Lunar Eclipse at 3° Aquarius 16 that occurred just after Dahmer's arrest on July 26, 1991, was quincunx his Pluto (ruling death) at 3:36 Virgo.

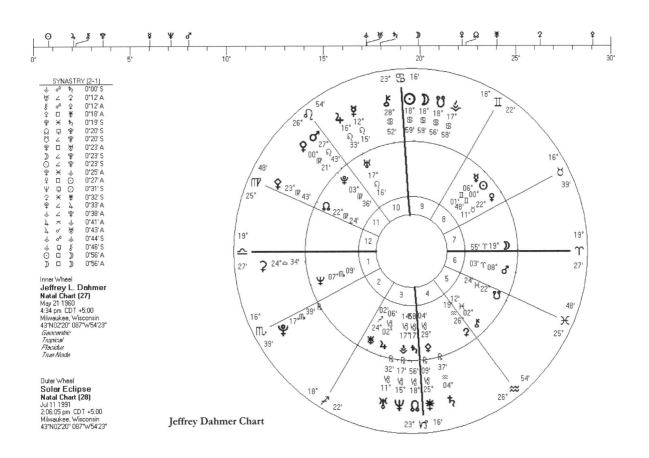

Jeffrey Dahmer Chart

South Node Solar Eclipse Through the Signs and Houses
The following are brief ideas about the impact of a South Node Solar Eclipse through the signs:

Aries or First House: You may discover a more holistic approach to self-care of body, mind and spirit because this is a time when a new approach to old physical conditions become available. It is an excellent time to experiment with homeopathic remedies, because you may notice a heightened sensitivity to physical responses. Since this is a time that engages the attention of others. your mate may be focused on your physical fitness. This would be a good time to employ a body-building trainer and nutritionist. Stress reduction techniques such as massage, stretching, acupuncture and regular exercise are very effective at this time. There is a side to this S. N. Solar Eclipse that can give one a strong desire to be free of all commitments, or your partner may be initiating freedom. This eclipse could be a time when you may experience some powerful education about your behaviors in relationships.

Taurus or Second House: Here, issues of finances and self-worth become the focus of your partner or significant other. Your personal possessions may become the property of another, such as when settling disputes of movable property from a terminated relationship. A mentor may encourage you to use your talents, leading to a change in the way you earn your money. You may receive outside confirmation of the value of your talents.

Gemini or Third House: This S. N. Solar Eclipse in Gemini or the third house has a strong focus on shared information or gossip. Any traveling back and forth is more likely to be done in pairs. Any decisions made become joint affairs and relationships could be tested on the basis of failure to honor one's word. Learning to be clear in how things are said may be the greatest lesson learned from this eclipse. Basic transportation issues are higher on the list where someone else is involved, such as a new car, or a car that may be owned by someone else. For example: a man without a car moved in to his girlfriend's house on the South Node Solar Eclipse in Gemini. At first, the woman enjoyed feeling generous by letting her boyfriend use her car, but eventually she resented the inconvenience it caused her. The boyfriend took advantage of her generosity, creating a situation which eventually led to the breakup of the relationship.

There could be a focus on the neighborhood or its deterioration. Problems with siblings and their mates or partnerships may surface. A sibling could get married or make a noticeable change in his or her career, or might be in the news or get a big career break. There may be a marked change in the way your mate relates to your siblings. Often, there is much more paperwork than usual, and this time it is directly concerned with someone else's matters. An important piece of information that could involve a significant other alters your relationship.

Cancer or Fourth House: This eclipse could pull you out of your safe environment and create a reason to move to a totally new area. There might be a series of moves instead of just one big one. Personal boundary issues may become very clear with a S. N. Solar Eclipse here. For example, a woman moved from New York to Boston with a South Node Solar Eclipse in her fourth house on her Mercury to follow a boyfriend. Another woman moved from Boston to Texas with a South Node eclipse in her fourth house in hopes of better career opportunities. And another young woman inherited $10,000 from her grandfather. She spent the money building a loft in a very temporary apartment she didn't own.

Leo or Fifth House: Romance may go sour with this eclipse or maybe you just see things clearly for the first time and realize that the relationship is not what you wanted. An old love from the past could return. Sometimes, it becomes clear a child's performance in school is off. A child could receive special attention or be brought into the public eye. You may let go of a hobby and regret it later. Vacations could be difficult, but they could also bring you close to someone.

Virgo or Sixth House: With this S. N. Solar Eclipse, coworker problems or unions are the focus. During this period, pets tend to be a major concern or expense. For example: With the S. N. Solar Eclipse in a woman's sixth house, she experienced a serious car accident at the time of a major relationship crisis. Her doctor insisted this relationship battle affected her judgment when driving. At the same time, her cat was trapped for two weeks in the foundation under her apartment building before it was freed. You may be forced to deal with chronic health issues, or to develop a new routine health maintenance program. Obsessive, compulsive habits can be broken at this time. The sixth house can be mentally disturbing. For example, family members prompted a man to enter a recovery program for substance abuse. He then began a structured program for mental and physical health maintenance.

Libra or Seventh House: The eclipse in Libra or the seventh house puts the focus on marriage, separation, divorce, partnership, your closest friend, legal affairs, or major social events and your social environment. Lawsuits begun at a S. N. Solar Eclipse could go on for long periods of time. You may feel forced into a lawsuit. The type of people you have been attracted to in the past may change. You may let go of an old social circle and seek out new people. There is a greater likelihood of long, involved disputes with mates and your best friends.

Scorpio or Eighth House: Since this is the house of death, sex, taxes, and other people's money the S.N. Solar Eclipse can bring new ways of helping you to work with others in these areas. Sometimes mortgages or bank loans become too difficult to manage and bankruptcy can occur with this eclipse. There can be a shared or lost inheritance, or a major change can occur concerning shared resources. A deep bonding with another could occur, or the sexual aspect of your relationship could significantly change. The birth of a child could transform a relationship. You may deal with old abandonment issues or engage in psychotherapy.

Sagittarius or Ninth House: You or your mate or a close personal relationship may undergo a major shift in philosophical or religious views. You could drop classes or education programs. You could change your major in college, or change colleges or return to or replace a guru. Foreign travel could become frequent due to a mate or career interests abroad. While traveling you may be dependent on a host. You may feel a greater need for space or may perceive a loss of freedom. You could be the focus of a news story or article. When publishing at this time, others may have too much control over your work. Make careful decisions when advertising.

Capricorn or Tenth House: Eclipses in the tenth house of Capricorn focus on small or big business structures, heads of company, immediate bosses, career, parents, active goals, reputation, credibility and projected image presentation. Changes in career direction or a shift in your career role may be the result of pressures from a significant other. For example, a woman left her job to stay home with her four-year-old child. Her irresponsible husband had not contributed to the household up to this point. Her decision changed her daily routine and his, as he then began working to support the family. In another example, a chiropractor opened her own office due to the unfair practices of her partner. She became worried about making ends meet and considered taking a new partner. The old business partner continued to be a source of her stress. You may find your boss's relationships are at the center of your attention. The company you work for may be undergoing reorganizations or change as a result of partnership agreements.

Matters of real estate as a business involving others are typical with this eclipse. For example, a woman had a S.N. Solar Eclipse in her tenth house. Her realtor/boyfriend encouraged her to purchase rental property. She knew nothing about property management and was dependent on the boyfriend's knowledge. Their relationship collapsed and the boyfriend easily and illegally manipulated the property from the woman seven years later. Parents' homes may have a legal complication or there may be concerns for their health with the S.N. Solar Eclipse in Capricorn or the tenth house.

Aquarius or Eleventh House: A S.N. Solar Eclipse in the eleventh house or Aquarius stimulates areas of acquaintances (one's closest friends are seventh house people), long-range plans, group associations and community participation all with the involvement of a significant other. Grown children who have moved away may come back home with partners. Children could have legal problems. This area is also likely to activate matters regarding adopted, foster or stepchildren with the involvement of a significant other. For example, a S.N. Solar Eclipse occurred in a woman's eleventh house and she made a serious attempt to adopt a girl. The girl had been adopted and in the custody of the woman's sister. The sister did not want the child any longer and had been abusive to the child. Social services decided to remove the child from the reach of the entire family.

Your circle of friends may change drastically, possibly due to marriage or a change regarding your closest friend. You may resign your position in a group, where there could be power struggles within the group.

Pisces or Twelfth House: With an eclipse in the twelfth house or Pisces can come a time of hard-to-diagnose health matters or prolonged illness, confusion and escapism. Circumstances involving isolation, substance abuse, art or music can be a focus. You may need to deal with matters that appear to be unexplained or strange situations. In the following example, a woman's estranged mother moved into her neighborhood from 400 miles away. The upset woman moved and changed her name to escape involvement with her emotionally-disturbed mother. Here's another example: a man had been ill and took his small son on a train trip. They experienced many strange encounters along the way, and there was a point of danger on the trip when the man became disoriented and lost his direction in a dangerous section of the city. The confused and vulnerable man attracted the concern of a couple who took the pair in for the night. Later, he said the incident allowed him to see how the safety of his son had been threatened by his illness.

Solar Eclipses To Natal Planets

An eclipse in aspect to your planets will not only trigger topics ruled by the planets, but also activates the matters pertaining to the house the planet rules. For instance, if the eclipse is conjunct your Venus, the matters of relationships, women, love and money are triggered. Locate the house cusps ruled by Venus (Taurus and Libra) because they are the ones activated. Consider the sign in which the eclipse occurs with regard to the kinds of activities that are common to that sign. For example, if the eclipse occurs in Virgo, there is an overall theme of work and health maintenance. The planet aspected by the eclipse may describe the "who" component of the work. For instance, a Virgo (work) eclipse (major change) aspected a woman's Sun (her environment and a primary male), and it was conjunct her Venus (love, gifts and money). Her limited funds did not cover the estimated cost of the work needed in her home. Her boyfriend generously donated his carpentry labor.

Sun

With an eclipse to the Sun or the house it rules, the greatest changes can occur in your life. The Sun represents the positive and masculine nature of your identity and the radiation of your personality. This Sun rules your vitality, outlook, ego, creative essence and self-expression. The Sun has a strong influence on your appearance, as well as a strong influence on your career direction. Activity to the Sun can reveal concerns of your bosses and the company for which you work. If you are self-employed, the Sun represents your business. For a man or a woman, the primary male characters in your life (husbands, brothers and father) are represented by the Sun. An eclipse in aspect to the natal Sun can be a major turning point in life. A N.N. Solar Eclipse can bring the focus to your core identity, vitality and your physical body. Your career or your bosses may undergo major changes in your workplace. A Solar Eclipse conjunct the Sun in a woman's chart can signify a major change of career and residence and, sometimes, marriage – all at the same time.

Example: A N.N. Solar Eclipse occurred October 24, 1995 at 0° Scorpio 18' conjoined to Hillary Clinton's Sun at 2° Scorpio 43. Clinton's actions fell under investigation after firing several employees in what was dubbed "Travelgate," thus making her the first "First Lady" to be subpoenaed. Her Sun had been under the influence of a Solar Eclipse on May 22, 1993. At that time, a S.N. Solar Eclipse was at 0° Gemini 31' (gossip, open information) quincunx (out of the blue) her Sun (career, important male figures) at 2° Scorpio 43'(death & taxes). She and her husband came under extreme scrutiny just before the death of their life-long friend Vincent Foster in July of 1993. The White Water Investigation was initiated around the death of Foster, and investigation of a stock investment that earned the Clinton's $100,000. Mrs. Clinton's activities in her law firm were also investigated.

A S.N. Solar Eclipse on December 4, 1983 at 11° Sagittarius 47' brought a pair of Scorpios together, both with Sagittarius Ascendants. With the eclipse conjunct their Ascendants, they married six months after the Sagittarius eclipse. You might think they would have been a perfect match, but they struggled for many years to make the relationship work. The October 24, 1995 eclipse at 0° Scorpio 18' was conjunct the woman's Sun and it brought an end to the marriage. The woman had met her second in the spring of '95 and they were married May 1996.

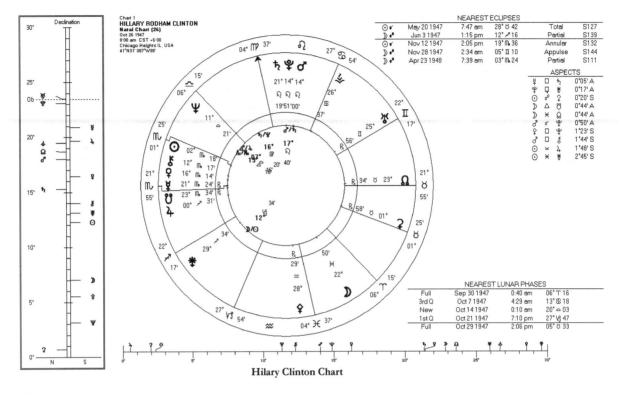

Hilary Clinton Chart

Moon

With an eclipse to one's Moon and the house it rules, the home and family structure can be affected. The Moon represents how you feel, what you need to feel secure, and your softer and receptive nature. An eclipse in aspect to your Moon can activate matters regarding babies, nurturing, automatic behaviors and habits. An eclipse's impact can bring attention to your brain, brain power, memories and psychological design. The Moon is an indicator of the important women in your life, such as wives, sisters and mother. The Moon rules the sign of Cancer. An eclipse in aspect to the Moon can bring changes in residence, accommodations and domestic preferences. Eclipses to the Moon can change matters of safety, security, and currency, and there could be fluctuations in finances. Catering, mothering or mothers can be a theme with an eclipse in aspect to the Moon.

In a man's chart, the Moon represents matters concerning his marriage partner as well as his mother and sisters. For a woman, the focus can be on mother, sisters and closest female friends. Relationships in general can be the issue, as with an eclipse on the Moon. The Moon is responsible for one-on-one relationships. The Moon is the Sun's mate and the symbol of male and female interaction. Example: a man experienced a Solar Eclipse at 0° Gemini conjunct his Moon 29° Taurus 9' and Nadir on May 21, 1993. He ended a ten-year relationship with a woman that had been very angry and non-productive for a long time. They both felt that they had stayed in the relationship beyond its end. They shared ownership of a condominium that held them together, but felt they could find no way to build a traditional Taurus future. He wanted children, and she did not. As another example, a woman experienced a S.N. Solar Eclipse at

7° Virgo 48' conjunct her Moon at 3° Virgo. She inherited a large piece of undeveloped land in Maine from her grandmother. (Grandparents are found on the first and seventh houses.) She began building a vacation spot on the land.

Mercury

An eclipse to Mercury or the houses it rules can bring much excitement and extremely big changes in your life. Mercury's rulership of neighborhoods often activates changes of a major relocation. Leaving home for the first time also falls into the realm of an eclipse to Mercury. I have seen many examples of people making moves across the country or to another country entirely. Animals may also be important themes. We also know that Mercury rules people, such as children, aunts and uncles. Many people reported losing their mother with a Solar or Lunar Eclipse to their Mercury. Two examples: Britain's Prince William lost his mother the day the Solar Eclipse at 8°Virgo squared his 8°Gemini Mercury. The same eclipse was conjunct Prince Harry's 5° Virgo Mercury and sharply squared his 9° Sagittarius Uranus. A Lunar Eclipse two weeks later occurred the day before Harry's birthday, nearly his solar return.

Activities such as running back and forth to the eye doctor, doctor, dentist, mechanic, shops and hardware stores for yourself or someone you are caring for are also featured. With an eclipse to Mercury, significant introductions can later bring about a change in relationship activity. Mercury's primary role as the ruler of information and communication can initiate important written material, instigate gossip, or publish your name in headlines. Ruminating and worrying about important decisions is common, as is a heavy schedule with many appointments and a great deal of paper shuffling.

As an example, looking again at Hillary Rodham Clinton's chart, there was an eclipse on November 13, 1993 at 21° Scorpio 32'. This was conjunct Mrs. Clinton's Mercury at 21° Scorpio 19'. The exhaustive questioning (ruled by Mercury) began covering various matters three months prior to the eclipse, which would have been near the Power Point New Moons we discussed earlier. There were many references to paperwork that Mrs. Clinton had to produce and explain. The Last Quarter Moon that occurred at 22° Scorpio 55' on February 12, 1996 belongs to the November 13, 1993 eclipse. At that time, Mrs. Clinton was ordered to "put in writing" (Mercury), her account of the Travelgate firings. In another example, a young Aquarius woman with Virgo rising and Mercury at 16° Capricorn 09' in the fourth house lived a fast life in New York City, when she and her best friend decided to pack it all in for a more sensible lifestyle in Boston. The big decision came about when a Solar Eclipse fell in her fourth house conjunct her Mercury on January 4, 1992 at 13° Capricorn 51'. Six months later, she met her husband-to-be in Boston. Eclipses that aspect Mercury can indicate a particularly big move, as well as important introductions. For example, a woman with her Mercury at 12° Scorpio 54 in the fourth house relocated to Texas from Boston just after the eclipse on November 3, 1994 at 10° Scorpio 54'. She later moved back when the eclipse at 0° Scorpio 18' occurred exactly conjunct her IC on October 24, 1995. Another client had an eclipse on her Mercury at 24° Virgo in her third house. She spent six months tending to routine check-ups, not only for herself but for her aging mother. She also adopted two great big gorgeous cats and bought a new car. In anothr example, a woman whose Mercury opposed a S.N. Solar Eclipse point was hired to write an article that was never published. When the Sun traveled around the zodiac to conjoin her Mercury, she received a "kill" fee for the article.

Venus

An eclipse on your Venus or the house it rules may or may not stimulate your love life. It does impact your closest personal relationships. You may find your value system is challenged in some way. You could develop sensitivities or cravings. Some make esthetic changes to their appearance, especially if Uranus is involved. This aspect might bring a focus on adornments and dressing up or changing one's style of dress. There is a desire for harmony, beauty and happiness in the territory of Venus. Venus also rules how we relate to others and share our worldly goods and affections. Pleasing others and cooperation are major Venus topics. Art, money and major purchases for the home are some areas that could change as a result of an eclipse to Venus, as are matters concerning young women and sisters. A man's idealized version of woman is his Venus. Look to Venus for a change in social activity, since the power of attraction and one's popularity can be altered by an eclipse aspected to Venus.

In actual case studies of eclipses conjunct Venus, there were more people splitting up in relationships than joining together. There was an overall theme of people being forced to have harmony and balance in their lives even if it meant ending a primary relationships or partnerships. Relationships that were not working either ended, or the couple totally changed the way they lived in their relationship. Many relationships with constant turmoil and struggle can be relationships that are working for them. Evaluation of the outcome of a relationship is a tedious task. Many couples work through their apparently impassable problems. I never advise a client to marry or split up. I don't consider it my job to make major life decisions for anyone but myself.

For example, a Capricorn woman, the mother of two young children, left her husband just after her own father died. The woman did not have much to do with her parents while the father was alive, but upon his death she left her home in New England. Taking her children with her, the woman stayed with her mother on a beautiful coastal area in New Jersey. It was to be a two-week visit to help her mother through a tough period, but the Capricorn woman decided to take the opportunity to end her troubled marriage. The woman's Capricorn Venus was conjoined with the eclipse at 13° Capricorn 51' on January 4, 1992. The husband lost contact with his small children and went through a long court battle for visitation rights.

Mars

An eclipse to Mars can be a real mixed bag of events. On the one hand, you could be making great headway with goals and career efforts. An eclipse to Mars can also bring a new job, because it rules how you apply your energy as well as courage, endurance, battles, competition, assertiveness, action and sex. Some might think that an eclipse on Mars would increase sexuality and sex life. I have found that in many cases, the effect of an eclipse to Mars actually has the opposite effect. Some people experience an eclipse to Mars as dramatic, while others find it has only mundane or mildly annoying effects. In all cases, the planetary aspects of the actual eclipse chart must be considered when evaluating the impact an eclipse will have on Mars, or on any other planet for that matter.

With an eclipse to Mars, you could find yourself fighting every cold and flu that comes along. It is not

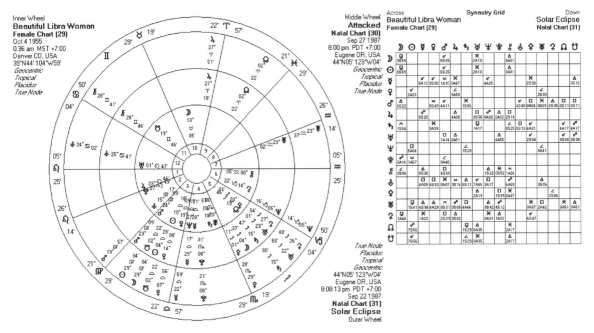

Inner Wheel
Beautiful Libra Woman
Female Chart (29)
Oct 4 1955
0:36 am MST +7:00
Denver CO, USA
39°N44' 104°W59'
Geocentric
Tropical
Placidus
True Node

Middle Wheel
Attacked
Natal Chart (30)
Sep 27 1987
8:00 pm PDT +7:00
Eugene OR, USA
44°N05' 123°W04'
Geocentric
Tropical
Placidus
True Node

Across
Beautiful Libra Woman
Female Chart (29)

Synastry Grid

Down
Solar Eclipse
Natal Chart (31)

True Node
Placidus
Tropical
Geocentric
44°N05' 123°W04'
8:08:13 pm PDT +7:00
Sep 22 1987
Natal Chart (31)
Solar Eclipse
Outer Wheel

uncommon with this aspect to have an over-abundance of energy that leaves you open to injury. Most times this eclipse advances your career or creates a job change. You may find yourself in a new creative vein.

Sometimes, an eclipse to Mars can bring violence if the natal chart has a predisposition to such. The next chart is an example of the eclipse at 29° Virgo, September 1987 that had a violent impact on a beautiful Libra woman. Her Mars at 24° Virgo 8' in her third house (ruler of short-distance travel) was the focus. It was just five days after the eclipse, and one week before her birthday, that this Libra woman was attacked while riding her bicycle home from the library. She sustained injuries mostly to her head and face, and was treated with several surgical procedures. The chart of the eclipse had many difficult aspects to the woman's chart. The transiting planets are very descriptive of the attack, since transiting Uranus was square her natal Mars, along with eclipse Mars conjunct her Mars and square her natal Nodes. The personal planets (☉, ☿, ♀ and ♂) of the eclipse chart activated her own personal planets as they each neared their natal returns.

The eclipse point at 29° Virgo 34' made a sesqui-square aspect to her Moon in the tenth house, creating a period of emotional distress, relationship problems and unease at home. This was expressed as her attacker parked himself on her doorstep after she returned from the hospital. Obviously, she did not feel safe. Also, her mate spent most of his hours away from the house because he could not deal with the extent of her trauma. This set of circumstances led to the end of the relationship.

The synastry grid shows the aspects from the solar eclipse to this woman's natal chart. This kind of bombardment from an eclipse suggests a need for caution. Most natal charts do not suffer such a heavy attack. This is an example of what the old astrology books considered "affliction." The accompanying grid shows the many major aspects from the eclipse planets, and several minor aspects that are more difficult to spot with the eye.

The woman had no insurance and was wiped out financially by her medical bills. This is partially explained by transiting Saturn (blocks and restrictions) square her natal Vesta (ruler of insurance) in her second house of money. Neptune quincunx her Ascendant created a case of mistaken identity to which major adjustments had to be made. The police assumed she was the girlfriend of the leader of the gang that had beat her, and they refused to be of any assistance; the crime went unpunished. The woman practiced a great process of forgiveness to release her rage around this nightmarish event.

In another example, another woman with Sun in Scorpio, Ascendant in Cancer, and Midheaven in Aries had a car accident within weeks of an eclipse that had formed a sextile to her Mars. Her Mars at 2° Virgo 51' sat close to the cusp of her third house at 4° Virgo 11. She too had injuries to the head and face, as well as short-term memory loss and dizziness, but she had no long-term complications. Also, in yet another example, a Libra Woman with Aquarius rising has Mars at 29° Libra conjunct her Scorpio Midheaven. The eclipse on October 24, 1995 at 0° Scorpio 18' was conjunct her Mars. She was sick with colds and viruses from August of that year (at the Power Point New Moon) through January of 1996. It was suspected that the woman's workplace was harboring a contaminant of some sort, since many workers had been sick far more than usual. In addition, this woman and her boyfriend battled over the direction their relationship was taking, after being together for nine years. It was finally agreed that they would get married in the spring of 1997.

Jupiter

Eclipses on Jupiter, or the house it rules, expand your social environment and bring you a sense of freedom. Several clients who had been feeling trapped in dead-end relationships got their chance for freedom with an eclipse to their Jupiter. Another individual had an eclipse on their Jupiter in the seventh house and actually met the man who would be her husband at that time. Others were brought out socially. Travel is definitely one of the benefits with an eclipse on Jupiter. Educational pursuits both large and small are very likely. Try advertising your talents or business. Publishing and publishers are prominent at the time of an eclipse on Jupiter. A religious experience or a change in religion could occur with an eclipse in aspect to Jupiter. Extreme emotional highs and lows are found with an eclipse to Jupiter. In some cases, there were people who were diagnosed with a manic depressive disorder. For some, legal matters were experienced with this eclipse.

Saturn

Contrary to popular belief about Saturn, I see a lot of positive effects of an eclipse to Saturn or the house it rules, especially with a N.N. Solar Eclipse. This is not to say that the reputation for hard times and struggle is unfounded. It can be a time of reward for your efforts. The work you have been doing, up until the time of an eclipse to your Saturn, now has the chance to be acknowledged. Consider it like a job review. If you have done a good job, you will get a good review and maybe even a raise in pay.

An eclipse in aspect to Saturn can put you in touch with your debts. Very often, people manage money problems more efficiently when their Saturn is involved at the eclipse. At the very least, they can get more serious about finances and work harder to lessen financial burdens. Work situations may come along that support better management of time and money. Heavy decisions regarding the responsibility of older family members are common with this eclipse. One could expect to assume greater responsibility on the job in your particular field. You may be asked to lend your expertise to a club or organization or you could be brought into a position of honor or recognition. If your deeds fall short of actual reward, you may find yourself answering to higher authorities.

An example of an eclipse conjunct a man's Saturn on November 3, 1994 gave him the ability to confront his irresponsible spending habits, since he had been living beyond his means most of his life. He hired a manager to help maintain control over his finances and stopped using his credit cards. His heavy Scorpio Saturn was conjunct the Nadir and ruled his Capricorn Moon.

Uranus

An eclipse to Uranus, or the house it rules, can bring an interesting and exciting six months. Clients describe eclipses with Uranus as giving them the feeling of great change, although often without external manifestation unless it comes much later. It can be a time of uneasiness and accelerated expectations. Uranus does rule astrologers and the study of astrology. Major changes in one's appearance are very often the case with Uranus aspected by the eclipse. Plastic surgery or large weight shifts have been noted with several of my clients. Often the desire to create security is thwarted by a constant change of events. It seems all areas of one's life are unpredictable, and the individual is searching for changes that will make his or her life work. This time period is much too unstable to try to nail things down. Relationships with others are most affected. People find themselves unable to make commitments at this time. If one is already involved in a relationship, one might experience annoying upsets and shifts in sentiment. Look for unique opportunities at the time of this eclipse. Naturally, the placement of one's Uranus will have a great influence on the types of events that arise.

The example found in the accompanying chart brought many changes from a series of eclipses to a Virgo woman who we will call Sara. Sara's natal Venus was unfavorably wedged between Saturn and Neptune and square to Uranus in Cancer. On July 11, 1991, a Solar Eclipse at 18° Cancer 59' made a conjunction to the ruler of her fourth house cusp, Uranus. Her father died. Sara and her brother became heirs of a small house. Her brother immediately took possession of the house with his wife and two children. (Saturn is the ruler

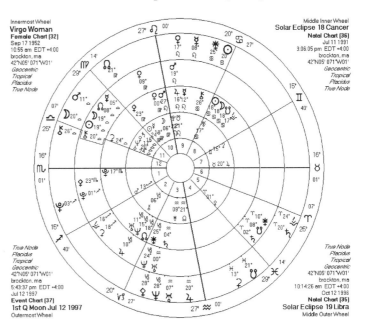

of the third house of siblings.) Sara was unable to remove her brother and to add insult to injury, the IRS seized any proceeds of her portion of the house. Sara and her mate owned a business that incurred the tax problems. She was not rid of her eighth house problems when a N.N. Solar Eclipse on October 24, 1995, 0° Scorpio 18' brought the IRS to Sara's door demanding back taxes (Scorpio, Pluto and the eighth house rules taxes and the IRS). That eclipse occurred in her twelfth house of hidden enemies and contacted Sara's Mars, perched on the cusp of her second house of money matters, with a semi-square. (A semi-square is labeled a minor aspect, a term not to be confused with its major impact.) All the natal aspects formed by natal Mars would then be activated. Natal Mars is sextile to Sara's eleventh house stellium in Libra with the Venus Saturn conjunction that then squared natal Uranus in the eighth house. There were signs of the IRS threatening her as early as two years prior, when a N. N. Solar Eclipse at 21° Scorpio 32' squared her Pluto near the Midheaven. Ignoring all warnings, she failed to secure her finances and suffered a loss of salary when the IRS garnished her wages in October 1996. The Solar Eclipse on October 12, 1996 at 19°Libra 32' was conjunct Sara's Venus stellium and square her trouble-making Uranus set in motion what, pre-warned, Sara described as a "surprise attack" on her paycheck. Near the First Quarter Moon, related to the 19° Libra eclipse's Moon Family July 12, 1997, the IRS released her wages.

Neptune

For some, an eclipse to Neptune can be a time period of fantasy and romance. The "Neptunian haze" (a cloud of euphoria) can be the general state of mind of an eclipse to Neptune. If all the necessary characters are present, there could be a marriage motivated by romance. In many instances of marriage in our modern culture, a strong focus of Neptune is apparent. Princess Diana's chart is a perfect example of this. An eclipse in the sign of romance (Leo) was square to her Neptune in her very public tenth house and semi-sextile her Sun at 9° Cancer 40'. Transiting Neptune at 22° Sagittarius was also present in her first house, conjunct her

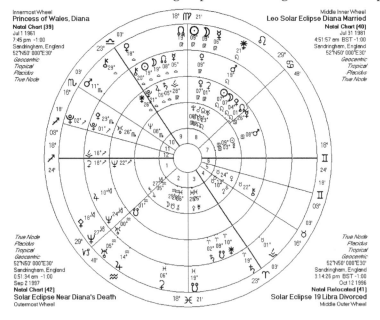

18° Sagittarius Ascendant. She and Charles both admitted adultery and divorced June, 28, 1996 when the Solar Eclipse at 19°Libra was applying that fall. That eclipse fell in Diana's ninth house and conjunct her MC, ruler of matters announced to the public. Diana died days before the solar eclipse at 9° Virgo fell in her eighth house of death, from a car crash in Paris. The crash occurred at 12:27 am on August 31, 1997. That last eclipse to impact her chart is seen conjunct her Pluto, at the midpoint of her 9° Cancer Sun and 8° Scorpio Neptune, and opposed natal Chiron.

Eclipses in aspect to Neptune can

also be a time of confusion or spiritual awareness. This eclipse can send you on a vision quest or mission, and it can be a time of great inspiration. For an artist, of any kind, this can be a period of significant, creative growth. Music and art can heal your mood swings and help to change your attitude. If there are health matters that arise when under the influence of an eclipse in aspect to your Neptune, they can be very difficult to diagnose or they can be chronic. Mostly, this aspect brings annoying health concerns but there can be matters of misdiagnosed illnesses or a prolonged recovery. This is a good time to have your eyes examined. Some people experience forgetfulness and a temporary memory loss. This eclipse can mark a noticeable beginning of menopause. Sleep can be restless, with many vivid dreams, and there can be an excessive need for sleep. Escapism through drugs and alcohol are some indicators of an eclipse to the natal Neptune. Your problem regarding substance abuse may be with your close association with someone who suffers from an addiction. You need to "let go" in order for others to find their own way, and this may be the hardest thing to do. There may also be issues regarding victims or victimization with an eclipse to Neptune. This is dream time in all its forms. Your imagination and creative mode will occupy your consciousness. You may have a visionary project or something special you want to do, but find yourself unable to make a move because of prior commitments and a trapped feeling. Your intuition may be heightened at this time and access to spiritual support will be broadened.

In the accompanying chart a Libra Man experienced a N.N. Solar Eclipse conjunct his second house Neptune. He had been restless and suffering a loss of sleep for a couple of months. He had an incredible vision to make a great deal of money. He also invested a large sum of money and received a settle-

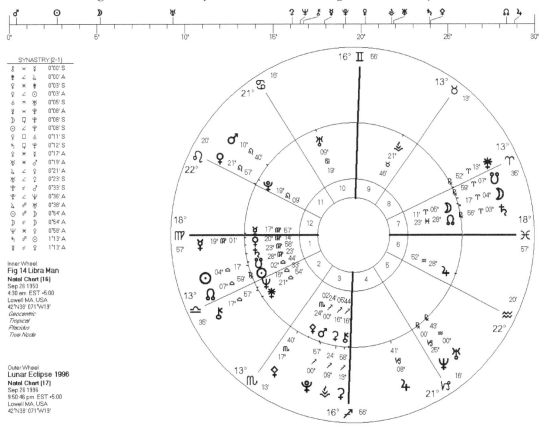

ment of several thousand dollars from an old lawsuit. This chart also impacted by the Lunar Eclipse 9/26/1996 at 4° Aries12' was opposite his Sun. At that time he and a business partner (seventh house cusp is Pisces, ruled by Neptune) began dividing their business due to issues surrounding the partner's substance abuse. With the eclipse also in aspect to his Neptune, the division of assets went through a torturous process that ended with the Lunar Eclipse at 22° Virgo conjunct his Venus/Saturn conjunction.

Pluto

This is a time for letting go and the exposure of matters that have been deeply hidden. You may experience an intensely gripping involvement, since eclipses to Pluto can be filled with power struggles that deal with facing your own inner demons. The surprise may be that there is no monster inside, but simply that your ideas of surrender and release must be addressed in order to reduce your resistance to change. A powerful drama involving you and another may arise, exposing someone else's inner monster. Some of the deepest emotional traumas can be exposed and transformed when an eclipse aspects natal Pluto. People around you are difficult and there seem to be few breaks. This is not a time for lightweights. This eclipse will leave you with a new set of tools for living. You will tap into your own external or internal power source. Naturally, Pluto rules death, sex and taxes, as well as insurance, estates, births and abandonment issues. All of these topics are prominent at an eclipse to Pluto. Your financial status could change significantly, for better or for worse, depending on the entire horoscope picture. These changes are not sudden, but they build slowly.

This is an example of a N.N. Solar Eclipse conjunct a woman's Pluto that seemed to change her entire life. We'll call her Cathy. Cathy had a wonderful job at a museum for eleven years when she was offered a job that would triple her income. She began her new job within a month of her marriage to a man she had been with for nine years. Weeks after her wedding her father died. The relationship with Cathy's father had been very difficult for many years since her parent's divorce. Cathy's mother, as well, was suffering the loss of her partner. Cathy also lost a very close friend from her old job a few weeks after the father passed away. Cathy's Pluto rules her eighth house and is located in her sixth house, square natal Saturn in her eighth.

The next chart is of a woman who was the victim of sexual abuse as a child.

One of her perpetrators was exposed in 1962, with a 7° Leo solar eclipse conjunct the woman's Pluto. Her natal Pluto is located at the leg of a "T" square, connecting her Mars on the cusp of her second house and her Moon in her eighth house. The Scorpio Moon is the ruler of her 5th house (childhood), and describes the secret abuse she endured since an infant from another perpetrator. Also affected by that eclipse was Saturn/Pluto midpoint at 8° Leo. This midpoint indicates permanent change to the foundation of her life.

Symbolism can vary from chart to chart regarding such intense midpoints one is Saturn/Pluto. For Hillary Rodham Clinton, an eclipse fell on her Saturn/Pluto midpoint in August 1999 at 18° Leo, when her husband, Bill Clinton, announced his wife's plan to run for the U.S. Senate. This changed the structure of her life in a very positive way.

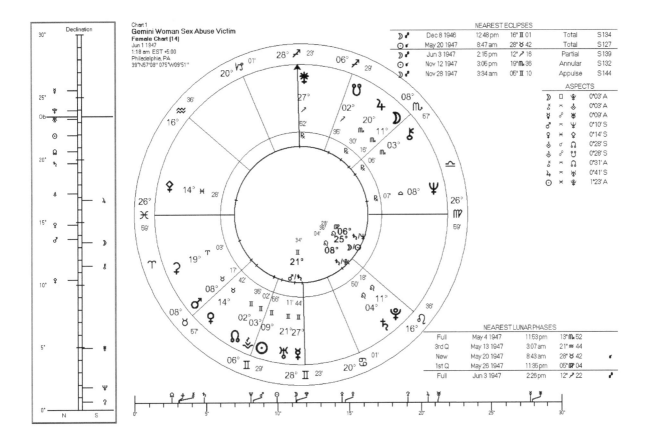

Chart 1
Gemini Woman Sex Abuse Victim
Female Chart [14]
Jun 1 1947
1:18 am EST +5:00
Philadelphia, PA
39°N57'08" 075°W09'51"

NEAREST ECLIPSES					
☽ ♐	Dec 8 1946	12:48 pm	16° ♊ 01	Total	S 134
☉ ♐	May 20 1947	8:47 am	28° ♉ 42	Total	S 127
☽ ♐	Jun 3 1947	2:15 pm	12° ♐ 16	Partial	S 139
☉ ♐	Nov 12 1947	3:06 pm	19° ♏ 36	Annular	S 132
☽ ♐	Nov 28 1947	3:34 am	05° ♊ 10	Appulse	S 144

ASPECTS			
☽	□ ⚷	0°03' A	
⚷	⚹ ⚷	0°03' A	
☿	⚹ ⚵	0°09' A	
♂	⚹ ♆	0°10' S	
♀	⚹ ♀	0°14' S	
⚷	☌ ☊	0°28' S	
⚷	☍ ☋	0°28' S	
⚷	⚹ ☊	0°31' A	
♃	⚹ ⚵	0°41' S	
☉	⚹ ⚷	1°23' A	

NEAREST LUNAR PHASES				
Full	May 4 1947	11:53 pm	13° ♏ 52	
3rd Q	May 13 1947	3:07 am	21° ♒ 44	
New	May 20 1947	8:43 am	28° ♉ 42	
1st Q	May 26 1947	11:35 pm	05° ♍ 04	
Full	Jun 3 1947	2:26 pm	12° ♐ 22	

☊ North Node

The North Node (N.N.) acts like an Ascendant/Midheaven midpoint and has a combination of a first house and tenth house quality in the way that it represents you, your physical body and your independent qualities. (It works so well as an Ascendant that the Draconic system was developed to view a chart from this perspective.) Eclipses to the Nodes of the Moon in your chart trigger relationship and health changes. Both marriage and divorce occur when the North Node is activated. If there are indications of weaknesses in the physical structure, there could be health problems. Jacqueline Kennedy died at the time of a Solar Eclipse at 19° Taurus 48. The eclipse was conjunct her North Node.

☋ South Node

The South Node (S.N.) represents significant others, the opposition, total strangers, and it is also a health indicator. This is a point of repeated patterns and a return of life themes. The South Node pulls familiar problems and people into your life. Matters of joining and separating, as well as legal matters are S.N. affairs. The South Node acts like a Descendant and has a seventh house quality to its interpretation. When in aspect to an eclipse, it will also indicate major health changes. It is said that the North Node is the point of receiving and the South Node the point of taking away.

Ascendant

An eclipse on your Ascendant, or to its ruler, puts the focus on your appearance, physical body and close personal relationships. You may find yourself craving a cosmetic makeover, which could include plastic surgery, engaging in an exercise routine, or a noticeable shift in weight and energy. Major changes to your overall health and care of your body are triggered with this eclipse. If an eclipse is combined with aspects to Mars, surgery could be indicated. A shift of any significance in physical status is more visible at this time. Slow down to avoid haphazard conditions that might be more prevalent. Magnetic attractions to others are more likely as your introductions to new people increase. A boost in identity awareness and enhancement can be a result of an eclipse on the Ascendant. This is a time when you are "on." A strong need for independence and self expression can also be expected. A fresh perspective or a new direction could be the result of an eclipse in aspect to your Ascendant.

A woman experienced a S.N. Solar Eclipse conjunct her Ascendant on June 30, 1992 at 8° Cancer 57'. Her 23° Sagittarius Moon, ruler of her Ascendant, 23° Sagittarius Jupiter and 23° Scorpio Mars were under the influence of the Lunar Eclipse on June 15, 1992 at 24° Sagittarius 20'. On the day of the Full Moon of May 16, 1992, conjunct natal Mars, she underwent an emergency hernia repair six weeks before she moved to a new apartment. Her natal Mars is 135° (sesquisquare) from her Ascendant and was exactly conjunct the Full Moon.

A Solar Eclipse nineteen years earlier (June 30, 1973) at 8° Cancer had not created health problems until a Solar Eclipse conjunct her Moon/Jupiter conjunction in her sixth house on December 13, 1974 at 21° Sagittarius. At that time she was badly injured in a car accident on Christmas Eve. Though she suffered many internal injuries, she made a full recovery. Her son suffered minor injuries in the accident as a result of her fifth house Mars in aspect to that eclipse.

Midheaven

The Midheaven represents the *outward* projection of who you are and where you are going. Any major astrological stimulation will activate this principle in your life, such as a transiting planetary station point, and will have an effect when and if you put yourself out to the world. A Mercury station, for example, that is conjunct the MC could indicate an important decision or announcement in regard to your career, family structure (including weddings and divorces) matters of real estate and other outer changes in the way you live your life. The reason weddings and divorces can be indicated from the MC is because this is an outer change to which unrelated persons would eventually become privy. The MC recognizes all matters that become public in one's life. Some times there are unwanted releases of personal information when the chart's MC is triggered by events such as eclipses and planetary stations. The MC is the highest and most visible point in your chart and its ruler is extremely prone to exposing matters that belong in the outer information batch files of life. Each time one changes their presentation to the world in some remarkable way, a cosmic notice goes out to all concerned parties. We will notice with a Mercury station that one's private affairs could become a topic of conversation or gossip. I find it helpful to advise a client when things are going to be particularly out in the open. This can be used to great advantage when it is the intention to release information to the public.

The most common result of an eclipse to the Midheaven is to create changes to one's career. The changes may affect one's job directly or the company itself. Sometimes, it is the hierarchy of upper management that changes under the influence of this eclipse. Look for a company going out of business or merging with another company. This is common with a Lunar Eclipse in aspect to the MC. Often you could find yourself in the midst of a career change, planned or unplanned.

Be sure to check the rulers of both the fourth and tenth house axis when an eclipse aspects the Midheaven. The entire polarity is always affected and makes way for major life changes. You may experience core changes that affect your entire life.

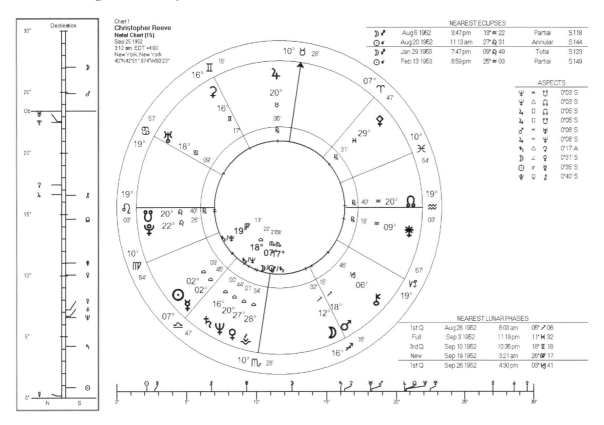

Such was the case with actor Christopher Reeve when his neck was broken because of a horse riding accident on May 27, 1995. This occurred one month after a Solar Eclipse at 8° Taurus made a conjunction to his Midheaven on April 29, 1995. Venus, the MC ruler, was the object of the Lunar Eclipse April 15, 1995. Christopher enjoyed a successful acting career and starred in the leading role as Superman in 1978, for which he won the BAFTA award for most promising newcomer. Sadly, he died on October 11, 2004. A Solar Eclipse at 21° Libra conjoined his natal Neptune and sextile Pluto. Both Saturn and Neptune had progressed to 22° Libra. The nodes of the Moon were still traveling through Scorpio and formed a closer connection to the up and coming Lunar Eclipse at 5° Taurus which was conjunct Christopher's MC. His Chiron received a trine from that Lunar Eclipse. In mythology, Chiron pleaded with the gods for the gift of death, which would release him from his pain. His wish was granted and his image was honored to be the centaur for the sign of Sagittarius.

On a happier note, buying and selling homes are likely, as well as a strong focus on parents and their needs. This can be a time when you find yourself in the public eye in one way or another. You may appreciate the attention if it is your desire to be the focus of attention, or you may be annoyed by gossip and unwanted press.

Another story is that of a young man who defended his home shooting 3 intruders who invaded his house at the time a Solar Eclipse at 9° Virgo that was conjunct his MC. The man was tried for murder and was found not guilty on grounds of self-defense. The highly-publicized case created so much attention the man moved away after the trial to secure a normal life.

Chapter 6

Lunar Eclipses

Lunar Eclipses: Hidden Treasure or Pandora's Box

The multifaceted study of Lunar Eclipses proves to be considerably more complex than the average Full Moon. A Lunar Eclipse can be described as a byproduct of a Solar Eclipse, but that fact does not diminish the effects of its impact on global and human affairs. The wake of a Lunar Eclipse can be as profound as that of a Solar Eclipse, creating drastic changes and leaving its mark on the chapters of our lives. At times a Lunar Eclipse can reveal a hidden treasure and, at other times, open a box of troubles and set them loose into the world. If your life has been hit with the unkind packages that can accompany a Lunar Eclipse, you may underestimate some of the benefits that can come your way.

The study of Lunar Eclipses begins with a more fixed focus on the Earth, the nodes of the Moon, and the obscuring of the Sun's light at least twice a year. By their nature, Lunar Eclipses are particularly fascinating Full Moons that have an added dimension – the Earth. The added component of the Earth, temporarily blocking the flow of light from the Sun, is the key to their mysterious nature. Lunar Eclipses occur two weeks before or after a Solar Eclipse, if they are within a twelve degree orb to the nodes of the Moon. There are times when two Lunar Eclipses will occur around a Solar Eclipse.

Some astrologers believe that a Lunar Eclipse will not deliver an outstanding impact unless you can actually see the eclipse. The October 27, 2004 Lunar Eclipse became the hidden treasure when the Red Sox won the World Series under the crimson cast of the disappearing eclipsed Moon during their winning game. It put an end to the 86-year losing streak for the team, a record they called "the curse." It seemed the heavens staged a public lesson about Lunar Eclipses on that night.

Using the tables of eclipses in the Appendix, we can easily view both columns of Solar and Lunar Eclipses and spot the zodiacal position of the eclipses. With additional astronomical research, you may find the path of the actual shadow of an eclipse. Many astrology software programs feature global maps with eclipse paths added for your study.

Some Lunar Eclipses share a relationship with Solar Eclipses of nearly-matching degree points. The related Lunar Eclipses will occur 18 months before or after the source Solar Eclipse, thus creating a very powerful family of Moons, discussed in the Lunar Gestation Cycle in Chapter 1. A very important Solar-Lunar Eclipse degree relationship occurs midway in the 19-year cycle that carries our storylines from one Solar Eclipse at a degree to the next, 19 years later. You can see this when you find a Lunar Eclipse degree close by or matching the Solar Eclipse 9.5 years earlier. This is midway through the Me-

A Solar Eclipse Moon Family Containing A Lunar Eclipse					
Solar Eclipse			18 months later a Lunar Eclipse		
1950	18-Mar	27♓28	1951	15-Sep	22♓19
1953	11-Jul	18♋30	1955	8-Jan	17♋57
1957	29-Apr	09♉23	1958	27-Oct	03♉43
1964	10-Jun	19♊19	1965	8-Dec	16♊25
1968	28-Mar	08♈19	1969	25-Sep	02♈25
1969	17-Mar	27♓25	1970	15-Sep	23♓12
1971	22-Jul	28♋56	1973	18-Jan	28♋40
1972	16-Jan	25♑25	1973	15-Jul	22♑51
1975	11-May	19♉59	1976	6-Nov	14♉41
1979	26-Feb	07♓29	1980	26-Aug	03♓03
1982	21-Jun	29♊47	1983	29-Dec	27♊36
1982	15-Dec	23♐04	1984	13-Jun	22♐45
1986	9-Apr	19♈06	1987	7-Oct	13♈22
1993	21-May	00♊32	1994	18-Nov	25♉42
1997	9-Mar	18♓31	1998	6-Sep	13♓40
2000	1-Jul	10♋14	2001	30-Dec	08♋48
2000	25-Dec	04♑14	2002	24-Jun	03♑11
2004	19-Apr	29♈49	2005	17-Oct	24♈13
2011	1-Jun	11♊02	2012	28-Nov	07♊09
2011	25-Nov	02♐37	2013	25-May	04♐36
2015	20-Mar	29♓28	2016	16-Sep	24♓49
2018	13-Jul	20♋42	2020	10-Jan	20♋28
2022	30-Apr	10♉29	2023	28-Oct	5♉38
2026	17-Feb	28♒50	2027	17-Aug	24♒34
2029	12-Jun	21♊30	2030	9-Dec	18♊17
2029	5-Dec	13♐46	2031	5-Jun	15♐07
2033	30-Mar	10♈21	2034	28-Sep	5♈34
2036	23-Jul	01♌10	2038	21-Jan	01♌40
2037	16-Jan	26♑36	2038	16-Jul	24♑30
2040	11-May	21♉04	2041	8-Nov	16♉38
2044	28-Feb	09♓54	2045	27-Aug	05♓05
2047	23-Jun	01♋56	2048	20-Dec	29♊26
2047	16-Dec	24♐56	2049	15-Jun	25♐36

tonic cycle. For an example of this, note the Solar Eclipse, February 26, 1998 at 7°55' Pisces and the Lunar Eclipse, August 28, 2007 at 4°46' Pisces, which occurs 9.5 years later (halfway through the 19-year cycle). Look for the connections in your personal stories as well as the news headlines. Another example of this Solar/Lunar eclipse relationship can be found midway in the Metonic cycle at the south node Solar Eclipse on April 17, 1996 and in a related Lunar Eclipse on October 17, 2005 at 24°17' Aries.

Another point of interest is to note the effects of **Lunar Eclipses that occur six months apart at close polar opposite points, creating a set of two eclipses.** This has an effect on the outcome of matters brought up at the first eclipse events, maintaining the pressure and attention of issues to conclude at the second eclipse of the pair. If one of the eclipses is a total eclipse, it will command a dominance over the issues regardless of the chronological order.

Planetary stations activate eclipse degrees before or after the actual eclipse occurs. The transiting nodes of the Moon are powerful triggers for eclipse events. They can set an eclipse degree into action as much as seven or eight months before or after the eclipse occurs. Polar opposites are activated with the dual occupation of the Sun and the Moon in the horoscope at any Full Moon or Lunar Eclipse.

Use the degrees of Solar and Lunar Eclipses to note the most outstanding points in any chart. This study need not be limited to just your natal chart, but can include event charts, lunar and solar returns, progressions and especially progressed angles. They may all show a heightened sensitivity in the areas occupied by an eclipse degree as far back or forth in time as nine to 19 years. Allow the eclipse degrees to become active points in your memory. This comes in very handy when you pick up a chart and your eye zooms in on the planets and points that occupy those degrees.

Document Eclipse Activity

To personalize the meaning of eclipses, refer to your journals or any document that may jog your memory. I find checkbooks and credit card statements can be good tools to encourage and stimulate memory. Keeping notes concurrent with the eclipse seasons is great for documentation at that time and obviously, for later. Note any increase in activity with the issues in your life and also a list of people around you during these times. You may notice they cycle back when eclipses are repeated at similar degrees. For instance, an old love from 1996 moved out of the country and was spoken about when visiting with a friend in 2004. The old flame was back in the U.S. at that time. Some of the major events in your life can be triggered by a Lunar Eclipse. The event may not occur exactly on the day of a Lunar Eclipse but instead, within the eclipse season. The heart of the story will be found in the symbolism of the planet hit by the eclipse. For instance, a woman's mother passed away when a Lunar Eclipse occurred in exact conjunction to her Saturn (serious event and can indicate parents). Saturn is also the ruler of her fourth house cusp (mother). The eclipse occurred a full six weeks after the mother's passing which is within the orb of influence for the impact of a Lunar Eclipse.

Look for the 19-year Metonic cycle for clues of the meaning in the larger cycle. Notice that the Lunar Eclipses that occur square to one another within the 19-year Metonic cycle will set off related life events. In addition, keep a close note of the position of the Moon's nodes to your planets. The eclipses that aspect your planets repeatedly at the 19-year cycle can be sorted further by measuring the intensity when the nodes of the Moon are closest to your planets. For instance, a solar eclipse in 1996 is repeated at the halfway point. Have fun connecting the dots between the eclipses and the stories in your life. Make a list of events that cluster around the dates of both Solar and Lunar Eclipses.

Watching mundane events of our times is a very interesting study. The *Volume Library Year Books* publishes lists of events for each year. For an example of outstanding events, let's look at the activity in the spring of 1996 surrounding the Lunar Eclipse at 14° Libra 30' on April 4, 1996. Keep in mind that Lunar Eclipse themes are crisis, exposure, closure, loss and endings. Look for activities requiring two sides, joining and separating, war and peace, etc.

* March 27, 1996: In Israel, a life sentence was imposed on Yigal Amir after he was convicted of Prime Minister Yitzkak Rabin's assassination on November 4, 1995. (The Lunar Eclipse symbolism is marking the end of a trial and bringing closure to the country's deep loss.)

* April 3, 1996: U.S. Secretary of Commerce Ronald Brown and a delegation of U.S. corporate executives were killed in a plane crash near the airport in Croatia. There were 36 aboard the U.S. military plane traveling on a trade mission. (Trading is a two-sided activity which falls under the symbolism of the Lunar Eclipse. Add Ron Brown to the list of those that met their death while serving under the Clinton administration.)

* April 4, 1996: A 53-year-old former mathematics professor, Theodore J. Kaczynski, was arrested and charged with possessing bomb materials in Helena, MT. He was suspected of being the Unabomber, killing three and injuring 23 since May 1978 with mail-bombs. (One does not need to look too deeply for the Lunar Eclipse symbolism in this example as the Unabomber is exposed at the obvious end of his career.)

* April 6, 1996: Fighting broke out again in Liberia between government soldiers and rebels after a

peace plan had been accepted in the African nation in August 1995. (The Lunar Eclipse symbolism is clear in a broken agreement between two sides. The fighting is also a Lunar Eclipse event, as the opposition of the Sun and Moon represent conflict when not joining opposing forces.)

Which Eclipse Did What? For Some it's Solar, for Others it's Lunar

Aside from global events, the Lunar Eclipse season (most active approximately six weeks before and after the eclipse) is likely to create some excitement in our personal lives. Since the Lunar Eclipse is never more than two weeks from the Solar Eclipse, it can be difficult to identify whether the results of an eclipse are those of a Solar or Lunar Eclipse. For one person it may be a Solar Eclipse event, whereas for another it may be a Lunar Eclipse event.

Here is an example of that thought. In 1976, the lives of a couple were forever changed when the man, then age 34, suffered a heart attack on May 29. In the man's chart, an exact 30-degree aspect to Mars received the impact of the April 29, 1976 Solar Eclipse at 9° Taurus. That Solar Eclipse also was square to his 6° Aquarius Ascendant. For the female, her 23° Scorpio Mars received a hit as well, but from the Lunar Eclipse two weeks later exactly at 23° Scorpio. For the man, it was his heart attack and a rather masculine Solar Eclipse event. This was an eclipse where something happened to him. For her, it was her partner's physical danger that caused a traumatic shift in her relationship. Therefore, from her perspective an event happened to them as a couple. At work were the relationship points to the Lunar Eclipse's dualistic symbolism and that of the unexpected element from the Earth.

Another couple experienced a series of eclipses that coincided with the end of their marriage. The woman was reclaiming her independence as the Solar Eclipse of October 1996 was conjunct natal Uranus. However, for the man, the Lunar Eclipse conjunct his MC and opposing his Venus described his loss of home and loved one. When evaluating the effect of an eclipse on a person's chart, consider the charts of those around them to fill in the blanks and add depth to your interpretation.

Some Eclipses Have A Grip On Time

A major news event with long-term consequences transpired on April 19, 1993 just over a month before the 0° Gemini Solar Eclipse. That was the day of a dramatic end to a 51-day standoff with the FBI and the Branch Davidians led by David Koresh. Janet Reno held the "top cop" position as U.S. Attorney General. The Koresh compound burned to the ground in Waco, Texas in what the FBI described as a mass suicide that took 86 lives. To many, it looked more like a fumbled FBI mission. Exactly two years later on April 19, 1995, in what was described as an act of revenge for the Waco deaths, Timothy McVeigh set off a massive bomb outside a federal building in Oklahoma. Many children were among the 168 fatalities that day in Oklahoma City.

The Lunar Eclipse that preceded the bombing of the Federal building in Oklahoma is an example of an eclipse that has a grip on time. That 25 Libra Lunar Eclipse was reactivated two years later with a Mercury retrograde station. It took two years to muddle through the legal details that would lead to a fair trial for Timothy McVeigh and much later for Terry Nichols.

It was that very Mercury retrograde station that brought to mind Mercury's mythological role as messenger of the gods. As astrologers, we must keep our detective skills sharp, hunting for clues, collecting important data and facts in pursuit of connections that fit the puzzle. Numbers begin to hold their own personal message as the 360 degrees of a wheel becomes a familiar playground for interpretation of astrology's cryptic messages from "the gods."

Mercury is named the trickster for its retrograde antics, causing mistakes, mishaps and problems. Perhaps it's Mercury's role as the "scout" that gives him the title of "Messenger of the Gods." As the scout, he seems to dart out ahead and plunk a red retrograde flag with his blatant zodiacal and numerical messages to call attention to events in the past or future. The retrograde or direct station degree often occurs at the same degree of another planetary station or eclipse point, and these are the points where we should be making numerical connections. Mercury sends an early warning sign or reactivates old red flags of significant events by zodiacal degree, thus creating a sensitive degree point.

The late astrologer Eleanor Bach kept a list of sensitive degrees where all the planetary retrograde and direct stationary points occurred. It is easy to agree with her tenet that these points remained sensitive for at least two years. After studying the charts of the stationary planets, it becomes clear there are messages in their horoscopes. Such is

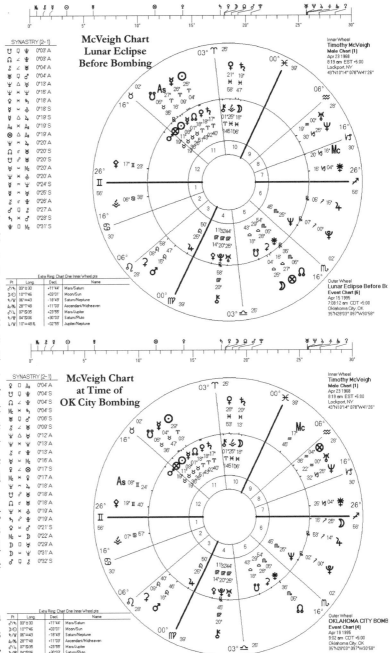

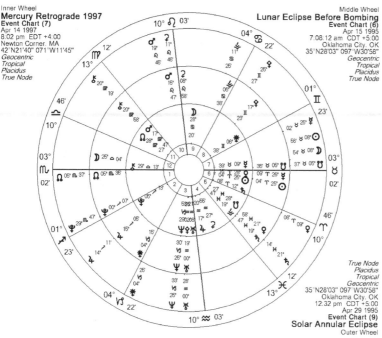

Inner Wheel
Mercury Retrograde 1997
Event Chart (7)
Apr 14 1997
8:02 pm EDT +4:00
Newton Corner, MA
42°N21'40" 071°W11'45"
Geocentric
Tropical
Placidus
True Node

Middle Wheel
Lunar Eclipse Before Bombing
Event Chart (6)
Apr 15 1995
7:08:12 am CDT +5:00
Oklahoma City, OK
35°N28'03" 097°W30'58"
Geocentric
Tropical
Placidus
True Node

True Node
Placidus
Tropical
Geocentric
35°N28'03" 097°W30'58"
Oklahoma City, OK
12:32 pm CDT +5:00
Apr 29 1995
Event Chart (9)
Solar Annular Eclipse
Outer Wheel

Mercury Retrograde at Time of Bombing

the case with the Mercury retrograde station chart that occurred two years after the Oklahoma bombing.

Source for Timothy McVeigh's birth time: from a broadcast of the ABC television show, *Prime Time* hosted by Diane Sawyer on 3/29/2001. Timothy McVeigh's baby book shows the time as 8:19am viewed on the screen during the show.

This Mercury retrograde station on April 14, 1997 placed its red flag at the same sensitive degree of the Solar Eclipse of 9° Taurus that occurred two years earlier on April 29, 1995. The horoscope of the Mercury station points to the Lunar Eclipse of the spring of 1995. Note the Sun's position at 25° Aries is involved in an active First Quarter square with the Cancer Moon. This is the same degree of the Sun's position for the April 15, 1995 Lunar Eclipse at 25° Libra, just four days before the Oklahoma City bombing.

The Moon is slightly past its 25° Cancer First Quarter phase but clearly in opposition to Neptune, the planet of religious fervor run amok. The Lunar Eclipse point on April 14, 1995, was exactly square to Neptune at its retrograde station of 25° Capricorn. They are all involved in a grand cardinal square, including the First Quarter's Sun and Moon, Neptune, Venus and Chiron. The symbolism of the First Quarter is becoming actively involved in a process initiated some time ago. Venus rules Libra and the legal council. There were many legal issues that needed to be settled before the Unabomber trial could begin. One of the legal technicalities was whether the bomber's wife would be allowed to testify. At the time of this Mercury station, the jury selection for the trial was just getting underway. A Lunar Eclipse occurred at the same degree just ten days before Timothy McVeigh's April 23, 1968 birth in Lockport, NY at 8:30 a.m. Neptune is often found in a prominent position in the event charts of terrorism with a religious platform. The David Koresh disaster on the same date in 1993 inspired this retaliation bombing by McVeigh.

Timing the Influence of a Lunar Eclipse

The timing of the impact of a Lunar Eclipse will vary from person to person and every eclipse is different. When studying a chart you may find an eclipse in exact aspect to a planet that ignites a very powerful event in someone's life. Then you may find another who also has an exact hit from an eclipse to their planet and nothing happens, at least not immediately. As I have advanced my astrological research, I find triggers are not one size fits all, as is true of most techniques in astrology. Further, the astronomical events that trigger global events may differ widely from the triggers to an individual's chart. As with Solar Eclipses, there are short- and long-range timers. The most immediate impact seen in the headlines and news stories close to you may be noticed within two weeks of the Lunar Eclipse.

* Three months before or after a Lunar Eclipse is a powerful ignition time because a Full Moon occurring at 90° from the eclipse point will square the Lunar Eclipse.
* The transiting node of the Moon will trigger a Lunar Eclipse up to eight months before the eclipse date.
* The first recurrence of the topics activated by a Lunar Eclipse will be evident in six months, when the Sun reaches the point where the Lunar Eclipse occurred.
* A related event will emerge in nine months at the Last Quarter in the Lunar Gestation Cycle.

I toggle between various techniques to seek a conclusion about the impact of an eclipse. I rely heavily on secondary progressions closely following the Mean Quotidian (Q2) rate of progressing the angles. Look for the day when a Solar or Lunar Eclipse degree pops up on client's angles to spot the trigger day.

Note that the long-term effects of a Lunar Eclipse can be related years beyond an eclipse date, noticeably triggered by the transiting phases of the Moon in the Lunar Gestation Cycle or a transiting planetary station. Another powerful degree connection to the Lunar Eclipse is found with the Solar Eclipse nine and a half years before or after the Lunar Eclipse.

Full Moon Eclipse = Full Exposure
During a Full Moon, the opposition of the Sun and Moon at a Lunar Eclipse speaks to the highest level of visibility possible. The full face of the Moon shines at its brightest in its 29-day cycle, making this a time of total exposure. Discretion may be futile during a Lunar Eclipse season, as clandestine affairs have fewer hiding places. The Earth's shadow across the face of the Moon is a symbol of the interference in the flow of matters during that time. It can be the voice of the people, the legal system, an objection or a major complication that changes the established flow of matters.

You might want to take advantage of the maximum exposure you gain during a Lunar Eclipse season with the possibilities of the added dimension of the Earth. You may attract more than you bargained for, but it may be just what you need. It could be a fine time to toast your endeavors with a grand opening. It's also a beneficial time to launch a website, promote new business or plan a show or an exhibit. Try having a block party or neighborhood yard sale. This can be a great time for grand parties and reunions and these events are more likely to be well-attended. Choose this time to announce a candidacy, or make your best presentation in the public eye. Even addressing major health matters at a Lunar Eclipse would lead to a more complete view of physical problems and to the most effective treatment. Matters that have been lacking in definition tend to shift with decisive clarity during a Lunar Eclipse season. The most pressing problems come out into the open. Marriages and divorces are common themes during a Lunar Eclipse season. You will do things differently. This is the natural time that major deadlines in your year become pressing.

The Impact on Relationships During Lunar Eclipses

The activation of polar opposites at a Lunar Eclipse may explain why Lunar Eclipses have so much to do with interpersonal relationships. The opposition of the Sun and Moon gives an Aries/Libra symbolism at any Full Moon or eclipse – yin/yang, him/her, here/there – all speaking to polarity. The Moon as a symbol in the Lunar Eclipse never operates alone, but always with its partner, the Sun. The Sun as a symbol can be experienced as a mate, a co-conspirator or an adversary. It is sometimes difficult to know if opposing forces are working in harmony or disharmony. At times, the oppositions see eye-to-eye as they join forces, while at other times they fight to remain separate. Many that are united find the ribbons of union during this time to be delicate. They can pray that the ties that bind them together are stronger than the forces that would tear them apart. At times, the probing spotlight of a Lunar Eclipse seems relentless in its inspections that expose the deepest fabric of existing relationships. The Lunar Eclipse season is often experienced as a time of cosmic airing-out that offers partnerships the opportunity to discard outworn behaviors that stand in the way of progress and happiness.

Marriages and divorce, as well as health issues, are topics for eclipses in tight aspect to the Ascendant/Descendant axis in a chart. The Sun can be included as a similar polarity, using the Sun's polar opposite point as a DSC. Use the North Node for the same observations. However, many of these types of topics are activated when the Midheaven receives a conjunction aspect from the eclipse, thus creating a square point that may or may not align with the horizon or the Ascendant. I find this also to be true when studying progressions. Activity to the Midheaven indicates serious or well-known matters brought out for general knowledge. This is the point that represents the public arena in your world.

Other major transits and progressions need to be identified to support this claim. Find at least three examples within each chart type to support your statement. When looking for validation of your theory, find three configurations of:
* transits to the natal chart
* progressed chart as a stand-alone
* solar arc chart to natal
* transits to the progressed charts
* group of solar return charts surrounding the matter

The ruling planet of the Midheaven may be the object to create the attention to the MC. If the Asc/Mc midpoint is the object of the eclipse, there will be core changes in the life of the individual or the primary focus for the chart, such as a relationship, your house chart, your company, etc. Very often people marry, move and start a new job all at the same time. At the same time, the native's parents may be experiencing a lot due to major stimulation of the Midheaven/Nadir axis.

The following story is of a couple married in the summer of '98, which was at the interesting point of nine and a half years after they met. The Solar Eclipse at 28° Leo was conjunct woman's Pluto and square to her natal Saturn. This was likely to be a greater life change than anticipated, as the Saturn and Pluto combination speaks to deep structural change in life. Certainly one expects to experience significant changes when one marries. Unfortunately her dad died that fall and her job changed, leaving her

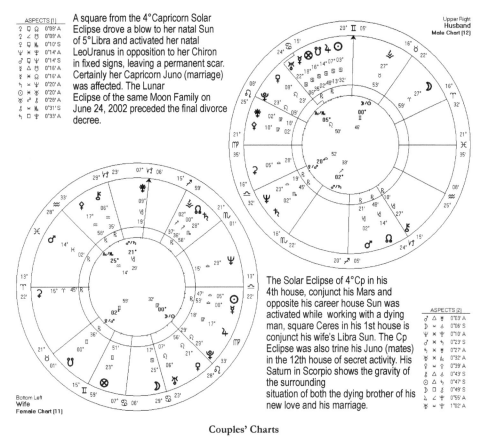

A square from the 4°Capricorn Solar Eclipse drove a blow to her natal Sun of 5°Libra and activated her natal Leo Uranus in opposition to her Chiron in fixed signs, leaving a permanent scar. Certainly her Capricorn Juno (marriage) was affected. The Lunar Eclipse of the same Moon Family on June 24, 2002 preceded the final divorce decree.

The Solar Eclipse of 4°Cp in his 4th house, conjunct his Mars and opposite his career house Sun was activated while working with a dying man, square Ceres in his 1st house is conjunct his wife's Libra Sun. The Cp Eclipse was also trine his Juno (mates) in the 12th house of secret activity. His Saturn in Scorpio shows the gravity of the surrounding situation of both the dying brother of his new love and his marriage.

Bottom Left
Wife
Female Chart [11]

Couples' Charts

in a stressful state of grief and disruption. She was not tending her new marriage in the way she had expected to. The real challenge was instigated by a 4°Capricorn December 2000 Solar Eclipse that set off the personal planets of both parties. She, a 5° Libra Sun, and he, a 3° Cancer Sun, would begin to undergo a drama that continues to this day.

On this page, are the couple's charts. With the influence from the 4°14' Capricorn Solar Eclipse that occurred at Christmas 2000, the husband began seeing another woman, much younger, three months before the Solar Eclipse — at the Power Point New Moon on September 27, 2000. This coincided with his wife's birthday — Mars his Sun (driven choices that affect his life), Saturn (commitment), Juno (marriage vs. mistress), Ceres (matters that are serious and affect the bond between two people. More Ceres symbolism was revealed about how the relationship began with the other women. As a doctor, the husband met the woman as the sister of one of his dying patients. By the time the Lunar Eclipse of the same Moon Family occurred eighteen months later, the divorce was finalized. The Lunar Eclipse point was conjunct the husband's Mars, and it appeared in his solar return chart. It was his birthday when the Lunar Eclipse occurred, and once again squared the wife's Sun. The now divorced couple remained connected, continuing with couples' therapy to heal their wounds. The man's mistress became his wife in March 2005. The eclipses that changed their lives are long past, but the drama continues. The original couple still maintains the commitment to heal their wounds. The woman continues yearning for the return of her husband, while the husband nurtures his new relationship. Many experience a pivotal change in their lives when the events are connected to such a powerful Moon Family.

The Lunar Eclipse in a Solar Eclipse Moon Family

We saw the impact for the above couple of a Lunar Eclipse in a Solar Eclipse Moon family. All eclipses belong to a Moon Family because they are Moon phases— extraordinary Moon phases. Some Lunar Eclipses belong to the same Moon family that began with a Solar Eclipse. Less notable Moon Families begin with a New Moon at the top of their family tree, producing a Lunar Eclipse a year and a half later.

Each Lunar Eclipse comes equipped with its unique set of lessons and awarenesses based on a list of variables.

* Polarities are the theme in a Lunar Eclipse because of the obvious Sun/Moon opposition at the polar opposite nodes of the Moon. Themes can be noticed that are particular to sign and polarity, such as the individuality/partnership theme of Libra/Aries or the acquisition/sharing theme of Taurus/Scorpio or the travel and learning curve theme with the Gemini/Sagittarius polarity.
* As with pairs of Solar Eclipses it is important to study the pairs of Lunar Eclipses. Like Solar Eclipses, you can find Lunar Eclipses occurring at opposite points of the zodiac and six months apart. These points of the zodiac appear as cosmic bookends containing an elongated focus of a particular theme.
* Planetary aspects of the eclipse chart give a Lunar Eclipse individuality. Conjunctions and oppositions and squares hold the strongest impact in a Lunar Eclipse chart. Planets in opposition are especially important as they match the harmonic of the already intense Sun Moon opposition of the Lunar Eclipse. They carry the same energy and draw added polarities into the arena of action. Parallels and contra-parallels in declination are powerfully dynamic aspects in any eclipse chart, as they are the vital component that allows the eclipse event to occur. Without the Sun/Moon parallel at a Solar Eclipse and the contra-parallel at the Lunar Eclipse, the overshadowing that occurs during an eclipse would not occur.
* Keep in mind the nature of the root member in the Lunar Eclipse Moon Family. Is it a New Moon or Solar Eclipse?
* Locate the Solar Eclipse 9.5 years before or after a Lunar Eclipse for the longer-range studies.

A Lunar Eclipse in a Solar Eclipse Moon Family carries a bigger punch and is more likely to ignite greater events over the 18 month period it takes to produce the Lunar Eclipse. We get the powerful beginning at the Solar Eclipse and the powerful ending or exposure at the Lunar Eclipse. Such a Super Moon Family set the political stage for the greatest shift in power in American government in forty years. The story begins during the Solar Eclipse season of May 21, 1993 with a big news story in the Clinton administration that would seed future events with major consequences. Hillary Rodham Clinton was the focus of attention. She took a highly-visible role in the administration and many were threatened by the power she had been given. They balked, complaining that she was not elected and should not have such a dynamic role in setting policy. The Republican Party was livid regarding her powerful role, and with enough attendant pressure pressed her into writing children's books and cookbooks, the intended role for all good first wives.

However you may think of her, Hillary Rodham Clinton represents a women in charge of her own destiny. Like Eleanor Roosevelt, the wife of President F.D.R., Hilary Clinton was ambitious and had her own agenda. She succeeded in taking on a more powerful political role when she won her seat in the Senate in the 2000 election.

Astrologically there were several interesting notes about this eclipse. For one, the Solar Eclipse at 0° Gemini 32' produced a Lunar Eclipse as a family member but in a different sign, Taurus. Often found when an eclipse occurs at 0° or 29° of a sign, the Moon phases may fall into the neighboring sign and still remain within orb of the Solar Eclipse. This eclipse at 0° Gemini bore these characteristics in its Moon Family.

Lunar Gestation Cycle Moon Family			
Solar Eclipse	First Quarter Moon	Lunar Eclipse	Last Quarter Moon
05/21/93 0 ♊ 32	02/18/94 29 ♉ 51	11/18/94 25 ♉ 42	08/18/95 24 ♉ 43

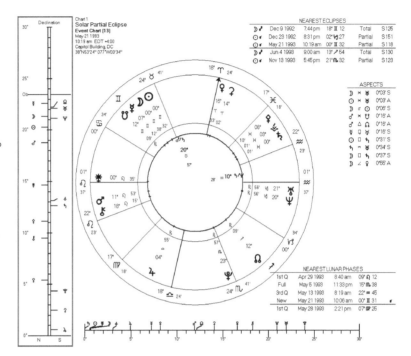

This configuration adds a dimension to any eclipse family and makes an interesting study at all four Moon phases. One can assume the changes set for the future might be fairly dramatic.

The zero degree symbolizes that a special point will be made. Gemini (the sign of stories often with many sides) at zero degrees indicates it will be a big story with ears, arms and legs. All of which fits perfectly with the Travelgate scandal mentioned earlier. Gemini, ruler of both travel and scandal, set the stage within hours of the May 21st eclipse when Hillary Rodham Clinton became the object of the Travelgate scandal. Seven employees were dismissed on May 19th from the White House travel office, five of which were reinstated by May 25th. Allegations had emerged suggesting President Clinton's family and friends had a vested interest in White House business. Travelgate was one of the topics targeted by the forty-million-dollar investigation by the White House's Independent Council, Ken Starr, who made many expensive investigations of the Clintons.

The 0° Gemini Solar Eclipse laid the groundwork for the coming political changes that would alter the control of the U.S. House and the Senate. Saturn at 0° Pisces is clearly square the eclipse point at 0°Gemini. Saturn represents the conservative party and Jupiter the liberals. This eclipse set the stage for the Republican party to take back the U.S. House and Senate majority at the '94 mid-term elections when

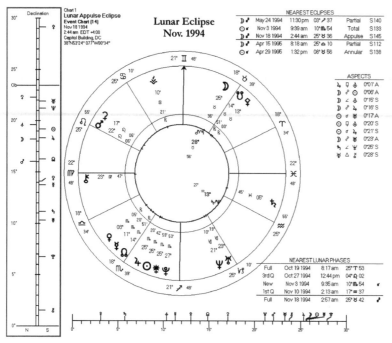

Chart 1
Lunar Appulse Eclipse
Event Chart (I4)
Nov 18 1994
2:44 am EDT +4:00
Capitol Building, DC
38°N53'24" 077°W00'34"

**Lunar Eclipse
Nov. 1994**

NEAREST ECLIPSES					
☽ ☊	May 24 1994	11:30 pm	03° ♐ 37	Partial	S140
☉ ☌	Nov 3 1994	9:39 am	10° ♏ 54	Total	S133
☽ ☋	Nov 18 1994	2:44 am	25° ♉ 36	Appulse	S145
☽ ☊	Apr 15 1995	8:18 am	25° ♎ 10	Partial	S112
☉ ☌	Apr 29 1995	1:32 pm	08° ♉ 56	Annular	S138

ASPECTS			
♃ ☌ ♅	0°01' A		
☽ ☍ ☉	0°06' A		
☽ ∠ ☉	0°15' S		
☽ ☍ ♃	0°16' S		
☉ ♂ ♅	0°17' A		
☉ ☌ ♃	0°20' S		
☉ ♂ ♃	0°21' S		
☽ ☍ ♅	0°23' A		
♄ ∠ ♀	0°26' S		
♅ △ ☋	0°28' S		

NEAREST LUNAR PHASES				
Full	Oct 19 1994	8:17 am	25° ♈ 53	
3rd Q	Oct 27 1994	12:44 pm	04° ♌ 02	
New	Nov 3 1994	9:35 am	10° ♏ 54	
1st Q	Nov 10 1994	2:13 am	17° ♒ 37	
Full	Nov 18 1994	2:57 am	25° ♉ 42	

a Lunar Eclipse in the same Moon Family occurred eighteen months later.

This Lunar Eclipse chart for November 18, 1994 dominated the U.S. 1994 mid-term elections on November 8, 1994. The Sun, both conjunct and parallel Jupiter, relates to the Democratic liberal party which was eclipsed by the conservative Republican party, indicated by Saturn. Saturn was exactly square the Solar eclipse point of this Moon Family.

Eighteen months later the related Lunar Eclipse on November 18, 1994 proved to hold a mighty punch in American government when the Republican Party scored its greatest victory in decades, winning control of both houses of Congress for the first time since the mid-term election on November 2, 1954.

These charts were cast for Washington, DC as the west coast polls closed at 11:00pm EST during the November 2, 1954 election on Capitol Hill, Washington, DC,. (A chart could be cast for the first vote for an election if that time and location is known. Votes for Elections nowadays can be cast days earlier, making the closing polls the most logical chart to cast.)

The chart shows the Sun/Saturn conjunction that placed the focus on the Republican Party – the conservative party and ruled by Saturn. Likewise, Jupiter rules the Democratic Party – the liberal party. The Saturn Mars square indicates a dead stop. Jupiter at the 29 degree of any sign would indicate a change because Jupiter would then soon change signs.

Looking back at the 1954 election, one Democratic seat was won, which made the small change that gave the Democrats control of the U. S. Senate. They then controlled Congress with 232 of the 435 available seats, an advantage they did not lose until the 1994 midterm election. The '94 Congress brought us Newt Gingrich of Georgia, who was nominated as Speaker of the House in the 104th Congress, and who became a major thorn in the side of the Clinton administration – so much so that the 106th House of Representatives impeached President Clinton four years later on December 19, 1998.

Comparison notes for the two elections:

* The 1954 Pluto reaches a square to the 1994 Pluto.
* Both charts show square type aspects between Saturn and Pluto, even though the square is out of sign in the '94 chart.
* The 1954 Jupiter at the last degree of Cancer is an indication of change for the liberal party. Certainly, the Uranus conjunction Jupiter indicates change.
* Interestingly, Venus played a part in both elections to the party's rulers. In 1954 Venus was trine the liberal party's ruling planet Jupiter. In 1994 Venus was trine the conservative party's ruler Saturn.
* Mars is square the Sun in both elections.
* Both charts have the Moons in Aquarius.

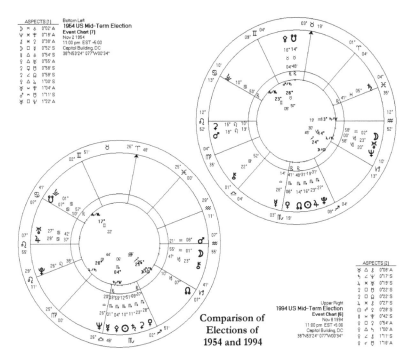

Comparison of
Elections of
1954 and 1994

The midpoints in the center of the wheels reveal stunning connections but are not noted here.

Newt Gingrich and his nominated successor Robert Livingston were described as casualties of the Clinton impeachment hearings. Gingrich resigned from Congress just after the November 1998 elections during which Republicans lost seats, in what was becoming an unpopular Republican House of Representatives. Bob Livingston resigned because a story about his marital indiscretions surfaced. Livingston admitted to his wife and the nation that he strayed in his marriage on several occasions. He unsuccessfully used his resignation as a ploy to taunt Clinton into resigning from the Presidency. This did not work.

The tables on the following page are lists of the Lunar Eclipses that are in the same family as a Solar Eclipse from 1950-2050. See if the following Lunar Eclipses dates coincide with special events that have changed your life.

The Solar Point of a Lunar Eclipse
When looking at a chart of a Solar or Lunar Eclipse, we do not want to overlook the obvious and miss the symbolic posture of each type of eclipse. The Solar/Lunar union at the Solar Eclipse occupies one

degree of the zodiac. On the other hand, a Lunar Eclipse has a dual occupation as it straddles the zodiac with the Sun and Moon at opposite posts, drawing our attention to polarity. This fact becomes important when delineating the symbolic effect of a Lunar Eclipse in a natal chart. Remember that the Sun always rules and that the greatest power of a Lunar Eclipse is located at the Solar point of the eclipse.

For example, if you are having a Lunar Eclipse conjunct your natal Sun, the Moon of the eclipse conjuncts your Sun and the Solar point of the eclipse would be opposite your Sun. This would occur six months after your birthday.

Eclipse' Solar point 14 ♈	opposite	Natal Sun 14 ♎ Lunar Eclipse 14 ♎

With the transiting Sun in opposition to your Sun, the power would be in the hands of a significant other. (A significant other can change with topics; this person does not always have to be a personal partner but rather a partner in a specific matter – the essential character in an opposing matter.) The opposition holds the power. If the opposition is working in your favor, this could benefit you. If you are involved in an adversarial situation, you could find yourself at a disadvantage. This could also be an indication that timing is the issue. You may be on the right track, but matters need time to develop.

The reverse scenario would show the Lunar Eclipse in opposition to your natal Sun. Coming at the time of a Solar return, which is your birthday, the eclipse's Solar point conjuncts your Sun. In this case, the Solar point of the Lunar Eclipse empowers the natal Sun that enables you to initiate change in your life.

Lunar Eclipse 14 ♈		natal Sun 14 ♎ Solar point 14 ♎

Lunar Eclipse Pairs
On occasion, a pair of Lunar Eclipses occurs. The eclipses are six months apart, in close opposition to one another. In the 1990s there were three such pairs of Lunar Eclipses; you will find pairs throughout the centuries. In recent times, there were two pairs in the late 1970s, and no pairs in the 1980s.

Let's look at the pairs of the 1990s. We will label them (A) or (B).

When eclipses occur in pairs they mark a period of prolonged scenarios common in complicated court battles. There can be great delays and matters hold their level of intensity as they drag on over extended periods. The double hits from eclipses, at the polar opposite points, offer plenty of ammunition to ignite a long-term saga. If you have experienced an eclipse (Solar or Lunar) in aspect to a planet with little to no noticeable influence, you will experience the opposite effect when a pair of Lunar Eclipses hits a planet. Eclipse pairs in aspect to a planet will show obvious signs of change related to the eclipse symbolism.

Lunar Eclipse A		Lunar Eclipse B
14 ♈ 54 on Oct. 8, 1995	followed in six months by	14 ♎ 31 on Apr. 4, 1996
4 ♈ 17 on Sep. 27, 1996	followed in six months by	03 ♎ 35 on Mar. 24, 1997
23 ♓ 56 on Sep. 16, 1997	followed in six months by	22 ♍ 24 on Mar. 13, 1998

In this section, we will break the pairs down to become more specific regarding the eclipse's influence and note whether eclipse (A) is conjunct or opposed your natal planet. Our anchor for delineation is the Sun, (Solar point) of the Lunar Eclipse, so keep your eye on the eclipse's Sun.

The following is an example of a Lunar Eclipse pair with the first eclipse, (A), conjunct the natal Sun. This places the eclipse's Solar Point in opposition to the natal Sun.

Here are a few possibilities when a pair of Lunar Eclipses aspect a natal Sun and, commencing with the first of the pair, conjunct the Sun. You could become involved in a matter that gains public attention. You may find your actions scrutinized by others. You may have a clear idea of what you want and how you will get it, but a major component is out of your reach. You may eventually find there is interference from a significant other, of which you may or may not be aware. It later becomes clear that you are not acting alone. This particular eclipse situation can also initiate separation of various sorts.

Many of these factors were clear in the situation of Anita Bryant, an outspoken Aries, born-again Christian singer and beauty queen of the seventies. Her anti-gay statements enraged millions. The first of a pair of Lunar Eclipses at 4:7 Aries in September 1977, was conjunct her Sun, placing the Solar Point in her Solar seventh house. She became involved in a civil rights conspiracy lawsuit. The fallout from her outspoken opinions eventually cost her an orange juice contract, her marriage and her church affiliation.

As another example, the following eclipses occurred with Jack and Jill. It was October 8, 1995 and Jill's birthday occurred on the day of a Lunar Eclipse (A), at 14° Aries. Six months later, when the Sun at 14 Aries opposed her Libra Sun, the (B) Lunar Eclipse occurred at 14° Libra, and was conjunct her Sun.

This was Jill's situation. In the fall, at the time of the Lunar Eclipse (A), she was unhappy in a relationship and began pulling away from her partner. Although she was successful at creating space in a close situation, Jack wanted very badly to save the relationship and was trying every-

Eclipse	Date	Lunar Eclipse			Solar Point			Eclipse Aspect
		Moon's Position			Sun's Position	Natal Planet		to Natal Point
A	Oct 28 2004	05° ♉ 02'			05° ♏ 02'			opposite
B	Apr 24 2005	04° ♏ 20'			04° ♉ 20'	Sun 5° ♉		conjunct

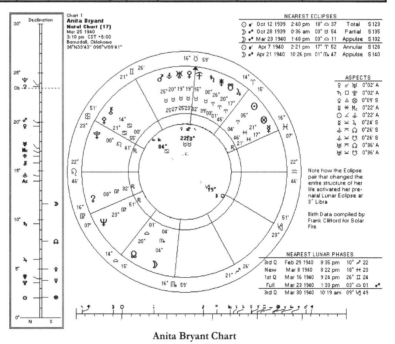

Anita Bryant Chart

thing. Jill could not end it and the inevitable just seemed to be dragging on. During the following winter, the midpoint between the pair of eclipses, the couple nearly resolved their differences. Then a drastic event made it clear that the relationship truly needed to end. It was not until the time of the (B) eclipse that Jack surrendered to the inevitable and got his own place. They parted as friends.

Some Notes When Considering The Solar Point of a Lunar Eclipse
When studying the impact of the Lunar Eclipse, keep an eye on the Sun opposite the Lunar Eclipse point. Because of the activation of the polar opposite, remember you are not doing this eclipse alone. Since you are not the single occupant on the planet, there *is* a significant other involved in the symbolism of a Lunar Eclipse.

I find the 30° sort allows me to locate most of the planets in aspect to the eclipse point. Then I can quickly note the houses that they rule. A planet conjunct or in opposition to a Lunar Eclipse will be affected as well as the house that planet rules. For example, a 25° Libra Lunar Eclipse conjunct a person's natal Sun would have an impact on the Sun, as well as the matters pertaining to the house with Leo on the cusp. Remember to include the nodes, MC, ASC, Sun/Moon midpoint and ASC/MC midpoint. If you have a cluster of planets at a degree hit by the eclipse, blend their meanings and list all the houses they rule. An eclipse degree is as important as a retrograde or direct planetary station point, in which cases you would normally use an orb of 5° when evaluating the impact. Following that same sense of importance, use an orb of five degrees for the conjunction or opposition for current Solar or Lunar Eclipses and an orb of one or two degrees for all other aspects. I use only one or two degrees when evaluating eclipses that occurred in the past.

Some older writings on eclipses don't consider a square from an eclipse to have importance. My experience has shown that the planet or point that receives the square is powerfully activated and not always contrary. There can be greater challenges, blind spots and broadside type events involved in the change stimulated by a square from an eclipse. You may find a Lunar Eclipse square to the Moon can create a change in address, sometimes with more complications than more harmonious address changes in the past. A good example of this occurred when a woman left a two family home that she and her sister had shared and where they began their families. The move into a larger home was brought about because her husband's mom suddenly passed away, and it made sense to take on the house. Everyone gained as a result of the loss, but all was bittersweet. The sister left behind was sad to lose the close family arrangements that supported their family in so many ways. The would-be purchasers of the home had trouble and delays passing papers on the house because the bank required the installation of separate gas meters. So, a square can get you moving but you may have to expect to make more adjustments and allow for more patience, as it could take a longer time than anticipated to adjust and satisfy all the necessary components that develop.

There are times when the square indicates a message of "no" or "no for now." If the "no" is the final answer to a question of long standing, as in a legal matter, you may feel compelled to continue to pursue your objective. This is still the chosen direction of the individual and his or her destiny is part of the journey. In one case there was a very unfortunate price paid with a Lunar Eclipse square to an eleventh house Saturn. His Saturn ruled his 12th house and he was arrested and sent to jail for possession of drugs.

When counseling someone on the impact of a difficult eclipse, I find it is not up to the astrologer to impose his or her belief systems or choose what is best. Helping someone find what is best for them provides a more useful service and honors the individual's path. I remove my opinions or any vested interest in the outcome and allow my skills to deliver unbiased guidance. This can be a challenge when it appears the client is pursuing a destructive path, but my primary objective as the astrologer is not to lose sight of the individual's freedom of choice. He or she has a right to make mistakes, which will probably lead them to the direction of his or her unique path. What appears like an avoidable problem to the astrologer may be a long-awaited opportunity for the client. The client may need hard aspects to set their life into action. In many cases that is exactly what the hard aspects produce, the action needed to bring about a forward shift in life. You may look at future eclipses, five years ahead, to see if there is a trend toward more harmonious energy. Overall, realizing the innate characteristic of an eclipse is a high-energy experience.

One person experienced a Lunar Eclipse square her Moon. She was relocating across the country to eventually marry. There were many complications and power struggles making the entire process grueling.

Let's look at another couple in the following example. A couple met on the telephone in response to a personal ad within days of a Lunar Eclipse that was square both their Suns. His Sun is 25° Leo and her Sun is 26° Aquarius. For this couple, this was a romantic Lunar Eclipse. The Lunar Eclipse at 25° Taurus 42 took place in her seventh house of marriage and in his fifth house of romance. Nine months later the couple began living together. The following Lunar Eclipse also occurred at the same degree, 25°, but was not part of a set or pair of eclipses. It was the Lunar Eclipse at 25° Libra and that created a trine to her Sun and a sextile to his Sun that helped them take the next step in their relationship. The Libra Lunar Eclipse also formed a square to his Cancer Ascendant. The relationship was faced with many major challenges, even a huge health issue when the woman had open-heart surgery in January 1998. At the time of her surgery, she experienced a Lunar Eclipse in Virgo conjunct her Mars and conjunct her Sun. She recovered nicely and went back to the business of their relationship. In 1999 they were planning a wedding and starting a business together with a pair of fixed Solar Eclipses that square his 16° Taurus Mars and her 18° Taurus Jupiter. The Lunar Eclipse in the summer of '99 was in opposition to her Leo Moon. This couple seemed to use the Solar and Lunar Eclipse squares very well. They expressed some minor problems in their relationship around the intensity of the relationship and control issues, but for the most part the relationship was successful.

The Lunar Eclipse as Interference

Ancient astrology studies used the Earth when studying a chart. The earth was placed in a chart opposite the Sun to represent what effects the heavens had on the Earth. The ancient sky watchers were well aware of the Earth when an astronomical event in the heavens coincided with an event on Earth. It was not considered a superstitious connection, but the law of nature. To the ancients, all things were connected; as above, so below. Living in harmony with your environment meant keeping a tender and observable balance of the delicate web of life.

When a Lunar Eclipse occurs, the Earth is positioned between the Sun and the Moon, interrupting the flow of light from the Sun and casting a shadow over the face of the Full Moon. This interference from the Earth blocks the light normally received by the Moon. Well, this is a surprise. The Sun's light is not reflected, therefore it is not represented. It is shunned or dismissed, made impotent and insignificant. The Moon normally brilliant in the night sky is darkened and obliterated. The creative and the receptive are both interrupted by another body with a halting voice. At times it's obvious when the eclipse coincides with a natural disaster. A greater force takes center stage when the magnetic field is polarized at a critical moment and the Earth shifts or a volcano blows. Then we get it.

But when a Lunar Eclipse nonchalantly appears in your chart like a big Full Moon— do we get it? It's not a big Full Moon. It's something different. The Earth is a player, a major player. This mark is energized with the full magnetic field running straight through the center and out the other end of the Earth. How fantastic to have two large bodies on either side of the globe, both pulling with their greatest powers, and the Earth sits in the middle. The symbolism is different than a Full Moon. A major statement is being made. The Earth at the time of the eclipse acts as a body of people that can be associated with the symbolism of the sign or house it occupies. The Earth takes on the role of busybody, mediator, imposition, and/or go-between, diffusing the Sun's grand, brilliant and directive power. The Earth's position breaks the actions projected by the Suns' intentions and original plan (set 18 months prior). A pause, a halt or a dramatic shift in activities occurs, interrupting the stride of activities that have been flowing along for good or ill.

Imagine that the Sun is temporarily exiled and filed into a line which virtually neutralizes its power. Who dares to interrupt the light from the mighty Sun? The inability to nourish its garden during this time leaves surrounding circumstances to the lesser gods. Often there is an element of surprise, as if stunned by the interruption of the flow of light, and rightfully so.

The Lunar Eclipse symbolizes the perfect equalizer or communal power. The Sun needs help to shine again. Perhaps the matters planted at the New Moon eighteen months earlier could have run amiss, with important clues overlooked. On the positive side, by temporarily setting the Sun back from the limelight, it is time to invite additional players.

The most obvious example catches someone amidst a period of reckless behavior. A close aspect from a Lunar Eclipse can call out the "public eye" to examine, scrutinize, warrant, indict and terminate questionable activities.

Look again at when Bill Clinton's most private affairs became public, as prosecutors forced Clinton to answer a deposition in January 1998 in the Paula Jones case. The busybody characteristic of the Lunar Eclipse at 22° Virgo formed a square to Clinton's Uranus and nodal axis. Surprises galore tormented his

Uranus at 21° Gemini, ruler of his fifth house of romance. The eclipse actually landed in his twelfth house of private affairs. The eclipse brought all out in the open – more than we needed to know. By the time the next Lunar Eclipse occurred, Clinton answered questions before the grand jury on August 8, 1998. The Lunar Eclipse the day before at 15°Aquarius brought his lover Monica Lewinsky to the stand as well. Before the attack from the political right, Bill Clinton was nearly unstoppable with few boundaries. He was brilliant, well educated and popular both at home and abroad. His presidential agenda was unfortunately derailed when he was forced to answer to the courts.

A Lunar Eclipse is a Grandstanding Event Evaluating the Impact of a Lunar Eclipse
There is a vital difference between a common Full Moon and a Lunar Eclipse; the light is blocked from the Sun and that temporarily cuts out the light of the Moon. The symbolism of being eclipsed carries through the stories in our lives as we move through our activities and are interrupted or derailed by an imposing force. Perhaps it's a mild adjustment of priorities.

The sign and degree of the Lunar Eclipse, as with any full Moon, has a characteristic all its own. The nature of a Leo Lunar Eclipse is obviously different than one in Pisces. The house that receives the eclipse is lit up and stimulated as it magnetically attracts attention to matters akin to the sign. You might experience a son or daughter's wedding when a Libra Lunar Eclipse occurs in your fifth house; your dog may need special travel gear when you have a Sagittarius Lunar Eclipse in your sixth house.

With a typical Full Moon, the Solar point holds the power. What I mean by this is that during the original New Moon eighteen months earlier, the seed was planted.

The lunar point of the eclipse shows where, what and who is being drawn onto the stage in the form of the significant other to play a role for the eclipse. Expect matters of the entire polarity (such as the Taurus / Scorpio polarity) to be enlightened, exposed or ended in some significant way. Everything under the rulership of the sign is subject to exposure, whether intended for public view or not. Lunar Eclipses imprint a mark and provoke change in our lives, suggesting, in effect: "You will do things differently from this point on."

If the New Moon, eighteen months earlier, was a Solar Eclipse then its Lunar Eclipse will have greater consequences. An ordinary New Moon as the parent of a Lunar Eclipse might be less problematic. When assessing the impact of any Moon phase, look to the solar point as the "director" in the chart; the Moon delivers the event. The recipient quality of the Moon is always in response to the Sun in some way. They are never without some sort of relationship. They are the dominant lights that fuel our existence as the cosmic king and queen; we keep our eye on both. They are always seen as a couple. Anything associated with the pair is significant. Their midpoint is key to understanding their common ground; their arc separation at any aspect is important as well as their sign placements.

The New Moon's seed chart for the Lunar Eclipse holds the clues for the hidden or underdeveloped issues which began 18 months before, and that are now in full bloom and subject to scrutiny by the public. Perhaps the creative drive represented by the Sun has gone off in the "wrong direction," and by the time it opposes the point of the parenting New Moon it is time for a realignment. If so, this is the time that fact will be revealed.

A First House Lunar Eclipse puts the solar point in the seventh house.
A Lunar Eclipse in the first house shows the Sun in the seventh house, exposing personal issues of your partner or some type of outer social affair that reaches into your first house and may draw you into the drama. This Lunar Eclipse can be present at the time of an engagement or beginning of a partnership or marriage planning, much like the Lunar Eclipse in the reverse position. Often legal matters begin and/or end with a Lunar Eclipse in the first house. The Sun in the seventh house may represent assistance to the significant other. Check the status of the ruler of the seventh house and evaluate how the Lunar Eclipse affects it. Often, but not always, seventh house people are calling the shots at the time of a first house Lunar Eclipse. Seventh house people are mates, best friends, lawyers, business partners or hired consultants. The seventh house person represents the significant other in any primary scenario in your life. For instance if you have a car accident involving another moving vehicle, the other driver becomes the significant other. One person was diagnosed with hepatitis C when a Lunar Eclipse was conjunct the Ascendant. Of course the partner became directly involved with the medical issue.

A Second House Lunar Eclipse puts the solar point in the eighth house.
The Sun in the eighth house shines light on your personal finances and holdings, but it is the eighth house people who are looking. Eighth house people could be the IRS, loan holders and mortgage lenders, estate lawyers or a person that represents the public at large. Your paycheck is in your second house and this could be good or bad. Since the eighth house rules mortgages, taxes, estates and other shared resources, you may be seeing a settlement (the end of the matter) that deposits (the *Lunar* point of the eclipse) money in your (second house) hand. So look at the rulers of your second house to see if it is receiving the eclipse in a favorable fashion. Do not always expect a trine to be your savior as it allows things to flow in a certain direction and not necessarily the way you think matters should proceed. Other second house topics that are not particularly financial are your talents. You could find someone in a public position (eighth house) drawn to your talents.

A Third House Lunar Eclipse puts the solar point in the ninth house.
The third house Lunar point of a Lunar Eclipse is likely to include the symbolism from ninth house affairs such as foreign travel, higher education and religious matters. The third house represents your neighborhood and that may change with a third house Lunar Eclipse. It may not be forever, but the Lunar Eclipse that activates your third and ninth houses is sure to take you outside your normal realm of experience and offer a new perspective on life.

This was the case for a woman whose life shifted drastically when she married in '94. An eclipse in her third house set her chart off when a Lunar Eclipse at 25° Taurus 42' was conjunct natal Jupiter at 25° Taurus 51'. Jupiter ruled her Sagittarius Midheaven and formed a sextile to her fifth house Venus in Cancer. She had graduated from a Boston school earlier and it was time for her husband to continue his education. Shortly after the wedding, the couple relocated to Pennsylvania for her husband's graduate school program. While away from home, the woman came to value her family and friends in a new way contrary to how she previously imagined her freedom. She actually hated living so far away from home. Her husband did not like the masters program at the new school and they returned when he was accepted at MIT in their hometown.

Other events may include a major event with a sibling, such as his or her marriage, birth of a child or health issues. This eclipse position could also affect involvement with immigration laws, or struggle with a customs department while traveling.

With a Lunar Eclipse in the third house and the solar point in the ninth, matters of the ninth house may reach out in a public way. A substantial advertising project may be indicated or a thesis deadline. It could be a time to bring in a new computer or other communication equipment.

A Fourth House Lunar Eclipse puts the solar point in the tenth house.
This Lunar Eclipse will certainly create major life change, especially if it occurs close to the Midheaven. You may find yourself changing career direction. A man was forced to make such a decision when a pair of Lunar Eclipses created a square to his Midheaven. He had started a company that he put his heart and soul energy into, when ten years later internal power struggles forced him to move on.

Another man had been committed to a Ph.D. program when he suddenly decided it was time for him and his wife to get on with the business of making their family. His chart received the Lunar Eclipse conjunct his fourth house cusp. He found a job in his field working as an engineer. The Solar point naturally was conjunct his Midheaven symbolizing career moves. At first his wife was concerned with what, at first, appeared to be quitting, but then she realized how important it was to finally start their family.

A Fifth House Lunar Eclipse puts the solar point in the eleventh house.
This eclipse can bring some happy events if the natal chart happily receives it. Many times people find love, get married or have a child with a Lunar Eclipse in the fifth house. It can also symbolize your child's wedding. This is the house of creativity. This can be great for an art show or cutting your first record. Do whatever fun thing that you would love to do more of. Children are often indicated with this Lunar Eclipse. The solar point in the eleventh house can bring stepchildren into your life.

The entire chart must be considered when evaluating the impact of any eclipse. Naturally, the symbolism will vary when with aspects to radical planets. For instance, one woman's life has experienced drastic shifts when a Lunar Eclipse occurs in her fifth or eleventh houses, because it squares her natal Saturn. One of the Lunar Eclipses brought the birth of her daughter. A pair of Lunar Eclipses timed first the beginning of her chiropractic business and then her father's bypass surgery. Her father's convalescence created a huge crisis in her life because she covered for all his chiropractic patients, as well as dealing with a medical emergency in the family.

Another client experienced the Sun in the eleventh house at the 2004 Taurus Lunar Eclipse. The Moon fell in her fifth house of children when her daughter became engaged to her long-term boyfriend.

A Sixth House Lunar Eclipse puts the solar point in the twelfth house.

This Lunar Eclipse can affect a number of matters that are work- or health-related. It really does depend on what planets occupy, oppose or square this house. This could be a time when deadlines press on major work projects. It could signify the end a job or the finding of the job that you've been hunting for some time. It could expose issues that have been brewing for the past year and a half with co-workers (remember there was a New Moon at this zodiacal address a year and a half ago.) This Lunar Eclipse could also expose a health matter. If it creates an aspect to Mars there could be a surgical procedure involved in the treatment. Pets are often a focus and you may decide to adopt a pet or tend to a convalescing animal. Mental health concerns are very common with a Lunar Eclipse in the sixth house. You may receive a diagnosis and seek treatment for depression with medication or acupuncture treatments. The sign on the cusps of the twelfth and sixth houses gives clues as to the type of health maintenance indicated. Then again, you may just find yourself working very hard.

For instance, one man experienced a Lunar Eclipse in the sixth house when he broke his hip cleaning his house's gutters. The 11° Leo Lunar Eclipse occurred exactly at the midpoint of his Saturn/Pluto conjunction. The eclipse also was square his eighth house Jupiter, ruler of his Midheaven. Ten days after his fall, his dad died suddenly of a heart attack. Saturn ruled his Capricorn 12th house cusp.

A Seventh House Lunar Eclipse puts the solar point in the first house.

This Lunar Eclipse is likely to "show you the way." You could become involved in a major social event. A younger recipient of this Lunar Eclipse found himself following others. With so many choices in today's world, this is a good time to introduce a regimen that leads you in a positive direction. If you are paying attention, this eclipse could put you in the right spot at the right time. For instance, if someone is particularly creative, this could lead him or her into a setting that promotes more creativity. Even if you are not one to party by nature, you may receive more invitations than usual or even give a party of your own. The seventh house focus is likely to draw you out and into a more social scene. You may initiate a law suit or seek council for a matter that has been your primary focus for some time. A major drama involving a loved one may dominate your attention. I had this eclipse six months after I began working as a 900-Line Astrologer. I met volumes of new people in a short period of time and began working for a very creative globe-trotting client and still do to this day. We have a very close working relationship that is productive and profitable for us both.

An Eighth House Lunar Eclipse puts the solar point in the second house.

A Pisces woman took an offer for a new job with a 25% increase in pay when the Taurus Lunar Eclipse fell in her eighth house. The solar point in her second house of talents was bringing her rewards and increased the cash in her pocket. Eighth house eclipses can accompany matters regarding death, sex, taxes and surgery. It also rules matters of insurance, estates and monies held in accounts in your name, like social security. It rules pregnancies and miscarriages.

Here is a story of a client who suffered a miscarriage after a Lunar Eclipse at 0°Leo occurred in her second house and the next Lunar Eclipse at 25°Capricorn was conjunct her eighth house. The 0° Leo eclipse formed aspects to her Venus (ruled her fifth) and Uranus (ruler of her eighth). The Capricorn eclipse formed aspects to her Mars in the fifth and the Moon in the sixth. The woman's sadness was compounded by the detached response from her mate. Naturally, she was expecting compassion, but instead her partner responded to her heartbreak with no support whatsoever. He didn't want a child, so for him this was a blessing. At a total loss for emotional support, she turned to a neighbor who had been visiting the couple over the past year and they began to bond over the issue. The next Lunar Eclipse occurred in her seventh house and through the support from the friend she found the strength to temporarily separate from her inconsiderate partner. The five-month separation ended with a Lunar Eclipse in her seventh house. The couple stayed together for another two years but these events marked the beginning of the end of this long-term relationship.

A Ninth House Lunar Eclipse puts the solar point in the third house.
Success is often the result of this eclipse. One man experienced his Saturn return at the time he graduated from an MIT Masters program at the top of his class in 1998. His chart received a Lunar Eclipse in the ninth house. Another man experienced great success when his ninth house Lunar Eclipse brought him the deal of a lifetime. He founded a dot com business that would assist lawyers and others when filing legal documents (ninth house topic). The Sun in his third house helped him sharpen his networking skills as he secured funding and technical support with ease and swiftly began moving forward. These things were initiated nearly two months before the Lunar Eclipse in the fall of 2004 at 5°Taurus.

A Tenth House Lunar Eclipse puts the solar point in the fourth house.
When a Lunar Eclipse occurs in the tenth house, fourth house matters are illuminated by the Sun's presence in this sensitive and most personal area of your chart. The fourth house is the private zone that is filled with your deepest feelings, personal concerns and the problems that you are most prone to keep to yourself. This zone is so personal, that as a professional astrologer, I tread very softly. After explaining the nature of the fourth house area, now under a spotlight, I invite my client to share what feels safe. I then offer my insights, still employing a delicate approach. Just because someone is in my office, I resist assuming anything. Nor do I stomp in private areas without asking first. I avoid a dogmatic approach, as so many times the clients sees themselves differently and they know best. I've been hired as a consultant and avoid the role of a "seer."

Often the issues surround major conclusions to matters concerning the home and housing, parents and family structure, brought into the open arena of the tenth house. But most often there are deeper matters that have been brewing steadily over the past year and a half since a New Moon or Solar Eclipse occurred in the fourth house.

One of the most difficult times for a man occurred when he experienced a Lunar Eclipse conjunct his tenth house. It was filled with emotional issues that hit, one right after another. First, he decided he made a big mistake by moving in with a friend. It was a very incompatible situation. His greatest source of moral support married and moved away. A dear friend died and another was sent to prison. The man had to learn to reach out (which was the result of the third and ninth house eclipses), but first went through a year of alternative healing practitioners to seek some balance.

In another case, a Lunar Eclipse occurred in a man's tenth house and he became involved in a public dispute over the name of his newfound business. He eventually chose a new name for his business.

A video producer launched a documentary project that placed him on the map in his field when a Lunar Eclipse was conjunct his Midheaven. However, during that time he became deeply upset about the power struggle with the mother of his daughter over their child. The Solar point was conjunct natal Pluto.

An Eleventh House puts the Solar point in the fifth house

This Lunar Eclipse puts the Solar point in the fifth house. The eleventh house is special because the Ascendant/Midheaven midpoint most often falls in this house. The Asc/Mc midpoint is what I call the toggle switch in your chart. If the eclipse occurs within 10° of this point, you will experience an event that has an impact on every house in the chart. If you have planets in the fifth or eleventh house, the planet will dominate the nature of the scenario activated by a lunar eclipse here. Donald Rumsfeld's chart is a good example of how an eclipse here proved to be highly troublesome in his life. It was reported in January 2004 that sexually explicit photographs were taken of the prisoners at the Abu Ghraib base on November 8, 2003. That was the day of a Lunar Eclipse that fell in Rumsfeld's fifth house. Three months later (at a Power Point Moon phase) Mr. Rumsfeld claimed that the photo reached his desk in January. The press did not get a strong hold on the story until the Lunar Eclipse on May 4, 2004. The American Gulf War Veterans Association had called for his resignation back in October 2002, and these calls accelerated from all sources through the presidential elections in 2004. Bush asked Rumsfeld to stay for a second term against popular opinion to let him go.

A Twelfth House Lunar Eclipse puts the Solar point in the sixth house

Another opportunity to refer to past presidential politics. The Lunar Eclipse at 22°24' Virgo on March 13, 1998 was the influencing eclipse when Bill Clinton answered the deposition in the Paula Jones case. That degree fell in the President's twelfth house, accusing him of inappropriate sexual behavior. The interference factor of a lunar eclipse was completely vivid in this example.

Most of you won't suffer the public humiliation and embarrassment that President Clinton did, but you may undergo a private battle with secrets that come to the surface. Perhaps matters with other employees invade your privacy. You may have a close relationship with a neighbor that turns from fond to foul.

For some it is a period of health maintenance appointments. One woman was remodeling her house by adding a large room. It turned into a fiasco with contractors that she claims nearly drove her insane. One man told a sad story that had a silver lining, of an acquaintance who willed him a large sum of money in a suicide note. As the designated heir and now a suspect for the possible murder of the poor fellow, the surviving man was left with the largest legal clean-up job of his life.

Lunar Eclipse To The Planets

As with all interpretations in astrology, assessment is relative to many factors. These notes are not intended to be taken as fact, but as suggestions that may inspire your own observations. These are simply my observations.

When any major event involves a planet in your chart, you must consider all of the natal aspects to that planet. Use this rule whenever a planet is under the direct influence of a Solar or Lunar Eclipse, an important progression, a planet station or a major transiting configuration. Another planet for close study is the house ruler. Follow the same rules when investigating the natal aspects to the house ruler. While a seventh house ruled by Venus may seem like a dream, if that Venus is involved in a T-square with Pluto and Mars, it may not be the best time for the person's relationships. It will certainly be a time that reveals what that T-square really means in the individual's life.

This could be described as a very public time period in your life, especially if a Lunar Eclipse contacts your personal planets. Because of the activation of polar opposites occupied by the 180° separation of the Sun and Moon, you are not likely to be isolated if your planets are directly involved. A 5° orb for the conjunction or opposition may hold the greatest impact; the square with a tight orb of 2.5° is next and the very small 1°-2° orb for the sextile and trine can show symbolism developing as well. You may be directly involved in a major life change or closely supportive or involved with someone who is the object of a significant event. A Lunar Eclipse in aspect to a planet or personal point brings far greater activity than a hit that occurs in a house without planet contact. A house is also activated when an eclipse aspects a *house ruler*. When the planet ruling the Ascendant or Midheaven is in aspect from the eclipse, there may be core changes to the structure of your body, relationships, and/or life direction.

Lunar Eclipse Point Conjunct the Natal Sun
This eclipse is a powerful event that will occur opposite your birthday. If this eclipse is square to your Sun, it is three months before or after your birthday. Each of these positions is highly dynamic and sure to bring elevated activity into your life. Besides an aspect from an eclipse (New or Full Moon) to your Sun, note the significant shifts in each year when the transiting Sun forms hard angles (conjunction, square and opposition) to your natal Sun. This is the case if a Lunar Eclipse is square the Sun. (For solar return charts: the last square of the Sun to the natal Sun, and three months before the birthday, marks the onset of the next solar return chart. This is similar to the onset and release point of the eclipse seasons.)

I use a method for looking more directly into the effects of a Lunar Eclipse (or any major transit event) to the Sun by casting the solar chart, derived by casting your chart with the Sun on the ASC and equal houses. This chart proves useful with all your chart studies and can be used in accompaniment with your charts that are cast with time and space house systems. I find any tool that brings you back to the basics of astrology delivers an uncomplicated view of the chart that will deepen your relationship with the most powerful planet in the chart, the Sun, and allow the symbolism to be obvious.

With the transiting Sun opposed your natal Sun, the power would be in the hands of a significant other (of any kind). If the opposition in your life holds the power, it is possible for it to work in your favor. If you are involved in an adversarial situation this could put you at a disadvantage. This could also be an indication that timing is the issue. You may be on the right track but need to give matters time to

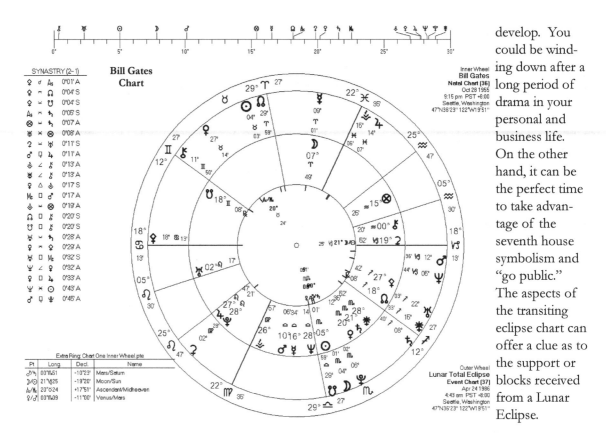

Bill Gates Chart

develop. You could be winding down after a long period of drama in your personal and business life. On the other hand, it can be the perfect time to take advantage of the seventh house symbolism and "go public." The aspects of the transiting eclipse chart can offer a clue as to the support or blocks received from a Lunar Eclipse.

A Lunar Eclipse in aspect to the natal Sun can bring an end to your career as you know it or the way you do your job. You may find matters of timing to be most significant. For example your timing could be excellent, or you may be faced with crucial timing deadlines. When you are working on a major project, the deadline seems to have a natural affinity for Lunar Eclipse dates. A Lunar Eclipse can bring projects to a point of full presentation and maximum exposure for success. Such was the case with billionaire Bill Gates who launched Microsoft on March 13, 1986, six weeks before the Lunar Eclipse at 4 Scorpio occurred conjunct his natal Sun. In the eclipse chart, transiting Jupiter broadened his public appeal as it reached out to the masses from his ninth house and formed a propitious grand trine to his Cancer Ascendant and Scorpio Saturn in the fifth house. To add stability to the promise of success, transiting Saturn formed another grand trine to his career's tenth house Aries Moon and to his Uranus in his first house. The transiting Saturn acted as an anchor for his personal endeavors. Six days after Microsoft's first trade chart, transiting Saturn made a retrograde station.

High Energy From Eclipses Acts as an Incentive for Change.
When the Solar point is conjunct your Sun at the eclipse, you become motivated to take matters into your own hands. If the eclipse opposes your Sun, others have the control and matters can operate in your favor if the situation draws the favor of others. Managing the surrounding business relationships can become your greatest challenge. Often Lunar Eclipses in aspect to the natal Sun may be an indica-

tion of internal company problems or changes in the chain of command, many of which can be traced directly to the boss. In this next example, we see a chart of a businessman who began a company with three other men in 1988. The prime directive of the company was to unite global commerce. The original consortium remained aligned but experienced continual power struggles with

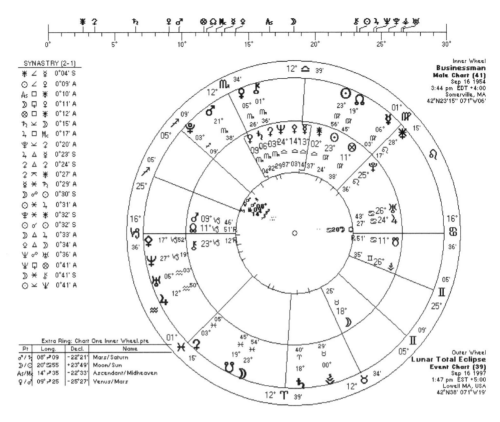

its financial backers. This businessman felt his efforts were thwarted at every move and suffered years of frustration with little financial reward.

Lunar Eclipse Point Opposite the Natal Sun

When a Lunar Eclipse occurs in opposition to your natal Sun, it may be your birthday. The solar point at its return to your Sun makes this a benchmark birthday. The events of this year are likely to be memorable and will mark a time period of many life changes. You could be empowered by this Lunar Eclipse. Cast your solar return chart and study its effects from this eclipse.

With the Lunar Eclipse solar point conjunct your Sun, you may be changing jobs or your career. Eventually, you will be privy to all that goes on around you. If you find yourself at the center of a drama and everyone seems to know your business, it is because this is such a public time. You could be presenting an important project for your work and find you are well-received.

A Lunar Eclipse point opposite the Sun is used in the next example of a Gemini woman's chart who we will call Carol. She came for a consultation one month before the Lunar Eclipse of June 4th, 1993, because of problems at work. Her job description was beginning to change and she became concerned

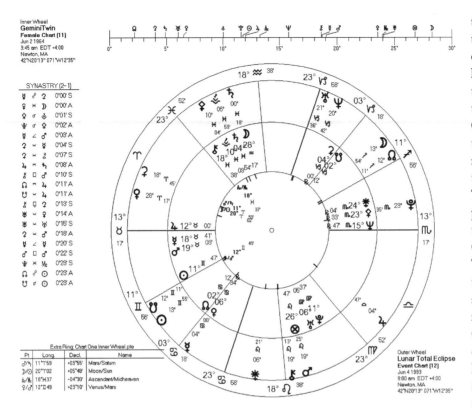

Inner Wheel
GeminiTwin
Female Chart (11)
Jun 2 1964
3:45 am EDT +4:00
Newton, MA
42°N20'13" 071°W12'35"

SYNASTRY (2-1)

☿ ☍ ♃	0°00' S	
♀ ⚹ ☽	0°00' A	
♀ ☌ ⚷	0°01' S	
♀ ☌ ♀	0°02' A	
☿ ∠ ♂	0°03' A	
♃ ⚺ ♅	0°04' S	
♃ ⚻ ⚷	0°07' A	
♄ ⚻ ♄	0°08' A	
⚷ □ ♂	0°10' S	
☊ ⚻ ♃	0°11' A	
☋ ⚻ ♃	0°11' A	
⚷ ⚼ ♃	0°13' S	
♅ ⚺ ♀	0°14' A	
♅ ⚺ ♅	0°16' S	
♃ ⚺ ♂	0°18' A	
☿ ∠ ♅	0°20' S	
♂ □ ♂	0°22' S	
♆ ⚹ Mc	0°23' S	
☊ ☍ ☉	0°23' A	
☋ ☌ ☉	0°23' A	

Extra Ring: Chart One Inner Wheel.pte

Pt	Long.	Decl.	Name
♂/♄	11°♈59	+03°55'	Mars/Saturn
☽/☉	20°♈02	+05°48'	Moon/Sun
As/Mc	18°♓37	-04°30'	Ascendant/Midheaven
♀/♂	12°♊49	+23°10'	Venus/Mars

Outer Wheel
Lunar Total Eclipse
Event Chart (12)
Jun 4 1993
9:00 am EDT +4:00
Newton, MA
42°N20'13" 071°W12'35"

that her job could be threatened. Coincidentally, Carol's husband was the top salesperson at the same company. Carol was very close to her boss and noticed changes in the boss's attitude. The Lunar Eclipse point at 13° Sagittarius was located in Carol's eighth house. This is usually a sign that finances are about to undergo a major shift. The 13° Gemini Sun of the eclipse in her second house suggested that she would continue to receive money. The eclipse Sun was conjunct her natal Sun within 2 degrees. An eclipse to the natal Sun is an indicator that the company was undergoing a major shift. The natal Sun represents the status of the company where you work. I thought it might be possible that her boss would leave the job and that there might be layoffs. Even though Carol's boss was a woman, she would still be represented by Carol's natal Sun. With transiting Uranus conjunct Carol's Midheaven, anything could have happened, even an extended vacation. This was beginning to look more and more probable, especially with transiting Jupiter at the Lunar Eclipse in her sixth house of jobs. The symbolism later proved to fit when she lost her job and began collecting unemployment benefits. Carol had more on her lists of concerns. Her pregnant twin sister was opening a New Age bookstore. The sister's dream was to have Carol quit her day job and join her as a partner to run the store. Carol was torn because she liked her current job and wanted to join her sister, but felt insecure about running a new business. I suggested she do nothing for a month and simply watch the changes at the office. I implied that her boss might leave and that the company would begin laying people off shortly thereafter. I told her there was a possibility she would be collecting unemployment by the middle of the summer and that she would be able to help her sister with the store by the Full Moon on August 2, 1993. As it turned out, the boss left the job, and the company revealed they were in trouble and began laying people off. Many employees were laid off before Carol, which made her worry that she would miss an opportunity to change careers. By August 2, Carol was laid off and joined her sister to run the new store.

Lunar Eclipse to the Natal Moon

The natal Moon in a horoscope is one of the richest points for the study of eclipses. The Moon, after all, is the brightest light in the night sky. Putting aside our scientific knowledge of the Moon's actual size, from Earth's vantage point the Moon is as large as the Sun itself. The importance of the Moon lies in the symbolism of this optical illusion. The Sun, representing our vital body, can not exist without the Moon to represent our soul or emotional body. The Sun by day, the Moon by night, both light the way to individuality. The Sun/Moon midpoint represents the integration point of the brilliant pair representing one's heart and soul.

The activation of the Moon by any eclipse can act as a trigger to one's deep personal relationships or set off a period of emotional land mines, creating not only a psychological statement but residual fallout carried over to new relationships. All relationships (including various types such as co-worker, sibling, etc.) become fair game for a period of upheaval whenever the natal Moon is triggered by an eclipse, major transit or progression.

A long list of Moon topics are likely to include a change in personal relationship status, changes to living situation, a new baby in your immediate or extended family, a focus on wife, mother or another women to whom you are close. At a minimum, a change in your daily routine can be expected. The changes effected by an eclipse can prove to be as momentous as those to the natal Sun. Expect any aspect to the Moon from any eclipse to set the Moon's natal promise into action. You may need adequate time to recover from an eclipse to your Moon. Not only is the stage set for a long time healing, but it can also indicate extended rewards that can manifest to add fulfillment in your life.

To be born with a Moon on an eclipse point often indicates that one has experienced a lifetime of extreme turmoil to the home base and one's emotional foundation has been under great challenge. To gain closure on the past and engage in solid emotional support is crucial to the individual's mental health. It is futile to avoid dealing with one's emotions with a natal Moon on an eclipse point. The memories held within the Moon are activated when aspected by an eclipse. A Lunar Eclipse might bring someone into your life to help you process your past and your memories. The pre-programmed material that one accepts as the facts of one's life is challenged every time an eclipse sets off that Moon, and you are given an opportunity to change. Of course you could opt to run in the other direction to avert any possible change but I don't think it will help. Somehow, some way, the old ways are being challenged.

Consider all aspects, no matter how small, to effect change when the Moon is involved with an eclipse. Watch for a set of eclipses in aspect to the Moon to generate a list of significant Moon-related events.

The first thing to assess is the nature of the eclipse by sign and the transiting planet most closely aspected. The aspects to your natal Moon color the activities you are likely to experience. A natal Moon/Saturn aspect may respond to eclipses by buying and selling real estate or making serious decisions in regard to elders, whereas a Moon/Jupiter natal aspect may respond to eclipses with expansion of extended family and travel. Certainly the Moon's natal house will be a major consideration. Look for a dominant transiting aspect such as a Pluto station conjunct your Moon or a Saturn Jupiter square in relationship to your Moon. Each eclipse is different.

If your **Moon is located in the first house,** the eclipse experience is likely to be very personal. You may be extremely emotional during this eclipse season. All your woes may be worn on your sleeve. If the **Moon is in the second house,** the eclipse could set off a financial drama that triggers emotions around having enough and feelings of not being enough. Your resources may change with strong emotional fluxes. When a Lunar Eclipse is in aspect to your **Moon in the third house,** your siblings could be affected. You may also move, since the third house rules neighborhood and the Moon rules home. A Lunar Eclipse to a fourth house Moon will surely create change in the home, and family is the focus. A **fifth house Moon** is likely to place the focus on children, vacations and creative projects as well as on personal relationships. With an eclipse in aspect to your **sixth house Moon,** the way you eat and work changes. Co-workers are a big topic with an eclipse to the sixth house Moon. A **seventh house Moon** will activate your personal relationships more deeply and involve your dearest friends and their mothers. An **eighth house Moon** will bring matters of shared resources that are connected with monthly cycles, such as shared payments of mortgages and other household expenses. You may experience changes with your maternal figures. You could become involved with some vast public event. A **ninth house Moon** will probably help you finish school or reach out into the foreign places of the world. With an eclipse to a **tenth house Moon** you may finally land a great job on your soul's path. Or you could again experience change with your mother or housing. With an eclipse to an **eleventh house Moon** you may realize a long-term goal. This Lunar Eclipse could bring children into your life, especially other people's children. An eclipse to a **twelfth house Moon** can seem almost magical as it attracts that soul mate feeling to relationships begun at this time. It can be a time of great spiritual growth or a time that draws you into a deeply-committed service position. You may also feel all your secrets are at risk for being exposed.

Some people report a change in food habits when a Lunar Eclipse is in aspect to the Moon. For example, a woman moved and her eating habits changed drastically because her new home had a poorly-operating electric range and she was attached to cooking with gas. She stopped cooking and began eating poorly. The stove may have become an issue as her natal Mars aspects her Moon. Another person became a vegetarian when an eclipse hit the Moon.

Lunar Eclipse to Mercury
A Lunar Eclipse in any aspect to Mercury may activate a series of events that involves trails of paperwork. Typically a sequel of activities is set up in a "next step" format (you must do this before you do that, etc.). This eclipse could be particularly annoying and tedious, or it could include a set of self-selected tasks. Areas of your life where you have avoided details give this eclipse season a bull's-eye target. You may find more things get lost or broken beyond repair if left untended. Animal stories are high on the list of Mercury eclipses as well as issues with children, regardless of age, and shifts in routine. One of the most interesting characteristics to an eclipse to Mercury is an increase in introductions to new people and invitations you may receive. Mercury can bring people together from your past with those that you have never met. It's a curious combination, compounded by the node of the Moon in proximity to Mercury. It often opens doors through the mother. Several people report the loss of

their mother with this eclipse.

In the case of Prince Charles, his Mercury at 6°Scorpio and south node of the Moon at 4°Scorpio received the 2005 Lunar Eclipse at 4°Scorpio the month he married Camilla Parker Bowles. The original plans for the wedding were scheduled for the day of the Solar Eclipse at 19°Aries on his MC, but the passing of Pope John Paul II caused them to delay the wedding for a day.

For one woman, a set of Lunar Eclipses to her fifth house Mercury brought a new car after someone hit her parked car during a snowstorm. Soon after, the reinstatement of her son's driver's license ended a long period of the mom driving for the family business. Then the woman's mother died, followed by the son's wedding. A new family member was welcomed, which then involved a series of details required by immigration since the bride was a citizen of another country. The second Lunar Eclipse continued the drama, bringing an end to the marriage with the foreign bride. The son had deeply fallen for the woman, but he discovered that she was only interested in a marriage to obtain U.S. citizenship. The son was devastated and he spiraled into a deep depression.

Lunar Eclipse to Venus

A Lunar Eclipse in aspect to Venus may not always create new activity in the relationship department, but may focus on how your relationships function. For many, you may have a period when all your friendships are shifting and the lesson is how you get along with others and how you have selected your friends. Perhaps you feel you've grown out of your friendships or they seem to operate in a one-way direction. At times people find a new mate if other factors are activated, such as the ascendant, descendant, and their rulers. Often it's the Solar Eclipse that coincides with a marriage. Of course, if your Venus is in your seventh house and rules that house, chances are very high that you will marry within six to nine months of an eclipse conjunct your Venus. With existing relationships, it may be a time when they are scrutinized, criticized and up for review as this bright light exposes a couple's trouble spots. Some have experienced a renewal to their marriage. An eclipse activating Venus is probably not a guarantee to happiness, but may stimulate friendship and acts of kindness from inside and out. Many people talk of how their friends have shown them unexpected support during a time in need. You may come into some money or increase your earnings. Your relationships with women could improve with a focus on sisters. For some, there was a change in their appearance. It doesn't always bring blessings, especially if Venus is involved in a difficult natal T-square or otherwise compromising position. One woman's mother died the year a set of Lunar Eclipses were conjunct/opposite her Venus.

A woman with her Venus at 14°Taurus who was living in a horrible marriage found that it became more loving after a set of Lunar Eclipses to her Venus. Her boys went off to college together and left the couple alone. They didn't have as much to argue over with the boys gone. Many times they nearly killed each other and now they are becoming more peaceful. She also received an increase in pay and ease to the turmoil she had been suffering at work.

America's first funny lady, Lucille Ball, was a Leo with a Libra MC showing the ruler Venus at 23°Virgo Her solar arc-progressed Sun reached 22°Virgo when a Lunar Eclipse occurred at 22° Pisces, leaving the eclipse Sun with her Venus. This eclipse set the stage just a month before her TV show "I Love Lucy" aired and lasted for ten years. Her Virgo Venus in its fall did not hold her back. Ms. Ball was a multi-talent in the industry and was president of the Desilu studio, which she ran. She brought shows to television such as *Mission Impossible* and *Star Trek*. This is another case where the Lunar Eclipse Sun is conjunct a planet that brings a benefit.

Lunar Eclipse to Mars

As you might expect, a Lunar Eclipse to your Mars can heat up your life. You may find yourself compelled and driven in a way that most directly speaks to the inherent meaning of your natal Mars. You could experience longer work days needing greater effort. Besides the potential for job changes, conflict, and anger issues, this eclipse brings your independent and willful nature right to the surface. You may find yourself taking a stand and venturing out into the world in a way that could change how you see yourself and the rest of the world. You may do something that becomes a well-known fact in your world. You may find you are willing to risk it all for your principals or desires. You may be more demonstrative and open in your behavior with actions that are straightforward, clear and highly motivated. A woman may expect direct attention from your man or young adult son, or another important man may draw you into an arena that involves the two of you. If you are unattached, you may become attached. If attached, you may end your relationship. If you maintain your current relationship, it may change dramatically. You may have to take on challenges you never thought you would encounter. Your courage becomes a factor.

When a Lunar Eclipse is conjunct your Mars, the Sun sits in opposition to your Mars. The area of the most control follows the Sun. This opposition to Mars can place your most important matters in the hands of another. The significant other in this case needs to be addressed directly. For instance, if you are involved in a legal matter, the opposition could have the upper hand. An eclipse to one's Mars often invites legal issues. Even with a simpler transit you could have to appear in court for one reason or another.

An excellent example of Mars in action can be seen in the story of Cassius Clay, who won the Olympic light-heavyweight championship in 1960. In 1964 he became Muhammad Ali, truly a Mars individual, won the crown of world heavyweight boxing champion, and continued to gain global attention. Three years later he refused to serve in the military for religious reasons (natal Mars in the ninth house). He failed to appear for his scheduled induction in Houston on April 18, 1967. The public involvement at a Lunar Eclipse came from the New York Athletic Commission who stripped Ali of his title and boxing in reaction to his stand as a conscientious objector to the Viet Nam war. The Lunar Eclipse occurred six days later in his third house and opposed his Mars, exactly. The Sun appeared proudly conjunct his ninth house Mars and the eclipse chart Venus was conjunct his Jupiter. The fortunate planets are a clue to the eventual favorable outcome, supported by transiting Jupiter in opposition to his Sun. Ali became the subject of extreme reactions, for there were those who loathed his actions and others who praised him. This began a highly publicized three-year court fiasco that eventually concluded in Ali's favor with a Supreme Court decision on October 26, 1970, when he returned to the ring again and knocked out each of his opponents. We see astrology in action with the transiting Sun on October 26th at 3° Scorpio conjoined the Lunar Eclipse point that began his fight as the conscientious objector in April 1967.

Four years later he regained his title. In the following chart the Lunar Eclipse, just days after he was stripped of his title, shows the Sun conjunct his ninth house Mars. The power of the Sun put these events in Ali's hands, and it was his choice to fight this battle that he eventually won. Here is an interesting note about the Lunar Eclipse prior to the Supreme Court decision in Ali's favor: it showed transiting Mars (the boxer) conjunct the Leo Sun (the star) opposed to the Aquarius Moon (the rights of the people), forming a grand fixed cross to Saturn (the

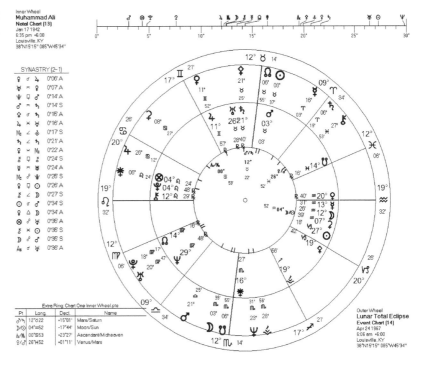

supreme court) in Taurus and Neptune (religious objection) in Scorpio. The August 16, 1970 Lunar Eclipse at 23°Aquarius laid across Ali's Ascendant into his seventh house and conjunct his natal Venus. Saturn had returned to its natal position in his 10th house.

Muhammad Ali is now fighting his battle with Parkinson's disease, diagnosed in 1984 when a Lunar Eclipse was conjunct transiting Mars and fell in his fourth house. His progressed Mars reached natal Uranus in the tenth house, and transiting Saturn was tightly conjunct his IC. He remains one of America's most beloved characters, and has received many awards throughout the years for his courage and convictions. I find it interesting that a fighter's message is that of peace.

An eclipse to your Mars ignites your driving force on all levels. This can mean your motivating force, as well as your physical energy, is needed to sustain your efforts. You will get a first hand lesson in what gets you "all fired up." What are you missing in regard to the Mars principal in your life? Are you disarmed in some way? Do you allow your anger to sabotage your progress? Do you prolong addressing underlying issues, causing resentments that block your path? Here's an interesting question: can you identify a blockage of the heat source in your life? What keeps your internal furnace running smoothly?

My observation has shown that the transiting Sun to natal Mars, or the reverse, occurs at a time when there is a build-up of heat in the body which often results in a run down condition, leaving you open to any virus that comes along.

In transit, an eclipse conjunct transiting Mars is noisy and riddled with blasts, fire or violence. It has been present as a positive boost, lighting the flame for invention, creating new designs such as for engines or tires for vehicles. Some of the most horrific events involving a streak of rage have shown a strong Mars influence in the eclipse chart. Mars has never been listed as benefic planet but nothing is ever all bad or all good. Mars brings the fire under the pot to get things cooking and working with a full head of steam.

This fire under the pot most commonly sets the stage for job issues; for some it's a job change or possibly a facet of work that comes under fire. For many, it's a time of completion. When the Lunar Eclipse activates your Mars your performance may be required to meet a major deadline. Maybe it will mark the end of a significant project or the close of a department.

One woman decided it was time to move on. Here is her story. A set of Lunar Eclipses hit a high-profile natal Mars at the cardinal axis of 15°Taurus in the chart of this Pisces female. Her Mars is in the eighth house and the Lunar Eclipses would fall in the second and eighth for a period from November 2003 through April 2005. Early 2004 she became dissatisfied with her comfortable supportive job of seven years when she got another offer from a head hunter. She was a high performer in a sales position and could set her terms, but her company had reached a ceiling on her pay. Her company truly wanted her to stay but she decided to take the new job. Upon resignation from her existing job, she became extremely ill. She suffered from multiple sclerosis. Too sick to start her new job for two months, she got off on the wrong foot. Finally five months into the new job and at the final Scorpio eclipse April 24, 2005, she decided to return to her old job. They were supportive to her when she had flare ups of her illness and had been there throughout her marriage, then divorce, and were an all around, caring company. A lesson of values and support became more important than an increase in pay. The last set of Scorpio/Taurus Lunar Eclipses fell at 5° which formed a tight square to her natal Nodes of the Moon. This speaks to the health crisis surrounding the change.

If you are job hunting and the Sun opposes your Mars, your goals may be out of your reach. If you get the job you want, you could be placed in a compromised position or lose it to an insider. If you really want to change jobs for something better, follow up in two months when the Sun is trine to your Mars. By waiting until the Sun moves into the sextile (opportunities and bridges) to your Mars, you can find the job you want.

Make sure there are not drastic changes coming up in the near future (six months to two years) that will upset the new job and place you in a position of looking for another job. I find Mars to be the best indicator for direct action. Mars is the number one planet to deliver action. It will thrust matters forward for good or ill.

When looking at the natal chart, use Mars as an indicator for a person, most likely a man. Look for someone between the ages of 20 and 40. To better define the person or characteristics of your Mars, consider the sign and house in which Mars occurs. If the individual represented by your Mars is not operating on the up-and-up, he or she may be stopped in his or her tracks, or be disarmed in some way. You can assess the character for this or any other planet hit with an eclipse. I have described the planets as characters in the chapter called **Eclipse Tools.**

In addition to the natal chart, assess the impact of eclipses to the angles and planets in a solar arc and secondary progressed charts. I find that progressed planets gain strength the older you get. An eclipse or any major transits to the progressed planets are powerful timers of events for predictive astrology.

This Lunar Eclipse heats the source of your energy as well as the fires that burn your causes and convictions. Issues may ignite into battles at times or you may thrust your support behind another, helping them with their battle. Look for how the Lunar Eclipse will draw others into your scenario. Your topics may be drawn into an arena for center-stage attention, seeking a major decision or deciding to end something or getting your ball rolling. Look for how a person or body of people may intrude in some way, invited or not. Those invited may include a team of specialists or a final hearing with a key planning board. Maybe an investigation begins, or action is taken by a governing body. Look for clues at the New Moon eighteen months earlier. You may gain added insight by studying all four charts of the Moon family members.

When evaluating a planet through the houses, check the rulership of the houses. In this case we are using Mars. Find the planet(s) that rule the house and sign where Mars is located. When there is an eclipse in another house and in aspect to Mars, begin your evaluation with the house and its ruler where the eclipse occurs. Look for the ruler of the house that Mars occupies. And finally, look to the house where Mars resides and the house he rules. The nature of the aspect may bring varied results such as an energizing square or an unfortunate litany of complications from the square. First note the hit and let the influence from the type of aspect be secondary to your delineation. A hit is a hit. Many times trines and sextiles are no less stressful or more beneficial than other aspects. Keep in mind that Mars is a strong indicator of the man in a woman's chart as well as her work. In a man's chart, besides his work, it is his actions that are attracting the attention. The following summary expresses a few ideas for a Lunar Eclipse conjunct Mars through the houses.

You become affected personally if your Mars occupies your **first house**. This Lunar Eclipse brings your opinions out in the open as well as unresolved anger. Bruises, cuts and surgeries may be a result of the additional physical activity you experience while you're under this influence. Protect your face, eyes and head and avoid anything that may be hazardous, including overexposure to the Sun's rays. Stories about accidents with flying objects, fires and hazards due to haste are all too common. If Uranus is also a factor, you may elect plastic surgery.

A Lunar Eclipse to Mars in your **second house** can activate your spending and earning power. Your actions may lead you to a soul awareness of your true values. Money is not everything. Having and holding may not be that rewarding. Your talents may be activated. You may be putting all your energy towards developing your talents or be highly motivated toward acquisition. If you are the proprietor of a business, you may have a period of gains. If you are unemployed, you may find a job. As a young child, you might learn how to prepare yourself for your future.

If the Lunar Eclipse to Mars is in your **third house,** you may be caught in a battle with siblings or be helping them to fight their battles. You may take a job that causes you to move to a new neighborhood.

Mars in the **fourth house** can attract fires, fireplaces or a new kitchen or workspace in the home. There may be more heated subjects at dinner. Someone close to home may go to war or become a fire fighter. There may be issues with a mother's health.

The **fifth house** attracts battles fought both with and for children. You may experience hot love affairs and battles with your lovers. You may light a fire under your creative pot. Mars can be highly creative and attract buyers for your wares. Mars is very important in the retail business. If you have a product to market, this is your best time to find a buyer.

The **sixth house** Lunar Eclipse on Mars brings contentious relationships at work. You could also become involved with great enthusiastic projects. You may receive recognition and honors for your labors.

The **seventh house** Lunar Eclipse on Mars may invite a legal battle or a physical challenge. Your partner could become an adversary or have trouble in his or her career. Your partners or mates could become famous or suffer casualties in their efforts to reach the top. You too may experience forceful actions or accusations from others.

Surgery is the first thing that comes to mind when Mars is hit by a Lunar Eclipse in the **eighth house** but it's not always something that scary. It depends on what your goals are. This eclipse beckons your Mars and springs it into action. One woman, with her eighth house Mars in Cancer, began a business. She sold her city home, moved to the Berkshire Mountains and opened a Bed and Breakfast. As a gourmet cook and brilliant hostess, she is highly successful. A similar story involved an Amtrak electrician who has an eighth house Mars in Scorpio; he left the city with his new bride, moved to the mountains and decided a 90-minute commute to work was worth it. Another man, a contractor with his Mars in Libra, made a million dollars that year.

A Lunar Eclipse in a **ninth house** Mars can send you traveling (often with others) if that is your greatest desire, but, more generally, I find it gives people courage. Muhammad Ali had his Mars in the ninth house. One man finally developed enough courage, with his Mars in Virgo, to begin an eleven month chemotherapy treatment for the hepatitis C virus that infected him 19 years earlier. A woman with a Capricorn Mars took her experience of a severe health crisis and turned it into the motivation to begin a very successful whole health practice. Another woman whose ninth house Mars ruled her seventh house got a divorce. Then there is the woman who became involved with a man after years of no personal relationships. Her Mars ruled the tenth house and her beau was a political advocate and in the public eye. Someone else relocated to another state. That makes sense because the Sun in the third house represents your neighborhood and the ninth house would take you to a new one.

Then there's the Lunar Eclipse in the **tenth house** Mars. A woman with her Mars in Aquarius in the tenth house quit her seven-year career as a lawyer in search of something less competitive. She entered the teaching field and found similar problems in that calling. Another woman quit her successful career writing software after the intended sale of the business. She went on to renovate houses with her partner. She is a Pisces with Mars in Taurus. A man was unjustly fired when a Lunar Eclipse was conjunct his tenth house Mars. He entered into a long drawn-out lawsuit to reclaim his job. A Scorpio woman married for the second time with this eclipse to her Mars. A Libra woman's husband lost his job and could not find another for years. She became very busy as a designer.

A Lunar Eclipse to your **eleventh house** Mars can put you to work in a special interest group or call you into political awareness or action, such becoming part of an environmental project. You may join a group of friends in a particular mission or fun activity. But the most outstanding point in the eleventh house is the presence of the ASC/MC, midpoint for most birth latitudes. If your Mars is located within five degrees of that midpoint, your entire life could be thrust into action. Every house in the chart is affected because the ASC/MC midpoint acts as a toggle switch for the entire wheel. You may be driven to change every detail of your life or an event occurs that places you in such a position. This is one of the most enlightening Lunar Eclipses that will lead the way to the flame in your torch.

The **twelfth house** Mars Lunar Eclipse may bring suppressed behaviors out in the open if you have been unaware of subconscious behavior that is causing problems. You could be involved in disarming yourself as a reaction to an early childhood event, and this eclipse can help to access a hidden strength. This eclipse could also present a confrontation with a problem such as drinking or substance abuse that becomes ripe for a therapeutic plan. Your spiritual world may be livened with an activity such as yoga, meditation or other body, mind and soul work. You could become engaged in an inner developmental process with a teacher or guru type of mentor.

Lunar Eclipse to Jupiter
We think of Jupiter as the great benefactor that will surely bestow bounty and gifts upon us. At times, and for some people, Jupiter may perform that way, but not for all. Some of us need a dose of Saturn to actualize our ability to thrive, and others are able to use the expansive energy of Jupiter to grow and explore. A Lunar Eclipse to Jupiter may or may not seem helpful in a tight situation. It may help those who are ill to take that long last journey to the other side if they are hanging on for dear life. The end may not always be as a result of a long illness. Great age can send you on that trip via an accident. For the most part, Jupiter will broaden your experience as a travel planet, taking you to new places on the globe or in your mind. You are bound to open up new avenues of interest and become familiar with new cultures. Maybe a family member (in-law) comes from another country, and you visit with their culture at your home and theirs. You could become engaged in a long process with government bodies that deal with foreign affairs. This Lunar Eclipse can activate the search for a publisher of your works. Perhaps you will lecture about your material both on the road and at home. If natal Jupiter is found in a personal house or tightly connected to a personal planet, you may come to a higher understanding of an important

key to your development. You may learn lessons about honoring another's choices or expanding your relationship with integrity. This is the time to expect a growth spurt, but not always in the direction that you imagined. Jupiter, as with the other planets, is strongly related to its sign and rulership.

An American Aries man, with 29°Sagittarius rising, fell in love with a woman from New Zealand. A Cancer Lunar Eclipse occurred in his seventh house when he met her at a party in the U.S. Six months later a Capricorn Lunar Eclipse was conjunct his Jupiter in his first house and he visited the woman in New Zealand. He became seriously interested in her and the notion of moving to New Zealand to be with her, and to begin to travel the world. First he brought her to the U.S. for a visit to his home, and then followed her back to her country for a few months. Nine months later he gave up his life in the U.S. to start a life with her. The Lunar Eclipses left the Cancer/Capricorn polarity and fell backward into Taurus/Scorpio, skipping the signs of Gemini/Sagittarius. The fixed sign Lunar Eclipses began at 27°Taurus (which is opposite the man's ASC/MC midpoint which we will explore in its own section). When the fixed sign eclipses moved backward to the set at 16°and 14° Scorpio/Taurus, they formed a square to his Uranus. Much to his surprise, when he arrived in New Zealand the woman wanted nothing to do with him. She had not informed him of her change of heart for some unkind reason. After five months of trying to turn things around, he surrendered and returned to the U.S. Four months later he took a job with a network news firm as a cameraman in Iraq and worked there through Iraq's elections. In 2005, he was scheduled to return to film the war in Iraq at three-month intervals.

Here is another Lunar Eclipse story to a man's Jupiter. A Sagittarius man had Sagittarius on the MC and he experienced a Lunar Eclipse in his sixth house that formed a square to his eighth house Jupiter. There was a Leo Lunar Eclipse that activated his sixth house Leo Saturn (father)/Pluto conjunction and square natal eighth house Scorpio Jupiter (ruler of the MC) when his father died suddenly from a heart attack. The father's death happened at the worst time, because a few days previously the Sagittarius man had fallen from a ladder while cleaning gutters and broken his hip (hip is ruled by Jupiter). He was unable to attend his dad's funeral six hours away. The Midheaven axis represents the parents.

Lunar Eclipse to Saturn

Astrologers have a strong respect for Saturn. For some it's feared when it appears at center stage during an eclipse, a planet station, a progression, or by strong placement in the solar return chart. Eventually after years of study, we all learn to appreciate its value when we observe how it adds security and strong base to our lives. If we are pulled from our greater purpose, Saturn's contribution can help to return us to sound living. For many, the stimulation of Saturn allows one to gain standing in their world or cement the foundation for primary relationships, and could bring the purchase of a home along with its long-term mortgage. It is surprising when it is present during a stroke of good luck, but I will show you one case to make the point. Whether you believe in karma or not, I have seen Saturn present during a full range of life changes, from doom to bliss. As with any planet, its natal condition is your best guide for assessing how your Saturn will respond to any eclipse or other activity.

Events that occur during a period when the angles of a chart are contacted by Saturn's transiting stations, progressions, a Saturn return or an eclipse to Saturn are often the times when people go through structural changes in their life. This can be why students of astrology get nervous when it shows up. I don't believe it brings harm, but it can act like a strong hand that will corral one onto the "right track." Saturn can emerge as a mentor, a board of authority figures, the law, a discipline or a practice to frame your routine and allow you to better meet your true goals. Many times it can be embodied as your mate. Eventually, when the foundations required to satisfy the needs of your natal Saturn are fulfilled, you are ready to become the author of your life. Look for ways that Saturn:

* Encourages resolution with internal father issues
* Develops worthiness
* Delivers the natal promise
* Builds foundation
* Actualizes and crystallizes
* Rewards efforts
* Supplies a forum for practical applications
* Manifests your creative efforts into product
* Secures your future
* Brings safety
* Challenges stagnation

Begin your assessment by slowly pondering over the usual list that includes Saturn's natal sign and house and closest natal aspects. Locate the house/s ruled by Saturn rule. What planets are in those houses? The natal aspects indicate the tone, support and stress from other planets. Check to see if the ruler of your Saturn forms an aspect to natal Saturn, and reflect on the phase of your Saturn cycle. Are you in the 270° reward phase when Saturn is at its last quarter and heading back to the return? Naturally any eclipse contacting either Saturn or the ruling planet can set the chart into a shift of structure.

Aspects from natal Saturn to your angles bring strong lessons from Saturn and may indicate you have a strong purpose and are required to pay attention and answer to your calling. With Saturn as the ruler of an angle you may find that area of your life is the most difficult to satisfy and carries the strongest lessons. A square from a Lunar Eclipse to Saturn does not always bring a negative experience. As with some trines, it can be a set-up to drop your guard and let something slide that holds you together. Your life might be taking an unwanted detour which you thought wouldn't be a problem. But then Saturn lays out a plan to a more productive future along with the lessons showing how to do the foot work. This happened to a young man who suffered from a severe substance abuse problem. During a year and a half, transiting Saturn (6°Cancer) stationed at the first quarter square his Saturn (6° Aries), then Saturn made a station on his ASC to bring him back on track, but not before he nearly died. His active participation in his recovery led to him rebuilding his business, and meeting the woman he married.

Eclipses that square your natal Saturn are not all bad, as they can energize your work setting or open the door of commerce for you. Eclipses that form conjunctions and oppositions that occur in pairs at six-month intervals put all the cards on the table and form conclusions and endings in those areas ruled by your Saturn.

Any eclipse that contains an aspect between transiting Saturn and another planet (i.e. natal Saturn sextile Uranus) is repeating a familiar harmonic of your natal Saturn, even when the aspect occurs at a different zodiacal location. The eclipse will activate your natal angle and leave a legacy that echoes to the intrinsic nature of your Saturn.

I will use my natal Saturn sextile Uranus as an example (aside from a tighter Venus/Saturn conjunction). Transiting Saturn and Uranus were sextile in March of 1997 and the eclipse season was also in March '97. With natal Saturn in my third house, I was working hard on *Lunar Shadows'* first edition and the preparations for my first international lecture, which took place in England six months later. So many other things took place that year, including a move to a new place upon my return from England. The Solar Eclipse Mar '97 was conjunct my MC; the lunar was conjunct my Vesta (housing) and square my Ascendant axis. The Lunar Eclipse in the fall was exactly square to my Moon. A move was evident. The (Saturn) structure of my life is supported by the unique gifts from Uranus, my astrology studies. When they repeated my natal angle during an eclipse conjunct my MC, I was given greater presence within the institution of astrological studies. That trip led to a book deal with the Russian National Council for Geocosmic Research and continues to influence my career today.

Researching your past is the best key for predicting your future.

What really makes us nervous about an eclipse to Saturn is the fear of the unknown. Reflect on the past when eclipses or major transit events such as a Saturn return and Saturn stations occurred. How did you survive those experiences? Did someone die every time Saturn was in the spotlight? Probably not; maybe you found greater satisfaction or gained reward for your efforts and accomplishments.

Record the positions of the outer planets from the past events. Astrologers get nervous that the signals may lead to the passing of someone close. I found that Pluto is usually involved in that scenario in a significant way. For example, a Lunar Eclipse to your Saturn while Pluto forms a strong aspect to a personal point may be more dramatic than a Lunar Eclipse to your Saturn when Pluto is in a benign position. A good clue: always check your Sun/Moon midpoint and ASC/MC midpoint, as they are largely important. At a Lunar Eclipse in 1969 a woman became involved with a man in a relationship that lasted sixteen years. The relationship ended in 1984. A Lunar Eclipse in 1988 conjunct her Saturn occurred when he died in 1988. Pluto was opposite her ASC/MC midpoint. Read more about the ASC/MC midpoint in its section.

If the Lunar Eclipse occurs in a loaded Moon family containing both a Solar Eclipse and Lunar Eclipse in the same family, then your experience may be different than that of a Moon family with only the Lunar Eclipse.

A Lunar Eclipse in aspect to Saturn can bring positions of heavy responsibility such as added workload or reaching an elevated position in one's work environment. This eclipse is useful for climbing the corporate ladder. If parents are elderly or ill, you may need to act on their behalf. Some people are put in the grueling position of arranging assisted living situations for their parents. If your business is your focus, you could be accumulating large debt or better yet, taking on large contracts. This eclipse could indicate the end of a long-term commitment such as the final payment of a thirty-year mortgage. You could end a marriage or enter a new one.

Did you ever know Saturn to be lucky? A Cancer man won $15,000 at a Full Moon exactly midway between a pair of Virgo/Pisces Lunar Eclipses. His Saturn was the object of the eclipses in Virgo and ruler of his twelfth house. In addition, transiting Saturn was conjunct his Jupiter in his second house. By keeping an open mind, we learn new things about astrological symbolism all the time. So don't count Saturn out of the realm of good luck. For this man it delivered and just in time. He won the exact figure he needed to get out of debt, no more and no less. Have a look at the chart.

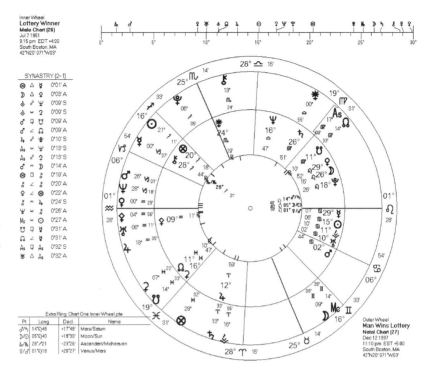

Of course not all eclipses to Saturn are so lucky. It really depends on the natal Saturn, the stage of your life and of course the rulership, sign and house. Younger people may not have the best experiences with eclipses to Saturn. Their world may seem to be demanding safety, structure and discipline. More mature experiences could include marriage, especially for men, appointment to a higher position, the beginning of a long period of parenting a difficult or sick child or family member, or any long-term commitment. Some people gain respect and recognition.

Lunar Eclipse to Uranus

This is an interesting Lunar Eclipse, to say the least. Expect the unexpected and look to be surprised. More than likely you will have a very full plate when everything seems to happen at once. A feeling of great expectation that seems to hold an electrical charge accompanies this time. Often people undergo a dramatic change to their personal appearance. There can be extreme shifts in weight or a period of weight fluctuations. Some people elect plastic surgery, choose a completely new hairstyle, or begin wearing a new style of clothing. Besides changing what you look like, anything could happen in a spontaneous way. Awakening, discovery and invention are brought to us by Uranus.

Alexander Graham Bell is a good example of someone born with Uranus near the degree of a Lunar

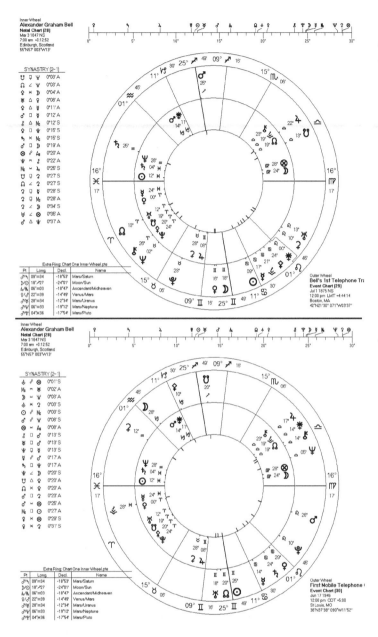

Eclipse. He was born with Uranus at 12° Aries conjunct his south node at 19° Aries; three weeks later a Lunar Eclipse opposed his Uranus. This was the perfect combination for the inventor who changed the world with the telephone. The north node reached Bell's natal Uranus in 1875 when he transmitted his first telecommunication on July 1st. Transiting Uranus was trine the transiting node. The Solar Eclipse that year occurred at 16°Aries.

"June 17, 1946 - A driver in St. Louis, Mo., pulled out a handset from under his car's dashboard, placed a phone call and made history. It was the first mobile telephone call." (*Source: From the website of AT&T 1946: First Mobile Telephone Call*) Even beyond the death of Mr. Bell, his chart was clearly activated at this event. A Lunar Eclipse occurred on June 14, 1946 at 23° Sagittarius opposite the Sun, Uranus and north node conjunct at Bell's IC.

No time was given for that first call from the mobile phone, but the transits for that day remain interesting.

Golf superstar Tiger Woods surprised his opponents in April 2005 when he won the Masters Tournament which he had also won in 1997, 2001 and 2002. Probably the best golfer of all time, his career as a professional golfer began in late summer of 1996. "With his second Masters victory in 2001, Tiger became the first ever to hold all four professional major championships at the same time." (Source: official Tiger Woods website). He is another who was born with Uranus at the node. 14° may seem wide for a conjunction, but the nodes hold a wider orb range than that for planets. Tiger is not an inventor, but he has radically raised the bar for the standards in the world of golf.

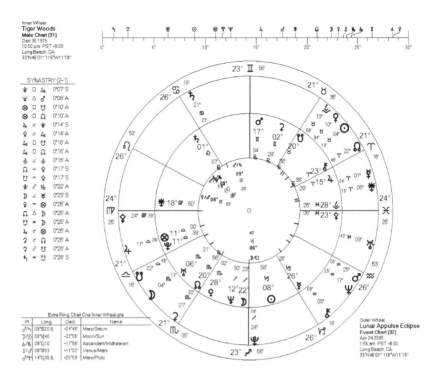

Inner Wheel
Tiger Woods
Male Chart [31]
Dec 30 1975
10:50 pm PST +8:00
Long Beach, CA
33°N46'01" 118°W11'18"

SYNASTRY (2-1)

♆	□	As	0°07' S
♀	△	♂	0°08' A
⊗	□	☋	0°10' A
⊗	□	☊	0°10' A
♃	♂	♆	0°14' S
♀	♂	As	0°14' A
As	□	☋	0°16' A
As	□	☊	0°16' A
⚷	⚼	⚷	0°16' A
☊	⚼	♀	0°17' S
☋	⚻	♀	0°17' S
♆	⚹	Mc	0°22' A
☽	∠	⚷	0°23' S
♀	⚻	⊗	0°25' A
☊	△	☽	0°25' A
☋	⚼	☽	0°25' A
♃	♂	⊗	0°26' A
♀	♂	☊	0°26' A
♀	♂	☋	0°26' A
♄	⚹	☋	0°28' S

Extra Ring, Chart One Inner Wheel.pte

Pt	Long.	Decl.	Name
♂/♄	09°♏20 R	+24°48'	Mars/Saturn
☽/⊙	00°♍40	-22°06'	Moon/Sun
As/Mc	09°♍10	+17°58'	Ascendant/Midheaven
♀/♂	08°♍03	+11°02'	Venus/Mars
♂/♇	14°♍36 R	+25°59'	Mars/Pluto

Outer Wheel
Lunar Appulse Eclipse
Event Chart [32]
Apr 24 2005
1:55 am PST +8:00
Long Beach, CA
33°N46'01" 118°W11'18"

Lunar Eclipse to Neptune

"Prayer from the heart can achieve what nothing else can
in the world." - *Mahatma Gandhi*

Divine gifts for the soul arrive with Neptune's blessings, lifting you to a level of inspirational bliss that
recharges the creative flame within your soul (a benefit from the god of the sea). When Neptune is
activated by an eclipse, it can produce the vision that motivates a work from your heart. Religious leaders
and motivational speakers utilize this special gift of inspiration when projecting their enthusiasm in order
to inspire others to follow them. Their inspiring nature is designed to take you on a spiritual journey that
reunites you with your soul's path. Inspiration at times is seductive, bringing a twist of fate that leads you
to a place you never imagined. A Lunar Eclipse in aspect to Neptune may send you on a mission, lead
you astray, or both. It can bring you crashing down to Earth after riding high on a pink cloud.

Neptune is a difficult planet to pin down, largely elusive and the author of denial. Neptune can bring
imagination, inspiration and illusion. But if not careful, one can build a fantasy that leads to delusion,
confusion and misconception. Neptune is the most misunderstood and overlooked planet, but it is
also most often the culprit amidst misunderstandings. How many times have you picked up a chart and
glossed right over Neptune? Under Neptune's influence, you can be the victim of misrepresentations or

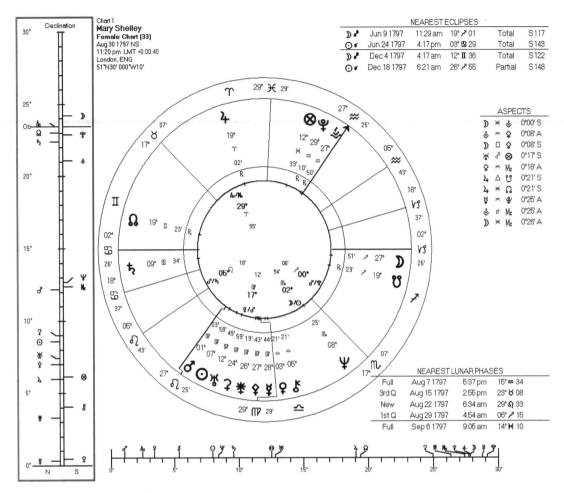

Chart 1
Mary Shelley
Female Chart [33]
Aug 30 1797 NS
11:20 pm LMT +0:00:40
London, ENG
51°N30' 000°W10'

	NEAREST ECLIPSES					
☽ ☋	Jun 9 1797	11:29 am	19° ♐ 01	Total	S117
☉ ☋	Jun 24 1797	4:17 pm	03° ♋ 29	Total	S143
☽ ☋	Dec 4 1797	4:17 pm	12° ♊ 36	Total	S122
☉ ☋	Dec 18 1797	6:21 am	26° ♐ 55	Partial	S148

	ASPECTS	
☽ ⚹ ⚷	0°00' S
⚷ ⚻ ♀	0°08' A
☽ □ ♀	0°08' S
♅ ☍ ⊗	0°17' S
♀ ⚻ Mc	0°18' A
♃ △ ☋	0°21' S
♃ ⚹ ☊	0°21' S
☿ ⚻ ♆	0°25' A
⚷ ♂ Mc	0°25' A
☽ ⚹ Mc	0°26' A

	NEAREST LUNAR PHASES			
Full	Aug 7 1797	5:37 pm	15° ♒ 34
3rd Q	Aug 15 1797	2:55 pm	23° ♉ 08
New	Aug 22 1797	6:34 am	29° ♌ 33
1st Q	Aug 29 1797	4:54 am	06° ♐ 15
Full	Sep 6 1797	9:05 am	14° ♓ 10

lead others astray despite your good intentions. The negative side of Neptune emerges in stories of the victim and victimizer. Eclipse charts with a hard aspect to Neptune often have stories laden with someone who has run amuck with their own dogma, fear or mission and wreaked havoc on others.

Neptune can be very strange. From the imagination of Mary Shelley came *Frankenstein,* published in 1818 when a Lunar Eclipse was conjunct her Scorpio Neptune. Can it get much stranger than that? See chart.

You often hear sad stories when Neptune has been activated by any eclipse. For one man a sad event occurred when his father, without asking his grown children, sold their lifelong summer house and told them all to come from around the country to gather their belongings from the house before the new owners came. The grown kids felt ripped off and disrespected when the place that held their childhood memories was virtually discarded.

A woman received a Lunar Eclipse conjunct her Neptune when she suffered a spiritual breakdown. She worked and lived in a spiritual community where her life revolved around the principals that she studied and serviced. Her life changed dramatically after a romance took an unfortunate turn. She went on a journey to India and when she returned, her roommate had taken up with her boyfriend. Feeling completely betrayed, she placed her home on the market, resigned her position within the community and moved away. She naturally became isolated, then depressed. She became very thin, giving the impression she was trying to disappear.

Surrender is often the theme with this eclipse. We're most familiar with stories of substance abuse. The most profound change can occur when the eclipse is conjunct or opposed natal Neptune. The addict surrenders, realizing that he or she must ask for help. Sometimes just the square will suffice to bring awareness a step closer to therapeutic recovery from any type of substance abuse, including gambling.

Lunar Eclipse to Pluto
"Forgiveness is not an occasional act; it is a permanent attitude." - *Martin Luther King Jr.*

A prayer for Pluto.
In my constant quest of new tools for survival in a world at times too cruel for my gentle spirit, may I continue to greet the world with wonder and love even after the torture of things real and imagined. May I assimilate the symbols in my life, those found in my dreams and dropped in my path, as keys from the masters, to break the shackles of my conscious and unconscious attachments and replace them with bonds of joy, love and a lightness of being. – *Dietrech Pessin*

A Lunar Eclipse involving your Pluto brings new tools for living, inherent to your survival. When studying natal Pluto in a contemplative fashion, you may find he represents your deepest and greatest area of growth as well as your soul's evolution. You want to consider Pluto in all forms of its symbolism, as with any planet. Look to the house it rules (Scorpio); study all of its natal aspects; note any change in direction (turning retrograde or direct), prenatal and the immediate post-natal stations, along with any time over your life when it was prominently placed in a solar return or received an eclipse or transiting planet station.

Like all the planets, Pluto has many faces. You may or may not be consciously aware of the consequences when you engage with the god of the underworld. You do understand this relationship when apply for a loan. Your application states your ability to fulfill the agreement, unlike the umbilical cord relationships with parents that maintain a child's financial security into their adult years. This type of support may or may not come at great cost. When developing dependent relationships with anyone, you enter into a Pluto relationship. Marriage bonds include the eighth house of shared resources, bringing joint bank accounts or shared property all under Pluto's domain. Irreconcilable differences over money are the most common cause for divorce.

When your financial security becomes the issue, all of your security issues can be challenged, tapping into your deepest fears and inner demons. For some it's a fear of being without. You can create a list of what being without means to you. Perhaps it's about losing your control over your existence. Control issues arise in most of our relationships where fear motivates the individuals and they constantly engage in power plays. Pluto will reveal the deepest profile of your psychological nature when a fear of losing control of a situation holds an unknown outcome. We all want to be in control of our destiny.

A fear of losing control of your destiny may come at a time of the greatest changes in your life, such as a marriage, birth of a child, loss of a parent, or a change in earnings. When under the influence of a Lunar eclipse, you will learn your ability to handle change. The changes are permanent, and there is no turning back from your new awareness to the virgin perspective prior to this eclipse.

Feelings of insanity often surround such changes. When you feel your security is threatened, you may approach these circumstances one step at a time, beginning with the wisdom found in the Serenity Prayer. Do all that you can to accept the things you cannot change and to change the things you can. Pray to know the difference. Then remove your investment from the outcome, and invite the generosity of the universe to bring you the best possible results. You then become a tool for the solution, and stand the best chance for success. The power that Pluto possesses wants you to succeed by bringing radical awareness that incites dramatic change to promote spiritual and evolutionary growth. Pluto's attachments are burrowed deeply beyond the principals of Venus. Once acquired, Pluto claims them, and has the capacity to turn the earth into gold. Not a simple task. Transiting Pluto's long journey around the zodiac never reaches a return in one lifetime.

A Lunar eclipse involving natal Pluto will bring to the surface issues that bond us to others and can offer clues to your ability to:
*   Maintain self-preservation from a center of balance
*   Rise above your fears and take on change
*   Let go of the things you can not change
*   Maintain a standing of your choice when engaged with those holding the reigns of power
*   Attain liberation without annihilating others
*   Engage in deep commitment
*   Navigate control issues of your own or those of another
*   Handle power
*   Manage money, credit and loans
*   Fearlessly face your psychological profile

A Lunar Eclipse to Pluto indicates a time for letting go of a something that has had formidable significance in your life. It could be a person, place or thing. Not always a tormenting event, it can accompany the release of a thirty-year mortgage. Alternatively, if may be time to let go of an old behavior or an unhealthy attachment to a bad experience. Nevertheless, it is likely to touch the deepest part of your being. You may be attached to your anger or pain connected to an issue that has confined you, and are now forced to grow past the event. Easier said then done. If you can ask for help, specifically for the willingness to let go, you might notice the process begin. There is probably a story in your life where your forgiveness is the key to move forward.

When an eclipse activates your Pluto, a fearless exercise might be helpful. Try something like this or make up your own.

* First, retrieve from your memory your first experience of complete powerlessness.
* Describe the surrounding situation and your role and ask a few questions that you might want to write down.
* What could/would you do differently now?
* In what area of your life does this memory motivate a need for change?
* Can you create a category in which you store this memory now and retrieve it later for further work?
* What is the name of this category?
* Do you have more recent memories you can store in this category?
* List any dates you can remember and investigate related Pluto principals.
* What are the valuable survival skills you can attribute to this experience?

This memory could originate at a time when someone imposed his or her will over you. It may not be a person at all; one person remembered a childhood experience in which a large dog pinned her down for what seemed like an eternity and overpowered her. Another person fell down the stairs as a child, and a china cabinet fell on top of him. He was trapped for what seemed like hours. Some remember an overpowering experience that was psychological. A woman describes a story as an eight-year-old who gagged when forced to eat something she thought was revolting. Two Pisces women have great fears and horrible nightmares. One woman suffers intense fear of death. The other fights the demons in her dreams. Both experienced lunar eclipses to their ascendants. My sister would fly out of bed screaming of attacks from monsters, slamming into the dresser or walls, often resulting in severe bruises and other injuries.

The heartbreaking stories are those of rape and oppressing force. Some people are given the gift of insight at the time of a Lunar eclipse to Pluto that becomes a vehicle for the release of embedded issues. When a lunar eclipse occurs, exposing the stories of your past, you may not only re-experience the offense but also learn new details by fleshing

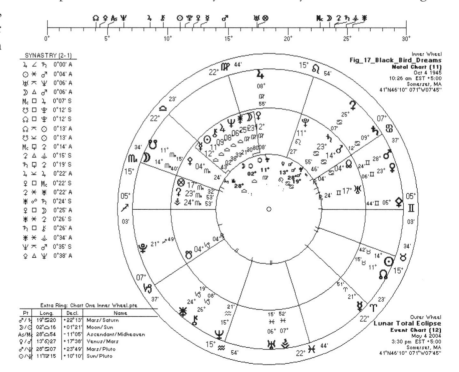

out a child's interpretation of the event. A dear friend remembers a large black bird hovering over her bed that would return repeatedly and flap his wings and was hurting her. A Lunar Eclipse occurred and she began experiencing bad dreams about the bird, shortness of breath and pains in her groin. She asked me to help sort it out. In my office she began to unravel the story and remembered her mother's lover, a priest dressed in his black suit. She then realized he was her sexual abuser after he got her mother drunk. The 14° 42' Scorpio Lunar Eclipse that occurred on the cusp of her twelfth house and square to her Pluto in Leo opened her story to find the family friend, the priest, as the twelfth house character in her life. Scorpio on that cusp rules sexual secrets. She found the most important person to forgive was herself, for being too small to fight back. She did not have the tools to defend herself as a child but now did have those tools.

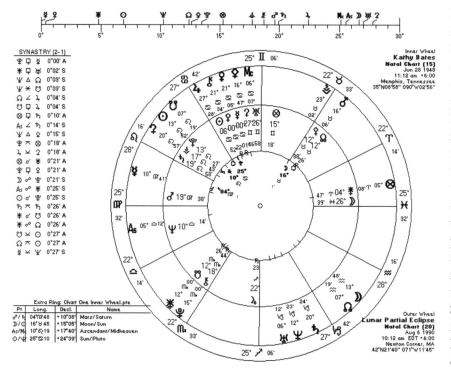

It's the psychological impression left so deep it becomes a root response and often is the source of conflict in close personal relationships. How we see ourselves in the embedded issues from those who have trespassed against us sets the stage for how we perceive others are treating us when under intense pressure. Some fight, some surrender, some return bitter with revenge to make the world pay. Some pray to be released from their personal hell. Bill Clinton awaited the decision of his impeachment trial when a Lunar Eclipse at 11° Leo was conjunct his Pluto. Others prey on the weak continuing the cycle of power plays. Do you remember Kathy Bates in *Misery*? In 1990 she won an Academy Award for her role as the psychotic nurse Annie Wilkes who captured her favorite writer, played by James Caan, as he awakened from a car accident. She kept him hostage, tortured unmercifully. The stars appear even to effect her star image. Ms. Bates also received a Lunar Eclipse in opposition to her eleventh house Pluto in 1990.

However your automatic reflex is expressed, a lunar eclipse to Pluto is just what the cosmic doctor ordered to teach you new skills. Many of us study and learn but still hold onto our past response, not wanting to let go of what defines us, like the physically abused woman who holds a taut banner saying "look at what I have survived." A secret understanding of the abuse may give this abused woman a low opinion of herself, and possibly the belief that on some level she deserves the treatment she received. It does not occur to her that she has free will, for she only relates to the trap. Invested in keeping a sad story alive, she returns to her torture chamber with apparent willingness.

As observers we ask of the physically abused woman, "Why doesn't she leave him?" "What is her perception of her choices?" "What stands in the way of her seeing things differently that allows for change?" As counselors, it is not our role to make choices for others, but only to guide them to discover that they, in fact, do have choices. This counselor does not pass judgment but seeks to unravel the puzzle, and find the right combination of insight and encourage that leads the individual to a loving self-image.

Infestations of vermin brought powerlessness home for one woman who lived in a beautiful home in the nicest section of town. She was mortified one day when she discovered her windows blackened by flies. The flies were not her only torment. The exterminator informed her that approximately 300 mice were living throughout her house. A Scorpio Lunar Eclipse was square to her natal twelfth house Pluto.

Internal power struggles may block your ability to reach your highest goals. With courage and faith you will discover an abundance of personal resources and inner strengths you failed to acknowledge, until the enlightened experience of a lunar eclipse to your Pluto. It may not always be painful. For some it is the deep love from another that allows the courage to make vital changes in one's life. To trust and feel safe for the first time opens the door for change. This was the case for a woman too attached to a grown child to allow him to suffer the losses of his own demise. When a deep love came into her life, a compelling need emerged to lovingly allow the son to find his own way, and release them both from the constant drama surrounding them. This was a desire to transform the shackles of self-induced traps, and bond with another as an equal – not the gatekeeper or prisoner as in past dysfunctional relationships.

Lunar Eclipse to the Natal Nodes of the Moon

1 nodal cycle 6793.39 days   (18.5997 years)

The nodes of the Moon are the hot spots where all the action takes place. They hold the key to the complex 18.6 year cycle of the Moon's orbit. This cycle is different from the 19-year Metonic cycle.   Research of this cycle links it to climate clocks, long-term herring cycles and tidal cycles.

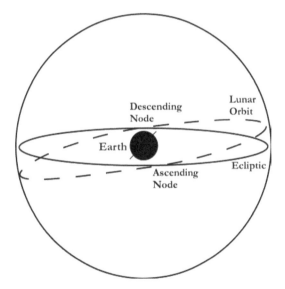

One lunar cycle, when the four phases the Moon are completed, is 29.5 days long. The Moon's orbit is located mostly in the northerly or southerly portions of the sky at a 5.2° incline from the celestial equator (Source: *The Secret Language of the Stars and Planets*, pg 18).

During a lunar cycle, the Moon appears to lie on the ecliptic twice a month at one of two points; the ascending or descending node as the Moon slips from the north to south declination. These points travel backwards through the signs from Aries to Pisces at the rate of about 18-20 months for each sign returning in approximately 18.6 years.

When the Sun travels close to a node, it too appears to lie on the ecliptic; when the Moon joins the Sun (at a New Moon) there will be a Solar Eclipse. When the Sun is at a node and the Moon is opposite the Sun at the other node, there will be a Lunar Eclipse. When a planet reaches the same zodiacal point as a node and is joined by the Moon, there will be an occultation.

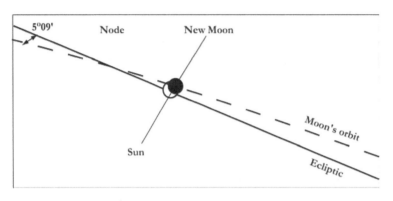

You can tell by looking at a natal chart if a person was born near an eclipse. If the Sun is conjunct a node, they are likely to be within two weeks of a Solar or Lunar Eclipse.

Metaphorically, I think of the nodes as intersections along two highways in the sky, the highway of the Moon's path around the Earth that crosses with the highway of the apparent path (celestial equator) of the Sun around the Earth. The celestial equator holds the quality of an ASC/DSC and the orbit of the Moon acts as a MC/IC. Combine the two planes at one point, the "knot" or the node, and they hold the quality of the ASC/MC midpoint. I refer to this point as the "toggle switch" of the horoscope. This is the reason why, when activated, they bring attention to the polarities of both the individual/partner and home/career. The nodes are the toggle switch to the greater cycles in one's life. Along the 18.6 year lunar cycle there is a repeat of the phases of the Moon, beginning with the repeat of an eclipse near the same degree every 19 years. Halfway through the cycle at 9.3 years, the cycle flips and the Moon phases appear at mirror reflective degrees on the opposite side of the zodiac. This is because the Moon's cycle of extreme southerly or northerly rising points appears to rise.

When studying a chart, a planet conjunct or square a node plays a prominent role in the life of the individual.

I think of them in a couple of ways, but one is as the Ascendant (north node)-Descendant (south node) for our solar system. We know them as intersection points where eclipses take place when a New or Full Moon is conjunct the nodes; within 18° for a Solar Eclipse and 12° for a Lunar Eclipse. The intersection point causes this overly-wide orb zone. This width allows greater opportunities for massive amounts of energy to enter. My personal belief is that the nodes are the doors where our souls enter this world. We come in with a group that chooses to work together for this lifetime with our special team. When the Sun is within orb of the intersection point, it is Sol's biannual time of the year. The Sun's presence at a node broadens our Earth's view into the universe. Have you noticed that when there are meteor showers within weeks of any eclipse, the showers are more spectacular? It happens when the meteors coincide with the eclipse season. With the Sun's close proximity to the intersection points, the nodes bring us closer to the universe, opening a wide-angle lens.

Looking at a birth chart with the **Sun close to the nodes** is a clue that person was born near the date of an eclipse. Their world may have a broader range than those born with the Sun more than 18° from the nodes. They might be drawn into a public lifestyle or make notable or infamous contributions in their community and beyond. Not all high-profile individuals have their Sun conjunct the nodes, but in the charts of a few popular musicians the distance of their Sun from the node falls within the eclipse orb. Elvis Presley has the Sun 14° from north node, John Lennon 5° to the north node and George Harrison 9° to the south node.

To be born close to a Lunar Eclipse may involve a partner as the notable or infamous contributor. Your ability to function may be strongly linked to partnership, making it difficult for you to feel complete without your partner. You may be constantly drawn into the limelight with them, as would be the life partner of a political figure. This may give you a high-profile lifestyle with many dramatic encounters.

When a Lunar Eclipse occurs close to your birthday, you are having an approximate nodal return at your solar return. The nodes don't actually return on your birthday for 1,638 years. However, they do return to the natal position sometime between 18 years + six months to 18 years + eight months from your birth date.

Planets Conjunct a Node
Looking at a chart that has a planet conjunct a node may indicate the person was born near an occultation. This happens when a planet, the Moon, and the Earth all line up at a node, creating a parallel between all three. This is an interesting point to investigate when preparing a chart or researching the finer details of your chart.

Planets Square the Node
When a planet squares the node, it draws on the intersection points with the high energy of the ninety-degree angle. We learned the Power Point New or Full Moon occurs when they square the eclipse points. The eclipse points conjunct the north or south node; therefore a planet square the Moon's nodes are prominently placed, and can be used as an important key to one's career choices, personality or life experiences.

Nodes travel through a sign in 18 to 20 months. The 18 months is the time it takes from a New Moon to Full Moon in a Moon Family. The nodes of the Moon in any chart are hot zones for action that are activated at their half cycle, nine plus years after the nodal return. At that time the transiting north node opposes the natal north node. A Lunar Eclipse to the natal nodes indicates an approximate return of the natal nodes. This may stimulate similar issues to that of the ASC/DSC, like the coming and going of partners/partnerships and physical changes within your/partner's body that may require medical care. It may include changes to your perspective and the manner in which you relate to others and how they relate to you. In my studies of charts with no birth time available, I find the use of the north node as an ASC and south node as the DSC to be an adequate tool. (The solar chart, using the Sun on the ASC with equal houses, is always useful even with a birth time.) There are significant points of shifts in each year when the Sun forms hard angles to the nodes. The same is true when the Sun forms hard angles to the natal Sun. You will notice how your yearly tone shifts at the last hard angle to your Sun, marking the onset of your next solar return chart. This is thrust into action three months before the birthday when the transiting Sun forms its last square to your natal Sun.

The nodal axis possesses an all-encompassing complexity that attracts/repels, comforts/antagonizes, makes public/private, personal/interpersonal, strengthens/weakens. In all cases when roused by an eclipse, the events touch your body, mind and soul, leading to a marked and greater level of individual awareness, attention and growth.

These extremely sensitive personal points are equal to the sensitivity of the ASC/DSC axis, and when activated you become directly engaged in activities concerned with your evolution.

The public quality of the nodes is likened to that of MC/IC axis, often indicating an accelerated emphasis on your deeds. When energized by an eclipse, there's an opportunity for your skills and talents to become popular. You can be drawn into a public role to share your gifts. This is your time and the world is your stage. The nodes are like a cosmic magnet seeking your special talents and enlisting your expertise. If you have been waiting for your reward, your powers of attraction draw you into your rightful occupational place. When the nodes are illuminated by any eclipse, you can be drawn into a spotlight or public zone of activity. A magnified level of attention is focused directly on you, your body and your relationship with others. It can be a time of appreciation for your accomplishments, such as with Clint Eastwood in 2005.

The Lunar Eclipse pair of Taurus/Scorpio in 2004/05 highlighted Clint Eastwood's nodal axis when the movie he directed, *Million Dollar Baby*, was released and won an Oscar on February 27, 2005. Eastwood's north node is located in his sixth house and forms a square to his Leo Moon in the ninth house of the director. The planet square the node can support the career direction. His Scorpio rising sign, co-ruled by Mars and Pluto, supported his success. Mars at 28 Aries received the 29°Aries Solar Eclipse in the spring of 2004 that also formed a beautiful trine to his Leo MC and Neptune at 0°54'Virgo. Natal Pluto in the eighth is trine his Ascendant.

We see this when people become deeply engaged in personal relationships that lead to long-term commitments. When people go through challenging periods with their health, there is often an eclipse activating natal nodes. A strong focus on how these topics affect you and your significant others may determine how you function in your world during that period.

A Love Story

An Aries woman married a Leo Man six days before a Lunar Eclipse at 4° Scorpio. The eclipse was conjunct her south node. She had met her husband nine months earlier. Other planets affected by the eclipse include Aries Mercury, Gemini Venus (attachment and love), Aries Saturn (commitment), Ceres (bonding), and the marriage asteroid Juno. The eclipse occurred in her eighth house, trine her Pisces ASC. This was her second marriage. Her progressed Sun at 5° Gemini was conjunct her natal Venus. For her husband, the Lunar Eclipse degree at 4° Scorpio showed up on his secondary progressed chart with solar arc angles. His progressed Jupiter and Neptune at the IC received the eclipse as well. His progressed ASC at 12°Leo is her natal Moon. The transiting nodes at the Lunar Eclipse were 22° Aries; his progressed south node was 22° Aries.

Another Love Story

A couple 9.5 years apart in age shared the same nodal polarity, she with her north node in Taurus and he with his north node in Scorpio at opposing degrees. This nodal arrangement is common with this kind of age difference. In this case it was also a lunar eclipse at their nodes that drew them together in the fall of 1985. They fell in love and knew in their hearts they had met their soul mate. But life took so many turns and interrupted their relationship. He followed his altruistic heart to help rebuild a hurricane-torn town 2000 miles away. She went on with her life and invested her energy into her career. Neither found another love that ever measured up.

Nine years later, he returned to the area, but the lovers did not reconnect until 1998 when their reunion coincided with a major life event for him. His children living 2000 miles away searched, found their dad, and asked to meet him after their 19-year separation (a nodal return). His heart allowed only one thing, and that was to relocate to where the children lived and establish a relationship. His girlfriend let go of the relationship again to allow him to follow his heart.

19 years after the couple first met, they ran into one another again. Very slowly they became friends again, until they could not deny they belonged together. They reestablished their relationship and when the Moon's south node and a Solar Eclipse conjoined the woman's Sun, they decided it was finally their time and they would commit to each other and build a home together.

Lunar Eclipse to the Ascendant
A Lunar Eclipse involving the Ascendant (used with the Davison Relationship chart)

By finding the exact moment midway between two births and the midpoint location between the two births, you can create a Relationship Chart. Different from a composite chart that creates a new chart from the midpoint between each planet of two charts, the time and space technique was created by astrologer Ronald Davison and is referred to as a Davison chart. It's a great chart most often used between two people, and you can study the chart with all the same techniques as you would with a natal chart. I have gone beyond casting relationship charts between two people, and have used them to study a solar or lunar eclipse or any major event. I find them to be a lot of fun. Most astrology programs have the option to create a Relationship Chart.

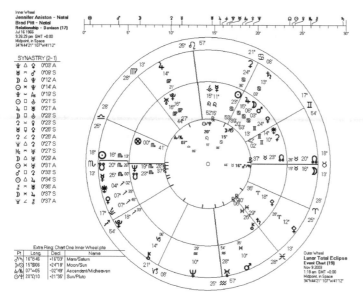

Inner Wheel
Jennifer Aniston - Natal
Brad Pitt - Natal
Relationship - Davison [17]
Jul 16 1966
9:26:25 pm GMT +0:00
Midpoint, in Space
34°N44'21" 107°W41'12"

SYNASTRY (2-1)

♀ △ ♀	0°03'	A
♅ ⚹ ♂	0°09'	S
☽ □ ♆	0°12'	A
♆ ⚹ ♃	0°14'	A
♀ ⚹ ♃	0°19'	S
☉ □ ♀	0°21'	S
♃ □ ♅	0°21'	A
☽ □ ♀	0°23'	A
☿ ∠ ♀	0°23'	S
♅ ⚹ ♀	0°26'	S
♀ ∠ ♀	0°26'	A
♆ △ ♀	0°27'	A
♏ ⚹ ♅	0°27'	S
☽ △ ♅	0°29'	A
☉ ⚹ ♅	0°31'	A
♂ □ ♀	0°33'	S
☉ △ ♃	0°34'	S
☽ ⚹ ♃	0°36'	A
☽ ⚹ ♃	0°37'	S
♆ ∠ ⚷	0°37'	A

Extra Ring: Chart One Inner Wheel.pts

Pt	Long.	Decl.	Name
♂/♄	16°♏46'	+16°03'	Mars/Saturn
☽/☉	15°♍06'	+24°1'8'	Moon/Sun
As/Mc	07°♏05'	-02°49'	Ascendant/Midheaven
☉/♇	20°♌10'	+21°35'	Sun/Pluto

Outer Wheel
Lunar Total Eclipse
Event Chart [19]
Nov 9 2003
1:18 am GMT +0:00
Midpoint, in Space
34°N44'21" 107°W41'12"

ASPECTS (1)

♂ △ ♅	0°03'	A
♆ ☌ ♅	0°09'	S
♂ □ ♃	0°12'	S
♀ △ ☊	0°12'	S
♀ ⚹ ☊	0°12'	S
♃ ⚹ ♅	0°14'	A
☽ ⚹ ⚷	0°19'	S
☉ ∠ ♀	0°30'	A
♅ ☍ ⚷	0°31'	S
♀ ⚹ As	0°33'	A
♂ ⚹ ⚷	0°33'	A
⚷ ⚹ ☊	0°35'	A

Upper Right
Jennifer Aniston
Female Chart [16]

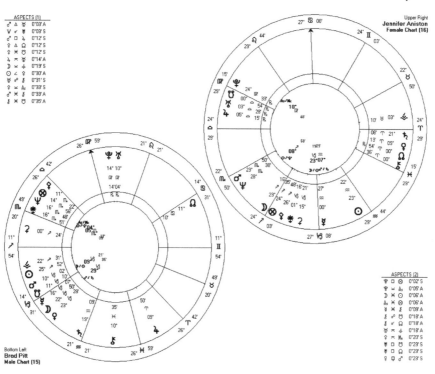

Bottom Left
Brad Pitt
Male Chart [15]

ASPECTS (2)

♇ □ ⊗	0°02'	S
♇ ⚹ As	0°05'	A
☽ ⚹ ☉	0°06'	A
As ⚹ ⊗	0°06'	A
♀ ⚹ ⚷	0°09'	A
⚷ ☍ ☊	0°18'	A
⚷ ☌ ☊	0°18'	A
♅ ⚹ ⚸	0°18'	A
♀ ⚹ ♏	0°20'	S
♇ □ ☊	0°23'	S
♅ □ ☊	0°23'	S
♀ □ ♂	0°23'	S

The Ascendant/Descendant axis of the Relationship Chart, for Hollywood couple Jennifer Aniston and Brad Pitt, took a couple hits from a pair of Lunar Eclipses November 2003 and May 2004 at 16° Taurus/14°Scorpio. Mr. Pitt began filming *Mr. and Mrs. Smith,* his movie with Angelina Jolie, November 2003. The end of the favorite couple's marriage was the talk of the tabloids after they announced their separation on January 7, 2005; this tabloid gossip continued for months to follow. They had a million dollar wedding on July 29, 2000, the day before the Solar Eclipse at 8° Leo. They filed for divorce, stating irreconcilable differences, on August 19, 2005 in Los Angeles CA. Their divorce will be final October 2, 2005, nine months after they announced they were separating. The Lunar Eclipse of October 17, 2005 is a major marker for endings within a six-month period, and it is conjunct Aniston's seventh house cusp of marriage. That eclipse also is square to the Moon's nodes (24° Capricorn) in the Solar Eclipse chart when they married. Brad's Moon and Venus conjunction is at 22°-23° Capricorn.

Of course, not everyone experiences divorce when a lunar eclipse falls upon their Relationship Chart Ascendant. Keep the pre-natal Solar and Lunar eclipses points up front when studying important changes over the years. Transiting activity often brings on a major event when the prenatal or close postnatal eclipses are stimulated.

Lunar Eclipse to the Midheaven

The Midheaven (MC) as the most public point in any chart attracts attention from the eyes and ears of anyone within range, reaching beyond your immediate circle. Many times people are noted for their accomplishments. We call this the point of fame, but most of the time it's the news that goes out into your world from the changes made in your life. Think of the public learning about your marriage or divorce. The Midheaven is activated when the world comes into your world – for instance, if you are renting an apartment and your property owner announces to you that he or she is selling the house and you need to move. Another example may occur when your surviving parent dismantles your childhood home and informs you he has sold it, and that you will need to return from across the country to collect any treasures you've left behind.

We most often relate the MC to our careers, and where we are headed in life. A couple of examples come to mind. The first is of a Malaysian woman who collaborated with a man in a high-tech software company who later became her fiancée. They were extremely successful and had sold their software to a leading computer company, when a 16° Taurus Lunar Eclipse conjoined her tenth House Mars. The couple decided to continue working as a team with the new owners of the company for a year. A Lunar Eclipse occurred at 5° Taurus on her MC when their year ended. They went into a very different direction when they bought a three-family house with the proceeds from the tech business. The both decided to roll up their sleeves and grab hammer and

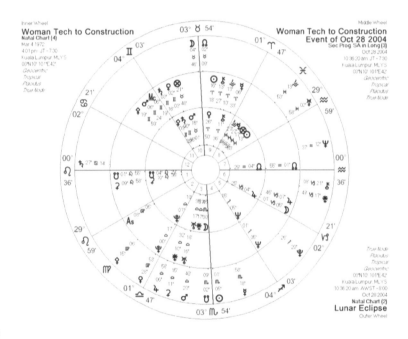

saw to renovate the apartments and sell them as condominiums. Again, they were successful. Now with that project behind them, they were looking for what is next. This time the Lunar Eclipse was conjunct her fourth House and the Sun occurred on her tenth House. Her sister had a music school in Malaysia that she no longer wanted. My client had spoken to me years ago about wanting her own music school. It seemed to be perfect timing as she and her mate looked for a new direction. She bought her sister's school, rented an apartment in Malaysia while her fiancée finished working on the second house, and planned to join her in the fall.

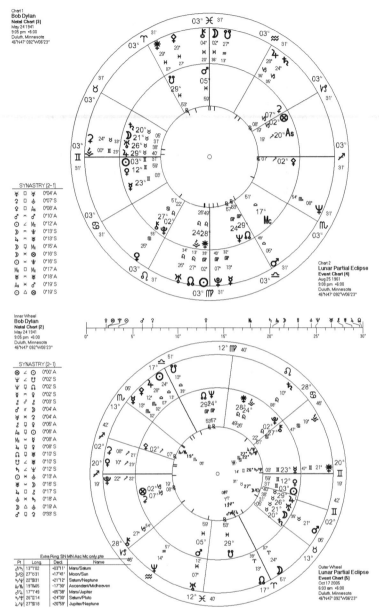

Chart 1
Bob Dylan
Natal Chart [3]
May 24 1941
9:05 pm +6:00
Duluth, Minnesota
46°N47' 092°W06'23"

SYNASTRY (2–1)

Chart 2
Lunar Partial Eclipse
Event Chart [4]
Aug 25 1961
9:08 pm +6:00
Duluth, Minnesota
46°N47' 092°W06'23"

Inner Wheel
Bob Dylan
Natal Chart [2]
May 24 1941
9:05 pm +6:00
Duluth, Minnesota
46°N47' 092°W06'23"

SYNASTRY (2–1)

Extra Ring: SN MN Asc Mc only.pts
Pt	Long	Decl	Name
♂/♄	13°♍02	+03°11'	Mars/Saturn
☽/⊙	27°♉31	+17°41'	Moon/Sun
♄/♆	22°♍31	+21°12'	Saturn/Neptune
Asc/Mc	19°♏05	–17°30'	Ascendant/Midheaven
♂/♃	17°↑49	+05°38'	Mars/Jupiter
♄/♇	26°♊14	+24°30'	Saturn/Pluto
♃/♆	27°♉18	+20°59'	Jupiter/Neptune

Outer Wheel
Lunar Partial Eclipse
Event Chart [5]
Oct 17 2005
6:03 am +6:00
Duluth, Minnesota
46°N47' 092°W06'23"

Bob Dylan's chart also appears to respond to lunar eclipses. Bob Dylan began gaining recognition on September 29, 1961 when the *New York Times* reviewed his work. The 2°39' Pisces Lunar Eclipse prior to the *New York Times* interview formed an activating square to Dylan's 3°Gemini Sun. That square stimulated his career by falling 10 signs from his natal Gemini Sun and creating his Solar tenth House.

Dylan was known as a master of picking up the mannerisms and accents of other artists and a quick study of instrumental styles. They called him "the sponge." Since Neptune rules water it also is ruler of this sponge label. As Dylan's Neptune was magnified heavily, being so close to the north node of the Moon, he became famous for illusions and theatrics. This complimented his poetic and musical talent when his prominently placed Neptune was conjunct his prominently placed nodal axis at 29° Virgo/Pisces, conjunct the point called the global axis (a point that gains world attention and is located at 0° of each of the cardinal signs, Aries, Cancer, Libra and Capricorn.) The release of his first album was on March 19, 1962, within two days of a 0°Aries Full Moon, announcing his arrival. The Lunar Eclipse one month prior occurred at 0° Pisces conjunct his Mars, bringing an amazing music man that would influence more musicians than any other in his own lifetime. His 29° Taurus Jupiter gladly received the Pisces Lunar Eclipse with a square.

July 29, 1966, a motorcycle accident interrupted Bob Dylan's concert tours. The accident occurred three months before the Lunar Eclipse of October 29, 1966 at 5° 32' Taurus. With the solar point of that eclipse in Dylan's tenth house, it is said he used the accident as an excuse to break away from the pressures of stardom. Natal Sun, Mars and Ceres were all hit by the degree of the eclipse. The combination of the three indicates a serious (Ceres) event involving speed (Mars) that affects the vitality of the individual (Sun). Also involved were Pallas and Pluto. Pallas would rule scheduling and bookings, and Pluto rules the masses of people waiting to see him perform.

Dylan was always a man of few words when interviewed. He claims his verses were never written as protest songs, or to incite revolution or speak for a generation. In spite of these denials, he did become an icon for a generation and the voice of a nation. He was nominated for a Nobel Prize of Literature, an honor which has never been awarded to a songwriter, in 1997, 1998, 1999, 2001 and 2002. He was also honored by a Martin Scorsese documentary titled *No Direction Home*, first broadcast in the fall of 2005. The October 2005 Lunar Eclipse at 24° Aries takes this Lunar Eclipse right to his home.

A Note About Lunar Eclipses and the Solar Return

The 5° Taurus Lunar eclipse degree was active in Bob's 1966 solar return, with 5°42' Taurus at the Nadir and the solar return Moon at 4°Leo. The return had 5°34 Capricorn rising, as it appears Jupiter was holding the cord of life at the DSC and in the sixth house at nearly 4°Cancer.

By casting a solar return chart at the natal location only, the signs on the Midheaven show a pattern that changes approximately at ten-year intervals. The pattern shows one modality at the MC for ten or so years. The modality changes by moving backwards from a high degree to a low degree on the MC from Mutable, Fixed to Cardinal Signs. 1966 was the last solar return with a fixed mode, since they appeared on the MC each solar return beginning 1957. In addition, the lunar eclipse opposite the MC adds to the symbolism of the end of a personal or public era. He took eight years to return to concert tours. Meanwhile he kept writing and recording.

Chapter 7
Astrological Tools

This chapter contains a collage of Astrological tools organized in a quick reference format. This section is designed to allow you, the reader, ease in managing basic astrological data and to supply you with perpetual support for your studies at any level. If this is your first astrology book, or if you are a seasoned astrologer, the information throughout the book will fascinate and facilitate a useful and practical application of this age-old study. Within the basic material, you will find information on signs, cycles, houses, horizons, and sign divisions. In this book, you will be introduced to the planets, depicted here, as characters at a party. Aspects, orbs, prominently placed planets, and developing themes in a chart are also described in detail.

The magic of astrology still enchants me. My understanding of this remarkable art/science is essentially a paradox of complex simplicity. The decoding process begins with simple lists of keywords for the meanings of signs, houses, planets, and aspects. The basic terms are best understood when holding them to their simplest symbolism and then blending the keywords to build an image or notion. I find that literal interpretations present uncomplicated information that allows for a broader application of astrology. Astrology can be explored on many different levels. Just as in the rules for living, in the study of astrology keep it simple and stick to the basics. You will be on your way to one of the richest studies of the human experience. The possibilities are endless.

Memorizing astrological language and symbols would be a daunting task were it not for its easy-to-remember glyphs in the original template zodiac wheel of twelve signs and their rulers. This template is where the core of astrology is found. Astrology's interpretation is built from the study of the symbolism of this simple wheel. With the ever-changing charts of the sky, the signs in their natural order remain constant. Sign symbolism can be found in the interpretations of houses and in the complex study of aspects.

By using planets as sign rulers, the planet's home is designated and helps organize a horoscope. With rulership, the planets lead your attention in a logical pattern right back to its home.

The original template of the zodiac remains as a guide to more complex details. The development of ideas for research, teaching, and technique in astrology is based on this ever-valuable picture on the following page.

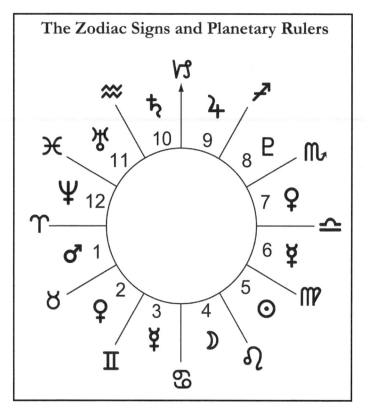

The Zodiac Signs and Planetary Rulers

The Zodiac Signs and Rulers

The Zodiac is a term commonly used to denote a "Circle of Animals." The Zodiac more correctly represents a "Circle of Living Beings" situated on an imaginary belt in the heavens, extending about eight degrees on either side of the apparent path of the Sun, and including the paths of the Moon and Planets. The circle is divided into twelve equal arcs, called signs, each named for a different constellation. Each of the twelve signs occupies an arc of 30 degrees. In the accompanying table are the twelve zodiac signs with their planetary rulers in natural zodiacal order, with keywords.

The ancient rulers – the Sun, the Moon, Mercury, Venus, Mars, Jupiter, and Saturn – are known as such because they were the only planets visible to the naked eye. With the use of telescopes came the discoveries of Uranus, Neptune, and Pluto. The system of ancient rulers worked for astrologers for over 500 years, and today many astrologers still use the ancient rulers for the signs.

Zodiac Sign	Ruling Planet		Keyword
♈ Aries	Mars	♂	action/force/man
♉ Taurus	Venus	♀	beauty/money/woman
♊ Gemini	Mercury	☿	thought/document/child
♋ Cancer	Moon	☽	Emotions/baby/mother
♌ Leo	Sun	☉	Vitality/creator/leader
♍ Virgo	Mercury	☿	analyze/organize/worker
♎ Libra	Venus	♀	Love/counselor
♏ Scorpio	Pluto	♇ ancient-ruler ♂	Transformation/power/lender
♐ Sagittarius	Jupiter	♃	Expansion/lawyer/clergy
♑ Capricorn	Saturn	♄	Structure/CEO
♒ Aquarius	Uranus	♅, ancient-ruler ♄	Awaken/invention/citizen
♓ Pisces	Neptune	♆, ancient-ruler ♃	Devine inspiration/isolation

Keywords and Dates of the Signs of the Zodiac

Aries ♈ March 20 to April 19

Aries the Ram is a creative, quick, aggressive, **cardinal fire sign**. It rules the head and eyes.

Taurus ♉ April 19 through May 20

Taurus the Bull is a strong, stable, **fixed earth sign**. Taurus rules the throat.

Gemini ♊ May 20 through June 20

Gemini, symbol of the Twins, represents a communicative, flexible, **mutable air sign**. It rules the larynx, hands and arms.

Cancer ♋ June 20/21 through July 22

Cancer the Crab is an emotional, protective, **cardinal water sign** ruling the breast, stomach and female reproductive organs.

Leo ♌ July 22 through August 22

Leo the Lion is a prideful, demonstrative, **fixed fire sign**, ruling the heart and the spine.

Virgo ♍ August 22 through September 22

Virgo, the Virgin with a shaft of wheat, is a dutiful, conscientious, **mutable earth sign**, ruler of the intestinal tract.

Libra ♎ September 22 through October 22/23

Libra the Scales are a symbol of balance and justice. Libra is a **cardinal air sign** ruling the kidneys and lower spine.

Scorpio ♏ October 22/23 through November 21/22

Represented by a Scorpion, Scorpio is a deep, intense, reactive, **fixed water sign** possessing power and stamina. It rules the reproductive system.

Sagittarius ♐ November 21/22 through December 21

Sagittarius the Archer is represented in heavens by the Centaur Chiron, and is an adventurous, freedom-loving, **mutable fire sign** ruling the hips and thighs.

Capricorn ♑ December 22 through January 20

Capricorn the Goat is an ambitious, steady, **cardinal earth sign** ruling teeth, bones, skin, and knees.

Aquarius ♒ January 20 through February 19

Aquarius represented by the Water Bearer is an innovative, unique, **fixed air sign** ruling the ankles and circulatory system.

Pisces ♓ February 19 through March 20

Pisces is a constellation of two fish swimming in opposite directions. It is an imaginative, inspirational, **mutable water sign,** ruling the feet.

Essential Dignities				
Planet	**Rules Home**	**Detriment**	**Exalted**	**Fall**
♂ Mars	Aries	Libra	Capricorn	Cancer
♀ Venus	Taurus/Libra	Scorpio/Aries	Pisces	Virgo
☿ Mercury	Gemini/Virgo	Sagittarius/Pisces	Aquarius	Leo
☽ Moon	Cancer	Capricorn	Taurus	Scorpio
☉ Sun	Leo	Aquarius	Aries	Libra
♇ Pluto	Scorpio	Taurus	Leo	Aquarius
♃ Jupiter	Sagittarius	Gemini	Cancer	Capricorn
♄ Saturn	Capricorn	Cancer	Libra	Aries
♅ Uranus	Aquarius	Leo	Scorpio	Taurus
♆ Neptune	Pisces	Virgo	Cancer	Capricorn
☊ North Node			Gemini	Sagittarius
☋ South Node			Sagittarius	Gemini

Essential Dignities

Essential Dignities is an evaluation list that sorts the planets according to their home rulership sign, which is an *essential dignity,* and their opposite position, called a *debility.* The sign of the planet's Exaltation is also an essential dignity placing the planet at a debility in the opposite sign and thus called its Fall. Dr. J. Lee Lehman has devoted an entire book on the subject titled *"Essential Dignities."*

Cardinal Signs	Fixed Signs	Mutable Signs
Aries ♈	Taurus ♉	Gemini ♊
Cancer ♋	Leo ♌	Virgo ♍
Libra ♎	Scorpio ♏	Sagittarius ♐
Capricorn ♑	Aquarius ♒	Pisces ♓

Planetary Modes

The signs of the Zodiac when grouped in fours are called **Modes**. Modes consist of three categories of behaviors, Cardinal, Fixed, and Mutable. Modes are the angular divisions of the zodiac.

Modes are also called Qualities or Quadruplicities, and they refer to a mode of expression. These modes of behavior indicate the way a sign operates. You learn what to expect from the four signs according to category or classification.

Cardinal signs are progressive and aggressive signs of action and initiation. They indicate the spark for the individual, draw upon the roots to collaborate and join, in order to govern its structures and rise as a pillar in the world.

Fixed signs are rooted in their original foundations of material and talents, to have and to hold, being resistant to change and display and perform its virtues in order to continue to commit to core matters and secure stability. .

Mutable signs are flexible, motion-oriented signs capable of alteration, communication and the process of information that takes thought, to tablet, to publication and finally to assimilation of cohesive information.

Planetary Elements

The following are called **Triplicitie**
divisions of the Zodiac. The energ
another.

	Fire	Earth	Air	Water
	♈	♉	♊	♋
	♌	♍	♎	♏
	♐	♑	♒	♓

Fire signs are creative and dramatic.   **Earth** signs are practical and stable.
Air signs are intellectual and communicative.   **Water** signs are emotional and permeating.

Personal Planets and Points

☊ The Nodes of the Moon ☋

The Nodes of the Moon are invisible spots on the celestial ecliptic (an equatorial line), that are points where the Sun and the Moon's orbital plane intersect. There are two nodes of the Moon, a North and South Node that sit on the zodiac belt in exact opposition to one another, and parallel the ecliptic in *declination*. Declination is the measurement of distance a celestial body sits from the celestial ecliptic, in a north or south position.

The symbol for the North Node is ☊ and the South Node symbol is ☋. They are considered Personal Points in a chart.

For delineation purposes, planets can be broken down into two categories:
The Inner Personal Planets - The Personal Planets are the Sun, Moon, Mercury, Venus and Mars.
The Outer Social Planets - Jupiter, Saturn, Uranus, Neptune and Pluto.
The Personal Points - The Ascendent, Mid-heaven and Nodes of the Moon.

Sun/Moon Midpoint— It's a "We" Thing

The Sun/Moon midpoint is an extremely revealing point in the natal chart and an exciting point to watch in all charts. Its rich symbolism runs deep into the heart of your natal chart. The symbolic list of this key point could go on at length. When found in a prominent position it can represent changes in your personal relationships and noteworthy developments in your creative growth. Watch for eclipse activity around this point. Think of the Moon as your internal thermometer and the Sun as your outer or obvious persona. The Moon is your private self and the Sun is your more public self. The midpoint help to explain your response mechanism or your personal take on situations, any given activity or events in your life. Certainly, this point can help to describe the types of interactions you may have with those on a personal level and shows how you approach the bonding process. It also shows what is going on inside when you are not in a comfortable personal situation but those that are casual.

If your Sun/Moon midpoint occurs in a water sign you may have difficulty in cold social settings. Maybe you prefer quiet one on one interaction where you can exchange something personal about with the other person. These people are more private and some are reserved with a private world. A few with the Sun/Moon midpoint in water signs are: Judy Garland, Nancy Reagan, Pope Benedict XVI, Dick Cheney, Tony Blair, Charlie Sheen, Leonardo DiCaprio in addition to a Daycare provider and an artist/antique dealer.

On the other hand, people with a Sun/Moon Midpoint in an air sign might be fully equipped in both close or casual relationships and well suited for public positions. Marlene Dietrich, Paul Newman, Whitney Houston also a Bed & Breakfast proprietor.

For those with their Sun/Moon midpoint in an earth sign They may posses standing through family associations or be driven by status or desire close associations to their roots. Pope John Paul II, Princess Diana, Tiger Woods, Mata Hari, Liza Minnelli, George W. Bush, Condeleesa Rice, Robert Downey, Jr. and a family court lawyer. Also with her Sun/Moon midpoint in an earth sign is a nun who left the convent to raise her child but never married.

With the midpoint in a fire sign the individual may have adventurous nature with showman qualities or a cavalier style. Henry Kissinger has his Sun/Moon midpoint in Leo. He was comfortable with interactions with heads of state. Johnny Carson, Rock Hudson, Jimmy Hoffa, Donald Rumsfeld, and Paula Abdul also have their Sun/Moon midpoint in a fire sign.

A few ideas for the for the Sun/Moon midpoint are as follows:

Sun/Moon Midpoint represents the point of :
*   Balance of an individual's inner and outer being.
*   Automatic response, as the individual's most sensitive zone. The proverbial "button".
*   Integration point of the male female principle within an individual.
*   How you integrate your emotional body with the activities in your life.
*   The point in your body most like the Sun/Moon midpoint is found at the solar plexus. – Your gut reaction is here.
*   Marriage functions.
*   Where your outer world meets your inner world.
*   Your emotional quotient is a term coined along the lines of intelligent quotient, IQ"or in this case the "EQ". *
    How well does your emotional body function with your intellectual capacity. A highly intellectual person may not
    posses the balance or feel they do not posses the balance to interact with others in appropriate or comfortable
    manner. They may retreat as with an introverted personality.
*   Intuitive response to anyone who qualifies as significant other whether in a temporary or permanent fashion..
*   The source for your creative outlet
*   Synthesis of your emotions and actions with daily living the individual's emotional response to the people and
    the situations
*   The bonding experience between two people.
*   Child vs. parental issues
*   an emotional self-image point

Divisions of the Sky— Ascendant/Midheaven

A "Horoscope" or natal chart of a person or event is the symbolic picture of the heavens at a specific moment in time and space.

Of the twelve divisions in a natal chart called "houses," four are of greater significance. The houses are partitioned by lines called "cusps," and the four most important ones are the Ascendant (ASC); its opposite, the Descendant (DSC); the Mid-heaven (MC); and its opposite, the Nadir (IC).

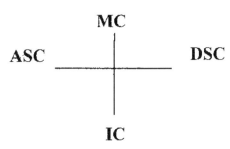

The point rising on the *eastern horizon* at the moment of birth is called the *Rising Sign* or Ascendant, referred to as a *Personal Point*. It usually falls on the first house cusp. Notice that while it is located on the western side of the page in the nine o'clock position, it represents the *eastern horizon*. In the original template of the zodiac, the sign Aries, which is ruled by Mars, occupies this position and, therefore, Aries' and Mars' basic principles are referenced and blended with the actual Ascendant sign. This point represents the beginning or the opening perspective of the horoscope wheel.

The opposite point to the Ascendant, the Descendent, is at the three o'clock position, and it's also the seventh house cusp. It represents the western horizon in a horoscope and the setting point of the Sun, called the <u>Descendent</u> (DSC). In the original template of the zodiac, the sign Libra, which is ruled by Venus, occupies this position and, therefore, Libra's and Venus' basic principles are referenced and blended with the actual Descendent sign. This point represents a point of social integration, partnering, and marriage.

The point highest in the heavens at the moment of birth is called the Mid-heaven, and it is another Personal Point. It is located at the top of the wheel in the noon time position. In the original template of the zodiac, the sign Capricorn, which is ruled by Saturn, occupies this position and, therefore, Capricorn's and Saturn's basic principles are referenced and blended with the actual Mid-heaven sign. Planets, and their symbolism, at the Mid-heaven represent issues that are most visible in the life of the native.

The lowest point in the heavens at the moment of birth is called the Nadir or IC. It is located at the bottom of the wheel at the six o'clock position. In the original template of the zodiac, the sign Cancer, which is ruled by the Moon, occupies this position and, therefore, Cancer's and the Moon's basic principles are referenced and blended with the actual Nadir/IC sign. This position represents private and family matters.

The axes of the ASC/DSC and the MC/IC form a cross which divides the horoscope wheel into quadrants. Each of the four quadrants is further divided into three sectors called Houses, representing the different areas of activity in life.

ASC/MC Midpoint – The Thread that Holds the Chart Together

The Ascendant/Midheaven midpoint is another highly sensitive point in any chart. If there were one point that represents a sort of toggle switch that activates all the houses in ones chart, it would be the ASC/MC midpoint.

The value of this point can be found in a brief review of house divisions used for horoscope chart construction. Bear with me while we draw a few connections. The chart wheel is comprised of 12 house divisions based on two primary points; the exact point on eastern horizon (the Ascendant) and the exact point of the highest center of the heavens (the Midheaven). These two points fall somewhere along the celestial belt of the 12 constellations. The MC has its polar opposite position the nadir or IC. The ASC has its polar opposite point the Descendant that divides the sky into quadrants that are further divided into sectors. The sectors are computed by various mathematical equations labeled as systems such as Placidus, Koch, Porphyry, Meridian etc. With one of the systems chosen the distance between the MC and the ASC is divided into three parts that give the cusps of houses 10, 11,and 12. Following the polar opposite points of these houses automatically gives houses 4,5,and 6 of the wheel. By the same method the distance between the ASC and the IC is divided by three which creates houses 1,2, and 3 matching the polar opposite points for houses 7, 8, and 9. We can see how the chart wheel is formed with the two important positions of the ASC and the MC.

The wheel and its houses represent the container for all the different departments in your life. This foundation adds the structure needed to house the planets that represent the players of our lives.

The point midway between the two major components required to form the wheel could be seen as the seam in the fabric of the wheel. Imagine a thread basted through each house along the edge of the wheel of your chart. Once the thread bastes together each house and is knotted at the ASC/MC midpoint at your birth it remains a very sensitive and personal point on the wheel that could be seen as holding it all together. Where it is the players that are the most sensitive at the Sun/Moon midpoint. It is the perspective and foundation or structure of the departments of your life when the Ascendant/Midheaven midpoint are activated by eclipses, transits and progressions. If a natal planet is conjunct, square or opposite this point you have additional trigger. The symbolism of that planet becomes the activating force when there is a major change in ones life.

A few ideas to describe the Asc/Midheaven midpoint are:
* Your physical being (ASC), personal relationships (DSC), integrated with your inner (nadir-IC) and outer
  (MC) life is equally sensitized to the outer activity and may prove to be dramatic.
* a powerful dynamic point—when impacted by an eclipse could "make or break" the status of your life in any
  given year.
* point at which your own personal core/world as it is:
     1) integrated with the larger world (your environment)
     2) perceived by the larger world
* A point when activated brings real world view in relationship to your endeavors.
* A sensitive point when activated that has the capacity to change your life as you know it.

Houses Divisions of a Chart

Calculations used to construct a natal chart, produce exact planetary locations at the time of birth as well as an Ascendant and Descendent, Midheaven and Nadir included in the twelve house divisions of the sky. Houses are derived by dividing the sky, using any number of different mathematical formulas.

Houses Can Be Big or Small — But Signs Are Always 30 degrees.

Each zodiac signs is exactly thirty degrees. Houses can vary in their size according to the mathematical formula used for horoscope house divisions and are not fixed in space, nor are they consistently 30° apart. The twelve zodiac signs are 30°apart and fall within houses of varying sizes and starting points.

Only some house systems are made up of twelve equal sections of which each house is exactly 30° apart which is true with Equal houses or Solar Sign houses Sun on First (Moon on the First, or other Planet on First such as Mercury on the First, or Point on First such as a Moon's node, etc). There is a significant difference between a chart cast with the Sun as a starting point for the houses or the Solar *sign* as a starting point.

For example of **Sun on 1st** or sometimes called Solar Houses: the Sun is located at 20° Taurus 32' and begins the chart with the first house at 20° Taurus 32' followed by the remaining eleven houses begin at 20° 32' of the next sign. Ie. The second house is 20°Gemini 32'. The third house is 20°Cancer 32', etc. You may choose any planet or point to begin the wheel in the same manner.

For an example of **Solar Signs**: The houses begin with whole signs therefore start with zero degrees of the same sign occupied by the Sun. Therefore, the chart that shows the Sun at 20°Taurus 32' will have 0° Taurus as the rising sign and the Sun falls in the that first house at 20°Taurus 32'. The second house begins at 0° Gemini, followed by the third house at 0° Cancer, etc.

Most other house systems are not equally spaced. The most popular house systems used are called Placidus and Koch houses. The following are some of the house systems found on Solar Fire: Campanus, Equal, Koch, Meridian, Morinus, Placidus, Porphyry, Regiomontanus, Topocentric, 0°Aries, Hindu Bhava, Alcabitius, Sun on 1st, Moon on 1st, Mercury on 1st, (etc).

Author's Preferences

Students often ask what do I use when casting a chart. My choice is not just one but a variety of house systems for different applications. I use the **Placidus House** system for my primary use when casting a chart for general purposes. For deeper client studies, I use a variety of house systems for charts. I use **Sun on First** most frequently along with **North Node on First**. When evaluating the impact of eclipses to a natal chart, I find the conjunction from the eclipse point to a planet. I then cast a **Planet on First** to view the wheel from the perspective of the planet hit by the eclipse
I apply 0°Aries Houses when writing about transits for my weekly report, studying Moon phases and eclipse charts (also for eclipses I use North Node Houses).

Find the Ruler of the House and Find the Secrets of the House.

Houses represent categories or departments of life. Each house represents a specific department of life. The planets found in a house bring strong influence to that house. Go back to the planet rulership list to find the signs that each planet rules. Find the house with that sign on its cusp. For the house not occupied by a planet they will always have a planet ruling that house. The aspects made to the ruling planet then describe the secrets of that house. Another secret

For example: In a chart with Cancer on the third house, that has *no planets in the third house*, hunt down the Moon which is Cancer's ruling planet.

* What is the Moon's sign and what planet rules that sign. (Moon in Aries is ruled by Mars.)
* As the ruler of the Moon, what are the aspects to (the example Aries — then see Mars aspects).
* What planet(s) does the Moon aspect?
* What is that aspect? (Conjunction, semi-sextile, semi-square, sextile, square, trine, sesqui- square, quincunx or
      opposition.)
* Is the Moon applying (moving closer) to that aspect or is it separating (pulling apart)? An aspect has a stronger
      effect when applying.

All of this adds up some very interesting information. Eventually you will be able to build a little storyline around your findings. It may help to take some notes. When preparing for a client, I draw every chart I read . I learn more from the hands on experience than just trying to sort it out.

Another thought to keep in mind is the natural order of the signs of the zodiac and the planet rulers. When looking at the third house always consider that Gemini holds that position in the natural order of the zodiac. Therefore, Mercury, ruler of Gemini is considered to have an influence on third house matters.

Planets in a House or On the Cusp

A planet *on the cusp* of a house is the object for action of that house. It further defines the cusp line and becomes more sensitive than planets more deeply in a house. In an example of the Moon in Aries, let's imagine it occurs exactly on the second house cusp. Each time there is a lunar return when the Moon comes back to the Moon each month there may be a little money drama. Maybe the person is an emotional spender that seeks a trigger to shop. Perhaps they are the opposite and are a compulsive saver that enjoys watching their savings account accumulate each month.

A planet *in a* house describes the conditions of that house. The Moon in Aries in the middle of the second house may describe someone who wants or receives a quick return for their efforts. A woman with her Aries Moon in the second house earns a living caring for children in her home. The renowned madam, Heidi Fleiss was born with her Moon in Aries in the second house. Perhaps her house was her place of work as well.

Expand Your Intuition with 30° House Lines.
Planets can create additional house divisions when they occur in multiple of 30° from the point of your attention. For instance when a planet is found exactly 30° beyond the Ascendant then it can be treated as another 2nd house indicator, even if found in the first house or more deeply into the actual second house. Any measurement in 30° increments will work as houses to the Ascendant. Try this with the Midheaven, Sun, and nodes of the Moon. Your understanding of the planets can benefit from this exercise.

The following are a brief description of the departments of life governed by each house.
The 1st house is the personal house, and represents the self, physical appearance, the condition of the body, and one's perspective in life.

The 2nd house is a material house and represents one's possessions, earnings, values, self worth, and salable talents. This is a money house without ties to other people, unlike the 8th house.

The 3rd house is a house of communication, transportation, neighborhood and siblings.

The 4th house is the house of roots and foundations, one's parents, home, and real estate. This is the foundation on which you are standing, your most private matters including your emotions.

The 5th house is the house of creation, children, play, love, speculation, and money from real estate.

The 6th house is the house of routine, jobs, health maintenance, co-workers, and pets.

The 7th house is the house of partnership and marriage. Legal matters and contracts can be found in the 7th house. This house also relates to roommates and your closest friend.

The 8th house is the house of shared resources, death, sex and taxes, estates, mortgages, and all money with ties to other people.

The 9th house is the house of religion, higher education, foreign matters, and in-laws.

The 10th house is the house of one's greatest direction in life, career matters, one's business and parents. Your boss can be found here and your public standing and reputation.

The 11th house is the house of friendship and comrades, social connections, and group activity. Stepchildren are found in the 11th house. This house contains the money from a self-owned business or business venture. This house most frequently contains the Ascendant /Mid-heaven midpoint and is a highly sensitive point I call the toggle switch or the chart.

The 12th house is the house of hidden, behind-the-scene matters, spiritual development, issues from the past, escapism, and addictions. Large stable animals are found here. This house sometimes contains the Ascendant /Mid-heaven midpoint the highly sensitive point I call the toggle switch or the chart.

Divisions of the Signs — Using Decanates and Dwads

A useful tool for looking more closely at a specific degree of the Zodiac is the following Decanate and Dwad Table. Each sign is divided into twelve, 2.5 degree parts called *dwads*. The twelve dwads in sign represent the twelve signs of the zodiac within one sign. *Decanates*, also called *decans*, divide a sign into three equal parts of 10 degrees each. The Decanates, in the shaded boxes, highlight the elemental divisions (Fire, Earth, Air and Water) of each sign, giving a sign three sub-rulers.

Decanate and Dwad Table

0° - 2.5°	♈	♉	♊	♋	♌	♍	♎	♏	♐	♑	♒	♓
2.5° - 5°	♉	♊	♋	♌	♍	♎	♏	♐	♑	♒	♓	♈
5° - 7.5°	♊	♋	♌	♍	♎	♏	♐	♑	♒	♓	♈	♉
7.5° - 10°	♋	♌	♍	♎	♏	♐	♑	♒	♓	♈	♉	♊
10° -12.5°	♌	♍	♎	♏	♐	♑	♒	♓	♈	♉	♊	♋
12.5° -15°	♍	♎	♏	♐	♑	♒	♓	♈	♉	♊	♋	♌
15° -17.5°	♎	♏	♐	♑	♒	♓	♈	♉	♊	♋	♌	♍
17.5° - 20°	♏	♐	♑	♒	♓	♈	♉	♊	♋	♌	♍	♎
20° - 22.5°	♐	♑	♒	♓	♈	♉	♊	♋	♌	♍	♎	♏
22.5° - 25°	♑	♒	♓	♈	♉	♊	♋	♌	♍	♎	♏	♐
25° -27.5°'	♒	♓	♈	♉	♊	♋	♌	♍	♎	♏	♐	♑
27.5°- 30°	♓	♈	♉	♊	♋	♌	♍	♎	♏	♐	♑	♒

Example: 0° Aries is a fire sign (the other fire signs are Leo and Sagittarius). The first ten degrees (0° to 10°) of Aries are under the major influence of Aries and its ruling planet Mars. The second ten degrees (10° to 20°) are shared with Aries and Leo, ruled by Mars and co-ruled by the Sun. The third ten degrees (20° to 30°) are a combined influence of Aries and Sagittarius, ruled by Mars and co-ruled by Jupiter.

The influence of dwads is blended with the ruler and sub-ruler. For example: 14 Aries is under the Leo decanate and Virgo dwad. Hence, when using the Decanate and Dwad Table, there are three signs, Aries, Leo and Virgo, to consider for the 14th degree of Aries. All three rulers of those signs, Mars, Sun, and Mercury, influence the 14th degree of Aries. To expand our understanding of any degree of the zodiac, use keywords associated with each of the signs and planetary rulers.

Planetary Cycles

The accompanying chart shows the planets and the average travel time it takes them to complete one revolution on the celestial equator:

Planetary Revolutions		
Moon 27 .5 days	☽	(0° Aries to 0° Aries)
Sun	☉	365 .5 days
Mercury	☿	88 days
Venus	♀	225 days
Mars	♂	2 years
Jupiter	♃	12 years
Saturn	♄	29.5 years
Uranus	♅	84 years
Neptune	♆	168 years
Pluto	♇	245 years
Moon's Nodes ☊/☋ 18.62 years		
(they back up through the signs at a rate of 20° a year)		
Asteroids		
Ceres	⚳	4.6 years
Pallas	⚴	4.6 years
Juno	⚵	4.4 years
Vesta	⚶	3.6 years
Chiron	⚷	50 years

Planetary Stations

As a planet travels through the zodiac, it will sometimes appear from our perspective on earth to make stops and reverse its direction. These stops are called Planetary Stations. Planetary Stations include the apparent stand-still position of a planet when it appears to reverse its direction and travel backward (**retrograde**), and then the stopping to turn forward again **(direct)**. During this process, a planet will visit the same degree on the zodiac three times – passing over point A, stopping and returning over point A in its retrograde motion, and lastly passing over point A again as it moves on in its direct motion. All planets and asteroids move in this fashion, with the exception of the Sun and the Moon, which are not planets.

Although the standing still, backward, and forward motions of these planets do not actually occur, since it is an optical illusion caused by our perspective here on earth, these effects are perceived as though this apparent motion were an absolute fact.

Retrograde motion is noted with an **R** or **℞** after a planet on a printed chart, and is found listed in an ephemeris (a book of planetary tables) under the planet column. This marks the planet's Retrograde Station date and degree.

Direct motion is signified with a **D** under a planet column in the ephemeris, which marks the planet's Stationary Direct date and degree.

The station date and degree is an essential tool in astrology. Stationary points are extremely important factors in the study of the planets. The dates of these stations mark major changes in life. The degree position is used to show where the change occurs, and its degree is measured to the other planets in the chart, to determine the impact it may have on one's life.

Lorraine Welsh has written an excellent description of Planetary Stations in the National Council for the Geocosmic Research (NCGR) textbook, *Essentials for Intermediate Astrology*.

Planets

The planets are named after the gods and goddesses in Greek and Roman Mythology. Their myths and characters are as relevant today as they were in ancient times, as we see these stories play out in our everyday lives. Myths reveal the nature and character of planets, their most likely behavior and typical attitude. A list of mythology books is found in the appendix of this book for further study.

As a method of introducing the planets, visualize meeting them as characters at a party. Imagine the planets walking into a room. How might they dress? What would they say, and what gestures would they use? This section is not a description of the signs, but of the planets themselves. The descriptions for each planet are broken down into four headings: The planet in mythology; How to recognize a planet at a party; what the planet represents in a chart; and the planet as a transiting planet.

The Sun in Mythology ☉

The Sun is a regal character, represented in Greek mythology by handsome and talented Apollo, ruler of prophecy, healing, and music. He was one of the Olympians born on Delos as the son of Zeus and Leto. His twin sister is Artemis, the goddess of the Moon.

How to Recognize the Sun at a Party

As a character at a party he would be approximately twenty-four to thirty-four years old, handsome, and bright with an aura of excitement. His chin is held high as he glances around the room to see who may recognize him. His voice is strong, articulate and baritone. He graciously thanks his hostess for the invitation. Of course, he is dressed like a king. You may catch him turning from one side to the other, the better to model his lavish costume. Everyone in the room stops what they are doing to welcome his commanding presence, for the Sun is a talented showman (or wants to be). He possesses dignity and demands attention. His most valued currencies are love and applause.

The Sun is generous with his light, and brings warmth and joy to all he touches. He takes charge and is at the top of the guest list. His executive abilities can lead a group in his direction. The Sun is the masculine, authoritative Emperor of the Sky.

What Does the Sun Represent in a Chart?

As a practical application in a chart, the Sun not only signifies characteristics of both masculinity and authority in actual people, but also directs the flow of energy in a chart. The light from the Sun is a strong magnetic source of energy, projected outward to the planets.

In a natal chart, the Sun represents the center of one's personality, identity, and vitality. The strength of the ego and the totality of its expression can be found in the house ruled by the Sun, in sign placement, and the relationship the Sun has with the planets and Personal Points in a chart. These relationships are determined by *aspects*. Planetary aspects are the distances measured between two bodies or points located on the zodiac wheel. The distances are derived by the division of 360° by multiples of two and three. Aspects will be discussed later in this chapter.

The Sun represents the vital core of the self. This is the symbol of the self's center in its purest sense. Here you are entitled to every quirk and identifying mark describing who you are. The Sun's contact with other points and planets, and the resulting picture, deliver the entire profile. The Sun represents the unifying principle, and thus the psychological integration, of human character. How the Sun relates to other points and bodies show where and how you shine or retract your light. The Sun has an aggressive outward quality, but may have an inward expression when located in a retiring and contemplative position (often noted by its house placement). Nonetheless, the Sun's position will always illuminate and magnetically pull life's events together for you. This is your source of self-importance, pride, creativity, and recognition.

The Sun's location represents the point of the greatest amount of illumination. It is here that you are most aware and interactive with your environment. Even introverts will find that their Sun point will bring them into the light from time to time. The Sun is the organizer of all the energies combined.

The Sun as a Transiting Planet

The *transiting** Sun will activate and stimulate any planet it contacts by bringing it into the center stage. It illuminates the concerns of the planet it is transiting. For example, the transiting Sun in conjunction with the natal (also called radical) Moon can bring enlightenment or awareness of current emotional issues. The current focus of attention is spotlighted by the Sun. It energizes, revives, and brings the return of issues regarding the natal planet transited by Sun, as its transit marks an anniversary. When the Sun transits its original position in a natal chart, it is called a *Solar Return,* which marks your birthday. A chart cast for the moment of the Solar Return describes the energy and events of the coming year. The Sun rules Sunday.

———————————————————

The Moon in Mythology ☽

The Moon is represented in Greek mythology by the goddess Artemis (she is called Diana in Roman mythology, also Isis, Luna, and Selene in other mythologies). As Diana, she is the twin sister of Apollo, a beautiful huntress clad in a short hunting dress, and carrying a bow and arrow. She was the daughter of Jove, or Jupiter, and Latona.

How to Recognize the Moon at a Party

At a party, you may find the Moon tastefully dressed, as tailored for comfort as she is elegant. The Moon radiates a feminine, mystical, shy, and soft light. She could be a newborn baby up to ninety-five years of age, for she encompasses the development of all four phases of the Moon. The Moon also represents the development of the infant to seven years of age. At the New Moon stage of her development, she is like a child with a childlike point of view. In her *First Quarter* stage, the Moon is like a young woman, engaged in education and travel. In her *Full Moon* stage, she represents the mother goddess, maternal, nurturing and supportive. In the Moon's *Last Quarter* stage, she is the honored crone, sharing her wisdom and knowledge.

At the party, you may find the Moon snuggled in a corner counseling a friend with a problem, or surrounded by her own little clan. She is intuitive and sensitive, and holds the memories of the past. She may carry a small family album with her, and shares stories of her heritage.

The Moon's strong boundaries allow only a few into her beautiful home, where she is at ease in her roles as wife, mother, nurturer, and caretaker. The Moon's moods are reflected in her luminous face, framed by her dramatic midnight blue aura. Her moods may last for two and a half days at a time, affecting her entire environment. She is the Empress of the sky, wife of the Sun.

What Does the Moon Represent in a Chart?

As a practical application, the Moon in the natal chart indicates one's emotional structure, and represents the foundation of an individual's needs – how a person operates in a relationship, how long he or she remains connected to others, freedom and intimacy issues, and the ability to give and take. These can all be examined by noting the Moon's sign and house placements, in relation to the other points and planets of the horoscope. The Moon also has an association with the Nadir and its ruling planet. Noting all of these indicators can offer insight into the emotional profile of an individual.

The Moon describes the first relationship an infant has with his/her mother or first primary caretaker. Any complications with the initial nurturing, mother/child bonding, feeding and digestion, would be apparent through a study of the Moon. All close personal relationships in a person's life are greatly influenced by this initial relationship, even before developing a sense of self. The integration of other nuclear family members into the infant's life are represented by the Sun (for father figures), and by Mercury (for siblings), when the child's awareness can already focus beyond the fulfillment of basic needs. The home environment is defined by the Moon as well, along with any changes in the home's location, or general fluctuations of family members and housing needs.

The Moon as a Transiting Planet
The transiting Moon will set a tone and a mood for the day, as it travels from one sign to another. This is explained in great depth throughout this book within several chapters on the Moon.. The aspects made by the Moon to other transiting planets color the mood of the Moon. The Moon absorbs and reflects the surrounding energies of the transiting planets, and projects a mood onto the planet. The interactions between the Moon and the planets may have a subtle impact on a natal chart, unless other major aspects between other transiting planets are involved, the impact of which may be more noticeable.

When the transiting Moon is in *exact hard aspect* (a separation of zero degrees, ninety degrees, 180 degrees or 270 degrees) to the transiting Sun, the position of the Moon is dramatically noticed. The Moon's monthly cycle in a natal chart is called a *Lunar Return*. A chart cast for that moment of the Lunar Return can describe the energy and events for the current month. A chart specifically cast to answer a question is called a *Horary chart*. In a Horary chart the Moon represents the querent. The day of the week ruled by the Moon is Monday.

Mercury in Mythology ☿
Mercury is the messenger of the Gods. He has winged feet and moves at lightning-fast speed. Mercury is the son of Jupiter, God of the Heavens and Maia, Goddess of the Plains. He grew to adult proportions just a few minutes after birth. From his cradle, Mercury flew to Apollo's stable, where he stole cattle (cattle represent clouds). Mercury's name is derived from the Sanskrit *Sarameias*, which means "the breeze of a summer morning." This breeze came in the morning to whisk away the souls of the dead. The ancient belief was that in the wind were the souls of the dead. Mercury also used the melody of the wind to invent music, which can awaken feelings of joy and sorrow, regret, and yearning. Mercury traveled in all circles, acting as a guide between their worlds. He represents information.[*]

How to Recognize Mercury at a Party.
Mercury might enter a room so quickly you that may miss the actual moment of his arrival. He has the ability to camouflage his adolescent-like appearance, so that he resembles a young child, as he represents

---

[*]*Myths of Greece and Rome by H.A. Guerber.*

ages between seven and fifteen years old. He is a rather androgynous character and is like a sibling to most people. His moods swing like those of a typical teenager. He may be wearing clothes best designed for travel as he is constantly in motion. Mercury probably ran a dozen errands before coming to the party, and is likely to be there to deliver some sort of message to someone.

Mercury needs no introduction, for he already knows at least a little about everyone in the room. In fact, if you are interested in meeting someone in particular at the party, Mercury is the person you want to talk to for that introduction. You may want to be careful with Mercury, however, for he can get some of his facts mixed up. Some people say he is a liar, but he insists there are two sides to every story. He feels gossip is information to be shared by all, and that secrets are public property.

Mercury is a social butterfly, and uses small talk to keep the party filled with ever-changing topics of conversation. Along with his gift for gab, he is chameleon-like and can change his mood as easily as the subject. Stories are Mercury's domain, words are his battleground, and information is his mission.

What Does Mercury Represent in a Chart?
Mercury is the point of information and motion, including transportation, in your chart. Mercury writes and receives letters, makes calls, and exchanges information – and misinformation. You have to be careful with Mercury; he is a fast talker with a quick tongue, who meddles, gossips, tricks, and is famous for telling fibs. His reporting style gives the facts, but you have to get the facts straight. Mercury gives two sides to every story.

Mercury is a connector, networker, medium, guide and spokesperson. All introductions come through Mercury, and the arrangement of meetings is also Mercury's department. Your decision-making process is ruled by Mercury. Mercury describes your neighborhood and sensory environment.

Mercury is like a radio transmitter and defines your personal style of communication. Mercury rules what is heard, what is seen and how things are said and written. The things you think about, your style of talking and writing, and even the types of communication equipment you have can be described by Mercury. Mercury rules your short trips on a day-to-day basis, and could give a clue to your means of transportation. Mercury administrates the mundane details of life, by making appointments and shuffling paper.

Mercury represents the androgynous people you meet in your life. Mercury points to relationships with children, siblings, aunts, and uncles. Mercury rules postal carriers and delivery persons, as well as secretaries, clerks, telephone operators, mechanics, technicians and store keepers, to name a few.

Mercury as a Transiting Planet
Mercury as a transiting planet makes its greatest impact on its retrograde and direct *planetary stations* (see footnote above). Mercury brings visitors and messages, and creates the need for decisions. Mercury brings attention to paper work, errands, and cleaning-up. Mercury takes on the nature of the sign it is in and the planets it most closely aspects. The sign which Mercury occupies indicates the type of informa-

tion apparent at the time of the transit. Our attention to tasks and details can be described by a Mercury transit. Mercury appropriately rules the middle of the week, specifically Wednesday.

Venus in Mythology ♀

Venus is the Goddess of beauty, love, laughter, and marriage. It is said she is the daughter of Jupiter and Dione, but Venus has also been said to have sprung from the foam of the sea.

How to Recognize Venus at a Party

Naturally, Venus is your hostess. Venus is every man's desire and is approximately fifteen to twenty-four years old. Her home is a beautiful expression of fine taste as she surrounds herself with objects d'art and lush foliage. She is refined yet seductive. Venus is pleasant to everyone and insists that everyone is pleasant to everyone else.

Venus is cultured and gracious, but can be "catty," for she also has a jealous nature. It is not necessary for her to be loved by all, but she does want to be liked by all, and has perfected the art of people pleasing. She has therefore anticipated your every need, has provided you with delectable treats, and various sensual delights.

Venus is dressed in the finest fabrics, adorned with only genuine jewels. She is dazzling and soft-spoken. Femininity is her domain. She is multi-talented, which includes her talent for material acquisition. She displays apparent wealth. Her colors are soft pinks and rich greens. Venus is the goddess of beauty.

What Does Venus Represent in a Chart?

How you keep the peace and mediate your surroundings is the realm of Venus. The things in life you desire, the colors you choose, and the clothes you wear are all in Venus' domain. She brings you comfort and soothes your pain, quiets discord, and gives you hope. Venus rules the throat, thyroid, and the lower back. Diabetes and venereal diseases are also Venus-ruled.

Venus describes how and on what you spend your money. She determines the things in life you value and your movable valuables. Venus shows the things to which you are attached.

Venus represents the Feminine ideal for a man and describes his choice of girlfriend and the characteristics of his spouse. Venus represents female friends for both men and woman. The professions Venus represents are counselors, lawyers, mediators, peacemakers, matchmakers, artists, and decorators. Venus is a partner in business, a sister, and a guardian angel.

Venus as a Transiting Planet

Venus in transit brings a soothing and softening energy to the planets and houses it transits. It can bring calm after a stormy period, making you feel appreciated and warm. Love, money, and abundance are more accessible during a Venus transit. Acquisition of goods and personal treasures are likely when her energy creates the desire to spend money. The pleasures of sleep, food, and relaxation are more likely with a visit from Venus. Venus brings women and feminine energy, often filling the air with harmony. Venus transits can bring counselors and lawyers. Venus rules relationships and can invite a union between two people.

Keywords for Venus are gentle, quiet, persuasive, smooth, flirtatious, self-indulgent, vain, and lazy. Venus is sensual, affectionate, sympathetic, intimate, mellow, graceful and tactful.

Venus is balancing, harmonizing, peacemaking, and people pleasing. Venus rules love, sentiment, romance, friendship, marriage, weddings, social events, social circles, etiquette, dances, theaters and all festivities. Venus rules personal value systems, appreciation, aesthetics, fashion, art, pleasure, music, and beauty parlors. Venus also rules flowers and flowering plants.

Venus is the ruler of treasures, money, cash, checks, banks, stocks, bonds, gems, furnishings and furniture, the day of Friday, gems, and attachments.

Venus rules females, all women in general, wives, mates, partnerships, sisters, and the woman in a man's chart, as well as counselors, mediators, peacemakers, and matchmakers.

Mars in Mythology ♂

In Greek and Roman mythology, Mars and Ares represent the same character. Mars is the God of War. He was the son of Jupiter (the sky) and Juno (the heavenly light) and brother to Vulcan (the celestial artist). Mars' name comes from the root Maruts, meaning "grinder" or "crusher." Mars and Venus were united by Love (Cupid).

How to Recognize Mars at a Party

Mars has just crashed the party. He wasn't invited because he and the hostess, Venus, have been arguing all week. He is her lover and wouldn't miss this for the world. He knows that as long as he is in her presence, she'll desire no one else. He has been brutal in battle, beating and bludgeoning his enemy for a month over his latest cause. He is a conqueror.

He is from thirty-four to forty-five years of age, courageous, usually noisy, and short on both patience and manners. He can be very charming to every woman in the room, but is quick to switch his machismo to jeer with the men. His dress is strictly masculine and up-to-date. His opinions are many and his punishment for injustice is swift and often merciless.

He is a man of the here and now, and yet prides himself on his foresight, though he never saves for the future. His ideas are brilliant and enterprising, but he lacks follow-through. He is the master of initiation, motivation and drive. Mars is dynamic; wherever he is, there is action. Mars is the god of war.

What does Mars Represent in a Chart?

Locate your tools for living by identifying where Mars is, its sign, and the house it occupies. Mars indicates survival skills, depicting one's style and ability to defend oneself. Mars in a natal chart is a powerful indicator of how to direct and apply energy, as well as what type of energy one has. Mars shows what drives and motivates an individual and how to be assertive. Even non-assertive individuals will manage to get what they want with the help of Mars.

As a professional indicator Mars identifies the source of direction and focuses on goals. Mars ignites, heats and "fires up." It points to the sources and triggers of anger, aggression, and force. Mars crusades, conquers and rules conflicts of all types. Mars points out where you are most opinionated and inconsiderate.

Mars rules muscles, and physical energy, power and stamina, described by the sign and the house it occupies. People represented by Mars are brothers, men in general, athletic competitors, armies or teams, enemies and aggressors.

Mars indicates work and job activity. It is a sex indicator and in a woman's chart, Mars can show the type of man to whom she is attracted. With questions related to the man in a woman's chart, Mars must definitely be considered.

Mars indicates the point of a knife at any surgical procedure. Head injuries and accidents are under the rulership of Mars. Heavy machinery and large trucks, fire engines and cars are Mars-ruled. Red is the color of Mars.

Mars as a Transiting Planet
Mars as a transiting planet is a point of ignition. Keeping a watchful eye on Mars will surely show where and what the action is. When Mars applies an aspect to a natal chart, it can spark the action needed to get things off the ground. It shows sexual activity, burning calories, and muscle exertion. Mars brings aggressive male energy to a situation and can cause conflict, battle and arguments. Mars may be found in a prominent position to the Sun or Ascendant on the day of a court appearance. Tuesday is ruled by Mars.

The following are keywords related to a Mars transit: ignition, pursuits, fire, hot, red, rashes, flashes, explosions, noise, head, blood, muscles, sexuality, fast, action, energy, speed, armed forces, guns, war, battle threats, violence, forcefulness, selfish, proud, passionate, ambitious, competition, discord, brute strength, anger, hatred, resentment, uproar, unruly, untidy, impatient, angry, incisive, wounds, inflammation, fevers, headaches, and burnout.

Jupiter in Mythology ♃
In mythology Jupiter (or Zeus) reigns as the God of Gods and of men. He is the son of Saturn and Rhea, husband of Juno, brother of Pluto and Neptune. Thunder was his weapon, the eagle, his favorite bird, bore his thunderbolt. The domains of the universe were divided between Jupiter and his two brothers. Jupiter was ruler of the heavens, Neptune ruled the ocean and Pluto ruled the realms of the

dead. The Earth was considered common property. Jupiter is the God of Knowledge.

How to Recognize Jupiter at a Party
Jupiter is a happy fellow. He is a large, jovial character between the ages of forty-five to fifty-seven years old. His clothes are a bit of a mess. He was probably playing ball with his dog before he came in to the party. He enters with a large laugh and slaps a buddy on the back with a warm hello. He loves women (or womanizing) and fun, and prizes his freedom. He has been labeled irresponsible and can charm others into paying his way even though he might buy the party a round of drinks.

He, too, is a story teller, but unlike Mercury, his tales are of his distant travels. He has met people from all over the world and exchanges letters from foreign places. It is possible he can speak more than one language, or grasp the language of grand concepts. He understands things without having studied them formally. He may posses a universal wisdom of hope and insight. He is a natural salesman, and has been a student, a teacher, an explorer, an entrepreneur, and even a minister. He enjoys good wine, good company, and sleeping under the stars. He frequents the theater and music halls. He loves to party. His education may or may not be formal for the world is his classroom, and he is a perpetual student. He will talk of gathering together again in the future, but he'll forget those plans as soon as he walks out the door.

What Does Jupiter Represent in a Chart?
On a practical level Jupiter is a symbol for broad, expanded vision and optimism. Jupiter will be particularly activated in one's most productive years, 35 through 55. Jupiter can broaden the perspective of the house it occupies as well as the planets it contacts. Jupiter has been labeled as a good luck planet, but actually needs the right combination of aspects to generate good fortune. Jupiter indicates a relaxed point in a chart and can promote a reclined position, and may be prone to missing opportunities due to a carefree sense of contentment.

Jupiter is not motivated unless stimulated by other planets such as Mars or Uranus. Jupiter acts like a valve, releasing steam from a kettle, diminishing pressure. The release of pressure serves to ease stress in order to bring an opportunity, or expand knowledge in the sign and house it occupies.

Jupiter's place in a chart describes one's greatest endeavor to reach beyond limits and boundaries in order to bring greater understanding. Here are persuasive powers, personal wisdom, and judgments.

Jupiter's house position, sign, and aspects will show how one's need for freedom is expressed. The house Jupiter occupies may show where the greatest amount of space is required in one's life and psychological structure.

Jupiter as a Transiting Planet
Jupiter as a transiting planet can expand social circles and/or the environment ruled by the house and sign it transits in a natal chart.

Jupiter creates space and denotes a need for freedom in the house it transits. It will have the same effect when contacting a planet. Jupiter brings a broadened perspective and expanded understanding to the concerns of the house or planet it transits. Jupiter can activate a new study in a particular area and create a new understanding or judgment in the house it transits. It may send you back to school or have you collecting unemployment. Its design is to open things up, not to have you lose your job, but to offer you a vacation or break. The break can be so comfortable that you may not be able to find any motivation to get things done. The people indicated by Jupiter in one's chart are represented by clergy, professors, lawyers, publishers, in-laws, people, and matters from foreign countries, universities, and cultural affairs.

Saturn in Mythology ♄

Gaea and Uranus bore the Titans – twelve gigantic children with great strength – six sons and six daughters. Saturn, also known as Cronus, was the youngest and most courageous of the sons. Uranus, fearful of his giant children, cruelly chained them in a cavern and ignored their cries for help. Gaea, who could not bear the sounds of their cries, urged the Titans to conspire against their father and escape. Saturn was the only one with enough courage to carry out his mother's plans. Saturn's siblings, joyous at their release, expressed willingness to be ruled by him.

Saturn, in turn fearful of losing his reign of Mount Olympus, swallowed up all of his children: Neptune, Pluto, Vesta, Ceres and Juno. When the last, Jupiter, was born he was saved by his mother and not swallowed by Saturn. After Jupiter grew up to overthrow his father as god of all the gods, Saturn threw up the rest of his swallowed children. Saturn was exiled to a prosperous kingdom and reigned in peace for many long years.

How to Recognize Saturn at a Party

Saturn accepted this invitation because it could be good for business. He may be fifty-seven through seventy. He has a sober look on his face as if he has just come in from the cold. He's probably suffering from arthritis. His hair is gray and his eyes are cautious and suspicious, which is his normal attitude. He has been labeled a pessimist, but he is seasoned with life's lessons. He is no longer enchanted with the johnny-come-lately's, but wants to see who and what has stood the test of time. Saturn is a wise old man with all the experience of the Sun, Moon, Mercury, Venus, Mars, and Jupiter put together. He is the head of his company or highly placed in government, and a smart businessman with none of the get-rich-quick schemes that Jupiter might offer. He's not for the new, but for the old. He is stable, concrete and reliable. He is a pillar of the community.

Saturn will tell you to take your time and do it right. His advice is to persevere, and do all your work so that you will reap the rewards of your efforts. You'll find Saturn being asked for his savvy business advice. He has been mentor to many young hopefuls at this party. He has tips on building strong foundations for long-standing projects. Saturn is never in a hurry, for Saturn is the god of Time.

What Does Saturn Represent In A Chart?

Saturn is the planet of structure, limitations, and debts. It shows where one's debts are located. Your fears or failures can be described by Saturn's placement. It represents your dedications, duties, and burdens. Saturn can bring you structure, stability, and efficiency. It rules anything that is old, permanent, and simple. It is where you are most cautious, patient, and laborious. This is your level of ambition or your greatest insecurities. When past the age of 42, Saturn will help you to be the author of your life. Heavy family matters and great responsibility are indicated by Saturn. This is where you are most likely to conform to the rules.

Saturn's sign and house position, along with the aspects made by other planets, can begin to describe one's purpose in this life. Saturn indicates your major career goals, bosses, and mentors. The people represented by Saturn are fathers, bosses, all authority figures, government figures and elderly people.

Saturn as a Transiting Planet
Saturn in transit can be a difficult experience or a time of long-awaited rewards. Saturn restructures and demands attention to responsibility in the house it transits. The planets it contacts will be players in the drama of responsibility.

At times, Saturn can bring problems to teeth and bones or a more focused attention to the body.

Saturn can supply you with help from elders and mentors. When transiting Saturn reaches a prominent position in the chart, it can bring you to the top of your field. At the same time you may find work seems harder than usual. Finances and supplies could be low, but more stable. The difficulty in relationships can bring about much needed reorganization. Saturn rules Saturday.

Uranus in Mythology ♅
Uranus, who represents the starry heaven, was created by Gaea, who represents earth, to be her husband. Together, they conceived the twelve Titans, of which Saturn was their youngest son.

How to Recognize Uranus at a Party
Uranus arrives at the party unexpectedly. Uranus surprises everyone by arriving with a three-ring circus in tow. If something is bizarre, it must belong to Uranus. Everyone knows who he is, but he looks different every time he walks in the room. It's the costumes that change. He is usually sudden and abrupt in whatever he does; however, it is bound to be unique and ingenious. He is out of this world, an alien. Rebellion is the wood that fuels his fire. He can be a mad scientist or a radical revolutionary. Uranus is an innovator and experimenter. He is always out of step with time, whether it's being extremely conventional and traditional in a new age setting, or radical and bizarre in more conventional, main stream setting. Uranus breaks limits and laws as he goes beyond Saturn's words to the wise.

Aloof and detached, Uranus is equipped with the right stuff for a true humanitarian; he changes social mores. Because he is not invested in illusion, he fearlessly exposes the truth as he sees it. He is an individualist. His goal is to self-actualize and maintain the rights of individuality for all. A humanitarian and champion of the oppressed, he has written the constitution to guarantee the rights of equality, life, liberty and the pursuit of happiness. He advocates the principles of one's right to freedom.

What Does Uranus Represent in a Chart?

In a natal chart, Uranus is an indicator of individuality and social objectives. Here is where your unique "take" on life can be expressed. A desire for excitement is prominent when Uranus is amplified in your chart. Likewise, an interest in subjects like astrology and abstract thought is indicated by Uranus. Uranus could make it difficult for you to work for others and may constantly be pulling you to do your own thing. Rebellion and issues of independence are often brought into focus by Uranus' position. Uranus represents friendship and acquaintances (your closest friends are indicated by Venus).

Uranus as a Transiting Planet

Uranus is the planet of sudden and abrupt change, and can shake up, stir up and conjure up a whole new look to your life. Depending on which planets it contacts or aspects, Uranus can rearrange your life. It can walk into your closet and throw out everything you thought you liked and demand a new wardrobe. It can radically change your appearance, shift your weight, and alter your environment. All of a sudden, you may have an unbelievable job offer across the country, or you may experience a restlessness compelling you to change.

Uranus rules astrology, erratic shifts, uniqueness, brilliance and the pulse of society. Uranus indicates things out of this world. Aliens and behaviors that alienate are associated with Uranus.

Uranus can bring an intuition of impending change. You may not be able to put your finger on the source or cause, but you can be sure that things will not remain the same. Uranus can upset life and create chaos. Out of chaos, a new pattern, the "strange attractor" of the process emerges. Wish fulfillment, desires and impulses toward positive growth and development are a common response to Uranus transits, unless you perceive change as a threat to your security. One thing you can count on is that Uranus, ultimately in the interest of your highest good. Uranus is the Great Awakener.
Uranus can be responsible for bringing the love of your life to you, such as getting married after a brief, whirlwind romance, even if the marriage is only short-lived. However, Uranus' impact is likely to leave as suddenly as it came.

Expect the unexpected during a Uranus transit. This is not the time to nail things down and anchor your plans for the future. Just when you thought the coast was clear, Uranus will more than likely be back your way again in a year and a half, triggering the same planets. This is the result of its *retrograde and direct planetary station* pattern).

Neptune in Mythology Ψ

Neptune also known as Poseidon, carries a trident. He is the God of the Sea and of all the waters on the face of the earth. His brothers are Jupiter and Pluto. Neptune is a tyrannical ruler with unrestricted power whose green hair encircles the earth that he loves. Neptune's vengeful nature created a monster that came upon shore, devouring all inhabitants within its reach and arousing great terror in all.

How to Recognize Neptune at A Party

A brisk wind pushes open the door and a mysterious character appears wearing a cape partially covering his face. He disguises his identity because even he does not know who he is. He is ageless. He is wearing the scent of patchouli or could it be the hemp he may have smoked on his way over to the party? He speaks in poetic phrases, his speech as musical as his ability to play haunting melodies on any instrument.

He's elusive, you can never pin him down. He is not prone to commitment, and his boundaries are changeable.

Neptune has a comfortable reflective nature that resonates with those in his company. As he mirrors your behavior and every thought, you feel as though you have found your soul mate.

Neptune is a seducer and a narcissist who may woo you, entice you, romance you, but may never touch you. Nevertheless, you may fall madly in love with him, even when he tells you are not what he is looking for. Neptune may attach himself to you especially if you spurn or reject him, for then he is likely to make you his next victim. Neptune's sweet, gentle face appears vulnerable and peaceful. But much to everyone's surprise, he is a warrior. Neptune's trident is his symbol of battle. Neptune is the God of the mighty and powerful sea.

What Does Neptune Represent in a Chart?

Neptune is a complex planet and one of the least understood. Its home sign of Pisces and twelfth house influence contributes to its wide range of expressions. You might say Neptune is the grand master of altered states, on a continuum ranging from psychosis and terror to high spirituality. And, while Neptune has been considered on the great benefics in astrology, it is also considered the ruler of misunderstandings. Therefore, Neptune's effects can be considered positive or negative, by looking at its sign, house placement, and aspects to planets and points in a chart.

Neptune's positive influence can be felt in the form of inspirations, divine interventions, sympathetic responses, and blind faith connections. Neptune can inspire pure, compassionate, and selfless love. One of Neptune's most beautiful expressions is the faith connection created when you surrender to a higher source for help. This great act of strength and faith creates a spiritual connection, the outpouring of which can be an ecstatic or prophetic experience.

This type of experience calls to mind the lives and experiences of the great mystics and saints, and Neptune can indicate an interest in formal religion. However, whether a person has an interest in formal religion or not, a study of Neptune in a chart indicates one's connection to a higher spiritual source.

While Neptune's influence is extremely private and positively personal, its influence can affect a whole generation collectively. Hence, the great interest in New Age spirituality along with the rise of vast numbers into fundamental religions in the "Boom" generation, for example.

Neptune is also prone to addictions of all kinds. This can apply to substances or relationships. A "Neptunian haze" drops a veil of intoxication over your normal state of being, inspiring a consuming passion for a particular person, project, or mission, propelling you into a larger and lighter space. You feel "madly in love," have twinkle toes, and all the warm and happy sensations that go along with this state. Everything becomes more easily tolerated and everyone is beautiful as glide on you cloud of enchantment. An abundance of hope is present, along with an all around sense of well-being. You may feel you could accomplish anything in this state of mind. But beware, because Neptune's great idealism can be the beginning of denial.

A not-so-positive side of Neptune can be one of victim and victimizer. When harboring the pain of being victimized, one can lash out and inflict pain and terror on others. The effect can be extremely violent. Think of Neptune, the God of the Sea, with his sea battles, tidal waves and undertow. Neptune often feels justified in his rage, and, like a hurricane, will blow anything away in his path.

And, finally, if Neptune's great passions overreach themselves, they can turn delusional. Whether on is experiencing the extremes of Neptune's passions or has become a victim of them, a variety of neuroses and psychoses can be identified. Perhaps, in the overall scheme of things, for one to be spiritually wise, one must experience the complete range of altered states. This could, on an esoteric level, give the mentally ill individual a spiritual advantage. Nonetheless, it is interesting to note that psychoses are starting to be looked at therapeutically as spiritual emergencies.

Neptune as a Transiting Planet

Neptune in transit can be a time of wonderful inspiration or great confusion. Neptune can bring a sense of divine purpose or can wash energy away. It has a mesmerizing, dissolving and elusive influence on the planets and the houses with which it comes into contact. It influences many kinds of altered states. It can bring sleep or sleeplessness, grogginess, or an intoxicated state of consciousness. A Neptune transit can cloud one's thinking and anesthetize suffering, as it has a numbing effect.

Metaphorically speaking a person is often under a "Neptunian haze" at the time of a wedding. This anesthetic veil, at the time of a marriage, may allow a couple to proceed with what ordinarily seems overwhelming or an unlikely course of action.

Neptune can bring deception, misunderstanding, and bad judgment. Losing possessions or unwise spending or lending can be its theme.

Neptune transits can represent medications and hospital care. Neptune can also bring aquarium fish into your life or water experiences like boating or beaches. Retreats and meditation ashrams are under the rulership of Neptune.

Neptune has also been present at times in acts of great violence that are motivated by religion or a mission-from-god theme. It is also prominent with the victim or victimizer. Neptune does not always represent a loving spiritual experience and must be respected for the havoc it can wreak. Major weather and terrestrial disasters are often under Neptune transits.

People ruled by Neptune are fishermen, nurses and caretakers, artists and poets, illicit characters and prisoners, visionaries, psychics, photographers, camera persons, chemists, dancers, poets, and musicians.

Pluto in Mythology ♇ or ♇

Pluto (Hades or Aïdes), meaning "wealth giver" or "the unseen," is the god of the Underworld. Pluto was given reign of the dead and riches. All precious metals are buried deep in the earth. This god was most feared of all the gods, for he surfaced only when in search of a victim to drag below. The emblem of his power was a two-pronged fork, and his vehicle was a chariot driven by four coal-black horses. Persephone was his bride and queen of the underworld. His domain, called Hades, was impossible to leave if visited unless accompanied by Mercury.*

How to Recognize Pluto at a Party

Pluto is the deepest, most intense character in the room. Pluto may not be the most handsome creature at the party, but he is by far the sexiest with his smoldering, dark looks. Pluto is the master of games, whether games of the mind, table, or paper. His humor, sometimes dry, sometimes corny, but usually funny, will boldly poke fun at sensitive and delicate matters of life. He is so intense you either run for your life, or are drawn to him like a moth to a flame. He is the master of the hidden agenda. What is dark and taboo to you is Pluto's playground.

Pluto's greatest game is he can manipulate your every thought and action, from the moment you become the object of his attention. He claims his territory and takes his prize without your conscious consent. You find yourself more willing than you imagined, just waiting for his next cue. Your better judgment has no authority when engaged in activity with Pluto. He will take you to a place that even your fantasies have considered taboo. However, you may have a mysterious feeling of protection, secure in a place filled with land mines. You will not even ask yourself if you have the courage to move forward, you simply go.

Pluto is rich with intrigue, big money connections, secret information, ancient rituals, and the keys to future success. Pluto is often in a position of power or associated with those in positions of great power. Pluto possesses a magnetic attraction, projects an aura of intrigue and sexuality which enhances his appearance, and tempts his admirers into submission. Whether you are repelled or attracted, your life is about to change in ways you had never imagined. Once this seducer captures your affection and attention, you may find it difficult to ever be released from his hypnotic grip. He has been called ruthless and uncompromising.

What Does Pluto Mean in Your Chart?

Pluto is the planet of deep change and transformation. Pluto in a chart can represent an arsenal of powers and secrets. Pluto's location indicates where you want to have the most control, and where you will find your deepest psychological attachments. Pluto can bring money or powerful people through the activities of the house it occupies. Pluto is deep and rich in its experience, and will engage the planets it contacts through manipulation and control. Pluto can represent your thoughts of the dead, of riches and of inheritance.

Pluto as a Transiting Planet

Through the association with Pluto, you will find you have tools for living of which you were previously unaware. These tools will equip you for a journey you had not considered taking. At the time of a Pluto transit you may need to rely on outside resources for support. You will learn to trust the process development of the issue that is under the rule of a Pluto transit.

A personal, dynamic, psychological and structural change will occur in your life as a result of contact with Pluto. At the time of a Pluto transit, the changes you have long desired in the most set patterns of your life will openly transform. The changes that occur as a result of your association with Pluto will be permanent. After becoming aware that your perspective has changed, you will notice that the tools and level of knowledge you've gathered have armed you with sharpened skills for living.

You will not return to your old familiar ways, but take on a deepened awareness of what you needed all along but never had the courage to initiate on your own. The most profound changes in your life will occur after engaging with Pluto.

People ruled by Pluto are psychiatrists, therapists, sex therapists, accountants, bankers, insurance agents and adjusters, funeral director, gangsters, occultists, researchers, security guards, surgeons, garbage collectors, junk collectors, and tax collectors.

Four Major Asteroids and Chiron

Ceres in Mythology ⚳

Ceres in mythology is the goddess of Agriculture. She was the mother of Persephone who was abducted by Pluto and taken as his bride to become queen of the underworld. Ceres is known as the "grieving mother," as the loss of her daughter caused the withering of vegetation and starvation on the earth. Jupiter intervened and forced Ceres and Pluto to negotiate a compromise. It was agreed that Persephone would return to the underworld six months of the year.

What Does Ceres Represent In A Chart?

In a chart, Ceres rules supplies, resources and nurturing as well as food, food issues, grains and their cycles. Ceres means deep bonding on an emotional and nurturing level. It represents one's sense of duty to children or parents. Ceres people are parents, mothers or children, and those with whom you are tightly bonded or are responsible for their caretaking.

Ceres in Transit

Ceres as a transiting asteroid represents matters of parenting, mother, caretaking of parents or children, pregnancy, babies, day care workers, nurses and doctors. Ceres is also evident at the time of abortions as well as labor in childbirth.

Ceres is an indicator of the contents of the refrigerator and pantry, food and food issues, cycles of food supplies, productivity, commodities, and grains.

Ceres also rules gardening, farms, farming, labor, workers, labor unions, labor strikes, and animals for labor.

A transit to natal Ceres represents the cerebral and is present in cases of skull or brain injuries, treatments or surgery. Ceres is also found in transit when any anatomical growth is present. Ceres rules growths. A slow-moving Ceres transit can be indicated at any period under a doctor's care.

The influence of a slow-moving or stationary Ceres transit can create a deep bonding between two people and therefore can be found present at engagements and marriages. At times, a Ceres union can be one of a particularly dependent couple. Persephone and Ceres were so tightly bonded that only Pluto's abduction could tear them apart. At the time of the abduction, Ceres entered a period of deep and serious withdrawal due to her intense grief. The planet's food source began to wither and die. This was the beginning of the change in seasons, with the cold dark months of winter. Not until Jupiter intervened did Pluto and Ceres strike a bargain to release Persephone to her mother for six months of the year.

Vesta in Mythology ⚶
Vesta in mythology (also Hestia) was goddess of the Hearth and Keeper of the Sacred Flame. She represented the household family altar, the sanctuary of peace, equity as well as the source of all happiness and wealth. She also ruled the hearth at the center of the earth which answered to the hearth at the center of the universe.

Conflicts of sexuality are addressed by the asteroid Vesta. For example, in ancient times, her temple priestesses participated in sacred sexual rituals. Later, however, her representatives, the vestal virgins, were known for their purity and sexual chastity. Vestal virgins were dedicated to maintaining the flame in the temple.

What Does Vesta Represent in a Chart?
Vesta is an indicator of your "internal flame" and "sacred space." This is the place where you find your greatest sense of commitment, purpose and work. Vesta represents any transactions related to your home, real estate matters and all investments. Vesta can be an indicator of sacrifice or denial of pleasure for commitment and investment. It also shows issues of security, safety and protection. Vesta has a strong association in your chart with your traditions, homeland, and family ties.

Vesta in Transit
Vesta as a transiting asteroid concerns herself with all types of commitments, work, investments, stocks and bonds, mortgages, insurance, real estate matters (even moving to a new apartment), protection, safety, locks, government protection agencies, stoves, fires, and sexual behavior. Nuns, priests, sanctuaries and

dome-shaped buildings are also Vesta concerns. Vesta represents issues concerning trust, credibility, and tradition, also vows, fidelity, home, family and heritage. Conservation, borders, maps and boundaries are Vesta territories.

A transit to one's natal Vesta can indicate a change in your assignments on the job or the job itself.

Vesta is bound to tradition and the sanctity of the family. A Vesta transit can be present when arranging family reunions or major family affairs.

Pallas in Mythology ♀

Pallas (Athena) in mythology was born fully-grown, clad in armor as she sprang from the head of Zeus. Pallas is goddess of Wisdom and Strategy. She is a warrior goddess and brain child. She was respected for her wisdom and justice. She was consulted by those in high places for advice on strategy and problem solving. Pallas was also known as a weaver.

What Does Pallas Represent in a Chart?

As the brainchild of Jupiter, Pallas shows where you are an authority on a subject or a specific field. She is the representative of fairness and firmness. She represents where you would repeat patterns, due to the fact that she was a weaver. The repeated patterns of DNA and the immune system are also ruled by Pallas.

Pallas in Transit

Pallas in transit brings about issues related to repeated patterns, and all matters of defending oneself. Look to Pallas for legal strategies and advisors, lawyers, and counselors. In creative work, see Pallas bring about video taping, reading lines as in singing or acting, as well as sewing, tailoring, arts and crafts. Someone may commission your talents to reproduce a work of your specialty when Pallas transits. Pallas rules anything related to intelligence, computers, problem solving, and brain. Pallas is the goddess of ingenuity, design, and invention. She rules precision tools, machines and engineering. You can also find her playing a role in interpersonal relationships, as she often indicates an exchange of likeness between people.

Juno in Mythology ✳

Juno is the Goddess of Marriage and Queen of the Heavens. She is the jealous and vengeful wife of Jupiter (God of the Heavens). Jupiter denied Juno her greatest desire for total union and fulfillment in her marriage. Jupiter's infidelities tortured Juno as she continually tried to enforce their contract of marriage.

What Does Juno Represent in a Chart?

Juno represents marriage, legal agreements, and contracts. She can show changes in personal relationships. Juno can indicate matters of infidelity. Juno fights for the rights of the underdog, particularly battered wives and children. Juno may represent matters of abuse in a natal chart. She is concerned with outside appearances and represents beauty as does Venus. Juno's concerns are often with clothing and appropriate presentations. Juno will decorate any house she occupies in a chart, therefore bringing improved appearances to the matters of the house. If Juno is close to another planet, she will enhance its presentation and improve its appearance, as well as bring honor to the planets involved.

Juno in Transit

Juno in transit can bring matters of relationship to the planet and the house it contacts. It can create a situation of partnership to an area of your life. There can also be an increase in jealousy, or topics of abuse to women. Children could be in the forefront.

Juno also adorns and decorates. When in aspect to Personal Points, Ascendant, and Node of the Moon or the Sun and Moon, Juno adorns your physical appearance.

Chiron ⚷

Chiron was discovered in November 1, 1977. It was first classified as a planetoid, but more recently is classified as a comet. It is considered to have significance in chart interpretation.

Chiron in Mythology

Chiron was the wisest of all the centaurs (half horse, half man) in Greek mythology. He was educated was conducted by Apollo and Diana. He became renowned for his skills in music, medicine, prophecy and hunting. He trained the young heroes of Greece in martial arts and hunting. Chiron taught Aesculapius the mysteries of the healing arts with herbs and surgery. Aesculapius became a famous physician who restored life to the dead. Chiron educated Hercules as well. In the study of mythology, several different tales can be found to explain one event. In one account, Hercules' deadly arrow accidentally shot his beloved tutor, Chiron. The mortal wound could not be healed, and Chiron died.

The word surgery is found in Chirurgery. Other Chiron words are chiropractor, and chiropody (a branch of medicine dealing with the diseases of the foot also called podiatry). Chiro means hand and chiromancy (meaning palmistry) as well as handwriting and the analysis of handwriting.

Chiron was badly wounded at a wedding feast when a conflict broke out and several centaurs were slain. From that day on Chiron endured constant pain. Even Chiron's great knowledge of medicine and healing could not cure his wound. From this legend, Chiron represents the "wounded healer."

Chiron married Charicles, one of the water goddesses. They had a daughter, Thea the Prophetess.

What Does Chiron Represent in a Chart?

Chiron's glyph (a letter k over a circle) represents a skeleton key. Chiron represents the key that opens any door, as in the key of knowledge. Chiron can identify the area of where you would have a thirst for knowledge and a special wisdom.

Chiron in a chart indicates disruption, rebellion and troublemaking related to the conflict that broke out at the wedding feast. Chiron, as an intellectual maverick, in a chart shows where you have a deep thirst for knowledge and identifies the key to your spiritual quest. There can also be a wish fulfillment quality to Chiron.

The Centaur's animal nature indicates sexual activity. Chiron, as a learned Centaur, was cause for him to be singled out and set apart from the others. In chart interpretation Chiron indicates where you stand apart from others, where you stand alone regarding major issues in life, as well as where you are on your own.

Saturn is Chiron's father. Because of Chiron's rejection by his mother, Philyra, he is an indicator of the abandoned child, adopted child or foster child. Chiron became both foster parent and teacher to his students. Chiron offered his students a curriculum of art, music, astrology, herbal medicine, surgery, hunting, riding and combat as well as ethical values; these qualities are therefore represented by Chiron in a chart.

Chiron is present in charts of injuries and major health matters, magicians, horses, doctors, surgery, risk takers and those who suffer consequences. Because Chiron reveals mysteries, the study of palmistry falls under his jurisdiction. As a great healer, all forms of alternative healing, chiropractors, acupuncturists and physical therapists are ruled by Chiron.

Chiron in Transit
Chiron in transit often brings a focus on sexual matters when in aspect to the personal planets; Sun, Moon, Mercury, Venus and Mars, or Personal Points; Ascendant, Mid-heaven or the Nodes of the Moon. Chiron in transit also brings enlightenment to the matters of the house, the sign it transits, and the planets it aspects. The message may deeply affect one's psyche as it has the capacity to open old wounds for healing process to begin.

Chiron's key symbolism can bring a period of lost or misplaced keys with this transit.

Only if other factors in the chart confirm, Chiron indicates health matters that may include surgery. A prominent Chiron creates a reliance on alternative methods of healing as in acupuncture, chiropractic, homeopathy and herbal treatments. Injuries in general have Chiron's aspect indicated in transit.

Chiron in transit can also bring an interest in horses, a study of astrology or palmistry. Chiron being the father of Prophetess could mark a period of prophetic dreams or psychic impressions.

In simpler terms, Chiron is an indicator of the healing process of old wounds and can be identified as the key to understanding oneself and one's spiritual path.

Aspects

Specifically, an aspect is the distance between two planets or personal points, defined by whether a 360° circle is divided by (commonly used) 0, 2, 3, 4, 6, 8, and 12. A division by 0 is a conjunction, by 2 is an opposition, by 3 is a trine, by 4 is a square, by 6 is a sextile, by 8 is either a semi-square or a sesqui-square, and by 12 is a semi-sextile. In this book, when speaking of planets, the personal points are also considered.

Aspects are the unifying principle in chart interpretation. Symbolically, an aspect has a specific inclination or mood, defined by the number of degrees of separation. An aspect draws a connection and conveys a mood between two seemingly unrelated points. You could then say that aspects are how planets speak to each other. Each aspect speaks with a different mood.

As we learned earlier, each planet has a basic identity. The planet's identity is blended with the meaning of the planet's sign. The sign gives the identity a certain expression or attitude. The identity's attitude is blended with the symbolism of the planet's house location in a chart. In the house, the identity receives an agenda for its operations. Therefore, a planet's identity expresses an attitude with a specific agenda. A faster-moving planet (the applying planet) casts a certain mood by its aspect to a slower-moving target planet. The identity applies a mood to a target planet. The identity with an attitude has an agenda and casts a mood to the target planet.

With this notion in mind, you could make sentences to connect the meaning of two planets in aspect in a chart. Making these sentences builds

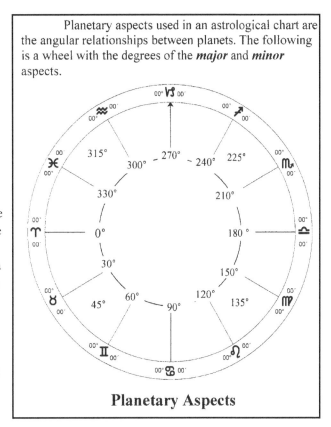

Planetary aspects used in an astrological chart are the angular relationships between planets. The following is a wheel with the degrees of the **major** and **minor** aspects.

Planetary Aspects

Aspect	Symbol	Angular Separation
conjunction	☌	0 °
semi-sextile	⚺	30 °
semi-square	∠	45°
sextile	✳	60°
square	□	90°
trine	△	120°
sesqui-square	⊓	135°
quincunx	⚻	150°
opposition	☍	180°

concepts for chart interpretation. As an over-simplification, a sentence structured in this way may look like the accompanying charts:

The planet has an identity.	♂	A man
The sign shows the planet's attitude	♉	An easy going man
The house gives the identity an agenda	6th House	An easy going man working
The aspects relates a *mood*	△	An easy going man enjoys working
The planet to the target planet	♃	A easy going man enjoys working with travelers.

With the aspect interpretation found later in this chapter, you can have fun building sentences for any two planets separated by any aspect.

The mood of the aspect describes the type of relationships planets have with each other. Some aspects between planets cast calm, soft moods, while others cast pressure with hard moods. A planet will be considered stressed or relaxed only if there is predominance of one type or another. Therefore the pressure from hard aspects creates stress and challenge. On the other hand, the influence from soft aspects is relaxed and harmonizing.

If we were to imagine two planets meeting with a soft aspect, one may say to the other, "Oh, hello, it's been so long since I've seen you." If we were to imagine two planets meeting with a hard aspect, the tone shifts to, "Oh, it's you again." That is an oversimplification because the tone is also set by the players. A trine (soft aspect) between Venus and Jupiter may bring about all the right combinations in a beautiful way. The sign keywords of each planet are layered into the delineation, but what if you see Mars and Neptune in a beautiful open trine? Mars and Neptune in combination may promote a spiritual setting, they are not the best company together. A tendency to allow a type of shifty behavior is encouraged by the openness of a trine. The presence of Jupiter tends to enlarge things, activities and related matters. I always think of the state of Texas when I think of Jupiter, hats are not just hats, they are ten gallon hats. The point is to consider the players, the signs they occupy and their house. A Venus in Virgo trine Saturn in Capricorn is serious and takes joy in productivity. By contrast, Venus in Aries and Saturn in Sagittarius might encourage a strong creative outlet that allows one to drop responsibility and travel the world.

My treatment of the aspects is just a guide to help you get started. Even a seasoned astrologer may find it easier to anchor his or her keywords to the symbolism of development of the entire 360°. I found that to use aspects interpretations with half a circle was telling only half the story and separating the aspects from the whole circle. By keeping the focus on the basics, astrology is a study of the full cycles of the Sun, Moon, nodes and planets.

I deliberately listed the node before the planets because the nature of the nodes of the Moon link the Moon to the path of Sun, which opens up the rest of the solar system through the wide porthole at the node. Anything in hard aspect to the nodes is hot, especially the conjunction and next the square. When the Sun and Moon form a conjunction or opposition at either the north or south node, there will be an eclipse. A similar effect is noted with a planet conjunct the nodes. Often there will be an occultation when the planet, Moon and earth align at either the north or south node of the Moon. It not just a mark that crosses two circles, it's a point of magnificence.

Hard Aspects ♂, □, ♂

Hard aspects are formed by primary geometric hard angles, and they can be found by dividing a circle by four. This division shows one conjunction (0°), two squares (90°), and one opposition (180°). Joining all four points creates a grand cross.

Divide the circle by eight to find the minor (hard) aspects: semi-squares ∠ (45°) and sesqui-square, also called sesqui-quadrate ⊡ (135°), formed by geometrically lesser-hard angles that are secondary to the 90° square. Join all eight points together to form an octagon. The angularity itself is a form of pressure that gives the hard aspects much energy. Hard aspects apply tension and are high-action aspects, promoting the greatest amount of both structure and change.

The hard aspects do not always indicate harsh problems, but more often they do define a more intense use of the planets involved. Many times, hard aspects are beneficial.

Difficulties that arise as the result of the influence of an aspect challenge us to allow change into our lives. An aspect once viewed as a liability may eventually become a great asset.

Squares are too-often interpreted as bad aspects. A carpenter explained that every building constructed is based on the 90° angle, forming the foundation for the roof. Apparently, we need squares in our lives.

I personally look forward to the clashing energy of squares from transiting planets, since they will make things happen and get things done. Squares initiate, motivate, instigate and generate. If you are bored and desire change in your life, a good square is the cure. Semi-squares and sesqui-squares also promote action and can harbor stubborn problems.

Soft Aspects

120° Trines △ are formed by dividing a 360 ° circle by three. Connecting the three trines in a circle creates a grand trine. Trines have a relaxed, gentle, and supportive energy filled with creative flow, expansion, and expression. Trines do not apply the pressure found in angular aspects, but they facilitate continuity through the flow of nature: "to go with the flow." The planets involved in a trine have been known to produce dynamic events in one's life if the planets are prominently placed. The aspect alone does not guarantee beauty, peace, and abundance. Depending on the planets involved, it can offer an environment for these things to exist. If the planets are known troublemakers, you may not be guaranteed their more positive side just because they're involved in a trine. My golden rule is to check what planets are participating, as their basic nature flows easily when involved in soft aspects.

A Sextile ✳ (60°) is formed by dividing the circle by six. Joining the six points creates a six-pointed star called a grand sextile. The influence of a sextile acts as a bridge to deliver information, communications and opportunities.

Although the semi-sextile ⊻ (30°) and the quincunx ⊼ (150°) are labeled as soft aspects by their geometrical positions, their natures can be set apart from the characteristics of the other soft aspects. They are at times difficult. The quincunx often produces a degree of stress and tension. It's the "life's messy, so clean it up" aspect.

A quincunx ⚹ located in the lower part of the circle is read differently than one found in the upper part of the circle. A lower circle quincunx can be measured 150° from point A to point B, and it is found 30° before an opposition. It's related to a sixth house-like influence. This is the aspect of adjustment. Metaphorically speaking, the quincunx is that of an arrow being shot through a window. Whatever you may have been doing, you must now stop to make adjustments for the strange development that so rudely broke your stride. Now you are called to make an adjustment: fixing, fine-tuning, adapting, improving, alleviating, and correcting.

An upper circle quincunx ⚹ is measured 210° from point A to point B, and it's found 30° after an opposition. It can be related to an eighth house-like influence. This is an aspect of settlement, arrangement, compromise, reconciliation, allotment, compensation, remuneration, and regulation.

As you can see, soft aspects do not always produce harmonizing effects, and hard aspects do not always cause trouble. If you are concerned about a certain aspect to your chart, do some research. Find the last time this aspect occurred and reflect on your experience. That might tell you more about what the aspect means to YOU. Your chart receives aspects differently because your natal arrangements create various possibilities.

Aspects Are Stages in a Cycle

The increasing sequential degrees of aspects are an indication that they form a cycle as their numbers increase around a wheel. Therefore, two planets separated by an aspect show where they are in their cycle, and they are viewed as part of an ongoing process.

The conjunction (a hard aspect) is the beginning of the cycle. The two planets of a conjunction experience a great impact at the beginning of their cycle. The degree of their conjunction is embedded in the memory of each planet, and remains a reference point between the two planets throughout the rest of their cycle. A chart cast for the moment of a conjunction is used to study the full cycle between any two planets.

For example: A Solar Eclipse is a very special conjunction of the Sun and the Moon. It's degree remains sensitive for nineteen years and is triggered with the phases of the Moon for at least 2.25 years.

The fact that conjunctions are hard aspects by geometric definition does not mean they are always harsh or difficult in expression. The planets involved in the conjunction partially determine the hard or soft expression of conjunction.

Many planetary pairs meet very seldom in a long span of time, as with Jupiter and Saturn who meet every twenty years. Such pairs offer material for generational studies. One of the interpretations of a Jupiter/Saturn aspect is social integration. In an individual's chart, the point where the Jupiter/Saturn conjunction occurred prior to their birth remains sensitive and may represent the individual's link (or lack of) with their generation and their ability to integrate with society. I view all aspects from the perceptive of their cycles and refer to the planets' most recent conjunction as an important tool for understanding the aspects.

Keeping in mind the value of cycles, consider the whole circle when locating aspects. An aspect differs in its interpretation when waxing, as it increases in light (the faster moving body is ahead of the slow planet), or when waning, as it decreases in light (the faster moving body is behind the slow planet). This is a clue why a square at the beginning of a cycle conveys a different action or expression than the square formed at the end of a cycle. For example: the hard aspects between the Sun and Mars and beyond mark the beginning and ending of the retrograde cycles for planets. Always when the Sun opposes a planet, it is retrograde. The retrograde planet can be read as compromised and a reflection period because of the retrograding motion. A brief review of each aspect is found following the next section.

Aspects can be measured visually by using the degree of the slower-moving body as an Ascendant point. The faster-moving body is the planet applying the aspect.

Are Aspects Good or Bad?

Warning: The interpretation of an isolated aspect is limited and is often misread without considering the chart as a whole.

To say an aspect is either good or bad is an oversimplification that narrows the true understanding of aspects. Aspects develop the relationships between planets with many levels of both pressure and ease. The entire chart is carefully investigated when assessing a favorable or unfavorable impact to the individual of the chart. It would be an over-generalization to say soft aspects offer only pleasant experiences and hard aspects offer only trouble. It is not that simple; refer back to the basic knowledge of the nature of the planets involved in any aspect.

The study of aspects is at the core for

Aspect	Symbol	Separation	Falls on House
conjunction	☌	0°	1st
waxing semi-sextile	⊻	30 °	2nd
waxing semi-square	∠	45°	mid 2nd
waxing sextile	✶	60°	3rd
waxing, first square	□	90°	4th
waxing trine	△	120°	5th
waxing sesqui-square	⊡	135°	mid 5th
waxing quincunx	⊼	150°	6th
opposition	☍	180°	7th
waning quincunx	⊼	210°	8th
waning sesqui-square	⊡	225°	mid 8th
waning trine	△	240°	9th
waning, last square	□	270°	10th
waning sextile	✶	300°	11th
waning semi-square	∠	315°	mid 11th
waning semi-sextile	⊻	330°	12th

waxing: building, collecting   **waning**: declining, ebbing decoding the messages hidden in this magnificent study of astrology. When I approach a chart I take the perspective of viewing an artists' work such as a painting. The focal point creates involvement between the painting and the viewer. The grasp of the astrologer's attention is often stimulated by something particularly eye-catching. A composition of intrigue and intensity can produce a beautiful work of art. The unique and seemingly-coincidental set of patterns of an astrological chart is not unlike a beautiful work of art. The combination of aspects, of tension and pressure, blended with aspects of harmony and release, could describe the motivated brilliance of the artist. Once the painting is viewed by someone other than the painter, the essence of the painting changes because an interpretation of the painting is a factor. The metaphor of the painting is considered when delineating a stressful aspect: maybe a key component is needed to create enough pressure to capture one's attention in order to invite change. As with many circumstances, the changes that follow a difficult period often leave us with not only a meaningful experience, but often a better way of life. The following is a **Whole Wheel Aspect Table**, which accounts for aspects that are waxing (increasing in light) and waning (diminishing in light). I use the concepts found with house symbolism as a tool for delineating aspects connect with all twelve house cusps, plus the minor hard aspects fall in the middle of houses two, five, eight and eleven. The house cusp symbolism used as a tool to assist with aspect delineation.

Conjunctions are two planets joined at the same degree and sign of the zodiac marking the beginning of a new cycle. The blended energies form a unique seed stage quality that begin to develop as the faster moving planet separates and forms new aspects to the slower moving planet. This high-impact aspect is one of the initiation that expresses variable amounts of stress or harmony., specific to the planets involved. The blending might create an excited reactionary impact such as with Mars and Uranus or a soft and subtle impression such as with Venus and Mercury. Not only the sign colors the interpretation but the degree of the conjunction holds potency.

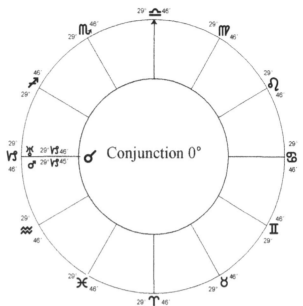

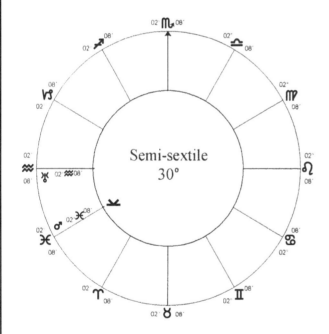

The first semi-sextile is an aspect of increase, gain & hope. It represents resources, talents and ownership as associated with the second house, accompanied by separation anxiety. Depending on the planets, this aspect can be difficult. The aspect holds an under-developed perspective when action is taken during this aspect..

Semi-squares are separated by a sign and a half. They are the first sign of tension and will trigger events & activities seeded at the conjunction. Semi-squares point to problems of a fixed nature. They indicate annoyances, often of a financial nature.

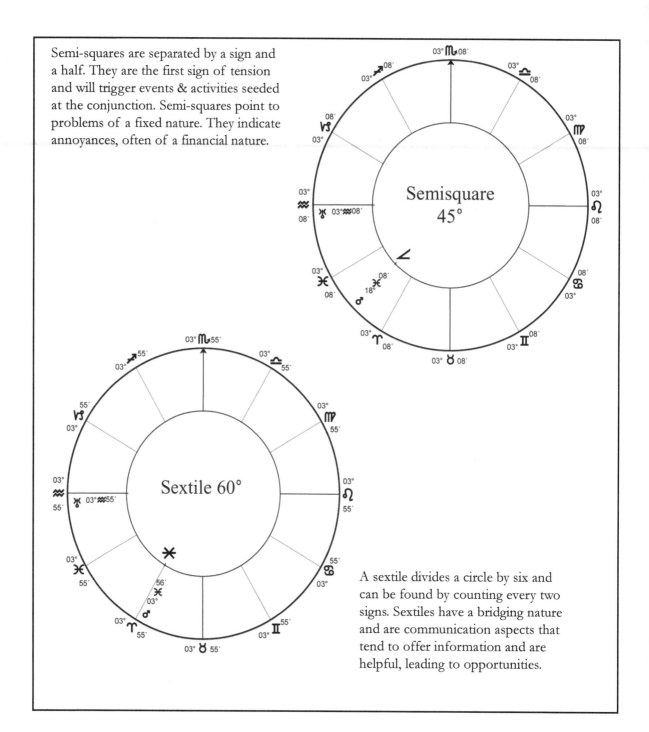

A sextile divides a circle by six and can be found by counting every two signs. Sextiles have a bridging nature and are communication aspects that tend to offer information and are helpful, leading to opportunities.

Squares are separated by three signs. This waxing aspect increases in light, bringing awareness. Expect action and tension with a square aspect. This aspect is often stressful and challenging. Squares produce the energy required to get projects off the ground. Squares are high impact aspects that call attention to problems and can bring chaos, but reveal the stumbling blocks in the process intended for development.

First Quarter
Square 90°

Trine 120°

Trines are four signs apart. The have a relaxed, supportive energy, often filled with a creative flow. The harmonizing influence of a trine allows an ease of energy to flow between the planets, with no resistance to their intent. Consider the nature of planets involved, before assuming this is a positive aspect.

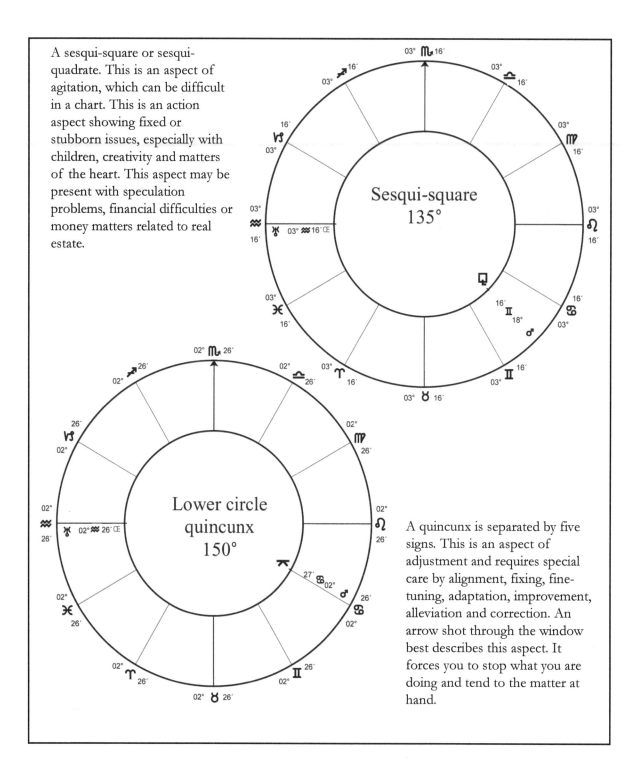

A sesqui-square or sesqui-quadrate. This is an aspect of agitation, which can be difficult in a chart. This is an action aspect showing fixed or stubborn issues, especially with children, creativity and matters of the heart. This aspect may be present with speculation problems, financial difficulties or money matters related to real estate.

Sesqui-square
135°

Lower circle
quincunx
150°

A quincunx is separated by five signs. This is an aspect of adjustment and requires special care by alignment, fixing, fine-tuning, adaptation, improvement, alleviation and correction. An arrow shot through the window best describes this aspect. It forces you to stop what you are doing and tend to the matter at hand.

Opposition brings two bodies in full view of each other at their greatest separation point often placing objects out of reach. It is a relationship aspect, being a point of conflict or compromise. This is an aspect of agreement or separation, marriage or divorce. This is an awareness aspect.

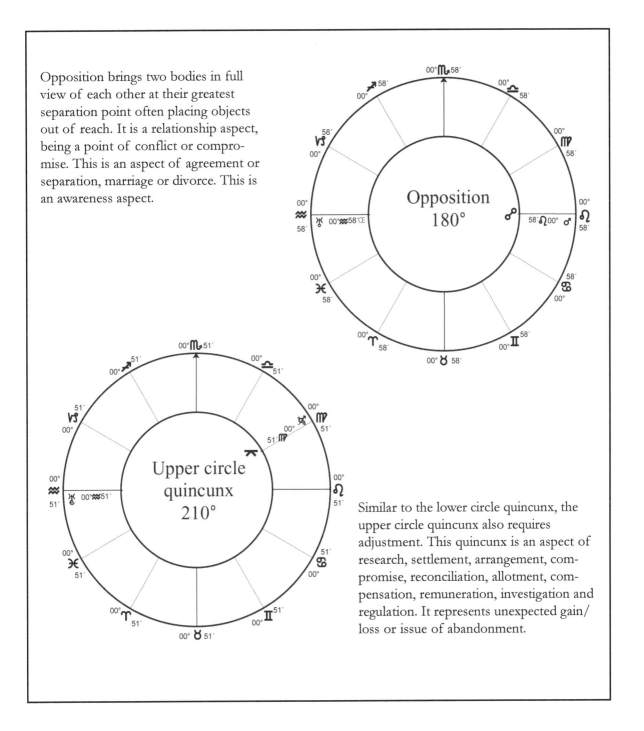

Similar to the lower circle quincunx, the upper circle quincunx also requires adjustment. This quincunx is an aspect of research, settlement, arrangement, compromise, reconciliation, allotment, compensation, remuneration, investigation and regulation. It represents unexpected gain/loss or issue of abandonment.

The 2nd sesqui-quadrate generates stress from a deep psychological level. Problems of a fixed nature can be slow or difficult to resolve. There can be money problems with this aspect, especially with borrowed or shared resources. It is a fundraising aspect.

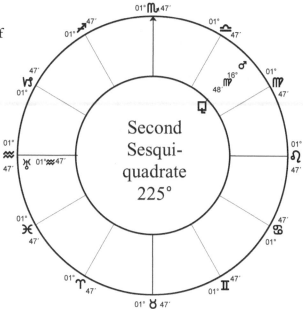

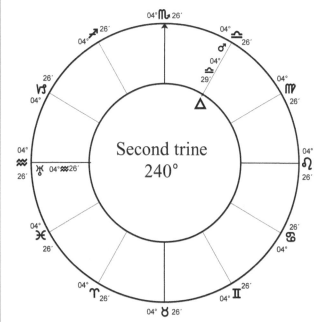

The second trine is an aspect as harmonious as the first, with an emphasis on expansion and broadening of perspective and integration. This trine seeks to complete the "whole picture" with a full breadth of knowledge, social and cultural development. This aspect enlightens and shares its talents and connects with the whole. It allows further developments to reach out into the world.

This is the last quarter square of a circle separated by nine signs. This square is also a high impact aspect. The types of activities are usually those from the past or authority figures. It brings reward or consequence, showing a time to pay or be paid.

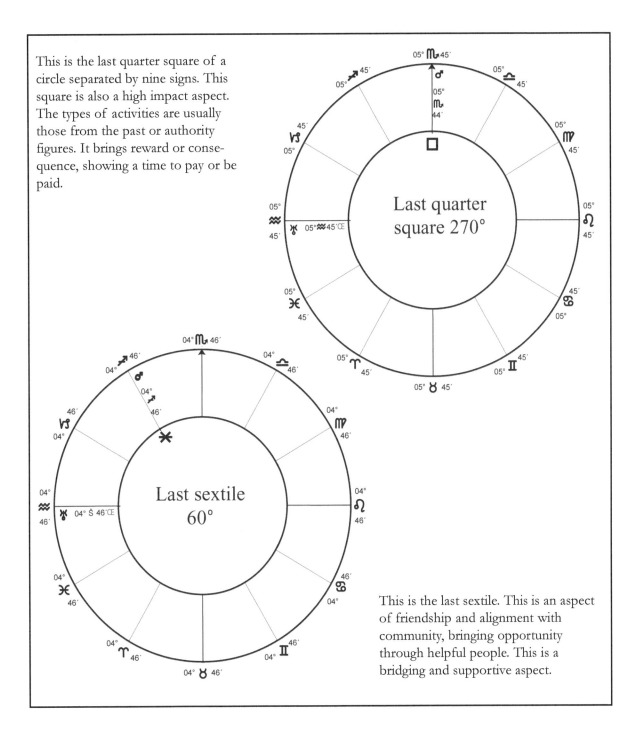

Last quarter square 270°

Last sextile 60°

This is the last sextile. This is an aspect of friendship and alignment with community, bringing opportunity through helpful people. This is a bridging and supportive aspect.

The last semi-square is a stubborn and difficult aspect with hidden problems. This aspect shows money problems with business or parents. There can be tension with management of organizations. This aspect can show stress in friendship and social or outer affairs. This aspect could draw one into community action.

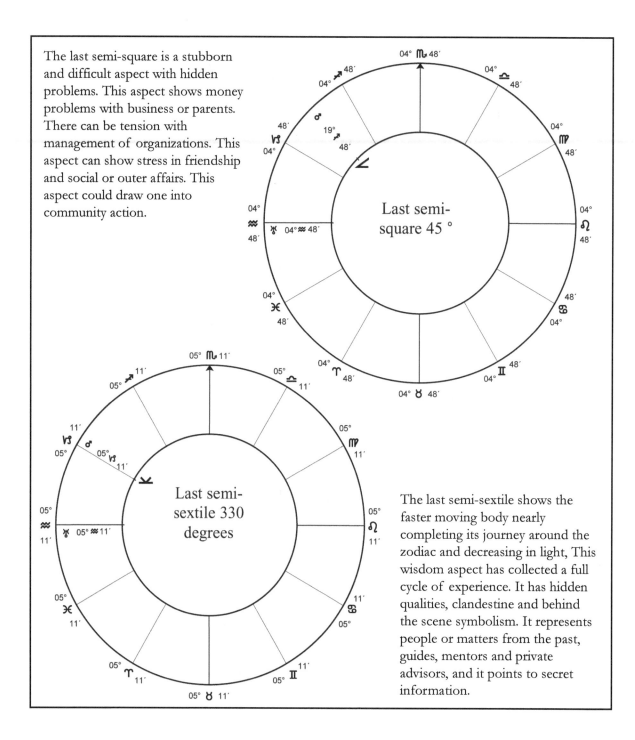

The last semi-sextile shows the faster moving body nearly completing its journey around the zodiac and decreasing in light, This wisdom aspect has collected a full cycle of experience. It has hidden qualities, clandestine and behind the scene symbolism. It represents people or matters from the past, guides, mentors and private advisors, and it points to secret information.

Aspect Orb of Influence

Orb, from Fred Gettings' *Dictionary of Astrology*: That area of influence (expressed in degrees of arc) within which planets in aspect may be said to exert and influence while still forming or separating.

Lorraine Welsh in the *NCGR's Essential of Intermediate Astrology* describes orbs as the distances allowed between planets when noting the effectiveness of an aspect.

Aspects between planets rarely occur exactly at the same degree in a natal chart. An orb allows for the field of influence to be considered. The number of degrees in an orb is added or subtracted from a given aspect.

The width of the orb used can vary from as little as 1 minute of arc to as much as 12° or wider, in special cases. When discussing transiting eclipses the allowable orb is specific to the Nodes of the Moon and can occur as much as 18°. Many factors are considered when determining the width of aspect orbs, and the more you study aspects the harder it is to offer a concise formula without seeming evasive. These are the way I use orbs. Your own experience and that of your teachers might vary and should be considered. Nothing I say is a hard and fast rule. I have learned 98% of my astrology from hands-on experience, and there is plenty of research that will prove to be different. I invite any new ideas and I love learning new things so please share your experience with me. Here are a few examples of how I use orbs:

Aspect type: Considered when determining the width of an orb. For use in a natal chart, orbs for hard aspects are 5° to 10°; soft aspects, 6° to 8°; minor aspects, 1° - 3°. When measuring hard aspects from a current transiting eclipse, t he orb is 5° all around. But when reviewing the impact of eclipses in the past or distant future, I use a small 1° orb. Sometimes because of translation of light, your orb will be expanded.

Applying Aspect orbs: Applying aspects use wider orbs of 2° to 10° relative to the nature of the chart. A transiting chart use smaller orbs. Transits applied to a natal chart can be larger if the planet is slow in its approach. Noting how the planets station points are a powerful factor here. A planet that turns retrograde and then direct while in aspect to a planet should include the entire range of retrograde travel. Use the points of the stations, and ask at what point did the retrograde occur, and what is the point of direct motion. After the retrograde planet has moved direct, include the point where the retrograde occurred. Wait until it is passes that point before it releases your planet.

Separating Aspect orbs: Very narrow orbs are used for separating aspects, only 5 minutes up to 1°. Transits to transit aspects fizzle out quickly, except the parallel and contra-parallel.
Planets: The planets involved in the aspect can be a factor in orb width; for instance, wider orbs are used for the Sun and Moon, sometimes as wide as 12°. Orbs used for aspects from all other planets are not usually more than 8°, and aspect orbs used for some asteroids may be even smaller, like 1° to 2°.

Transits: Very narrow aspect orbs are used in faster-moving transit charts (1° to 5° for applying transiting aspects, and 30 minutes - 1° for separating aspects).

Progressed charts: Orbs used for progressed charts are generally very small, not greater than 1° but with a slightly wider separating orb of 1.5°.

Eclipses: Orbs used for aspects from the point of a current eclipse is 5°. For a past or distant future eclipse, use small orbs 1°.

When calculating aspects of Moon Phases to your natal planets and Personal Points, small orbs must be used. The orb of influence of a Moon Phase is determined by the 7 ° to 8° that the Sun travels between traditional Moon Phases in a calendar month. Therefore, use an orb of only 3.5° to 4°; wider orbs overlap the degree of the next Moon Phase.

Prominently-Placed Planets

A prominently-placed planet has an amplified importance. A planet can be attributed strength by its connection to key points in a horoscope. Conjunctions to the Sun, Moon, Ascendant, Midheaven and their opposite points would qualify as prominently placed. Any of the four angles add strength to a planet's significance in a chart. If a planet captures your attention when you pick up a chart, it is probably in a prominent place, in some way. To determine if one planet stands out from the others, we are looking for something special about its location in a chart, as well as its relationship to the other planets. Any two or more planets in exact aspect to one another become very important. Any natal chart planet in exact aspect to a natal solar or lunar eclipse point remains hot for most of one's life. As time goes by and other planets are closely aspected by transiting eclipses, they will become activated during the period that the eclipse is effective.

Certain areas of a chart are simply more important that others. The Ascendant and Midheaven areas are important. A planet conjunct the Ascendant or Midheaven would be prominent or if it was in their respective first and tenth houses. This rule also applies to any planet conjunct the Sun or Moon. If a planet creates a hard aspect to the Sun or Moon, it also becomes prominently placed.

Other prominently-placed planetary positions are:
*   Planets in angular houses 1, 4, 7, 10, or Planets conjunct the Ascendant, Descendant, Midheaven, or Nadir (IC).
*   Planets in hard aspect to the Sun, Moon, or Nodes.
*   Planets parallel (equally aligned in north or south declination) to the Sun or Moon. Or contraparallel (one planet north declination and the other at a south declination at the same degree).
*   Planets at extreme North or South declination, considered out of bounds.
*   A Stationary Planet at the time of birth.
*   A natal planet conjunct a planetary station degree.
*   Planet at the apex (the point) of a T-square or yod.
*   The two planets at either edge of a stellium (a conjunction of three or more planets).
*   The two planets of either edge holding the remaining planets in a bowl shape configuration in a chart.
*   The one planet at the midpoint of a stellium.

* A singleton planet isolated on one side of a chart.
* Any Planet or personal points at either 0° or 29° of any sign.
* Any planets in exact aspect to another planet.
* Planets conjunct or in exact aspect to a natal planetary station position (within nine months of birth).

Find Planet Groups with a 30-Degree Sort

Planet groups show a cluster of planets found at the same number in a horoscope chart. By using a 30° sorted list, the horoscope wheel is organized to show all whole aspects occurring at 30° intervals, conjunction, semi-sextile, sextile, square, trine, quincunx (inconjunct) and opposition.

30° sort: A list of planets in a horoscope from 0° to 30°, designed to show planets at the same number around the zodiac wheel.

A Moon Phase or an eclipse at a particular degree of a sign impacts all signs at that degree. Therefore, a Moon Phase at 21° of a sign impacts 21° of all signs. Look around the wheel and find all the planets at 21°. Do this by making a 30° sort in a list from 0° to 30°. List planets and points by the nearest whole degree, using the 30-minute point to designate the lower or higher number. Example: Mars at 6° Libra 21'

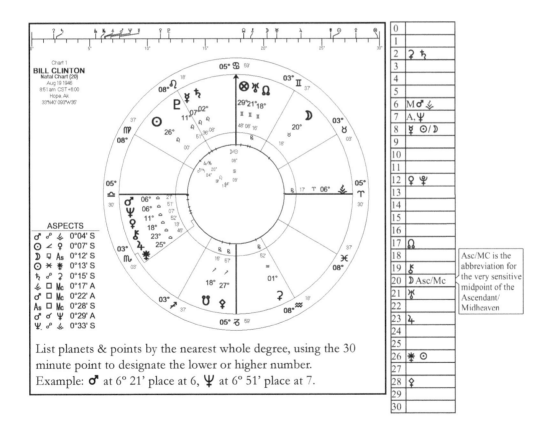

List planets & points by the nearest whole degree, using the 30 minute point to designate the lower or higher number.
Example: ♂ at 6° 21' place at 6, ♆ at 6° 51' place at 7.

is placed at 6, Neptune at 6° Libra 51 is placed at 7. This sort allows a quick spot of every planet near the same degree. A 30° sort will pick up the conjunction, semi-sextile, square, trine, quincunx, and opposition aspects. This sort does not pick up the semi-square at 45° and sesqui-square at 135° aspects, as found in a 45° sort. These very valuable minor aspects overlap the degrees of the Moon Phases and defeat the purpose of this particular sort. It is helpful to use the 45° sort separately.

The 30° sort lists planets by degree number only; their zodiac sign is not a factor on the list. This sort organizes the zodiac wheel to give a picture of planets by group; this picture is referred to as planet groups. Major astrological events, such as eclipses and planetary stations occurring within an orb of plus or minus 5° of the natal planet groups, affect it immensely. Smaller orbs of 3.5° to 4° are used for hits from transiting Moon Phases.

With the 30° sort, listing the planets for other work becomes more manageable. When studying transits, eclipses, Moon phases and progressions, you can spot the heavy activity areas very quickly. On September 6, 2004, Mr. Clinton underwent a quadruple bypass surgery to head off a likely heart attack in the future. A last quarter Moon occurred on that very day at 14° Gemini.

The Phases of the Moon
The Sun travels through the Zodiac in approximately 365 days. The Moon travels through the Zodiac approximately every 29 days, completing a full cycle once a month, called a lunation. In approximately one month, the Moon will make four important angles to the Sun. These angles are the Phases of the Moon. The cycle begins with the conjunction of the Sun and the Moon at the New Moon. The time lapse between each Phase of the Moon is approximately one week, during which time the Moon will travel through three zodiac signs. Example: A New Moon at 0° Aries on March 20th will reach the First Quarter Moon seven days later. The Sun then moved forward at an approximate rate of 1° each day. The Moon's daily motion moves an average of 12.5°. In 2.5 days the Moon will pass through one zodiac sign. (2½ days times 12.5° = 30° = one sign) occur approximately at 7° Cancer.

When the Moon separates 90° distance from the Sun, it will have passed through the signs Taurus and Gemini before reaching its 90° square to the Sun in Cancer. This square (90°) is the First Quarter Moon and the Sun, a First Quarter Moon occurs, at approximately 7° Cancer. The Full Moon occurs two weeks after a New Moon at 14° of Libra. The Last Quarter Moon is 270° from the Sun and would occur one week after the Full Moon, or three weeks after the New Moon at 21° Capricorn. The Moon conjoins the Sun again, sharing the same degree for the next New Moon at approximately 28° Aries.

How to find eclipses and Moon Phases in the Ephemeris

Example: Using Neil Michelsen's *American Ephemeris for the 20th Century*, look to the page headed July 1989. At the bottom of the page there are six columns filled with various data. The Moon Phases are listed in the fifth column. The fifth column is separated to show Moon phases for two months. In the top section are the Moon phases for July 1989, and in the bottom section are the phases for August 1989.

A New Moon is identified with a solid black circle (●) on July 3, 1989 at 11 Cancer 15'. It is printed as the following:
3 4:49 ● 11 ♋ 15. It translates as: July 3, 1989 at 4:49 am Greenwich Mean Time (all times in the ephemeris are for Greenwich, England unless your ephemeris states differently) there was a New Moon at eleven degrees of Cancer and fifteen minutes.

The First Quarter Moon identified as a left facing crescent (☽) and is listed on July 11, 1989 at 18 Libra 42. It is printed as the following:
11 0:19 ☽ 18 ♎ 42 It translates as: July 11, 1989 at 12:19 am Greenwich Mean Time there was a First Quarter Moon at eighteen degrees of Libra and forty two minutes.

The Full Moon is indicated as an open circle (○) in the ephemeris and is show on July 18, 1989 at 26 Capricorn 4'. It is printed as the following:
18 17:42 ○ 26 ♑ 4 It translates as: July 18, 1989, at 5:42 PM Greenwich Mean Time, a Full Moon occurred at twenty six degrees of Capricorn and 4 minutes.

The Last Quarter Moon, identified as a right facing crescent (☾) is listed as July 25 at 2 Taurus 35. It is printed as the following:
25 13:31 ☾ 2 ♉ 35 This translates as: July 25, 1989 at 1:31 PM Greenwich Mean Time, a Last Quarter Moon occurred at two degrees of Taurus and thirty five minutes.

Note that in the month of August, there is an extra symbol after the Full Moon on August 17, 1989 which reads as the following:
17 3: 7 ○ ☋ 24 ♒ 12. This means there was a Lunar Eclipse at that Full Moon on August 17, 1989 at 3:07 AM GMT at 24= Aquarius 12.

Note another strange symbol at the New Moon on August 31, 1989 that looks like the following:
31 5:45 ● ☌ 7 ♍ 48. This means there was a Solar Eclipse at that New Moon at 5:45 AM GMT at 7= Virgo 48'.
Solar and Lunar Eclipse Tables at their North and South Node Positions are listed for years 1950-1990. Eclipses for the years 1990-2010 are found in bold print throughout the next set of tables containing the Traditional Moon Phases.

Appendix

Tables of Solar and Lunar Eclipses

- **Table I.** Solar and Lunar Eclipses in Chronological Order 1900-2099 at the North and South Node.

  There are two columns in the table of **Solar and Lunar Eclipses** that appear in chronological order. The solar eclipse is noted with a column indicating the eclipse's relationship to the north or south node. The Lunar Eclipse column occurs within two weeks of the Solar Eclipse.

- **Table II.** Solar and Lunar Eclipses in zodiacal order before 1900-2099 in Metonic Cycle Groups which includes a Lunar Eclipse at the 9.5 year mark that is midway through the nineteen-year Metonic cycle. This table is outlined in-depth after Table I.

These tables are shown in various formats, designed to help research your life through the window of eclipses and lunar phase patterns. Choose a news story, historic topic or any astrological or non-astrological study to test the patterns. Yes you can study the cycles of Eclipses and the Moon phases with or without actual horoscope charts. For the novice or the non-astrologer the tables work great with things like journal studies, family histories, maybe a marketing study for your business or a business you are watching for investment. With just the dates you can scan through the tables to research the history of the object of your attention and marking events. Or with knowledge of your chart you can line up the zodiacal position of these events with the planets and points in your natal, progressed, relationship charts and return charts.

Eclipses in Chronological Order -
North and South Node noted for Solar Eclipses

Solar Eclipses at North or South Node						Lunar Eclipses			
28/May/1900	06°	♊	47	S		13/Jun/1900	21°	♐	38
22/Nov/1900	29°	♏	33	N		6/Dec/1900	13°	♊	53
18/May/1901	26°	♉	34	S		3/May/1901	12°	♏	35
11/Nov/1901	18°	♏	13	N		27/Oct/1901	03°	♉	30
8/Apr/1902	17°	♈	47	S		22/Apr/1902	01°	♏	41
7/May/1902	16°	♉	24	S					
31/Oct/1902	06°	♏	58	N		17/Oct/1902	22°	♈	56
29/Mar/1903	07°	♈	11	S		12/Apr/1903	20°	♎	55
21/Sep/1903	27°	♍	0	N		6/Oct/1903	12°	♈	11
17/Mar/1904	26°	♓	12	S		2/Mar/1904	11°	♍	6
						31/Mar/1904	10°	♎	22
9/Sep/1904	16°	♍	42	N		24/Sep/1904	01°	♈	13
6/Mar/1905	14°	♓	58	S		19/Feb/1905	00°	♍	28
30/Aug/1905	06°	♍	28	N		15/Aug/1905	21°	♒	37
23/Feb/1906	03°	♓	48	S		9/Feb/1906	19°	♌	40
21/Jul/1906	27°	♋	49	N					
20/Aug/1906	26°	♌	6	N		4/Aug/1906	11°	♒	12
14/Jan/1907	22°	♑	55	S		29/Jan/1907	08°	♌	31
10/Jul/1907	17°	♋	11	N		25/Jul/1907	01°	♒	4
3/Jan/1908	12°	♑	8	S		18/Jan/1908	27°	♋	4
28/Jun/1908	06°	♋	31	N		14/Jun/1908	23°	♐	3
						13/Jul/1908	21°	♑	2
23/Dec/1908	01°	♑	17	S		7/Dec/1908	15°	♊	25
17/Jun/1909	26°	♊	4	N		4/Jun/1909	12°	♐	46
12/Dec/1909	20°	♐	11	S		27/Nov/1909	04°	♊	29
9/May/1910	17°	♉	42	N		24/May/1910	02°	♐	9
2/Nov/1910	08°	♏	46	S		17/Nov/1910	23°	♉	47
28/Apr/1911	07°	♉	29	N		13/May/1911	21°	♏	21
22/Oct/1911	27°	♎	38	S		6/Nov/1911	13°	♉	7
17/Apr/1912	27°	♈	5	N		1/Apr/1912	11°	♎	48
10/Oct/1912	16°	♎	52	S		26/Sep/1912	03°	♈	0
6/Apr/1913	16°	♈	19	N		22/Mar/1913	01°	♎	15
31/Aug/1913	07°	♍	48	S		15/Sep/1913	22°	♓	3
30/Sep/1913	06°	♎	25	S		12/Mar/1914	20°	♍	45
25/Feb/1914	05°	♓	33	N		4/Sep/1914	11°	♓	10
21/Aug/1914	27°	♌	35	S		31/Jan/1915	10°	♌	14
14/Feb/1915	24°	♒	24	N		1/Mar/1915	10°	♍	6
10/Aug/1915	17°	♌	12	S		26/Jul/1915	02°	♒	25
						24/Aug/1915	00°	♓	37
3/Feb/1916	13°	♒	30	N		20/Jan/1916	28°	♋	57
30/Jul/1916	06°	♌	34	S		15/Jul/1916	22°	♑	20
24/Dec/1916	02°	♑	44	N		8/Jan/1917	17°	♋	29
23/Jan/1917	02°	♒	45	N					
19/Jun/1917	27°	♊	38	S		4/Jul/1917	12°	♑	17
19/Jul/1917	25°	♋	51	S					
14/Dec/1917	21°	♐	50	N		28/Dec/1917	06°	♋	6
8/Jun/1918	17°	♊	15	S		24/Jun/1918	02°	♑	5
3/Dec/1918	10°	♐	39	N		17/Dec/1918	25°	♊	3
29/May/1919	07°	♊	6	S		15/May/1919	23°	♏	9
22/Nov/1919	29°	♏	16	N		7/Nov/1919	14°	♉	31
18/May/1920	26°	♉	59	S		3/May/1920	12°	♏	19
10/Nov/1920	17°	♏	58	N		27/Oct/1920	03°	♉	51
8/Apr/1921	17°	♈	59	S		22/Apr/1921	01°	♏	37
1/Oct/1921	07°	♎	46	N		16/Oct/1921	23°	♈	2
28/Mar/1922	07°	♈	4	S		13/Mar/1922	22°	♍	6
21/Sep/1922	27°	♍	24	N		11/Apr/1922	21°	♎	9

Eclipses in Chronological Order –
North and South Node noted for Solar Eclipses

Solar Eclipses at North or South Node						Lunar Eclipses			
						6/Oct/1922	11°	♈	59
17/Mar/1923	25°	♓	54	S		3/Mar/1923	11°	♍	32
10/Sep/1923	17°	♍	6	N		26/Aug/1923	02°	♓	9
5/Mar/1924	14°	♓	49	S		20/Feb/1924	00°	♍	45
31/Jul/1924	08°	♌	16	N		14/Aug/1924	21°	♒	43
30/Aug/1924	06°	♍	40	N					
24/Jan/1925	04°	♒	7	S		8/Feb/1925	19°	♌	39
20/Jul/1925	27°	♋	36	N		4/Aug/1925	11°	♒	33
14/Jan/1926	23°	♑	21	S		28/Jan/1926	08°	♌	13
10/Jul/1926	16°	♋	56	N		25/Jun/1926	03°	♑	31
3/Jan/1927	12°	♑	28	S		25/Jul/1926	01°	♒	30
						19/Dec/1926	26°	♊	35
29/Jun/1927	06°	♋	31	N		15/Jun/1927	23°	♐	14
24/Dec/1927	01°	♑	21	S		8/Dec/1927	15°	♊	38
19/May/1928	28°	♉	17	N		3/Jun/1928	12°	♐	38
17/Jun/1928	26°	♊	21	N					
12/Nov/1928	19°	♏	46	S		27/Nov/1928	04°	♊	53
9/May/1929	18°	♉	7	N		23/May/1929	01°	♐	52
1/Nov/1929	08°	♏	35	S		17/Nov/1929	24°	♉	10
28/Apr/1930	07°	♉	45	N		13/Apr/1930	22°	♎	34
21/Oct/1930	27°	♎	46	S		7/Oct/1930	13°	♈	46
18/Apr/1931	27°	♈	2	N		2/Apr/1931	12°	♎	6
12/Sep/1931	18°	♍	27	S		26/Sep/1931	02°	♈	45
11/Oct/1931	17°	♎	15	S					
7/Mar/1932	16°	♓	32	N		22/Mar/1932	01°	♎	40
31/Aug/1932	08°	♍	10	S		14/Sep/1932	21°	♓	48
24/Feb/1933	05°	♓	28	N		10/Feb/1933	21°	♌	21
						12/Mar/1933	21°	♍	5
21/Aug/1933	27°	♌	42	S		5/Aug/1933	12°	♒	53
						4/Sep/1933	11°	♓	12
14/Feb/1934	24°	♒	38	N		30/Jan/1934	10°	♌	6
10/Aug/1934	17°	♌	1	S		26/Jul/1934	02°	♒	48
5/Jan/1935	13°	♑	57	N		19/Jan/1935	28°	♋	39
3/Feb/1935	13°	♒	55	N					
30/Jun/1935	08°	♋	4	S		16/Jul/1935	22°	♑	44
30/Jul/1935	06°	♌	17	S					
25/Dec/1935	03°	♑	1	N		8/Jan/1936	17°	♋	18
19/Jun/1936	27°	♊	43	S		4/Jul/1936	12°	♑	31
13/Dec/1936	21°	♐	48	N		28/Dec/1936	06°	♋	15
8/Jun/1937	17°	♊	36	S		25/May/1937	03°	♐	40
2/Dec/1937	10°	♐	22	N		18/Nov/1937	25°	♉	34
29/May/1938	07°	♊	31	S		14/May/1938	22°	♏	53
22/Nov/1938	29°	♏	1	N		7/Nov/1938	14°	♉	51
19/Apr/1939	28°	♈	43	S		3/May/1939	12°	♏	17
12/Oct/1939	18°	♎	36	N		28/Oct/1939	03°	♉	56
7/Apr/1940	17°	♈	51	S		23/Mar/1940	03°	♎	1
						22/Apr/1940	01°	♏	53
1/Oct/1940	08°	♎	10	N		16/Oct/1940	22°	♈	49
27/Mar/1941	06°	♈	45	S		13/Mar/1941	22°	♍	30
21/Sep/1941	27°	♍	48	N		5/Sep/1941	12°	♓	44
17/Mar/1942	25°	♓	45	S		3/Mar/1942	11°	♍	47
12/Aug/1942	18°	♌	45	N		26/Aug/1942	02°	♓	17
10/Sep/1942	17°	♍	18	N					
5/Feb/1943	15°	♒	17	S		20/Feb/1943	00°	♍	42
1/Aug/1943	08°	♌	2	N		15/Aug/1943	22°	♒	5
25/Jan/1944	04°	♒	32	S		9/Feb/1944	19°	♌	20

Eclipses in Chronological Order - North and South Node noted for Solar Eclipses

Solar Eclipses at North or South Node						Lunar Eclipses			
20/Jul/1944	27°	♋	21	N		6/Jul/1944	13°	♑	57
						4/Aug/1944	11°	♒	58
14/Jan/1945	23°	♑	41	S		29/Dec/1944	07°	♋	47
9/Jul/1945	16°	♋	57	N		25/Jun/1945	03°	♑	39
3/Jan/1946	12°	♑	32	S		19/Dec/1945	26°	♊	49
30/May/1946	08°	♊	48	N		14/Jun/1946	23°	♐	4
29/Jun/1946	06°	♋	48	N					
23/Nov/1946	00°	♐	49	S		8/Dec/1946	16°	♊	3
20/May/1947	28°	♉	41	N		3/Jun/1947	12°	♐	21
12/Nov/1947	19°	♏	35	S		28/Nov/1947	05°	♊	16
9/May/1948	18°	♉	22	N		23/Apr/1948	03°	♏	17
1/Nov/1948	08°	♏	43	S		18/Oct/1948	24°	♈	37
28/Apr/1949	07°	♉	41	N		13/Apr/1949	22°	♎	54
21/Oct/1949	28°	♎	8	S		7/Oct/1949	13°	♈	30
18/Mar/1950	27°	♓	27	N		2/Apr/1950	12°	♎	32
12/Sep/1950	18°	♍	48	S		26/Sep/1950	02°	♈	31
						21/Feb/1951	02°	♍	26
7/Mar/1951	16°	♓	28	N		23/Mar/1951	01°	♎	59
						17/Aug/1951	23°	♒	24
1/Sep/1951	08°	♍	16	S		15/Sep/1951	21°	♓	51
25/Feb/1952	05°	♓	43	N		11/Feb/1952	21°	♌	13
20/Aug/1952	27°	♌	31	S		5/Aug/1952	13°	♒	17
14/Feb/1953	25°	♒	3	N		29/Jan/1953	09°	♌	47
11/Jul/1953	18°	♋	29	S		26/Jul/1953	03°	♒	12
9/Aug/1953	16°	♌	45	S					
5/Jan/1954	14°	♑	13	N		19/Jan/1954	28°	♋	29
30/Jun/1954	08°	♋	10	S		16/Jul/1954	22°	♑	57
25/Dec/1954	02°	♑	58	N		8/Jan/1955	17°	♋	28
20/Jun/1955	28°	♊	4	S		5/Jun/1955	14°	♐	8
14/Dec/1955	21°	♐	30	N		29/Nov/1955	06°	♊	41
8/Jun/1956	18°	♊	1	S		24/May/1956	03°	♐	24
2/Dec/1956	10°	♐	8	N		18/Nov/1956	25°	♉	55
30/Apr/1957	09°	♉	22			13/May/1957	22°	♏	52
23/Oct/1957	29°	♎	31	N		7/Nov/1957	14°	♉	55
19/Apr/1958	28°	♈	34	S		4/Apr/1958	13°	♎	52
						3/May/1958	12°	♏	33
12/Oct/1958	19°	♎	1	N		27/Oct/1958	03°	♉	43
8/Apr/1959	17°	♈	33	S		24/Mar/1959	03°	♎	25
2/Oct/1959	08°	♎	34	N		17/Sep/1959	23°	♓	23
27/Mar/1960	06°	♈	38	S		13/Mar/1960	22°	♍	46
21/Sep/1960	27°	♍	58	N		5/Sep/1960	12°	♓	52
15/Feb/1961	26°	♒	25	S		2/Mar/1961	11°	♍	44
11/Aug/1961	18°	♌	30	N		26/Aug/1961	02°	♓	38
5/Feb/1962	15°	♒	42	S		19/Feb/1962	00°	♍	25
31/Jul/1962	07°	♌	48	N		17/Jul/1962	24°	♑	24
						15/Aug/1962	22°	♒	30
25/Jan/1963	04°	♒	51	S		9/Jan/1963	18°	♋	58
20/Jul/1963	27°	♋	24	N		6/Jul/1963	14°	♑	5
14/Jan/1964	23°	♑	43	S		30/Dec/1963	08°	♋	1
10/Jun/1964	19°	♊	18	N		25/Jun/1964	03°	♑	30
9/Jul/1964	17°	♋	15	N					
4/Dec/1964	11°	♐	55	S		19/Dec/1964	27°	♊	14
30/May/1965	09°	♊	13	N		14/Jun/1965	22°	♐	48
23/Nov/1965	00°	♐	39	S		8/Dec/1965	16°	♊	25
20/May/1966	28°	♉	55	N		4/May/1966	13°	♏	55
12/Nov/1966	19°	♏	45	S		29/Oct/1966	05°	♉	32
9/May/1967	18°	♉	17	N		24/Apr/1967	03°	♏	37

Eclipses in Chronological Order -
North and South Node noted for Solar Eclipses

Solar Eclipses at North or South Node						Lunar Eclipses			
2/Nov/1967	09°	♏	7	S		18/Oct/1967	24°	♈	20
28/Mar/1968	08°	♈	18	N		13/Apr/1968	23°	♎	19
22/Sep/1968	29°	♍	29	S		6/Oct/1968	13°	♈	16
18/Mar/1969	27°	♓	25	N		2/Apr/1969	12°	♎	50
						27/Aug/1969	03°	♓	58
11/Sep/1969	18°	♍	53	S		25/Sep/1969	02°	♈	35
7/Mar/1970	16°	♓	44	N		21/Feb/1970	02°	♍	17
31/Aug/1970	08°	♍	4	S		17/Aug/1970	23°	♒	48
25/Feb/1971	06°	♓	8	N		10/Feb/1971	20°	♌	55
22/Jul/1971	28°	♋	55	S		6/Aug/1971	13°	♒	41
20/Aug/1971	27°	♌	15	S					
16/Jan/1972	25°	♑	24	N		30/Jan/1972	09°	♌	39
10/Jul/1972	18°	♋	36	S		26/Jul/1972	03°	♒	23
4/Jan/1973	14°	♑	9	N		18/Jan/1973	28°	♋	40
30/Jun/1973	08°	♋	31	S		15/Jun/1973	24°	♐	34
						15/Jul/1973	22°	♑	50
24/Dec/1973	02°	♑	40	N		10/Dec/1973	17°	♊	51
20/Jun/1974	28°	♊	29	S		4/Jun/1974	13°	♐	53
13/Dec/1974	21°	♐	17	N		29/Nov/1974	07°	♊	1
11/May/1975	19°	♉	59	S		25/May/1975	03°	♐	25
3/Nov/1975	10°	♏	29	N		18/Nov/1975	25°	♉	57
29/Apr/1976	09°	♉	13	S		13/May/1976	23°	♏	9
23/Oct/1976	29°	♎	55	N		6/Nov/1976	14°	♉	40
18/Apr/1977	28°	♈	16	S		4/Apr/1977	14°	♎	16
12/Oct/1977	19°	♎	24	N		27/Sep/1977	04°	♈	7
7/Apr/1978	17°	♈	26	S		24/Mar/1978	03°	♎	39
2/Oct/1978	08°	♎	43	N		16/Sep/1978	23°	♓	33
26/Feb/1979	07°	♓	29	S		13/Mar/1979	22°	♍	41
22/Aug/1979	29°	♌	0	N		6/Sep/1979	13°	♓	15
16/Feb/1980	26°	♒	50	S		1/Mar/1980	11°	♍	26
						27/Jul/1980	04°	♒	51
10/Aug/1980	18°	♌	16	N		26/Aug/1980	03°	♓	3
4/Feb/1981	16°	♒	1	S		20/Jan/1981	00°	♌	10
31/Jul/1981	07°	♌	51	N		17/Jul/1981	24°	♑	30
25/Jan/1982	04°	♒	53	S		9/Jan/1982	19°	♋	14
21/Jun/1982	29°	♊	46	N		6/Jul/1982	13°	♑	54
20/Jul/1982	27°	♋	43	N					
15/Dec/1982	23°	♐	4	S		30/Dec/1982	08°	♋	26
11/Jun/1983	19°	♊	42	N		25/Jun/1983	03°	♑	14
4/Dec/1983	11°	♐	46	S		20/Dec/1983	27°	♊	36
30/May/1984	09°	♊	26	N		15/May/1984	24°	♏	31
						13/Jun/1984	22°	♐	44
22/Nov/1984	00°	♐	50	S		8/Nov/1984	16°	♉	30
19/May/1985	28°	♉	50	N		4/May/1985	14°	♏	16
12/Nov/1985	20°	♏	8	S		28/Oct/1985	05°	♉	14
9/Apr/1986	19°	♈	5	N		24/Apr/1986	04°	♏	2
3/Oct/1986	10°	♎	16	S		17/Oct/1986	24°	♈	7
29/Mar/1987	08°	♈	17	N		14/Apr/1987	23°	♎	37
23/Sep/1987	29°	♍	34	S		7/Oct/1987	13°	♈	22
18/Mar/1988	27°	♓	41	N		3/Mar/1988	13°	♍	17
11/Sep/1988	18°	♍	40	S		27/Aug/1988	04°	♓	22
7/Mar/1989	17°	♓	9	N		20/Feb/1989	01°	♍	58
31/Aug/1989	07°	♍	48	S		17/Aug/1989	24°	♒	12
26/Jan/1990	06°	♒	34	N		9/Feb/1990	20°	♌	46
22/Jul/1990	29°	♋	4	S		6/Aug/1990	13°	♒	51
15/Jan/1991	25°	♑	19	N		30/Jan/1991	09°	♌	50
11/Jul/1991	18°	♋	59	S		27/Jun/1991	04°	♑	59

Eclipses in Chronological Order -
North and South Node noted for Solar Eclipses

Solar Eclipses at North or South Node						Lunar Eclipses			
						26/Jul/1991	03°	♒	16
4/Jan/1992	13°	♑	51	N		21/Dec/1991	29°	♊	2
30/Jun/1992	08°	♋	56	S		15/Jun/1992	24°	♐	20
24/Dec/1992	02°	♑	27	N		9/Dec/1992	18°	♊	10
21/May/1993	00°	♊	31	S		4/Jun/1993	13°	♐	54
13/Nov/1993	21°	♏	31	N		29/Nov/1993	07°	♊	3
10/May/1994	19°	♉	48	S		25/May/1994	03°	♐	42
3/Nov/1994	10°	♏	54	N		18/Nov/1994	25°	♉	42
29/Apr/1995	08°	♉	56	S		15/Apr/1995	25°	♎	3
24/Oct/1995	00°	♏	17	N		8/Oct/1995	14°	♈	53
17/Apr/1996	28°	♈	11	S		4/Apr/1996	14°	♎	30
12/Oct/1996	19°	♎	31	N		27/Sep/1996	04°	♈	16
9/Mar/1997	18°	♓	30	S		24/Mar/1997	03°	♎	35
2/Sep/1997	09°	♍	33	N		16/Sep/1997	23°	♓	56
26/Feb/1998	07°	♓	54	S		13/Mar/1998	22°	♍	23
						8/Aug/1998	15°	♒	21
22/Aug/1998	28°	♌	47	N		6/Sep/1998	13°	♓	40
16/Feb/1999	27°	♒	7	S		31/Jan/1999	11°	♌	19
11/Aug/1999	18°	♌	21	N		28/Jul/1999	04°	♒	57
5/Feb/2000	16°	♒	1	S		21/Jan/2000	00°	♌	26
1/Jul/2000	10°	♋	14	N		16/Jul/2000	24°	♑	19
31/Jul/2000	08°	♌	11	N					
25/Dec/2000	04°	♑	14	S		9/Jan/2001	19°	♋	39
21/Jun/2001	00°	♋	10	N		5/Jul/2001	13°	♑	38
14/Dec/2001	22°	♐	56	S		30/Dec/2001	08°	♋	47
11/Jun/2002	19°	♊	54	N		26/May/2002	05°	♐	3
						24/Jun/2002	03°	♑	11
4/Dec/2002	11°	♐	58	S		20/Nov/2002	27°	♉	32
31/May/2003	09°	♊	19	N		16/May/2003	24°	♏	52
23/Nov/2003	01°	♐	13	S		9/Nov/2003	16°	♉	12
19/Apr/2004	29°	♈	48	N		4/May/2004	14°	♏	41
14/Oct/2004	21°	♎	6	S		28/Oct/2004	05°	♉	2
8/Apr/2005	19°	♈	5	N		24/Apr/2005	04°	♏	19
3/Oct/2005	10°	♎	18	S		17/Oct/2005	24°	♈	13
29/Mar/2006	08°	♈	34	N		14/Mar/2006	24°	♍	14
22/Sep/2006	29°	♍	20	S		7/Sep/2006	15°	♓	0
19/Mar/2007	28°	♓	7	N		3/Mar/2007	12°	♍	59
11/Sep/2007	18°	♍	24	S		28/Aug/2007	04°	♓	45
7/Feb/2008	17°	♒	44	N		21/Feb/2008	01°	♍	52
1/Aug/2008	09°	♌	31	S		16/Aug/2008	24°	♒	21
26/Jan/2009	06°	♒	29	N		9/Feb/2009	20°	♌	59
22/Jul/2009	29°	♋	26	S		7/Jul/2009	15°	♑	24
						6/Aug/2009	13°	♒	43
15/Jan/2010	25°	♑	1	N		31/Dec/2009	10°	♋	14
11/Jul/2010	19°	♋	23	S		26/Jun/2010	04°	♑	46
4/Jan/2011	13°	♑	38	N		21/Dec/2010	29°	♊	20
1/Jun/2011	11°	♊	1	S		15/Jun/2011	24°	♐	23
1/Jul/2011	09°	♋	12	S					
25/Nov/2011	02°	♐	36	N		10/Dec/2011	18°	♊	10
20/May/2012	00°	♊	20	S		4/Jun/2012	14°	♐	13
13/Nov/2012	21°	♏	56	N		28/Nov/2012	06°	♊	46
						25/Apr/2013	05°	♏	45
10/May/2013	19°	♉	31	S		25/May/2013	04°	♐	7
3/Nov/2013	11°	♏	15	N		18/Oct/2013	25°	♈	45
29/Apr/2014	08°	♉	51	S		15/Apr/2014	25°	♎	15
23/Oct/2014	00°	♏	25	N		8/Oct/2014	15°	♈	5
20/Mar/2015	29°	♓	27	S		4/Apr/2015	14°	♎	24

Eclipses in Chronological Order -
North and South Node noted for Solar Eclipses

Solar Eclipses at North or South Node						Lunar Eclipses			
13/Sep/2015	20°	♍	10	N		28/Sep/2015	04°	♈	40
9/Mar/2016	18°	♓	55	S		23/Mar/2016	03°	♎	17
1/Sep/2016	09°	♍	21	N		18/Aug/2016	25°	♒	51
						16/Sep/2016	24°	♓	20
26/Feb/2017	08°	♓	12	S		11/Feb/2017	22°	♌	27
21/Aug/2017	28°	♌	52	N		7/Aug/2017	15°	♒	25
15/Feb/2018	27°	♒	7	S		31/Jan/2018	11°	♌	36
13/Jul/2018	20°	♋	41	N					
11/Aug/2018	18°	♌	41	N		27/Jul/2018	04°	♒	44
6/Jan/2019	15°	♑	25	S		21/Jan/2019	00°	♌	51
2/Jul/2019	10°	♋	37	N		16/Jul/2019	24°	♑	4
26/Dec/2019	04°	♑	6	S		10/Jan/2020	20°	♋	0
						5/Jun/2020	15°	♐	33
21/Jun/2020	00°	♋	21	N		5/Jul/2020	13°	♑	37
14/Dec/2020	23°	♐	8	S		30/Nov/2020	08°	♊	38
10/Jun/2021	19°	♊	47	N		26/May/2021	05°	♐	25
4/Dec/2021	12°	♐	22	S		19/Nov/2021	27°	♉	14
30/Apr/2022	10°	♉	28	N		16/May/2022	25°	♏	17
25/Oct/2022	02°	♏	0	S		8/Nov/2022	16°	♉	1
20/Apr/2023	29°	♈	49	N		5/May/2023	14°	♏	58
14/Oct/2023	21°	♎	7	S		28/Oct/2023	05°	♉	9
8/Apr/2024	19°	♈	23	N		25/Mar/2024	05°	♎	7
2/Oct/2024	10°	♎	4	S		18/Sep/2024	25°	♓	40
29/Mar/2025	08°	♈	59	N		14/Mar/2025	23°	♍	56
21/Sep/2025	29°	♍	5	S		7/Sep/2025	15°	♓	22
17/Feb/2026	28°	♒	49	N		3/Mar/2026	12°	♍	53
12/Aug/2026	20°	♌	2	S		28/Aug/2026	04°	♓	54
6/Feb/2027	17°	♒	37	N		20/Feb/2027	02°	♍	5
						18/Jul/2027	25°	♑	48
2/Aug/2027	09°	♌	55	S		17/Aug/2027	24°	♒	11
26/Jan/2028	06°	♒	10	N		12/Jan/2028	21°	♋	27
22/Jul/2028	29°	♋	50	S		6/Jul/2028	15°	♑	11
14/Jan/2029	24°	♑	50	N		31/Dec/2028	10°	♋	32
12/Jun/2029	21°	♊	29	S		26/Jun/2029	04°	♑	49
11/Jul/2029	19°	♋	37	S					
5/Dec/2029	13°	♐	45	N		20/Dec/2029	29°	♊	20
1/Jun/2030	10°	♊	49	S		15/Jun/2030	24°	♐	43
25/Nov/2030	03°	♐	2	N		9/Dec/2030	17°	♊	54
						7/May/2031	16°	♏	24
21/May/2031	00°	♊	4	S		5/Jun/2031	14°	♐	39
14/Nov/2031	22°	♏	17	N		30/Oct/2031	06°	♉	40
9/May/2032	19°	♉	29	S		25/Apr/2032	05°	♏	57
3/Nov/2032	11°	♏	21	N		18/Oct/2032	25°	♈	57
30/Mar/2033	10°	♈	20	S		14/Apr/2033	25°	♎	9
23/Sep/2033	00°	♎	51	N		8/Oct/2033	15°	♈	29
20/Mar/2034	29°	♓	52	S		3/Apr/2034	14°	♎	6
12/Sep/2034	19°	♍	58	N		28/Sep/2034	05°	♈	4
9/Mar/2035	19°	♓	12	S		22/Feb/2035	03°	♍	33
2/Sep/2035	09°	♍	27	N		19/Aug/2035	25°	♒	55
27/Feb/2036	08°	♓	10	S		11/Feb/2036	22°	♌	45
23/Jul/2036	01°	♌	9	N					
21/Aug/2036	29°	♌	14	N		7/Aug/2036	15°	♒	12
16/Jan/2037	26°	♑	35	S		31/Jan/2037	12°	♌	2
13/Jul/2037	21°	♋	3	N		27/Jul/2037	04°	♒	29
5/Jan/2038	15°	♑	18	S		21/Jan/2038	01°	♌	11
2/Jul/2038	10°	♋	47	N		17/Jun/2038	26°	♐	2
						16/Jul/2038	24°	♑	4

Eclipses in Chronological Order -
North and South Node noted for Solar Eclipses

Solar Eclipses at North or South Node						Lunar Eclipses			
26/Dec/2038	04°	♑	19	S		11/Dec/2038	19°	♊	45
21/Jun/2039	00°	♋	12	N		6/Jun/2039	15°	♐	56
15/Dec/2039	23°	♐	32	S		30/Nov/2039	08°	♊	19
11/May/2040	21°	♉	3	N		26/May/2040	05°	♐	50
4/Nov/2040	12°	♏	58	S		18/Nov/2040	27°	♉	3
30/Apr/2041	10°	♉	30	N		16/May/2041	25°	♏	32
25/Oct/2041	02°	♏	0	S		8/Nov/2041	16°	♉	9
20/Apr/2042	00°	♉	8	N		5/Apr/2042	15°	♎	55
						29/Sep/2042	06°	♈	25
14/Oct/2042	20°	♎	52	S		28/Oct/2042	05°	♉	31
9/Apr/2043	19°	♈	49	N		25/Mar/2043	04°	♎	49
3/Oct/2043	09°	♎	49	S		19/Sep/2043	26°	♓	2
28/Feb/2044	09°	♓	53	N		13/Mar/2044	23°	♍	52
23/Aug/2044	00°	♍	34	S		7/Sep/2044	15°	♓	29
16/Feb/2045	28°	♒	42	N		3/Mar/2045	13°	♍	8
12/Aug/2045	20°	♌	25	S		27/Aug/2045	04°	♓	43
5/Feb/2046	17°	♒	18	N		22/Jan/2046	02°	♌	39
2/Aug/2046	10°	♌	19	S		18/Jul/2046	25°	♑	37
26/Jan/2047	06°	♒	0	N		12/Jan/2047	21°	♋	44
23/Jun/2047	01°	♋	55	S		7/Jul/2047	15°	♑	16
22/Jul/2047	00°	♌	4	S					
16/Dec/2047	24°	♐	55	N		1/Jan/2048	10°	♋	31
11/Jun/2048	21°	♊	16	S		26/Jun/2048	05°	♑	10
5/Dec/2048	14°	♐	10	N		20/Dec/2048	29°	♊	3
						17/May/2049	26°	♏	59
31/May/2049	10°	♊	33	S		15/Jun/2049	25°	♐	8
25/Nov/2049	03°	♐	23	N		9/Nov/2049	17°	♉	40
20/May/2050	00°	♊	2	S		6/May/2050	16°	♏	35
14/Nov/2050	22°	♏	22	N		30/Oct/2050	06°	♉	53
11/Apr/2051	21°	♈	9	S		26/Apr/2051	05°	♏	49
4/Oct/2051	11°	♎	35	N		19/Oct/2051	26°	♈	21
30/Mar/2052	10°	♈	45	S		14/Apr/2052	24°	♎	51
22/Sep/2052	00°	♎	39	N		8/Oct/2052	15°	♈	52
20/Mar/2053	00°	♈	8	S		4/Mar/2053	14°	♍	35
12/Sep/2053	20°	♍	6	N		29/Aug/2053	06°	♓	27
9/Mar/2054	19°	♓	9	S		22/Feb/2054	03°	♍	51
3/Aug/2054	11°	♌	38	N		18/Aug/2054	25°	♒	41
2/Sep/2054	09°	♍	49	N					
27/Jan/2055	07°	♒	44	S		11/Feb/2055	23°	♌	10
24/Jul/2055	01°	♌	31	N		7/Aug/2055	14°	♒	57
16/Jan/2056	26°	♑	30	S		1/Feb/2056	12°	♌	22
12/Jul/2056	21°	♋	12	N		27/Jun/2056	06°	♑	29
						26/Jul/2056	04°	♒	31
5/Jan/2057	15°	♑	32	S		22/Dec/2056	00°	♋	55
1/Jul/2057	10°	♋	37	N		17/Jun/2057	26°	♐	25
26/Dec/2057	04°	♑	44	S		11/Dec/2057	19°	♊	27
22/May/2058	01°	♊	36	N		6/Jun/2058	16°	♐	20
21/Jun/2058	29°	♊	56	N					
16/Nov/2058	24°	♏	0	S		30/Nov/2058	08°	♊	9
11/May/2059	21°	♉	7	N		27/May/2059	06°	♐	5
5/Nov/2059	12°	♏	57	S		19/Nov/2059	27°	♉	12
30/Apr/2060	10°	♉	49	N		15/Apr/2060	26°	♎	39
						9/Oct/2060	17°	♈	14
24/Oct/2060	01°	♏	44	S		8/Nov/2060	16°	♉	31
20/Apr/2061	00°	♉	33	N		4/Apr/2061	15°	♎	38
13/Oct/2061	20°	♎	37	S		29/Sep/2061	06°	♈	46
11/Mar/2062	20°	♓	51	N		25/Mar/2062	04°	♎	46

Eclipses in Chronological Order -
North and South Node noted for Solar Eclipses

Solar Eclipses at North or South Node						Lunar Eclipses			
3/Sep/2062	11°	♍	9	S		18/Sep/2062	26°	♓	8
28/Feb/2063	09°	♓	44	N		14/Mar/2063	24°	♍	7
24/Aug/2063	00°	♍	58	S		7/Sep/2063	15°	♓	17
17/Feb/2064	28°	♒	24	N		2/Feb/2064	13°	♌	49
12/Aug/2064	20°	♌	49	S		28/Jul/2064	06°	♒	2
5/Feb/2065	17°	♒	9	N		22/Jan/2065	02°	♌	55
3/Jul/2065	12°	♋	20	S					
2/Aug/2065	10°	♌	31	S		17/Jul/2065	25°	♑	43
27/Dec/2065	06°	♑	7	N		11/Jan/2066	21°	♋	42
22/Jun/2066	01°	♋	42	S		7/Jul/2066	15°	♑	37
17/Dec/2066	25°	♐	21	N		31/Dec/2066	10°	♋	13
11/Jun/2067	21°	♊	2	S		28/May/2067	07°	♐	32
						27/Jun/2067	05°	♑	36
6/Dec/2067	14°	♐	30	N		20/Nov/2067	28°	♉	43
31/May/2068	10°	♊	33	S		17/May/2068	27°	♏	9
24/Nov/2068	03°	♐	26	N		9/Nov/2068	17°	♉	54
21/Apr/2069	01°	♉	53	S					
20/May/2069	00°	♊	19	S		6/May/2069	16°	♏	26
15/Oct/2069	22°	♎	24	N		30/Oct/2069	07°	♉	18
11/Apr/2070	21°	♈	33	S		25/Apr/2070	05°	♏	32
4/Oct/2070	11°	♎	25	N		19/Oct/2070	26°	♈	44
31/Mar/2071	11°	♈	0	S		16/Mar/2071	25°	♍	33
23/Sep/2071	00°	♎	48	N		9/Sep/2071	17°	♓	3
19/Mar/2072	00°	♈	4	S		4/Mar/2072	14°	♍	53
12/Sep/2072	20°	♍	28	N		28/Aug/2072	06°	♓	12
7/Feb/2073	18°	♒	52	S		22/Feb/2073	04°	♍	16
3/Aug/2073	11°	♌	59	N		17/Aug/2073	25°	♒	27
27/Jan/2074	07°	♒	40	S		11/Feb/2074	23°	♌	29
24/Jul/2074	01°	♌	38	N		8/Jul/2074	16°	♑	56
						7/Aug/2074	14°	♒	59
16/Jan/2075	26°	♑	44	S		2/Jan/2075	12°	♋	6
13/Jul/2075	21°	♋	2	N		28/Jun/2075	06°	♑	52
6/Jan/2076	15°	♑	57	S		22/Dec/2075	00°	♋	36
1/Jun/2076	12°	♊	5	N		17/Jun/2076	26°	♐	49
1/Jul/2076	10°	♋	21	N					
26/Nov/2076	05°	♐	5	S		10/Dec/2076	19°	♊	17
22/May/2077	01°	♊	40	N		6/Jun/2077	16°	♐	34
15/Nov/2077	23°	♏	58	S		29/Nov/2077	08°	♊	18
11/May/2078	21°	♉	27	N		27/Apr/2078	07°	♏	20
						21/Oct/2078	28°	♈	7
4/Nov/2078	12°	♏	40	S		19/Nov/2078	27°	♉	35
1/May/2079	11°	♉	15	N		16/Apr/2079	26°	♎	23
24/Oct/2079	01°	♏	30	S		10/Oct/2079	17°	♈	34
21/Mar/2080	01°	♈	47	N		4/Apr/2080	15°	♎	36
13/Sep/2080	21°	♍	48	S		29/Sep/2080	06°	♈	51
10/Mar/2081	20°	♓	43	N		25/Mar/2081	05°	♎	2
3/Sep/2081	11°	♍	34	S		18/Sep/2081	25°	♓	56
27/Feb/2082	09°	♓	25	N		13/Feb/2082	24°	♌	57
24/Aug/2082	01°	♍	22	S		8/Aug/2082	16°	♒	31
16/Feb/2083	28°	♒	15	N		2/Feb/2083	14°	♌	5
14/Jul/2083	22°	♋	46	S		29/Jul/2083	06°	♒	11
13/Aug/2083	21°	♌	1	S					
7/Jan/2084	17°	♑	20	N		22/Jan/2084	02°	♌	52
3/Jul/2084	12°	♋	7	S		17/Jul/2084	26°	♑	5
27/Dec/2084	06°	♑	33	N		10/Jan/2085	21°	♋	23
22/Jun/2085	01°	♋	27	S		8/Jun/2085	18°	♐	2
						7/Jul/2085	16°	♑	2

Eclipses in Chronological Order -
North and South Node noted for Solar Eclipses

Solar Eclipses at North or South Node						Lunar Eclipses			
16/Dec/2085	25°	♐	40	N		1/Dec/2085	09°	♊	50
11/Jun/2086	21°	♊	2	S		28/May/2086	07°	♐	41
6/Dec/2086	14°	♐	33	N		20/Nov/2086	28°	♉	58
2/May/2087	12°	♉	34	S		17/May/2087	27°	♏	0
1/Jun/2087	10°	♊	51	S					
26/Oct/2087	03°	♏	17	N		10/Nov/2087	18°	♉	19
21/Apr/2088	02°	♉	18	S		5/May/2088	16°	♏	9
14/Oct/2088	22°	♎	14	N		30/Oct/2088	07°	♉	41
10/Apr/2089	21°	♈	48	S		26/Mar/2089	06°	♎	27
4/Oct/2089	11°	♎	34	N		19/Sep/2089	27°	♓	42
31/Mar/2090	10°	♈	55	S		15/Mar/2090	25°	♍	52
23/Sep/2090	01°	♎	11	N		8/Sep/2090	16°	♓	48
18/Feb/2091	29°	♒	58	S		5/Mar/2091	15°	♍	19
15/Aug/2091	22°	♌	29	N		29/Aug/2091	05°	♓	59
7/Feb/2092	18°	♒	49	S		23/Feb/2092	04°	♍	35
						19/Jul/2092	27°	♑	23
3/Aug/2092	12°	♌	5	N		17/Aug/2092	25°	♒	30
27/Jan/2093	07°	♒	55	S		12/Jan/2093	23°	♋	16
23/Jul/2093	01°	♌	27	N		8/Jul/2093	17°	♑	19
16/Jan/2094	27°	♑	9	S		1/Jan/2094	11°	♋	46
13/Jun/2094	22°	♊	34	N		28/Jun/2094	07°	♑	17
12/Jul/2094	20°	♋	46	N					
7/Dec/2094	16°	♐	12	S		21/Dec/2094	00°	♋	27
2/Jun/2095	12°	♊	12	N		17/Jun/2095	27°	♐	2
27/Nov/2095	05°	♐	2	S		11/Dec/2095	19°	♊	27
						7/May/2096	17°	♏	56
22/May/2096	02°	♊	1	N		6/Jun/2096	16°	♐	28
15/Nov/2096	23°	♏	40	S		31/Oct/2096	09°	♉	4
						29/Nov/2096	08°	♊	42
11/May/2097	21°	♉	52	N		26/Apr/2097	07°	♏	3
4/Nov/2097	12°	♏	27	S		21/Oct/2097	28°	♈	27
1/Apr/2098	12°	♈	38	N		15/Apr/2098	26°	♎	22
25/Sep/2098	02°	♎	31	S					
24/Oct/2098	01°	♏	35	S		10/Oct/2098	17°	♈	38
21/Mar/2099	01°	♈	38	N		5/Apr/2099	15°	♎	53
14/Sep/2099	22°	♍	13	S		29/Sep/2099	06°	♈	38

The Metonic Cycle Eclipse Groups as They Travel Through a Lifetime

Discovered by the ancient Greek mathematician Meton, the metonic cycle measures the repetition of eclipses occurring on or near the same day every nineteen years. Since these eclipse points repeat four to five times in succession, a complete string of these eclipse points may span 76 to 95 years. This is the metonic cycle. It offers a means to track related events spanning generations. Wars, famine, economic highs and lows, and the lifetime narrative of you and your family may all be tracked within the metonic cycle.

The tables of the metonic-cycle eclipses are grouped by zodiacal degree, each box contains both solar and lunar eclipses. In the left column you will find the solar eclipses related by their zodiacal position. In the right column, you will find the *related* lunar eclipses. Both lunar and solar eclipses with similar degree points are associated together. More importantly, these lunar eclipses occur at the halfway point on the 19-year metonic cycle. These lunar eclipses occur 9.5 years before or after a solar eclipse when the nodes of the Moon have reversed position to transit halfway around the zodiac. The monthly Moon phases also repeat in an identical pattern every nineteen years. It is no wonder that we become creatures of habit.

Put another way, nodes are where eclipses take place. When a new or full moon occurs close by a lunar node there will be a solar or lunar eclipse. A solar or lunar eclipse is a major astronomical event that happens only when there is a new or full moon 12 to18 degrees from the lunar nodes. When looking at the chart of a solar eclipse you will notice that the north and south lunar nodes are in exact opposition to one another. The nodes are intersection points in the sky and not celestial bodies. The node can be as far as 12 degrees from a full moon for there to be a lunar eclipse or 18 degrees from a new moon for there to be a solar eclipse. Therefore, the node may not exactly conjunct the eclipse point. This is something to keep in mind when you are researching eclipse triggers to assess the impact of an eclipse chart related to a birth, relationship, or business chart, etc.

Here is where the fun begins. The tables of the metonic-cycle eclipse groups can be used as a powerful tool to reconstruct a timeline in your personal narrative and project your story into the future. The solar and lunar eclipses are linked to one another, showing when the major events in your life most likely occurred. Eclipses have a six month range of influence, three months before and three months after. So you have plenty of leeway to tag your events. Many people tell of an eventful year when their prenatal eclipse returns.

I have grouped eclipses and moons phase occurring at similar degrees into what I've termed *Moon Families*. You will find your story ties to the related Moon Family Tables associated throughout the nineteen year cycle. Each new moon and eclipse carries the seeds of change for your body, mind and spirit. Each moon phase marks an evolution of associated events. New beginnings are seeded at a New Moon. The First Quarter Moon is a strong action time when you are highly motivated or called to move forward. Full Moons bring events into the full light of awareness. Finally, the Last Quarter Moon is the wind down stage where you reap the rewards for your efforts or face paying the bill. In the Last Quarter you will also take something away with you to seed the future.

Whether your stories are minor tales or major events the Moon families thread your narrative along a timeline. The dates of these cosmic events can be used as markers for the stages in your life or significant changes to your inner landscape. From your earliest memories to your plans for your future, there are eclipses and Moon phases that mark your progress. Studying your metonic cycle will be eye opening and perhaps cathartic. You may find it restorative as you gather up the threads of your life to reveal recurring themes and patterns. By taking a wider view, you'll also have an opportunity to gain perspective on habitual patterns even as a related Moon phase is approaching. There may be a date when your life took a major turn. And this event may be tied to other events seemingly less memorable or important. If a date is not the first thing that comes to mind, then perhaps both the metonic-cycle and Moon family tables will inspire deeper insight into surrounding events.

Begin with your most powerful eclipse, your prenatal solar eclipse. Follow the developments in your life at key points over the years. Track events back to the astrological degree of the last solar eclipse before your birth. If your metonic-cycle group should end at any point in your life, don't fret, another begins in eight years to pick up your life story. What you might realize or look forward to at that time is a noticeable shift along your path, a complete change of direction or an obvious maturation when your eclipse group ends and another begins. Realize that these metonic-cycle groups weave their tapestry through their related Moon Families. As you draw connections between the Moon phases, solar eclipses, mid-metonic-cycle lunar eclipses, and the next solar eclipse, you will also draw connections between events. The timing of events will begin to appear more than coincidental. You may begin to wonder why you hadn't seen these patterns before.

Within the metonic cycle, the lunar eclipse revives the storyline seeded at the solar eclipse. This 9.5-year marker points to an important pivot in your 19-year narrative. A related lunar eclipse often arrives before the new solar eclipse metonic-cycle begins. With the exception of the cycles end, when you see a lunar eclipse occurring two weeks before a solar eclipse, you can now be aware of the secret relationship that that this lunar eclipse has to a distant solar eclipse 9.5 years away.

Remember to consider the eclipse triggers.

Keep an eye on the transiting lunar nodes. There are a couple of very hot days in a year when the transiting node reaches the eclipse point and you will notice increased activity. You will find this to be true with either the mean or true node. The node of the Moon will reach the point of a solar or lunar eclipse at different times. The news is more stunning in either personal or public formats. The node conjunct the solar eclipse point seems to be dominant.

When the eclipse occurs very close to the eclipse point it indicates a total eclipse but, most eclipses are partial showing the node of the Moon several degrees from the eclipse point. The node may reach the actual eclipse degree months before of after the eclipse. For instance, the solar eclipse on August 1, 2008 at 9°31' Leo and the south node at 18°31' Leo. The mean node reaches the same point on January 27, 2009. The transiting true node reaches 9°31' Leo on December 27, 2008. For many eclipses, this is the date when the promise of eclipse is fulfilled.

Think of eclipses as seasonal events. Notice the strength of events at the New or Full Moon three months before and after an eclipse. Look for *any Moon phase* in hard aspect to the solar or lunar eclipse point to continue the story. Most often six months after an eclipse there is an eclipse in very close opposition. Use this eclipse to notice how the others in your life are experiencing the eclipse.

There is a connection between the micro 29 day lunar cycle and the macro 29-year Saturn cycle. Watch for a new chapter in your story when Saturn forms a hard aspect to your prenatal eclipse. This is true when transiting Saturn forms a hard aspect to any transiting eclipse.

Begin your study of Metonic cycle groups with your Prenatal Solar Eclipse and then move onto each of your planets, Ascendant and Midheaven. This method works great with a marriage or home purchase; a business or any event of your interest.

Here are a couple of Prenatal Eclipse stories that weave throughout two Metonic cycle groups.

Aries Eclipses in Metonic Cycle Groups

Solar Eclipses		Lunar Eclipses	
Mar 29 1903	07 ♈ 12	Sep 26 1912	03 ♈ 00
Mar 28 1922	07 ♈ 4	Sep 26 1931	02 ♈ 45
Mar 27 1941	06 ♈ 46	Sep 26 1950	02 ♈ 30
Mar 27 1960	06 ♈ 38	Sep 25 1969	02 ♈ 34

Mar 28 1968	08 ♈ 19	Sep 27 1977	04 ♈ 07
Mar 29 1987	08 ♈ 18	Sep 27 1996	04 ♈ 16
Mar 29 2006	08 ♈ 35	Sep 28 2015	04 ♈ 40
Mar 29 2025	08 ♈ 59	Sep 28 2034	05 ♈ 03

The table above contains two Aries Metonic cycle groups. The dates related to the table are noted in bold print in this story. You will notice the strong Aries theme in this story of a Cancer man named Jack, born with an Aries prenatal eclipse in 1941. This eclipse was conjunct his Mars ruling his third house of siblings. This Metonic cycle group ended with the solar eclipse in 1960. A new Aries Metonic cycle group began in 1968. Jack was the younger of two boys and was a high mischievous, high spirited and difficult child to parent. His parents placed him in a military academy for structure and discipline. In 1960 Jack was married and the couple had three children. His older brother was a scholar and excelled as a prominent lawyer at a young age. Jack and his father, born in 1912, were business partners and the brother was their lawyer. Sadly the brother was killed in a car accident in 1968 on the day of a First Quarter Moon at 5° Aries at the north node of the Moon also at 5° Aries. There had been a lunar eclipse at 13° Aries early that fall but that eclipse was unrelated to Jack's Metonic cycle group. However the lunar eclipse was conjunct Jack's 9° Aries Mars. For Jack, the ruler of siblings, Mercury was 7° Cancer and square to his Mars. This not only changed Jack's life dramatically but the family tragically fell apart. Jack's marriage also broke up after he began a new relationship in September of 1969. The family lost their fortune of $16+million in 1977 as a result of lawsuits resulting from a grief driven violent episode that also took place in 1969. He survived a major coronary in 1976, eighteen months before the '77 lunar eclipse, while trying to stave off the eventual loss of the last piece of real estate in the family. His heart attack occurred at the New Moon at the start of the Moon Family leading to the 1977 lunar eclipse. Jack's life ended with a heart attack in 1988 leaving his three children, his mother and father.

18°-19° Taurus Eclipses in Metonic Cycle Groups

Solar Eclipses

May 9 1910	17 ♉ 43
May 9 1929	18 ♉ 07
May 9 1948	18 ♉ 22
May 9 1967	18 ♉ 17

May 11 1975	19 ♉ 59
May 10 1994	19 ♉ 48
May 10 2013	19 ♉ 31
May 9 2032	19 ♉ 28

Lunar Eclipses

Nov 8 1919	14 ♉ 31
Nov 7 1938	14 ♉ 51
Nov 7 1957	14 ♉ 55
Nov 7 1976	14 ♉ 40

Nov 8 1984	16 ♉ 30
Nov 9 2003	16 ♉ 12
Nov 8 2022	16 ♉ 00
Nov 8 2041	16 ♉ 08
Nov 8 2060	16 ♉ 30

Moon Family Dates

Solar Eclipse May 9 1948	Feb 6 1949	Nov 5 1949	Aug 5 1950
May 5 1951	Feb 2 1952	Nov 1 1952	Aug 1 1953
May 10 1956	Feb 7 1957	Lunar Eclipse Nov 7 1957	Aug 7 1958
May 7 1959	Feb 4 1960	Nov 3 1960	Aug 3 1961
Solar Eclipse May 9 1967	Feb 6 1968	Nov 4 1968	Aug 4 1969

The table above contains two tables for the following story.

Metonic cycle groups are noted in bold throughout the following story. Also noted are a few related Moon Families (here italicized).

The next story follows some of the significant events over the life of Bessie, born in the fall of **1948** with the prenatal eclipse at 18°22 Taurus in May 1948. Taurus is associated with tradition and the bonds of the family. Often we see the sign symbolism develop in an individual's life not as gifts but as challenges and issues to be worked out over a lifetime. Think of the prenatal eclipse point as a sort of ascendant.

In this case the Taurus solar eclipse applied a few hard aspects in Bessie's chart that defined the experiences in her life. She was born within an hour of a Mars-Chiron conjunction at 23°Scorpio that was in opposition to the prenatal eclipse point (the imaginary Descendant). Pluto at 16° Leo was square to the prenatal eclipse point (the imaginary nadir). Many of the major events in her life occurred in the same months of Feb, May, August and November, as the Moon Family pattern.

Bessie's Mercury is conjunct the south node at her birth, foregrounding the issues of health and siblings. Interestingly, Bessie's mother was born near the November **1919** Taurus mid-Metonic lunar eclipse. Bessie's older sister Alice was born in June of 1947 with a 28°Taurus prenatal eclipse that carried a similar theme throughout her life. A third sister Peggy was born with tuberculosis in *August of 1950*. Peggy's birth came near the Last Quarter Moon in Taurus. This was the last Moon Family member that began with the prenatal 18° Taurus solar eclipse.

Peggy was removed from the family at birth because of her illness. Her older sisters saw Peggy only once in *November of 1952*. Soon after Peggy's birth, their mother had to be forced into treatment. Her diseased lung was removed and she was transferred to a tuberculosis sanitarium until her disease came under control. But, Bessie and Alice never lived with their mother once they were placed in state care by their father. He was unable to care for his girls and took them to an orphanage in February of 1951 (three months before the Solar Eclipse anniversary New Moon of May 1951. The two girls were moved to another temporary holding in *May of 1951* where they both remember being sadly abused.

In August 1951 the girls were finally placed in a long-term foster home with the Wilson's who were a childless couple with no idea about raising children. The Wilson's did not want to become attached to the girls and did not express affection for the little girls but put them on a rigid routine and taught them chores that would occupy their time and eliminate any playing in the house.

An important new Moon family began on May 10, 1956 that would bring forth the mid-Metonic Lunar Eclipse in November 1957. On May 8 1956, Mrs. Wilson gave birth to a son. Her pregnancy was a surprise to her until she was nearly full term. The birth of this child was the seed of great change for the fate of Bessie and her sister.

There are several events the girls remember about their infancy but, one event stands out the summer after the baby was born. The story was remembered only later as a horrific nightmare. Both girls recall the same scary dream of a hot summer night in August of 1956. On many occasions they recalled the thickness in the dead air of that summer night. They remember the room turning red with a light bouncing around the room. The window between their twin beds rose and two devils entered their room. As they screamed the devils covered their mouths and began to operate on them one at a time. The nightmare was identical from each girl, which should have been a clue. For years they imagined they must have been abducted by aliens or something like that.

Finally Bessie remembered the details of that night and it wasn't a dream. Her memory came when the transiting north node was 18° Aquarius. Chiron and Neptune were both conjunct the node in Aquarius and all were square her prenatal solar eclipse degree. Chiron as the wounded healer was the theme for an awakening (Aquarius) to access this memory (Moon's node) thought to have been a dream (Neptune). Here is what happened. The Wilson's sent the girls to bed and took their infant across the street to the neighbor's house for a game of cards. This was a common practice, as no harm was expected to come to the girls sleeping alone in the house where the front door was in clear view. But someone was very aware of this weekend routine. Two male intruders were able to gain easy access to the little girls by climbing through an open window between the twin beds in the girl's bedroom. They silenced the girl's screams and perpetrated their hideous deeds out of sight and sound of the card players. More than likely the young men were related to the family across the street.

This was the summer of 1956. Bessie's New Moon Family began in May and that Moon family packed a punch with a lunar eclipse to follow. For Bessie's sister Alice this horrible event occurred three months before her first mid-Metonic cycle Lunar Eclipse in November 1956. The girls were left speechless and terrified and the event became a blur. The memory was transformed into a nightmare that the girls shared only between themselves years later. It was only days after the event that anyone noticed there was something physically wrong with the girls. Questions remain to this day. Why were their screams not heard? The room must have been a horrible sight. But no one asked the girls what happened, even as they were most obviously too frightened to talk. They were taken to the doctor and treated for injuries and gross infections but sadly, no further investigation was conducted nor was counseling to follow such a horrifying event.

Alice became noticeably angry and mean after the event and Bessie withdrew. Three months before Bessie's first mid-metonic Lunar Eclipse of 1957, the Wilson's took the three children and a niece to California to visit Mrs. Wilson's family. The girls were not aware that their family would soon move to California. A year later, in November 1958, the girls were left behind when the family moved. The social worker was able to place the girls in the home of Mrs. Wilson's brother and his wife. The girls were severely damaged without hope of being understood since their story was a mystery even to them.

Unfortunately, their new foster father lost his job in May, nine-months after the girls moved in. As hard as he and his wife tried, they could not keep the girls. The girls were devastated as this was a good home. That August 1959, they were placed with a total stranger, in the home of a 64 year old widowed woman who could not deal with the needs of two preadolescent girls with problems. It was no surprise that the home lasted only three months.

Four new foster homes followed until the girls were placed with a family that had a set of parents and four kids in August of 1960. There was a serious problem at that home; the foster father was a sexual abuser. His behavior escalated over a three year period. Once again the girls were too terrified to speak but were forced to explain what was wrong during a routine psychological checkup. The ink blot tests were highly suspicious of sexual problems. The girls were forced to tell what was going on. They had never discussed what had gone on even with each other prior to the doctor visit. Once the issues were out in the open, the doctor concluded the girls were lying and sent them back home to work things out. The social worker tossed the girls at the foster father and said, "the girls are claiming you are making passes at them." The foster father was a born again Christian and did not lie and confessed to the accusations. The social worker was shocked and removed the girls from that home after a few days.

This episode took place mid-November in 1963. The transiting Scorpio Sun (the light on the subject), was conjunct both Ceres (serious) and Neptune (secrets) and all were square to the Aquarius Saturn (the father). The transiting set of planets completed a T-square to Bessie's prenatal Taurus solar eclipse.

The November '63 foster home was the last one with a couple with a 26 year age difference. The foster mother managed to split the girls. They were each sent to separate orphanages in rough areas of a major city where Bessie was raped coming home from school on the anniversary of the prenatal solar eclipse.

Her Metonic cycle group was coming to a close in May 1967. Bessie had a son in 1967. There was a lot of healing that came from having her own child but her marriage was a disaster. It ended in divorce in February 1972.

January 31, 1974 Bessie read her first astrology book that resonated with her soul. She began to study astrology and took her first lesson in chart construction in May 1974. This was the year before the first solar eclipse in the new Metonic cycle.

Bessie had a new relationship for a few years before a mid-Metonic cycle lunar eclipse in **1976** made a powerful impact. Her boyfriend suffered a major heart attack.

In many ways that relationship was a destructive force in Bessie's life and by the mid-Metonic cycle Lunar Eclipse of 1984 the relationship ended. With what she describes as a liberating period she recalls feeling she had a new lease on life.

With the prompting of a close friend she began writing over the course of 1993/94 within nine months of a new Metonic cycle solar eclipse in May **1994**. Many stories of growth and positive development can be told about the years that followed with her primary focus on her work.

By finding your stories within the Metonic cycles you might notice a significant theme revealed in the patterns drawn by the events in your life. Those events may not define who you are but the patterns that emerge might be a key to a healthier you in the future. A wise man said, "It's easy to believe that an event has only happened to us once, when it's really part of a pattern . . . especially when the pattern includes missing the pattern."

How are your stories found in the cycles of the Moon Families and Eclipses? By looking at events in time periods related by moon phases within the metonic cycle, you have the opportunity to gain a view of psychologically powerful events otherwise clouded by emotion intensity. What were the seeds of a crescendo event? How might seemingly unrelated events be tied together at an emotional level? Are you entering or exiting an emotionally charged time period? How far back do its roots stretch?

Enjoy the phases of your life.

Metonic Cycle Groups

On the left, the Solar Eclipses are grouped with the 19-year Metonic cycle. On the right, are the related Lunar Eclipses that are found midway through the 19-year Metonic cycle or 9.5-years before or after the Solar Eclipse. This midway point Lunar Eclipse occurs when the lunar nodes are opposite the nodes of the Solar Eclipse. This Lunar Eclipse revives an older storyline for an important pivot in the 19-yr narrative. Realize that the Metonic cycle dovetails with their related Moon Families that carry the story along Moon phase lines from Solar Eclipse to the mid-Metonic cycle Lunar eclipse to the next Solar Eclipse in the Metonic cycle group. When one group ends often another begins eight years later.

Aries Eclipses in Metonic Cycle Groups

Solar Eclipses / Lunar Eclipses

Solar Eclipses			Lunar Eclipses		
Mar 20 2015	29	♓ 28	Sep 18 2024	25	♓ 41
Mar 20 2034	29	♓ 52	Sep 19 2043	26	♓ 02
Mar 20 2053	00	♈ 08	Sep 18 2062	26	♓ 08
Mar 19 2072	00	♈ 04	Sep 18 2081	25	♓ 55
Mar 21 2080	01	♈ 48	Sep 19 2089	27	♓ 42
Mar 21 2099	01	♈ 38	Sep 20 2108	27	♓ 26
Mar 22 2118	01	♈ 20	Sep 20 2127	27	♓ 26
Mar 22 2137	01	♈ 14	Sep 20 2146	27	♓ 20
Mar 29 1903	07	♈ 12	Sep 26 1912	03	♈ 00
Mar 28 1922	07	♈ 4	Sep 26 1931	02	♈ 45
Mar 27 1941	06	♈ 46	Sep 26 1950	02	♈ 30
Mar 27 1960	06	♈ 38	Sep 25 1969	02	♈ 34
Mar 28 1968	08	♈ 19	Sep 27 1977	04	♈ 07
Mar 29 1987	08	♈ 18	Sep 27 1996	04	♈ 16
Mar 29 2006	08	♈ 35	Sep 28 2015	04	♈ 40
Mar 29 2025	08	♈ 59	Sep 28 2034	05	♈ 03
Mar 30 2033	10	♈ 21	Sep 29 2042	06	♈ 25
Mar 30 2052	10	♈ 45	Sep 29 2061	06	♈ 46
Mar 31 2071	11	♈ 0	Sep 29 2080	06	♈ 51
Mar 31 2090	10	♈ 56	Sep 29 2099	06	♈ 37
Apr 6 1856	15	♈ 39	Oct 4 1865	11	♈ 41
Apr 6 1875	15	♈ 4	Oct 4 1884	12	♈ 04
Apr 6 1894	16	♈ 20	Oct 6 1903	12	♈ 11
Apr 6 1913	16	♈ 18	Oct 6 1922	11	♈ 58
Apr 8 1902	17	♈ 48			
Apr 8 1921	18	♈ 0	Oct 7 1930	13	♈ 47
Apr 7 1940	17	♈ 51	Oct 7 1949	13	♈ 30
Apr 8 1959	17	♈ 33	Oct 6 1968	13	♈ 16
Apr 7 1978	17	♈ 26	Oct 7 1987	13	♈ 21
Apr 9 1986	19	♈ 6	Oct 8 1995	14	♈ 54
Apr 8 2005	19	♈ 6	Oct 8 2014	15	♈ 05
Apr 8 2024	19	♈ 24	Oct 8 2033	15	♈ 28
Apr 9 2043	19	♈ 49	Oct 8 2052	15	♈ 52
Apr 11 2051	21	♈ 10	Oct 9 2060	17	♈ 14
Apr 11 2070	21	♈ 34	Oct 10 2079	17	♈ 34
Apr 10 2089	21	♈ 48	Oct 10 2098	17	♈ 38
Apr 11 2108	21	♈ 42	Oct 10 2117	17	♈ 24
Apr 16 1874	26	♈ 24	Oct 16 1883	22	♈ 04
Apr 16 1893	26	♈ 49	Oct 17 1902	22	♈ 56
Apr 17 1912	27	♈ 5	Oct 16 1921	23	♈ 02
Apr 18 1931	27	♈ 2	Oct 16 1940	22	♈ 48
Apr 19 1939	28	♈ 44	Oct 18 1948	24	♈ 37
Apr 19 1958	28	♈ 34	Oct 18 1967	24	♈ 20
Apr 18 1977	28	♈ 16	Oct 17 1986	24	♈ 07
Apr 17 1996	28	♈ 11	Oct 17 2005	24	♈ 13
Apr 19 2004	29	♈ 49	Oct 19 2013	25	♈ 45
Apr 20 2023	29	♈ 50	Oct 18 2032	25	♈ 57
Apr 20 2042	00	♉ 9	Oct 19 2051	26	♈ 21
Apr 20 2061	00	♉ 34	Oct 19 2070	26	♈ 44

Libra Eclipses in Metonic Cycle Groups

Solar Eclipses / Lunar Eclipses

Solar Eclipses			Lunar Eclipses		
			Mar 25 2024	05	♎ 07
Sep 23 2033	00	♎ 52	Mar 25 2043	04	♎ 50
Sep 22 2052	00	♎ 40	Mar 25 2062	04	♎ 46
Sep 23 2071	00	♎ 48	Mar 25 2081	05	♎ 02
Sep 23 2090	01	♎ 11			
			Mar 31 1847	10	♎ 32
Sep 29 1856	06	♎ 11	Mar 31 1866	10	♎ 14
Sep 29 1875	05	♎ 58	Mar 30 1885	10	♎ 08
Sep 29 1894	06	♎ 04	Mar 31 1904	10	♎ 22
Sep 30 1913	06	♎ 25			
			Apr 1 1912	11	♎ 49
Oct 1 1921	7	♎ 47	Apr 2 1931	12	♎ 07
Oct 1 1940	8	♎ 11	Apr 2 1950	12	♎ 32
Oct 2 1959	8	♎ 34	Apr 2 1969	12	♎ 50
Oct 2 1978	8	♎ 43			
			Apr 4 1958	13	♎ 53
			Apr 4 1977	14	♎ 16
Oct 3 1986	10	♎ 16	Apr 4 1996	14	♎ 30
Oct 3 2005	10	♎ 19	Apr 4 2015	14	♎ 23
Oct 2 2024	10	♎ 04	Apr 3 2034	14	♎ 05
Oct 3 2043	09	♎ 49			
			Apr 5 2042	15	♎ 56
Oct 4 2051	11	♎ 36	Apr 4 2061	15	♎ 38
Oct 4 2070	11	♎ 25	Apr 4 2080	15	♎ 36
Oct 4 2089	11	♎ 35	Apr 5 2099	15	♎ 53
Oct 5 2108	11	♎ 57			
			Apr 11 1865	21	♎ 17
Oct 10 1874	16	♎ 59	Apr 10 1884	21	♎ 00
Oct 10 1893	16	♎ 46	Apr 12 1903	20	♎ 55
Oct 10 1912	16	♎ 52	Apr 11 1922	21	♎ 09
Oct 11 1931	17	♎ 15			
			Apr 13 1930	22	♎ 34
Oct 12 1939	18	♎ 37	Apr 13 1949	22	♎ 54
Oct 12 1958	19	♎ 02	Apr 13 1968	23	♎ 19
Oct 12 1977	19	♎ 24	Apr 14 1987	23	♎ 37
Oct 12 1996	19	♎ 31			
			Apr 15 1995	25	♎ 04
Oct 14 2004	21	♎ 06	Apr 15 2014	25	♎ 16
Oct 14 2023	21	♎ 08	Apr 14 2033	25	♎ 09
Oct 14 2042	20	♎ 52	Apr 14 2052	24	♎ 51
Oct 13 2061	20	♎ 37			
			Apr 15 2060	26	♎ 40
Oct 15 2069	22	♎ 25	Apr 16 2079	26	♎ 23
Oct 14 2088	22	♎ 15	Apr 15 2098	26	♎ 22
Oct 16 2107	22	♎ 25	Apr 16 2117	26	♎ 40
Oct 16 2126	22	♎ 48			
			Apr 22 1883	01	♏ 58
Oct 20 1882	27	♎ 51	Apr 22 1902	01	♏ 41
Oct 22 1911	27	♎ 39	Apr 22 1921	01	♏ 37
Oct 21 1930	27	♎ 46	Apr 22 1940	01	♏ 53
Oct 21 1949	28	♎ 08			
			Apr 23 1948	03	♏ 17
Oct 23 1957	29	♎ 31	Apr 24 1967	03	♏ 37
Oct 23 1976	29	♎ 56	Apr 24 1986	04	♏ 02
Oct 24 1995	00	♏ 18	Apr 24 2005	04	♏ 19
Oct 23 2014	00	♏ 24			

Taurus Eclipses in Metonic Cycle Groups

Solar Eclipses | Lunar Eclipses

Solar Eclipses			Lunar Eclipses		
Apr 19 2004	29	♈ 49	Oct 19 2013	25	♈ 45
Apr 20 2023	29	♈ 50	Oct 18 2032	25	♈ 57
Apr 20 2042	00	♉ 09	Oct 19 2051	26	♈ 21
Apr 20 2061	00	♉ 34	Oct 19 2070	26	♈ 44
Apr 21 2069	01	♉ 54	Oct 21 2078	28	♈ 07
Apr 21 2088	02	♉ 19	Oct 21 2097	28	♈ 27
Apr 22 2107	02	♉ 32	Oct 21 2116	28	♈ 29
Apr 22 2126	02	♉ 26	Oct 21 2135	28	♈ 14
Apr 26 1892	07	♉ 05	Oct 27 1901	03	♉ 30
Apr 28 1911	07	♉ 30	Oct 27 1920	03	♉ 51
Apr 28 1930	07	♉ 45	Oct 28 1939	03	♉ 56
Apr 28 1949	07	♉ 41	Oct 27 1958	03	♉ 42
Apr 30 1957	09	♉ 23	Oct 29 1966	05	♉ 32
Apr 29 1976	09	♉ 14	Oct 28 1985	05	♉ 14
Apr 29 1995	08	♉ 56	Oct 28 2004	05	♉ 02
Apr 29 2014	08	♉ 51	Oct 28 2023	05	♉ 08
			Oct 28 2042	05	♉ 30
Apr 30 2022	10	♉ 29	Oct 30 2031	06	♉ 41
Apr 30 2041	10	♉ 30	Oct 30 2050	06	♉ 54
Apr 30 2060	10	♉ 50	Oct 30 2069	07	♉ 18
May 1 2079	11	♉ 15	Oct 30 2088	07	♉ 40
May 7 1845	15	♉ 42	Nov 4 1854	12	♉ 09
May 7 1864	15	♉ 42	Nov 4 1873	12	♉ 19
May 7 1883	15	♉ 59	Nov 4 1892	12	♉ 43
May 7 1902	16	♉ 24	Nov 6 1911	13	♉ 06
May 9 1910	17	♉ 43	Nov 8 1919	14	♉ 31
May 9 1929	18	♉ 07	Nov 7 1938	14	♉ 51
May 9 1948	18	♉ 22	Nov 7 1957	14	♉ 55
May 9 1967	18	♉ 17	Nov 7 1976	14	♉ 40
May 11 1975	19	♉ 59	Nov 8 1984	16	♉ 30
May 10 1994	19	♉ 48	Nov 9 2003	16	♉ 12
May 10 2013	19	♉ 31	Nov 8 2022	16	♉ 00
May 9 2032	19	♉ 28	Nov 8 2041	16	♉ 08
			Nov 8 2060	16	♉ 30
May 11 2040	21	♉ 04	Nov 9 2049	17	♉ 41
May 11 2059	21	♉ 08	Nov 9 2068	17	♉ 54
May 11 2078	21	♉ 28	Nov 10 2087	18	♉ 18
May 11 2097	21	♉ 52	Nov 11 2106	18	♉ 41
May 17 1863	26	♉ 15	Nov 15 1872	23	♉ 11
May 17 1882	26	♉ 16	Nov 16 1891	23	♉ 22
May 18 1901	26	♉ 34	Nov 17 1910	23	♉ 46
May 18 1920	26	♉ 59	Nov 17 1929	24	♉ 09
May 19 1928	28	♉ 18	Nov 18 1937	25	♉ 35
May 20 1947	28	♉ 42	Nov 18 1956	25	♉ 55
May 20 1966	28	♉ 55	Nov 18 1975	25	♉ 57
May 19 1985	28	♉ 50	Nov 18 1994	25	♉ 41

Scorpio Eclipses in Metonic Cycle Groups

Solar Eclipses | Lunar Eclipses

Solar Eclipses			Lunar Eclipses		
			Apr 25 2013	05	♏ 46
Oct 25 2022	02	♏ 01	Apr 25 2032	05	♏ 58
Oct 25 2041	02	♏ 01	Apr 26 2051	05	♏ 49
Oct 24 2060	01	♏ 44	Apr 25 2070	05	♏ 32
Oct 24 2079	01	♏ 30			
Oct 30 1826	07	♏ 07	May 1 1836	10	♏ 56
Oct 30 1845	07	♏ 27	May 2 1855	11	♏ 10
Oct 30 1864	07	♏ 29	May 1 1874	11	♏ 04
Oct 30 1883	07	♏ 14	Apr 30 1893	10	♏ 47
Oct 31 1902	06	♏ 58			
			May 3 1901	12	♏ 36
Nov 2 1910	08	♏ 47	May 3 1920	12	♏ 19
Nov 1 1929	08	♏ 36	May 3 1939	12	♏ 17
Nov 1 1948	08	♏ 44	May 3 1958	12	♏ 33
Nov 2 1967	09	♏ 07			
			May 4 1966	13	♏ 56
Nov 3 1975	10	♏ 30	May 4 1985	14	♏ 16
Nov 3 1994	10	♏ 54	May 4 2004	14	♏ 41
Nov 3 2013	10	♏ 16	May 5 2023	14	♏ 57
Nov 3 2032	10	♏ 21			
			May 7 2031	16	♏ 25
Nov 4 2040	12	♏ 59	May 6 2050	16	♏ 35
Nov 5 2059	12	♏ 58	May 6 2069	16	♏ 26
Nov 4 2078	12	♏ 40	May 5 2088	16	♏ 09
Nov 4 2097	12	♏ 27			
Nov 10 1844	18	♏ 08	May 12 1854	21	♏ 32
Nov 10 1863	18	♏ 28	May 12 1873	21	♏ 45
Nov 10 1882	18	♏ 13	May 12 1892	21	♏ 39
Nov 11 1901	18	♏ 13	May 13 1911	21	♏ 21
Nov 10 1920	17	♏ 58			
			May 15 1919	23	♏ 09
Nov 12 1928	19	♏ 47	May 14 1938	22	♏ 53
Nov 12 1947	19	♏ 36	May 13 1957	22	♏ 52
Nov 12 1966	19	♏ 45	May 13 1976	23	♏ 09
Nov 12 1985	20	♏ 08			
			May 15 1984	24	♏ 31
Nov 13 1993	21	♏ 32	May 16 2003	24	♏ 52
Nov 13 2012	21	♏ 57	May 16 2022	25	♏ 17
Nov 14 2031	22	♏ 17	May 16 2041	25	♏ 32
Nov 14 2050	22	♏ 22			
			May 17 2049	27	♏ 00
Nov 16 2058	24	♏ 01	May 17 2068	27	♏ 10
Nov 15 2077	23	♏ 59	May 17 2087	27	♏ 00
Nov 15 2096	23	♏ 40	May 17 2106	26	♏ 43
Nov 15 2115	23	♏ 27	May 17 2125	26	♏ 39
Nov 15 2134	23	♏ 34			
Nov 21 1862	29	♏ 15	May 22 1872	02	♐ 09
Nov 21 1881	29	♏ 33	May 24 1891	02	♐ 17
Nov 22 1900	29	♏ 34	May 24 1910	02	♐ 09
Nov 22 1919	29	♏ 17	May 23 1929	01	♐ 52
Nov 21 1938	29	♏ 01			

Gemini Eclipses in Metonic Cycle Groups

Solar Eclipses				Lunar Eclipses			
May 21 1993	00	♊	32	Nov 20 2002	27	♉	33
May 20 2012	00	♊	21	Nov 19 2021	27	♉	14
May 21 2031	00	♊	04	Nov 18 2040	27	♉	03
May 20 2050	00	♊	02	Nov 19 2059	27	♉	11
May 20 2069	00	♊	19	Nov 19 2078	27	♉	34

Solar Eclipses				Lunar Eclipses			
May 22 2058	01	♊	37	Nov 21 2067	28	♉	43
May 22 2077	01	♊	41	Nov 20 2086	28	♉	58
May 22 2096	02	♊	02	Nov 21 2105	29	♉	23
May 24 2115	02	♊	27	Nov 21 2124	29	♉	45
May 23 2134	02	♊	43				

Solar Eclipses				Lunar Eclipses			
May 27 1881	06	♊	47	Nov 26 1890	04	♊	16
May 28 1900	06	♊	47	Nov 27 1909	04	♊	29
May 29 1919	07	♊	06	Nov 27 1928	04	♊	53
May 29 1938	07	♊	31	Nov 28 1947	05	♊	15

Solar Eclipses				Lunar Eclipses			
May 30 1946	08	♊	49	Nov 29 1955	06	♊	42
May 30 1965	09	♊	13	Nov 29 1974	07	♊	01
May 30 1984	09	♊	26	Nov 29 1993	07	♊	03
May 31 2003	09	♊	19	Nov 28 2012	06	♊	46

Solar Eclipses				Lunar Eclipses			
Jun 1 2011	10	♊	02	Nov 30 2020	08	♊	38
Jun 1 2030	10	♊	50	Nov 30 2039	08	♊	19
May 31 2049	10	♊	34	Nov 30 2058	08	♊	08
May 31 2068	10	♊	33	Nov 29 2077	08	♊	18
Jun 1 2087	10	♊	51	Nov 29 2096	08	♊	41

Solar Eclipses				Lunar Eclipses			
Jun 8 1899	17	♊	13	Dec 7 1908	15	♊	25
Jun 8 1918	17	♊	16	Dec 8 1927	15	♊	38
Jun 8 1937	17	♊	36	Dec 8 1946	16	♊	02
Jun 8 1956	18	♊	01	Dec 8 1965	16	♊	24

Solar Eclipses				Lunar Eclipses			
Jun 10 1964	19	♊	19	Dec 10 1973	17	♊	51
Jun 11 1983	19	♊	43	Dec 10 1992	18	♊	10
Jun 10 2002	19	♊	54	Dec 10 2011	18	♊	10
Jun 10 2021	19	♊	47	Dec 9 2030	17	♊	53

Solar Eclipses				Lunar Eclipses			
Jun 12 2029	21	♊	30	Dec 11 2038	19	♊	46
Jun 11 2048	21	♊	17	Dec 11 2057	19	♊	27
Jun 11 2067	21	♊	02	Dec 10 2076	19	♊	17
Jun 11 2086	21	♊	02	Dec 11 2095	19	♊	27

Solar Eclipses				Lunar Eclipses			
				Dec 17 1842	25	♊	03
Jun 17 1852	26	♊	34	Dec 17 1861	25	♊	26
Jun 17 1871	26	♊	23	Dec 17 1880	25	♊	08
Jun 17 1890	26	♊	06	Dec 17 1899	24	♊	56
Jun 17 1909	26	♊	04	Dec 17 1918	25	♊	03
Jun 17 1928	26	♊	21				

Solar Eclipses				Lunar Eclipses			
Jun 19 1917	27	♊	39	Dec 19 1926	26	♊	35
Jun 19 1936	27	♊	44	Dec 19 1945	26	♊	49
Jun 20 1955	28	♊	05	Dec 19 1964	27	♊	14
Jun 20 1974	28	♊	30	Dec 20 1983	27	♊	35

Solar Eclipses				Lunar Eclipses			
Jun 21 1982	29	♊	47	Dec 21 1991	29	♊	03
Jun 21 2001	00	♋	11	Dec 21 2010	29	♊	20
Jun 21 2020	00	♋	21	Dec 20 2029	29	♊	20
Jun 21 2039	00	♋	12	Dec 20 2048	29	♊	02
Jun 21 2058	29	♊	56				

Sagittarius Eclipses in Metonic Cycle Groups

Solar Eclipses				Lunar Eclipses			
				May 25 1937	03	♐	40
Nov 23 1946	00	♐	50	May 24 1956	03	♐	24
Nov 23 1965	00	♐	40	May 25 1975	03	♐	25
Nov 22 1984	00	♐	50	May 25 1994	03	♐	42
Nov 23 2003	01	♐	14	May 25 2013	04	♐	07

Solar Eclipses				Lunar Eclipses			
				May 26 2002	05	♐	04
Nov 25 2011	02	♐	37	May 26 2021	05	♐	25
Nov 25 2030	03	♐	02	May 26 2040	05	♐	50
Nov 25 2049	03	♐	23	May 27 2059	06	♐	04
Nov 24 2068	03	♐	26				

Solar Eclipses				Lunar Eclipses			
				May 28 2067	07	♐	33
Nov 26 2076	05	♐	06	May 28 2086	07	♐	41
Nov 27 2095	05	♐	03	May 28 2105	07	♐	31
Nov 26 2114	04	♐	44	May 28 2124	07	♐	14
Nov 26 2133	04	♐	32	May 28 2143	07	♐	12
Nov 26 2152	04	♐	39				

Solar Eclipses				Lunar Eclipses			
Dec 3 1880	10	♐	23	Jun 4 1890	12	♐	35
Dec 3 1899	10	♐	41	Jun 4 1909	12	♐	46
Dec 3 1918	10	♐	40	Jun 3 1928	12	♐	38
Dec 2 1937	10	♐	22	Jun 3 1947	12	♐	21
Dec 2 1956	10	♐	08				

Solar Eclipses				Lunar Eclipses			
				Jun 5 1955	14	♐	08
Dec 4 1964	11	♐	56	Jun 4 1974	13	♐	53
Dec 4 1983	11	♐	47	Jun 4 1993	13	♐	54
Dec 4 2002	11	♐	58	Jun 4 2012	14	♐	13
Dec 4 2021	12	♐	21	Jun 5 2031	14	♐	38

Solar Eclipses				Lunar Eclipses			
				Jun 5 2020	15	♐	34
Dec 5 2029	13	♐	46	Jun 6 2039	15	♐	56
Dec 5 2048	14	♐	11	Jun 6 2058	16	♐	20
Dec 6 2067	14	♐	31	Jun 6 2077	16	♐	33
Dec 6 2086	14	♐	33				

Solar Eclipses				Lunar Eclipses			
				Jun 12 1843	20	♐	37
Dec 12 1852	19	♐	20	Jun 12 1862	20	♐	58
Dec 12 1871	19	♐	44	Jun 12 1881	21	♐	23
Dec 12 1890	20	♐	11	Jun 13 1900	21	♐	38
Dec 12 1909	20	♐	11				

Solar Eclipses				Lunar Eclipses			
				Jun 14 1908	23	♐	04
Dec 14 1917	21	♐	50	Jun 15 1927	23	♐	14
Dec 13 1936	21	♐	49	Jun 14 1946	23	♐	04
Dec 14 1955	21	♐	31	Jun 14 1965	22	♐	47
Dec 13 1974	21	♐	16	Jun 13 1984	22	♐	44

Solar Eclipses				Lunar Eclipses			
				Jun 15 1973	24	♐	35
Dec 15 1982	23	♐	05	Jun 15 1992	24	♐	20
Dec 14 2001	22	♐	56	Jun 15 2011	24	♐	23
Dec 14 2020	23	♐	08	Jun 15 2030	24	♐	42
Dec 15 2039	23	♐	32	Jun 15 2049	25	♐	07

Solar Eclipses				Lunar Eclipses			
				Jun 17 2038	26	♐	02
Dec 16 2047	24	♐	56	Jun 17 2057	26	♐	25
Dec 17 2066	25	♐	22	Jun 17 2076	26	♐	49
Dec 16 2085	25	♐	41	Jun 17 2095	27	♐	01
Dec 17 2104	25	♐	42				

Cancer Eclipses in Metonic Cycle Groups

Solar Eclipses / Lunar Eclipses

Solar Eclipses				Lunar Eclipses			
Jun 23 2047	01	♋	56	Dec 22 2056	00	♋	55
Jun 22 2066	01	♋	43	Dec 22 2075	00	♋	36
Jun 22 2085	01	♋	28	Dec 21 2094	00	♋	27
Jun 22 2104	01	♋	30	Dec 22 2113	00	♋	38
Jun 23 2123	01	♋	49				
Jun 28 1870	06	♋	59	Dec 28 1879	06	♋	36
Jun 28 1899	06	♋	47	Dec 27 1898	06	♋	18
Jun 28 1908	06	♋	32	Dec 28 1917	06	♋	06
Jun 29 1927	06	♋	31	Dec 28 1936	06	♋	15
Jun 29 1946	06	♋	48				
Jun 30 1935	08	♋	5	Dec 29 1944	07	♋	47
Jun 30 1954	08	♋	10	Dec 30 1963	08	♋	01
Jun 30 1973	08	♋	32	Dec 30 1982	08	♋	26
Jun 30 1992	08	♋	56	Dec 30 2001	08	♋	47
Jul 1 2011	09	♋	12				
Jul 1 2000	10	♋	15	Dec 31 2009	10	♋	15
Jul 2 2019	10	♋	38	Dec 31 2028	10	♋	32
Jul 2 2038	10	♋	47	Jan 1 2048	10	♋	30
Jul 1 2057	10	♋	38	Dec 31 2066	10	♋	13
Jul 1 2076	10	♋	21				
Jul 3 2065	12	♋	22	Jan 2 2075	12	♋	06
Jul 3 2084	12	♋	08	Jan 2 2094	11	♋	46
Jul 4 2103	11	♋	54	Jan 1 2113	11	♋	32
Jul 4 2122	11	♋	56	Jan 1 2132	11	♋	50
Jul 9 1907	17	♋	24	Jan 8 1898	17	♋	48
Jul 10 1907	17	♋	12	Jan 8 1917	17	♋	29
Jul 9 1926	16	♋	57	Jan 8 1936	17	♋	18
Jul 9 1945	16	♋	57	Jan 8 1955	17	♋	27
Jul 9 1964	17	♋	15				
Jul 11 1953	18	♋	30	Jan 10 1963	18	♋	59
Jul 10 1972	18	♋	37	Jan 9 1982	19	♋	14
Jul 11 1991	18	♋	59	Jan 9 2001	19	♋	38
Jul 11 2010	19	♋	24	Jan 10 2020	19	♋	59
Jul 11 2029	19	♋	37				
Jul 13 2018	20	♋	42	Jan 12 2028	21	♋	27
Jul 13 2037	21	♋	4	Jan 12 2047	21	♋	44
Jul 12 2056	21	♋	13	Jan 11 2066	21	♋	41
Jul 13 2075	21	♋	2	Jan 10 2085	21	♋	23
Jul 12 2094	20	♋	46				
				Jan 17 1850	27	♋	03
Jul 19 1860	26	♋	6	Jan 17 1870	27	♋	21
Jul 19 1879	26	♋	17	Jan 17 1889	27	♋	22
Jul 18 1898	26	♋	7	Jan 18 1908	27	♋	04
Jul 19 1917	25	♋	51				
Jul 21 1906	27	♋	50	Jan 20 1916	28	♋	58
Jul 20 1925	27	♋	37	Jan 19 1935	28	♋	39
Jul 20 1944	27	♋	22	Jan 19 1954	28	♋	29
Jul 20 1963	27	♋	24	Jan 18 1973	28	♋	39
Jul 20 1982	27	♋	43				
Jul 22 1971	28	♋	56	Jan 20 1981	00	♌	10
Jul 22 1990	29	♋	4	Jan 21 2000	00	♌	26
Jul 22 2009	29	♋	27	Jan 21 2019	00	♌	51
Jul 22 2028	29	♋	51	Jan 21 2038	01	♌	11
Jul 22 2047	00	♌	4				

Capricorn Eclipses in Metonic Cycle Groups

Solar Eclipses / Lunar Eclipses

Solar Eclipses				Lunar Eclipses			
				Jun 22 1861	01	♑	03
Dec 22 1870	00	♑	31	Jun 22 1880	01	♑	26
Dec 22 1889	00	♑	56	Jun 24 1899	01	♑	51
Dec 23 1908	01	♑	17	Jun 24 1918	02	♑	05
Dec 24 1927	01	♑	21				
Dec 24 1916	02	♑	45	Jun 25 1926	03	♑	31
Dec 25 1935	03	♑	02	Jun 25 1945	03	♑	40
Dec 25 1954	02	♑	59	Jun 25 1964	03	♑	30
Dec 24 1973	02	♑	40	Jun 25 1983	03	♑	13
Dec 24 1992	02	♑	27	Jun 24 2002	03	♑	10
				Jun 27 1991	05	♑	00
Dec 25 2000	04	♑	15	Jun 26 2010	04	♑	46
Dec 26 2019	04	♑	07	Jun 26 2029	04	♑	49
Dec 26 2038	04	♑	20	Jun 26 2048	05	♑	10
Dec 26 2057	04	♑	44	Jun 27 2067	05	♑	35
Dec 27 2065	06	♑	08	Jun 27 2056	06	♑	29
Dec 27 2084	06	♑	34	Jun 28 2075	06	♑	53
Dec 28 2103	06	♑	52	Jun 28 2094	07	♑	17
Dec 28 2122	06	♑	52	Jun 29 2113	07	♑	28
				Jul 4 1879	11	♑	30
Jan 1 1889	11	♑	44	Jul 4 1898	12	♑	52
Jan 3 1908	12	♑	8	Jul 4 1917	12	♑	17
Jan 3 1927	12	♑	29	Jul 4 1936	12	♑	30
Jan 3 1946	12	♑	32				
Jan 5 1935	13	♑	58	Jul 6 1944	13	♑	58
Jan 5 1954	14	♑	14	Jul 6 1963	14	♑	06
Jan 4 1973	14	♑	10	Jul 6 1982	13	♑	54
Jan 4 1992	13	♑	51	Jul 5 2001	13	♑	38
Jan 4 2011	13	♑	38	Jul 5 2020	13	♑	37
				Jul 7 2009	15	♑	24
Jan 6 2019	15	♑	26	Jul 6 2028	15	♑	11
Jan 5 2038	15	♑	19	Jul 7 2047	15	♑	16
Jan 5 2057	15	♑	32	Jul 7 2066	15	♑	37
Jan 6 2076	15	♑	57	Jul 7 2085	16	♑	02
				Jul 12 1832	20	♑	28
Jan 11 1842	20	♑	14	Jul 13 1851	20	♑	14
Jan 10 1861	20	♑	14	Jul 12 1870	21	♑	17
Jan 11 1880	21	♑	09	Jul 12 1889	20	♑	36
Jan 11 1899	21	♑	33	Jul 13 1908	21	♑	01
Jan 14 1907	22	♑	56	Jul 15 1916	22	♑	20
Jan 14 1926	23	♑	21	Jul 16 1935	22	♑	44
Jan 14 1945	23	♑	41	Jul 16 1954	22	♑	56
Jan 14 1964	23	♑	43	Jul 15 1973	22	♑	50
				Jul 17 1962	24	♑	25
Jan 16 1972	25	♑	25	Jul 17 1981	24	♑	31
Jan 15 1991	25	♑	20	Jul 16 2000	24	♑	19
Jan 15 2010	25	♑	01	Jul 16 2019	24	♑	03
Jan 14 2029	24	♑	50	Jul 16 2038	24	♑	03
				Jul 18 2027	25	♑	49
Jan 16 2037	26	♑	36	Jul 18 2046	25	♑	37
Jan 16 2056	26	♑	30	Jul 17 2065	25	♑	43
Jan 16 2075	26	♑	45	Jul 17 2084	26	♑	04
Jan 16 2094	27	♑	09				

Leo Eclipses in Metonic Cycle Groups

Solar Eclipses
Jul 23 2036	01 ♌ 10
Jul 24 2055	01 ♌ 32
Jul 24 2074	01 ♌ 39
Jul 23 2093	01 ♌ 27
Jul 29 1859	06 ♌ 11
Jul 29 1878	06 ♌ 34
Jul 29 1897	06 ♌ 43
Jul 30 1916	06 ♌ 34
Jul 30 1935	06 ♌ 17
Jul 31 1924	08 ♌ 17
Aug 1 1943	08 ♌ 03
Jul 31 1962	07 ♌ 49
Jul 31 1981	07 ♌ 51
Jul 31 2000	08 ♌ 11
Aug 1 2008	09 ♌ 32
Aug 2 2027	09 ♌ 55
Aug 2 2046	10 ♌ 19
Aug 2 2065	10 ♌ 31
Aug 3 2054	11 ♌ 39
Aug 3 2073	12 ♌ 00
Aug 3 2092	12 ♌ 06
Aug 4 2111	11 ♌ 54
Aug 10 1877	16 ♌ 41
Aug 9 1896	17 ♌ 03
Aug 10 1915	17 ♌ 12
Aug 10 1934	17 ♌ 01
Aug 9 1953	16 ♌ 45
Aug 12 1942	18 ♌ 46
Aug 11 1961	18 ♌ 31
Aug 10 1980	18 ♌ 17
Aug 11 1999	18 ♌ 21
Aug 11 2018	18 ♌ 41
Aug 12 2026	20 ♌ 02
Aug 12 2045	20 ♌ 26
Aug 12 2064	20 ♌ 49
Aug 13 2083	21 ♌ 01
Aug 18 1849	25 ♌ 06
Aug 18 1868	25 ♌ 29
Aug 19 1887	25 ♌ 53
Aug 20 1906	26 ♌ 06
Aug 20 1895	27 ♌ 14
Aug 21 1914	27 ♌ 36
Aug 21 1933	27 ♌ 43
Aug 20 1952	27 ♌ 31
Aug 20 1971	27 ♌ 15
Aug 22 1979	29 ♌ 01
Aug 22 1998	28 ♌ 48
Aug 21 2017	28 ♌ 53
Aug 21 2036	29 ♌ 14

Lunar Eclipses
Jan 22 2046	02 ♌ 39
Jan 22 2065	02 ♌ 55
Jan 23 2084	02 ♌ 51
Jan 23 2103	02 ♌ 33
Jan 28 1869	08 ♌ 13
Jan 28 1888	08 ♌ 32
Jan 29 1907	08 ♌ 31
Jan 28 1926	08 ♌ 13
Jan 31 1915	10 ♌ 14
Jan 30 1934	10 ♌ 07
Jan 30 1953	09 ♌ 48
Jan 30 1972	09 ♌ 39
Jan 30 1991	09 ♌ 50
Jan 31 1999	11 ♌ 20
Jan 31 2018	11 ♌ 37
Jan 31 2037	12 ♌ 02
Feb 1 2056	12 ♌ 21
Feb 2 2064	13 ♌ 50
Feb 2 2083	14 ♌ 05
Feb 2 2102	14 ♌ 01
Feb 2 2121	13 ♌ 42
Feb 8 1887	19 ♌ 22
Feb 9 1906	19 ♌ 40
Feb 8 1925	19 ♌ 38
Feb 9 1944	19 ♌ 20
Feb 10 1933	21 ♌ 22
Feb 11 1952	21 ♌ 14
Feb 10 1971	20 ♌ 55
Feb 9 1990	20 ♌ 46
Feb 9 2009	20 ♌ 59
Feb 11 2017	22 ♌ 28
Feb 11 2036	22 ♌ 45
Feb 11 2055	23 ♌ 10
Feb 11 2074	23 ♌ 29
Feb 17 1840	28 ♌ 02
Feb 17 1859	28 ♌ 17
Feb 17 1878	28 ♌ 42
Feb 17 1897	29 ♌ 03
Feb 19 1905	00 ♍ 29
Feb 20 1924	00 ♍ 46
Feb 20 1943	00 ♍ 42
Feb 19 1962	00 ♍ 24
Feb 21 1951	02 ♍ 26
Feb 21 1970	02 ♍ 18
Feb 20 1989	01 ♍ 59
Feb 21 2008	01 ♍ 52
Feb 21 2027	02 ♍ 05

Aquarius Eclipses in Metonic Cycle Groups

Solar Eclipses
Jan 23 1860	02 ♒ 17
Jan 23 1879	02 ♒ 09
Jan 23 1898	02 ♒ 21
Jan 23 1917	02 ♒ 45
Jan 24 1925	04 ♒ 08
Jan 25 1944	04 ♒ 33
Jan 25 1963	04 ♒ 52
Jan 25 1982	04 ♒ 53
Jan 26 1990	06 ♒ 35
Jan 26 2009	06 ♒ 30
Jan 26 2028	06 ♒ 11
Jan 26 2047	06 ♒ 00
Jan 27 2055	07 ♒ 46
Jan 27 2074	07 ♒ 41
Jan 27 2093	07 ♒ 56
Jan 29 2112	08 ♒ 21
Feb 2 1878	13 ♒ 25
Feb 1 1897	13 ♒ 18
Feb 3 1916	13 ♒ 31
Feb 3 1935	13 ♒ 55
Feb 4 1943	15 ♒ 18
Feb 5 1962	15 ♒ 43
Feb 4 1981	16 ♒ 01
Feb 5 2000	16 ♒ 01
Feb 7 2008	17 ♒ 45
Feb 6 2027	17 ♒ 38
Feb 5 2046	17 ♒ 18
Feb 5 2065	17 ♒ 09
Feb 7 2073	18 ♒ 53
Feb 7 2092	18 ♒ 50
Feb 8 2111	18 ♒ 50
Feb 8 2130	19 ♒ 30
Feb 13 1896	24 ♒ 31
Feb 14 1915	24 ♒ 25
Feb 14 1934	24 ♒ 38
Feb 14 1953	25 ♒ 03
Feb 15 1961	26 ♒ 26
Feb 16 1980	26 ♒ 50
Feb 16 1999	27 ♒ 08
Feb 15 2018	27 ♒ 07
Feb 17 2026	28 ♒ 50
Feb 16 2045	28 ♒ 43
Feb 17 2064	28 ♒ 24
Feb 16 2083	28 ♒ 15

Lunar Eclipses
Jul 24 1850	00 ♒ 53
Jul 23 1869	00 ♒ 40
Jul 23 1888	00 ♒ 44
Jul 25 1907	01 ♒ 04
Jul 25 1926	01 ♒ 29
Jul 26 1915	02 ♒ 25
Jul 26 1934	02 ♒ 48
Jul 26 1953	03 ♒ 12
Jul 26 1972	03 ♒ 23
Jul 26 1991	03 ♒ 15
Jul 27 1980	04 ♒ 52
Jul 28 1999	04 ♒ 58
Jul 27 2018	04 ♒ 44
Jul 27 2037	04 ♒ 29
Jul 26 2056	04 ♒ 30
Jul 28 2064	06 ♒ 03
Jul 29 2083	06 ♒ 11
Jul 30 2102	06 ♒ 33
Jul 30 2121	06 ♒ 57
Aug 3 1887	11 ♒ 07
Aug 4 1906	11 ♒ 12
Aug 4 1925	11 ♒ 33
Aug 4 1944	11 ♒ 58
Aug 5 1933	12 ♒ 53
Aug 5 1952	13 ♒ 17
Aug 6 1971	13 ♒ 41
Aug 6 1990	13 ♒ 51
Aug 6 2009	13 ♒ 42
Aug 8 1998	15 ♒ 21
Aug 7 2017	15 ♒ 25
Aug 7 2036	15 ♒ 12
Aug 7 2055	14 ♒ 57
Aug 7 2074	14 ♒ 59
Aug 8 2082	16 ♒ 31
Aug 9 2101	16 ♒ 39
Aug 9 2120	17 ♒ 02
Aug 10 2139	17 ♒ 27
Aug 15 1905	21 ♒ 37
Aug 14 1924	21 ♒ 43
Aug 15 1943	22 ♒ 04
Aug 15 1962	22 ♒ 29
Aug 17 1951	23 ♒ 25
Aug 17 1970	23 ♒ 49
Aug 17 1989	24 ♒ 12
Aug 16 2008	24 ♒ 21
Aug 17 2027	24 ♒ 11
Aug 18 2016	25 ♒ 52
Aug 19 2035	25 ♒ 55
Aug 18 2054	25 ♒ 41
Aug 17 2073	25 ♒ 26
Aug 17 2092	25 ♒ 29

Virgo Eclipses in Metonic Cycle Groups

Solar Eclipses	Lunar Eclipses
	Feb 22 2035 03 ♍ 33
Aug 23 2044 00 ♍ 35	Feb 22 2054 03 ♍ 51
Aug 24 2063 00 ♍ 58	Feb 22 2073 04 ♍ 16
Aug 24 2082 01 ♍ 22	Feb 23 2092 04 ♍ 35
Aug 24 2101 01 ♍ 32	

Solar Eclipses	Lunar Eclipses
	Feb 27 1858 09 ♍ 04
Aug 29 1867 05 ♍ 41	Feb 27 1877 09 ♍ 21
Aug 29 1886 06 ♍ 04	Feb 27 1896 09 ♍ 45
Aug 30 1905 06 ♍ 28	Mar 01 1915 10 ♍ 06
Aug 30 1924 06 ♍ 40	

Solar Eclipses	Lunar Eclipses
Aug 31 1913 07 ♍ 49	Mar 2 1904 11 ♍ 07
Aug 31 1932 08 ♍ 10	Mar 3 1923 11 ♍ 32
Sep 1 1951 08 ♍ 17	Mar 3 1942 11 ♍ 47
Aug 31 1970 08 ♍ 04	Mar 2 1961 11 ♍ 44
Aug 31 1989 07 ♍ 48	Mar 1 1980 11 ♍ 25

Solar Eclipses	Lunar Eclipses
	Mar 3 1988 13 ♍ 18
Sep 2 1997 9 ♍ 34	Mar 4 2007 12 ♍ 59
Sep 1 2016 9 ♍ 21	Mar 3 2026 12 ♍ 53
Sep 2 2035 9 ♍ 28	Mar 3 2045 13 ♍ 07
Sep 2 2054 9 ♍ 49	

Solar Eclipses	Lunar Eclipses
	Mar 4 2053 14 ♍ 35
Sep 3 2062 11 ♍ 09	Mar 4 2072 14 ♍ 54
Sep 3 2081 11 ♍ 34	Mar 5 2091 15 ♍ 19
Sep 3 2100 11 ♍ 57	Mar 6 2110 15 ♍ 37
Sep 4 2119 12 ♍ 06	

Solar Eclipses	Lunar Eclipses
	Mar 10 1876 20 ♍ 03
Sep 8 1885 16 ♍ 19	Mar 11 1895 20 ♍ 19
Sep 9 1904 16 ♍ 42	Mar 12 1914 20 ♍ 45
Sep 10 1923 17 ♍ 06	Mar 12 1933 21 ♍ 04
Sep 10 1942 17 ♍ 17	

Solar Eclipses	Lunar Eclipses
	Mar 13 1922 22 ♍ 06
Sep 12 1931 18 ♍ 28	Mar 13 1941 22 ♍ 31
Sep 12 1950 18 ♍ 49	Mar 13 1960 22 ♍ 46
Sep 11 1969 18 ♍ 53	Mar 13 1979 22 ♍ 41
Sep 11 1988 18 ♍ 40	Mar 13 1998 22 ♍ 23
Sep 11 2007 18 ♍ 24	

Solar Eclipses	Lunar Eclipses
	Mar 15 2006 24 ♍ 15
Sep 13 2015 20 ♍ 11	Mar 14 2025 23 ♍ 56
Sep 12 2034 19 ♍ 59	Mar 13 2044 23 ♍ 52
Sep 12 2053 20 ♍ 06	Mar 14 2063 24 ♍ 06
Sep 12 2072 20 ♍ 28	

Solar Eclipses	Lunar Eclipses
	Mar 16 2071 25 ♍ 33
Sep 13 2080 21 ♍ 48	Mar 16 2090 25 ♍ 53
Sep 14 2099 22 ♍ 13	Mar 17 2109 26 ♍ 18
Sep 15 2118 22 ♍ 36	Mar 17 2128 26 ♍ 35
Sep 15 2137 22 ♍ 44	

Solar Eclipses	Lunar Eclipses
	Mar 21 1894 00 ♎ 57
Sep 21 1903 27 ♍ 01	Mar 22 1913 00 ♎ 15
Sep 21 1922 27 ♍ 25	Mar 22 1932 00 ♎ 40
Sep 21 1941 27 ♍ 48	Mar 23 1951 02 ♎ 00
Sep 20 1960 27 ♍ 58	

Solar Eclipses	Lunar Eclipses
	Mar 23 1940 03 ♎ 01
	Mar 24 1959 03 ♎ 26
Sep 22 1968 29 ♍ 30	Mar 24 1978 03 ♎ 40
Sep 23 1987 29 ♍ 34	Mar 24 1997 03 ♎ 35
Sep 22 2006 29 ♍ 20	Mar 23 2016 03 ♎ 16
Sep 21 2025 29 ♍ 05	

Pisces Eclipses in Metonic Cycle Groups

Solar Eclipses	Lunar Eclipses
	Aug 24 1839 00 ♓ 58
Feb 23 1849 04 ♓ 23	Aug 24 1858 01 ♓ 04
Feb 23 1868 04 ♓ 18	Aug 23 1877 00 ♓ 51
Feb 22 1887 03 ♓ 59	Aug 23 1896 00 ♓ 36
Feb 23 1906 03 ♓ 48	Aug 24 1915 00 ♓ 37

Solar Eclipses	Lunar Eclipses
Feb 25 1914 05 ♓ 34	Aug 26 1923 02 ♓ 09
Feb 24 1933 05 ♓ 29	Aug 26 1942 02 ♓ 16
Feb 25 1952 05 ♓ 43	Aug 26 1961 02 ♓ 38
Feb 25 1971 06 ♓ 8	Aug 26 1980 03 ♓ 02

Solar Eclipses	Lunar Eclipses
	Aug 27 1969 03 ♓ 58
Feb 26 1979 07 ♓ 30	Aug 27 1988 04 ♓ 23
Feb 26 1998 07 ♓ 55	Aug 28 2007 04 ♓ 45
Feb 26 2017 08 ♓ 12	Aug 28 2026 04 ♓ 53
Feb 27 2036 08 ♓ 10	Aug 27 2045 04 ♓ 42

Solar Eclipses	Lunar Eclipses
Feb 28 2044 09 ♓ 53	Aug 29 2053 06 ♓ 28
Feb 28 2063 09 ♓ 45	Aug 28 2072 06 ♓ 12
Feb 27 2082 09 ♓ 26	Aug 29 2091 05 ♓ 59
Feb 28 2101 09 ♓ 18	Aug 29 2110 06 ♓ 03

Solar Eclipses	Lunar Eclipses
Mar 6 1867 15 ♓ 23	Sep 4 1876 11 ♓ 38
Mar 6 1886 15 ♓ 17	Sep 4 1895 11 ♓ 25
Mar 6 1905 14 ♓ 58	Sep 4 1914 11 ♓ 10
Mar 5 1924 14 ♓ 49	Sep 4 1933 11 ♓ 11

Solar Eclipses	Lunar Eclipses
Mar 7 1932 16 ♓ 33	Sep 5 1941 12 ♓ 45
Mar 7 1951 16 ♓ 29	Sep 5 1960 12 ♓ 52
Mar 7 1970 16 ♓ 44	Sep 6 1979 13 ♓ 15
Mar 7 1989 17 ♓ 09	Sep 6 1998 13 ♓ 39

Solar Eclipses	Lunar Eclipses
Mar 9 1997 18 ♓ 31	Sep 7 2006 15 ♓ 00
Mar 9 2016 18 ♓ 56	Sep 7 2025 15 ♓ 22
Mar 9 2035 19 ♓ 12	Sep 7 2044 15 ♓ 29
Mar 9 2054 19 ♓ 09	Sep 7 2063 15 ♓ 17

Solar Eclipses	Lunar Eclipses
Mar 11 2062 20 ♓ 52	Sep 9 2071 17 ♓ 03
Mar 10 2081 20 ♓ 43	Sep 8 2090 16 ♓ 48
Mar 10 2100 20 ♓ 25	Sep 9 2109 16 ♓ 34
Mar 10 2119 20 ♓ 18	Sep 9 2128 16 ♓ 40

Solar Eclipses	Lunar Eclipses
Mar 17 1904 26 ♓ 13	Sep 15 1913 22 ♓ 17
Mar 17 1923 25 ♓ 54	Sep 15 1913 22 ♓ 03
Mar 16 1942 25 ♓ 45	Sep 14 1932 21 ♓ 48
Mar 17 1904 26 ♓ 13	Sep 15 1951 21 ♓ 51

Solar Eclipses	Lunar Eclipses
Mar 18 1950 27 ♓ 28	Sep 17 1959 23 ♓ 24
Mar 18 1969 27 ♓ 25	Sep 16 1978 23 ♓ 33
Mar 18 1988 27 ♓ 42	Sep 16 1997 23 ♓ 55
Mar 19 2007 28 ♓ 06	Sep 16 2016 24 ♓ 19

Table III. Moon Families Linked with the Lunar Gestation Cycle 1927-2050.

Moon Family tables show groups of four Moon phases that follow across the page from left to right beginning with the New Moon through the Last Quarter Moon but are not found in a calendar month. These Moon phases are related to one another by their zodiacal position and are separated by nine-month intervals. Each group forms a Moon Family. The nine month separation is called the Lunar Gestation Cycle. Note how this table is different from the example of Traditional Moon Phases.

New Moon	First Quarter Moon	Full Moon	Last Quarter Moon
26-Jan-2009	25-Oct-2009	25-Jul-2010	24-Apr-2011
06° ≈ 30'	02° ≈ 44'	03° ≈ 00'	04° ≈ 34'

The dates of a Moon Family can be used to follow the major changes in a storyline or be used to project the next major event of the given story. Older Moon Families are perfect for historic studies, journal studies and any number of reflective studies.

The Moon Families cluster around Eclipses and can be found to repeat in three years from the Solar Eclipse date. A Moon Family that clusters around a Lunar Eclipse at times will repeat in three years from the Lunar Eclipse date or can precede the Lunar Eclipse by three years. Solar and Lunar Eclipses are printed in bold fonts it is with this example of a Solar Eclipse on January 26, 2009.

The quickest way to find a Moon Family is to begin with the Moon phase closest to your issue in **Table IV - Traditional Monthly Moon Phases**. Then hold that phase and its date in your mind and turn to **Table III- Moon Families with the Lunar Gestation Cycle**.

- First match the Moon phase to its corresponding column.
- Then match the date to quickly find your Moon Family.
- Read the entire row for the complete Moon family.

Investigate how the four dates that you find in that same row are embedded in your story.

If the story begins with a New Moon, it is possible there was a Solar Eclipse or New Moon near this date. Check at three year intervals. If you look nine-months before any New Moon you will find a Last Quarter Moon near the same sign and degree that shares a lineage to the New Moon (or Solar Eclipse) in your story and may have carried the seed from the past cycle into this new cycle beginning at the New Moon.

By searching through Moon families you may find a powerful Moon Family with both a Solar and Lunar eclipse at the New Moon and Full Moon phase. Another note to consider when finding a Lunar Eclipse in a Moon Family that it has a relationship to a Solar Eclipse found 9.5 years earlier or later. You can find match the Lunar Eclipse to its Solar Eclipse in **Table II. Metonic Cycle Groups**.

A note to keep in mind when matching up a New Moon Family to the next or previous family member is that Moon Families cluster around *Solar and Lunar Eclipses*. Moon Families begin breaking down when more than 6°-7° from the Solar Eclipse degree and after the Moon Family completes its second repeat of the cycle. However your storyline may continue to be recognized throughout the phases of a more distant Moon Family.

There are times when Moon Families fade out all together because the 76 to 95 year old **Metonic Cycle Group (Table II)** is coming to an end. Look for a Moon Family that begins three years before a brand new Solar Eclipse Metonic Cycle Group at a near by degree.

Moon Families - Eclipses in Bold Print

New Moon				First Quarter Moon				Full Moon				Last Quarter Moon			
3/Jan/1927	**12°**	**♑**	**28**	3/Oct/1927	09°	♑	51	2/Jul/1928	10°	♑	54	2/Apr/1929	12°	♑	4
2/Feb/1927	12°	♒	31	2/Nov/1927	09°	♒	12	1/Aug/1928	09°	♒	5	1/May/1929	11°	♒	9
3/Mar/1927	12°	♓	13	1/Dec/1927	08°	♓	54	30/Aug/1928	07°	♓	25	31/May/1929	09°	♓	41
1/Apr/1927	11°	♈	26	31/Dec/1927	08°	♈	47	29/Sep/1928	06°	♈	6	29/Jun/1929	07°	♈	51
1/May/1927	10°	♉	8	29/Jan/1928	08°	♉	39	28/Oct/1928	05°	♉	16	29/Jul/1929	05°	♉	53
30/May/1927	08°	♊	26	27/Feb/1928	08°	♊	18	**27/Nov/1928**	**04°**	**♊**	**53**	27/Aug/1929	04°	♊	2
29/Jun/1927	**06°**	**♋**	**31**	28/Mar/1928	07°	♋	33	26/Dec/1928	04°	♋	49	25/Sep/1929	02°	♋	30
28/Jul/1927	04°	♌	37	26/Apr/1928	06°	♌	23	25/Jan/1929	04°	♌	50	25/Oct/1929	01°	♌	26
27/Aug/1927	03°	♍	0	26/May/1928	04°	♍	51	23/Feb/1929	04°	♍	41	23/Nov/1929	00°	♍	53
25/Sep/1927	01°	♎	50	24/Jun/1928	03°	♎	7	25/Mar/1929	04°	♎	10	22/Dec/1929	00°	♎	47
25/Oct/1927	01°	♏	13	24/Jul/1928	01°	♏	25	23/Apr/1929	03°	♏	13	21/Jan/1930	00°	♏	54
24/Nov/1927	01°	♐	8	23/Aug/1928	29°	♏	56	**23/May/1929**	**01°**	**♐**	**53**	20/Feb/1930	00°	♐	59
23/Dec/1927	**01°**	**♑**	**21**	21/Sep/1928	28°	♐	51	21/Jun/1929	00°	♑	14	21/Mar/1930	00°	♑	46
22/Jan/1928	01°	♒	35	21/Oct/1928	28°	♑	13	21/Jul/1929	28°	♑	30	20/Apr/1930	00°	♒	4
21/Feb/1928	01°	♓	31	20/Nov/1928	28°	♒	0	20/Aug/1929	26°	♒	52	20/May/1930	28°	♒	54
21/Mar/1928	00°	♈	58	19/Dec/1928	28°	♓	1	18/Sep/1929	25°	♓	32	19/Jun/1930	27°	♓	20
20/Apr/1928	29°	♈	52	18/Jan/1929	28°	♈	4	18/Oct/1929	24°	♈	37	18/Jul/1930	25°	♈	34
19/May/1928	**28°**	**♉**	**17**	16/Feb/1929	27°	♉	52	**16/Nov/1929**	**24°**	**♉**	**10**	17/Aug/1930	23°	♉	49
17/Jun/1928	**26°**	**♊**	**21**	18/Mar/1929	27°	♊	13	16/Dec/1929	24°	♊	3	15/Sep/1930	22°	♊	17
16/Jul/1928	24°	♋	20	16/Apr/1929	26°	♋	5	14/Jan/1930	24°	♋	3	15/Oct/1930	21°	♋	7
15/Aug/1928	22°	♌	27	15/May/1929	24°	♌	30	13/Feb/1930	23°	♌	55	13/Nov/1930	20°	♌	24
13/Sep/1928	20°	♍	58	14/Jun/1929	22°	♍	39	14/Mar/1930	23°	♍	28	12/Dec/1930	20°	♍	5
13/Oct/1928	20°	♎	3	13/Jul/1929	20°	♎	44	**13/Apr/1930**	**22°**	**♎**	**34**	11/Jan/1931	20°	♎	1
12/Nov/1928	**19°**	**♏**	**46**	12/Aug/1929	19°	♏	2	12/May/1930	21°	♏	14	9/Feb/1931	19°	♏	57
12/Dec/1928	19°	♐	56	10/Sep/1929	17°	♐	43	11/Jun/1930	19°	♐	35	11/Mar/1931	19°	♐	40
10/Jan/1929	20°	♑	18	10/Oct/1929	16°	♑	56	10/Jul/1930	17°	♑	48	9/Apr/1931	19°	♑	0
9/Feb/1929	20°	♒	31	9/Nov/1929	16°	♒	42	9/Aug/1930	16°	♒	7	9/May/1931	17°	♒	55
11/Mar/1929	20°	♓	17	9/Dec/1929	16°	♓	51	7/Sep/1930	14°	♓	43	8/Jun/1931	16°	♓	29
9/Apr/1929	19°	♈	29	7/Jan/1930	17°	♈	7	**7/Oct/1930**	**13°**	**♈**	**46**	7/Jul/1931	14°	♈	52
9/May/1929	**18°**	**♉**	**7**	6/Feb/1930	17°	♉	13	6/Nov/1930	13°	♉	17	6/Aug/1931	13°	♉	13
7/Jun/1929	16°	♊	18	7/Mar/1930	16°	♊	51	5/Dec/1930	13°	♊	10	5/Sep/1931	11°	♊	45
6/Jul/1929	14°	♋	15	6/Apr/1930	15°	♋	56	4/Jan/1931	13°	♋	13	4/Oct/1931	10°	♋	37
4/Aug/1929	12°	♌	13	5/May/1930	14°	♌	27	2/Feb/1931	13°	♌	12	3/Nov/1931	09°	♌	54
3/Sep/1929	10°	♍	28	3/Jun/1930	12°	♍	33	4/Mar/1931	12°	♍	53	2/Dec/1931	09°	♍	33
2/Oct/1929	09°	♎	13	2/Jul/1930	10°	♎	30	**2/Apr/1931**	**12°**	**♎**	**7**	31/Dec/1931	09°	♎	25
1/Nov/1929	**08°**	**♏**	**35**	1/Aug/1930	08°	♏	30	2/May/1931	10°	♏	50	30/Jan/1932	09°	♏	17
30/Nov/1929	08°	♐	31	30/Aug/1930	06°	♐	51	31/May/1931	09°	♐	10	28/Feb/1932	08°	♐	57
30/Dec/1929	08°	♑	49	29/Sep/1930	05°	♑	44	29/Jun/1931	07°	♑	16	28/Mar/1932	08°	♑	14
29/Jan/1930	09°	♒	10	29/Oct/1930	05°	♒	14	29/Jul/1931	05°	♒	25	27/Apr/1932	07°	♒	7
28/Feb/1930	09°	♓	14	28/Nov/1930	05°	♓	18	27/Aug/1931	03°	♓	51	26/May/1932	05°	♓	40
30/Mar/1930	08°	♈	48	27/Dec/1930	05°	♈	42	**26/Sep/1931**	**02°**	**♈**	**44**	25/Jun/1932	04°	♈	1
28/Apr/1930	**07°**	**♉**	**45**	26/Jan/1931	06°	♉	5	26/Oct/1931	02°	♉	10	25/Jul/1932	02°	♉	21
28/May/1930	06°	♊	9	25/Feb/1931	06°	♊	7	25/Nov/1931	02°	♊	3	24/Aug/1932	00°	♊	53
26/Jun/1930	04°	♋	12	27/Mar/1931	05°	♋	34	24/Dec/1931	02°	♋	12	22/Sep/1932	29°	♊	46
25/Jul/1930	02°	♌	9	25/Apr/1931	04°	♌	23	23/Jan/1932	02°	♌	21	22/Oct/1932	29°	♋	5
23/Aug/1930	00°	♍	14	24/May/1931	02°	♍	39	21/Feb/1932	02°	♍	15	21/Nov/1932	28°	♌	48
22/Sep/1930	28°	♍	44	22/Jun/1931	00°	♎	35	**22/Mar/1932**	**01°**	**♎**	**40**	20/Dec/1932	28°	♍	46
21/Oct/1930	**27°**	**♎**	**46**	22/Jul/1931	28°	♎	26	20/Apr/1932	00°	♏	34	19/Jan/1933	28°	♎	44
20/Nov/1930	27°	♏	22	20/Aug/1931	26°	♏	29	20/May/1932	28°	♏	57	17/Feb/1933	28°	♏	28
19/Dec/1930	27°	♐	26	18/Sep/1931	24°	♐	57	18/Jun/1932	27°	♐	1	18/Mar/1933	27°	♐	49
18/Jan/1931	27°	♑	43	18/Oct/1931	24°	♑	2	17/Jul/1932	25°	♑	1	16/Apr/1933	26°	♑	42
17/Feb/1931	27°	♒	55	16/Nov/1931	23°	♒	46	16/Aug/1932	23°	♒	12	16/May/1933	25°	♒	10
19/Mar/1931	27°	♓	45	16/Dec/1931	24°	♓	1	**14/Sep/1932**	**21°**	**♓**	**48**	14/Jun/1933	23°	♓	24
17/Apr/1931	**27°**	**♈**	**2**	15/Jan/1932	24°	♈	31	14/Oct/1932	20°	♈	58	14/Jul/1933	21°	♈	34
17/May/1931	25°	♉	45	14/Feb/1932	24°	♉	51	13/Nov/1932	20°	♉	43	12/Aug/1933	19°	♉	55

Moon Families - Eclipses in Bold Print

New Moon				First Quarter Moon				Full Moon				Last Quarter Moon			
15/Jun/1931	24°	♊	0	15/Mar/1932	24°	♊	43	12/Dec/1932	20°	♊	53	11/Sep/1933	18°	♊	40
15/Jul/1931	22°	♋	2	13/Apr/1932	23°	♋	57	11/Jan/1933	21°	♋	12	11/Oct/1933	17°	♋	54
13/Aug/1931	20°	♌	6	13/May/1932	22°	♌	34	**10/Feb/1933**	**21°**	♌	**21**	10/Nov/1933	17°	♌	39
11/Sep/1931	**18°**	♍	**27**	11/Jun/1932	20°	♍	42	**11/Mar/1933**	**21°**	♍	**5**	10/Dec/1933	17°	♍	45
11/Oct/1931	**17°**	♎	**15**	10/Jul/1932	18°	♎	35	10/Apr/1933	20°	♎	13	8/Jan/1934	17°	♎	56
9/Nov/1931	16°	♏	34	9/Aug/1932	16°	♏	29	9/May/1933	18°	♏	48	7/Feb/1934	17°	♏	55
9/Dec/1931	16°	♐	22	7/Sep/1932	14°	♐	40	8/Jun/1933	16°	♐	56	8/Mar/1934	17°	♐	29
7/Jan/1932	16°	♑	28	6/Oct/1932	13°	♑	21	7/Jul/1933	14°	♑	53	6/Apr/1934	16°	♑	31
6/Feb/1932	16°	♒	37	5/Nov/1932	12°	♒	39	**5/Aug/1933**	**12°**	♒	**53**	6/May/1934	15°	♒	2
7/Mar/1932	**16°**	♓	**32**	4/Dec/1932	12°	♓	33	**4/Sep/1933**	**11°**	♓	**12**	4/Jun/1934	13°	♓	11
5/Apr/1932	16°	♈	2	3/Jan/1933	12°	♈	52	3/Oct/1933	10°	♈	1	3/Jul/1934	11°	♈	11
5/May/1932	15°	♉	0	2/Feb/1933	13°	♉	16	2/Nov/1933	09°	♉	27	2/Aug/1934	09°	♉	16
4/Jun/1932	13°	♊	30	4/Mar/1933	13°	♊	24	1/Dec/1933	09°	♊	25	31/Aug/1934	07°	♊	41
3/Jul/1932	11°	♋	43	3/Apr/1933	13°	♋	2	31/Dec/1933	09°	♋	45	30/Sep/1934	06°	♋	39
2/Aug/1932	09°	♌	51	2/May/1933	12°	♌	3	**30/Jan/1934**	**10°**	♌	**7**	30/Oct/1934	06°	♌	13
31/Aug/1932	**08°**	♍	**9**	1/Jun/1933	10°	♍	31	1/Mar/1934	10°	♍	9	29/Nov/1934	06°	♍	19
30/Sep/1932	06°	♎	50	30/Jun/1933	08°	♎	36	30/Mar/1934	09°	♎	38	28/Dec/1934	06°	♎	40
29/Oct/1932	05°	♏	59	29/Jul/1933	06°	♏	33	29/Apr/1934	08°	♏	30	27/Jan/1935	06°	♏	58
27/Nov/1932	05°	♐	35	28/Aug/1933	04°	♐	38	28/May/1934	06°	♐	50	26/Feb/1935	06°	♐	53
27/Dec/1932	05°	♑	31	26/Sep/1933	03°	♑	5	27/Jun/1934	04°	♑	51	27/Mar/1935	06°	♑	15
25/Jan/1933	05°	♒	34	25/Oct/1933	02°	♒	3	**26/Jul/1934**	**02°**	♒	**48**	25/Apr/1935	05°	♒	0
24/Feb/1933	**05°**	♓	**28**	24/Nov/1933	01°	♓	35	24/Aug/1934	00°	♓	55	25/May/1935	03°	♓	15
25/Mar/1933	05°	♈	1	23/Dec/1933	01°	♈	34	22/Sep/1934	29°	♓	27	23/Jun/1935	01°	♈	10
24/Apr/1933	04°	♉	6	22/Jan/1934	01°	♉	47	22/Oct/1934	28°	♈	31	22/Jul/1935	29°	♈	3
24/May/1933	02°	♊	46	21/Feb/1934	01°	♊	56	20/Nov/1934	28°	♉	10	20/Aug/1935	27°	♉	8
22/Jun/1933	01°	♋	7	22/Mar/1934	01°	♋	44	20/Dec/1934	28°	♊	18	19/Sep/1935	25°	♊	42
22/Jul/1933	29°	♋	21	21/Apr/1934	01°	♌	4	**19/Jan/1935**	**28°**	♋	**39**	19/Oct/1935	24°	♋	54
21/Aug/1933	**27°**	♌	**42**	21/May/1934	29°	♌	52	18/Feb/1935	28°	♌	53	17/Nov/1935	24°	♌	44
19/Sep/1933	26°	♍	20	20/Jun/1934	28°	♍	14	20/Mar/1935	28°	♍	41	17/Dec/1935	25°	♍	2
19/Oct/1933	25°	♎	23	19/Jul/1934	26°	♎	23	18/Apr/1935	27°	♎	53	16/Jan/1936	25°	♎	31
17/Nov/1933	24°	♏	53	17/Aug/1934	24°	♏	32	18/May/1935	26°	♏	32	15/Feb/1936	25°	♏	48
16/Dec/1933	24°	♐	44	16/Sep/1934	22°	♐	56	16/Jun/1935	24°	♐	44	16/Mar/1936	25°	♐	35
15/Jan/1934	24°	♑	44	15/Oct/1934	21°	♑	45	**15/Jul/1935**	**22°**	♑	**44**	14/Apr/1936	24°	♑	44
13/Feb/1934	**24°**	♒	**38**	13/Nov/1934	21°	♒	2	14/Aug/1935	20°	♒	47	14/May/1936	23°	♒	15
15/Mar/1934	24°	♓	13	13/Dec/1934	20°	♓	45	12/Sep/1935	19°	♓	7	12/Jun/1936	21°	♓	18
13/Apr/1934	23°	♈	21	11/Jan/1935	20°	♈	43	11/Oct/1935	17°	♈	55	11/Jul/1936	19°	♈	9
13/May/1934	22°	♉	2	10/Feb/1935	20°	♉	43	10/Nov/1935	17°	♉	16	9/Aug/1936	17°	♉	2
11/Jun/1934	20°	♊	25	11/Mar/1935	20°	♊	30	9/Dec/1935	17°	♊	8	7/Sep/1936	15°	♊	16
11/Jul/1934	18°	♋	41	10/Apr/1935	19°	♋	55	**8/Jan/1936**	**17°**	♋	**18**	7/Oct/1936	14°	♋	3
10/Aug/1934	**17°**	♌	**1**	10/May/1935	18°	♌	53	7/Feb/1936	17°	♌	31	5/Nov/1936	13°	♌	27
8/Sep/1934	15°	♍	38	9/Jun/1935	17°	♍	28	8/Mar/1936	17°	♍	28	5/Dec/1936	13°	♍	27
8/Oct/1934	14°	♎	38	8/Jul/1935	15°	♎	48	6/Apr/1936	16°	♎	57	4/Jan/1937	13°	♎	50
6/Nov/1934	14°	♏	5	7/Aug/1935	14°	♏	6	6/May/1936	15°	♏	53	3/Feb/1937	14°	♏	15
6/Dec/1934	13°	♐	55	5/Sep/1935	12°	♐	34	5/Jun/1936	14°	♐	21	5/Mar/1937	14°	♐	23
5/Jan/1935	**13°**	♑	**56**	5/Oct/1935	11°	♑	23	**4/Jul/1936**	**12°**	♑	**31**	3/Apr/1937	13°	♑	58
3/Feb/1935	**13°**	♒	**55**	3/Nov/1935	10°	♒	36	2/Aug/1936	10°	♒	36	3/May/1937	12°	♒	53
4/Mar/1935	13°	♓	36	3/Dec/1935	10°	♓	12	1/Sep/1936	08°	♓	52	2/Jun/1937	11°	♓	14
3/Apr/1935	12°	♈	48	1/Jan/1936	10°	♈	3	30/Sep/1936	07°	♈	30	1/Jul/1937	09°	♈	14
2/May/1935	11°	♉	32	30/Jan/1936	09°	♉	55	30/Oct/1936	06°	♉	38	30/Jul/1937	07°	♉	9
1/Jun/1935	09°	♊	53	29/Feb/1936	09°	♊	38	28/Nov/1936	06°	♊	16	28/Aug/1937	05°	♊	13
30/Jun/1935	**08°**	♋	**4**	29/Mar/1936	09°	♋	0	**27/Dec/1936**	**06°**	♋	**15**	27/Sep/1937	03°	♋	41

Moon Families - Eclipses in Bold Print

New Moon				First Quarter Moon				Full Moon				Last Quarter Moon			
30/Jul/1935	**06°**	♌	**17**	28/Apr/1936	07°	♌	59	26/Jan/1937	06°	♌	21	26/Oct/1937	02°	♌	42
28/Aug/1935	04°	♍	46	27/May/1936	06°	♍	35	25/Feb/1937	06°	♍	18	24/Nov/1937	02°	♍	18
27/Sep/1935	03°	♎	40	26/Jun/1936	04°	♎	58	26/Mar/1937	05°	♎	52	24/Dec/1937	02°	♎	22
27/Oct/1935	03°	♏	3	26/Jul/1936	03°	♏	18	25/Apr/1937	04°	♏	59	23/Jan/1938	02°	♏	40
25/Nov/1935	02°	♐	54	25/Aug/1936	01°	♐	50	**25/May/1937**	**03°**	♐	**40**	21/Feb/1938	02°	♐	54
25/Dec/1935	**03°**	♑	**1**	23/Sep/1936	00°	♑	41	23/Jun/1937	02°	♑	1	23/Mar/1938	02°	♑	44
24/Jan/1936	03°	♒	8	23/Oct/1936	29°	♑	56	23/Jul/1937	00°	♒	13	22/Apr/1938	02°	♒	1
22/Feb/1936	02°	♓	59	21/Nov/1936	29°	♒	34	21/Aug/1937	28°	♒	30	22/May/1938	00°	♓	45
22/Mar/1936	02°	♈	22	21/Dec/1936	29°	♓	27	20/Sep/1937	27°	♓	4	20/Jun/1938	29°	♓	2
21/Apr/1936	01°	♉	13	19/Jan/1937	29°	♈	21	19/Oct/1937	26°	♈	5	20/Jul/1938	27°	♈	6
20/May/1936	29°	♉	37	17/Feb/1937	29°	♉	5	**18/Nov/1937**	**25°**	♉	**34**	18/Aug/1938	25°	♉	12
19/Jun/1936	**27°**	♊	**43**	19/Mar/1937	28°	♊	28	17/Dec/1937	25°	♊	26	16/Sep/1938	23°	♊	34
18/Jul/1936	25°	♋	47	17/Apr/1937	27°	♋	24	16/Jan/1938	25°	♋	27	16/Oct/1938	22°	♋	21
16/Aug/1936	24°	♌	1	17/May/1937	25°	♌	56	14/Feb/1938	25°	♌	22	14/Nov/1938	21°	♌	38
15/Sep/1936	22°	♍	40	15/Jun/1937	24°	♍	13	16/Mar/1938	24°	♍	58	13/Dec/1938	21°	♍	23
15/Oct/1936	21°	♎	52	15/Jul/1937	22°	♎	27	14/Apr/1938	24°	♎	8	12/Jan/1939	21°	♎	26
13/Nov/1936	21°	♏	38	13/Aug/1937	20°	♏	52	**14/May/1938**	**22°**	♏	**53**	10/Feb/1939	21°	♏	32
13/Dec/1936	**21°**	♐	**48**	12/Sep/1937	19°	♐	39	12/Jun/1938	21°	♐	19	12/Mar/1939	21°	♐	25
12/Jan/1937	22°	♑	5	12/Oct/1937	18°	♑	53	12/Jul/1938	19°	♑	35	11/Apr/1939	20°	♑	52
11/Feb/1937	22°	♒	10	11/Nov/1937	18°	♒	35	11/Aug/1938	17°	♒	54	11/May/1939	19°	♒	50
12/Mar/1937	21°	♓	49	10/Dec/1937	18°	♓	35	9/Sep/1938	16°	♓	28	9/Jun/1939	18°	♓	23
11/Apr/1937	20°	♈	54	9/Jan/1938	18°	♈	40	9/Oct/1938	15°	♈	26	9/Jul/1939	16°	♈	41
10/May/1937	19°	♉	27	7/Feb/1938	18°	♉	36	**7/Nov/1938**	**14°**	♉	**51**	8/Aug/1939	14°	♉	55
8/Jun/1937	**17°**	♊	**36**	9/Mar/1938	18°	♊	7	7/Dec/1938	14°	♊	39	6/Sep/1939	13°	♊	19
7/Jul/1937	15°	♋	34	7/Apr/1938	17°	♋	8	5/Jan/1939	14°	♋	39	6/Oct/1939	12°	♋	3
6/Aug/1937	13°	♌	36	6/May/1938	15°	♌	40	4/Feb/1939	14°	♌	36	4/Nov/1939	11°	♌	12
4/Sep/1937	11°	♍	57	4/Jun/1938	13°	♍	51	5/Mar/1939	14°	♍	16	3/Dec/1939	10°	♍	47
4/Oct/1937	10°	♎	50	4/Jul/1938	11°	♎	54	3/Apr/1939	13°	♎	30	1/Jan/1940	10°	♎	38
2/Nov/1937	10°	♏	19	2/Aug/1938	10°	♏	5	**3/May/1939**	**12°**	♏	**17**	31/Jan/1940	10°	♏	35
2/Dec/1937	**10°**	♐	**22**	1/Sep/1938	08°	♐	36	1/Jun/1939	10°	♐	42	29/Feb/1940	10°	♐	22
1/Jan/1938	10°	♑	43	1/Oct/1938	07°	♑	38	1/Jul/1939	08°	♑	55	30/Mar/1940	09°	♑	48
31/Jan/1938	11°	♒	2	31/Oct/1938	07°	♒	13	31/Jul/1939	07°	♒	9	29/Apr/1940	08°	♒	50
2/Mar/1938	10°	♓	59	29/Nov/1938	07°	♓	17	29/Aug/1939	05°	♓	39	28/May/1940	07°	♓	29
31/Mar/1938	10°	♈	24	29/Dec/1938	07°	♈	35	28/Sep/1939	04°	♈	33	27/Jun/1940	05°	♈	54
30/Apr/1938	09°	♉	12	28/Jan/1939	07°	♉	48	**28/Oct/1939**	**03°**	♉	**56**	27/Jul/1940	04°	♉	15
29/May/1938	**07°**	♊	**31**	26/Feb/1939	07°	♊	38	26/Nov/1939	03°	♊	44	25/Aug/1940	02°	♊	44
27/Jun/1938	05°	♋	31	28/Mar/1939	06°	♋	55	26/Dec/1939	03°	♋	47	24/Sep/1940	01°	♋	30
26/Jul/1938	03°	♌	27	26/Apr/1939	05°	♌	37	24/Jan/1940	03°	♌	50	24/Oct/1940	00°	♌	40
25/Aug/1938	01°	♍	35	25/May/1939	03°	♍	50	23/Feb/1940	03°	♍	38	22/Nov/1940	00°	♍	14
23/Sep/1938	00°	♎	8	23/Jun/1939	01°	♎	47	**23/Mar/1940**	**03°**	♎	**1**	21/Dec/1940	00°	♎	4
23/Oct/1938	29°	♎	17	23/Jul/1939	29°	♎	43	**21/Apr/1940**	**01°**	♏	**54**	20/Jan/1941	29°	♎	58
21/Nov/1938	**29°**	♏	**1**	21/Aug/1939	27°	♏	54	21/May/1940	00°	♐	19	18/Feb/1941	29°	♏	42
21/Dec/1938	29°	♐	13	20/Sep/1939	26°	♐	33	19/Jun/1940	28°	♐	28	19/Mar/1941	29°	♐	6
20/Jan/1939	29°	♑	36	19/Oct/1939	25°	♑	50	19/Jul/1940	26°	♑	33	18/Apr/1941	28°	♑	5
19/Feb/1939	29°	♒	48	18/Nov/1939	25°	♒	43	17/Aug/1940	24°	♒	50	17/May/1941	26°	♒	42
20/Mar/1939	29°	♓	33	18/Dec/1939	26°	♓	3	16/Sep/1940	23°	♓	33	16/Jun/1941	25°	♓	4
19/Apr/1939	**28°**	♈	**43**	17/Jan/1940	26°	♈	30	**16/Oct/1940**	**22°**	♈	**49**	16/Jul/1941	23°	♈	23
18/May/1939	27°	♉	18	16/Feb/1940	26°	♉	42	14/Nov/1940	22°	♉	34	14/Aug/1941	21°	♉	49
17/Jun/1939	25°	♊	27	16/Mar/1940	26°	♊	23	14/Dec/1940	22°	♊	41	13/Sep/1941	20°	♊	35
16/Jul/1939	23°	♋	24	15/Apr/1940	25°	♋	26	13/Jan/1941	22°	♋	53	13/Oct/1941	19°	♋	47
14/Aug/1939	21°	♌	25	14/May/1940	23°	♌	52	11/Feb/1941	22°	♌	54	11/Nov/1941	19°	♌	25

Moon Families - Eclipses in Bold Print

New Moon				First Quarter Moon				Full Moon				Last Quarter Moon			
13/Sep/1939	19°	♍	46	12/Jun/1940	21°	♍	54	**13/Mar/1941**	**22°**	**♍**	**30**	11/Dec/1941	19°	♍	21
12/Oct/1939	**18°**	**♎**	**36**	12/Jul/1940	19°	♎	44	11/Apr/1941	21°	♎	34	10/Jan/1942	19°	♎	22
11/Nov/1939	18°	♏	1	10/Aug/1940	17°	♏	41	11/May/1941	20°	♏	7	8/Feb/1942	19°	♏	13
10/Dec/1939	17°	♐	56	8/Sep/1940	15°	♐	58	9/Jun/1941	18°	♐	15	9/Mar/1942	18°	♐	42
9/Jan/1940	18°	♑	9	8/Oct/1940	14°	♑	49	8/Jul/1941	16°	♑	14	7/Apr/1942	17°	♑	43
8/Feb/1940	18°	♒	24	6/Nov/1940	14°	♒	19	7/Aug/1941	14°	♒	19	7/May/1942	16°	♒	17
8/Mar/1940	18°	♓	22	6/Dec/1940	14°	♓	24	**5/Sep/1941**	**12°**	**♓**	**44**	5/Jun/1942	14°	♓	33
7/Apr/1940	**17°**	**♈**	**51**	5/Jan/1941	14°	♈	51	5/Oct/1941	11°	♈	42	5/Jul/1942	12°	♈	42
7/May/1940	16°	♉	46	4/Feb/1941	15°	♉	17	3/Nov/1941	11°	♉	15	3/Aug/1942	10°	♉	57
5/Jun/1940	15°	♊	10	6/Mar/1941	15°	♊	21	3/Dec/1941	11°	♊	19	2/Sep/1942	09°	♊	31
5/Jul/1940	13°	♋	15	4/Apr/1941	14°	♋	49	2/Jan/1942	11°	♋	37	2/Oct/1942	08°	♋	35
3/Aug/1940	11°	♌	17	4/May/1941	13°	♌	39	1/Feb/1942	11°	♌	53	1/Nov/1942	08°	♌	11
1/Sep/1940	09°	♍	32	2/Jun/1941	11°	♍	56	**2/Mar/1942**	**11°**	**♍**	**47**	30/Nov/1942	08°	♍	13
1/Oct/1940	**08°**	**♎**	**10**	1/Jul/1941	09°	♎	53	1/Apr/1942	11°	♎	8	30/Dec/1942	08°	♎	26
30/Oct/1940	07°	♏	20	31/Jul/1941	07°	♏	45	30/Apr/1942	09°	♏	54	29/Jan/1943	08°	♏	33
29/Nov/1940	06°	♐	59	29/Aug/1941	05°	♐	49	30/May/1942	08°	♐	10	27/Feb/1943	08°	♐	17
28/Dec/1940	07°	♑	0	27/Sep/1941	04°	♑	18	28/Jun/1942	06°	♑	9	28/Mar/1943	07°	♑	30
27/Jan/1941	07°	♒	8	27/Oct/1941	03°	♒	23	27/Jul/1942	04°	♒	6	27/Apr/1943	06°	♒	10
25/Feb/1941	07°	♓	8	25/Nov/1941	03°	♓	5	**25/Aug/1942**	**02°**	**♓**	**16**	26/May/1943	04°	♓	25
27/Mar/1941	**06°**	**♈**	**46**	25/Dec/1941	03°	♈	16	24/Sep/1942	00°	♈	54	24/Jun/1943	02°	♈	25
26/Apr/1941	05°	♉	54	24/Jan/1942	03°	♉	39	23/Oct/1942	00°	♉	7	23/Jul/1943	00°	♉	25
26/May/1941	04°	♊	33	22/Feb/1942	03°	♊	53	22/Nov/1942	29°	♉	54	22/Aug/1943	28°	♉	40
24/Jun/1941	02°	♋	51	24/Mar/1942	03°	♋	42	22/Dec/1942	00°	♋	8	21/Sep/1943	27°	♊	25
24/Jul/1941	01°	♌	0	23/Apr/1942	02°	♌	56	21/Jan/1943	00°	♌	31	20/Oct/1943	26°	♋	47
22/Aug/1941	29°	♌	14	23/May/1942	01°	♍	36	**20/Feb/1943**	**00°**	**♍**	**42**	19/Nov/1943	26°	♌	43
20/Sep/1941	**27°**	**♍**	**48**	21/Jun/1942	29°	♍	49	21/Mar/1943	00°	♎	25	19/Dec/1943	27°	♍	3
20/Oct/1941	26°	♎	47	21/Jul/1942	27°	♎	48	20/Apr/1943	29°	♎	29	18/Jan/1944	27°	♎	25
18/Nov/1941	26°	♏	16	19/Aug/1942	25°	♏	50	19/May/1943	28°	♏	0	17/Feb/1944	27°	♏	31
18/Dec/1941	26°	♐	7	17/Sep/1942	24°	♐	9	18/Jun/1943	26°	♐	6	17/Mar/1944	27°	♐	6
16/Jan/1942	26°	♑	8	16/Oct/1942	22°	♑	56	17/Jul/1943	24°	♑	2	15/Apr/1944	26°	♑	4
15/Feb/1942	26°	♒	6	15/Nov/1942	22°	♒	17	**15/Aug/1943**	**22°**	**♒**	**5**	15/May/1944	24°	♒	28
16/Mar/1942	**25°**	**♓**	**45**	14/Dec/1942	22°	♓	7	13/Sep/1943	20°	♓	27	13/Jun/1944	22°	♓	28
15/Apr/1942	24°	♈	59	13/Jan/1943	22°	♈	15	13/Oct/1943	19°	♈	20	12/Jul/1944	20°	♈	19
15/May/1942	23°	♉	45	11/Feb/1943	22°	♉	25	11/Nov/1943	18°	♉	47	10/Aug/1944	18°	♉	17
13/Jun/1942	22°	♊	11	13/Mar/1943	22°	♊	21	11/Dec/1943	18°	♊	45	9/Sep/1944	16°	♊	39
13/Jul/1942	20°	♋	27	12/Apr/1943	21°	♋	49	10/Jan/1944	19°	♋	3	8/Oct/1944	15°	♋	37
11/Aug/1942	**18°**	**♌**	**45**	12/May/1943	20°	♌	48	**9/Feb/1944**	**19°**	**♌**	**21**	7/Nov/1944	15°	♌	14
10/Sep/1942	**17°**	**♍**	**17**	10/Jun/1943	19°	♍	18	9/Mar/1944	19°	♍	19	7/Dec/1944	15°	♍	24
9/Oct/1942	16°	♎	13	10/Jul/1943	17°	♎	32	8/Apr/1944	18°	♎	44	6/Jan/1945	15°	♎	51
8/Nov/1942	15°	♏	35	8/Aug/1943	15°	♏	41	8/May/1944	17°	♏	34	5/Feb/1945	16°	♏	14
7/Dec/1942	15°	♐	20	7/Sep/1943	14°	♐	0	6/Jun/1944	15°	♐	54	6/Mar/1945	16°	♐	14
6/Jan/1943	15°	♑	19	6/Oct/1943	12°	♑	41	**5/Jul/1944**	**13°**	**♑**	**57**	5/Apr/1945	15°	♑	37
4/Feb/1943	**15°**	**♒**	**17**	4/Nov/1943	11°	♒	50	**4/Aug/1944**	**11°**	**♒**	**58**	5/May/1945	14°	♒	22
6/Mar/1943	14°	♓	58	4/Dec/1943	11°	♓	25	2/Sep/1944	10°	♓	12	3/Jun/1945	12°	♓	34
4/Apr/1943	14°	♈	14	2/Jan/1944	11°	♈	19	1/Oct/1944	08°	♈	50	2/Jul/1945	10°	♈	27
4/May/1943	13°	♉	3	1/Feb/1944	11°	♉	18	31/Oct/1944	08°	♉	0	31/Jul/1945	08°	♉	18
2/Jun/1943	11°	♊	29	1/Mar/1944	11°	♊	9	29/Nov/1944	07°	♊	42	29/Aug/1945	06°	♊	24
2/Jul/1943	09°	♋	45	31/Mar/1944	10°	♋	40	**29/Dec/1944**	**07°**	**♋**	**47**	28/Sep/1945	04°	♋	57
31/Jul/1943	**08°**	**♌**	**2**	30/Apr/1944	09°	♌	46	28/Jan/1945	07°	♌	59	27/Oct/1945	04°	♌	8
30/Aug/1943	06°	♍	33	29/May/1944	08°	♍	27	26/Feb/1945	08°	♍	2	26/Nov/1945	03°	♍	56
29/Sep/1943	05°	♎	26	28/Jun/1944	06°	♎	51	28/Mar/1945	07°	♎	40	26/Dec/1945	04°	♎	11

Moon Families - Eclipses in Bold Print

New Moon				First Quarter Moon				Full Moon				Last Quarter Moon			
28/Oct/1943	04°	♏	46	28/Jul/1944	05°	♏	9	27/Apr/1945	06°	♏	47	25/Jan/1946	04°	♏	37
27/Nov/1943	04°	♐	30	26/Aug/1944	03°	♐	34	26/May/1945	05°	♐	24	23/Feb/1946	04°	♐	53
26/Dec/1943	04°	♑	30	25/Sep/1944	02°	♑	17	**25/Jun/1945**	**03°**	♑	**39**	25/Mar/1946	04°	♑	40
25/Jan/1944	**04°**	♒	**32**	24/Oct/1944	01°	♒	24	24/Jul/1945	01°	♒	46	24/Apr/1946	03°	♒	49
23/Feb/1944	04°	♓	20	23/Nov/1944	00°	♓	54	23/Aug/1945	29°	♒	58	23/May/1946	02°	♓	22
24/Mar/1944	03°	♈	42	22/Dec/1944	00°	♈	42	21/Sep/1945	28°	♓	29	22/Jun/1946	00°	♈	29
22/Apr/1944	02°	♉	34	20/Jan/1945	00°	♉	35	21/Oct/1945	27°	♈	27	21/Jul/1946	28°	♈	25
22/May/1944	01°	♊	1	19/Feb/1945	00°	♊	21	19/Nov/1945	26°	♉	56	19/Aug/1946	26°	♉	25
20/Jun/1944	29°	♊	12	20/Mar/1945	29°	♊	49	**18/Dec/1945**	**26°**	♊	**49**	18/Sep/1946	24°	♊	44
20/Jul/1944	**27°**	♋	**21**	19/Apr/1945	28°	♋	53	17/Jan/1946	26°	♋	54	17/Oct/1946	23°	♋	34
18/Aug/1944	25°	♌	43	18/May/1945	27°	♌	34	15/Feb/1946	26°	♌	54	15/Nov/1946	22°	♌	58
17/Sep/1944	24°	♍	28	17/Jun/1945	25°	♍	59	17/Mar/1946	26°	♍	35	15/Dec/1946	22°	♍	52
17/Oct/1944	23°	♎	43	17/Jul/1945	24°	♎	19	16/Apr/1946	25°	♎	50	13/Jan/1947	23°	♎	6
15/Nov/1944	23°	♏	27	15/Aug/1945	22°	♏	46	15/May/1946	24°	♏	38	12/Feb/1947	23°	♏	21
15/Dec/1944	23°	♐	31	14/Sep/1945	21°	♐	31	**14/Jun/1946**	**23°**	♐	**4**	14/Mar/1947	23°	♐	20
14/Jan/1945	**23°**	♑	**41**	14/Oct/1945	20°	♑	40	14/Jul/1946	21°	♑	19	13/Apr/1947	22°	♑	48
12/Feb/1945	23°	♒	39	12/Nov/1945	20°	♒	14	12/Aug/1946	19°	♒	34	13/May/1947	21°	♒	43
13/Mar/1945	23°	♓	12	12/Dec/1945	20°	♓	4	11/Sep/1946	18°	♓	3	11/Jun/1947	20°	♓	9
12/Apr/1945	22°	♈	13	10/Jan/1946	20°	♈	1	10/Oct/1946	16°	♈	56	11/Jul/1947	18°	♈	17
11/May/1945	20°	♉	45	8/Feb/1946	19°	♉	49	9/Nov/1946	16°	♉	17	9/Aug/1947	16°	♉	23
9/Jun/1945	18°	♊	55	10/Mar/1946	19°	♊	19	**8/Dec/1946**	**16°**	♊	**3**	7/Sep/1947	14°	♊	39
9/Jul/1945	**16°**	♋	**57**	8/Apr/1946	18°	♋	22	6/Jan/1947	16°	♋	2	7/Oct/1947	13°	♋	18
7/Aug/1945	15°	♌	5	8/May/1946	17°	♌	0	5/Feb/1947	16°	♌	0	5/Nov/1947	12°	♌	26
6/Sep/1945	13°	♍	35	6/Jun/1946	15°	♍	19	6/Mar/1947	15°	♍	42	4/Dec/1947	12°	♍	2
6/Oct/1945	12°	♎	35	6/Jul/1946	13°	♎	32	5/Apr/1947	15°	♎	0	3/Jan/1948	11°	♎	59
4/Nov/1945	12°	♏	10	4/Aug/1946	11°	♏	50	4/May/1947	13°	♏	51	1/Feb/1948	12°	♏	4
4/Dec/1945	12°	♐	14	3/Sep/1946	10°	♐	29	**3/Jun/1947**	**12°**	♐	**21**	2/Mar/1948	12°	♐	1
3/Jan/1946	**12°**	♑	**32**	3/Oct/1946	09°	♑	35	3/Jul/1947	10°	♑	39	1/Apr/1948	11°	♑	36
1/Feb/1946	12°	♒	44	1/Nov/1946	09°	♒	9	1/Aug/1947	08°	♒	56	30/Apr/1948	10°	♒	42
3/Mar/1946	12°	♓	33	1/Dec/1946	09°	♓	6	31/Aug/1947	07°	♓	25	30/May/1948	09°	♓	23
1/Apr/1946	11°	♈	50	31/Dec/1946	09°	♈	14	30/Sep/1947	06°	♈	15	29/Jun/1948	07°	♈	45
1/May/1946	10°	♉	33	29/Jan/1947	09°	♉	15	29/Oct/1947	05°	♉	33	29/Jul/1948	06°	♉	0
30/May/1946	**08°**	♊	**48**	28/Feb/1947	08°	♊	56	**28/Nov/1947**	**05°**	♊	**16**	27/Aug/1948	04°	♊	22
28/Jun/1946	**06°**	♋	**48**	29/Mar/1947	08°	♋	8	27/Dec/1947	05°	♋	15	26/Sep/1948	03°	♋	0
28/Jul/1946	04°	♌	47	27/Apr/1947	06°	♌	48	26/Jan/1948	05°	♌	14	25/Oct/1948	02°	♌	3
26/Aug/1946	03°	♍	0	26/May/1947	05°	♍	3	24/Feb/1948	05°	♍	1	23/Nov/1948	01°	♍	30
25/Sep/1946	01°	♎	40	25/Jun/1947	03°	♎	6	24/Mar/1948	04°	♎	23	23/Dec/1948	01°	♎	18
24/Oct/1946	00°	♏	57	24/Jul/1947	01°	♏	10	**23/Apr/1948**	**03°**	♏	**17**	21/Jan/1949	01°	♏	13
23/Nov/1946	**00°**	♐	**49**	23/Aug/1947	29°	♏	32	22/May/1948	01°	♐	47	19/Feb/1949	01°	♐	3
23/Dec/1946	01°	♑	6	22/Sep/1947	28°	♐	22	21/Jun/1948	00°	♑	1	21/Mar/1949	00°	♑	35
22/Jan/1947	01°	♒	29	21/Oct/1947	27°	♑	47	20/Jul/1948	28°	♑	13	19/Apr/1949	29°	♑	43
20/Feb/1947	01°	♓	36	20/Nov/1947	27°	♒	43	19/Aug/1948	26°	♒	36	19/May/1949	28°	♒	27
22/Mar/1947	01°	♈	12	20/Dec/1947	28°	♓	0	18/Sep/1948	25°	♓	22	18/Jun/1949	26°	♓	54
20/Apr/1947	00°	♉	13	19/Jan/1948	28°	♈	18	**17/Oct/1948**	**24°**	♈	**37**	18/Jul/1949	25°	♈	16
20/May/1947	**28°**	♉	**42**	17/Feb/1948	28°	♉	19	16/Nov/1948	24°	♉	19	16/Aug/1949	23°	♉	42
18/Jun/1947	26°	♊	46	18/Mar/1948	27°	♊	49	16/Dec/1948	24°	♊	20	15/Sep/1949	22°	♊	24
17/Jul/1947	24°	♋	42	16/Apr/1948	26°	♋	42	14/Jan/1949	24°	♋	26	14/Oct/1949	21°	♋	28
16/Aug/1947	22°	♌	44	15/May/1948	25°	♌	3	13/Feb/1949	24°	♌	21	13/Nov/1949	20°	♌	56
14/Sep/1947	21°	♍	7	14/Jun/1948	23°	♍	3	14/Mar/1949	23°	♍	52	12/Dec/1949	20°	♍	43
14/Oct/1947	20°	♎	3	13/Jul/1948	20°	♎	57	**12/Apr/1949**	**22°**	♎	**54**	11/Jan/1950	20°	♎	38
12/Nov/1947	**19°**	♏	**35**	11/Aug/1948	19°	♏	0	12/May/1949	21°	♏	27	9/Feb/1950	20°	♏	27

Moon Families - Eclipses in Bold Print

New Moon

Date	°	Sign	'
12/Dec/1947	19°	♐	39
11/Jan/1948	20°	♑	0
9/Feb/1948	20°	♒	17
10/Mar/1948	20°	♓	13
9/Apr/1948	19°	♈	35
8/May/1948	**18°**	♉	**22**
7/Jun/1948	16°	♊	39
6/Jul/1948	14°	♋	39
4/Aug/1948	12°	♌	38
3/Sep/1948	10°	♍	50
2/Oct/1948	09°	♎	30
1/Nov/1948	**08°**	♏	**43**
30/Nov/1948	08°	♐	29
30/Dec/1948	08°	♑	37
28/Jan/1949	08°	♒	52
27/Feb/1949	08°	♓	57
29/Mar/1949	08°	♈	36
28/Apr/1949	**07°**	♉	**42**
27/May/1949	06°	♊	16
26/Jun/1949	04°	♋	27
25/Jul/1949	02°	♌	29
23/Aug/1949	00°	♍	39
22/Sep/1949	29°	♍	9
21/Oct/1949	**28°**	♎	**8**
20/Nov/1949	27°	♏	39
19/Dec/1949	27°	♐	33
18/Jan/1950	27°	♑	39
16/Feb/1950	27°	♒	42
18/Mar/1950	**27°**	♓	**27**
17/Apr/1950	26°	♈	45
16/May/1950	25°	♉	33
15/Jun/1950	23°	♊	57
15/Jul/1950	22°	♋	8
13/Aug/1950	20°	♌	21
11/Sep/1950	**18°**	♍	**48**
11/Oct/1950	17°	♎	39
9/Nov/1950	16°	♏	59
9/Dec/1950	16°	♐	44
7/Jan/1951	16°	♑	43
6/Feb/1951	16°	♒	43
7/Mar/1951	**16°**	♓	**28**
6/Apr/1951	15°	♈	50
5/May/1951	14°	♉	44
4/Jun/1951	13°	♊	14
4/Jul/1951	11°	♋	32
2/Aug/1951	09°	♌	48
1/Sep/1951	**08°**	♍	**16**
30/Sep/1951	07°	♎	5
30/Oct/1951	06°	♏	20
28/Nov/1951	05°	♐	59
28/Dec/1951	05°	♑	56

First Quarter Moon

Date	°	Sign	'
10/Sep/1948	17°	♐	28
9/Oct/1948	16°	♑	31
8/Nov/1948	16°	♒	11
8/Dec/1948	16°	♓	24
7/Jan/1949	16°	♈	52
6/Feb/1949	17°	♉	13
7/Mar/1949	17°	♊	7
6/Apr/1949	16°	♋	24
5/May/1949	15°	♌	2
3/Jun/1949	13°	♍	10
3/Jul/1949	11°	♎	3
1/Aug/1949	08°	♏	55
30/Aug/1949	07°	♐	3
28/Sep/1949	05°	♑	41
28/Oct/1949	04°	♒	56
27/Nov/1949	04°	♓	50
27/Dec/1949	05°	♈	11
25/Jan/1950	05°	♉	39
24/Feb/1950	05°	♊	53
26/Mar/1950	05°	♋	36
25/Apr/1950	04°	♌	39
24/May/1950	03°	♍	7
23/Jun/1950	01°	♎	10
22/Jul/1950	29°	♎	3
20/Aug/1950	27°	♏	2
18/Sep/1950	25°	♐	21
17/Oct/1950	24°	♑	13
16/Nov/1950	23°	♒	41
16/Dec/1950	23°	♓	42
14/Jan/1951	24°	♈	2
13/Feb/1951	24°	♉	21
15/Mar/1951	24°	♊	19
14/Apr/1951	23°	♋	46
14/May/1951	22°	♌	37
12/Jun/1951	20°	♍	59
11/Jul/1951	19°	♎	3
10/Aug/1951	17°	♏	4
8/Sep/1951	15°	♐	16
7/Oct/1951	13°	♑	54
6/Nov/1951	13°	♒	3
5/Dec/1951	12°	♓	43
3/Jan/1952	12°	♈	46
2/Feb/1952	12°	♉	56
3/Mar/1952	12°	♊	56
2/Apr/1952	12°	♋	33
1/May/1952	11°	♌	41
31/May/1952	10°	♍	21
30/Jun/1952	08°	♎	39
29/Jul/1952	06°	♏	50
28/Aug/1952	05°	♐	6
26/Sep/1952	03°	♑	40

Full Moon

Date	°	Sign	'
10/Jun/1949	19°	♐	38
10/Jul/1949	17°	♑	42
8/Aug/1949	15°	♒	53
7/Sep/1949	14°	♓	26
6/Oct/1949	**13°**	♈	**30**
5/Nov/1949	13°	♉	7
5/Dec/1949	13°	♊	10
4/Jan/1950	13°	♋	23
2/Feb/1950	13°	♌	31
4/Mar/1950	13°	♍	17
2/Apr/1950	**12°**	♎	**32**
2/May/1950	11°	♏	14
31/May/1950	09°	♐	29
29/Jun/1950	07°	♑	29
28/Jul/1950	05°	♒	29
27/Aug/1950	03°	♓	45
25/Sep/1950	**02°**	♈	**30**
25/Oct/1950	01°	♉	52
24/Nov/1950	01°	♊	46
24/Dec/1950	02°	♋	2
22/Jan/1951	02°	♌	22
21/Feb/1951	**02°**	♍	**26**
23/Mar/1951	**02°**	♎	**0**
21/Apr/1951	00°	♏	57
21/May/1951	29°	♏	22
19/Jun/1951	27°	♐	25
18/Jul/1951	25°	♑	20
16/Aug/1951	**23°**	♒	**24**
15/Sep/1951	**21°**	♓	**51**
14/Oct/1951	20°	♈	51
13/Nov/1951	20°	♉	27
13/Dec/1951	20°	♊	33
11/Jan/1952	20°	♋	55
10/Feb/1952	**21°**	♌	**13**
11/Mar/1952	21°	♍	7
10/Apr/1952	20°	♎	25
9/May/1952	19°	♏	7
8/Jun/1952	17°	♐	20
7/Jul/1952	15°	♑	18
5/Aug/1952	**13°**	♒	**17**
3/Sep/1952	11°	♓	31
3/Oct/1952	10°	♈	13
1/Nov/1952	09°	♉	28
1/Dec/1952	09°	♊	16
31/Dec/1952	09°	♋	28
29/Jan/1953	**09°**	♌	**48**
28/Feb/1953	09°	♍	54
30/Mar/1953	09°	♎	31
28/Apr/1953	08°	♏	33
28/May/1953	07°	♐	2
26/Jun/1953	05°	♑	11

Last Quarter Moon

Date	°	Sign	'
10/Mar/1950	19°	♐	57
9/Apr/1950	19°	♑	3
8/May/1950	17°	♒	44
7/Jun/1950	16°	♓	8
6/Jul/1950	14°	♈	25
5/Aug/1950	12°	♉	48
4/Sep/1950	11°	♊	27
4/Oct/1950	10°	♋	31
2/Nov/1950	10°	♌	2
2/Dec/1950	09°	♍	55
1/Jan/1951	09°	♎	58
30/Jan/1951	09°	♏	55
28/Feb/1951	09°	♐	32
30/Mar/1951	08°	♑	42
28/Apr/1951	07°	♒	24
27/May/1951	05°	♓	43
26/Jun/1951	03°	♈	51
25/Jul/1951	02°	♉	0
24/Aug/1951	00°	♊	26
22/Sep/1951	29°	♊	19
22/Oct/1951	28°	♋	46
21/Nov/1951	28°	♌	42
21/Dec/1951	28°	♍	55
20/Jan/1952	29°	♎	7
18/Feb/1952	29°	♏	2
18/Mar/1952	28°	♐	26
17/Apr/1952	27°	♑	17
16/May/1952	25°	♒	39
14/Jun/1952	23°	♓	41
13/Jul/1952	21°	♈	37
12/Aug/1952	19°	♉	45
10/Sep/1952	18°	♊	17
10/Oct/1952	17°	♋	25
9/Nov/1952	17°	♌	11
9/Dec/1952	17°	♍	25
8/Jan/1953	17°	♎	51
6/Feb/1953	18°	♏	5
8/Mar/1953	17°	♐	53
6/Apr/1953	17°	♑	4
6/May/1953	15°	♒	39
4/Jun/1953	13°	♓	46
3/Jul/1953	11°	♈	38
1/Aug/1953	09°	♉	31
31/Aug/1953	07°	♊	43
29/Sep/1953	06°	♋	26
29/Oct/1953	05°	♌	49
28/Nov/1953	05°	♍	48
28/Dec/1953	06°	♎	12
26/Jan/1954	06°	♏	39
25/Feb/1954	06°	♐	50
27/Mar/1954	06°	♑	27

Moon Families - Eclipses in Bold Print

New Moon				First Quarter Moon				Full Moon				Last Quarter Moon			
26/Jan/1952	05°	≈	55	25/Oct/1952	02°	≈	41	**26/Jul/1953**	**03°**	**≈**	**12**	25/Apr/1954	05°	≈	25
25/Feb/1952	**05°**	**♓**	**43**	24/Nov/1952	02°	♓	8	24/Aug/1953	01°	♓	20	25/May/1954	03°	♓	48
25/Mar/1952	05°	♈	7	23/Dec/1952	01°	♈	57	22/Sep/1953	29°	♓	50	23/Jun/1954	01°	♈	47
24/Apr/1952	04°	♉	3	22/Jan/1953	01°	♉	55	22/Oct/1953	28°	♈	49	22/Jul/1954	29°	♈	37
23/May/1952	02°	♊	34	20/Feb/1953	01°	♊	48	20/Nov/1953	28°	♉	21	20/Aug/1954	27°	♉	36
22/Jun/1952	00°	♋	51	22/Mar/1953	01°	♋	24	20/Dec/1953	28°	♊	18	19/Sep/1954	25°	♊	58
21/Jul/1952	29°	♋	6	20/Apr/1953	00°	♌	37	**18/Jan/1954**	**28°**	**♋**	**29**	18/Oct/1954	24°	♋	55
20/Aug/1952	**27°**	**♌**	**31**	20/May/1953	29°	♌	25	17/Feb/1954	28°	♌	36	17/Nov/1954	24°	♌	30
19/Sep/1952	26°	♍	17	19/Jun/1953	27°	♍	53	19/Mar/1954	28°	♍	22	16/Dec/1954	24°	♍	36
18/Oct/1952	25°	♎	29	18/Jul/1953	26°	♎	13	18/Apr/1954	27°	♎	39	15/Jan/1955	25°	♎	0
17/Nov/1952	25°	♏	7	17/Aug/1953	24°	♏	35	17/May/1954	26°	♏	25	14/Feb/1955	25°	♏	20
16/Dec/1952	25°	♐	5	16/Sep/1953	23°	♐	13	16/Jun/1954	24°	♐	47	16/Mar/1955	25°	♐	19
15/Jan/1953	25°	♑	9	15/Oct/1953	22°	♑	14	**15/Jul/1954**	**22°**	**♑**	**57**	15/Apr/1955	24°	♑	42
13/Feb/1953	**25°**	**≈**	**3**	14/Nov/1953	21°	≈	39	14/Aug/1954	21°	≈	7	14/May/1955	23°	≈	28
15/Mar/1953	24°	♓	34	13/Dec/1953	21°	♓	23	12/Sep/1954	19°	♓	31	13/Jun/1955	21°	♓	43
13/Apr/1953	23°	♈	35	11/Jan/1954	21°	♈	16	12/Oct/1954	18°	♈	20	12/Jul/1955	19°	♈	42
13/May/1953	22°	♉	8	10/Feb/1954	21°	♉	4	10/Nov/1954	17°	♉	39	10/Aug/1955	17°	♉	39
11/Jun/1953	20°	♊	22	11/Mar/1954	20°	♊	37	9/Dec/1954	17°	♊	25	9/Sep/1955	15°	♊	52
10/Jul/1953	**18°**	**♋**	**29**	10/Apr/1954	19°	♋	47	**8/Jan/1955**	**17°**	**♋**	**28**	8/Oct/1955	14°	♋	30
9/Aug/1953	**16°**	**♌**	**45**	9/May/1954	18°	♌	34	6/Feb/1955	17°	♌	30	6/Nov/1955	13°	♌	42
8/Sep/1953	15°	♍	21	8/Jun/1954	17°	♍	2	8/Mar/1955	17°	♍	17	6/Dec/1955	13°	♍	26
7/Oct/1953	14°	♎	26	7/Jul/1954	15°	♎	22	7/Apr/1955	16°	♎	40	4/Jan/1956	13°	♎	33
6/Nov/1953	14°	♏	2	6/Aug/1954	13°	♏	45	6/May/1955	15°	♏	36	3/Feb/1956	13°	♏	48
6/Dec/1953	14°	♐	2	5/Sep/1954	12°	♐	24	**5/Jun/1955**	**14°**	**♐**	**8**	4/Mar/1956	13°	♐	53
4/Jan/1954	**14°**	**♑**	**13**	5/Oct/1954	11°	♑	26	5/Jul/1955	12°	♑	26	3/Apr/1956	13°	♑	32
3/Feb/1954	14°	≈	17	3/Nov/1954	10°	≈	54	3/Aug/1955	10°	≈	40	2/May/1956	12°	≈	38
4/Mar/1954	14°	♓	0	3/Dec/1954	10°	♓	42	2/Sep/1955	09°	♓	4	1/Jun/1956	11°	♓	14
3/Apr/1954	13°	♈	12	1/Jan/1955	10°	♈	39	1/Oct/1955	07°	♈	49	1/Jul/1956	09°	♈	27
2/May/1954	11°	♉	52	31/Jan/1955	10°	♉	33	31/Oct/1955	07°	♉	2	30/Jul/1956	07°	♉	34
31/May/1954	10°	♊	7	1/Mar/1955	10°	♊	9	**29/Nov/1955**	**06°**	**♊**	**41**	28/Aug/1956	05°	♊	47
30/Jun/1954	**08°**	**♋**	**10**	30/Mar/1955	09°	♋	21	28/Dec/1955	06°	♋	38	27/Sep/1956	04°	♋	19
29/Jul/1954	06°	♌	14	28/Apr/1955	08°	♌	5	27/Jan/1956	06°	♌	38	26/Oct/1956	03°	♌	18
28/Aug/1954	04°	♍	34	28/May/1955	06°	♍	28	25/Feb/1956	06°	♍	26	24/Nov/1956	02°	♍	45
26/Sep/1954	03°	♎	23	26/Jun/1955	04°	♎	39	26/Mar/1956	05°	♎	51	24/Dec/1956	02°	♎	35
26/Oct/1954	02°	♏	46	26/Jul/1955	02°	♏	53	24/Apr/1956	04°	♏	49	22/Jan/1957	02°	♏	38
25/Nov/1954	02°	♐	42	25/Aug/1955	01°	♐	23	**24/May/1956**	**03°**	**♐**	**24**	21/Feb/1957	02°	♐	37
25/Dec/1954	**02°**	**♑**	**58**	23/Sep/1955	00°	♑	19	23/Jun/1956	01°	♑	44	23/Mar/1957	02°	♑	18
23/Jan/1955	03°	≈	16	23/Oct/1955	29°	♑	45	22/Jul/1956	00°	≈	0	21/Apr/1957	01°	≈	33
22/Feb/1955	03°	♓	15	22/Nov/1955	29°	≈	38	21/Aug/1956	28°	≈	24	21/May/1957	00°	♓	21
23/Mar/1955	02°	♈	44	22/Dec/1955	29°	♓	45	19/Sep/1956	27°	♓	8	20/Jun/1957	28°	♓	48
22/Apr/1955	01°	♉	37	20/Jan/1956	29°	♈	52	19/Oct/1956	26°	♈	18	19/Jul/1957	27°	♈	5
21/May/1955	00°	♊	1	19/Feb/1956	29°	♉	43	**18/Nov/1956**	**25°**	**♉**	**54**	18/Aug/1957	25°	♉	25
19/Jun/1955	**28°**	**♊**	**4**	19/Mar/1956	29°	♊	5	17/Dec/1956	25°	♊	50	16/Sep/1957	23°	♊	59
19/Jul/1955	26°	♋	1	17/Apr/1956	27°	♋	54	16/Jan/1957	25°	♋	52	16/Oct/1957	22°	♋	55
17/Aug/1955	24°	♌	7	17/May/1956	26°	♌	16	14/Feb/1957	25°	♌	44	14/Nov/1957	22°	♌	16
16/Sep/1955	22°	♍	36	15/Jun/1956	24°	♍	20	15/Mar/1957	25°	♍	14	14/Dec/1957	21°	♍	58
15/Oct/1955	21°	♎	40	14/Jul/1956	22°	♎	20	14/Apr/1957	24°	♎	16	12/Jan/1958	21°	♎	52
14/Nov/1955	21°	♏	20	13/Aug/1956	20°	♏	33	**13/May/1957**	**22°**	**♏**	**52**	10/Feb/1958	21°	♏	44
14/Dec/1955	**21°**	**♐**	**30**	11/Sep/1956	19°	♐	12	12/Jun/1957	21°	♐	9	12/Mar/1958	21°	♐	21
12/Jan/1956	21°	♑	54	11/Oct/1956	18°	♑	25	11/Jul/1957	19°	♑	19	10/Apr/1958	20°	♑	35
11/Feb/1956	22°	≈	9	10/Nov/1956	18°	≈	12	10/Aug/1957	17°	≈	37	10/May/1958	19°	≈	25

Moon Families - Eclipses in Bold Print

New Moon		First Quarter Moon		Full Moon		Last Quarter Moon	
12/Mar/1956	21° ♓ 57	10/Dec/1956	18° ♓ 25	8/Sep/1957	16° ♓ 14	9/Jun/1958	17° ♓ 56
10/Apr/1956	21° ♈ 11	9/Jan/1957	18° ♈ 46	8/Oct/1957	15° ♈ 20	8/Jul/1958	16° ♈ 18
10/May/1956	19° ♉ 50	7/Feb/1957	18° ♉ 56	**7/Nov/1957**	**14° ♉ 55**	7/Aug/1958	14° ♉ 42
8/Jun/1956	**18° ♊ 1**	9/Mar/1957	18° ♊ 39	7/Dec/1957	14° ♊ 53	6/Sep/1958	13° ♊ 19
7/Jul/1956	15° ♋ 58	7/Apr/1957	17° ♋ 45	5/Jan/1958	15° ♋ 0	5/Oct/1958	12° ♋ 17
6/Aug/1956	13° ♌ 57	6/May/1957	16° ♌ 16	4/Feb/1958	15° ♌ 0	4/Nov/1958	11° ♌ 39
4/Sep/1956	12° ♍ 11	5/Jun/1957	14° ♍ 21	5/Mar/1958	14° ♍ 40	3/Dec/1958	11° ♍ 23
3/Oct/1956	10° ♎ 55	4/Jul/1957	12° ♎ 14	**3/Apr/1958**	**13° ♎ 52**	2/Jan/1959	11° ♎ 17
2/Nov/1956	10° ♏ 14	2/Aug/1957	10° ♏ 11	**3/May/1958**	**12° ♏ 33**	31/Jan/1959	11° ♏ 10
2/Dec/1956	**10° ♐ 8**	31/Aug/1957	08° ♐ 28	1/Jun/1958	10° ♐ 50	1/Mar/1959	10° ♐ 46
31/Dec/1956	10° ♑ 24	30/Sep/1957	07° ♑ 17	1/Jul/1958	08° ♑ 54	31/Mar/1959	09° ♑ 59
30/Jan/1957	10° ♒ 45	30/Oct/1957	06° ♒ 45	30/Jul/1958	07° ♒ 0	29/Apr/1959	08° ♒ 46
1/Mar/1957	10° ♓ 49	29/Nov/1957	06° ♓ 48	29/Aug/1958	05° ♓ 23	29/May/1959	07° ♓ 13
31/Mar/1957	10° ♈ 23	28/Dec/1957	07° ♈ 13	27/Sep/1958	04° ♈ 16	27/Jun/1959	05° ♈ 29
29/Apr/1957	**09° ♉ 22**	27/Jan/1958	07° ♉ 39	**27/Oct/1958**	**03° ♉ 43**	27/Jul/1959	03° ♉ 48
29/May/1957	07° ♊ 49	26/Feb/1958	07° ♊ 45	26/Nov/1958	03° ♊ 39	26/Aug/1959	02° ♊ 20
27/Jun/1957	05° ♋ 54	28/Mar/1958	07° ♋ 16	25/Dec/1958	03° ♋ 52	24/Sep/1959	01° ♋ 16
26/Jul/1957	03° ♌ 52	26/Apr/1958	06° ♌ 8	24/Jan/1959	04° ♌ 4	24/Oct/1959	00° ♌ 40
25/Aug/1957	01° ♍ 59	25/May/1958	04° ♍ 26	23/Feb/1959	03° ♍ 59	23/Nov/1959	00° ♍ 29
23/Sep/1957	00° ♎ 29	24/Jun/1958	02° ♎ 22	**24/Mar/1959**	**03° ♎ 26**	22/Dec/1959	00° ♎ 32
22/Oct/1957	**29° ♎ 30**	23/Jul/1958	00° ♏ 13	23/Apr/1959	02° ♏ 18	21/Jan/1960	00° ♏ 35
21/Nov/1957	29° ♏ 6	21/Aug/1958	28° ♏ 13	22/May/1959	00° ♐ 41	19/Feb/1960	00° ♐ 21
21/Dec/1957	29° ♐ 7	19/Sep/1958	26° ♐ 39	20/Jun/1959	28° ♐ 44	20/Mar/1960	29° ♐ 40
19/Jan/1958	29° ♑ 20	19/Oct/1958	25° ♑ 41	19/Jul/1959	26° ♑ 41	18/Apr/1960	28° ♑ 29
18/Feb/1958	29° ♒ 29	17/Nov/1958	25° ♒ 21	18/Aug/1959	24° ♒ 49	17/May/1960	26° ♒ 53
20/Mar/1958	29° ♓ 17	17/Dec/1958	25° ♓ 33	**16/Sep/1959**	**23° ♓ 23**	15/Jun/1960	25° ♓ 1
18/Apr/1958	**28° ♈ 34**	16/Jan/1959	26° ♈ 1	16/Oct/1959	22° ♈ 32	15/Jul/1960	23° ♈ 7
18/May/1958	27° ♉ 19	15/Feb/1959	26° ♉ 22	15/Nov/1959	22° ♉ 16	14/Aug/1960	21° ♉ 25
17/Jun/1958	25° ♊ 37	17/Mar/1959	26° ♊ 17	14/Dec/1959	22° ♊ 27	12/Sep/1960	20° ♊ 7
16/Jul/1958	23° ♋ 42	16/Apr/1959	25° ♋ 34	13/Jan/1960	22° ♋ 49	12/Oct/1960	19° ♋ 22
14/Aug/1958	21° ♌ 48	15/May/1959	24° ♌ 14	12/Feb/1960	23° ♌ 0	11/Nov/1960	19° ♌ 10
13/Sep/1958	20° ♍ 11	14/Jun/1959	22° ♍ 25	**13/Mar/1960**	**22° ♍ 46**	11/Dec/1960	19° ♍ 21
12/Oct/1958	**19° ♎ 1**	13/Jul/1959	20° ♎ 21	11/Apr/1960	21° ♎ 56	9/Jan/1961	19° ♎ 38
11/Nov/1958	18° ♏ 21	11/Aug/1959	18° ♏ 16	11/May/1960	20° ♏ 31	8/Feb/1961	19° ♏ 42
10/Dec/1958	18° ♐ 9	9/Sep/1959	16° ♐ 28	9/Jun/1960	18° ♐ 40	9/Mar/1961	19° ♐ 18
9/Jan/1959	18° ♑ 12	8/Oct/1959	15° ♑ 7	8/Jul/1960	16° ♑ 36	8/Apr/1961	18° ♑ 20
7/Feb/1959	18° ♒ 16	7/Nov/1959	14° ♒ 23	6/Aug/1960	14° ♒ 35	7/May/1961	16° ♒ 50
9/Mar/1959	18° ♓ 7	6/Dec/1959	14° ♓ 13	**5/Sep/1960**	**12° ♓ 52**	5/Jun/1961	14° ♓ 56
7/Apr/1959	**17° ♈ 33**	5/Jan/1960	14° ♈ 27	4/Oct/1960	11° ♈ 40	4/Jul/1961	12° ♈ 52
7/May/1959	16° ♉ 30	4/Feb/1960	14° ♉ 47	3/Nov/1960	11° ♉ 4	3/Aug/1961	10° ♉ 53
6/Jun/1959	15° ♊ 2	5/Mar/1960	14° ♊ 53	2/Dec/1960	11° ♊ 0	1/Sep/1961	09° ♊ 14
5/Jul/1959	13° ♋ 16	4/Apr/1960	14° ♋ 31	1/Jan/1961	11° ♋ 19	1/Oct/1961	08° ♋ 9
4/Aug/1959	11° ♌ 27	3/May/1960	13° ♌ 34	31/Jan/1961	11° ♌ 40	31/Oct/1961	07° ♌ 42
2/Sep/1959	09° ♍ 49	2/Jun/1960	12° ♍ 5	**2/Mar/1961**	**11° ♍ 44**	30/Nov/1961	07° ♍ 48
2/Oct/1959	**08° ♎ 33**	1/Jul/1960	10° ♎ 15	1/Apr/1961	11° ♎ 16	29/Dec/1961	08° ♎ 13
31/Oct/1959	07° ♏ 45	31/Jul/1960	08° ♏ 17	30/Apr/1961	10° ♏ 10	28/Jan/1962	08° ♏ 35
30/Nov/1959	07° ♐ 23	29/Aug/1960	06° ♐ 25	29/May/1961	08° ♐ 31	27/Feb/1962	08° ♐ 34
29/Dec/1959	07° ♑ 19	27/Sep/1960	04° ♑ 54	28/Jun/1961	06° ♑ 33	28/Mar/1962	07° ♑ 59
28/Jan/1960	07° ♒ 20	27/Oct/1960	03° ♒ 53	27/Jul/1961	04° ♒ 30	27/Apr/1962	06° ♒ 46
26/Feb/1960	07° ♓ 10	25/Nov/1960	03° ♓ 23	**25/Aug/1961**	**02° ♓ 38**	26/May/1962	05° ♓ 2
27/Mar/1960	**06° ♈ 38**	24/Dec/1960	03° ♈ 18	24/Sep/1961	01° ♈ 10	24/Jun/1962	02° ♈ 57
25/Apr/1960	05° ♉ 40	23/Jan/1961	03° ♉ 26	23/Oct/1961	00° ♉ 14	23/Jul/1962	00° ♉ 47

Moon Families - Eclipses in Bold Print

New Moon				First Quarter Moon				Full Moon				Last Quarter Moon			
25/May/1960	04°	♊	16	22/Feb/1961	03°	♊	29	22/Nov/1961	29°	♉	51	22/Aug/1962	28°	♉	50
23/Jun/1960	02°	♋	36	23/Mar/1961	03°	♋	14	21/Dec/1961	29°	♊	55	20/Sep/1962	27°	♊	21
23/Jul/1960	00°	♌	52	22/Apr/1961	02°	♌	30	20/Jan/1962	00°	♌	13	20/Oct/1962	26°	♋	28
22/Aug/1960	29°	♌	15	22/May/1961	01°	♍	19	**19/Feb/1962**	**00°**	**♍**	**25**	18/Nov/1962	26°	♌	15
20/Sep/1960	**27°**	**♍**	**58**	21/Jun/1961	29°	♍	44	21/Mar/1962	00°	♎	13	18/Dec/1962	26°	♍	32
20/Oct/1960	27°	♎	5	20/Jul/1961	27°	♎	57	19/Apr/1962	29°	♎	27	17/Jan/1963	27°	♎	0
18/Nov/1960	26°	♏	39	19/Aug/1961	26°	♏	12	19/May/1962	28°	♏	7	16/Feb/1963	27°	♏	19
18/Dec/1960	26°	♐	32	17/Sep/1961	24°	♐	41	17/Jun/1962	26°	♐	22	18/Mar/1963	27°	♐	10
16/Jan/1961	26°	♑	32	16/Oct/1961	23°	♑	34	**17/Jul/1962**	**24°**	**♑**	**24**	16/Apr/1963	26°	♑	23
15/Feb/1961	**26°**	**♒**	**25**	15/Nov/1961	22°	♒	53	**15/Aug/1962**	**22°**	**♒**	**30**	16/May/1963	24°	♒	58
16/Mar/1961	25°	♓	57	14/Dec/1961	22°	♓	36	13/Sep/1962	20°	♓	52	14/Jun/1963	23°	♓	4
15/Apr/1961	25°	♈	1	13/Jan/1962	22°	♈	32	13/Oct/1962	19°	♈	41	13/Jul/1963	20°	♈	55
14/May/1961	23°	♉	38	11/Feb/1962	22°	♉	26	11/Nov/1962	19°	♉	2	12/Aug/1963	18°	♉	49
13/Jun/1961	21°	♊	57	12/Mar/1962	22°	♊	7	11/Dec/1962	18°	♊	51	10/Sep/1963	17°	♊	2
12/Jul/1961	20°	♋	10	11/Apr/1962	21°	♋	26	**9/Jan/1963**	**18°**	**♋**	**58**	9/Oct/1963	15°	♋	46
11/Aug/1961	**18°**	**♌**	**30**	11/May/1962	20°	♌	20	8/Feb/1963	19°	♌	7	8/Nov/1963	15°	♌	7
9/Sep/1961	17°	♍	9	10/Jun/1962	18°	♍	53	10/Mar/1963	19°	♍	1	7/Dec/1963	15°	♍	3
9/Oct/1961	16°	♎	14	9/Jul/1962	17°	♎	15	8/Apr/1963	18°	♎	28	6/Jan/1964	15°	♎	21
8/Nov/1961	15°	♏	45	8/Aug/1962	15°	♏	36	8/May/1963	17°	♏	23	5/Feb/1964	15°	♏	44
7/Dec/1961	15°	♐	39	7/Sep/1962	14°	♐	10	7/Jun/1963	15°	♐	53	6/Mar/1964	15°	♐	51
6/Jan/1962	15°	♑	43	6/Oct/1962	13°	♑	4	**6/Jul/1963**	**14°**	**♑**	**5**	5/Apr/1964	15°	♑	28
4/Feb/1962	**15°**	**♒**	**42**	5/Nov/1962	12°	♒	23	5/Aug/1963	12°	♒	15	4/May/1964	14°	♒	27
6/Mar/1962	15°	♓	22	4/Dec/1962	12°	♓	3	3/Sep/1963	10°	♓	34	3/Jun/1964	12°	♓	52
4/Apr/1962	14°	♈	33	2/Jan/1963	11°	♈	55	2/Oct/1963	09°	♈	15	2/Jul/1964	10°	♈	56
3/May/1962	13°	♉	14	1/Feb/1963	11°	♉	46	1/Nov/1963	08°	♉	25	31/Jul/1964	08°	♉	54
2/Jun/1962	11°	♊	31	2/Mar/1963	11°	♊	24	30/Nov/1963	08°	♊	3	30/Aug/1964	07°	♊	0
1/Jul/1962	09°	♋	38	31/Mar/1963	10°	♋	41	**30/Dec/1963**	**08°**	**♋**	**1**	28/Sep/1964	05°	♋	30
31/Jul/1962	**07°**	**♌**	**48**	30/Apr/1963	09°	♌	33	28/Jan/1964	08°	♌	4	27/Oct/1964	04°	♌	30
29/Aug/1962	06°	♍	16	29/May/1963	08°	♍	5	27/Feb/1964	07°	♍	57	26/Nov/1964	04°	♍	4
28/Sep/1962	05°	♎	11	28/Jun/1963	06°	♎	24	27/Mar/1964	07°	♎	27	25/Dec/1964	04°	♎	3
28/Oct/1962	04°	♏	37	28/Jul/1963	04°	♏	44	26/Apr/1964	06°	♏	30	24/Jan/1965	04°	♏	15
27/Nov/1962	04°	♐	31	27/Aug/1963	03°	♐	17	26/May/1964	05°	♐	8	23/Feb/1965	04°	♐	24
26/Dec/1962	04°	♑	42	25/Sep/1963	02°	♑	12	**24/Jun/1964**	**03°**	**♑**	**30**	24/Mar/1965	04°	♑	11
25/Jan/1963	**04°**	**♒**	**52**	25/Oct/1963	01°	♒	34	24/Jul/1964	01°	♒	45	23/Apr/1965	03°	♒	28
23/Feb/1963	04°	♓	44	24/Nov/1963	01°	♓	18	23/Aug/1964	00°	♓	6	23/May/1965	02°	♓	14
25/Mar/1963	04°	♈	7	23/Dec/1963	01°	♈	16	21/Sep/1964	28°	♓	44	22/Jun/1965	00°	♈	35
23/Apr/1963	02°	♉	57	22/Jan/1964	01°	♉	13	20/Oct/1964	27°	♈	49	21/Jul/1965	28°	♈	43
22/May/1963	01°	♊	19	20/Feb/1964	00°	♊	56	19/Nov/1964	27°	♉	21	19/Aug/1965	26°	♉	54
21/Jun/1963	29°	♊	23	20/Mar/1964	00°	♋	16	**18/Dec/1964**	**27°**	**♊**	**14**	18/Sep/1965	25°	♊	20
20/Jul/1963	**27°**	**♋**	**24**	18/Apr/1964	29°	♋	8	17/Jan/1965	27°	♋	15	17/Oct/1965	24°	♋	11
19/Aug/1963	25°	♌	36	18/May/1964	27°	♌	35	15/Feb/1965	27°	♌	7	15/Nov/1965	23°	♌	29
17/Sep/1963	24°	♍	14	16/Jun/1964	25°	♍	47	17/Mar/1965	26°	♍	39	15/Dec/1965	23°	♍	13
17/Oct/1963	23°	♎	25	16/Jul/1964	23°	♎	57	15/Apr/1965	25°	♎	45	13/Jan/1966	23°	♎	11
16/Nov/1963	23°	♏	11	14/Aug/1964	22°	♏	19	15/May/1965	24°	♏	25	12/Feb/1966	23°	♏	11
15/Dec/1963	23°	♐	23	13/Sep/1964	21°	♐	5	**13/Jun/1965**	**22°**	**♐**	**48**	13/Mar/1966	22°	♐	58
14/Jan/1964	**23°**	**♑**	**43**	13/Oct/1964	20°	♑	22	13/Jul/1965	21°	♑	3	12/Apr/1966	22°	♑	20
13/Feb/1964	23°	♒	51	12/Nov/1964	20°	♒	9	12/Aug/1965	19°	♒	24	12/May/1966	21°	♒	16
13/Mar/1964	23°	♓	32	12/Dec/1964	20°	♓	15	10/Sep/1965	18°	♓	1	10/Jun/1966	19°	♓	49
12/Apr/1964	22°	♈	37	10/Jan/1965	20°	♈	26	10/Oct/1965	17°	♈	3	10/Jul/1966	18°	♈	9
11/May/1964	21°	♉	10	9/Feb/1965	20°	♉	24	8/Nov/1965	16°	♉	33	9/Aug/1966	16°	♉	28
9/Jun/1964	**19°**	**♊**	**18**	10/Mar/1965	19°	♊	57	**8/Dec/1965**	**16°**	**♊**	**25**	7/Sep/1966	14°	♊	58

Moon Families - Eclipses in Bold Print

New Moon			First Quarter Moon			Full Moon			Last Quarter Moon		
9/Jul/1964	**17° ♋**	**15**	8/Apr/1965	18° ♋	57	7/Jan/1966	16° ♋	27	7/Oct/1966	13° ♋	48
7/Aug/1964	15° ♌	16	8/May/1965	17° ♌	26	5/Feb/1966	16° ♌	24	5/Nov/1966	13° ♌	3
5/Sep/1964	13° ♍	36	6/Jun/1965	15° ♍	33	6/Mar/1966	16° ♍	2	5/Dec/1966	12° ♍	39
5/Oct/1964	12° ♎	26	5/Jul/1965	13° ♎	32	5/Apr/1966	15° ♎	12	3/Jan/1967	12° ♎	30
4/Nov/1964	11° ♏	54	4/Aug/1965	11° ♏	38	**4/May/1966**	**13° ♏**	**55**	1/Feb/1967	12° ♏	24
3/Dec/1964	**11° ♐**	**55**	2/Sep/1965	10° ♐	5	3/Jun/1966	12° ♐	16	3/Mar/1967	12° ♐	5
2/Jan/1965	12° ♑	17	2/Oct/1965	09° ♑	6	2/Jul/1966	10° ♑	27	1/Apr/1967	11° ♑	26
1/Feb/1965	12° ♒	37	1/Nov/1965	08° ♒	42	1/Aug/1966	08° ♒	40	1/May/1967	10° ♒	21
3/Mar/1965	12° ♓	37	1/Dec/1965	08° ♓	48	30/Aug/1966	07° ♓	9	30/May/1967	08° ♓	56
1/Apr/1965	12° ♈	3	30/Dec/1965	09° ♈	10	29/Sep/1966	06° ♈	5	29/Jun/1967	07° ♈	19
1/May/1965	10° ♉	53	29/Jan/1966	09° ♉	28	**29/Oct/1966**	**05° ♉**	**31**	29/Jul/1967	05° ♉	41
30/May/1965	**09° ♊**	**13**	28/Feb/1966	09° ♊	22	27/Nov/1966	05° ♊	24	28/Aug/1967	04° ♊	14
28/Jun/1965	07° ♋	13	29/Mar/1966	08° ♋	42	27/Dec/1966	05° ♋	31	26/Sep/1967	03° ♋	6
28/Jul/1965	05° ♌	10	27/Apr/1966	07° ♌	24	26/Jan/1967	05° ♌	36	26/Oct/1967	02° ♌	22
26/Aug/1965	03° ♍	18	27/May/1966	05° ♍	37	24/Feb/1967	05° ♍	25	24/Nov/1967	02° ♍	2
24/Sep/1965	01° ♎	50	25/Jun/1966	03° ♎	31	25/Mar/1967	04° ♎	46	24/Dec/1967	01° ♎	55
24/Oct/1965	**00° ♏**	**57**	24/Jul/1966	01° ♏	25	**24/Apr/1967**	**03° ♏**	**37**	22/Jan/1968	01° ♏	51
22/Nov/1965	00° ♐	39	22/Aug/1966	29° ♏	32	23/May/1967	02° ♐	0	20/Feb/1968	01° ♐	34
22/Dec/1965	00° ♑	49	21/Sep/1966	28° ♐	9	21/Jun/1967	00° ♑	6	21/Mar/1968	00° ♑	54
21/Jan/1966	01° ♒	9	21/Oct/1966	27° ♑	22	21/Jul/1967	28° ♑	8	19/Apr/1968	29° ♑	47
20/Feb/1966	01° ♓	21	19/Nov/1966	27° ♒	13	19/Aug/1967	26° ♒	23	19/May/1968	28° ♒	18
21/Mar/1966	01° ♈	6	19/Dec/1966	27° ♓	32	18/Sep/1967	25° ♓	5	17/Jun/1968	26° ♓	34
20/Apr/1966	00° ♉	18	18/Jan/1967	28° ♈	1	**18/Oct/1967**	**24° ♈**	**20**	17/Jul/1968	24° ♈	49
20/May/1966	**28° ♉**	**55**	17/Feb/1967	28° ♉	17	16/Nov/1967	24° ♉	8	15/Aug/1968	23° ♉	16
18/Jun/1966	27° ♊	7	19/Mar/1967	28° ♊	3	16/Dec/1967	24° ♊	19	14/Sep/1968	22° ♊	3
17/Jul/1966	25° ♋	6	17/Apr/1967	27° ♋	8	15/Jan/1968	24° ♋	35	14/Oct/1968	21° ♋	19
16/Aug/1966	23° ♌	9	17/May/1967	25° ♌	37	14/Feb/1968	24° ♌	38	13/Nov/1968	21° ♌	2
14/Sep/1966	21° ♍	30	15/Jun/1967	23° ♍	40	14/Mar/1968	24° ♍	15	12/Dec/1968	21° ♍	5
13/Oct/1966	20° ♎	21	14/Jul/1967	21° ♎	31	**12/Apr/1968**	**23° ♎**	**19**	11/Jan/1969	21° ♎	11
12/Nov/1966	**19° ♏**	**45**	12/Aug/1967	19° ♏	26	12/May/1968	21° ♏	51	9/Feb/1969	21° ♏	5
11/Dec/1966	19° ♐	38	10/Sep/1967	17° ♐	42	10/Jun/1968	19° ♐	58	11/Mar/1969	20° ♐	33
10/Jan/1967	19° ♑	48	10/Oct/1967	16° ♑	30	9/Jul/1968	17° ♑	55	9/Apr/1969	19° ♑	32
9/Feb/1967	19° ♒	59	8/Nov/1967	15° ♒	56	8/Aug/1968	15° ♒	57	8/May/1969	18° ♒	2
10/Mar/1967	19° ♓	54	8/Dec/1967	15° ♓	57	6/Sep/1968	14° ♓	21	6/Jun/1969	16° ♓	12
9/Apr/1967	19° ♈	22	7/Jan/1968	16° ♈	21	**6/Oct/1968**	**13° ♈**	**16**	6/Jul/1969	14° ♈	16
9/May/1967	**18° ♉**	**17**	6/Feb/1968	16° ♉	47	4/Nov/1968	12° ♉	49	4/Aug/1969	12° ♉	27
8/Jun/1967	16° ♊	44	7/Mar/1968	16° ♊	52	4/Dec/1968	12° ♊	53	3/Sep/1969	10° ♊	59
7/Jul/1967	14° ♋	53	5/Apr/1968	16° ♋	23	3/Jan/1969	13° ♋	13	3/Oct/1969	10° ♋	3
5/Aug/1967	12° ♌	58	5/May/1968	15° ♌	16	2/Feb/1969	13° ♌	31	2/Nov/1969	09° ♌	41
4/Sep/1967	11° ♍	15	3/Jun/1968	13° ♍	37	4/Mar/1969	13° ♍	27	1/Dec/1969	09° ♍	47
3/Oct/1967	09° ♎	55	3/Jul/1968	11° ♎	37	**2/Apr/1969**	**12° ♎**	**50**	31/Dec/1969	10° ♎	6
2/Nov/1967	**09° ♏**	**6**	1/Aug/1968	09° ♏	32	2/May/1969	11° ♏	37	30/Jan/1970	10° ♏	18
1/Dec/1967	08° ♐	46	30/Aug/1968	07° ♐	37	31/May/1969	09° ♐	53	28/Feb/1970	10° ♐	5
30/Dec/1967	08° ♑	45	29/Sep/1968	06° ♑	7	29/Jun/1969	07° ♑	52	30/Mar/1970	09° ♑	19
29/Jan/1968	08° ♒	50	28/Oct/1968	05° ♒	9	28/Jul/1969	05° ♒	48	28/Apr/1970	07° ♒	59
28/Feb/1968	08° ♓	45	26/Nov/1968	04° ♓	47	**27/Aug/1969**	**03° ♓**	**58**	27/May/1970	06° ♓	11
28/Mar/1968	**08° ♈**	**19**	26/Dec/1968	04° ♈	53	**25/Sep/1969**	**02° ♈**	**34**	25/Jun/1970	04° ♈	8
27/Apr/1968	07° ♉	24	25/Jan/1969	05° ♉	12	25/Oct/1969	01° ♉	45	25/Jul/1970	02° ♉	5
27/May/1968	06° ♊	3	23/Feb/1969	05° ♊	23	23/Nov/1969	01° ♊	31	23/Aug/1970	00° ♊	16
25/Jun/1968	04° ♋	22	25/Mar/1969	05° ♋	11	23/Dec/1969	01° ♋	44	22/Sep/1970	28° ♊	58
25/Jul/1968	02° ♌	34	24/Apr/1969	04° ♌	26	22/Jan/1970	02° ♌	5	21/Oct/1970	28° ♋	17

Moon Families - Eclipses in Bold Print

New Moon				First Quarter Moon				Full Moon				Last Quarter Moon			
23/Aug/1968	00°	♍	52	24/May/1969	03°	♍	8	**21/Feb/1970**	**02°**	**♍**	**17**	20/Nov/1970	28°	♌	13
22/Sep/1968	**29°**	**♍**	**29**	22/Jun/1969	01°	♎	25	22/Mar/1970	02°	♎	1	20/Dec/1970	28°	♍	34
21/Oct/1968	28°	♎	33	22/Jul/1969	29°	♎	29	21/Apr/1970	01°	♏	8	19/Jan/1971	29°	♎	1
20/Nov/1968	28°	♏	4	20/Aug/1969	27°	♏	36	20/May/1970	29°	♏	40	18/Feb/1971	29°	♏	11
19/Dec/1968	27°	♐	55	18/Sep/1969	25°	♐	58	19/Jun/1970	27°	♐	48	19/Mar/1971	28°	♐	50
17/Jan/1969	27°	♑	56	18/Oct/1969	24°	♑	47	18/Jul/1970	25°	♑	45	18/Apr/1971	27°	♑	50
16/Feb/1969	27°	♒	50	16/Nov/1969	24°	♒	7	**16/Aug/1970**	**23°**	**♒**	**48**	17/May/1971	26°	♒	16
17/Mar/1969	**27°**	**♓**	**25**	15/Dec/1969	23°	♓	54	15/Sep/1970	22°	♓	11	15/Jun/1971	24°	♓	16
16/Apr/1969	26°	♈	34	14/Jan/1970	23°	♈	58	14/Oct/1970	21°	♈	4	15/Jul/1971	22°	♈	6
16/May/1969	25°	♉	17	12/Feb/1970	24°	♉	2	13/Nov/1970	20°	♉	30	13/Aug/1971	20°	♉	2
14/Jun/1969	23°	♊	40	14/Mar/1970	23°	♊	52	12/Dec/1970	20°	♊	26	11/Sep/1971	18°	♊	21
14/Jul/1969	21°	♋	56	13/Apr/1970	23°	♋	17	11/Jan/1971	20°	♋	40	11/Oct/1971	17°	♋	14
13/Aug/1969	20°	♌	16	13/May/1970	22°	♌	14	**10/Feb/1971**	**20°**	**♌**	**55**	9/Nov/1971	16°	♌	47
11/Sep/1969	**18°**	**♍**	**53**	11/Jun/1970	20°	♍	47	11/Mar/1971	20°	♍	52	9/Dec/1971	16°	♍	55
11/Oct/1969	17°	♎	53	11/Jul/1970	19°	♎	4	10/Apr/1971	20°	♎	18	8/Jan/1972	17°	♎	22
9/Nov/1969	17°	♏	20	10/Aug/1970	17°	♏	18	10/May/1971	19°	♏	9	7/Feb/1972	17°	♏	46
9/Dec/1969	17°	♐	9	8/Sep/1970	15°	♐	43	8/Jun/1971	17°	♐	32	8/Mar/1972	17°	♐	49
7/Jan/1970	17°	♑	8	7/Oct/1970	14°	♑	29	8/Jul/1971	15°	♑	37	6/Apr/1972	17°	♑	15
6/Feb/1970	17°	♒	5	6/Nov/1970	13°	♒	41	**6/Aug/1971**	**13°**	**♒**	**41**	6/May/1972	16°	♒	3
7/Mar/1970	**16°**	**♓**	**44**	5/Dec/1970	13°	♓	18	4/Sep/1971	11°	♓	57	4/Jun/1972	14°	♓	19
5/Apr/1970	15°	♈	56	3/Jan/1971	13°	♈	10	4/Oct/1971	10°	♈	37	3/Jul/1972	12°	♈	14
5/May/1970	14°	♉	41	2/Feb/1971	13°	♉	6	2/Nov/1971	09°	♉	47	2/Aug/1972	10°	♉	6
3/Jun/1970	13°	♊	3	3/Mar/1971	12°	♊	50	2/Dec/1971	09°	♊	28	31/Aug/1972	08°	♊	11
3/Jul/1970	11°	♋	16	2/Apr/1971	12°	♋	15	31/Dec/1971	09°	♋	30	29/Sep/1972	06°	♋	43
2/Aug/1970	09°	♌	32	2/May/1971	11°	♌	15	**30/Jan/1972**	**09°**	**♌**	**39**	28/Oct/1972	05°	♌	51
31/Aug/1970	**08°**	**♍**	**4**	31/May/1971	09°	♍	54	28/Feb/1972	09°	♍	38	27/Nov/1972	05°	♍	35
30/Sep/1970	07°	♎	0	30/Jun/1971	08°	♎	18	29/Mar/1972	09°	♎	13	27/Dec/1972	05°	♎	46
30/Oct/1970	06°	♏	25	30/Jul/1971	06°	♏	38	28/Apr/1972	08°	♏	19	26/Jan/1973	06°	♏	9
28/Nov/1970	06°	♐	14	28/Aug/1971	05°	♐	8	27/May/1972	06°	♐	56	24/Feb/1973	06°	♐	22
28/Dec/1970	06°	♑	17	27/Sep/1971	03°	♑	56	26/Jun/1972	05°	♑	13	26/Mar/1973	06°	♑	10
26/Jan/1971	06°	♒	20	27/Oct/1971	03°	♒	9	**26/Jul/1972**	**03°**	**♒**	**23**	25/Apr/1973	05°	♒	22
25/Feb/1971	**06°**	**♓**	**8**	25/Nov/1971	02°	♓	45	24/Aug/1972	01°	♓	39	25/May/1973	03°	♓	59
26/Mar/1971	05°	♈	29	24/Dec/1971	02°	♈	35	22/Sep/1972	00°	♈	13	23/Jun/1973	02°	♈	10
24/Apr/1971	04°	♉	18	23/Jan/1972	02°	♉	28	22/Oct/1972	29°	♈	14	22/Jul/1973	00°	♉	9
24/May/1971	02°	♊	41	21/Feb/1972	02°	♊	11	20/Nov/1972	28°	♉	44	21/Aug/1973	28°	♉	12
22/Jun/1971	00°	♋	49	21/Mar/1972	01°	♋	33	20/Dec/1972	28°	♊	37	19/Sep/1973	26°	♊	34
22/Jul/1971	**28°**	**♋**	**55**	20/Apr/1972	00°	♌	32	**18/Jan/1973**	**28°**	**♋**	**40**	18/Oct/1973	25°	♋	24
20/Aug/1971	**27°**	**♌**	**15**	19/May/1972	29°	♌	7	17/Feb/1973	28°	♌	37	17/Nov/1973	24°	♌	46
19/Sep/1971	26°	♍	0	18/Jun/1972	27°	♍	28	18/Mar/1973	28°	♍	14	16/Dec/1973	24°	♍	36
19/Oct/1971	25°	♎	16	18/Jul/1972	25°	♎	46	17/Apr/1973	27°	♎	24	15/Jan/1974	24°	♎	45
17/Nov/1971	25°	♏	3	16/Aug/1972	24°	♏	13	16/May/1973	26°	♏	9	13/Feb/1974	24°	♏	54
17/Dec/1971	25°	♐	11	15/Sep/1972	23°	♐	1	**15/Jun/1973**	**24°**	**♐**	**34**	15/Mar/1974	24°	♐	49
16/Jan/1972	**25°**	**♑**	**24**	15/Oct/1972	22°	♑	16	**15/Jul/1973**	**22°**	**♑**	**50**	14/Apr/1974	24°	♑	16
14/Feb/1972	25°	♒	25	14/Nov/1972	21°	♒	55	13/Aug/1973	21°	♒	9	14/May/1974	23°	♒	12
15/Mar/1972	24°	♓	59	13/Dec/1972	21°	♓	52	12/Sep/1973	19°	♓	42	12/Jun/1974	21°	♓	41
13/Apr/1972	24°	♈	0	12/Jan/1973	21°	♈	52	11/Oct/1973	18°	♈	39	12/Jul/1974	19°	♈	53
12/May/1972	22°	♉	29	10/Feb/1973	21°	♉	42	10/Nov/1973	18°	♉	3	10/Aug/1974	18°	♉	4
11/Jun/1972	20°	♊	37	11/Mar/1973	21°	♊	10	**9/Dec/1973**	**17°**	**♊**	**51**	9/Sep/1974	16°	♊	25
10/Jul/1972	**18°**	**♋**	**36**	9/Apr/1973	20°	♋	10	8/Jan/1974	17°	♋	51	8/Oct/1974	15°	♋	8
9/Aug/1972	16°	♌	43	9/May/1973	18°	♌	43	6/Feb/1974	17°	♌	48	6/Nov/1974	14°	♌	18

Moon Families - Eclipses in Bold Print

New Moon	°			First Quarter Moon	°			Full Moon	°			Last Quarter Moon	°		
7/Sep/1972	15°	♍	10	7/Jun/1973	16°	♍	57	8/Mar/1974	17°	♍	27	6/Dec/1974	13°	♍	54
7/Oct/1972	14°	♎	9	7/Jul/1973	15°	♎	4	6/Apr/1974	16°	♎	40	4/Jan/1975	13°	♎	48
5/Nov/1972	13°	♏	43	5/Aug/1973	13°	♏	19	6/May/1974	15°	♏	27	3/Feb/1975	13°	♏	47
5/Dec/1972	13°	♐	49	4/Sep/1973	11°	♐	56	**4/Jun/1974**	**13°**	**♐**	**53**	4/Mar/1975	13°	♐	37
4/Jan/1973	**14°**	**♑**	**9**	4/Oct/1973	11°	♑	3	4/Jul/1974	12°	♑	9	3/Apr/1975	13°	♑	7
3/Feb/1973	14°	♒	25	3/Nov/1973	10°	♒	41	2/Aug/1974	10°	♒	27	3/May/1975	12°	♒	11
4/Mar/1973	14°	♓	17	2/Dec/1973	10°	♓	44	1/Sep/1974	08°	♓	58	1/Jun/1975	10°	♓	50
3/Apr/1973	13°	♈	35	1/Jan/1974	10°	♈	57	1/Oct/1974	07°	♈	52	1/Jul/1975	09°	♈	13
2/May/1973	12°	♉	17	31/Jan/1974	11°	♉	3	30/Oct/1974	07°	♉	14	31/Jul/1975	07°	♉	32
31/May/1973	10°	♊	32	1/Mar/1974	10°	♊	46	**29/Nov/1974**	**07°**	**♊**	**1**	29/Aug/1975	05°	♊	59
30/Jun/1973	**08°**	**♋**	**31**	30/Mar/1974	09°	♋	58	28/Dec/1974	07°	♋	2	28/Sep/1975	04°	♋	43
29/Jul/1973	06°	♌	29	29/Apr/1974	08°	♌	37	27/Jan/1975	07°	♌	3	27/Oct/1975	03°	♌	51
27/Aug/1973	04°	♍	41	28/May/1974	06°	♍	49	25/Feb/1975	06°	♍	48	26/Nov/1975	03°	♍	23
26/Sep/1973	03°	♎	19	26/Jun/1974	04°	♎	47	27/Mar/1975	06°	♎	8	25/Dec/1975	03°	♎	11
25/Oct/1973	02°	♏	33	25/Jul/1974	02°	♏	48	25/Apr/1975	04°	♏	59	23/Jan/1976	03°	♏	4
24/Nov/1973	02°	♐	24	24/Aug/1974	01°	♐	5	**25/May/1975**	**03°**	**♐**	**25**	22/Feb/1976	02°	♐	50
24/Dec/1973	**02°**	**♑**	**40**	23/Sep/1974	29°	♐	53	23/Jun/1975	01°	♑	36	22/Mar/1976	02°	♑	16
23/Jan/1974	03°	♒	3	22/Oct/1974	29°	♑	16	23/Jul/1975	29°	♑	45	21/Apr/1976	01°	♒	18
22/Feb/1974	03°	♓	13	21/Nov/1974	29°	♒	14	21/Aug/1975	28°	♒	7	20/May/1976	29°	♒	57
23/Mar/1974	02°	♈	51	21/Dec/1974	29°	♓	34	20/Sep/1975	26°	♓	54	19/Jun/1976	28°	♓	21
22/Apr/1974	01°	♉	54	20/Jan/1975	29°	♈	56	20/Oct/1975	26°	♈	11	19/Jul/1976	26°	♈	42
21/May/1974	00°	♊	23	19/Feb/1975	00°	♊	2	**18/Nov/1975**	**25°**	**♉**	**57**	17/Aug/1976	25°	♉	10
19/Jun/1974	**28°**	**♊**	**30**	20/Mar/1975	29°	♊	35	18/Dec/1975	26°	♊	3	16/Sep/1976	23°	♊	57
19/Jul/1974	26°	♋	26	18/Apr/1975	28°	♋	31	16/Jan/1976	26°	♋	11	16/Oct/1976	23°	♋	7
17/Aug/1974	24°	♌	29	18/May/1975	26°	♌	52	15/Feb/1976	26°	♌	8	14/Nov/1976	22°	♌	41
15/Sep/1974	22°	♍	51	16/Jun/1975	24°	♍	51	15/Mar/1976	25°	♍	39	14/Dec/1976	22°	♍	33
15/Oct/1974	21°	♎	46	15/Jul/1975	22°	♎	42	14/Apr/1976	24°	♎	39	12/Jan/1977	22°	♎	31
13/Nov/1974	21°	♏	16	13/Aug/1975	20°	♏	42	**13/May/1976**	**23°**	**♏**	**10**	10/Feb/1977	22°	♏	19
13/Dec/1974	**21°**	**♐**	**16**	12/Sep/1975	19°	♐	6	11/Jun/1976	21°	♐	19	12/Mar/1977	21°	♐	46
12/Jan/1975	21°	♑	35	11/Oct/1975	18°	♑	5	11/Jul/1976	19°	♑	20	10/Apr/1977	20°	♑	47
11/Feb/1975	21°	♒	51	10/Nov/1975	17°	♒	44	9/Aug/1976	17°	♒	28	9/May/1977	19°	♒	23
12/Mar/1975	21°	♓	46	10/Dec/1975	17°	♓	54	8/Sep/1976	15°	♓	59	8/Jun/1977	17°	♓	41
11/Apr/1975	21°	♈	10	9/Jan/1976	18°	♈	23	7/Oct/1976	15°	♈	2	7/Jul/1977	15°	♈	54
11/May/1975	**19°**	**♉**	**59**	8/Feb/1976	18°	♉	46	**6/Nov/1976**	**14°**	**♉**	**40**	6/Aug/1977	14°	♉	14
9/Jun/1975	18°	♊	18	8/Mar/1976	18°	♊	44	6/Dec/1976	14°	♊	46	5/Sep/1977	12°	♊	54
8/Jul/1975	16°	♋	21	7/Apr/1976	18°	♋	5	5/Jan/1977	15°	♋	3	5/Oct/1977	12°	♋	1
7/Aug/1975	14°	♌	22	7/May/1976	16°	♌	46	3/Feb/1977	15°	♌	13	3/Nov/1977	11°	♌	37
5/Sep/1975	12°	♍	36	5/Jun/1976	14°	♍	57	5/Mar/1977	15°	♍	1	3/Dec/1977	11°	♍	36
4/Oct/1975	11°	♎	16	4/Jul/1976	12°	♎	50	**3/Apr/1977**	**14°**	**♎**	**16**	2/Jan/1978	11°	♎	44
3/Nov/1975	**10°**	**♏**	**29**	2/Aug/1976	10°	♏	42	3/May/1977	12°	♏	58	31/Jan/1978	11°	♏	45
2/Dec/1975	10°	♐	13	31/Aug/1976	08°	♐	49	1/Jun/1977	11°	♐	12	2/Mar/1978	11°	♐	24
1/Jan/1976	10°	♑	18	30/Sep/1976	07°	♑	25	30/Jun/1977	09°	♑	11	31/Mar/1978	10°	♑	32
31/Jan/1976	10°	♒	30	29/Oct/1976	06°	♒	37	30/Jul/1977	07°	♒	9	29/Apr/1978	09°	♒	10
29/Feb/1976	10°	♓	30	28/Nov/1976	06°	♓	26	28/Aug/1977	05°	♓	23	28/May/1978	07°	♓	25
30/Mar/1976	10°	♈	7	28/Dec/1976	06°	♈	43	**27/Sep/1977**	**04°**	**♈**	**6**	27/Jun/1978	05°	♈	28
29/Apr/1976	**09°**	**♉**	**13**	27/Jan/1977	07°	♉	9	26/Oct/1977	03°	♉	26	26/Jul/1978	03°	♉	33
28/May/1976	07°	♊	49	25/Feb/1977	07°	♊	23	25/Nov/1977	03°	♊	20	25/Aug/1978	01°	♊	56
27/Jun/1976	06°	♋	3	27/Mar/1977	07°	♋	8	25/Dec/1977	03°	♋	37	24/Sep/1978	00°	♋	48
26/Jul/1976	04°	♌	9	26/Apr/1977	06°	♌	14	24/Jan/1978	03°	♌	58	23/Oct/1978	00°	♌	14
25/Aug/1976	02°	♍	21	25/May/1977	04°	♍	46	22/Feb/1978	04°	♍	4	22/Nov/1978	00°	♍	13
23/Sep/1976	00°	♎	54	24/Jun/1977	02°	♎	52	**24/Mar/1978**	**03°**	**♎**	**40**	22/Dec/1978	00°	♎	31

Moon Families - Eclipses in Bold Print

New Moon				First Quarter Moon				Full Moon				Last Quarter Moon			
23/Oct/1976	**29°**	♎	**55**	23/Jul/1977	00°	♏	49	22/Apr/1978	02°	♏	39	21/Jan/1979	00°	♏	49
21/Nov/1976	29°	♏	26	21/Aug/1977	28°	♏	50	22/May/1978	01°	♐	5	19/Feb/1979	00°	♐	48
20/Dec/1976	29°	♐	20	20/Sep/1977	27°	♐	10	20/Jun/1978	29°	♐	8	21/Mar/1979	00°	♑	14
19/Jan/1977	29°	♑	24	19/Oct/1977	26°	♑	1	19/Jul/1978	27°	♑	3	19/Apr/1979	29°	♑	6
17/Feb/1977	29°	♒	22	17/Nov/1977	25°	♒	26	18/Aug/1978	25°	♒	7	18/May/1979	27°	♒	26
19/Mar/1977	29°	♓	2	17/Dec/1977	25°	♓	23	**16/Sep/1978**	**23°**	♓	**33**	17/Jun/1979	25°	♓	25
18/Apr/1977	**28°**	♈	**16**	15/Jan/1978	25°	♈	37	16/Oct/1978	22°	♈	31	16/Jul/1979	23°	♈	19
17/May/1977	27°	♉	3	14/Feb/1978	25°	♉	52	14/Nov/1978	22°	♉	5	14/Aug/1979	21°	♉	23
16/Jun/1977	25°	♊	28	16/Mar/1978	25°	♊	48	14/Dec/1978	22°	♊	9	13/Sep/1979	19°	♊	52
16/Jul/1977	23°	♋	41	15/Apr/1978	25°	♋	14	13/Jan/1979	22°	♋	29	12/Oct/1979	18°	♋	56
14/Aug/1977	21°	♌	57	15/May/1978	24°	♌	7	11/Feb/1979	22°	♌	46	11/Nov/1979	18°	♌	40
13/Sep/1977	20°	♍	28	13/Jun/1978	22°	♍	32	**13/Mar/1979**	**22°**	♍	**41**	11/Dec/1979	18°	♍	55
12/Oct/1977	**19°**	♎	**24**	13/Jul/1978	20°	♎	41	12/Apr/1979	22°	♎	2	10/Jan/1980	19°	♎	23
11/Nov/1977	18°	♏	47	11/Aug/1978	18°	♏	47	11/May/1979	20°	♏	46	9/Feb/1980	19°	♏	42
10/Dec/1977	18°	♐	33	9/Sep/1978	17°	♐	4	10/Jun/1979	19°	♐	1	9/Mar/1980	19°	♐	33
8/Jan/1978	18°	♑	32	9/Oct/1978	15°	♑	44	9/Jul/1979	17°	♑	0	8/Apr/1980	18°	♑	48
7/Feb/1978	18°	♒	28	7/Nov/1978	14°	♒	54	7/Aug/1979	15°	♒	0	7/May/1980	17°	♒	25
8/Mar/1978	18°	♓	10	6/Dec/1978	14°	♓	32	**6/Sep/1979**	**13°**	♓	**15**	5/Jun/1980	15°	♓	33
7/Apr/1978	**17°**	♈	**26**	5/Jan/1979	14°	♈	31	5/Oct/1979	11°	♈	57	5/Jul/1980	13°	♈	24
6/May/1978	16°	♉	16	3/Feb/1979	14°	♉	35	4/Nov/1979	11°	♉	12	3/Aug/1980	11°	♉	16
5/Jun/1978	14°	♊	44	5/Mar/1979	14°	♊	30	3/Dec/1979	10°	♊	58	1/Sep/1980	09°	♊	26
5/Jul/1978	13°	♋	1	4/Apr/1979	14°	♋	2	2/Jan/1980	11°	♋	7	30/Sep/1980	08°	♋	5
3/Aug/1978	11°	♌	18	3/May/1979	13°	♌	7	31/Jan/1980	11°	♌	22	30/Oct/1980	07°	♌	24
2/Sep/1978	09°	♍	49	2/Jun/1979	11°	♍	47	**1/Mar/1980**	**11°**	♍	**26**	29/Nov/1980	07°	♍	20
2/Oct/1978	**08°**	♎	**43**	2/Jul/1979	10°	♎	9	31/Mar/1980	11°	♎	3	29/Dec/1980	07°	♎	42
31/Oct/1978	08°	♏	2	1/Aug/1979	08°	♏	24	30/Apr/1980	10°	♏	6	27/Jan/1981	08°	♏	9
30/Nov/1978	07°	♐	46	30/Aug/1979	06°	♐	46	29/May/1980	08°	♐	37	26/Feb/1981	08°	♐	21
29/Dec/1978	07°	♑	44	28/Sep/1979	05°	♑	26	28/Jun/1980	06°	♑	48	28/Mar/1981	08°	♑	1
28/Jan/1979	07°	♒	43	28/Oct/1979	04°	♒	30	**27/Jul/1980**	**04°**	♒	**51**	27/Apr/1981	07°	♒	3
26/Feb/1979	**07°**	♓	**29**	26/Nov/1979	04°	♓	0	**25/Aug/1980**	**03°**	♓	**3**	26/May/1981	05°	♓	29
27/Mar/1979	06°	♈	50	26/Dec/1979	03°	♈	49	24/Sep/1980	01°	♈	35	24/Jun/1981	03°	♈	31
26/Apr/1979	05°	♉	42	24/Jan/1980	03°	♉	44	23/Oct/1980	00°	♉	36	24/Jul/1981	01°	♉	23
25/May/1979	04°	♊	10	22/Feb/1980	03°	♊	32	22/Nov/1980	00°	♊	7	22/Aug/1981	29°	♉	22
24/Jun/1979	02°	♋	23	23/Mar/1980	03°	♋	2	21/Dec/1980	00°	♋	3	20/Sep/1981	27°	♊	44
23/Jul/1979	00°	♌	35	21/Apr/1980	02°	♌	8	**20/Jan/1981**	**00°**	♌	**10**	19/Oct/1981	26°	♋	39
22/Aug/1979	**29°**	♌	**0**	21/May/1980	00°	♍	51	18/Feb/1981	00°	♍	12	18/Nov/1981	26°	♌	11
21/Sep/1979	27°	♍	49	20/Jun/1980	29°	♍	18	20/Mar/1981	29°	♍	55	18/Dec/1981	26°	♍	13
20/Oct/1979	27°	♎	5	20/Jul/1980	27°	♎	39	19/Apr/1981	29°	♎	10	16/Jan/1982	26°	♎	32
19/Nov/1979	26°	♏	48	18/Aug/1980	26°	♏	5	18/May/1981	27°	♏	55	15/Feb/1982	26°	♏	49
19/Dec/1979	26°	♐	49	17/Sep/1980	24°	♐	49	17/Jun/1981	26°	♐	18	17/Mar/1982	26°	♐	46
17/Jan/1980	26°	♑	55	16/Oct/1980	23°	♑	55	**16/Jul/1981**	**24°**	♑	**30**	16/Apr/1982	26°	♑	11
16/Feb/1980	**26°**	♒	**50**	15/Nov/1980	23°	♒	26	15/Aug/1981	22°	♒	44	16/May/1982	25°	♒	0
16/Mar/1980	26°	♓	20	14/Dec/1980	23°	♓	15	13/Sep/1981	21°	♓	12	14/Jun/1982	23°	♓	20
14/Apr/1980	25°	♈	19	13/Jan/1981	23°	♈	9	13/Oct/1981	20°	♈	5	13/Jul/1982	21°	♈	23
14/May/1980	23°	♉	49	11/Feb/1981	22°	♉	55	11/Nov/1981	19°	♉	26	12/Aug/1982	19°	♉	24
12/Jun/1980	21°	♊	59	12/Mar/1981	22°	♊	24	11/Dec/1981	19°	♊	13	10/Sep/1982	17°	♊	39
12/Jul/1980	20°	♋	3	11/Apr/1981	21°	♋	28	**9/Jan/1982**	**19°**	♋	**14**	9/Oct/1982	16°	♋	20
10/Aug/1980	**18°**	♌	**16**	10/May/1981	20°	♌	9	8/Feb/1982	19°	♌	13	8/Nov/1982	15°	♌	31
9/Sep/1980	16°	♍	52	9/Jun/1981	18°	♍	32	9/Mar/1982	18°	♍	57	7/Dec/1982	15°	♍	12
8/Oct/1980	15°	♎	58	8/Jul/1981	16°	♎	48	8/Apr/1982	18°	♎	15	5/Jan/1983	15°	♎	15
7/Nov/1980	15°	♏	36	7/Aug/1981	15°	♏	10	7/May/1982	17°	♏	6	4/Feb/1983	15°	♏	24

Moon Families - Eclipses in Bold Print

New Moon			First Quarter Moon			Full Moon			Last Quarter Moon		
7/Dec/1980	15°	♐ 39	6/Sep/1981	13°	♐ 51	6/Jun/1982	15°	♐ 36	6/Mar/1983	15°	♐ 23
6/Jan/1981	15°	♑ 54	6/Oct/1981	12°	♑ 58	**6/Jul/1982**	**13°**	**♑ 54**	5/Apr/1983	14°	♑ 59
4/Feb/1981	**16°**	**♒ 1**	4/Nov/1981	12°	♒ 32	4/Aug/1982	12°	♒ 12	4/May/1983	14°	♒ 5
6/Mar/1981	15°	♓ 46	4/Dec/1981	12°	♓ 26	3/Sep/1982	10°	♓ 40	3/Jun/1983	12°	♓ 42
4/Apr/1981	14°	♈ 58	2/Jan/1982	12°	♈ 28	2/Oct/1982	09°	♈ 30	3/Jul/1983	11°	♈ 0
3/May/1981	13°	♉ 36	1/Feb/1982	12°	♉ 24	1/Nov/1982	08°	♉ 46	1/Aug/1983	09°	♉ 11
2/Jun/1981	11°	♊ 49	2/Mar/1982	12°	♊ 0	30/Nov/1982	08°	♊ 28	31/Aug/1983	07°	♊ 29
1/Jul/1981	09°	♋ 49	1/Apr/1982	11°	♋ 9	**30/Dec/1982**	**08°**	**♋ 26**	29/Sep/1983	06°	♋ 6
30/Jul/1981	**07°**	**♌ 51**	30/Apr/1982	09°	♌ 49	28/Jan/1983	08°	♌ 26	28/Oct/1983	05°	♌ 8
29/Aug/1981	06°	♍ 9	29/May/1982	08°	♍ 6	27/Feb/1983	08°	♍ 11	27/Nov/1983	04°	♍ 36
27/Sep/1981	04°	♎ 56	28/Jun/1982	06°	♎ 13	28/Mar/1983	07°	♎ 32	26/Dec/1983	04°	♎ 25
27/Oct/1981	04°	♏ 19	27/Jul/1982	04°	♏ 22	27/Apr/1983	06°	♏ 26	24/Jan/1984	04°	♏ 23
26/Nov/1981	04°	♐ 15	26/Aug/1982	02°	♐ 50	26/May/1983	04°	♐ 57	23/Feb/1984	04°	♐ 16
26/Dec/1981	04°	♑ 33	24/Sep/1982	01°	♑ 46	**25/Jun/1983**	**03°**	**♑ 14**	24/Mar/1984	03°	♑ 52
24/Jan/1982	**04°**	**♒ 53**	24/Oct/1982	01°	♒ 15	24/Jul/1983	01°	♒ 29	22/Apr/1984	03°	♒ 2
23/Feb/1982	04°	♓ 55	23/Nov/1982	01°	♓ 12	23/Aug/1983	29°	♒ 54	22/May/1984	01°	♓ 47
25/Mar/1982	04°	♈ 26	23/Dec/1982	01°	♈ 25	22/Sep/1983	28°	♓ 41	21/Jun/1984	00°	♈ 14
23/Apr/1982	03°	♉ 20	22/Jan/1983	01°	♉ 37	21/Oct/1983	27°	♈ 55	20/Jul/1984	28°	♈ 34
22/May/1982	01°	♊ 44	20/Feb/1983	01°	♊ 30	20/Nov/1983	27°	♉ 36	19/Aug/1984	26°	♉ 58
21/Jun/1982	**29°**	**♊ 46**	21/Mar/1983	00°	♋ 54	**19/Dec/1983**	**27°**	**♊ 36**	18/Sep/1984	25°	♊ 38
20/Jul/1982	**27°**	**♋ 43**	20/Apr/1983	29°	♋ 43	18/Jan/1984	27°	♋ 40	17/Oct/1984	24°	♋ 40
18/Aug/1982	25°	♌ 48	19/May/1983	28°	♌ 2	16/Feb/1984	27°	♌ 32	16/Nov/1984	24°	♌ 6
17/Sep/1982	24°	♍ 16	17/Jun/1983	26°	♍ 2	17/Mar/1984	27°	♍ 0	15/Dec/1984	23°	♍ 50
16/Oct/1982	23°	♎ 17	16/Jul/1983	23°	♎ 59	15/Apr/1984	25°	♎ 59	13/Jan/1985	23°	♎ 44
15/Nov/1982	22°	♏ 55	15/Aug/1983	22°	♏ 7	**14/May/1984**	**24°**	**♏ 31**	12/Feb/1985	23°	♏ 33
15/Dec/1982	**23°**	**♐ 4**	13/Sep/1983	20°	♐ 42	**13/Jun/1984**	**22°**	**♐ 44**	13/Mar/1985	23°	♐ 5
14/Jan/1983	23°	♑ 27	13/Oct/1983	19°	♑ 53	12/Jul/1984	20°	♑ 52	11/Apr/1985	22°	♑ 13
12/Feb/1983	23°	♒ 43	12/Nov/1983	19°	♒ 41	11/Aug/1984	19°	♒ 7	11/May/1985	20°	♒ 57
14/Mar/1983	23°	♓ 34	12/Dec/1983	19°	♓ 56	10/Sep/1984	17°	♓ 44	10/Jun/1985	19°	♓ 23
13/Apr/1983	22°	♈ 49	11/Jan/1984	20°	♈ 21	9/Oct/1984	16°	♈ 51	9/Jul/1985	17°	♈ 43
12/May/1983	21°	♉ 29	9/Feb/1984	20°	♉ 36	**8/Nov/1984**	**16°**	**♉ 30**	8/Aug/1985	16°	♉ 8
10/Jun/1983	**19°**	**♊ 42**	10/Mar/1984	20°	♊ 22	8/Dec/1984	16°	♊ 32	7/Sep/1985	14°	♊ 48
10/Jul/1983	17°	♋ 41	8/Apr/1984	19°	♋ 31	6/Jan/1985	16°	♋ 43	7/Oct/1985	13°	♋ 52
8/Aug/1983	15°	♌ 40	8/May/1984	18°	♌ 3	5/Feb/1985	16°	♌ 46	5/Nov/1985	13°	♌ 21
6/Sep/1983	13°	♍ 55	6/Jun/1984	16°	♍ 8	6/Mar/1985	16°	♍ 27	5/Dec/1985	13°	♍ 10
6/Oct/1983	12°	♎ 37	5/Jul/1984	13°	♎ 59	5/Apr/1985	15°	♎ 37	3/Jan/1986	13°	♎ 8
4/Nov/1983	11°	♏ 55	3/Aug/1984	11°	♏ 53	**4/May/1985**	**14°**	**♏ 16**	1/Feb/1986	13°	♏ 2
4/Dec/1983	**11°**	**♐ 46**	2/Sep/1984	10°	♐ 7	2/Jun/1985	12°	♐ 31	3/Mar/1986	12°	♐ 37
3/Jan/1984	12°	♑ 0	1/Oct/1984	08°	♑ 53	2/Jul/1985	10°	♑ 32	1/Apr/1986	11°	♑ 46
1/Feb/1984	12°	♒ 18	31/Oct/1984	08°	♒ 17	31/Jul/1985	08°	♒ 36	30/Apr/1986	10°	♒ 28
2/Mar/1984	12°	♓ 22	30/Nov/1984	08°	♓ 18	30/Aug/1985	06°	♓ 57	30/May/1986	08°	♓ 49
1/Apr/1984	11°	♈ 57	30/Dec/1984	08°	♈ 42	28/Sep/1985	05°	♈ 48	28/Jun/1986	07°	♈ 0
30/Apr/1984	10°	♉ 57	28/Jan/1985	09°	♉ 10	**28/Oct/1985**	**05°**	**♉ 14**	28/Jul/1986	05°	♉ 15
30/May/1984	**09°**	**♊ 26**	27/Feb/1985	09°	♊ 20	27/Nov/1985	05°	♊ 13	27/Aug/1986	03°	♊ 47
28/Jun/1984	07°	♋ 33	29/Mar/1985	08°	♋ 55	27/Dec/1985	05°	♋ 29	25/Sep/1986	02°	♋ 44
28/Jul/1984	05°	♌ 34	27/Apr/1985	07°	♌ 50	25/Jan/1986	05°	♌ 45	25/Oct/1986	02°	♌ 12
26/Aug/1984	03°	♍ 42	27/May/1985	06°	♍ 10	24/Feb/1986	05°	♍ 42	24/Nov/1986	02°	♍ 6
24/Sep/1984	02°	♎ 13	25/Jun/1985	04°	♎ 8	25/Mar/1986	05°	♎ 9	24/Dec/1986	02°	♎ 15
24/Oct/1984	01°	♏ 15	24/Jul/1985	01°	♏ 59	**24/Apr/1986**	**04°**	**♏ 2**	22/Jan/1987	02°	♏ 22
22/Nov/1984	**00°**	**♐ 49**	22/Aug/1985	00°	♐ 0	23/May/1986	02°	♐ 24	21/Feb/1987	02°	♐ 11
22/Dec/1984	00°	♑ 49	21/Sep/1985	28°	♐ 24	21/Jun/1986	00°	♑ 26	22/Mar/1987	01°	♑ 30

Moon Families - Eclipses in Bold Print

New Moon				First Quarter Moon				Full Moon				Last Quarter Moon			
20/Jan/1985	00°	♒	59	20/Oct/1985	27°	♑	22	21/Jul/1986	28°	♑	22	20/Apr/1987	00°	♒	17
19/Feb/1985	01°	♓	4	19/Nov/1985	26°	♒	58	19/Aug/1986	26°	♒	29	19/May/1987	28°	♒	37
21/Mar/1985	00°	♈	49	18/Dec/1985	27°	♓	6	18/Sep/1986	25°	♓	0	18/Jun/1987	26°	♓	41
20/Apr/1985	00°	♉	4	17/Jan/1986	27°	♈	31	**17/Oct/1986**	**24°**	♈	**7**	17/Jul/1987	24°	♈	43
19/May/1985	**28°**	♉	**50**	16/Feb/1986	27°	♉	51	16/Nov/1986	23°	♉	50	16/Aug/1987	22°	♉	57
18/Jun/1985	27°	♊	11	18/Mar/1986	27°	♊	47	16/Dec/1986	24°	♊	1	14/Sep/1987	21°	♊	36
17/Jul/1985	25°	♋	19	17/Apr/1986	27°	♋	7	14/Jan/1987	24°	♋	23	14/Oct/1987	20°	♋	51
16/Aug/1985	23°	♌	28	16/May/1986	25°	♌	51	13/Feb/1987	24°	♌	37	13/Nov/1987	20°	♌	40
14/Sep/1985	21°	♍	54	15/Jun/1986	24°	♍	5	15/Mar/1987	24°	♍	25	13/Dec/1987	20°	♍	55
13/Oct/1985	20°	♎	46	14/Jul/1986	22°	♎	4	**13/Apr/1987**	**23°**	♎	**37**	12/Jan/1988	21°	♎	17
12/Nov/1985	**20°**	♏	**8**	12/Aug/1986	20°	♏	3	13/May/1987	22°	♏	14	10/Feb/1988	21°	♏	25
11/Dec/1985	19°	♐	56	11/Sep/1986	18°	♐	17	11/Jun/1987	20°	♐	23	11/Mar/1988	21°	♐	5
10/Jan/1986	19°	♑	57	10/Oct/1986	16°	♑	56	10/Jul/1987	18°	♑	19	9/Apr/1988	20°	♑	8
8/Feb/1986	19°	♒	58	8/Nov/1986	16°	♒	10	9/Aug/1987	16°	♒	18	8/May/1988	18°	♒	38
10/Mar/1986	19°	♓	44	8/Dec/1986	15°	♓	55	7/Sep/1987	14°	♓	35	7/Jun/1988	16°	♓	43
9/Apr/1986	**19°**	♈	**6**	6/Jan/1987	16°	♈	4	**6/Oct/1987**	**13°**	♈	**21**	6/Jul/1988	14°	♈	36
8/May/1986	18°	♉	0	5/Feb/1987	16°	♉	19	5/Nov/1987	12°	♉	43	4/Aug/1988	12°	♉	33
7/Jun/1986	16°	♊	31	7/Mar/1987	16°	♊	22	5/Dec/1987	12°	♊	38	2/Sep/1988	10°	♊	51
6/Jul/1986	14°	♋	47	6/Apr/1987	15°	♋	59	3/Jan/1988	12°	♋	54	2/Oct/1988	09°	♋	42
5/Aug/1986	13°	♌	2	5/May/1987	15°	♌	3	2/Feb/1988	13°	♌	13	1/Nov/1988	09°	♌	12
4/Sep/1986	11°	♍	28	4/Jun/1987	13°	♍	37	**3/Mar/1988**	**13°**	♍	**17**	1/Dec/1988	09°	♍	18
3/Oct/1986	**10°**	♎	**15**	4/Jul/1987	11°	♎	51	2/Apr/1988	12°	♎	51	30/Dec/1988	09°	♎	44
2/Nov/1986	09°	♏	31	2/Aug/1987	09°	♏	58	1/May/1988	11°	♏	47	29/Jan/1989	10°	♏	9
1/Dec/1986	09°	♐	11	31/Aug/1987	08°	♐	11	31/May/1988	10°	♐	11	28/Feb/1989	10°	♐	13
30/Dec/1986	09°	♑	8	30/Sep/1987	06°	♑	44	29/Jun/1988	08°	♑	15	30/Mar/1989	09°	♑	41
29/Jan/1987	09°	♒	6	29/Oct/1987	05°	♒	44	28/Jul/1988	06°	♒	13	28/Apr/1989	08°	♒	31
27/Feb/1987	08°	♓	53	27/Nov/1987	05°	♓	13	**27/Aug/1988**	**04°**	♓	**22**	27/May/1989	06°	♓	48
29/Mar/1987	**08°**	♈	**17**	27/Dec/1987	05°	♈	6	25/Sep/1988	02°	♈	55	26/Jun/1989	04°	♈	44
27/Apr/1987	07°	♉	15	25/Jan/1988	05°	♉	9	24/Oct/1988	01°	♉	59	25/Jul/1989	02°	♉	34
27/May/1987	05°	♊	48	24/Feb/1988	05°	♊	6	23/Nov/1988	01°	♊	35	23/Aug/1989	00°	♊	35
26/Jun/1987	04°	♋	6	24/Mar/1988	04°	♋	45	23/Dec/1988	01°	♋	36	21/Sep/1989	29°	♊	3
25/Jul/1987	02°	♌	22	23/Apr/1988	03°	♌	58	21/Jan/1989	01°	♌	50	21/Oct/1989	28°	♋	7
24/Aug/1987	00°	♍	47	23/May/1988	02°	♍	45	**20/Feb/1989**	**01°**	♍	**58**	19/Nov/1989	27°	♌	50
22/Sep/1987	**29°**	♍	**34**	22/Jun/1988	01°	♎	12	22/Mar/1989	01°	♎	45	19/Dec/1989	28°	♍	4
22/Oct/1987	28°	♎	46	21/Jul/1988	29°	♎	29	20/Apr/1989	00°	♏	59	18/Jan/1990	28°	♎	31
21/Nov/1987	28°	♏	24	20/Aug/1988	27°	♏	49	20/May/1989	29°	♏	41	17/Feb/1990	28°	♏	50
20/Dec/1987	28°	♐	19	18/Sep/1988	26°	♐	24	19/Jun/1989	27°	♐	58	19/Mar/1990	28°	♐	43
19/Jan/1988	28°	♑	20	18/Oct/1988	25°	♑	22	18/Jul/1989	26°	♑	3	18/Apr/1990	27°	♑	59
17/Feb/1988	28°	♒	12	16/Nov/1988	24°	♒	45	**16/Aug/1989**	**24°**	♒	**11**	17/May/1990	26°	♒	38
17/Mar/1988	**27°**	♓	**41**	16/Dec/1988	24°	♓	29	15/Sep/1989	22°	♓	36	15/Jun/1990	24°	♓	47
16/Apr/1988	26°	♈	42	14/Jan/1989	24°	♈	23	14/Oct/1989	21°	♈	28	15/Jul/1990	22°	♈	42
15/May/1988	25°	♉	16	12/Feb/1989	24°	♉	14	13/Nov/1989	20°	♉	49	13/Aug/1990	20°	♉	38
14/Jun/1988	23°	♊	31	14/Mar/1989	23°	♊	48	12/Dec/1989	20°	♊	38	11/Sep/1990	18°	♊	51
13/Jul/1988	21°	♋	41	12/Apr/1989	23°	♋	0	10/Jan/1990	20°	♋	42	10/Oct/1990	17°	♋	33
12/Aug/1988	20°	♌	0	12/May/1989	21°	♌	49	**9/Feb/1990**	**20°**	♌	**47**	9/Nov/1990	16°	♌	52
10/Sep/1988	**18°**	♍	**40**	11/Jun/1989	20°	♍	20	11/Mar/1990	20°	♍	36	8/Dec/1990	16°	♍	43
10/Oct/1988	17°	♎	48	10/Jul/1989	18°	♎	41	9/Apr/1990	20°	♎	0	7/Jan/1991	16°	♎	57
9/Nov/1988	17°	♏	24	9/Aug/1989	17°	♏	5	9/May/1990	18°	♏	54	6/Feb/1991	17°	♏	16
9/Dec/1988	17°	♐	22	8/Sep/1989	15°	♐	43	8/Jun/1990	17°	♐	24	8/Mar/1991	17°	♐	20
7/Jan/1989	17°	♑	29	7/Oct/1989	14°	♑	43	7/Jul/1990	15°	♑	39	7/Apr/1991	16°	♑	57
6/Feb/1989	17°	♒	30	6/Nov/1989	14°	♒	8	**6/Aug/1990**	**13°**	♒	**51**	7/May/1991	15°	♒	58

Moon Families - Eclipses in Bold Print

New Moon				First Quarter Moon				Full Moon				Last Quarter Moon			
7/Mar/1989	**17°**	♓	**9**	5/Dec/1989	13°	♓	54	4/Sep/1990	12°	♓	15	5/Jun/1991	14°	♓	28
5/Apr/1989	16°	♈	18	4/Jan/1990	13°	♈	48	4/Oct/1990	11°	♈	0	5/Jul/1991	12°	♈	36
5/May/1989	14°	♉	57	2/Feb/1990	13°	♉	39	2/Nov/1990	10°	♉	12	3/Aug/1991	10°	♉	38
3/Jun/1989	13°	♊	11	3/Mar/1990	13°	♊	14	2/Dec/1990	09°	♊	52	1/Sep/1991	08°	♊	48
2/Jul/1989	11°	♋	15	2/Apr/1990	12°	♋	25	31/Dec/1990	09°	♋	49	1/Oct/1991	07°	♋	20
1/Aug/1989	09°	♌	22	1/May/1990	11°	♌	11	**30/Jan/1991**	**09°**	♌	**50**	30/Oct/1991	06°	♌	21
31/Aug/1989	**07°**	♍	**48**	31/May/1990	09°	♍	37	28/Feb/1991	09°	♍	39	28/Nov/1991	05°	♍	53
29/Sep/1989	06°	♎	43	29/Jun/1990	07°	♎	53	30/Mar/1991	09°	♎	5	28/Dec/1991	05°	♎	48
29/Oct/1989	06°	♏	11	29/Jul/1990	06°	♏	11	28/Apr/1991	08°	♏	4	26/Jan/1992	05°	♏	55
28/Nov/1989	06°	♐	8	28/Aug/1990	04°	♐	45	28/May/1991	06°	♐	39	25/Feb/1992	05°	♐	58
27/Dec/1989	06°	♑	22	26/Sep/1990	03°	♑	43	**27/Jun/1991**	**04°**	♑	**59**	26/Mar/1992	05°	♑	41
26/Jan/1990	**06°**	♒	**35**	26/Oct/1990	03°	♒	9	**26/Jul/1991**	**03°**	♒	**16**	24/Apr/1992	04°	♒	56
25/Feb/1990	06°	♓	29	25/Nov/1990	03°	♓	0	25/Aug/1991	01°	♓	40	24/May/1992	03°	♓	42
26/Mar/1990	05°	♈	53	24/Dec/1990	03°	♈	3	23/Sep/1991	00°	♈	24	23/Jun/1992	02°	♈	6
24/Apr/1990	04°	♉	42	23/Jan/1991	03°	♉	4	23/Oct/1991	29°	♈	32	22/Jul/1992	00°	♉	19
24/May/1990	03°	♊	3	21/Feb/1991	02°	♊	48	21/Nov/1991	29°	♉	7	21/Aug/1992	28°	♉	35
22/Jun/1990	01°	♋	5	23/Mar/1991	02°	♋	6	**21/Dec/1991**	**29°**	♊	**2**	19/Sep/1992	27°	♊	6
21/Jul/1990	**29°**	♋	**4**	21/Apr/1991	00°	♌	54	19/Jan/1992	29°	♋	3	19/Oct/1992	26°	♋	1
20/Aug/1990	27°	♌	14	20/May/1991	29°	♌	17	18/Feb/1992	28°	♌	55	17/Nov/1992	25°	♌	22
18/Sep/1990	25°	♍	50	19/Jun/1991	27°	♍	24	18/Mar/1992	28°	♍	24	16/Dec/1992	25°	♍	5
18/Oct/1990	25°	♎	0	18/Jul/1991	25°	♎	30	17/Apr/1992	27°	♎	25	15/Jan/1993	25°	♎	1
17/Nov/1990	24°	♏	45	17/Aug/1991	23°	♏	49	16/May/1992	26°	♏	1	13/Feb/1993	24°	♏	55
16/Dec/1990	24°	♐	57	15/Sep/1991	22°	♐	33	**15/Jun/1992**	**24°**	♐	**20**	15/Mar/1993	24°	♐	35
15/Jan/1991	**25°**	♑	**20**	15/Oct/1991	21°	♑	51	14/Jul/1992	22°	♑	33	13/Apr/1993	23°	♑	52
14/Feb/1991	25°	♒	31	14/Nov/1991	21°	♒	41	13/Aug/1992	20°	♒	54	13/May/1993	22°	♒	44
16/Mar/1991	25°	♓	14	14/Dec/1991	21°	♓	53	12/Sep/1992	19°	♓	34	12/Jun/1993	21°	♓	16
14/Apr/1991	24°	♈	21	13/Jan/1992	22°	♈	9	11/Oct/1992	18°	♈	40	11/Jul/1993	19°	♈	37
14/May/1991	22°	♉	54	11/Feb/1992	22°	♉	11	10/Nov/1992	18°	♉	14	10/Aug/1993	17°	♉	59
12/Jun/1991	21°	♊	2	12/Mar/1992	21°	♊	46	**9/Dec/1992**	**18°**	♊	**10**	9/Sep/1993	16°	♊	35
11/Jul/1991	**18°**	♋	**59**	10/Apr/1992	20°	♋	47	8/Jan/1993	18°	♋	15	8/Oct/1993	15°	♋	31
10/Aug/1991	16°	♌	59	9/May/1992	19°	♌	15	6/Feb/1993	18°	♌	13	7/Nov/1993	14°	♌	52
8/Sep/1991	15°	♍	18	7/Jun/1992	17°	♍	19	8/Mar/1993	17°	♍	50	6/Dec/1993	14°	♍	32
7/Oct/1991	14°	♎	7	7/Jul/1992	15°	♎	14	6/Apr/1993	16°	♎	58	5/Jan/1994	14°	♎	24
6/Nov/1991	13°	♏	32	5/Aug/1992	13°	♏	15	6/May/1993	15°	♏	37	3/Feb/1994	14°	♏	15
6/Dec/1991	13°	♐	31	3/Sep/1992	11°	♐	39	**4/Jun/1993**	**13°**	♐	**54**	4/Mar/1994	13°	♐	53
4/Jan/1992	**13°**	♑	**51**	3/Oct/1992	10°	♑	37	3/Jul/1993	12°	♑	1	3/Apr/1994	13°	♑	7
3/Feb/1992	14°	♒	12	2/Nov/1992	10°	♒	12	2/Aug/1993	10°	♒	12	2/May/1994	11°	♒	57
4/Mar/1992	14°	♓	13	2/Dec/1992	10°	♓	19	1/Sep/1993	08°	♓	40	1/Jun/1994	10°	♓	26
3/Apr/1992	13°	♈	41	1/Jan/1993	10°	♈	44	30/Sep/1993	07°	♈	37	30/Jun/1994	08°	♈	46
2/May/1992	12°	♉	33	30/Jan/1993	11°	♉	5	30/Oct/1993	07°	♉	6	30/Jul/1994	07°	♉	7
1/Jun/1992	10°	♊	54	1/Mar/1993	11°	♊	4	**29/Nov/1993**	**07°**	♊	**3**	29/Aug/1994	05°	♊	42
30/Jun/1992	**08°**	♋	**56**	31/Mar/1993	10°	♋	27	28/Dec/1993	07°	♋	14	28/Sep/1994	04°	♋	39
29/Jul/1992	06°	♌	54	29/Apr/1993	09°	♌	12	27/Jan/1994	07°	♌	22	27/Oct/1994	04°	♌	2
28/Aug/1992	05°	♍	2	28/May/1993	07°	♍	25	26/Feb/1994	07°	♍	12	26/Nov/1994	03°	♍	47
26/Sep/1992	03°	♎	35	26/Jun/1993	05°	♎	18	27/Mar/1994	06°	♎	33	25/Dec/1994	03°	♎	45
25/Oct/1992	02°	♏	41	26/Jul/1993	03°	♏	10	25/Apr/1994	05°	♏	21	24/Jan/1995	03°	♏	43
24/Nov/1992	02°	♐	20	24/Aug/1993	01°	♐	15	**25/May/1994**	**03°**	♐	**43**	22/Feb/1995	03°	♐	26
24/Dec/1992	**02°**	♑	**27**	22/Sep/1993	29°	♐	48	23/Jun/1994	01°	♑	46	23/Mar/1995	02°	♑	43
22/Jan/1993	02°	♒	45	22/Oct/1993	28°	♑	58	22/Jul/1994	29°	♑	47	22/Apr/1995	01°	♒	32
21/Feb/1993	02°	♓	55	21/Nov/1993	28°	♒	46	21/Aug/1994	27°	♒	59	21/May/1995	29°	♒	57
23/Mar/1993	02°	♈	40	20/Dec/1993	29°	♓	4	19/Sep/1994	26°	♓	38	19/Jun/1995	28°	♓	8

Moon Families - Eclipses in Bold Print

New Moon			First Quarter Moon			Full Moon			Last Quarter Moon		
21/Apr/1993	01° ♉	52	19/Jan/1994	29° ♈	32	19/Oct/1994	25° ♈	53	19/Jul/1995	26° ♈	19
21/May/1993	**00° ♊**	**31**	18/Feb/1994	29° ♉	51	**18/Nov/1994**	**25° ♉**	**42**	18/Aug/1995	24° ♉	43
20/Jun/1993	28° ♊	45	20/Mar/1994	29° ♊	39	18/Dec/1994	25° ♊	55	16/Sep/1995	23° ♊	31
19/Jul/1993	26° ♋	47	19/Apr/1994	28° ♋	49	16/Jan/1995	26° ♋	14	16/Oct/1995	22° ♋	49
17/Aug/1993	24° ♌	53	18/May/1994	27° ♌	21	15/Feb/1995	26° ♌	20	15/Nov/1995	22° ♌	37
16/Sep/1993	23° ♍	16	16/Jun/1994	25° ♍	25	17/Mar/1995	25° ♍	59	15/Dec/1995	22° ♍	45
15/Oct/1993	22° ♎	7	16/Jul/1994	23° ♎	18	**15/Apr/1995**	**25° ♎**	**3**	13/Jan/1996	22° ♎	56
13/Nov/1993	**21° ♏**	**31**	14/Aug/1994	21° ♏	13	14/May/1995	23° ♏	35	12/Feb/1996	22° ♏	54
13/Dec/1993	21° ♐	23	12/Sep/1994	19° ♐	28	13/Jun/1995	21° ♐	42	12/Mar/1996	22° ♐	24
11/Jan/1994	21° ♑	30	11/Oct/1994	18° ♑	14	12/Jul/1995	19° ♑	38	10/Apr/1996	21° ♑	22
10/Feb/1994	21° ♒	37	10/Nov/1994	17° ♒	37	10/Aug/1995	17° ♒	39	10/May/1996	19° ♒	49
12/Mar/1994	21° ♓	28	9/Dec/1994	17° ♓	34	9/Sep/1995	16° ♓	0	8/Jun/1996	17° ♓	55
11/Apr/1994	20° ♈	53	8/Jan/1995	17° ♈	53	**8/Oct/1995**	**14° ♈**	**53**	7/Jul/1996	15° ♈	54
10/May/1994	**19° ♉**	**48**	7/Feb/1995	18° ♉	16	7/Nov/1995	14° ♉	24	6/Aug/1996	14° ♉	1
9/Jun/1994	18° ♊	17	9/Mar/1995	18° ♊	22	7/Dec/1995	14° ♊	27	4/Sep/1996	12° ♊	30
8/Jul/1994	16° ♋	28	8/Apr/1995	17° ♋	55	5/Jan/1996	14° ♋	48	4/Oct/1996	11° ♋	32
7/Aug/1994	14° ♌	37	7/May/1995	16° ♌	51	4/Feb/1996	15° ♌	7	3/Nov/1996	11° ♌	10
5/Sep/1994	12° ♍	57	6/Jun/1995	15° ♍	16	5/Mar/1996	15° ♍	5	3/Dec/1996	11° ♍	18
5/Oct/1994	11° ♎	41	5/Jul/1995	13° ♎	19	**4/Apr/1996**	**14° ♎**	**30**	2/Jan/1997	11° ♎	42
3/Nov/1994	**10° ♏**	**54**	4/Aug/1995	11° ♏	18	3/May/1996	13° ♏	19	31/Jan/1997	11° ♏	58
2/Dec/1994	10° ♐	34	2/Sep/1995	09° ♐	26	1/Jun/1996	11° ♐	36	2/Mar/1997	11° ♐	50
1/Jan/1995	10° ♑	33	1/Oct/1995	07° ♑	56	1/Jul/1996	09° ♑	35	31/Mar/1997	11° ♑	7
30/Jan/1995	10° ♒	35	30/Oct/1995	06° ♒	58	30/Jul/1996	07° ♒	32	30/Apr/1997	09° ♒	47
1/Mar/1995	10° ♓	25	29/Nov/1995	06° ♓	33	28/Aug/1996	05° ♓	41	29/May/1997	07° ♓	59
31/Mar/1995	09° ♈	54	28/Dec/1995	06° ♈	34	**27/Sep/1996**	**04° ♈**	**16**	27/Jun/1997	05° ♈	53
29/Apr/1995	**08° ♉**	**56**	27/Jan/1996	06° ♉	47	26/Oct/1996	03° ♉	26	26/Jul/1997	03° ♉	47
29/May/1995	07° ♊	33	26/Feb/1996	06° ♊	55	25/Nov/1996	03° ♊	10	25/Aug/1997	01° ♊	55
28/Jun/1995	05° ♋	53	27/Mar/1996	06° ♋	40	24/Dec/1996	03° ♋	20	23/Sep/1997	00° ♋	33
27/Jul/1995	04° ♌	7	25/Apr/1996	05° ♌	54	23/Jan/1997	03° ♌	39	23/Oct/1997	29° ♋	48
26/Aug/1995	02° ♍	29	25/May/1996	04° ♍	38	22/Feb/1997	03° ♍	50	21/Nov/1997	29° ♌	42
24/Sep/1995	01° ♎	10	24/Jun/1996	02° ♎	58	**24/Mar/1997**	**03° ♎**	**35**	21/Dec/1997	00° ♎	4
24/Oct/1995	**00° ♏**	**17**	23/Jul/1996	01° ♏	8	22/Apr/1997	02° ♏	44	20/Jan/1998	00° ♏	32
22/Nov/1995	29° ♏	51	22/Aug/1996	29° ♏	19	22/May/1997	01° ♐	19	19/Feb/1998	00° ♐	46
22/Dec/1995	29° ♐	44	20/Sep/1996	27° ♐	46	20/Jun/1997	29° ♐	28	21/Mar/1998	00° ♑	29
20/Jan/1996	29° ♑	44	19/Oct/1996	26° ♑	38	20/Jul/1997	27° ♑	27	19/Apr/1998	29° ♑	32
18/Feb/1996	29° ♒	36	18/Nov/1996	25° ♒	58	18/Aug/1997	25° ♒	31	19/May/1998	28° ♒	0
19/Mar/1996	29° ♓	7	17/Dec/1996	25° ♓	44	**16/Sep/1997**	**23° ♓**	**55**	17/Jun/1998	26° ♓	2
17/Apr/1996	**28° ♈**	**11**	15/Jan/1997	25° ♈	43	16/Oct/1997	22° ♈	49	16/Jul/1998	23° ♈	53
17/May/1996	26° ♉	50	14/Feb/1997	25° ♉	42	14/Nov/1997	22° ♉	14	14/Aug/1998	21° ♉	48
16/Jun/1996	25° ♊	11	16/Mar/1997	25° ♊	26	14/Dec/1997	22° ♊	8	13/Sep/1998	20° ♊	5
15/Jul/1996	23° ♋	26	14/Apr/1997	24° ♋	47	12/Jan/1998	22° ♋	18	12/Oct/1998	18° ♋	55
14/Aug/1996	21° ♌	47	14/May/1997	23° ♌	41	11/Feb/1998	22° ♌	29	11/Nov/1998	18° ♌	24
12/Sep/1996	20° ♍	26	13/Jun/1997	22° ♍	13	**13/Mar/1998**	**22° ♍**	**23**	10/Dec/1998	18° ♍	27
12/Oct/1996	**19° ♎**	**31**	12/Jul/1997	20° ♎	33	11/Apr/1998	21° ♎	49	9/Jan/1999	18° ♎	52
11/Nov/1996	19° ♏	3	11/Aug/1997	18° ♏	52	11/May/1998	20° ♏	41	8/Feb/1999	19° ♏	15
10/Dec/1996	18° ♐	55	10/Sep/1997	17° ♐	23	10/Jun/1998	19° ♐	6	10/Mar/1999	19° ♐	19
9/Jan/1997	18° ♑	57	9/Oct/1997	16° ♑	14	9/Jul/1998	17° ♑	14	9/Apr/1999	18° ♑	48
7/Feb/1997	18° ♒	53	7/Nov/1997	15° ♒	31	**8/Aug/1998**	**15° ♒**	**21**	8/May/1999	17° ♒	40
9/Mar/1997	**18° ♓**	**30**	7/Dec/1997	15° ♓	10	**6/Sep/1998**	**13° ♓**	**40**	7/Jun/1999	16° ♓	0
7/Apr/1997	17° ♈	40	5/Jan/1998	15° ♈	2	5/Oct/1998	12° ♈	22	6/Jul/1999	13° ♈	59
6/May/1997	16° ♉	21	3/Feb/1998	14° ♉	54	4/Nov/1998	11° ♉	34	4/Aug/1999	11° ♉	53

Moon Families - Eclipses in Bold Print

New Moon

Date	Degree	Sign	Min
5/Jun/1997	14°	♊	39
4/Jul/1997	12°	♋	48
3/Aug/1997	11°	♌	1
1/Sep/1997	**09°**	♍	**33**
1/Oct/1997	08°	♎	32
31/Oct/1997	08°	♏	1
30/Nov/1997	07°	♐	54
29/Dec/1997	08°	♑	1
28/Jan/1998	08°	♒	6
26/Feb/1998	**07°**	♓	**54**
28/Mar/1998	07°	♈	14
26/Apr/1998	06°	♉	2
25/May/1998	04°	♊	23
24/Jun/1998	02°	♋	27
23/Jul/1998	00°	♌	30
22/Aug/1998	**28°**	♌	**47**
20/Sep/1998	27°	♍	31
20/Oct/1998	26°	♎	48
19/Nov/1998	26°	♏	37
18/Dec/1998	26°	♐	48
17/Jan/1999	27°	♑	4
16/Feb/1999	**27°**	♒	**8**
17/Mar/1999	26°	♓	43
16/Apr/1999	25°	♈	44
15/May/1999	24°	♉	13
13/Jun/1999	22°	♊	19
13/Jul/1999	20°	♋	17
11/Aug/1999	**18°**	♌	**21**
9/Sep/1999	16°	♍	46
9/Oct/1999	15°	♎	43
8/Nov/1999	15°	♏	17
7/Dec/1999	15°	♐	22
6/Jan/2000	15°	♑	43
5/Feb/2000	**16°**	♒	**1**
6/Mar/2000	15°	♓	56
4/Apr/2000	15°	♈	16
4/May/2000	14°	♉	0
2/Jun/2000	12°	♊	15
1/Jul/2000	**10°**	♋	**14**
31/Jul/2000	**08°**	♌	**11**
29/Aug/2000	06°	♍	22
27/Sep/2000	05°	♎	0
27/Oct/2000	04°	♏	12
25/Nov/2000	03°	♐	59
25/Dec/2000	**04°**	♑	**14**
24/Jan/2001	04°	♒	36
23/Feb/2001	04°	♓	46
25/Mar/2001	04°	♈	27
23/Apr/2001	03°	♉	31
23/May/2001	02°	♊	2
21/Jun/2001	**00°**	♋	**10**

First Quarter Moon

Date	Degree	Sign	Min
5/Mar/1998	14°	♊	34
3/Apr/1998	13°	♋	52
3/May/1998	12°	♌	46
2/Jun/1998	11°	♍	21
1/Jul/1998	09°	♎	43
31/Jul/1998	08°	♏	5
30/Aug/1998	06°	♐	38
28/Sep/1998	05°	♑	32
28/Oct/1998	04°	♒	51
27/Nov/1998	04°	♓	32
26/Dec/1998	04°	♈	26
24/Jan/1999	04°	♉	21
23/Feb/1999	04°	♊	1
24/Mar/1999	03°	♋	19
22/Apr/1999	02°	♌	12
22/May/1999	00°	♍	42
20/Jun/1999	28°	♍	58
20/Jul/1999	27°	♎	13
19/Aug/1999	25°	♏	39
17/Sep/1999	24°	♐	29
17/Oct/1999	23°	♑	47
16/Nov/1999	23°	♒	33
16/Dec/1999	23°	♓	36
14/Jan/2000	23°	♈	41
12/Feb/2000	23°	♉	33
13/Mar/2000	23°	♊	0
11/Apr/2000	21°	♋	57
10/May/2000	20°	♌	27
9/Jun/2000	18°	♍	36
8/Jul/2000	16°	♎	39
7/Aug/2000	14°	♏	50
5/Sep/2000	13°	♐	24
5/Oct/2000	12°	♑	30
4/Nov/2000	12°	♒	11
4/Dec/2000	12°	♓	18
2/Jan/2001	12°	♈	36
1/Feb/2001	12°	♉	47
3/Mar/2001	12°	♊	33
1/Apr/2001	11°	♋	46
30/Apr/2001	10°	♌	24
29/May/2001	08°	♍	35
28/Jun/2001	06°	♎	30
27/Jul/2001	04°	♏	26
25/Aug/2001	02°	♐	40
24/Sep/2001	01°	♑	24
24/Oct/2001	00°	♒	46
22/Nov/2001	00°	♓	43
22/Dec/2001	01°	♈	5
21/Jan/2002	01°	♉	30
20/Feb/2002	01°	♊	40
22/Mar/2002	01°	♋	17

Full Moon

Date	Degree	Sign	Min
3/Dec/1998	11°	♊	15
2/Jan/1999	11°	♋	14
31/Jan/1999	**11°**	♌	**19**
2/Mar/1999	11°	♍	14
31/Mar/1999	10°	♎	46
30/Apr/1999	09°	♏	49
30/May/1999	08°	♐	26
28/Jun/1999	06°	♑	44
28/Jul/1999	**04°**	♒	**57**
26/Aug/1999	03°	♓	17
25/Sep/1999	01°	♈	55
24/Oct/1999	01°	♉	0
23/Nov/1999	00°	♊	31
22/Dec/1999	00°	♋	24
21/Jan/2000	**00°**	♌	**26**
19/Feb/2000	00°	♍	19
20/Mar/2000	29°	♍	52
18/Apr/2000	28°	♎	59
18/May/2000	27°	♏	39
16/Jun/2000	26°	♐	3
16/Jul/2000	**24°**	♑	**19**
15/Aug/2000	22°	♒	40
13/Sep/2000	21°	♓	18
13/Oct/2000	20°	♈	19
11/Nov/2000	19°	♉	47
11/Dec/2000	19°	♊	37
9/Jan/2001	**19°**	♋	**39**
8/Feb/2001	19°	♌	35
9/Mar/2001	19°	♍	12
8/Apr/2001	18°	♎	21
7/May/2001	17°	♏	3
6/Jun/2001	15°	♐	25
5/Jul/2001	**13°**	♑	**38**
4/Aug/2001	11°	♒	55
2/Sep/2001	10°	♓	28
2/Oct/2001	09°	♈	25
1/Nov/2001	08°	♉	52
30/Nov/2001	08°	♊	43
30/Dec/2001	**08°**	♋	**47**
28/Jan/2002	08°	♌	50
27/Feb/2002	08°	♍	35
28/Mar/2002	07°	♎	53
27/Apr/2002	06°	♏	41
26/May/2002	**05°**	♐	**3**
24/Jun/2002	**03°**	♑	**11**
24/Jul/2002	01°	♒	18
22/Aug/2002	29°	♒	38
21/Sep/2002	28°	♓	24
21/Oct/2002	27°	♈	43
20/Nov/2002	**27°**	♉	**32**
19/Dec/2002	27°	♊	42

Last Quarter Moon

Date	Degree	Sign	Min
2/Sep/1999	09°	♊	59
2/Oct/1999	08°	♋	31
31/Oct/1999	07°	♌	36
29/Nov/1999	07°	♍	17
29/Dec/1999	07°	♎	23
28/Jan/2000	07°	♏	41
27/Feb/2000	07°	♐	51
28/Mar/2000	07°	♑	37
26/Apr/2000	06°	♒	51
26/May/2000	05°	♓	31
25/Jun/2000	03°	♈	47
24/Jul/2000	01°	♉	50
22/Aug/2000	29°	♉	57
21/Sep/2000	28°	♊	22
20/Oct/2000	27°	♋	13
18/Nov/2000	26°	♌	35
18/Dec/2000	26°	♍	23
16/Jan/2001	26°	♎	26
15/Feb/2001	26°	♏	30
16/Mar/2001	26°	♐	19
15/Apr/2001	25°	♑	43
15/May/2001	24°	♒	38
14/Jun/2001	23°	♓	8
13/Jul/2001	21°	♈	25
12/Aug/2001	19°	♉	40
10/Sep/2001	18°	♊	7
10/Oct/2001	16°	♋	55
8/Nov/2001	16°	♌	9
7/Dec/2001	15°	♍	46
6/Jan/2002	15°	♎	38
4/Feb/2002	15°	♏	33
6/Mar/2002	15°	♐	17
4/Apr/2002	14°	♑	40
4/May/2002	13°	♒	39
3/Jun/2002	12°	♓	15
2/Jul/2002	10°	♈	38
1/Aug/2002	09°	♉	0
31/Aug/2002	07°	♊	31
29/Sep/2002	06°	♋	22
29/Oct/2002	05°	♌	36
27/Nov/2002	05°	♍	13
27/Dec/2002	05°	♎	3
25/Jan/2003	04°	♏	56
23/Feb/2003	04°	♐	38
25/Mar/2003	04°	♑	0
23/Apr/2003	02°	♒	56
23/May/2003	01°	♓	29
21/Jun/2003	29°	♓	49
21/Jul/2003	28°	♈	7
20/Aug/2003	26°	♉	36
18/Sep/2003	25°	♊	26

Moon Families - Eclipses in Bold Print

New Moon				First Quarter Moon				Full Moon				Last Quarter Moon			
20/Jul/2001	28°	♋	8	20/Apr/2002	00°	♌	15	18/Jan/2003	27°	♋	55	18/Oct/2003	24°	♋	42
19/Aug/2001	26°	♌	12	19/May/2002	28°	♌	38	16/Feb/2003	27°	♌	53	17/Nov/2003	24°	♌	23
17/Sep/2001	24°	♍	35	18/Jun/2002	26°	♍	37	18/Mar/2003	27°	♍	24	16/Dec/2003	24°	♍	20
16/Oct/2001	23°	♎	29	17/Jul/2002	24°	♎	27	16/Apr/2003	26°	♎	23	15/Jan/2004	24°	♎	21
15/Nov/2001	22°	♏	57	15/Aug/2002	22°	♏	25	**16/May/2003**	**24°**	♏	**52**	13/Feb/2004	24°	♏	11
14/Dec/2001	**22°**	♐	**56**	13/Sep/2002	20°	♐	46	14/Jun/2003	23°	♐	0	13/Mar/2004	23°	♐	37
13/Jan/2002	23°	♑	11	13/Oct/2002	19°	♑	42	13/Jul/2003	20°	♑	59	12/Apr/2004	22°	♑	34
12/Feb/2002	23°	♒	24	11/Nov/2002	19°	♒	17	12/Aug/2003	19°	♒	5	11/May/2004	21°	♒	5
14/Mar/2002	23°	♓	18	11/Dec/2002	19°	♓	25	10/Sep/2003	17°	♓	33	9/Jun/2004	19°	♓	17
12/Apr/2002	22°	♈	42	10/Jan/2003	19°	♈	52	10/Oct/2003	16°	♈	34	9/Jul/2004	17°	♈	25
12/May/2002	21°	♉	32	9/Feb/2003	20°	♉	16	**9/Nov/2003**	**16°**	♉	**12**	7/Aug/2004	15°	♉	42
10/Jun/2002	**19°**	♊	**54**	11/Mar/2003	20°	♊	18	8/Dec/2003	16°	♊	20	6/Sep/2004	14°	♊	21
10/Jul/2002	18°	♋	0	9/Apr/2003	19°	♋	42	7/Jan/2004	16°	♋	40	6/Oct/2004	13°	♋	29
8/Aug/2002	16°	♌	3	9/May/2003	18°	♌	27	6/Feb/2004	16°	♌	53	5/Nov/2004	13°	♌	9
7/Sep/2002	14°	♍	20	7/Jun/2003	16°	♍	40	6/Mar/2004	16°	♍	43	5/Dec/2004	13°	♍	13
6/Oct/2002	13°	♎	1	7/Jul/2003	14°	♎	36	5/Apr/2004	15°	♎	59	3/Jan/2005	13°	♎	27
4/Nov/2002	12°	♏	14	5/Aug/2003	12°	♏	29	**4/May/2004**	**14°**	♏	**41**	2/Feb/2005	13°	♏	33
4/Dec/2002	**11°**	♐	**58**	3/Sep/2003	10°	♐	36	3/Jun/2004	12°	♐	55	3/Mar/2005	13°	♐	14
2/Jan/2003	12°	♑	1	2/Oct/2003	09°	♑	10	2/Jul/2004	10°	♑	53	2/Apr/2005	12°	♑	22
1/Feb/2003	12°	♒	9	1/Nov/2003	08°	♒	19	31/Jul/2004	08°	♒	50	1/May/2005	10°	♒	58
3/Mar/2003	12°	♓	5	30/Nov/2003	08°	♓	4	30/Aug/2004	07°	♓	3	30/May/2005	09°	♓	9
1/Apr/2003	11°	♈	38	30/Dec/2003	08°	♈	16	28/Sep/2004	05°	♈	44	28/Jun/2005	07°	♈	8
1/May/2003	10°	♉	43	29/Jan/2004	08°	♉	39	**28/Oct/2004**	**05°**	♉	**2**	28/Jul/2005	05°	♉	9
31/May/2003	**09°**	♊	**19**	28/Feb/2004	08°	♊	52	26/Nov/2004	04°	♊	55	26/Aug/2005	03°	♊	28
29/Jun/2003	07°	♋	36	28/Mar/2004	08°	♋	37	26/Dec/2004	05°	♋	11	25/Sep/2005	02°	♋	17
29/Jul/2003	05°	♌	45	27/Apr/2004	07°	♌	47	25/Jan/2005	05°	♌	33	25/Oct/2005	01°	♌	43
27/Aug/2003	04°	♍	1	27/May/2004	06°	♍	21	24/Feb/2005	05°	♍	40	23/Nov/2005	01°	♍	43
26/Sep/2003	02°	♎	37	25/Jun/2004	04°	♎	32	25/Mar/2005	05°	♎	18	23/Dec/2005	02°	♎	4
25/Oct/2003	01°	♏	41	25/Jul/2004	02°	♏	32	**24/Apr/2005**	**04°**	♏	**19**	22/Jan/2006	02°	♏	27
23/Nov/2003	**01°**	♐	**13**	23/Aug/2004	00°	♐	36	23/May/2005	02°	♐	47	21/Feb/2006	02°	♐	30
23/Dec/2003	01°	♑	7	21/Sep/2004	28°	♐	59	22/Jun/2005	00°	♑	51	22/Mar/2006	02°	♑	1
21/Jan/2004	01°	♒	9	20/Oct/2004	27°	♑	51	21/Jul/2005	28°	♑	46	21/Apr/2006	00°	♒	53
20/Feb/2004	01°	♓	4	19/Nov/2004	27°	♒	14	19/Aug/2005	26°	♒	50	20/May/2006	29°	♒	13
20/Mar/2004	00°	♈	39	18/Dec/2004	27°	♓	6	18/Sep/2005	25°	♓	15	18/Jun/2006	27°	♓	12
19/Apr/2004	**29°**	♈	**49**	17/Jan/2005	27°	♈	16	**17/Oct/2005**	**24°**	♈	**13**	17/Jul/2006	25°	♈	3
19/May/2004	28°	♉	33	16/Feb/2005	27°	♉	25	16/Nov/2005	23°	♉	46	16/Aug/2006	23°	♉	4
17/Jun/2004	26°	♊	57	17/Mar/2005	27°	♊	17	15/Dec/2005	23°	♊	47	14/Sep/2006	21°	♊	30
17/Jul/2004	25°	♋	12	16/Apr/2005	26°	♋	42	14/Jan/2006	24°	♋	5	14/Oct/2006	20°	♋	31
16/Aug/2004	23°	♌	31	16/May/2005	25°	♌	35	13/Feb/2006	24°	♌	20	12/Nov/2006	20°	♌	11
14/Sep/2004	22°	♍	6	15/Jun/2005	24°	♍	3	**14/Mar/2006**	**24°**	♍	**14**	12/Dec/2006	20°	♍	25
14/Oct/2004	**21°**	♎	**6**	14/Jul/2005	22°	♎	16	13/Apr/2006	23°	♎	36	11/Jan/2007	20°	♎	54
12/Nov/2004	20°	♏	32	13/Aug/2005	20°	♏	27	13/May/2006	22°	♏	23	10/Feb/2007	21°	♏	16
12/Dec/2004	20°	♐	21	11/Sep/2005	18°	♐	50	11/Jun/2006	20°	♐	40	12/Mar/2007	21°	♐	11
10/Jan/2005	20°	♑	21	10/Oct/2005	17°	♑	34	11/Jul/2006	18°	♑	42	10/Apr/2007	20°	♑	29
8/Feb/2005	20°	♒	16	9/Nov/2005	16°	♒	46	9/Aug/2006	16°	♒	43	10/May/2007	19°	♒	9
10/Mar/2005	19°	♓	53	8/Dec/2005	16°	♓	23	**7/Sep/2006**	**15°**	♓	**0**	8/Jun/2007	17°	♓	19
8/Apr/2005	**19°**	♈	**5**	6/Jan/2006	16°	♈	19	7/Oct/2006	13°	♈	43	7/Jul/2007	15°	♈	12
8/May/2005	17°	♉	51	5/Feb/2006	16°	♉	18	5/Nov/2006	12°	♉	58	5/Aug/2007	13°	♉	4
6/Jun/2005	16°	♊	16	6/Mar/2006	16°	♊	7	5/Dec/2006	12°	♊	42	4/Sep/2007	11°	♊	12
6/Jul/2005	14°	♋	30	5/Apr/2006	15°	♋	33	3/Jan/2007	12°	♋	48	3/Oct/2007	09°	♋	49
5/Aug/2005	12°	♌	48	5/May/2006	14°	♌	35	2/Feb/2007	12°	♌	59	1/Nov/2007	09°	♌	3

Moon Families - Eclipses in Bold Print

New Moon				First Quarter Moon				Full Moon				Last Quarter Moon			
3/Sep/2005	11°	♍	21	3/Jun/2006	13°	♍	13	**3/Mar/2007**	12°	♍	**59**	1/Dec/2007	08°	♍	55
3/Oct/2005	**10°**	**♎**	**18**	3/Jul/2006	11°	♎	36	2/Apr/2007	12°	♎	35	31/Dec/2007	09°	♎	14
2/Nov/2005	09°	♏	43	2/Aug/2006	09°	♏	56	2/May/2007	11°	♏	38	30/Jan/2008	09°	♏	40
1/Dec/2005	09°	♐	31	31/Aug/2006	08°	♐	23	1/Jun/2007	10°	♐	11	29/Feb/2008	09°	♐	52
31/Dec/2005	09°	♑	32	30/Sep/2006	07°	♑	9	30/Jun/2007	08°	♑	24	29/Mar/2008	09°	♑	34
29/Jan/2006	09°	♒	32	29/Oct/2006	06°	♒	19	30/Jul/2007	06°	♒	31	28/Apr/2008	08°	♒	39
28/Feb/2006	09°	♓	16	28/Nov/2006	05°	♓	52	**28/Aug/2007**	**04°**	**♓**	**45**	28/May/2008	07°	♓	9
29/Mar/2006	**08°**	**♈**	**35**	27/Dec/2006	05°	♈	42	26/Sep/2007	03°	♈	20	26/Jun/2008	05°	♈	15
27/Apr/2006	07°	♉	24	25/Jan/2007	05°	♉	35	26/Oct/2007	02°	♉	23	25/Jul/2008	03°	♉	10
27/May/2006	05°	♊	48	24/Feb/2007	05°	♊	19	24/Nov/2007	01°	♊	55	23/Aug/2008	01°	♊	11
25/Jun/2006	03°	♋	57	25/Mar/2007	04°	♋	43	24/Dec/2007	01°	♋	49	22/Sep/2008	29°	♊	33
25/Jul/2006	02°	♌	7	24/Apr/2007	03°	♌	43	22/Jan/2008	01°	♌	54	21/Oct/2008	28°	♋	27
23/Aug/2006	00°	♍	30	23/May/2007	02°	♍	21	**21/Feb/2008**	**01°**	**♍**	**52**	19/Nov/2008	27°	♌	55
22/Sep/2006	**29°**	**♍**	**20**	22/Jun/2007	00°	♎	45	21/Mar/2008	01°	♎	31	19/Dec/2008	27°	♍	53
22/Oct/2006	28°	♎	39	22/Jul/2007	29°	♎	6	20/Apr/2008	00°	♏	42	18/Jan/2009	28°	♎	8
20/Nov/2006	28°	♏	27	20/Aug/2007	27°	♏	34	20/May/2008	29°	♏	26	16/Feb/2009	28°	♏	21
20/Dec/2006	28°	♐	32	19/Sep/2007	26°	♐	22	18/Jun/2008	27°	♐	50	18/Mar/2009	28°	♐	15
19/Jan/2007	28°	♑	41	19/Oct/2007	25°	♑	34	18/Jul/2008	26°	♑	4	17/Apr/2009	27°	♑	40
17/Feb/2007	28°	♒	36	17/Nov/2007	25°	♒	11	**16/Aug/2008**	**24°**	**♒**	**21**	17/May/2009	26°	♒	31
19/Mar/2007	**28°**	**♓**	**7**	17/Dec/2007	25°	♓	5	15/Sep/2008	22°	♓	54	15/Jun/2009	24°	♓	55
17/Apr/2007	27°	♈	5	15/Jan/2008	25°	♈	2	14/Oct/2008	21°	♈	50	15/Jul/2009	23°	♈	3
16/May/2007	25°	♉	33	14/Feb/2008	24°	♉	48	13/Nov/2008	21°	♉	14	13/Aug/2009	21°	♉	9
15/Jun/2007	23°	♊	40	14/Mar/2008	24°	♊	14	12/Dec/2008	21°	♊	2	12/Sep/2009	19°	♊	27
14/Jul/2007	21°	♋	41	12/Apr/2008	23°	♋	13	11/Jan/2009	21°	♋	2	11/Oct/2009	18°	♋	10
12/Aug/2007	19°	♌	51	12/May/2008	21°	♌	48	**9/Feb/2009**	**20°**	**♌**	**59**	9/Nov/2009	17°	♌	23
11/Sep/2007	**18°**	**♍**	**24**	10/Jun/2008	20°	♍	5	11/Mar/2009	20°	♍	39	9/Dec/2009	17°	♍	2
11/Oct/2007	17°	♎	30	10/Jul/2008	18°	♎	18	9/Apr/2009	19°	♎	53	7/Jan/2010	17°	♎	1
9/Nov/2007	17°	♏	9	8/Aug/2008	16°	♏	38	9/May/2009	18°	♏	40	5/Feb/2010	17°	♏	4
9/Dec/2007	17°	♐	15	7/Sep/2008	15°	♐	19	7/Jun/2009	17°	♐	7	7/Mar/2010	16°	♐	57
8/Jan/2008	17°	♑	33	7/Oct/2008	14°	♑	28	**7/Jul/2009**	**15°**	**♑**	**24**	6/Apr/2010	16°	♑	28
7/Feb/2008	**17°**	**♒**	**44**	6/Nov/2008	14°	♒	7	**6/Aug/2009**	**13°**	**♒**	**43**	6/May/2010	15°	♒	32
7/Mar/2008	17°	♓	30	5/Dec/2008	14°	♓	7	4/Sep/2009	12°	♓	15	4/Jun/2010	14°	♓	10
6/Apr/2008	16°	♈	43	4/Jan/2009	14°	♈	15	4/Oct/2009	11°	♈	9	4/Jul/2010	12°	♈	31
5/May/2008	15°	♉	22	2/Feb/2009	14°	♉	15	2/Nov/2009	10°	♉	30	3/Aug/2010	10°	♉	46
3/Jun/2008	13°	♊	34	4/Mar/2009	13°	♊	52	2/Dec/2009	10°	♊	15	1/Sep/2010	09°	♊	10
3/Jul/2008	11°	♋	32	2/Apr/2009	12°	♋	59	**31/Dec/2009**	**10°**	**♋**	**14**	1/Oct/2010	07°	♋	52
1/Aug/2008	**09°**	**♌**	**31**	1/May/2009	11°	♌	36	30/Jan/2010	10°	♌	14	30/Oct/2010	06°	♌	59
30/Aug/2008	07°	♍	48	31/May/2009	09°	♍	49	28/Feb/2010	09°	♍	58	28/Nov/2010	06°	♍	30
29/Sep/2008	06°	♎	33	29/Jun/2009	07°	♎	51	30/Mar/2010	09°	♎	17	28/Dec/2010	06°	♎	18
28/Oct/2008	05°	♏	54	28/Jul/2009	05°	♏	56	28/Apr/2010	08°	♏	6	26/Jan/2011	06°	♏	12
27/Nov/2008	05°	♐	49	27/Aug/2009	04°	♐	20	27/May/2010	06°	♐	32	24/Feb/2011	06°	♐	0
27/Dec/2008	06°	♑	7	26/Sep/2009	03°	♑	14	**26/Jun/2010**	**04°**	**♑**	**46**	26/Mar/2011	05°	♑	29
26/Jan/2009	**06°**	**♒**	**29**	26/Oct/2009	02°	♒	44	26/Jul/2010	02°	♒	59	25/Apr/2011	04°	♒	34
25/Feb/2009	06°	♓	35	24/Nov/2009	02°	♓	44	24/Aug/2010	01°	♓	25	24/May/2011	03°	♓	15
26/Mar/2009	06°	♈	7	24/Dec/2009	03°	♈	2	23/Sep/2010	00°	♈	15	23/Jun/2011	01°	♈	41
25/Apr/2009	05°	♉	3	23/Jan/2010	03°	♉	19	23/Oct/2010	29°	♈	32	23/Jul/2011	00°	♉	2
24/May/2009	03°	♊	27	22/Feb/2010	03°	♊	16	21/Nov/2010	29°	♉	17	21/Aug/2011	28°	♉	29
22/Jun/2009	01°	♋	30	23/Mar/2010	02°	♋	42	**21/Dec/2010**	**29°**	**♊**	**20**	20/Sep/2011	27°	♊	15
22/Jul/2009	**29°**	**♋**	**26**	21/Apr/2010	01°	♌	32	19/Jan/2011	29°	♋	27	20/Oct/2011	26°	♋	23
20/Aug/2009	27°	♌	31	20/May/2010	29°	♌	50	18/Feb/2011	29°	♌	20	18/Nov/2011	25°	♌	55
18/Sep/2009	25°	♍	59	19/Jun/2010	27°	♍	48	19/Mar/2011	28°	♍	47	18/Dec/2011	25°	♍	43

Moon Families - Eclipses in Bold Print

New Moon				First Quarter Moon				Full Moon				Last Quarter Moon			
18/Oct/2009	24°	♎	58	18/Jul/2010	25°	♎	41	18/Apr/2011	27°	♎	44	16/Jan/2012	25°	♎	37
16/Nov/2009	24°	♏	34	16/Aug/2010	23°	♏	46	17/May/2011	26°	♏	13	14/Feb/2012	25°	♏	24
16/Dec/2009	24°	♐	39	15/Sep/2010	22°	♐	17	**15/Jun/2011**	**24°**	♐	**23**	15/Mar/2012	24°	♐	51
15/Jan/2010	**25°**	♑	**1**	14/Oct/2010	21°	♑	25	15/Jul/2011	22°	♑	27	13/Apr/2012	23°	♑	54
14/Feb/2010	25°	♒	17	13/Nov/2010	21°	♒	11	13/Aug/2011	20°	♒	41	12/May/2012	22°	♒	33
15/Mar/2010	25°	♓	10	13/Dec/2010	21°	♓	27	12/Sep/2011	19°	♓	17	11/Jun/2012	20°	♓	54
14/Apr/2010	24°	♈	27	12/Jan/2011	21°	♈	54	12/Oct/2011	18°	♈	24	11/Jul/2012	19°	♈	10
14/May/2010	23°	♉	9	11/Feb/2011	22°	♉	12	10/Nov/2011	18°	♉	4	9/Aug/2012	17°	♉	34
12/Jun/2010	21°	♊	23	12/Mar/2011	22°	♊	3	**10/Dec/2011**	**18°**	♊	**10**	8/Sep/2012	16°	♊	17
11/Jul/2010	**19°**	♋	**23**	11/Apr/2011	21°	♋	15	9/Jan/2012	18°	♋	25	8/Oct/2012	15°	♋	25
10/Aug/2010	17°	♌	24	10/May/2011	19°	♌	50	7/Feb/2012	18°	♌	31	7/Nov/2012	15°	♌	0
8/Sep/2010	15°	♍	40	9/Jun/2011	17°	♍	56	8/Mar/2012	18°	♍	13	6/Dec/2012	14°	♍	55
7/Oct/2010	14°	♎	23	8/Jul/2011	15°	♎	47	6/Apr/2012	17°	♎	23	5/Jan/2013	14°	♎	58
6/Nov/2010	13°	♏	40	6/Aug/2011	13°	♏	39	6/May/2012	16°	♏	1	3/Feb/2013	14°	♏	54
5/Dec/2010	13°	♐	28	4/Sep/2011	11°	♐	51	**4/Jun/2012**	**14°**	♐	**13**	4/Mar/2013	14°	♐	29
4/Jan/2011	**13°**	♑	**38**	4/Oct/2011	10°	♑	33	3/Jul/2012	12°	♑	13	3/Apr/2013	13°	♑	35
3/Feb/2011	13°	♒	53	2/Nov/2011	09°	♒	54	2/Aug/2012	10°	♒	15	2/May/2013	12°	♒	12
4/Mar/2011	13°	♓	55	2/Dec/2011	09°	♓	51	31/Aug/2012	08°	♓	33	31/May/2013	10°	♓	28
3/Apr/2011	13°	♈	29	1/Jan/2012	10°	♈	13	30/Sep/2012	07°	♈	22	30/Jun/2013	08°	♈	34
3/May/2011	12°	♉	30	31/Jan/2012	10°	♉	40	29/Oct/2012	06°	♉	47	29/Jul/2013	06°	♉	45
1/Jun/2011	**11°**	♊	**1**	1/Mar/2012	10°	♊	51	**28/Nov/2012**	**06°**	♊	**46**	28/Aug/2013	05°	♊	14
1/Jul/2011	**09°**	♋	**12**	30/Mar/2012	10°	♋	30	28/Dec/2012	07°	♋	5	27/Sep/2013	04°	♋	12
30/Jul/2011	07°	♌	15	29/Apr/2012	09°	♌	29	27/Jan/2013	07°	♌	24	26/Oct/2013	03°	♌	43
29/Aug/2011	05°	♍	27	28/May/2012	07°	♍	53	25/Feb/2013	07°	♍	24	25/Nov/2013	03°	♍	41
27/Sep/2011	04°	♎	0	27/Jun/2012	05°	♎	53	27/Mar/2013	06°	♎	52	25/Dec/2013	03°	♎	55
26/Oct/2011	03°	♏	2	26/Jul/2012	03°	♏	46	**25/Apr/2013**	**05°**	♏	**45**	24/Jan/2014	04°	♏	7
25/Nov/2011	**02°**	♐	**36**	24/Aug/2012	01°	♐	47	**25/May/2013**	**04°**	♐	**8**	22/Feb/2014	03°	♐	59
24/Dec/2011	02°	♑	34	22/Sep/2012	00°	♑	11	23/Jun/2013	02°	♑	9	24/Mar/2014	03°	♑	20
23/Jan/2012	02°	♒	41	22/Oct/2012	29°	♑	8	22/Jul/2013	00°	♒	5	22/Apr/2014	02°	♒	6
21/Feb/2012	02°	♓	42	20/Nov/2012	28°	♒	40	21/Aug/2013	28°	♒	10	21/May/2014	00°	♓	24
22/Mar/2012	02°	♈	22	20/Dec/2012	28°	♓	43	19/Sep/2013	26°	♓	40	19/Jun/2014	28°	♓	24
21/Apr/2012	01°	♉	35	18/Jan/2013	29°	♈	3	**18/Oct/2013**	**25°**	♈	**45**	19/Jul/2014	26°	♈	21
20/May/2012	**00°**	♊	**20**	17/Feb/2013	29°	♉	20	17/Nov/2013	25°	♉	26	17/Aug/2014	24°	♉	31
19/Jun/2012	28°	♊	43	19/Mar/2013	29°	♊	16	17/Dec/2013	25°	♊	36	16/Sep/2014	23°	♊	8
19/Jul/2012	26°	♋	54	18/Apr/2013	28°	♋	38	16/Jan/2014	25°	♋	58	15/Oct/2014	22°	♋	21
17/Aug/2012	25°	♌	8	18/May/2013	27°	♌	24	14/Feb/2014	26°	♌	12	14/Nov/2014	22°	♌	9
16/Sep/2012	23°	♍	37	16/Jun/2013	25°	♍	43	16/Mar/2014	26°	♍	1	14/Dec/2014	22°	♍	26
15/Oct/2012	22°	♎	32	16/Jul/2013	23°	♎	46	**15/Apr/2014**	**25°**	♎	**15**	13/Jan/2015	22°	♎	52
13/Nov/2012	**21°**	♏	**56**	14/Aug/2013	21°	♏	49	14/May/2014	23°	♏	54	12/Feb/2015	23°	♏	5
13/Dec/2012	21°	♐	45	12/Sep/2013	20°	♐	5	13/Jun/2014	22°	♐	5	13/Mar/2015	22°	♐	49
11/Jan/2013	21°	♑	45	11/Oct/2013	18°	♑	47	12/Jul/2014	20°	♑	3	12/Apr/2015	21°	♑	55
10/Feb/2013	21°	♒	43	10/Nov/2013	18°	♒	0	10/Aug/2014	18°	♒	2	11/May/2015	20°	♒	25
11/Mar/2013	21°	♓	24	9/Dec/2013	17°	♓	42	9/Sep/2014	16°	♓	19	9/Jun/2015	18°	♓	29
10/Apr/2013	20°	♈	40	8/Jan/2014	17°	♈	46	**8/Oct/2014**	**15°**	♈	**5**	8/Jul/2015	16°	♈	21
10/May/2013	**19°**	♉	**31**	6/Feb/2014	17°	♉	55	6/Nov/2014	14°	♉	25	7/Aug/2015	14°	♉	16
8/Jun/2013	18°	♊	0	8/Mar/2014	17°	♊	53	6/Dec/2014	14°	♊	17	5/Sep/2015	12°	♊	31
8/Jul/2013	16°	♋	17	7/Apr/2014	17°	♋	27	5/Jan/2015	14°	♋	30	4/Oct/2015	11°	♋	19
6/Aug/2013	14°	♌	34	7/May/2014	16°	♌	30	3/Feb/2015	14°	♌	47	3/Nov/2015	10°	♌	45
5/Sep/2013	13°	♍	4	5/Jun/2014	15°	♍	6	5/Mar/2015	14°	♍	50	3/Dec/2015	10°	♍	48
5/Oct/2013	11°	♎	56	5/Jul/2014	13°	♎	24	**4/Apr/2015**	**14°**	♎	**24**	2/Jan/2016	11°	♎	14
3/Nov/2013	**11°**	♏	**15**	4/Aug/2014	11°	♏	35	4/May/2015	13°	♏	22	1/Feb/2016	11°	♏	41

Moon Families - Eclipses in Bold Print

New Moon				First Quarter Moon				Full Moon				Last Quarter Moon			
3/Dec/2013	10°	♐	59	2/Sep/2014	09°	♐	55	2/Jun/2015	11°	♐	49	1/Mar/2016	11°	♐	48
1/Jan/2014	10°	♑	57	1/Oct/2014	08°	♑	32	2/Jul/2015	09°	♑	55	31/Mar/2016	11°	♑	20
30/Jan/2014	10°	♒	55	31/Oct/2014	07°	♒	36	31/Jul/2015	07°	♒	55	30/Apr/2016	10°	♒	13
1/Mar/2014	10°	♓	39	29/Nov/2014	07°	♓	6	29/Aug/2015	06°	♓	6	29/May/2016	08°	♓	32
30/Mar/2014	09°	♈	58	28/Dec/2014	06°	♈	56	**28/Sep/2015**	**04°**	**♈**	**40**	27/Jun/2016	06°	♈	30
29/Apr/2014	**08°**	**♉**	**51**	27/Jan/2015	06°	♉	54	27/Oct/2015	03°	♉	44	26/Jul/2016	04°	♉	21
28/May/2014	07°	♊	21	25/Feb/2015	06°	♊	46	25/Nov/2015	03°	♊	20	25/Aug/2016	02°	♊	22
27/Jun/2014	05°	♋	37	27/Mar/2015	06°	♋	19	25/Dec/2015	03°	♋	19	23/Sep/2016	00°	♋	47
26/Jul/2014	03°	♌	51	25/Apr/2015	05°	♌	27	24/Jan/2016	03°	♌	29	22/Oct/2016	29°	♋	48
25/Aug/2014	02°	♍	18	25/May/2015	04°	♍	11	22/Feb/2016	03°	♍	33	21/Nov/2016	29°	♌	27
24/Sep/2014	01°	♎	7	24/Jun/2015	02°	♎	38	**23/Mar/2016**	**03°**	**♎**	**17**	21/Dec/2016	29°	♍	37
23/Oct/2014	**00°**	**♏**	**24**	24/Jul/2015	00°	♏	58	22/Apr/2016	02°	♏	30	19/Jan/2017	00°	♏	2
22/Nov/2014	00°	♐	7	22/Aug/2015	29°	♏	23	21/May/2016	01°	♐	13	18/Feb/2017	00°	♐	20
22/Dec/2014	00°	♑	6	21/Sep/2015	28°	♐	4	20/Jun/2016	29°	♐	32	20/Mar/2017	00°	♑	13
20/Jan/2015	00°	♒	8	20/Oct/2015	27°	♑	7	19/Jul/2016	27°	♑	40	19/Apr/2017	29°	♑	31
18/Feb/2015	29°	♒	59	19/Nov/2015	26°	♒	35	**18/Aug/2016**	**25°**	**♒**	**51**	19/May/2017	28°	♒	14
20/Mar/2015	**29°**	**♓**	**27**	18/Dec/2015	26°	♓	22	**16/Sep/2016**	**24°**	**♓**	**19**	17/Jun/2017	26°	♓	27
18/Apr/2015	28°	♈	25	16/Jan/2016	26°	♈	16	16/Oct/2016	23°	♈	14	16/Jul/2017	24°	♈	26
18/May/2015	26°	♉	55	15/Feb/2016	26°	♉	3	14/Nov/2016	22°	♉	37	15/Aug/2017	22°	♉	25
16/Jun/2015	25°	♊	7	15/Mar/2016	25°	♊	32	14/Dec/2016	22°	♊	25	13/Sep/2017	20°	♊	39
16/Jul/2015	23°	♋	14	14/Apr/2016	24°	♋	38	12/Jan/2017	22°	♋	27	12/Oct/2017	19°	♋	22
14/Aug/2015	21°	♌	30	13/May/2016	23°	♌	21	**11/Feb/2017**	**22°**	**♌**	**28**	10/Nov/2017	18°	♌	38
13/Sep/2015	**20°**	**♍**	**10**	12/Jun/2016	21°	♍	47	12/Mar/2017	22°	♍	13	10/Dec/2017	18°	♍	26
13/Oct/2015	19°	♎	20	12/Jul/2016	20°	♎	7	11/Apr/2017	21°	♎	32	8/Jan/2018	18°	♎	35
11/Nov/2015	19°	♏	0	10/Aug/2016	18°	♏	32	10/May/2017	20°	♏	24	7/Feb/2018	18°	♏	49
11/Dec/2015	19°	♐	2	9/Sep/2016	17°	♐	13	9/Jun/2017	18°	♐	53	9/Mar/2018	18°	♐	49
10/Jan/2016	19°	♑	13	9/Oct/2016	16°	♑	18	9/Jul/2017	17°	♑	9	8/Apr/2018	18°	♑	24
8/Feb/2016	19°	♒	15	7/Nov/2016	15°	♒	50	**7/Aug/2017**	**15°**	**♒**	**25**	8/May/2018	17°	♒	26
9/Mar/2016	**18°**	**♓**	**55**	7/Dec/2016	15°	♓	41	6/Sep/2017	13°	♓	53	6/Jun/2018	15°	♓	59
7/Apr/2016	18°	♈	4	5/Jan/2017	15°	♈	40	5/Oct/2017	12°	♈	42	6/Jul/2018	14°	♈	12
6/May/2016	16°	♉	41	4/Feb/2017	15°	♉	32	4/Nov/2017	11°	♉	58	4/Aug/2018	12°	♉	19
5/Jun/2016	14°	♊	53	5/Mar/2017	15°	♊	5	3/Dec/2017	11°	♊	40	3/Sep/2018	10°	♊	33
4/Jul/2016	12°	♋	53	3/Apr/2017	14°	♋	11	2/Jan/2018	11°	♋	37	2/Oct/2018	09°	♋	8
2/Aug/2016	10°	♌	57	3/May/2017	12°	♌	52	**31/Jan/2018**	**11°**	**♌**	**37**	31/Oct/2018	08°	♌	12
1/Sep/2016	**09°**	**♍**	**21**	1/Jun/2017	11°	♍	12	2/Mar/2018	11°	♍	23	30/Nov/2018	07°	♍	43
1/Oct/2016	08°	♎	15	1/Jul/2017	09°	♎	24	31/Mar/2018	10°	♎	44	29/Dec/2018	07°	♎	36
30/Oct/2016	07°	♏	43	30/Jul/2017	07°	♏	39	30/Apr/2018	09°	♏	38	27/Jan/2019	07°	♏	38
29/Nov/2016	07°	♐	42	29/Aug/2017	06°	♐	11	29/May/2018	08°	♐	10	26/Feb/2019	07°	♐	34
29/Dec/2016	07°	♑	59	28/Sep/2017	05°	♑	10	28/Jun/2018	06°	♑	28	28/Mar/2019	07°	♑	11
28/Jan/2017	08°	♒	15	27/Oct/2017	04°	♒	41	**27/Jul/2018**	**04°**	**♒**	**44**	26/Apr/2019	06°	♒	23
26/Feb/2017	**08°**	**♓**	**12**	26/Nov/2017	04°	♓	38	26/Aug/2018	03°	♓	12	26/May/2019	05°	♓	8
28/Mar/2017	07°	♈	37	26/Dec/2017	04°	♈	47	25/Sep/2018	01°	♈	59	25/Jun/2019	03°	♈	34
26/Apr/2017	06°	♉	27	24/Jan/2018	04°	♉	53	24/Oct/2018	01°	♉	13	25/Jul/2019	01°	♉	50
25/May/2017	04°	♊	46	23/Feb/2018	04°	♊	39	23/Nov/2018	00°	♊	52	23/Aug/2019	00°	♊	11
24/Jun/2017	02°	♋	47	24/Mar/2018	03°	♋	56	22/Dec/2018	00°	♋	49	22/Sep/2019	28°	♊	48
23/Jul/2017	00°	♌	44	22/Apr/2018	02°	♌	42	**21/Jan/2019**	**00°**	**♌**	**51**	21/Oct/2019	27°	♋	48
21/Aug/2017	**28°**	**♌**	**52**	22/May/2018	01°	♍	1	19/Feb/2019	00°	♍	42	19/Nov/2019	27°	♌	13
20/Sep/2017	27°	♍	27	20/Jun/2018	29°	♍	4	21/Mar/2019	00°	♎	9	19/Dec/2019	26°	♍	58
19/Oct/2017	26°	♎	35	19/Jul/2018	27°	♎	5	19/Apr/2019	29°	♎	6	17/Jan/2020	26°	♎	51
18/Nov/2017	26°	♏	19	18/Aug/2018	25°	♏	20	18/May/2019	27°	♏	38	15/Feb/2020	26°	♏	41
18/Dec/2017	26°	♐	31	16/Sep/2018	24°	♐	1	17/Jun/2019	25°	♐	53	16/Mar/2020	26°	♐	15

Moon Families - Eclipses in Bold Print

New Moon				First Quarter Moon				Full Moon				Last Quarter Moon			
17/Jan/2018	26°	♑	54	16/Oct/2018	23°	♑	19	**16/Jul/2019**	**24°**	**♑**	**4**	14/Apr/2020	25°	♑	26
15/Feb/2018	**27°**	**♒**	**7**	15/Nov/2018	23°	♒	11	15/Aug/2019	22°	♒	24	14/May/2020	24°	♒	13
17/Mar/2018	26°	♓	53	15/Dec/2018	23°	♓	26	14/Sep/2019	21°	♓	5	13/Jun/2020	22°	♓	42
16/Apr/2018	26°	♈	2	14/Jan/2019	23°	♈	47	13/Oct/2019	20°	♈	13	12/Jul/2020	21°	♈	2
15/May/2018	24°	♉	36	12/Feb/2019	23°	♉	54	12/Nov/2019	19°	♉	51	11/Aug/2020	19°	♉	27
13/Jun/2018	22°	♊	44	14/Mar/2019	23°	♊	33	12/Dec/2019	19°	♊	51	10/Sep/2020	18°	♊	7
13/Jul/2018	**20°**	**♋**	**41**	12/Apr/2019	22°	♋	35	**10/Jan/2020**	**20°**	**♋**	**0**	10/Oct/2020	17°	♋	10
11/Aug/2018	**18°**	**♌**	**41**	12/May/2019	21°	♌	3	9/Feb/2020	20°	♌	0	8/Nov/2020	16°	♌	36
9/Sep/2018	17°	♍	0	10/Jun/2019	19°	♍	6	9/Mar/2020	19°	♍	37	8/Dec/2020	16°	♍	22
9/Oct/2018	15°	♎	48	9/Jul/2019	16°	♎	58	8/Apr/2020	18°	♎	43	6/Jan/2021	16°	♎	17
7/Nov/2018	15°	♏	11	7/Aug/2019	14°	♏	55	7/May/2020	17°	♏	20	4/Feb/2021	16°	♏	7
7/Dec/2018	15°	♐	7	6/Sep/2019	13°	♐	15	**5/Jun/2020**	**15°**	**♐**	**34**	6/Mar/2021	15°	♐	41
6/Jan/2019	**15°**	**♑**	**25**	5/Oct/2019	12°	♑	9	**5/Jul/2020**	**13°**	**♑**	**37**	4/Apr/2021	14°	♑	51
4/Feb/2019	15°	♒	45	4/Nov/2019	11°	♒	41	3/Aug/2020	11°	♒	45	3/May/2021	13°	♒	35
6/Mar/2019	15°	♓	47	4/Dec/2019	11°	♓	48	2/Sep/2020	10°	♓	12	2/Jun/2021	11°	♓	59
5/Apr/2019	15°	♈	17	3/Jan/2020	12°	♈	15	1/Oct/2020	09°	♈	8	1/Jul/2021	10°	♈	14
4/May/2019	14°	♉	10	2/Feb/2020	12°	♉	39	31/Oct/2020	08°	♉	38	31/Jul/2021	08°	♉	33
3/Jun/2019	12°	♊	33	2/Mar/2020	12°	♊	42	**30/Nov/2020**	**08°**	**♊**	**38**	30/Aug/2021	07°	♊	8
2/Jul/2019	**10°**	**♋**	**37**	1/Apr/2020	12°	♋	9	30/Dec/2020	08°	♋	53	29/Sep/2021	06°	♋	8
1/Aug/2019	08°	♌	36	30/Apr/2020	10°	♌	57	28/Jan/2021	09°	♌	5	28/Oct/2021	05°	♌	37
30/Aug/2019	06°	♍	46	30/May/2020	09°	♍	11	27/Feb/2021	08°	♍	57	27/Nov/2021	05°	♍	28
28/Sep/2019	05°	♎	20	28/Jun/2020	07°	♎	5	28/Mar/2021	08°	♎	18	27/Dec/2021	05°	♎	32
28/Oct/2019	04°	♏	25	27/Jul/2020	04°	♏	56	27/Apr/2021	07°	♏	6	25/Jan/2022	05°	♏	33
26/Nov/2019	04°	♐	3	25/Aug/2020	02°	♐	58	**26/May/2021**	**05°**	**♐**	**25**	23/Feb/2022	05°	♐	16
26/Dec/2019	**04°**	**♑**	**6**	24/Sep/2020	01°	♑	29	24/Jun/2021	03°	♑	27	25/Mar/2022	04°	♑	33
24/Jan/2020	04°	♒	21	23/Oct/2020	00°	♒	35	24/Jul/2021	01°	♒	26	23/Apr/2022	03°	♒	18
23/Feb/2020	04°	♓	28	22/Nov/2020	00°	♓	20	22/Aug/2021	29°	♒	37	22/May/2022	01°	♓	39
24/Mar/2020	04°	♈	12	21/Dec/2020	00°	♈	34	20/Sep/2021	28°	♓	13	21/Jun/2022	29°	♓	45
23/Apr/2020	03°	♉	24	20/Jan/2021	01°	♉	2	20/Oct/2021	27°	♈	26	20/Jul/2022	27°	♈	51
22/May/2020	02°	♊	4	19/Feb/2021	01°	♊	20	**19/Nov/2021**	**27°**	**♉**	**14**	19/Aug/2022	26°	♉	12
21/Jun/2020	**00°**	**♋**	**21**	21/Mar/2021	01°	♋	12	19/Dec/2021	27°	♊	28	17/Sep/2022	24°	♊	59
20/Jul/2020	28°	♋	26	20/Apr/2021	00°	♌	25	17/Jan/2022	27°	♋	50	17/Oct/2022	24°	♋	18
19/Aug/2020	26°	♌	35	19/May/2021	29°	♌	1	16/Feb/2022	27°	♌	59	16/Nov/2022	24°	♌	9
17/Sep/2020	25°	♍	0	18/Jun/2021	27°	♍	9	18/Mar/2022	27°	♍	40	16/Dec/2022	24°	♍	21
16/Oct/2020	23°	♎	53	17/Jul/2021	25°	♎	3	16/Apr/2022	26°	♎	45	15/Jan/2023	24°	♎	38
15/Nov/2020	23°	♏	17	15/Aug/2021	23°	♏	0	**16/May/2022**	**25°**	**♏**	**18**	13/Feb/2023	24°	♏	40
14/Dec/2020	**23°**	**♐**	**8**	13/Sep/2021	21°	♐	16	14/Jun/2022	23°	♐	25	15/Mar/2023	24°	♐	13
13/Jan/2021	23°	♑	13	13/Oct/2021	20°	♑	0	13/Jul/2022	21°	♑	21	13/Apr/2023	23°	♑	11
11/Feb/2021	23°	♒	16	11/Nov/2021	19°	♒	20	12/Aug/2022	19°	♒	21	12/May/2023	21°	♒	36
13/Mar/2021	23°	♓	3	11/Dec/2021	19°	♓	13	10/Sep/2022	17°	♓	41	10/Jun/2023	19°	♓	40
12/Apr/2021	22°	♈	24	9/Jan/2022	19°	♈	27	9/Oct/2022	16°	♈	32	10/Jul/2023	17°	♈	35
11/May/2021	21°	♉	17	8/Feb/2022	19°	♉	46	**8/Nov/2022**	**16°**	**♉**	**0**	8/Aug/2023	15°	♉	38
10/Jun/2021	**19°**	**♊**	**47**	10/Mar/2022	19°	♊	50	8/Dec/2022	16°	♊	1	6/Sep/2023	14°	♊	3
10/Jul/2021	18°	♋	1	9/Apr/2022	19°	♋	24	6/Jan/2023	16°	♋	21	6/Oct/2023	13°	♋	2
8/Aug/2021	16°	♌	14	9/May/2022	18°	♌	23	5/Feb/2023	16°	♌	40	5/Nov/2023	12°	♌	39
7/Sep/2021	14°	♍	38	7/Jun/2022	16°	♍	50	7/Mar/2023	16°	♍	40	5/Dec/2023	12°	♍	48
6/Oct/2021	13°	♎	24	7/Jul/2022	14°	♎	59	6/Apr/2023	16°	♎	7	4/Jan/2024	13°	♎	14
4/Nov/2021	12°	♏	40	5/Aug/2022	13°	♏	1	**5/May/2023**	**14°**	**♏**	**58**	2/Feb/2024	13°	♏	35
4/Dec/2021	**12°**	**♐**	**22**	3/Sep/2022	11°	♐	13	4/Jun/2023	13°	♐	18	3/Mar/2024	13°	♐	32
2/Jan/2022	12°	♑	20	3/Oct/2022	09°	♑	46	3/Jul/2023	11°	♑	18	2/Apr/2024	12°	♑	52
1/Feb/2022	12°	♒	19	1/Nov/2022	08°	♒	49	1/Aug/2023	09°	♒	15	1/May/2024	11°	♒	34

Moon Families - Eclipses in Bold Print

New Moon				First Quarter Moon				Full Moon				Last Quarter Moon			
2/Mar/2022	12°	♓	6	30/Nov/2022	08°	♓	21	31/Aug/2023	07°	♓	25	30/May/2024	09°	♓	46
1/Apr/2022	11°	♈	30	30/Dec/2022	08°	♈	18	29/Sep/2023	06°	♈	0	28/Jun/2024	07°	♈	40
30/Apr/2022	**10°**	♉	**28**	28/Jan/2023	08°	♉	25	**28/Oct/2023**	**05°**	♉	**9**	28/Jul/2024	05°	♉	32
30/May/2022	09°	♊	3	27/Feb/2023	08°	♊	27	27/Nov/2023	04°	♊	51	26/Aug/2024	03°	♊	38
29/Jun/2022	07°	♋	22	29/Mar/2023	08°	♋	8	27/Dec/2023	04°	♋	58	24/Sep/2024	02°	♋	12
28/Jul/2022	05°	♌	38	27/Apr/2023	07°	♌	21	25/Jan/2024	05°	♌	14	24/Oct/2024	01°	♌	24
27/Aug/2022	04°	♍	3	27/May/2023	06°	♍	5	24/Feb/2024	05°	♍	23	23/Nov/2024	01°	♍	14
25/Sep/2022	02°	♎	48	26/Jun/2023	04°	♎	29	**25/Mar/2024**	**05°**	♎	**7**	22/Dec/2024	01°	♎	34
25/Oct/2022	**02°**	♏	**0**	25/Jul/2023	02°	♏	43	23/Apr/2024	04°	♏	17	21/Jan/2025	02°	♏	3
23/Nov/2022	01°	♐	37	24/Aug/2023	01°	♐	0	23/May/2024	02°	♐	55	20/Feb/2025	02°	♐	19
23/Dec/2022	01°	♑	32	22/Sep/2023	29°	♐	32	22/Jun/2024	01°	♑	7	22/Mar/2025	02°	♑	5
21/Jan/2023	01°	♒	32	22/Oct/2023	28°	♑	28	21/Jul/2024	29°	♑	8	21/Apr/2025	01°	♒	12
20/Feb/2023	01°	♓	22	20/Nov/2023	27°	♒	50	19/Aug/2024	27°	♒	15	20/May/2025	29°	♒	43
21/Mar/2023	00°	♈	49	19/Dec/2023	27°	♓	35	**18/Sep/2024**	**25°**	♓	**40**	18/Jun/2025	27°	♓	47
20/Apr/2023	**29°**	♈	**50**	18/Jan/2024	27°	♈	31	17/Oct/2024	24°	♈	35	18/Jul/2025	25°	♈	40
19/May/2023	28°	♉	25	16/Feb/2024	27°	♉	25	15/Nov/2024	24°	♉	0	16/Aug/2025	23°	♉	36
18/Jun/2023	26°	♊	43	17/Mar/2024	27°	♊	3	15/Dec/2024	23°	♊	52	14/Sep/2025	21°	♊	52
17/Jul/2023	24°	♋	56	15/Apr/2024	26°	♋	18	13/Jan/2025	23°	♋	59	13/Oct/2025	20°	♋	39
16/Aug/2023	23°	♌	17	15/May/2024	25°	♌	8	12/Feb/2025	24°	♌	6	12/Nov/2025	20°	♌	4
15/Sep/2023	21°	♍	58	14/Jun/2024	23°	♍	39	**14/Mar/2025**	**23°**	♍	**56**	11/Dec/2025	20°	♍	4
14/Oct/2023	**21°**	♎	**7**	13/Jul/2024	22°	♎	0	13/Apr/2025	23°	♎	19	10/Jan/2026	20°	♎	24
13/Nov/2023	20°	♏	43	12/Aug/2024	20°	♏	24	12/May/2025	22°	♏	12	9/Feb/2026	20°	♏	46
12/Dec/2023	20°	♐	40	11/Sep/2024	19°	♐	0	11/Jun/2025	20°	♐	39	11/Mar/2026	20°	♐	49
11/Jan/2024	20°	♑	44	10/Oct/2024	17°	♑	57	10/Jul/2025	18°	♑	50	10/Apr/2026	20°	♑	20
9/Feb/2024	20°	♒	40	9/Nov/2024	17°	♒	19	9/Aug/2025	16°	♒	59	9/May/2026	19°	♒	14
10/Mar/2024	20°	♓	16	8/Dec/2024	17°	♓	2	**7/Sep/2025**	**15°**	♓	**22**	8/Jun/2026	17°	♓	38
8/Apr/2024	**19°**	♈	**24**	6/Jan/2025	16°	♈	55	7/Oct/2025	14°	♈	8	7/Jul/2026	15°	♈	41
8/May/2024	18°	♉	2	5/Feb/2025	16°	♉	46	5/Nov/2025	13°	♉	22	6/Aug/2026	13°	♉	40
6/Jun/2024	16°	♊	17	6/Mar/2025	16°	♊	21	4/Dec/2025	13°	♊	3	4/Sep/2026	11°	♊	48
5/Jul/2024	14°	♋	23	5/Apr/2025	15°	♋	33	3/Jan/2026	13°	♋	1	3/Oct/2026	10°	♋	21
4/Aug/2024	12°	♌	34	4/May/2025	14°	♌	21	1/Feb/2026	13°	♌	3	1/Nov/2026	09°	♌	25
3/Sep/2024	11°	♍	4	3/Jun/2025	12°	♍	50	**3/Mar/2026**	**12°**	♍	**53**	1/Dec/2026	09°	♍	3
2/Oct/2024	**10°**	♎	**3**	2/Jul/2025	11°	♎	9	2/Apr/2026	12°	♎	21	30/Dec/2026	09°	♎	5
1/Nov/2024	09°	♏	35	1/Aug/2025	09°	♏	31	1/May/2026	11°	♏	20	29/Jan/2027	09°	♏	17
1/Dec/2024	09°	♐	32	31/Aug/2025	08°	♐	7	31/May/2026	09°	♐	55	28/Feb/2027	09°	♐	22
30/Dec/2024	09°	♑	43	29/Sep/2025	07°	♑	5	29/Jun/2026	08°	♑	14	30/Mar/2027	09°	♑	6
29/Jan/2025	09°	♒	51	29/Oct/2025	06°	♒	30	29/Jul/2026	06°	♒	30	28/Apr/2027	08°	♒	19
28/Feb/2025	09°	♓	40	28/Nov/2025	06°	♓	17	**28/Aug/2026**	**04°**	♓	**54**	28/May/2027	07°	♓	1
29/Mar/2025	**09°**	♈	**0**	27/Dec/2025	06°	♈	17	26/Sep/2026	03°	♈	37	27/Jun/2027	05°	♈	21
27/Apr/2025	07°	♉	46	26/Jan/2026	06°	♉	14	26/Oct/2026	02°	♉	45	26/Jul/2027	03°	♉	29
27/May/2025	06°	♊	5	24/Feb/2026	05°	♊	54	24/Nov/2026	02°	♊	20	25/Aug/2027	01°	♊	41
25/Jun/2025	04°	♋	7	25/Mar/2026	05°	♋	8	24/Dec/2026	02°	♋	13	23/Sep/2027	00°	♋	10
24/Jul/2025	02°	♌	8	24/Apr/2026	03°	♌	56	22/Jan/2027	02°	♌	14	22/Oct/2027	29°	♋	5
23/Aug/2025	00°	♍	23	23/May/2026	02°	♍	20	**20/Feb/2027**	**02°**	♍	**5**	21/Nov/2027	28°	♌	27
21/Sep/2025	**29°**	♍	**5**	21/Jun/2026	00°	♎	32	22/Mar/2027	01°	♎	35	20/Dec/2027	28°	♍	14
21/Oct/2025	28°	♎	21	21/Jul/2026	28°	♎	43	20/Apr/2027	00°	♏	36	18/Jan/2028	28°	♎	13
20/Nov/2025	28°	♏	11	20/Aug/2026	27°	♏	7	20/May/2027	29°	♏	13	17/Feb/2028	28°	♏	10
20/Dec/2025	28°	♐	24	18/Sep/2026	25°	♐	57	19/Jun/2027	27°	♐	33	17/Mar/2028	27°	♐	53
18/Jan/2026	28°	♑	43	18/Oct/2026	25°	♑	18	**18/Jul/2027**	**25°**	♑	**48**	16/Apr/2028	27°	♑	12
17/Feb/2026	**28°**	♒	**49**	17/Nov/2026	25°	♒	8	**17/Aug/2027**	**24°**	♒	**11**	16/May/2028	26°	♒	5
19/Mar/2026	28°	♓	27	17/Dec/2026	25°	♓	17	15/Sep/2027	22°	♓	52	15/Jun/2028	24°	♓	36

Moon Families - Eclipses in Bold Print

New Moon

Date	Deg	Sign	Min
17/Apr/2026	27°	♈	28
16/May/2026	25°	♉	57
15/Jun/2026	24°	♊	3
14/Jul/2026	21°	♋	59
12/Aug/2026	**20°**	**♌**	**1**
11/Sep/2026	18°	♍	25
10/Oct/2026	17°	♎	21
9/Nov/2026	16°	♏	53
9/Dec/2026	16°	♐	56
7/Jan/2027	17°	♑	18
6/Feb/2027	**17°**	**♒**	**37**
8/Mar/2027	17°	♓	34
6/Apr/2027	16°	♈	57
6/May/2027	15°	♉	42
4/Jun/2027	13°	♊	58
4/Jul/2027	11°	♋	57
2/Aug/2027	**09°**	**♌**	**55**
31/Aug/2027	08°	♍	6
30/Sep/2027	06°	♎	43
29/Oct/2027	05°	♏	54
28/Nov/2027	05°	♐	39
27/Dec/2027	05°	♑	50
26/Jan/2028	**06°**	**♒**	**11**
25/Feb/2028	06°	♓	20
26/Mar/2028	06°	♈	2
24/Apr/2028	05°	♉	8
24/May/2028	03°	♊	41
22/Jun/2028	01°	♋	50
22/Jul/2028	**29°**	**♋**	**50**
20/Aug/2028	27°	♌	56
18/Sep/2028	26°	♍	21
18/Oct/2028	25°	♎	15
16/Nov/2028	24°	♏	43
16/Dec/2028	24°	♐	38
14/Jan/2029	**24°**	**♑**	**50**
13/Feb/2029	25°	♒	0
15/Mar/2029	24°	♓	52
13/Apr/2029	24°	♈	14
13/May/2029	23°	♉	4
12/Jun/2029	**21°**	**♊**	**29**
11/Jul/2029	**19°**	**♋**	**37**
10/Aug/2029	17°	♌	44
8/Sep/2029	16°	♍	4
7/Oct/2029	14°	♎	48
6/Nov/2029	14°	♏	2
5/Dec/2029	**13°**	**♐**	**45**
4/Jan/2030	13°	♑	46
2/Feb/2030	13°	♒	51
4/Mar/2030	13°	♓	43
2/Apr/2030	13°	♈	12
2/May/2030	12°	♉	13

First Quarter Moon

Date	Deg	Sign	Min
15/Jan/2027	25°	♈	27
14/Feb/2027	25°	♉	23
15/Mar/2027	24°	♊	51
13/Apr/2027	23°	♋	47
13/May/2027	22°	♌	13
11/Jun/2027	20°	♍	19
10/Jul/2027	18°	♎	17
9/Aug/2027	16°	♏	24
7/Sep/2027	14°	♐	55
7/Oct/2027	13°	♑	59
6/Nov/2027	13°	♒	40
6/Dec/2027	13°	♓	50
5/Jan/2028	14°	♈	13
3/Feb/2028	14°	♉	28
4/Mar/2028	14°	♊	18
2/Apr/2028	13°	♋	34
2/May/2028	12°	♌	13
31/May/2028	10°	♍	23
29/Jun/2028	08°	♎	16
28/Jul/2028	06°	♏	9
27/Aug/2028	04°	♐	19
25/Sep/2028	02°	♑	59
25/Oct/2028	02°	♒	18
24/Nov/2028	02°	♓	14
23/Dec/2028	02°	♈	36
22/Jan/2029	03°	♉	4
21/Feb/2029	03°	♊	16
23/Mar/2029	02°	♋	57
21/Apr/2029	01°	♌	59
21/May/2029	00°	♍	24
19/Jun/2029	28°	♍	24
18/Jul/2029	26°	♎	14
16/Aug/2029	24°	♏	11
15/Sep/2029	22°	♐	30
14/Oct/2029	21°	♑	23
13/Nov/2029	20°	♒	55
12/Dec/2029	20°	♓	59
11/Jan/2030	21°	♈	23
10/Feb/2030	21°	♉	47
12/Mar/2030	21°	♊	49
11/Apr/2030	21°	♋	16
10/May/2030	20°	♌	5
9/Jun/2030	18°	♍	23
8/Jul/2030	16°	♎	21
6/Aug/2030	14°	♏	16
4/Sep/2030	12°	♐	24
4/Oct/2030	10°	♑	58
2/Nov/2030	10°	♒	6
1/Dec/2030	09°	♓	47
31/Dec/2030	09°	♈	54
30/Jan/2031	10°	♉	12

Full Moon

Date	Deg	Sign	Min
15/Oct/2027	21°	♈	58
14/Nov/2027	21°	♉	31
13/Dec/2027	21°	♊	24
12/Jan/2028	**21°**	**♋**	**27**
10/Feb/2028	21°	♌	23
11/Mar/2028	20°	♍	59
9/Apr/2028	20°	♎	5
8/May/2028	18°	♏	44
7/Jun/2028	17°	♐	1
6/Jul/2028	**15°**	**♑**	**11**
5/Aug/2028	13°	♒	26
3/Sep/2028	11°	♓	59
3/Oct/2028	10°	♈	59
2/Nov/2028	10°	♉	29
2/Dec/2028	10°	♊	24
31/Dec/2028	**10°**	**♋**	**32**
30/Jan/2029	10°	♌	38
28/Feb/2029	10°	♍	24
30/Mar/2029	09°	♎	40
28/Apr/2029	08°	♏	25
27/May/2029	06°	♐	45
26/Jun/2029	**04°**	**♑**	**49**
25/Jul/2029	02°	♒	53
24/Aug/2029	01°	♓	12
22/Sep/2029	29°	♓	57
22/Oct/2029	29°	♈	16
21/Nov/2029	29°	♉	7
20/Dec/2029	**29°**	**♊**	**20**
19/Jan/2030	29°	♋	37
18/Feb/2030	29°	♌	38
19/Mar/2030	29°	♍	10
18/Apr/2030	28°	♎	9
17/May/2030	26°	♏	36
15/Jun/2030	**24°**	**♐**	**43**
15/Jul/2030	22°	♑	40
13/Aug/2030	20°	♒	45
11/Sep/2030	19°	♓	11
11/Oct/2030	18°	♈	10
10/Nov/2030	17°	♉	46
9/Dec/2030	**17°**	**♊**	**54**
8/Jan/2031	18°	♋	16
7/Feb/2031	18°	♌	32
9/Mar/2031	18°	♍	24
7/Apr/2031	17°	♎	42
7/May/2031	**16°**	**♏**	**24**
5/Jun/2031	**14°**	**♐**	**39**
4/Jul/2031	12°	♑	37
3/Aug/2031	10°	♒	34
1/Sep/2031	08°	♓	45
30/Sep/2031	07°	♈	25
30/Oct/2031	**06°**	**♉**	**40**

Last Quarter Moon

Date	Deg	Sign	Min
14/Jul/2028	22°	♈	55
13/Aug/2028	21°	♉	14
12/Sep/2028	19°	♊	47
11/Oct/2028	18°	♋	41
9/Nov/2028	18°	♌	0
9/Dec/2028	17°	♍	40
7/Jan/2029	17°	♎	32
5/Feb/2029	17°	♏	23
7/Mar/2029	17°	♐	1
5/Apr/2029	16°	♑	18
5/May/2029	15°	♒	11
4/Jun/2029	13°	♓	43
3/Jul/2029	12°	♈	5
2/Aug/2029	10°	♉	27
1/Sep/2029	09°	♊	2
30/Sep/2029	07°	♋	58
30/Oct/2029	07°	♌	19
28/Nov/2029	07°	♍	2
28/Dec/2029	06°	♎	56
26/Jan/2030	06°	♏	50
25/Feb/2030	06°	♐	30
26/Mar/2030	05°	♑	47
24/Apr/2030	04°	♒	37
24/May/2030	03°	♓	5
22/Jun/2030	01°	♈	20
22/Jul/2030	29°	♈	35
21/Aug/2030	28°	♉	3
19/Sep/2030	26°	♊	55
19/Oct/2030	26°	♋	15
18/Nov/2030	26°	♌	2
18/Dec/2030	26°	♍	5
16/Jan/2031	26°	♎	10
14/Feb/2031	26°	♏	2
16/Mar/2031	25°	♐	28
14/Apr/2031	24°	♑	23
13/May/2031	22°	♒	50
12/Jun/2031	20°	♓	58
11/Jul/2031	19°	♈	0
10/Aug/2031	17°	♉	13
8/Sep/2031	15°	♊	49
8/Oct/2031	14°	♋	57
7/Nov/2031	14°	♌	39
7/Dec/2031	14°	♍	48
5/Jan/2032	15°	♎	7
4/Feb/2032	15°	♏	17
5/Mar/2032	15°	♐	2
3/Apr/2032	14°	♑	12
2/May/2032	12°	♒	48
31/May/2032	10°	♓	56
30/Jun/2032	08°	♈	51
29/Jul/2032	06°	♉	49

Moon Families - Eclipses in Bold Print

New Moon				First Quarter Moon				Full Moon				Last Quarter Moon			
1/Jun/2030	**10°**	**♊**	**49**	1/Mar/2031	10°	♊	22	28/Nov/2031	06°	♊	31	27/Aug/2032	05°	♊	4
30/Jun/2030	09°	♋	8	31/Mar/2031	10°	♋	6	28/Dec/2031	06°	♋	46	26/Sep/2032	03°	♋	50
30/Jul/2030	07°	♌	21	29/Apr/2031	09°	♌	17	27/Jan/2032	07°	♌	8	26/Oct/2032	03°	♌	13
28/Aug/2030	05°	♍	41	29/May/2031	07°	♍	55	26/Feb/2032	07°	♍	16	24/Nov/2032	03°	♍	12
27/Sep/2030	04°	♎	20	28/Jun/2031	06°	♎	9	27/Mar/2032	06°	♎	54	24/Dec/2032	03°	♎	35
26/Oct/2030	03°	♏	27	27/Jul/2031	04°	♏	14	**25/Apr/2032**	**05°**	**♏**	**58**	23/Jan/2033	04°	♏	2
25/Nov/2030	**03°**	**♐**	**2**	25/Aug/2031	02°	♐	22	25/May/2032	04°	♐	27	22/Feb/2033	04°	♐	10
24/Dec/2030	02°	♑	56	24/Sep/2031	00°	♑	49	23/Jun/2032	02°	♑	33	24/Mar/2033	03°	♑	44
23/Jan/2031	02°	♒	57	23/Oct/2031	29°	♑	42	22/Jul/2032	00°	♒	30	22/Apr/2033	02°	♒	39
21/Feb/2031	02°	♓	48	21/Nov/2031	29°	♒	4	21/Aug/2032	28°	♒	34	21/May/2033	01°	♓	0
23/Mar/2031	02°	♈	19	21/Dec/2031	28°	♓	54	19/Sep/2032	27°	♓	0	19/Jun/2033	28°	♈	59
21/Apr/2031	01°	♉	24	19/Jan/2032	28°	♈	58	**18/Oct/2032**	**25°**	**♈**	**56**	19/Jul/2033	26°	♈	49
21/May/2031	**00°**	**♊**	**4**	18/Feb/2032	29°	♉	1	17/Nov/2032	25°	♉	28	17/Aug/2033	24°	♉	48
19/Jun/2031	28°	♊	27	18/Mar/2032	28°	♊	49	16/Dec/2032	25°	♊	27	15/Sep/2033	23°	♊	11
19/Jul/2031	26°	♋	43	17/Apr/2032	28°	♋	10	15/Jan/2033	25°	♋	41	15/Oct/2033	22°	♋	8
18/Aug/2031	25°	♌	4	17/May/2032	27°	♌	3	14/Feb/2033	25°	♌	53	13/Nov/2033	21°	♌	45
16/Sep/2031	23°	♍	42	16/Jun/2032	25°	♍	32	16/Mar/2033	25°	♍	46	13/Dec/2033	21°	♍	55
16/Oct/2031	22°	♎	46	15/Jul/2032	23°	♎	49	**14/Apr/2033**	**25°**	**♎**	**9**	12/Jan/2034	22°	♎	23
14/Nov/2031	**22°**	**♏**	**17**	14/Aug/2032	22°	♏	5	14/May/2033	23°	♏	57	11/Feb/2034	22°	♏	47
14/Dec/2031	22°	♐	9	12/Sep/2032	20°	♐	33	12/Jun/2033	22°	♐	17	13/Mar/2034	22°	♐	45
12/Jan/2032	22°	♑	10	12/Oct/2032	19°	♑	22	12/Jul/2033	20°	♑	21	11/Apr/2034	22°	♑	6
11/Feb/2032	22°	♒	4	10/Nov/2032	18°	♒	37	10/Aug/2033	18°	♒	25	11/May/2034	20°	♒	50
11/Mar/2032	21°	♓	39	9/Dec/2032	18°	♓	16	9/Sep/2033	16°	♓	44	9/Jun/2034	19°	♓	3
10/Apr/2032	20°	♈	47	8/Jan/2033	18°	♈	9	**8/Oct/2033**	**15°**	**♈**	**28**	9/Jul/2034	16°	♈	58
9/May/2032	**19°**	**♉**	**29**	6/Feb/2033	18°	♉	4	6/Nov/2033	14°	♉	44	7/Aug/2034	14°	♉	52
8/Jun/2032	17°	♊	50	8/Mar/2033	17°	♊	47	6/Dec/2033	14°	♊	28	5/Sep/2034	12°	♊	59
7/Jul/2032	16°	♋	2	6/Apr/2033	17°	♋	8	4/Jan/2034	14°	♋	31	4/Oct/2034	11°	♋	35
6/Aug/2032	14°	♌	18	6/May/2033	16°	♌	4	3/Feb/2034	14°	♌	38	3/Nov/2034	10°	♌	46
4/Sep/2032	12°	♍	52	4/Jun/2033	14°	♍	39	5/Mar/2034	14°	♍	34	2/Dec/2034	10°	♍	34
4/Oct/2032	11°	♎	52	4/Jul/2033	13°	♎	2	**3/Apr/2034**	**14°**	**♎**	**6**	1/Jan/2035	10°	♎	47
3/Nov/2032	**11°**	**♏**	**21**	3/Aug/2033	11°	♏	24	3/May/2034	13°	♏	8	31/Jan/2035	11°	♏	10
2/Dec/2032	11°	♐	14	2/Sep/2033	09°	♐	57	2/Jun/2034	11°	♐	43	2/Mar/2035	11°	♐	21
1/Jan/2033	11°	♑	18	1/Oct/2033	08°	♑	49	1/Jul/2034	09°	♑	58	31/Mar/2035	11°	♑	3
30/Jan/2033	11°	♒	19	31/Oct/2033	08°	♒	4	31/Jul/2034	08°	♒	7	30/Apr/2035	10°	♒	11
1/Mar/2033	11°	♓	3	29/Nov/2033	07°	♓	42	29/Aug/2034	06°	♓	25	30/May/2035	08°	♓	45
30/Mar/2033	**10°**	**♈**	**20**	29/Dec/2033	07°	♈	34	**28/Sep/2034**	**05°**	**♈**	**4**	28/Jun/2035	06°	♈	55
29/Apr/2033	09°	♉	7	27/Jan/2034	07°	♉	27	27/Oct/2034	04°	♉	10	28/Jul/2035	04°	♉	54
28/May/2033	07°	♊	27	25/Feb/2034	07°	♊	8	25/Nov/2034	03°	♊	43	26/Aug/2035	02°	♊	59
26/Jun/2033	05°	♋	34	27/Mar/2034	06°	♋	27	25/Dec/2034	03°	♋	37	24/Sep/2035	01°	♋	23
26/Jul/2033	03°	♌	40	25/Apr/2034	05°	♌	20	23/Jan/2035	03°	♌	38	23/Oct/2035	00°	♌	16
24/Aug/2033	02°	♍	2	24/May/2034	03°	♍	53	**22/Feb/2035**	**03°**	**♍**	**33**	22/Nov/2035	29°	♌	42
23/Sep/2033	**00°**	**♎**	**50**	23/Jun/2034	02°	♎	13	23/Mar/2035	03°	♎	7	21/Dec/2035	29°	♍	36
23/Oct/2033	00°	♏	12	23/Jul/2034	00°	♏	32	22/Apr/2035	02°	♏	15	20/Jan/2036	29°	♎	46
22/Nov/2033	00°	♐	3	22/Aug/2034	29°	♏	2	22/May/2035	00°	♐	57	18/Feb/2036	29°	♏	53
21/Dec/2033	00°	♑	12	20/Sep/2034	27°	♐	52	20/Jun/2035	29°	♐	19	19/Mar/2036	29°	♐	44
20/Jan/2034	00°	♒	24	20/Oct/2034	27°	♑	10	20/Jul/2035	27°	♑	34	18/Apr/2036	29°	♑	6
18/Feb/2034	00°	♓	21	19/Nov/2034	26°	♒	53	**19/Aug/2035**	**25°**	**♒**	**55**	18/May/2036	27°	♒	59
20/Mar/2034	**29°**	**♓**	**52**	18/Dec/2034	26°	♓	52	17/Sep/2035	24°	♓	32	17/Jun/2036	26°	♓	26
18/Apr/2034	28°	♈	50	17/Jan/2035	26°	♈	53	17/Oct/2035	23°	♈	33	16/Jul/2036	24°	♈	38
18/May/2034	27°	♉	16	15/Feb/2035	26°	♉	40	15/Nov/2035	23°	♉	0	15/Aug/2036	22°	♉	49
16/Jun/2034	25°	♊	22	16/Mar/2035	26°	♊	4	15/Dec/2035	22°	♊	50	13/Sep/2036	21°	♊	13

Moon Families - Eclipses in Bold Print

New Moon				First Quarter Moon				Full Moon				Last Quarter Moon			
15/Jul/2034	23°	♋	20	15/Apr/2035	24°	♋	59	13/Jan/2036	22°	♋	50	12/Oct/2036	19°	♋	59
14/Aug/2034	21°	♌	27	14/May/2035	23°	♌	29	**11/Feb/2036**	**22°**	**♌**	**45**	11/Nov/2036	19°	♌	14
12/Sep/2034	**19°**	**♍**	**58**	12/Jun/2035	21°	♍	41	12/Mar/2036	22°	♍	22	10/Dec/2036	18°	♍	53
12/Oct/2034	19°	♎	3	12/Jul/2035	19°	♎	49	10/Apr/2036	21°	♎	32	8/Jan/2037	18°	♎	49
11/Nov/2034	18°	♏	42	10/Aug/2035	18°	♏	6	10/May/2036	20°	♏	15	7/Feb/2037	18°	♏	46
10/Dec/2034	18°	♐	50	9/Sep/2035	16°	♐	46	8/Jun/2036	18°	♐	38	8/Mar/2037	18°	♐	33
9/Jan/2035	19°	♑	10	9/Oct/2035	15°	♑	56	8/Jul/2036	16°	♑	52	7/Apr/2037	17°	♑	58
8/Feb/2035	19°	♒	23	8/Nov/2035	15°	♒	38	**7/Aug/2036**	**15°**	**♒**	**11**	7/May/2037	16°	♒	58
9/Mar/2035	**19°**	**♓**	**12**	8/Dec/2035	15°	♓	44	5/Sep/2036	13°	♓	46	5/Jun/2037	15°	♓	35
8/Apr/2035	18°	♈	26	6/Jan/2036	15°	♈	58	5/Oct/2036	12°	♈	45	5/Jul/2037	13°	♈	58
7/May/2035	17°	♉	6	5/Feb/2036	16°	♉	2	4/Nov/2036	12°	♉	10	4/Aug/2037	12°	♉	17
6/Jun/2035	15°	♊	17	5/Mar/2036	15°	♊	41	3/Dec/2036	11°	♊	59	2/Sep/2037	10°	♊	46
5/Jul/2035	13°	♋	15	4/Apr/2036	14°	♋	48	2/Jan/2037	12°	♋	1	2/Oct/2037	09°	♋	34
3/Aug/2035	11°	♌	13	3/May/2036	13°	♌	23	**31/Jan/2037**	**12°**	**♌**	**2**	31/Oct/2037	08°	♌	46
2/Sep/2035	**09°**	**♍**	**27**	1/Jun/2036	11°	♍	33	2/Mar/2037	11°	♍	45	30/Nov/2037	08°	♍	21
1/Oct/2035	08°	♎	11	30/Jun/2036	09°	♎	31	31/Mar/2037	11°	♎	1	29/Dec/2037	08°	♎	11
31/Oct/2035	07°	♏	30	30/Jul/2036	07°	♏	32	29/Apr/2037	09°	♏	47	27/Jan/2038	08°	♏	3
29/Nov/2035	07°	♐	24	28/Aug/2036	05°	♐	52	29/May/2037	08°	♐	9	26/Feb/2038	07°	♐	45
29/Dec/2035	07°	♑	41	27/Sep/2036	04°	♑	43	27/Jun/2037	06°	♑	19	27/Mar/2038	07°	♑	8
28/Jan/2036	08°	♒	3	27/Oct/2036	04°	♒	12	**27/Jul/2037**	**04°**	**♒**	**29**	26/Apr/2038	06°	♒	7
27/Feb/2036	**08°**	**♓**	**10**	25/Nov/2036	04°	♓	14	25/Aug/2037	02°	♓	55	25/May/2038	04°	♓	44
27/Mar/2036	07°	♈	45	25/Dec/2036	04°	♈	36	24/Sep/2037	01°	♈	45	24/Jun/2038	03°	♈	7
26/Apr/2036	06°	♉	44	24/Jan/2037	04°	♉	57	24/Oct/2037	01°	♉	6	24/Jul/2038	01°	♉	27
25/May/2036	05°	♊	9	23/Feb/2037	04°	♊	59	22/Nov/2037	00°	♊	55	22/Aug/2038	29°	♉	57
24/Jun/2036	03°	♋	12	24/Mar/2037	04°	♋	27	22/Dec/2037	01°	♋	2	21/Sep/2038	28°	♊	47
23/Jul/2036	**01°**	**♌**	**9**	23/Apr/2037	03°	♌	18	**21/Jan/2038**	**01°**	**♌**	**11**	21/Oct/2038	28°	♋	2
21/Aug/2036	**29°**	**♌**	**14**	22/May/2037	01°	♍	37	19/Feb/2038	01°	♍	6	19/Nov/2038	27°	♌	40
20/Sep/2036	27°	♍	41	20/Jun/2037	29°	♍	34	21/Mar/2038	00°	♎	33	19/Dec/2038	27°	♍	33
19/Oct/2036	26°	♎	40	19/Jul/2037	27°	♎	25	19/Apr/2038	29°	♎	28	17/Jan/2039	27°	♎	29
18/Nov/2036	26°	♏	14	18/Aug/2037	25°	♏	27	18/May/2038	27°	♏	54	16/Feb/2039	27°	♏	15
17/Dec/2036	26°	♐	16	16/Sep/2037	23°	♐	54	**17/Jun/2038**	**26°**	**♐**	**2**	17/Mar/2039	26°	♐	40
16/Jan/2037	**26°**	**♑**	**35**	16/Oct/2037	22°	♑	58	**16/Jul/2038**	**24°**	**♑**	**4**	15/Apr/2039	25°	♑	37
15/Feb/2037	26°	♒	50	14/Nov/2037	22°	♒	42	14/Aug/2038	22°	♒	15	15/May/2039	24°	♒	10
16/Mar/2037	26°	♓	42	14/Dec/2037	22°	♓	56	13/Sep/2038	20°	♓	49	13/Jun/2039	22°	♓	27
15/Apr/2037	26°	♈	1	13/Jan/2038	23°	♈	24	13/Oct/2038	19°	♈	56	13/Jul/2039	20°	♈	38
15/May/2037	24°	♉	45	12/Feb/2038	23°	♉	45	11/Nov/2038	19°	♉	37	11/Aug/2039	19°	♉	0
13/Jun/2037	23°	♊	1	14/Mar/2038	23°	♊	39	**11/Dec/2038**	**19°**	**♊**	**45**	10/Sep/2039	17°	♊	43
13/Jul/2037	**21°**	**♋**	**3**	12/Apr/2038	22°	♋	55	10/Jan/2039	20°	♋	4	10/Oct/2039	16°	♋	55
11/Aug/2037	19°	♌	6	12/May/2038	21°	♌	33	9/Feb/2039	20°	♌	13	9/Nov/2039	16°	♌	35
9/Sep/2037	17°	♍	24	10/Jun/2038	19°	♍	41	10/Mar/2039	19°	♍	57	8/Dec/2039	16°	♍	36
9/Oct/2037	16°	♎	9	9/Jul/2038	17°	♎	33	9/Apr/2039	19°	♎	7	7/Jan/2040	16°	♎	44
7/Nov/2037	15°	♏	25	7/Aug/2038	15°	♏	26	8/May/2039	17°	♏	44	5/Feb/2040	16°	♏	43
6/Dec/2037	15°	♐	11	6/Sep/2038	13°	♐	36	**6/Jun/2039**	**15°**	**♐**	**56**	6/Mar/2040	16°	♐	19
5/Jan/2038	**15°**	**♑**	**18**	5/Oct/2038	12°	♑	16	6/Jul/2039	13°	♑	54	4/Apr/2040	15°	♑	24
4/Feb/2038	15°	♒	29	3/Nov/2038	11°	♒	33	4/Aug/2039	11°	♒	54	3/May/2040	13°	♒	59
5/Mar/2038	15°	♓	28	3/Dec/2038	11°	♓	26	2/Sep/2039	10°	♓	11	2/Jun/2040	12°	♓	10
4/Apr/2038	15°	♈	0	2/Jan/2039	11°	♈	44	2/Oct/2039	08°	♈	58	1/Jul/2040	10°	♈	11
4/May/2038	14°	♉	1	1/Feb/2039	12°	♉	9	31/Oct/2039	08°	♉	21	30/Jul/2040	08°	♉	17
3/Jun/2038	12°	♊	33	3/Mar/2039	12°	♊	20	**30/Nov/2039**	**08°**	**♊**	**19**	29/Aug/2040	06°	♊	43
2/Jul/2038	**10°**	**♋**	**47**	1/Apr/2039	12°	♋	1	30/Dec/2039	08°	♋	39	28/Sep/2040	05°	♋	40
1/Aug/2038	08°	♌	54	1/May/2039	11°	♌	4	29/Jan/2040	09°	♌	0	28/Oct/2040	05°	♌	11

Moon Families - Eclipses in Bold Print

New Moon				First Quarter Moon				Full Moon				Last Quarter Moon			
30/Aug/2038	07°	♍	9	31/May/2039	09°	♍	32	28/Feb/2040	09°	♍	2	26/Nov/2040	05°	♍	13
28/Sep/2038	05°	♎	45	29/Jun/2039	07°	♎	36	28/Mar/2040	08°	♎	32	26/Dec/2040	05°	♎	32
28/Oct/2038	04°	♏	49	28/Jul/2039	05°	♏	32	27/Apr/2040	07°	♏	27	25/Jan/2041	05°	♏	49
26/Nov/2038	04°	♐	23	26/Aug/2039	03°	♐	35	**26/May/2040**	**05°**	**♐**	**50**	24/Feb/2041	05°	♐	45
26/Dec/2038	**04°**	**♑**	**19**	25/Sep/2039	02°	♑	0	24/Jun/2040	03°	♑	52	25/Mar/2041	05°	♑	8
24/Jan/2039	04°	♒	24	24/Oct/2039	00°	♒	55	24/Jul/2040	01°	♒	48	23/Apr/2041	03°	♒	55
23/Feb/2039	04°	♓	20	22/Nov/2039	00°	♓	25	22/Aug/2040	29°	♒	53	22/May/2041	02°	♓	11
24/Mar/2039	03°	♈	56	22/Dec/2039	00°	♈	23	20/Sep/2040	28°	♓	22	21/Jun/2041	00°	♈	8
23/Apr/2039	03°	♉	6	21/Jan/2040	00°	♉	38	20/Oct/2040	27°	♈	24	20/Jul/2041	28°	♈	2
23/May/2039	01°	♊	49	19/Feb/2040	00°	♊	50	**18/Nov/2040**	**27°**	**♉**	**3**	18/Aug/2041	26°	♉	9
21/Jun/2039	**00°**	**♋**	**12**	20/Mar/2040	00°	♋	44	18/Dec/2040	27°	♊	11	17/Sep/2041	24°	♊	42
21/Jul/2039	28°	♋	27	19/Apr/2040	00°	♌	6	17/Jan/2041	27°	♋	32	16/Oct/2041	23°	♋	52
19/Aug/2039	26°	♌	44	19/May/2040	28°	♌	55	16/Feb/2041	27°	♌	46	15/Nov/2041	23°	♌	39
18/Sep/2039	25°	♍	17	17/Jun/2040	27°	♍	17	17/Mar/2041	27°	♍	36	15/Dec/2041	23°	♍	56
17/Oct/2039	24°	♎	16	17/Jul/2040	25°	♎	24	16/Apr/2041	26°	♎	52	14/Jan/2042	24°	♎	24
16/Nov/2039	23°	♏	43	15/Aug/2040	23°	♏	32	**16/May/2041**	**25°**	**♏**	**32**	13/Feb/2042	24°	♏	42
15/Dec/2039	**23°**	**♐**	**32**	14/Sep/2040	21°	♐	53	14/Jun/2041	23°	♐	46	14/Mar/2042	24°	♐	30
14/Jan/2040	23°	♑	33	13/Oct/2040	20°	♑	37	13/Jul/2041	21°	♑	45	13/Apr/2042	23°	♑	39
12/Feb/2040	23°	♒	28	11/Nov/2040	19°	♒	51	12/Aug/2041	19°	♒	45	12/May/2042	22°	♒	11
13/Mar/2040	23°	♓	5	10/Dec/2040	19°	♓	31	10/Sep/2041	18°	♓	3	11/Jun/2042	20°	♓	16
11/Apr/2040	22°	♈	17	9/Jan/2041	19°	♈	30	9/Oct/2041	16°	♈	49	10/Jul/2042	18°	♈	7
11/May/2040	**21°**	**♉**	**3**	7/Feb/2041	19°	♉	34	**8/Nov/2041**	**16°**	**♉**	**8**	8/Aug/2042	16°	♉	2
9/Jun/2040	19°	♊	30	9/Mar/2041	19°	♊	26	7/Dec/2041	15°	♊	59	6/Sep/2042	14°	♊	14
9/Jul/2040	17°	♋	46	8/Apr/2041	18°	♋	55	6/Jan/2042	16°	♋	9	6/Oct/2042	12°	♋	58
8/Aug/2040	16°	♌	5	8/May/2041	17°	♌	56	5/Feb/2042	16°	♌	23	4/Nov/2042	12°	♌	21
6/Sep/2040	14°	♍	38	6/Jun/2041	16°	♍	32	6/Mar/2042	16°	♍	22	4/Dec/2042	12°	♍	20
6/Oct/2040	13°	♎	34	6/Jul/2041	14°	♎	53	**5/Apr/2042**	**15°**	**♎**	**55**	3/Jan/2043	12°	♎	44
4/Nov/2040	**12°**	**♏**	**58**	5/Aug/2041	13°	♏	10	5/May/2042	14°	♏	55	2/Feb/2043	13°	♏	11
4/Dec/2040	12°	♐	45	3/Sep/2041	11°	♐	35	3/Jun/2042	13°	♐	24	4/Mar/2043	13°	♐	20
2/Jan/2041	12°	♑	45	3/Oct/2041	10°	♑	18	3/Jul/2042	11°	♑	33	2/Apr/2043	12°	♑	55
1/Feb/2041	12°	♒	43	1/Nov/2041	09°	♒	26	1/Aug/2042	09°	♒	36	2/May/2043	11°	♒	52
2/Mar/2041	12°	♓	25	30/Nov/2041	08°	♓	58	31/Aug/2042	07°	♓	49	31/May/2043	10°	♓	15
1/Apr/2041	11°	♈	41	30/Dec/2041	08°	♈	48	**29/Sep/2042**	**06°**	**♈**	**25**	30/Jun/2043	08°	♈	15
30/Apr/2041	**10°**	**♉**	**30**	28/Jan/2042	08°	♉	43	**28/Oct/2042**	**05°**	**♉**	**31**	29/Jul/2043	06°	♉	8
29/May/2041	08°	♊	55	26/Feb/2042	08°	♊	29	27/Nov/2042	05°	♊	6	27/Aug/2043	04°	♊	10
28/Jun/2041	07°	♋	8	28/Mar/2042	07°	♋	56	26/Dec/2042	05°	♋	4	25/Sep/2043	02°	♋	35
28/Jul/2041	05°	♌	21	27/Apr/2042	06°	♌	58	25/Jan/2043	05°	♌	10	25/Oct/2043	01°	♌	33
26/Aug/2041	03°	♍	48	26/May/2042	05°	♍	38	23/Feb/2043	05°	♍	10	23/Nov/2043	01°	♍	8
25/Sep/2041	02°	♎	39	25/Jun/2042	04°	♎	3	**25/Mar/2043**	**04°**	**♎**	**50**	23/Dec/2043	01°	♎	13
25/Oct/2041	**02°**	**♏**	**0**	25/Jul/2042	02°	♏	25	24/Apr/2043	04°	♏	1	21/Jan/2044	01°	♏	34
23/Nov/2041	01°	♐	48	23/Aug/2042	00°	♐	54	23/May/2043	02°	♐	44	20/Feb/2044	01°	♐	50
23/Dec/2041	01°	♑	51	22/Sep/2042	29°	♐	40	22/Jun/2043	01°	♑	5	21/Mar/2044	01°	♑	43
21/Jan/2042	01°	♒	56	22/Oct/2042	28°	♑	50	22/Jul/2043	29°	♑	15	20/Apr/2044	01°	♒	2
20/Feb/2042	01°	♓	47	20/Nov/2042	28°	♒	23	20/Aug/2043	27°	♒	30	20/May/2044	29°	♒	47
21/Mar/2042	01°	♈	13	20/Dec/2042	28°	♓	14	**19/Sep/2043**	**26°**	**♓**	**2**	18/Jun/2044	28°	♓	5
20/Apr/2042	**00°**	**♉**	**8**	18/Jan/2043	28°	♈	9	18/Oct/2043	24°	♈	59	18/Jul/2044	26°	♈	8
19/May/2042	28°	♉	36	16/Feb/2043	27°	♉	54	16/Nov/2043	24°	♉	25	16/Aug/2044	24°	♉	11
17/Jun/2042	26°	♊	45	18/Mar/2043	27°	♊	19	16/Dec/2043	24°	♊	14	14/Sep/2044	22°	♊	28
17/Jul/2042	24°	♋	49	16/Apr/2043	26°	♋	19	14/Jan/2044	24°	♋	14	13/Oct/2044	21°	♋	12
15/Aug/2042	23°	♌	3	15/May/2043	24°	♌	56	13/Feb/2044	24°	♌	11	12/Nov/2044	20°	♌	27
14/Sep/2042	21°	♍	41	14/Jun/2043	23°	♍	17	**13/Mar/2044**	**23°**	**♍**	**52**	11/Dec/2044	20°	♍	12

Moon Families - Eclipses in Bold Print

New Moon				First Quarter Moon				Full Moon				Last Quarter Moon			
14/Oct/2042	**20°**	♎	**51**	14/Jul/2043	21°	♎	34	12/Apr/2044	23°	♎	7	10/Jan/2045	20°	♎	17
12/Nov/2042	20°	♏	35	12/Aug/2043	19°	♏	58	12/May/2044	21°	♏	56	8/Feb/2045	20°	♏	25
12/Dec/2042	20°	♐	41	11/Sep/2043	18°	♐	42	10/Jun/2044	20°	♐	23	10/Mar/2045	20°	♐	21
11/Jan/2043	20°	♑	55	11/Oct/2043	17°	♑	51	10/Jul/2044	18°	♑	39	9/Apr/2045	19°	♑	52
9/Feb/2043	21°	♒	0	10/Nov/2043	17°	♒	28	8/Aug/2044	16°	♒	57	9/May/2045	18°	♒	54
11/Mar/2043	20°	♓	41	9/Dec/2043	17°	♓	26	**7/Sep/2044**	**15°**	♓	**29**	7/Jun/2045	17°	♓	29
9/Apr/2043	**19°**	♈	**49**	8/Jan/2044	17°	♈	29	7/Oct/2044	14°	♈	23	7/Jul/2045	15°	♈	46
9/May/2043	18°	♉	25	6/Feb/2044	17°	♉	24	5/Nov/2044	13°	♉	44	5/Aug/2045	13°	♉	57
7/Jun/2043	16°	♊	36	6/Mar/2044	16°	♊	57	4/Dec/2044	13°	♊	28	4/Sep/2045	12°	♊	17
6/Jul/2043	14°	♋	34	5/Apr/2044	16°	♋	0	3/Jan/2045	13°	♋	26	3/Oct/2045	10°	♋	57
5/Aug/2043	12°	♌	36	4/May/2044	14°	♌	36	1/Feb/2045	13°	♌	24	2/Nov/2045	10°	♌	3
3/Sep/2043	10°	♍	57	2/Jun/2044	12°	♍	51	**3/Mar/2045**	**13°**	♍	**8**	1/Dec/2045	09°	♍	35
3/Oct/2043	**09°**	♎	**48**	2/Jul/2044	10°	♎	58	1/Apr/2045	12°	♎	26	30/Dec/2045	09°	♎	26
1/Nov/2043	09°	♏	16	31/Jul/2044	09°	♏	9	1/May/2045	11°	♏	16	29/Jan/2046	09°	♏	24
1/Dec/2043	09°	♐	16	30/Aug/2044	07°	♐	39	30/May/2045	09°	♐	43	27/Feb/2046	09°	♐	13
31/Dec/2043	09°	♑	35	29/Sep/2044	06°	♑	38	29/Jun/2045	07°	♑	58	29/Mar/2046	08°	♑	45
30/Jan/2044	09°	♒	53	28/Oct/2044	06°	♒	11	28/Jul/2045	06°	♒	14	27/Apr/2046	07°	♒	52
28/Feb/2044	**09°**	♓	**53**	27/Nov/2044	06°	♓	12	**27/Aug/2045**	**04°**	♓	**43**	27/May/2046	06°	♓	35
29/Mar/2044	09°	♈	20	27/Dec/2044	06°	♈	27	26/Sep/2045	03°	♈	34	26/Jun/2046	05°	♈	1
27/Apr/2044	08°	♉	11	26/Jan/2045	06°	♉	38	25/Oct/2045	02°	♉	52	26/Jul/2046	03°	♉	20
27/May/2044	06°	♊	30	24/Feb/2045	06°	♊	28	24/Nov/2045	02°	♊	35	24/Aug/2046	01°	♊	46
25/Jun/2044	04°	♋	30	26/Mar/2045	05°	♋	46	24/Dec/2045	02°	♋	35	23/Sep/2046	00°	♋	29
24/Jul/2044	02°	♌	26	24/Apr/2045	04°	♌	31	**22/Jan/2046**	**02°**	♌	**39**	22/Oct/2046	29°	♋	35
23/Aug/2044	**00°**	♍	**34**	23/May/2045	02°	♍	48	20/Feb/2046	02°	♍	29	21/Nov/2046	29°	♌	5
21/Sep/2044	29°	♍	6	21/Jun/2045	00°	♎	47	22/Mar/2046	01°	♎	55	20/Dec/2046	28°	♍	51
20/Oct/2044	28°	♎	13	21/Jul/2045	28°	♎	44	20/Apr/2046	00°	♏	50	18/Jan/2047	28°	♎	44
19/Nov/2044	27°	♏	55	19/Aug/2045	26°	♏	55	20/May/2046	29°	♏	18	17/Feb/2047	28°	♏	30
19/Dec/2044	28°	♐	5	18/Sep/2045	25°	♐	33	18/Jun/2046	27°	♐	29	18/Mar/2047	27°	♐	58
18/Jan/2045	28°	♑	28	17/Oct/2045	24°	♑	48	**18/Jul/2046**	**25°**	♑	**37**	17/Apr/2047	27°	♑	3
16/Feb/2045	**28°**	♒	**42**	16/Nov/2045	24°	♒	40	16/Aug/2046	23°	♒	55	16/May/2047	25°	♒	45
18/Mar/2045	28°	♓	30	16/Dec/2045	24°	♓	58	15/Sep/2046	22°	♓	36	15/Jun/2047	24°	♓	10
17/Apr/2045	27°	♈	42	15/Jan/2046	25°	♈	23	14/Oct/2046	21°	♈	47	15/Jul/2047	22°	♈	29
16/May/2045	26°	♉	17	14/Feb/2046	25°	♉	35	13/Nov/2046	21°	♉	28	13/Aug/2047	20°	♉	55
15/Jun/2045	24°	♊	26	15/Mar/2046	25°	♊	17	13/Dec/2046	21°	♊	32	12/Sep/2047	19°	♊	38
14/Jul/2045	22°	♋	24	14/Apr/2046	24°	♋	21	**12/Jan/2047**	**21°**	♋	**44**	12/Oct/2047	18°	♋	46
12/Aug/2045	**20°**	♌	**25**	13/May/2046	22°	♌	51	10/Feb/2047	21°	♌	46	10/Nov/2047	18°	♌	19
11/Sep/2045	18°	♍	44	11/Jun/2046	20°	♍	53	12/Mar/2047	21°	♍	23	10/Dec/2047	18°	♍	11
10/Oct/2045	17°	♎	32	10/Jul/2046	18°	♎	44	10/Apr/2047	20°	♎	29	8/Jan/2048	18°	♎	9
8/Nov/2045	16°	♏	53	9/Aug/2046	16°	♏	39	9/May/2047	19°	♏	4	7/Feb/2048	18°	♏	0
8/Dec/2045	16°	♐	46	7/Sep/2046	14°	♐	56	8/Jun/2047	17°	♐	15	7/Mar/2048	17°	♐	32
7/Jan/2046	17°	♑	1	6/Oct/2046	13°	♑	45	**7/Jul/2047**	**15°**	♑	**16**	5/Apr/2048	16°	♑	37
5/Feb/2046	**17°**	♒	**18**	5/Nov/2046	13°	♒	15	5/Aug/2047	13°	♒	22	5/May/2048	15°	♒	16
7/Mar/2046	17°	♓	20	5/Dec/2046	13°	♓	20	4/Sep/2047	11°	♓	46	3/Jun/2048	13°	♓	35
6/Apr/2046	16°	♈	51	4/Jan/2047	13°	♈	45	3/Oct/2047	10°	♈	41	2/Jul/2048	11°	♈	45
6/May/2046	15°	♉	46	3/Feb/2047	14°	♉	11	2/Nov/2047	10°	♉	11	1/Aug/2048	10°	♉	1
4/Jun/2046	14°	♊	11	4/Mar/2047	14°	♊	16	2/Dec/2047	10°	♊	12	31/Aug/2048	08°	♊	35
4/Jul/2046	12°	♋	17	3/Apr/2047	13°	♋	47	**1/Jan/2048**	**10°**	♋	**31**	30/Sep/2048	07°	♋	37
2/Aug/2046	**10°**	♌	**19**	3/May/2047	12°	♌	39	31/Jan/2048	10°	♌	46	29/Oct/2048	07°	♌	10
31/Aug/2046	08°	♍	31	1/Jun/2047	10°	♍	57	29/Feb/2048	10°	♍	41	28/Nov/2048	07°	♍	7
30/Sep/2046	07°	♎	6	30/Jun/2047	08°	♎	53	30/Mar/2048	10°	♎	3	28/Dec/2048	07°	♎	16
29/Oct/2046	06°	♏	12	29/Jul/2047	06°	♏	44	28/Apr/2048	08°	♏	50	26/Jan/2049	07°	♏	22

Moon Families - Eclipses in Bold Print

New Moon

Date	Deg	Sign	Min
27/Nov/2046	05°	♐	48
27/Dec/2046	05°	♑	49
26/Jan/2047	**06°**	**♒**	**0**
24/Feb/2047	06°	♓	3
26/Mar/2047	05°	♈	44
25/Apr/2047	04°	♉	55
24/May/2047	03°	♊	36
23/Jun/2047	**01°**	**♋**	**55**
22/Jul/2047	**00°**	**♌**	**4**
21/Aug/2047	28°	♌	16
19/Sep/2047	26°	♍	45
19/Oct/2047	25°	♎	40
17/Nov/2047	25°	♏	5
16/Dec/2047	**24°**	**♐**	**55**
15/Jan/2048	24°	♑	58
14/Feb/2048	24°	♒	58
14/Mar/2048	24°	♓	41
13/Apr/2048	23°	♈	57
12/May/2048	22°	♉	48
11/Jun/2048	**21°**	**♊**	**16**
11/Jul/2048	19°	♋	33
9/Aug/2048	17°	♌	49
8/Sep/2048	16°	♍	17
7/Oct/2048	15°	♎	8
6/Nov/2048	14°	♏	26
5/Dec/2048	**14°**	**♐**	**10**
4/Jan/2049	14°	♑	9
2/Feb/2049	14°	♒	7
4/Mar/2049	13°	♓	51
2/Apr/2049	13°	♈	10
2/May/2049	12°	♉	2
31/May/2049	**10°**	**♊**	**33**
30/Jun/2049	08°	♋	52
29/Jul/2049	07°	♌	8
28/Aug/2049	05°	♍	36
27/Sep/2049	04°	♎	25
26/Oct/2049	03°	♏	41
25/Nov/2049	**03°**	**♐**	**22**
24/Dec/2049	03°	♑	21
23/Jan/2050	03°	♒	22

First Quarter Moon

Date	Deg	Sign	Min
28/Aug/2047	04°	♐	46
26/Sep/2047	03°	♑	14
25/Oct/2047	02°	♒	17
24/Nov/2047	01°	♓	58
24/Dec/2047	02°	♈	9
22/Jan/2048	02°	♉	33
21/Feb/2048	02°	♊	50
22/Mar/2048	02°	♋	42
21/Apr/2048	01°	♌	58
21/May/2048	00°	♍	38
19/Jun/2048	28°	♍	50
18/Jul/2048	26°	♎	48
17/Aug/2048	24°	♏	48
15/Sep/2048	23°	♐	5
14/Oct/2048	21°	♑	50
12/Nov/2048	21°	♒	8
12/Dec/2048	20°	♓	56
10/Jan/2049	21°	♈	6
9/Feb/2049	21°	♉	19
11/Mar/2049	21°	♊	19
10/Apr/2049	20°	♋	52
10/May/2049	19°	♌	52
8/Jun/2049	18°	♍	23
8/Jul/2049	16°	♎	35
6/Aug/2049	14°	♏	42
5/Sep/2049	12°	♐	59
4/Oct/2049	11°	♑	36
2/Nov/2049	10°	♒	41
1/Dec/2049	10°	♓	13
31/Dec/2049	10°	♈	6
29/Jan/2050	10°	♉	8
28/Feb/2050	10°	♊	3
30/Mar/2050	09°	♋	39
28/Apr/2050	08°	♌	49
28/May/2050	07°	♍	32
27/Jun/2050	05°	♎	57
27/Jul/2050	04°	♏	14
25/Aug/2050	02°	♐	37
24/Sep/2050	01°	♑	16
23/Oct/2050	00°	♒	17

Full Moon

Date	Deg	Sign	Min
27/May/2048	07°	♐	9
26/Jun/2048	**05°**	**♑**	**10**
25/Jul/2048	03°	♒	8
23/Aug/2048	01°	♓	17
22/Sep/2048	29°	♓	52
21/Oct/2048	29°	♈	2
20/Nov/2048	28°	♉	48
20/Dec/2048	**29°**	**♊**	**3**
19/Jan/2049	29°	♋	26
17/Feb/2049	29°	♌	37
19/Mar/2049	29°	♍	20
18/Apr/2049	28°	♎	26
17/May/2049	**26°**	**♏**	**59**
15/Jun/2049	**25°**	**♐**	**8**
15/Jul/2049	23°	♑	4
13/Aug/2049	21°	♒	5
11/Sep/2049	19°	♓	24
11/Oct/2049	18°	♈	14
9/Nov/2049	**17°**	**♉**	**40**
9/Dec/2049	17°	♊	39
8/Jan/2050	17°	♋	57
6/Feb/2050	18°	♌	15
8/Mar/2050	18°	♍	14
7/Apr/2050	17°	♎	42
6/May/2050	**16°**	**♏**	**35**
5/Jun/2050	14°	♐	57
4/Jul/2050	13°	♑	0
3/Aug/2050	10°	♒	59
1/Sep/2050	09°	♓	10
30/Sep/2050	07°	♈	45
30/Oct/2050	**06°**	**♉**	**53**
28/Nov/2050	06°	♊	34
28/Dec/2050	06°	♋	38
26/Jan/2051	06°	♌	51
25/Feb/2051	06°	♍	56
27/Mar/2051	06°	♎	39
26/Apr/2051	**05°**	**♏**	**50**
25/May/2051	04°	♐	29
24/Jun/2051	02°	♑	44
23/Jul/2051	00°	♒	48

Last Quarter Moon

Date	Deg	Sign	Min
25/Feb/2049	07°	♐	7
26/Mar/2049	06°	♑	23
24/Apr/2049	05°	♒	7
24/May/2049	03°	♓	23
22/Jun/2049	01°	♈	25
21/Jul/2049	29°	♈	27
20/Aug/2049	27°	♉	43
18/Sep/2049	26°	♊	28
18/Oct/2049	25°	♋	47
17/Nov/2049	25°	♌	40
17/Dec/2049	25°	♍	56
16/Jan/2050	26°	♎	17
14/Feb/2050	26°	♏	24
16/Mar/2050	26°	♐	0
14/Apr/2050	25°	♑	0
14/May/2050	23°	♒	25
12/Jun/2050	21°	♓	26
11/Jul/2050	19°	♈	19
9/Aug/2050	17°	♉	18
8/Sep/2050	15°	♊	40
7/Oct/2050	14°	♋	36
6/Nov/2050	14°	♌	10
6/Dec/2050	14°	♍	18
5/Jan/2051	14°	♎	45
4/Feb/2051	15°	♏	10
5/Mar/2051	15°	♐	11
4/Apr/2051	14°	♑	35
3/May/2051	13°	♒	19
2/Jun/2051	11°	♓	33
1/Jul/2051	09°	♈	27
30/Jul/2051	07°	♉	18
28/Aug/2051	05°	♊	23
27/Sep/2051	03°	♋	54
26/Oct/2051	03°	♌	2
25/Nov/2051	02°	♍	49
24/Dec/2051	03°	♎	5
23/Jan/2052	03°	♏	33
22/Feb/2052	03°	♐	50
23/Mar/2052	03°	♑	38
22/Apr/2052	02°	♒	49

IV. The Table of Traditional Moon Phases

The Table of Traditional Moon Phases is compiled of four columns reading from left to right in the order of their appearance beginning at each New Moon. Each New Moon (● symbol) begins a period called the synodic month that cycles from New Moon to New Moon. A synodic month can begin at any point within a calendar month which increases in light after the New Moon to a First Quarter Moon in about a week and it will appear as a left facing (☽) half-moon which swells to the Full Moon phase a week later (○ symbol). After the Full Moon the light begins to shrink in about a week and then appears as a right (☾) facing half-moon at its Last Quarter phase. In approximately a week the Moon will disappear completely into the next New Moon. These four phases are completed in any four week period and *all occur at different points along the zodiac.*

Traditional Moon Phases

New Moon Solar Eclipse	First Quarter Moon	Full Moon	Last Quarter Moon
26-Jan-2009 06°≈30'	2-Feb-2009 14°♉15'	9-Feb-2009 21°♌00'	16-Feb-2009 28°♏21'

The fact that each Moon phase occurs at a different degree and zodiac sign is a clue that they are not related to each other but share a chronological relationship. Think of the degree and sign of each Moon phase as its unique address or location linking to another time when a particular zodiacal location appears again. The patterns found with these locations perform as highly significant platforms where your storyline pivots or evolves. These points are place holders and markers for your research that weave through a 76-95 year period. This simple format of the dates and phases allows you to review the events of your study and match it up to one Moon phase.

You can also use this table for immediate assessment of the stage of any given event. For instance is this a new development or an older matter resurfacing. Realize that all Moon phases are dynamic events between the Moon and Sun that push matters out to the surface in some way; some more dynamic than others.

Getting the Most out of The Table of Traditional Moon Phases

This is the same table format I used when I discovered the nine-month interval I call the Lunar Gestation Cycle. As a counseling astrologer my job is to listen carefully and assist people to find the best route to their own way. As people tell their stories or recount an important event I always ask "when did this story begin?" That date becomes the *onset date of the story* that I use to research the history and future of the storyline. Sometimes the person doesn't know the onset date of their story which is fine. You can use the date they come to you with their story. The first story in this book is a perfect example of how this works also the story I told in the article, "What I Learned As a 900 Line Astrologer." Every story has a life of its own and a thread is found in the current Moon phase when you hear the story. Another way to find an onset date is to note when an event triggers an older storyline by a phone call, a letter, a court date, a marriage or merger, or simply bumping into a player in the story, etc.

By using the onset date of a storyline you then determine which Moon phase is closest to your topic. A few guidelines are easy to remember;

- When the onset date of a story falls within a week of a Solar or Lunar Eclipse then choose the Eclipse date as your Moon phase. **Eclipses are marked in bold print.**

- When the onset date of a story falls equally between two phases I often choose the future phase and keep in mind that the New Moon and Full Moon have a longer range of influence but does not mitigate the power of a First and Last Quarter Moon.

- Most often events that occur at First and Last Quarter Moon are within a day of that phase. The sharp 90° quality of the quarter Moons cut directly to the story. Look for any event on these phases to indicate a strong link to the storyline.

For now assign the symbolism of one of four Moon phases to determine the *stage of development* it represents in relationship to your story. Each Moon phase produces its own type of action:

- A New Moon – this is a dark period when a seed is planted. More will be revealed when the light increases. Do not initiate three days before or after a New Moon. A wait and see period.
- A First Quarter Moon-this is a high energy period. It is a time to put plans into action and respond to new beginnings. Waxing Moon.
- A Full Moon- this is a time of complete awareness. Matters come to a head and confusion is cleared and events are conducted in the open. This is a not a time to conceal or hold back but to finish a project.
- A Last Quarter Moon- this is a winding down time when you reap the rewards of your efforts. It is time to pay and get paid. Waning Moon.

The zodiac sign describes and defines the nature of the action at the Moon phase.

The Type of Action for each Sign at a Moon Phase		
High action time with initiating forward action. Now.	Basic life essentials and structures. Infrastructure. Matters requiring time to mature.	Evolution of Information; gathering, preparation, education, distribution and assimilation. Matters in motion as with errands and travel.
Aries	Taurus	Gemini
Cancer	Leo	Virgo
Libra	Scorpio	Sagittarius
Capricorn	Aquarius	Pisces

The following are a few key phases to apply to any Eclipse or Moon phase:

Aries = "right now" energy; matters move forward quickly. Fresh starts and new ideas. Aggressive, self-focused and motivated to solve problems. Intolerant and single-minded. Impatient, noisy, fiery and macho. Entrepreneurial.

Taurus = slow steady progress. Matters of money, possessions and traditions. Concerns of things valued or where you have a vested interest. The bull is more sensitive than he appears, beyond being stubborn. This is a feminine sign. Appease the bull with persuasion. Manners are crucial. Apply for a loan or request special attention.

Gemini = darting and changeable. Data collection and exchange information. The giving and receiving of notices. Networking. Scouting around town for errands, short trips and visits. An important story is told. Word gets out in a profound manner. Check your sources for errors as talk is abundant but not all always reliable. Topics regarding siblings can be an issue. The greatest gains are made in networking.

Cancer = important matters of home, family, babies, mothers and issues of nurturing. Real estate and house matters. Concerns of cash, safety and security. Nesting time but not reclining. Activities or events requiring a retreat to the clan. Subjects regarding insider information. Issues involving dependency or defensiveness and patriotism. Survival needs.

Leo = children, all creative projects, appreciation and applause. Performance and the stage. Demanding issues for both business and personal life. Confidence is up to proceed with a goal in mind. Matters of pride as an asset or liability. It is a time of securitization and harsh judgment.

Virgo = pronounced work, labor, health and food issues. Packed agendas focused on details, a specific task, or workers. Clean up and organization energy. Repair and adjust for specific needs. Service calls. Pets call for attention.

Libra = matters of peace and compromise. Legal issues. Relationship issues including marriage and divorce. Cooperate and establish partnership for common goals. Important major social events.

Scorpio = notices of death and taxes. Issues concerning sex, pregnancy, abortion and birth announcement. Dealings with accountants, money lenders and their officers. Anything that qualifies as red-tape. Meet with people in position of power. Pertains to matters with insurance companies and Human Resources. Requires a tough exterior. Be prepared. Psychological twists run rampant. If all other matters agree, retail business often thrives as purchases tend to be significant.

Sagittarius = a dramatic shift in perspective. Expanded awareness. Class registration. Book or take a trip. Events that release responsibility, as with job layoff or vacation; arguments made are philosophical and or political; cultural events such as concerts; matters of foreign policy and foreign places. Travel and immigration policies. Advertising marketing and publishing matters. Religion as an issue.

Capricorn = business, corporate and executive activities. Judicial decisions. Hire and fire. Hard-working and dead serious. Pressure for job performance with criticism and evaluations. Cold and calculated. The "rules" command the day. Progress and status are important. Important people that "count" are topics, also people you can count on. The exposure of parental issues, low self-esteem and gloomy feelings. Emotions drawn inward result in coldness. Fathers, bosses, and authority figures are the main characters. Architecture.

Aquarius = scientific, unusual, perhaps bizarre at this Moon phase. Ideas merge into collective opinions. A social event with the unexpected. Someone "acts out". Strange or alienating behaviors– this runs true with nations, and companies, etc. A sense or expectation or change, may feel like impending doom or a strong surge of hope that motivates. Revelations and awakenings. Mirrors and voice recorders. Reflection and repetitiveness reveal patterns. Invention and modernization. Medical appointments lead to treatments with the latest techniques and equipment.

Pisces = inspiration and composition. Critical pivot for food and substance abuse. Tasks with a mission. From brutality to gentle compassion. Wild weather, hurricanes, tidal waves and blizzards. Events of cosmetic and superficial appearances. Imposing or lifting a heavy black cloud. The emergence of the vehicle of divine intervention. Expect 'Murphy's Law" to be in full swing. Exposure of secrets. Life changing events through cinema, music and the arts. The rule of thumb with a Pisces Moon is that you will land in a different place than you expect.

When you tag a Moon phase at the onset of your story you are ready to match it up with its **Moon Family**, The Table of **Moon Families** and the Lunar Gestation Cycle hold four dates related to the various stages of the story.

Traditional Monthly Moon Phases - Eclipses in Bold Print

New Moon		First Quarter Moon		Full Moon		Last Quarter Moon	
26/Jan/1990	**06° ♒ 35'**	2/Feb/1990	13° ♉ 40'	**9/Feb/1990**	**20° ♌ 47'**	17/Feb/1990	28° ♏ 51'
25/Feb/1990	06° ♓ 30'	3/Mar/1990	13° ♊ 14'	11/Mar/1990	20° ♍ 37'	19/Mar/1990	28° ♐ 43'
26/Mar/1990	05° ♈ 53'	2/Apr/1990	12° ♋ 25'	9/Apr/1990	20° ♎ 00'	18/Apr/1990	27° ♑ 59'
25/Apr/1990	04° ♉ 43'	1/May/1990	11° ♌ 12'	9/May/1990	18° ♏ 54'	17/May/1990	26° ♒ 38'
24/May/1990	03° ♊ 03'	31/May/1990	09° ♍ 38'	8/Jun/1990	17° ♐ 24'	16/Jun/1990	24° ♓ 48'
22/Jun/1990	**01° ♋ 05'**	29/Jun/1990	07° ♎ 54'	7/Jul/1990	15° ♑ 39'	15/Jul/1990	22° ♈ 43'
21/Jul/1990	29° ♋ 04'	29/Jul/1990	06° ♏ 12'	**6/Aug/1990**	**13° ♒ 52'**	13/Aug/1990	20° ♉ 38'
20/Aug/1990	27° ♌ 15'	28/Aug/1990	04° ♐ 45'	4/Sep/1990	12° ♓ 15'	11/Sep/1990	18° ♊ 51'
18/Sep/1990	25° ♍ 50'	26/Sep/1990	03° ♑ 43'	4/Oct/1990	11° ♈ 00'	10/Oct/1990	17° ♋ 34'
18/Oct/1990	25° ♎ 00'	26/Oct/1990	03° ♒ 10'	2/Nov/1990	10° ♉ 13'	9/Nov/1990	16° ♌ 52'
17/Nov/1990	24° ♏ 45'	25/Nov/1990	03° ♓ 00'	2/Dec/1990	09° ♊ 52'	8/Dec/1990	16° ♍ 44'
17/Dec/1990	24° ♐ 58'	24/Dec/1990	03° ♈ 04'	31/Dec/1990	09° ♋ 50'	7/Jan/1991	16° ♎ 58'
16/Jan/1991	**25° ♑ 20'**	23/Jan/1991	03° ♉ 05'	**30/Jan/1991**	**09° ♌ 51'**	6/Feb/1991	17° ♏ 16'
14/Feb/1991	25° ♒ 31'	21/Feb/1991	02° ♊ 49'	28/Feb/1991	09° ♍ 40'	8/Mar/1991	17° ♐ 21'
16/Mar/1991	25° ♓ 14'	23/Mar/1991	02° ♋ 07'	30/Mar/1991	09° ♎ 06'	7/Apr/1991	16° ♑ 57'
14/Apr/1991	24° ♈ 21'	21/Apr/1991	00° ♌ 55'	28/Apr/1991	08° ♏ 04'	6/May/1991	15° ♒ 59'
14/May/1991	22° ♉ 54'	20/May/1991	29° ♌ 18'	28/May/1991	06° ♐ 39'	5/Jun/1991	14° ♓ 29'
12/Jun/1991	21° ♊ 02'	19/Jun/1991	27° ♍ 25'	**27/Jun/1991**	**05° ♑ 00'**	4/Jul/1991	12° ♈ 37'
11/Jul/1991	**18° ♋ 59'**	18/Jul/1991	25° ♎ 30'	**26/Jul/1991**	**03° ♒ 16'**	3/Aug/1991	10° ♉ 38'
9/Aug/1991	17° ♌ 00'	17/Aug/1991	23° ♏ 49'	25/Aug/1991	01° ♓ 41'	1/Sep/1991	08° ♊ 49'
8/Sep/1991	15° ♍ 18'	15/Sep/1991	22° ♐ 34'	23/Sep/1991	00° ♈ 24'	30/Sep/1991	07° ♋ 21'
7/Oct/1991	14° ♎ 07'	15/Oct/1991	21° ♑ 52'	23/Oct/1991	29° ♈ 33'	30/Oct/1991	06° ♌ 22'
6/Nov/1991	13° ♏ 32'	14/Nov/1991	21° ♒ 42'	21/Nov/1991	29° ♉ 08'	28/Nov/1991	05° ♍ 53'
5/Dec/1991	13° ♐ 31'	14/Dec/1991	21° ♓ 53'	**21/Dec/1991**	**29° ♊ 03'**	27/Dec/1991	05° ♎ 49'
5/Jan/1992	**13° ♑ 51'**	12/Jan/1992	22° ♈ 09'	19/Jan/1992	29° ♋ 04'	26/Jan/1992	05° ♏ 56'
3/Feb/1992	14° ♒ 12'	11/Feb/1992	22° ♉ 12'	18/Feb/1992	28° ♌ 55'	25/Feb/1992	05° ♐ 58'
4/Mar/1992	14° ♓ 14'	11/Mar/1992	21° ♊ 47'	18/Mar/1992	28° ♍ 24'	25/Mar/1992	05° ♑ 41'
3/Apr/1992	13° ♈ 42'	10/Apr/1992	20° ♋ 47'	17/Apr/1992	27° ♎ 26'	24/Apr/1992	04° ♒ 57'
2/May/1992	12° ♉ 34'	9/May/1992	19° ♌ 15'	16/May/1992	26° ♏ 01'	24/May/1992	03° ♓ 43'
31/May/1992	10° ♊ 55'	7/Jun/1992	17° ♍ 20'	**15/Jun/1992**	**24° ♐ 20'**	23/Jun/1992	02° ♈ 06'
30/Jun/1992	**08° ♋ 57'**	6/Jul/1992	15° ♎ 14'	14/Jul/1992	22° ♑ 34'	22/Jul/1992	00° ♉ 19'
29/Jul/1992	06° ♌ 54'	5/Aug/1992	13° ♏ 16'	13/Aug/1992	20° ♒ 55'	21/Aug/1992	28° ♉ 35'
27/Aug/1992	05° ♍ 03'	3/Sep/1992	11° ♐ 40'	11/Sep/1992	19° ♓ 34'	19/Sep/1992	27° ♊ 07'
26/Sep/1992	03° ♎ 36'	3/Oct/1992	10° ♑ 37'	11/Oct/1992	18° ♈ 40'	19/Oct/1992	26° ♋ 02'
25/Oct/1992	02° ♏ 41'	2/Nov/1992	10° ♒ 12'	10/Nov/1992	18° ♉ 14'	17/Nov/1992	25° ♌ 23'
24/Nov/1992	02° ♐ 21'	2/Dec/1992	10° ♓ 20'	**10/Dec/1992**	**18° ♊ 10'**	16/Dec/1992	25° ♍ 06'
24/Dec/1992	**02° ♑ 28'**	31/Dec/1992	10° ♈ 44'	8/Jan/1993	18° ♋ 15'	15/Jan/1993	25° ♎ 01'
22/Jan/1993	02° ♒ 46'	30/Jan/1993	11° ♉ 06'	6/Feb/1993	18° ♌ 13'	13/Feb/1993	24° ♏ 56'
21/Feb/1993	02° ♓ 55'	1/Mar/1993	11° ♊ 05'	8/Mar/1993	17° ♍ 50'	15/Mar/1993	24° ♐ 36'
23/Mar/1993	02° ♈ 40'	31/Mar/1993	10° ♋ 28'	6/Apr/1993	16° ♎ 58'	13/Apr/1993	23° ♑ 53'
21/Apr/1993	01° ♉ 52'	29/Apr/1993	09° ♌ 12'	5/May/1993	15° ♏ 38'	13/May/1993	22° ♒ 45'
21/May/1993	**00° ♊ 31'**	28/May/1993	07° ♍ 25'	**4/Jun/1993**	**13° ♐ 55'**	12/Jun/1993	21° ♓ 16'
19/Jun/1993	28° ♊ 46'	26/Jun/1993	05° ♎ 19'	3/Jul/1993	12° ♑ 02'	11/Jul/1993	19° ♈ 37'
19/Jul/1993	26° ♋ 48'	25/Jul/1993	03° ♏ 10'	2/Aug/1993	10° ♒ 12'	10/Aug/1993	18° ♉ 00'
17/Aug/1993	24° ♌ 53'	24/Aug/1993	01° ♐ 15'	31/Aug/1993	08° ♓ 41'	9/Sep/1993	16° ♊ 35'
15/Sep/1993	23° ♍ 16'	22/Sep/1993	29° ♐ 48'	30/Sep/1993	07° ♈ 37'	8/Oct/1993	15° ♋ 32'
15/Oct/1993	22° ♎ 08'	22/Oct/1993	28° ♑ 58'	30/Oct/1993	07° ♉ 06'	7/Nov/1993	14° ♌ 52'
13/Nov/1993	**21° ♏ 32'**	20/Nov/1993	28° ♒ 47'	**29/Nov/1993**	**07° ♊ 03'**	6/Dec/1993	14° ♍ 33'
13/Dec/1993	21° ♐ 23'	20/Dec/1993	29° ♓ 04'	28/Dec/1993	07° ♋ 15'	4/Jan/1994	14° ♎ 25'
11/Jan/1994	21° ♑ 31'	19/Jan/1994	29° ♈ 33'	27/Jan/1994	07° ♌ 23'	3/Feb/1994	14° ♏ 16'
10/Feb/1994	21° ♒ 38'	18/Feb/1994	29° ♉ 51'	25/Feb/1994	07° ♍ 13'	4/Mar/1994	13° ♐ 53'

Traditional Monthly Moon Phases - Eclipses in Bold Print

New Moon			First Quarter Moon			Full Moon			Last Quarter Moon		
12/Mar/1994	21° ♓	29'	20/Mar/1994	29° ♊	40'	27/Mar/1994	06° ♎	33'	2/Apr/1994	13° ♑	08'
10/Apr/1994	20° ♈	53'	18/Apr/1994	28° ♋	49'	25/Apr/1994	05° ♏	22'	2/May/1994	11° ♒	57'
10/May/1994	**19° ♉**	**48'**	18/May/1994	27° ♌	21'	**25/May/1994**	**03° ♐**	**43'**	1/Jun/1994	10° ♓	27'
9/Jun/1994	18° ♊	17'	16/Jun/1994	25° ♍	26'	23/Jun/1994	01° ♑	47'	30/Jun/1994	08° ♈	46'
8/Jul/1994	16° ♋	29'	15/Jul/1994	23° ♎	18'	22/Jul/1994	29° ♑	47'	30/Jul/1994	07° ♉	07'
7/Aug/1994	14° ♌	38'	14/Aug/1994	21° ♏	14'	21/Aug/1994	28° ♒	00'	29/Aug/1994	05° ♊	42'
5/Sep/1994	12° ♍	58'	12/Sep/1994	19° ♐	29'	19/Sep/1994	26° ♓	39'	27/Sep/1994	04° ♋	39'
4/Oct/1994	11° ♎	41'	11/Oct/1994	18° ♑	15'	19/Oct/1994	25° ♈	53'	27/Oct/1994	04° ♌	02'
3/Nov/1994	**10° ♏**	**54'**	10/Nov/1994	17° ♒	37'	**18/Nov/1994**	**25° ♉**	**42'**	26/Nov/1994	03° ♍	47'
2/Dec/1994	10° ♐	35'	9/Dec/1994	17° ♓	34'	17/Dec/1994	25° ♊	55'	25/Dec/1994	03° ♎	46'
1/Jan/1995	10° ♑	33'	8/Jan/1995	17° ♈	54'	16/Jan/1995	26° ♋	15'	24/Jan/1995	03° ♏	44'
30/Jan/1995	10° ♒	35'	7/Feb/1995	18° ♉	17'	15/Feb/1995	26° ♌	21'	22/Feb/1995	03° ♐	26'
1/Mar/1995	10° ♓	26'	9/Mar/1995	18° ♊	23'	16/Mar/1995	25° ♍	59'	23/Mar/1995	02° ♑	44'
30/Mar/1995	09° ♈	54'	8/Apr/1995	17° ♋	56'	**15/Apr/1995**	**25° ♎**	**04'**	21/Apr/1995	01° ♒	33'
29/Apr/1995	**08° ♉**	**56'**	7/May/1995	16° ♌	52'	14/May/1995	23° ♏	35'	21/May/1995	29° ♒	58'
29/May/1995	07° ♊	34'	6/Jun/1995	15° ♍	16'	13/Jun/1995	21° ♐	42'	19/Jun/1995	28° ♓	09'
27/Jun/1995	05° ♋	54'	5/Jul/1995	13° ♎	20'	12/Jul/1995	19° ♑	38'	19/Jul/1995	26° ♈	20'
27/Jul/1995	04° ♌	08'	3/Aug/1995	11° ♏	18'	10/Aug/1995	17° ♒	39'	17/Aug/1995	24° ♉	43'
26/Aug/1995	02° ♍	29'	2/Sep/1995	09° ♐	26'	8/Sep/1995	16° ♓	00'	16/Sep/1995	23° ♊	31'
24/Sep/1995	01° ♎	10'	1/Oct/1995	07° ♑	57'	**8/Oct/1995**	**14° ♈**	**54'**	16/Oct/1995	22° ♋	50'
24/Oct/1995	**00° ♏**	**18'**	30/Oct/1995	06° ♒	59'	7/Nov/1995	14° ♉	24'	15/Nov/1995	22° ♌	38'
22/Nov/1995	29° ♏	52'	29/Nov/1995	06° ♓	33'	6/Dec/1995	14° ♊	27'	15/Dec/1995	22° ♍	45'
21/Dec/1995	29° ♐	45'	28/Dec/1995	06° ♈	35'	5/Jan/1996	14° ♋	48'	13/Jan/1996	22° ♎	57'
20/Jan/1996	29° ♑	45'	27/Jan/1996	06° ♉	48'	4/Feb/1996	15° ♌	07'	12/Feb/1996	22° ♏	55'
18/Feb/1996	29° ♒	36'	26/Feb/1996	06° ♊	55'	5/Mar/1996	15° ♍	06'	12/Mar/1996	22° ♐	25'
19/Mar/1996	29° ♓	07'	26/Mar/1996	06° ♋	40'	**4/Apr/1996**	**14° ♎**	**31'**	10/Apr/1996	21° ♑	22'
17/Apr/1996	**28° ♈**	**12'**	25/Apr/1996	05° ♌	55'	3/May/1996	13° ♏	19'	10/May/1996	19° ♒	49'
17/May/1996	26° ♉	51'	25/May/1996	04° ♍	38'	1/Jun/1996	11° ♐	37'	8/Jun/1996	17° ♓	56'
15/Jun/1996	25° ♊	12'	24/Jun/1996	02° ♎	59'	30/Jun/1996	09° ♑	36'	7/Jul/1996	15° ♈	55'
15/Jul/1996	23° ♋	26'	23/Jul/1996	01° ♏	08'	30/Jul/1996	07° ♒	32'	6/Aug/1996	14° ♉	02'
14/Aug/1996	21° ♌	47'	21/Aug/1996	29° ♏	20'	28/Aug/1996	05° ♓	41'	4/Sep/1996	12° ♊	31'
12/Sep/1996	20° ♍	27'	20/Sep/1996	27° ♐	46'	**27/Sep/1996**	**04° ♈**	**17'**	4/Oct/1996	11° ♋	32'
12/Oct/1996	**19° ♎**	**32'**	19/Oct/1996	26° ♑	38'	26/Oct/1996	03° ♉	26'	3/Nov/1996	11° ♌	10'
11/Nov/1996	19° ♏	03'	17/Nov/1996	25° ♒	59'	25/Nov/1996	03° ♊	10'	3/Dec/1996	11° ♍	19'
10/Dec/1996	18° ♐	56'	17/Dec/1996	25° ♓	44'	24/Dec/1996	03° ♋	20'	1/Jan/1997	11° ♎	42'
9/Jan/1997	18° ♑	57'	15/Jan/1997	25° ♈	44'	23/Jan/1997	03° ♌	40'	31/Jan/1997	11° ♏	59'
7/Feb/1997	18° ♒	53'	14/Feb/1997	25° ♉	43'	22/Feb/1997	03° ♍	51'	2/Mar/1997	11° ♐	51'
9/Mar/1997	**18° ♓**	**31'**	15/Mar/1997	25° ♊	27'	**24/Mar/1997**	**03° ♎**	**35'**	31/Mar/1997	11° ♑	08'
7/Apr/1997	17° ♈	40'	14/Apr/1997	24° ♋	47'	22/Apr/1997	02° ♏	45'	29/Apr/1997	09° ♒	48'
6/May/1997	16° ♉	21'	14/May/1997	23° ♌	41'	22/May/1997	01° ♐	19'	29/May/1997	07° ♓	59'
5/Jun/1997	14° ♊	40'	13/Jun/1997	22° ♍	14'	20/Jun/1997	29° ♐	29'	27/Jun/1997	05° ♈	54'
4/Jul/1997	12° ♋	49'	12/Jul/1997	20° ♎	34'	19/Jul/1997	27° ♑	27'	26/Jul/1997	03° ♉	47'
3/Aug/1997	11° ♌	02'	11/Aug/1997	18° ♏	53'	18/Aug/1997	25° ♒	32'	24/Aug/1997	01° ♊	56'
2/Sep/1997	**09° ♍**	**34'**	9/Sep/1997	17° ♐	23'	**16/Sep/1997**	**23° ♓**	**56'**	23/Sep/1997	00° ♋	33'
1/Oct/1997	08° ♎	33'	9/Oct/1997	16° ♑	15'	15/Oct/1997	22° ♈	49'	23/Oct/1997	29° ♋	49'
31/Oct/1997	08° ♏	01'	7/Nov/1997	15° ♒	31'	14/Nov/1997	22° ♉	15'	21/Nov/1997	29° ♌	43'
29/Nov/1997	07° ♐	54'	7/Dec/1997	15° ♓	10'	13/Dec/1997	22° ♊	08'	21/Dec/1997	00° ♎	04'
29/Dec/1997	08° ♑	01'	5/Jan/1998	15° ♈	03'	12/Jan/1998	22° ♋	18'	20/Jan/1998	00° ♏	33'
28/Jan/1998	08° ♒	06'	3/Feb/1998	14° ♉	55'	11/Feb/1998	22° ♌	29'	19/Feb/1998	00° ♐	47'
26/Feb/1998	**07° ♓**	**55'**	5/Mar/1998	14° ♊	34'	**13/Mar/1998**	**22° ♍**	**24'**	21/Mar/1998	00° ♑	29'
27/Mar/1998	07° ♈	15'	3/Apr/1998	13° ♋	52'	11/Apr/1998	21° ♎	49'	19/Apr/1998	29° ♑	33'

Traditional Monthly Moon Phases - Eclipses in Bold Print

New Moon		First Quarter Moon		Full Moon		Last Quarter Moon	
26/Apr/1998	06° ♉ 03'	3/May/1998	12° ♌ 47'	11/May/1998	20° ♏ 42'	19/May/1998	28° ♒ 01'
25/May/1998	04° ♊ 23'	1/Jun/1998	11° ♍ 21'	10/Jun/1998	19° ♐ 06'	17/Jun/1998	26° ♓ 03'
23/Jun/1998	02° ♋ 27'	1/Jul/1998	09° ♎ 44'	9/Jul/1998	17° ♑ 15'	16/Jul/1998	23° ♈ 53'
23/Jul/1998	00° ♌ 31'	31/Jul/1998	08° ♏ 05'	**8/Aug/1998**	**15° ♒ 21'**	14/Aug/1998	21° ♉ 49'
22/Aug/1998	**28° ♌ 48'**	30/Aug/1998	06° ♐ 38'	**6/Sep/1998**	**13° ♓ 40'**	12/Sep/1998	20° ♊ 05'
20/Sep/1998	27° ♍ 32'	28/Sep/1998	05° ♑ 32'	5/Oct/1998	12° ♈ 23'	12/Oct/1998	18° ♋ 55'
20/Oct/1998	26° ♎ 49'	28/Oct/1998	04° ♒ 51'	4/Nov/1998	11° ♉ 35'	10/Nov/1998	18° ♌ 24'
19/Nov/1998	26° ♏ 38'	26/Nov/1998	04° ♓ 33'	3/Dec/1998	11° ♊ 15'	10/Dec/1998	18° ♍ 28'
18/Dec/1998	26° ♐ 48'	26/Dec/1998	04° ♈ 27'	1/Jan/1999	11° ♋ 15'	9/Jan/1999	18° ♎ 52'
17/Jan/1999	27° ♑ 05'	24/Jan/1999	04° ♉ 21'	**31/Jan/1999**	**11° ♌ 20'**	8/Feb/1999	19° ♏ 16'
16/Feb/1999	**27° ♒ 08'**	22/Feb/1999	04° ♊ 02'	2/Mar/1999	11° ♍ 15'	10/Mar/1999	19° ♐ 19'
17/Mar/1999	26° ♓ 44'	24/Mar/1999	03° ♋ 20'	31/Mar/1999	10° ♎ 46'	8/Apr/1999	18° ♑ 49'
16/Apr/1999	25° ♈ 45'	22/Apr/1999	02° ♌ 12'	30/Apr/1999	09° ♏ 49'	8/May/1999	17° ♒ 41'
15/May/1999	24° ♉ 14'	22/May/1999	00° ♍ 43'	30/May/1999	08° ♐ 26'	7/Jun/1999	16° ♓ 00'
13/Jun/1999	22° ♊ 20'	20/Jun/1999	28° ♍ 59'	28/Jun/1999	06° ♑ 45'	6/Jul/1999	13° ♈ 59'
12/Jul/1999	20° ♋ 17'	20/Jul/1999	27° ♎ 14'	**28/Jul/1999**	**04° ♒ 58'**	4/Aug/1999	11° ♉ 54'
11/Aug/1999	**18° ♌ 21'**	18/Aug/1999	25° ♏ 40'	26/Aug/1999	03° ♓ 17'	2/Sep/1999	10° ♊ 00'
9/Sep/1999	16° ♍ 47'	17/Sep/1999	24° ♐ 29'	25/Sep/1999	01° ♈ 56'	2/Oct/1999	08° ♋ 31'
9/Oct/1999	15° ♎ 44'	17/Oct/1999	23° ♑ 48'	24/Oct/1999	01° ♉ 00'	31/Oct/1999	07° ♌ 37'
7/Nov/1999	15° ♏ 17'	16/Nov/1999	23° ♒ 33'	23/Nov/1999	00° ♊ 32'	29/Nov/1999	07° ♍ 17'
7/Dec/1999	15° ♐ 22'	15/Dec/1999	23° ♓ 36'	22/Dec/1999	00° ♋ 25'	29/Dec/1999	07° ♎ 24'
6/Jan/2000	15° ♑ 44'	14/Jan/2000	23° ♈ 41'	**21/Jan/2000**	**00° ♌ 26'**	28/Jan/2000	07° ♏ 42'
5/Feb/2000	**16° ♒ 02'**	12/Feb/2000	23° ♉ 33'	19/Feb/2000	00° ♍ 20'	26/Feb/2000	07° ♐ 51'
6/Mar/2000	15° ♓ 56'	13/Mar/2000	23° ♊ 01'	20/Mar/2000	29° ♍ 53'	27/Mar/2000	07° ♑ 38'
4/Apr/2000	15° ♈ 16'	11/Apr/2000	21° ♋ 58'	18/Apr/2000	28° ♎ 59'	26/Apr/2000	06° ♒ 51'
4/May/2000	14° ♉ 00'	10/May/2000	20° ♌ 27'	18/May/2000	27° ♏ 40'	26/May/2000	05° ♓ 32'
2/Jun/2000	12° ♊ 15'	8/Jun/2000	18° ♍ 37'	16/Jun/2000	26° ♐ 03'	24/Jun/2000	03° ♈ 47'
1/Jul/2000	**10° ♋ 14'**	8/Jul/2000	16° ♎ 39'	**16/Jul/2000**	**24° ♑ 19'**	24/Jul/2000	01° ♉ 51'
31/Jul/2000	**08° ♌ 12'**	6/Aug/2000	14° ♏ 50'	15/Aug/2000	22° ♒ 41'	22/Aug/2000	29° ♉ 58'
29/Aug/2000	06° ♍ 23'	5/Sep/2000	13° ♐ 24'	13/Sep/2000	21° ♓ 18'	20/Sep/2000	28° ♊ 22'
27/Sep/2000	05° ♎ 00'	5/Oct/2000	12° ♑ 30'	13/Oct/2000	20° ♈ 19'	20/Oct/2000	27° ♋ 14'
27/Oct/2000	04° ♏ 12'	4/Nov/2000	12° ♒ 11'	11/Nov/2000	19° ♉ 47'	18/Nov/2000	26° ♌ 36'
25/Nov/2000	04° ♐ 00'	3/Dec/2000	12° ♓ 18'	11/Dec/2000	19° ♊ 38'	17/Dec/2000	26° ♍ 24'
25/Dec/2000	**04° ♑ 14'**	2/Jan/2001	12° ♈ 37'	**9/Jan/2001**	**19° ♋ 39'**	16/Jan/2001	26° ♎ 27'
24/Jan/2001	04° ♒ 37'	1/Feb/2001	12° ♉ 47'	8/Feb/2001	19° ♌ 35'	14/Feb/2001	26° ♏ 30'
23/Feb/2001	04° ♓ 47'	2/Mar/2001	12° ♊ 33'	9/Mar/2001	19° ♍ 12'	16/Mar/2001	26° ♐ 19'
24/Mar/2001	04° ♈ 28'	1/Apr/2001	11° ♋ 46'	7/Apr/2001	18° ♎ 22'	15/Apr/2001	25° ♑ 43'
23/Apr/2001	03° ♉ 32'	30/Apr/2001	10° ♌ 25'	7/May/2001	17° ♏ 04'	15/May/2001	24° ♒ 38'
22/May/2001	02° ♊ 03'	29/May/2001	08° ♍ 35'	5/Jun/2001	15° ♐ 26'	13/Jun/2001	23° ♓ 09'
21/Jun/2001	**00° ♋ 10'**	27/Jun/2001	06° ♎ 31'	**5/Jul/2001**	**13° ♑ 39'**	13/Jul/2001	21° ♈ 25'
20/Jul/2001	28° ♋ 08'	27/Jul/2001	04° ♏ 27'	4/Aug/2001	11° ♒ 56'	12/Aug/2001	19° ♉ 40'
18/Aug/2001	26° ♌ 12'	25/Aug/2001	02° ♐ 40'	2/Sep/2001	10° ♓ 28'	10/Sep/2001	18° ♊ 07'
17/Sep/2001	24° ♍ 36'	24/Sep/2001	01° ♑ 24'	2/Oct/2001	09° ♈ 26'	10/Oct/2001	16° ♋ 56'
16/Oct/2001	23° ♎ 30'	23/Oct/2001	00° ♒ 46'	1/Nov/2001	08° ♉ 52'	8/Nov/2001	16° ♌ 10'
15/Nov/2001	22° ♏ 58'	22/Nov/2001	00° ♓ 44'	30/Nov/2001	08° ♊ 43'	7/Dec/2001	15° ♍ 47'
14/Dec/2001	**22° ♐ 56'**	22/Dec/2001	01° ♈ 05'	**30/Dec/2001**	**08° ♋ 48'**	5/Jan/2002	15° ♎ 39'
13/Jan/2002	23° ♑ 11'	21/Jan/2002	01° ♉ 31'	28/Jan/2002	08° ♌ 51'	4/Feb/2002	15° ♏ 33'
12/Feb/2002	23° ♒ 25'	20/Feb/2002	01° ♊ 40'	27/Feb/2002	08° ♍ 36'	5/Mar/2002	15° ♐ 17'
13/Mar/2002	23° ♓ 19'	21/Mar/2002	01° ♋ 17'	28/Mar/2002	07° ♎ 54'	4/Apr/2002	14° ♑ 41'
12/Apr/2002	22° ♈ 42'	20/Apr/2002	00° ♌ 16'	26/Apr/2002	06° ♏ 41'	4/May/2002	13° ♒ 39'
12/May/2002	21° ♉ 32'	19/May/2002	28° ♌ 39'	**26/May/2002**	**05° ♐ 04'**	2/Jun/2002	12° ♓ 16'

Traditional Monthly Moon Phases - Eclipses in Bold Print

New Moon				First Quarter Moon				Full Moon				Last Quarter Moon			
11/Jun/2002	**19°**	♊	**54'**	17/Jun/2002	26°	♍	37'	**24/Jun/2002**	**03°**	♑	**11'**	2/Jul/2002	10°	♈	39'
10/Jul/2002	18°	♋	00'	17/Jul/2002	24°	♎	27'	24/Jul/2002	01°	♒	18'	1/Aug/2002	09°	♉	00'
8/Aug/2002	16°	♌	04'	15/Aug/2002	22°	♏	25'	22/Aug/2002	29°	♒	39'	30/Aug/2002	07°	♊	32'
6/Sep/2002	14°	♍	20'	13/Sep/2002	20°	♐	47'	21/Sep/2002	28°	♓	25'	29/Sep/2002	06°	♋	23'
6/Oct/2002	13°	♎	02'	13/Oct/2002	19°	♑	43'	21/Oct/2002	27°	♈	43'	29/Oct/2002	05°	♌	37'
4/Nov/2002	12°	♏	15'	11/Nov/2002	19°	♒	18'	**20/Nov/2002**	**27°**	♉	**33'**	27/Nov/2002	05°	♍	13'
4/Dec/2002	**11°**	♐	**58'**	11/Dec/2002	19°	♓	26'	19/Dec/2002	27°	♊	42'	26/Dec/2002	05°	♎	04'
2/Jan/2003	12°	♑	01'	10/Jan/2003	19°	♈	53'	18/Jan/2003	27°	♋	55'	25/Jan/2003	04°	♏	57'
1/Feb/2003	12°	♒	09'	9/Feb/2003	20°	♉	17'	16/Feb/2003	27°	♌	54'	23/Feb/2003	04°	♐	39'
2/Mar/2003	12°	♓	06'	11/Mar/2003	20°	♊	18'	18/Mar/2003	27°	♍	25'	24/Mar/2003	04°	♑	00'
1/Apr/2003	11°	♈	39'	9/Apr/2003	19°	♋	42'	16/Apr/2003	26°	♎	24'	23/Apr/2003	02°	♒	56'
1/May/2003	10°	♉	43'	9/May/2003	18°	♌	27'	**26/May/2003**	**24°**	♏	**53'**	22/May/2003	01°	♓	30'
31/May/2003	**09°**	♊	**20'**	7/Jun/2003	16°	♍	41'	14/Jun/2003	23°	♐	00'	21/Jun/2003	29°	♓	49'
29/Jun/2003	07°	♋	37'	6/Jul/2003	14°	♎	36'	13/Jul/2003	20°	♑	59'	21/Jul/2003	28°	♈	08'
29/Jul/2003	05°	♌	46'	5/Aug/2003	12°	♏	29'	12/Aug/2003	19°	♒	05'	19/Aug/2003	26°	♉	37'
27/Aug/2003	04°	♍	02'	3/Sep/2003	10°	♐	36'	10/Sep/2003	17°	♓	34'	18/Sep/2003	25°	♊	27'
25/Sep/2003	02°	♎	38'	2/Oct/2003	09°	♑	11'	10/Oct/2003	16°	♈	35'	18/Oct/2003	24°	♋	43'
25/Oct/2003	01°	♏	41'	1/Nov/2003	08°	♒	20'	**9/Nov/2003**	**16°**	♉	**13'**	17/Nov/2003	24°	♌	23'
23/Nov/2003	**01°**	♐	**14'**	30/Nov/2003	08°	♓	05'	8/Dec/2003	16°	♊	20'	16/Dec/2003	24°	♍	20'
23/Dec/2003	01°	♑	08'	30/Dec/2003	08°	♈	17'	7/Jan/2004	16°	♋	40'	15/Jan/2004	24°	♎	21'
21/Jan/2004	01°	♒	10'	29/Jan/2004	08°	♉	40'	6/Feb/2004	16°	♌	54'	13/Feb/2004	24°	♏	11'
20/Feb/2004	01°	♓	04'	27/Feb/2004	08°	♊	53'	6/Mar/2004	16°	♍	43'	13/Mar/2004	23°	♐	37'
20/Mar/2004	00°	♈	39'	28/Mar/2004	08°	♋	38'	5/Apr/2004	16°	♎	00'	11/Apr/2004	22°	♑	35'
19/Apr/2004	**29°**	♈	**49'**	27/Apr/2004	07°	♌	47'	**4/May/2004**	**14°**	♏	**42'**	11/May/2004	21°	♒	05'
19/May/2004	28°	♉	33'	27/May/2004	06°	♍	22'	3/Jun/2004	12°	♐	56'	9/Jun/2004	19°	♓	18'
17/Jun/2004	26°	♊	57'	25/Jun/2004	04°	♎	32'	2/Jul/2004	10°	♑	54'	9/Jul/2004	17°	♈	26'
17/Jul/2004	25°	♋	13'	24/Jul/2004	02°	♏	32'	31/Jul/2004	08°	♒	51'	7/Aug/2004	15°	♉	42'
15/Aug/2004	23°	♌	31'	23/Aug/2004	00°	♐	37'	29/Aug/2004	07°	♓	03'	6/Sep/2004	14°	♊	21'
14/Sep/2004	22°	♍	06'	21/Sep/2004	29°	♐	00'	28/Sep/2004	05°	♈	45'	6/Oct/2004	13°	♋	30'
13/Oct/2004	**21°**	♎	**06'**	20/Oct/2004	27°	♑	51'	**28/Oct/2004**	**05°**	♉	**02'**	5/Nov/2004	13°	♌	09'
12/Nov/2004	20°	♏	33'	19/Nov/2004	27°	♒	15'	26/Nov/2004	04°	♊	55'	4/Dec/2004	13°	♍	14'
11/Dec/2004	20°	♐	22'	18/Dec/2004	27°	♓	07'	26/Dec/2004	05°	♋	12'	3/Jan/2005	13°	♎	27'
10/Jan/2005	20°	♑	21'	17/Jan/2005	27°	♈	16'	25/Jan/2005	05°	♌	34'	2/Feb/2005	13°	♏	33'
8/Feb/2005	20°	♒	16'	15/Feb/2005	27°	♉	25'	24/Feb/2005	05°	♍	41'	3/Mar/2005	13°	♐	14'
10/Mar/2005	19°	♓	54'	17/Mar/2005	27°	♊	18'	25/Mar/2005	05°	♎	18'	1/Apr/2005	12°	♑	23'
8/Apr/2005	**19°**	♈	**06'**	16/Apr/2005	26°	♋	42'	**24/Apr/2005**	**04°**	♏	**20'**	1/May/2005	10°	♒	59'
8/May/2005	17°	♉	52'	16/May/2005	25°	♌	36'	23/May/2005	02°	♐	47'	30/May/2005	09°	♓	10'
6/Jun/2005	16°	♊	16'	14/Jun/2005	24°	♍	04'	22/Jun/2005	00°	♑	51'	28/Jun/2005	07°	♈	08'
6/Jul/2005	14°	♋	31'	14/Jul/2005	22°	♎	16'	21/Jul/2005	28°	♑	47'	27/Jul/2005	05°	♉	10'
4/Aug/2005	12°	♌	48'	12/Aug/2005	20°	♏	28'	19/Aug/2005	26°	♒	50'	26/Aug/2005	03°	♊	29'
3/Sep/2005	11°	♍	21'	11/Sep/2005	18°	♐	50'	17/Sep/2005	25°	♓	16'	25/Sep/2005	02°	♋	18'
3/Oct/2005	**10°**	♎	**19'**	10/Oct/2005	17°	♑	34'	**17/Oct/2005**	**24°**	♈	**13'**	24/Oct/2005	01°	♌	44'
1/Nov/2005	09°	♏	43'	8/Nov/2005	16°	♒	46'	15/Nov/2005	23°	♉	46'	23/Nov/2005	01°	♍	43'
1/Dec/2005	09°	♐	31'	8/Dec/2005	16°	♓	24'	15/Dec/2005	23°	♊	48'	23/Dec/2005	02°	♎	05'
30/Dec/2005	09°	♑	32'	6/Jan/2006	16°	♈	19'	14/Jan/2006	24°	♋	05'	22/Jan/2006	02°	♏	27'
29/Jan/2006	09°	♒	32'	5/Feb/2006	16°	♉	19'	13/Feb/2006	24°	♌	20'	21/Feb/2006	02°	♐	31'
27/Feb/2006	09°	♓	16'	6/Mar/2006	16°	♊	07'	**15/Mar/2006**	**24°**	♍	**15'**	22/Mar/2006	02°	♑	01'
29/Mar/2006	**08°**	♈	**35'**	5/Apr/2006	15°	♋	34'	13/Apr/2006	23°	♎	37'	20/Apr/2006	00°	♒	54'
27/Apr/2006	07°	♉	24'	5/May/2006	14°	♌	35'	13/May/2006	22°	♏	23'	20/May/2006	29°	♒	14'
27/May/2006	05°	♊	48'	3/Jun/2006	13°	♍	13'	11/Jun/2006	20°	♐	40'	18/Jun/2006	27°	♓	12'
25/Jun/2006	03°	♋	58'	3/Jul/2006	11°	♎	37'	10/Jul/2006	18°	♑	42'	17/Jul/2006	25°	♈	04'

Traditional Monthly Moon Phases - Eclipses in Bold Print

New Moon	First Quarter Moon	Full Moon	Last Quarter Moon
25/Jul/2006 02° ♌ 07'	2/Aug/2006 09° ♏ 56'	9/Aug/2006 16° ♒ 44'	15/Aug/2006 23° ♉ 05'
23/Aug/2006 00° ♍ 31'	31/Aug/2006 08° ♐ 24'	**7/Sep/2006 15° ♓ 00'**	14/Sep/2006 21° ♊ 30'
22/Sep/2006 29° ♍ 20'	30/Sep/2006 07° ♑ 09'	6/Oct/2006 13° ♈ 43'	13/Oct/2006 20° ♋ 31'
22/Oct/2006 28° ♎ 40'	29/Oct/2006 06° ♒ 19'	5/Nov/2006 12° ♉ 58'	12/Nov/2006 20° ♌ 12'
20/Nov/2006 28° ♏ 27'	28/Nov/2006 05° ♓ 53'	4/Dec/2006 12° ♊ 43'	12/Dec/2006 20° ♍ 25'
20/Dec/2006 28° ♐ 32'	27/Dec/2006 05° ♈ 42'	3/Jan/2007 12° ♋ 48'	11/Jan/2007 20° ♎ 54'
18/Jan/2007 28° ♑ 41'	25/Jan/2007 05° ♉ 36'	2/Feb/2007 12° ♌ 59'	10/Feb/2007 21° ♏ 16'
17/Feb/2007 28° ♒ 37'	24/Feb/2007 05° ♊ 19'	**4/Mar/2007 13° ♍ 00'**	11/Mar/2007 21° ♐ 11'
19/Mar/2007 28° ♓ 07'	25/Mar/2007 04° ♋ 43'	2/Apr/2007 12° ♎ 35'	10/Apr/2007 20° ♑ 29'
17/Apr/2007 27° ♈ 05'	24/Apr/2007 03° ♌ 43'	2/May/2007 11° ♏ 38'	10/May/2007 19° ♒ 09'
16/May/2007 25° ♉ 33'	23/May/2007 02° ♍ 22'	31/May/2007 10° ♐ 12'	8/Jun/2007 17° ♓ 19'
14/Jun/2007 23° ♊ 41'	22/Jun/2007 00° ♎ 46'	30/Jun/2007 08° ♑ 25'	7/Jul/2007 15° ♈ 12'
14/Jul/2007 21° ♋ 41'	22/Jul/2007 29° ♎ 06'	29/Jul/2007 06° ♒ 31'	5/Aug/2007 13° ♉ 05'
12/Aug/2007 19° ♌ 51'	20/Aug/2007 27° ♏ 35'	**28/Aug/2007 04° ♓ 46'**	3/Sep/2007 11° ♊ 12'
11/Sep/2007 18° ♍ 25'	19/Sep/2007 26° ♐ 22'	26/Sep/2007 03° ♈ 20'	3/Oct/2007 09° ♋ 49'
11/Oct/2007 17° ♎ 30'	19/Oct/2007 25° ♑ 35'	26/Oct/2007 02° ♉ 23'	1/Nov/2007 09° ♌ 04'
9/Nov/2007 17° ♏ 10'	17/Nov/2007 25° ♒ 12'	24/Nov/2007 01° ♊ 55'	1/Dec/2007 08° ♍ 56'
9/Dec/2007 17° ♐ 16'	17/Dec/2007 25° ♓ 05'	23/Dec/2007 01° ♋ 50'	31/Dec/2007 09° ♎ 14'
8/Jan/2008 17° ♑ 33'	15/Jan/2008 25° ♈ 02'	22/Jan/2008 01° ♌ 54'	30/Jan/2008 09° ♏ 40'
7/Feb/2008 17° ♒ 44'	13/Feb/2008 24° ♉ 49'	**21/Feb/2008 01° ♍ 53'**	28/Feb/2008 09° ♐ 52'
7/Mar/2008 17° ♓ 31'	14/Mar/2008 24° ♊ 14'	21/Mar/2008 01° ♎ 32'	29/Mar/2008 09° ♑ 34'
5/Apr/2008 16° ♈ 44'	12/Apr/2008 23° ♋ 13'	20/Apr/2008 00° ♏ 43'	28/Apr/2008 08° ♒ 39'
5/May/2008 15° ♉ 22'	11/May/2008 21° ♌ 48'	19/May/2008 29° ♏ 27'	27/May/2008 07° ♓ 10'
3/Jun/2008 13° ♊ 34'	10/Jun/2008 20° ♍ 06'	18/Jun/2008 27° ♐ 50'	26/Jun/2008 05° ♈ 15'
2/Jul/2008 11° ♋ 32'	10/Jul/2008 18° ♎ 18'	18/Jul/2008 26° ♑ 04'	25/Jul/2008 03° ♉ 10'
1/Aug/2008 09° ♌ 32'	8/Aug/2008 16° ♏ 38'	**16/Aug/2008 24° ♒ 21'**	23/Aug/2008 01° ♊ 12'
30/Aug/2008 07° ♍ 48'	7/Sep/2008 15° ♐ 19'	15/Sep/2008 22° ♓ 54'	22/Sep/2008 29° ♊ 34'
29/Sep/2008 06° ♎ 33'	7/Oct/2008 14° ♑ 28'	14/Oct/2008 21° ♈ 51'	21/Oct/2008 28° ♋ 27'
28/Oct/2008 05° ♏ 54'	6/Nov/2008 14° ♒ 07'	13/Nov/2008 21° ♉ 15'	19/Nov/2008 27° ♌ 56'
27/Nov/2008 05° ♐ 49'	5/Dec/2008 14° ♓ 08'	12/Dec/2008 21° ♊ 02'	19/Dec/2008 27° ♍ 54'
27/Dec/2008 06° ♑ 08'	4/Jan/2009 14° ♈ 16'	10/Jan/2009 21° ♋ 02'	17/Jan/2009 28° ♎ 08'
26/Jan/2009 06° ♒ 30'	2/Feb/2009 14° ♉ 15'	**9/Feb/2009 21° ♌ 00'**	16/Feb/2009 28° ♏ 21'
24/Feb/2009 06° ♓ 35'	4/Mar/2009 13° ♊ 52'	10/Mar/2009 20° ♍ 40'	18/Mar/2009 28° ♐ 16'
26/Mar/2009 06° ♈ 08'	2/Apr/2009 12° ♋ 59'	9/Apr/2009 19° ♎ 53'	17/Apr/2009 27° ♑ 40'
24/Apr/2009 05° ♉ 04'	1/May/2009 11° ♌ 36'	9/May/2009 18° ♏ 41'	17/May/2009 26° ♒ 32'
24/May/2009 03° ♊ 28'	30/May/2009 09° ♍ 50'	7/Jun/2009 17° ♐ 07'	15/Jun/2009 24° ♓ 56'
22/Jun/2009 01° ♋ 30'	29/Jun/2009 07° ♎ 52'	**7/Jul/2009 15° ♑ 24'**	15/Jul/2009 23° ♈ 03'
22/Jul/2009 29° ♋ 27'	28/Jul/2009 05° ♏ 57'	**6/Aug/2009 13° ♒ 43'**	13/Aug/2009 21° ♉ 09'
20/Aug/2009 27° ♌ 32'	27/Aug/2009 04° ♐ 21'	4/Sep/2009 12° ♓ 15'	11/Sep/2009 19° ♊ 28'
18/Sep/2009 25° ♍ 59'	26/Sep/2009 03° ♑ 15'	4/Oct/2009 11° ♈ 10'	11/Oct/2009 18° ♋ 11'
18/Oct/2009 24° ♎ 59'	25/Oct/2009 02° ♒ 44'	2/Nov/2009 10° ♉ 30'	9/Nov/2009 17° ♌ 23'
16/Nov/2009 24° ♏ 34'	24/Nov/2009 02° ♓ 45'	2/Dec/2009 10° ♊ 15'	8/Dec/2009 17° ♍ 03'
16/Dec/2009 24° ♐ 40'	24/Dec/2009 03° ♈ 03'	**31/Dec/2009 10° ♋ 15'**	7/Jan/2010 17° ♎ 01'
15/Jan/2010 25° ♑ 01'	23/Jan/2010 03° ♉ 20'	30/Jan/2010 10° ♌ 15'	5/Feb/2010 17° ♏ 04'
13/Feb/2010 25° ♒ 18'	21/Feb/2010 03° ♊ 17'	28/Feb/2010 09° ♍ 59'	7/Mar/2010 16° ♐ 57'
15/Mar/2010 25° ♓ 10'	23/Mar/2010 02° ♋ 42'	29/Mar/2010 09° ♎ 17'	6/Apr/2010 16° ♑ 29'
14/Apr/2010 24° ♈ 27'	21/Apr/2010 01° ♌ 32'	28/Apr/2010 08° ♏ 07'	6/May/2010 15° ♒ 33'
13/May/2010 23° ♉ 09'	20/May/2010 29° ♌ 51'	27/May/2010 06° ♐ 33'	4/Jun/2010 14° ♓ 11'
12/Jun/2010 21° ♊ 24'	19/Jun/2010 27° ♍ 49'	**26/Jun/2010 04° ♑ 46'**	4/Jul/2010 12° ♈ 31'
11/Jul/2010 19° ♋ 24'	18/Jul/2010 25° ♎ 42'	25/Jul/2010 03° ♒ 00'	3/Aug/2010 10° ♉ 46'
9/Aug/2010 17° ♌ 25'	16/Aug/2010 23° ♏ 47'	24/Aug/2010 01° ♓ 26'	1/Sep/2010 09° ♊ 10'

Traditional Monthly Moon Phases - Eclipses in Bold Print

New Moon				First Quarter Moon				Full Moon				Last Quarter Moon			
8/Sep/2010	15°	♍	41'	15/Sep/2010	22°	♐	18'	23/Sep/2010	00°	♈	15'	30/Sep/2010	07°	♋	52'
7/Oct/2010	14°	♎	24'	14/Oct/2010	21°	♑	26'	22/Oct/2010	29°	♈	33'	30/Oct/2010	06°	♌	59'
6/Nov/2010	13°	♏	40'	13/Nov/2010	21°	♒	12'	21/Nov/2010	29°	♉	18'	28/Nov/2010	06°	♍	30'
5/Dec/2010	13°	♐	29'	13/Dec/2010	21°	♓	27'	**21/Dec/2010**	**29°**	**♊**	**21'**	28/Dec/2010	06°	♎	19'
4/Jan/2011	**13°**	**♑**	**39'**	12/Jan/2011	21°	♈	54'	19/Jan/2011	29°	♋	27'	26/Jan/2011	06°	♏	13'
2/Feb/2011	13°	♒	54'	11/Feb/2011	22°	♉	13'	18/Feb/2011	29°	♌	20'	24/Feb/2011	06°	♐	00'
4/Mar/2011	13°	♓	56'	12/Mar/2011	22°	♊	03'	19/Mar/2011	28°	♍	48'	26/Mar/2011	05°	♑	29'
3/Apr/2011	13°	♈	30'	11/Apr/2011	21°	♋	16'	17/Apr/2011	27°	♎	44'	24/Apr/2011	04°	♒	34'
3/May/2011	12°	♉	31'	10/May/2011	19°	♌	51'	17/May/2011	26°	♏	13'	24/May/2011	03°	♓	16'
1/Jun/2011	**11°**	**♊**	**02'**	8/Jun/2011	17°	♍	56'	**15/Jun/2011**	**24°**	**♐**	**23'**	23/Jun/2011	01°	♈	41'
1/Jul/2011	**09°**	**♋**	**12'**	8/Jul/2011	15°	♎	47'	15/Jul/2011	22°	♑	28'	23/Jul/2011	00°	♉	02'
30/Jul/2011	07°	♌	16'	6/Aug/2011	13°	♏	40'	13/Aug/2011	20°	♒	41'	21/Aug/2011	28°	♉	30'
28/Aug/2011	05°	♍	27'	4/Sep/2011	11°	♐	51'	12/Sep/2011	19°	♓	17'	20/Sep/2011	27°	♊	15'
27/Sep/2011	04°	♎	00'	3/Oct/2011	10°	♑	34'	11/Oct/2011	18°	♈	24'	19/Oct/2011	26°	♋	24'
26/Oct/2011	03°	♏	03'	2/Nov/2011	09°	♒	55'	10/Nov/2011	18°	♉	05'	18/Nov/2011	25°	♌	55'
25/Nov/2011	**02°**	**♐**	**37'**	2/Dec/2011	09°	♓	52'	**10/Dec/2011**	**18°**	**♊**	**11'**	17/Dec/2011	25°	♍	44'
24/Dec/2011	02°	♑	34'	1/Jan/2012	10°	♈	13'	9/Jan/2012	18°	♋	26'	16/Jan/2012	25°	♎	38'
23/Jan/2012	02°	♒	42'	31/Jan/2012	10°	♉	41'	7/Feb/2012	18°	♌	32'	14/Feb/2012	25°	♏	24'
21/Feb/2012	02°	♓	42'	29/Feb/2012	10°	♊	52'	8/Mar/2012	18°	♍	13'	14/Mar/2012	24°	♐	52'
22/Mar/2012	02°	♈	22'	30/Mar/2012	10°	♋	30'	6/Apr/2012	17°	♎	23'	13/Apr/2012	23°	♑	55'
21/Apr/2012	01°	♉	35'	29/Apr/2012	09°	♌	29'	5/May/2012	16°	♏	01'	12/May/2012	22°	♒	33'
21/May/2012	**00°**	**♊**	**21'**	28/May/2012	07°	♍	53'	**4/Jun/2012**	**14°**	**♐**	**14'**	11/Jun/2012	20°	♓	54'
19/Jun/2012	28°	♊	43'	26/Jun/2012	05°	♎	54'	3/Jul/2012	12°	♑	14'	10/Jul/2012	19°	♈	11'
19/Jul/2012	26°	♋	55'	26/Jul/2012	03°	♏	47'	1/Aug/2012	10°	♒	15'	9/Aug/2012	17°	♉	34'
17/Aug/2012	25°	♌	08'	24/Aug/2012	01°	♐	48'	31/Aug/2012	08°	♓	34'	8/Sep/2012	16°	♊	17'
15/Sep/2012	23°	♍	37'	22/Sep/2012	00°	♑	12'	29/Sep/2012	07°	♈	22'	8/Oct/2012	15°	♋	26'
15/Oct/2012	22°	♎	32'	21/Oct/2012	29°	♑	09'	29/Oct/2012	06°	♉	48'	6/Nov/2012	15°	♌	00'
13/Nov/2012	**21°**	**♏**	**57'**	20/Nov/2012	28°	♒	41'	**28/Nov/2012**	**06°**	**♊**	**47'**	6/Dec/2012	14°	♍	55'
13/Dec/2012	21°	♐	45'	20/Dec/2012	28°	♓	44'	28/Dec/2012	07°	♋	06'	4/Jan/2013	14°	♎	58'
11/Jan/2013	21°	♑	46'	18/Jan/2013	29°	♈	04'	27/Jan/2013	07°	♌	24'	3/Feb/2013	14°	♏	54'
10/Feb/2013	21°	♒	43'	17/Feb/2013	29°	♉	21'	25/Feb/2013	07°	♍	24'	4/Mar/2013	14°	♐	29'
11/Mar/2013	21°	♓	24'	19/Mar/2013	29°	♊	16'	27/Mar/2013	06°	♎	52'	3/Apr/2013	13°	♑	35'
10/Apr/2013	20°	♈	41'	18/Apr/2013	28°	♋	38'	**25/Apr/2013**	**05°**	**♏**	**46'**	2/May/2013	12°	♒	13'
10/May/2013	**19°**	**♉**	**31'**	18/May/2013	27°	♌	25'	**25/May/2013**	**04°**	**♐**	**08'**	31/May/2013	10°	♓	28'
8/Jun/2013	18°	♊	01'	16/Jun/2013	25°	♍	43'	23/Jun/2013	02°	♑	10'	30/Jun/2013	08°	♈	35'
8/Jul/2013	16°	♋	18'	15/Jul/2013	23°	♎	46'	22/Jul/2013	00°	♒	06'	29/Jul/2013	06°	♉	45'
6/Aug/2013	14°	♌	35'	14/Aug/2013	21°	♏	49'	20/Aug/2013	28°	♒	11'	28/Aug/2013	05°	♊	15'
5/Sep/2013	13°	♍	04'	12/Sep/2013	20°	♐	06'	19/Sep/2013	26°	♓	41'	26/Sep/2013	04°	♋	13'
4/Oct/2013	11°	♎	56'	11/Oct/2013	18°	♑	47'	**19/Oct/2013**	**25°**	**♈**	**45'**	26/Oct/2013	03°	♌	43'
3/Nov/2013	**11°**	**♏**	**16'**	10/Nov/2013	18°	♒	00'	17/Nov/2013	25°	♉	26'	25/Nov/2013	03°	♍	41'
2/Dec/2013	10°	♐	59'	9/Dec/2013	17°	♓	43'	17/Dec/2013	25°	♊	36'	25/Dec/2013	03°	♎	56'
1/Jan/2014	10°	♑	57'	7/Jan/2014	17°	♈	46'	16/Jan/2014	25°	♋	58'	24/Jan/2014	04°	♏	08'
30/Jan/2014	10°	♒	55'	6/Feb/2014	17°	♉	56'	14/Feb/2014	26°	♌	13'	22/Feb/2014	04°	♐	00'
1/Mar/2014	10°	♓	39'	8/Mar/2014	17°	♊	54'	16/Mar/2014	26°	♍	02'	23/Mar/2014	03°	♑	20'
30/Mar/2014	09°	♈	59'	7/Apr/2014	17°	♋	27'	**15/Apr/2014**	**25°**	**♎**	**16'**	22/Apr/2014	02°	♒	07'
29/Apr/2014	**08°**	**♉**	**52'**	6/May/2014	16°	♌	30'	14/May/2014	23°	♏	55'	21/May/2014	00°	♓	24'
28/May/2014	07°	♊	21'	5/Jun/2014	15°	♍	06'	13/Jun/2014	22°	♐	06'	19/Jun/2014	28°	♓	24'
27/Jun/2014	05°	♋	37'	5/Jul/2014	13°	♎	24'	12/Jul/2014	20°	♑	03'	18/Jul/2014	26°	♈	22'
26/Jul/2014	03°	♌	52'	3/Aug/2014	11°	♏	36'	10/Aug/2014	18°	♒	02'	17/Aug/2014	24°	♉	32'
25/Aug/2014	02°	♍	19'	2/Sep/2014	09°	♐	55'	8/Sep/2014	16°	♓	19'	15/Sep/2014	23°	♊	09'
24/Sep/2014	01°	♎	08'	1/Oct/2014	08°	♑	33'	**8/Oct/2014**	**15°**	**♈**	**05'**	15/Oct/2014	22°	♋	21'

Traditional Monthly Moon Phases - Eclipses in Bold Print

New Moon				First Quarter Moon				Full Moon				Last Quarter Moon			
23/Oct/2014	**00°**	♏	**25'**	30/Oct/2014	07°	♒	36'	6/Nov/2014	14°	♉	26'	14/Nov/2014	22°	♌	10'
22/Nov/2014	00°	♐	07'	29/Nov/2014	07°	♓	06'	6/Dec/2014	14°	♊	18'	14/Dec/2014	22°	♍	26'
21/Dec/2014	00°	♑	06'	28/Dec/2014	06°	♈	56'	5/Jan/2015	14°	♋	31'	13/Jan/2015	22°	♎	52'
20/Jan/2015	00°	♒	09'	27/Jan/2015	06°	♉	55'	3/Feb/2015	14°	♌	48'	11/Feb/2015	23°	♏	06'
18/Feb/2015	00°	♓	00'	25/Feb/2015	06°	♊	47'	5/Mar/2015	14°	♍	50'	13/Mar/2015	22°	♐	49'
20/Mar/2015	**29°**	♓	**27'**	27/Mar/2015	06°	♋	19'	**4/Apr/2015**	**14°**	♎	**24'**	11/Apr/2015	21°	♑	55'
18/Apr/2015	28°	♈	25'	25/Apr/2015	05°	♌	27'	3/May/2015	13°	♏	23'	11/May/2015	20°	♒	26'
18/May/2015	26°	♉	56'	25/May/2015	04°	♍	11'	2/Jun/2015	11°	♐	49'	9/Jun/2015	18°	♓	30'
16/Jun/2015	25°	♊	07'	24/Jun/2015	02°	♎	38'	1/Jul/2015	09°	♑	55'	8/Jul/2015	16°	♈	22'
15/Jul/2015	23°	♋	14'	24/Jul/2015	00°	♏	59'	31/Jul/2015	07°	♒	56'	6/Aug/2015	14°	♉	17'
14/Aug/2015	21°	♌	31'	22/Aug/2015	29°	♏	24'	29/Aug/2015	06°	♓	06'	5/Sep/2015	12°	♊	32'
13/Sep/2015	**20°**	♍	**10'**	21/Sep/2015	28°	♐	04'	**28/Sep/2015**	**04°**	♈	**40'**	4/Oct/2015	11°	♋	19'
12/Oct/2015	19°	♎	20'	20/Oct/2015	27°	♑	08'	27/Oct/2015	03°	♉	45'	3/Nov/2015	10°	♌	45'
11/Nov/2015	19°	♏	01'	19/Nov/2015	26°	♒	36'	25/Nov/2015	03°	♊	20'	3/Dec/2015	10°	♍	48'
11/Dec/2015	19°	♐	03'	18/Dec/2015	26°	♓	22'	25/Dec/2015	03°	♋	20'	2/Jan/2016	11°	♎	14'
9/Jan/2016	19°	♑	13'	16/Jan/2016	26°	♈	16'	23/Jan/2016	03°	♌	29'	31/Jan/2016	11°	♏	41'
8/Feb/2016	19°	♒	16'	15/Feb/2016	26°	♉	03'	22/Feb/2016	03°	♍	34'	1/Mar/2016	11°	♐	48'
9/Mar/2016	**18°**	♓	**56'**	15/Mar/2016	25°	♊	33'	**23/Mar/2016**	**03°**	♎	**17'**	31/Mar/2016	11°	♑	20'
7/Apr/2016	18°	♈	04'	14/Apr/2016	24°	♋	39'	22/Apr/2016	02°	♏	31'	29/Apr/2016	10°	♒	13'
6/May/2016	16°	♉	41'	13/May/2016	23°	♌	21'	21/May/2016	01°	♐	14'	29/May/2016	08°	♓	33'
4/Jun/2016	14°	♊	53'	12/Jun/2016	21°	♍	47'	20/Jun/2016	29°	♐	32'	27/Jun/2016	06°	♈	30'
4/Jul/2016	12°	♋	54'	11/Jul/2016	20°	♎	07'	19/Jul/2016	27°	♑	40'	26/Jul/2016	04°	♉	21'
2/Aug/2016	10°	♌	58'	10/Aug/2016	18°	♏	32'	**18/Aug/2016**	**25°**	♒	**52'**	24/Aug/2016	02°	♊	22'
1/Sep/2016	**09°**	♍	**21'**	9/Sep/2016	17°	♐	13'	**16/Sep/2016**	**24°**	♓	**20'**	23/Sep/2016	00°	♋	48'
30/Sep/2016	08°	♎	15'	9/Oct/2016	16°	♑	19'	16/Oct/2016	23°	♈	14'	22/Oct/2016	29°	♋	49'
30/Oct/2016	07°	♏	44'	7/Nov/2016	15°	♒	50'	14/Nov/2016	22°	♉	38'	21/Nov/2016	29°	♌	28'
29/Nov/2016	07°	♐	43'	7/Dec/2016	15°	♓	42'	13/Dec/2016	22°	♊	26'	20/Dec/2016	29°	♍	38'
29/Dec/2016	07°	♑	59'	5/Jan/2017	15°	♈	40'	12/Jan/2017	22°	♋	27'	19/Jan/2017	00°	♏	02'
27/Jan/2017	08°	♒	15'	4/Feb/2017	15°	♉	32'	**11/Feb/2017**	**22°**	♌	**28'**	18/Feb/2017	00°	♐	20'
26/Feb/2017	**08°**	♓	**12'**	5/Mar/2017	15°	♊	05'	12/Mar/2017	22°	♍	13'	20/Mar/2017	00°	♑	14'
27/Mar/2017	07°	♈	37'	3/Apr/2017	14°	♋	12'	11/Apr/2017	21°	♎	33'	19/Apr/2017	29°	♑	32'
26/Apr/2017	06°	♉	27'	2/May/2017	12°	♌	52'	10/May/2017	20°	♏	24'	18/May/2017	28°	♒	14'
25/May/2017	04°	♊	47'	1/Jun/2017	11°	♍	13'	9/Jun/2017	18°	♐	53'	17/Jun/2017	26°	♓	28'
23/Jun/2017	02°	♋	47'	30/Jun/2017	09°	♎	24'	9/Jul/2017	17°	♑	09'	16/Jul/2017	24°	♈	26'
23/Jul/2017	00°	♌	44'	30/Jul/2017	07°	♏	39'	**7/Aug/2017**	**15°**	♒	**25'**	14/Aug/2017	22°	♉	25'
21/Aug/2017	**28°**	♌	**53'**	29/Aug/2017	06°	♐	11'	6/Sep/2017	13°	♓	53'	13/Sep/2017	20°	♊	40'
20/Sep/2017	27°	♍	27'	27/Sep/2017	05°	♑	11'	5/Oct/2017	12°	♈	43'	12/Oct/2017	19°	♋	22'
19/Oct/2017	26°	♎	35'	27/Oct/2017	04°	♒	41'	4/Nov/2017	11°	♉	59'	10/Nov/2017	18°	♌	38'
18/Nov/2017	26°	♏	19'	26/Nov/2017	04°	♓	38'	3/Dec/2017	11°	♊	40'	10/Dec/2017	18°	♍	26'
18/Dec/2017	26°	♐	31'	26/Dec/2017	04°	♈	47'	1/Jan/2018	11°	♋	38'	8/Jan/2018	18°	♎	36'
16/Jan/2018	26°	♑	54'	24/Jan/2018	04°	♉	53'	**31/Jan/2018**	**11°**	♌	**37'**	7/Feb/2018	18°	♏	49'
15/Feb/2018	**27°**	♒	**08'**	23/Feb/2018	04°	♊	39'	1/Mar/2018	11°	♍	23'	9/Mar/2018	18°	♐	50'
17/Mar/2018	26°	♓	53'	24/Mar/2018	03°	♋	57'	31/Mar/2018	10°	♎	45'	8/Apr/2018	18°	♑	24'
15/Apr/2018	26°	♈	02'	22/Apr/2018	02°	♌	42'	29/Apr/2018	09°	♏	39'	7/May/2018	17°	♒	27'
15/May/2018	24°	♉	36'	21/May/2018	01°	♍	02'	29/May/2018	08°	♐	10'	6/Jun/2018	16°	♓	00'
13/Jun/2018	22°	♊	44'	20/Jun/2018	29°	♍	04'	28/Jun/2018	06°	♑	28'	6/Jul/2018	14°	♈	13'
13/Jul/2018	**20°**	♋	**41'**	19/Jul/2018	27°	♎	06'	**27/Jul/2018**	**04°**	♒	**45'**	4/Aug/2018	12°	♉	19'
11/Aug/2018	**18°**	♌	**42'**	18/Aug/2018	25°	♏	20'	26/Aug/2018	03°	♓	12'	2/Sep/2018	10°	♊	34'
9/Sep/2018	17°	♍	00'	16/Sep/2018	24°	♐	02'	24/Sep/2018	02°	♈	00'	2/Oct/2018	09°	♋	09'
8/Oct/2018	15°	♎	48'	16/Oct/2018	23°	♑	19'	24/Oct/2018	01°	♉	13'	31/Oct/2018	08°	♌	12'
7/Nov/2018	15°	♏	11'	15/Nov/2018	23°	♒	11'	23/Nov/2018	00°	♊	52'	29/Nov/2018	07°	♍	43'

Traditional Monthly Moon Phases - Eclipses in Bold Print

New Moon				First Quarter Moon				Full Moon				Last Quarter Moon			
7/Dec/2018	15°	♐	07'	15/Dec/2018	23°	♓	27'	22/Dec/2018	00°	♋	49'	29/Dec/2018	07°	♎	36'
6/Jan/2019	**15°**	**♑**	**25'**	14/Jan/2019	23°	♈	48'	**21/Jan/2019**	**00°**	**♌**	**52'**	27/Jan/2019	07°	♏	38'
4/Feb/2019	15°	♒	45'	12/Feb/2019	23°	♉	55'	19/Feb/2019	00°	♍	42'	26/Feb/2019	07°	♐	34'
6/Mar/2019	15°	♓	47'	14/Mar/2019	23°	♊	33'	20/Mar/2019	00°	♎	09'	28/Mar/2019	07°	♑	12'
5/Apr/2019	15°	♈	17'	12/Apr/2019	22°	♋	35'	19/Apr/2019	29°	♎	07'	26/Apr/2019	06°	♒	23'
4/May/2019	14°	♉	11'	11/May/2019	21°	♌	03'	18/May/2019	27°	♏	39'	26/May/2019	05°	♓	09'
3/Jun/2019	12°	♊	34'	10/Jun/2019	19°	♍	06'	17/Jun/2019	25°	♐	53'	25/Jun/2019	03°	♈	34'
2/Jul/2019	**10°**	**♋**	**38'**	9/Jul/2019	16°	♎	58'	**16/Jul/2019**	**24°**	**♑**	**04'**	24/Jul/2019	01°	♉	51'
31/Jul/2019	08°	♌	37'	7/Aug/2019	14°	♏	56'	15/Aug/2019	22°	♒	24'	23/Aug/2019	00°	♊	12'
30/Aug/2019	06°	♍	47'	5/Sep/2019	13°	♐	16'	14/Sep/2019	21°	♓	05'	21/Sep/2019	28°	♊	49'
28/Sep/2019	05°	♎	20'	5/Oct/2019	12°	♑	09'	13/Oct/2019	20°	♈	14'	21/Oct/2019	27°	♋	49'
27/Oct/2019	04°	♏	25'	4/Nov/2019	11°	♒	42'	12/Nov/2019	19°	♉	52'	19/Nov/2019	27°	♌	14'
26/Nov/2019	04°	♐	03'	4/Dec/2019	11°	♓	49'	12/Dec/2019	19°	♊	52'	19/Dec/2019	26°	♍	58'
26/Dec/2019	**04°**	**♑**	**07'**	3/Jan/2020	12°	♈	15'	**10/Jan/2020**	**20°**	**♋**	**00'**	17/Jan/2020	26°	♎	52'
24/Jan/2020	04°	♒	22'	1/Feb/2020	12°	♉	40'	9/Feb/2020	20°	♌	00'	15/Feb/2020	26°	♏	41'
23/Feb/2020	04°	♓	29'	2/Mar/2020	12°	♊	42'	9/Mar/2020	19°	♍	37'	16/Mar/2020	26°	♐	16'
24/Mar/2020	04°	♈	12'	1/Apr/2020	12°	♋	09'	7/Apr/2020	18°	♎	44'	14/Apr/2020	25°	♑	27'
22/Apr/2020	03°	♉	24'	30/Apr/2020	10°	♌	57'	7/May/2020	17°	♏	20'	14/May/2020	24°	♒	14'
22/May/2020	02°	♊	05'	29/May/2020	09°	♍	12'	**5/Jun/2020**	**15°**	**♐**	**34'**	13/Jun/2020	22°	♓	42'
21/Jun/2020	**00°**	**♋**	**21'**	28/Jun/2020	07°	♎	06'	**5/Jul/2020**	**13°**	**♑**	**38'**	12/Jul/2020	21°	♈	03'
20/Jul/2020	28°	♋	27'	27/Jul/2020	04°	♏	56'	3/Aug/2020	11°	♒	46'	11/Aug/2020	19°	♉	28'
18/Aug/2020	26°	♌	35'	25/Aug/2020	02°	♐	59'	2/Sep/2020	10°	♓	12'	10/Sep/2020	18°	♊	08'
17/Sep/2020	25°	♍	01'	23/Sep/2020	01°	♑	29'	1/Oct/2020	09°	♈	08'	9/Oct/2020	17°	♋	10'
16/Oct/2020	23°	♎	53'	23/Oct/2020	00°	♒	36'	31/Oct/2020	08°	♉	38'	8/Nov/2020	16°	♌	37'
15/Nov/2020	23°	♏	18'	22/Nov/2020	00°	♓	20'	**30/Nov/2020**	**08°**	**♊**	**38'**	7/Dec/2020	16°	♍	22'
14/Dec/2020	**23°**	**♐**	**08'**	21/Dec/2020	00°	♈	35'	29/Dec/2020	08°	♋	53'	6/Jan/2021	16°	♎	17'
13/Jan/2021	23°	♑	13'	20/Jan/2021	01°	♉	02'	28/Jan/2021	09°	♌	06'	4/Feb/2021	16°	♏	08'
11/Feb/2021	23°	♒	17'	19/Feb/2021	01°	♊	21'	27/Feb/2021	08°	♍	57'	5/Mar/2021	15°	♐	42'
13/Mar/2021	23°	♓	04'	21/Mar/2021	01°	♋	12'	28/Mar/2021	08°	♎	18'	4/Apr/2021	14°	♑	51'
11/Apr/2021	22°	♈	25'	20/Apr/2021	00°	♌	25'	26/Apr/2021	07°	♏	06'	3/May/2021	13°	♒	35'
11/May/2021	21°	♉	18'	19/May/2021	29°	♌	01'	**26/May/2021**	**05°**	**♐**	**26'**	2/Jun/2021	11°	♓	59'
10/Jun/2021	**19°**	**♊**	**47'**	17/Jun/2021	27°	♍	09'	24/Jun/2021	03°	♑	28'	1/Jul/2021	10°	♈	14'
9/Jul/2021	18°	♋	02'	17/Jul/2021	25°	♎	04'	23/Jul/2021	01°	♒	26'	31/Jul/2021	08°	♉	33'
8/Aug/2021	16°	♌	14'	15/Aug/2021	23°	♏	01'	22/Aug/2021	29°	♒	37'	30/Aug/2021	07°	♊	09'
6/Sep/2021	14°	♍	38'	13/Sep/2021	21°	♐	16'	20/Sep/2021	28°	♓	14'	28/Sep/2021	06°	♋	09'
6/Oct/2021	13°	♎	25'	12/Oct/2021	20°	♑	01'	20/Oct/2021	27°	♈	26'	28/Oct/2021	05°	♌	37'
4/Nov/2021	12°	♏	40'	11/Nov/2021	19°	♒	21'	**19/Nov/2021**	**27°**	**♉**	**14'**	27/Nov/2021	05°	♍	28'
4/Dec/2021	**12°**	**♐**	**22'**	10/Dec/2021	19°	♓	13'	19/Dec/2021	27°	♊	29'	26/Dec/2021	05°	♎	32'
2/Jan/2022	12°	♑	20'	9/Jan/2022	19°	♈	28'	17/Jan/2022	27°	♋	51'	25/Jan/2022	05°	♏	33'
1/Feb/2022	12°	♒	20'	8/Feb/2022	19°	♉	46'	16/Feb/2022	27°	♌	59'	23/Feb/2022	05°	♐	17'
2/Mar/2022	12°	♓	07'	10/Mar/2022	19°	♊	50'	18/Mar/2022	27°	♍	40'	25/Mar/2022	04°	♑	33'
1/Apr/2022	11°	♈	31'	9/Apr/2022	19°	♋	24'	16/Apr/2022	26°	♎	46'	23/Apr/2022	03°	♒	19'
30/Apr/2022	**10°**	**♉**	**28'**	8/May/2022	18°	♌	23'	**16/May/2022**	**25°**	**♏**	**18'**	22/May/2022	01°	♓	39'
30/May/2022	09°	♊	03'	7/Jun/2022	16°	♍	51'	14/Jun/2022	23°	♐	25'	20/Jun/2022	29°	♓	46'
28/Jun/2022	07°	♋	23'	6/Jul/2022	14°	♎	59'	13/Jul/2022	21°	♑	21'	20/Jul/2022	27°	♈	52'
28/Jul/2022	05°	♌	39'	5/Aug/2022	13°	♏	02'	11/Aug/2022	19°	♒	22'	19/Aug/2022	26°	♉	12'
27/Aug/2022	04°	♍	04'	3/Sep/2022	11°	♐	14'	10/Sep/2022	17°	♓	41'	17/Sep/2022	24°	♊	59'
25/Sep/2022	02°	♎	49'	2/Oct/2022	09°	♑	47'	9/Oct/2022	16°	♈	33'	17/Oct/2022	24°	♋	19'
25/Oct/2022	**02°**	**♏**	**00'**	1/Nov/2022	08°	♒	49'	**8/Nov/2022**	**16°**	**♉**	**01'**	16/Nov/2022	24°	♌	10'
23/Nov/2022	01°	♐	38'	30/Nov/2022	08°	♓	22'	8/Dec/2022	16°	♊	02'	16/Dec/2022	24°	♍	22'
23/Dec/2022	01°	♑	33'	29/Dec/2022	08°	♈	18'	6/Jan/2023	16°	♋	22'	14/Jan/2023	24°	♎	38'

Traditional Monthly Moon Phases - Eclipses in Bold Print

New Moon				First Quarter Moon				Full Moon				Last Quarter Moon			
21/Jan/2023	01°	♒	33'	28/Jan/2023	08°	♉	26'	5/Feb/2023	16°	♌	41'	13/Feb/2023	24°	♏	40'
20/Feb/2023	01°	♓	22'	27/Feb/2023	08°	♊	27'	7/Mar/2023	16°	♍	40'	14/Mar/2023	24°	♐	13'
21/Mar/2023	00°	♈	50'	28/Mar/2023	08°	♋	09'	6/Apr/2023	16°	♎	07'	13/Apr/2023	23°	♑	11'
20/Apr/2023	**29°**	**♈**	**50'**	27/Apr/2023	07°	♌	21'	**5/May/2023**	**14°**	**♏**	**58'**	12/May/2023	21°	♒	37'
19/May/2023	28°	♉	26'	27/May/2023	06°	♍	06'	3/Jun/2023	13°	♐	18'	10/Jun/2023	19°	♓	40'
18/Jun/2023	26°	♊	43'	26/Jun/2023	04°	♎	29'	3/Jul/2023	11°	♑	19'	9/Jul/2023	17°	♈	36'
17/Jul/2023	24°	♋	56'	25/Jul/2023	02°	♏	43'	1/Aug/2023	09°	♒	16'	8/Aug/2023	15°	♉	39'
16/Aug/2023	23°	♌	17'	24/Aug/2023	01°	♐	00'	30/Aug/2023	07°	♓	25'	6/Sep/2023	14°	♊	04'
14/Sep/2023	21°	♍	59'	22/Sep/2023	29°	♐	32'	29/Sep/2023	06°	♈	00'	6/Oct/2023	13°	♋	03'
14/Oct/2023	**21°**	**♎**	**08'**	21/Oct/2023	28°	♑	28'	**28/Oct/2023**	**05°**	**♉**	**09'**	5/Nov/2023	12°	♌	40'
13/Nov/2023	20°	♏	44'	20/Nov/2023	27°	♒	51'	27/Nov/2023	04°	♊	51'	5/Dec/2023	12°	♍	49'
12/Dec/2023	20°	♐	40'	19/Dec/2023	27°	♓	35'	26/Dec/2023	04°	♋	58'	3/Jan/2024	13°	♎	15'
11/Jan/2024	20°	♑	44'	17/Jan/2024	27°	♈	32'	25/Jan/2024	05°	♌	15'	2/Feb/2024	13°	♏	36'
9/Feb/2024	20°	♒	41'	16/Feb/2024	27°	♉	26'	24/Feb/2024	05°	♍	23'	3/Mar/2024	13°	♐	32'
10/Mar/2024	20°	♓	17'	17/Mar/2024	27°	♊	04'	**25/Mar/2024**	**05°**	**♎**	**07'**	1/Apr/2024	12°	♑	52'
8/Apr/2024	**19°**	**♈**	**24'**	15/Apr/2024	26°	♋	18'	23/Apr/2024	04°	♏	18'	1/May/2024	11°	♒	35'
7/May/2024	18°	♉	02'	15/May/2024	25°	♌	08'	23/May/2024	02°	♐	55'	30/May/2024	09°	♓	46'
6/Jun/2024	16°	♊	18'	14/Jun/2024	23°	♍	39'	21/Jun/2024	01°	♑	07'	28/Jun/2024	07°	♈	40'
5/Jul/2024	14°	♋	23'	13/Jul/2024	22°	♎	01'	21/Jul/2024	29°	♑	09'	27/Jul/2024	05°	♉	32'
4/Aug/2024	12°	♌	34'	12/Aug/2024	20°	♏	24'	19/Aug/2024	27°	♒	15'	26/Aug/2024	03°	♊	38'
2/Sep/2024	11°	♍	04'	11/Sep/2024	19°	♐	00'	**17/Sep/2024**	**25°**	**♓**	**41'**	24/Sep/2024	02°	♋	12'
2/Oct/2024	**10°**	**♎**	**04'**	10/Oct/2024	17°	♑	58'	17/Oct/2024	24°	♈	35'	24/Oct/2024	01°	♌	24'
1/Nov/2024	09°	♏	35'	9/Nov/2024	17°	♒	20'	15/Nov/2024	24°	♉	01'	22/Nov/2024	01°	♍	15'
1/Dec/2024	09°	♐	33'	8/Dec/2024	17°	♓	02'	15/Dec/2024	23°	♊	53'	22/Dec/2024	01°	♎	34'
30/Dec/2024	09°	♑	44'	6/Jan/2025	16°	♈	56'	13/Jan/2025	24°	♋	00'	21/Jan/2025	02°	♏	03'
29/Jan/2025	09°	♒	51'	5/Feb/2025	16°	♉	46'	12/Feb/2025	24°	♌	06'	20/Feb/2025	02°	♐	20'
27/Feb/2025	09°	♓	40'	6/Mar/2025	16°	♊	21'	**14/Mar/2025**	**23°**	**♍**	**57'**	22/Mar/2025	02°	♑	05'
29/Mar/2025	**09°**	**♈**	**00'**	4/Apr/2025	15°	♋	33'	12/Apr/2025	23°	♎	20'	20/Apr/2025	01°	♒	12'
27/Apr/2025	07°	♉	47'	4/May/2025	14°	♌	21'	12/May/2025	22°	♏	13'	20/May/2025	29°	♒	43'
26/May/2025	06°	♊	06'	2/Jun/2025	12°	♍	50'	11/Jun/2025	20°	♐	39'	18/Jun/2025	27°	♓	48'
25/Jun/2025	04°	♋	08'	2/Jul/2025	11°	♎	10'	10/Jul/2025	18°	♑	50'	17/Jul/2025	25°	♈	40'
24/Jul/2025	02°	♌	08'	1/Aug/2025	09°	♏	32'	9/Aug/2025	17°	♒	00'	16/Aug/2025	23°	♉	37'
23/Aug/2025	00°	♍	23'	31/Aug/2025	08°	♐	07'	**7/Sep/2025**	**15°**	**♓**	**22'**	14/Sep/2025	21°	♊	52'
21/Sep/2025	**29°**	**♍**	**05'**	29/Sep/2025	07°	♑	06'	6/Oct/2025	14°	♈	08'	13/Oct/2025	20°	♋	40'
21/Oct/2025	28°	♎	22'	29/Oct/2025	06°	♒	30'	5/Nov/2025	13°	♉	23'	12/Nov/2025	20°	♌	05'
20/Nov/2025	28°	♏	12'	28/Nov/2025	06°	♓	18'	4/Dec/2025	13°	♊	04'	11/Dec/2025	20°	♍	04'
19/Dec/2025	28°	♐	25'	27/Dec/2025	06°	♈	17'	3/Jan/2026	13°	♋	02'	10/Jan/2026	20°	♎	25'
18/Jan/2026	28°	♑	44'	26/Jan/2026	06°	♉	14'	1/Feb/2026	13°	♌	04'	9/Feb/2026	20°	♏	46'
17/Feb/2026	**28°**	**♒**	**50'**	24/Feb/2026	05°	♊	54'	**3/Mar/2026**	**12°**	**♍**	**54'**	11/Mar/2026	20°	♐	49'
18/Mar/2026	28°	♓	27'	25/Mar/2026	05°	♋	09'	1/Apr/2026	12°	♎	21'	10/Apr/2026	20°	♑	20'
17/Apr/2026	27°	♈	29'	23/Apr/2026	03°	♌	56'	1/May/2026	11°	♏	21'	9/May/2026	19°	♒	15'
16/May/2026	25°	♉	58'	23/May/2026	02°	♍	21'	31/May/2026	09°	♐	56'	8/Jun/2026	17°	♓	38'
14/Jun/2026	24°	♊	03'	21/Jun/2026	00°	♎	32'	29/Jun/2026	08°	♑	15'	7/Jul/2026	15°	♈	42'
14/Jul/2026	21°	♋	59'	21/Jul/2026	28°	♎	43'	29/Jul/2026	06°	♒	30'	5/Aug/2026	13°	♉	40'
12/Aug/2026	**20°**	**♌**	**02'**	19/Aug/2026	27°	♏	08'	**28/Aug/2026**	**04°**	**♓**	**54'**	4/Sep/2026	11°	♊	49'
10/Sep/2026	18°	♍	26'	18/Sep/2026	25°	♐	57'	26/Sep/2026	03°	♈	37'	3/Oct/2026	10°	♋	21'
10/Oct/2026	17°	♎	22'	18/Oct/2026	25°	♑	18'	26/Oct/2026	02°	♉	46'	1/Nov/2026	09°	♌	26'
9/Nov/2026	16°	♏	53'	17/Nov/2026	25°	♒	08'	24/Nov/2026	02°	♊	20'	1/Dec/2026	09°	♍	03'
8/Dec/2026	16°	♐	57'	17/Dec/2026	25°	♓	17'	23/Dec/2026	02°	♋	14'	30/Dec/2026	09°	♎	05'
7/Jan/2027	17°	♑	18'	15/Jan/2027	25°	♈	28'	22/Jan/2027	02°	♌	14'	29/Jan/2027	09°	♏	18'
6/Feb/2027	**17°**	**♒**	**38'**	14/Feb/2027	25°	♉	23'	**21/Feb/2027**	**02°**	**♍**	**06'**	28/Feb/2027	09°	♐	23'

Traditional Monthly Moon Phases - Eclipses in Bold Print															
New Moon				**First Quarter Moon**				**Full Moon**				**Last Quarter Moon**			
8/Mar/2027	17°	♓	35'	15/Mar/2027	24°	♊	52'	22/Mar/2027	01°	♎	35'	29/Mar/2027	09°	♑	06'
6/Apr/2027	16°	♈	57'	13/Apr/2027	23°	♋	47'	20/Apr/2027	00°	♏	37'	28/Apr/2027	08°	♒	19'
6/May/2027	15°	♉	43'	13/May/2027	22°	♌	14'	20/May/2027	29°	♏	14'	28/May/2027	07°	♓	02'
4/Jun/2027	13°	♊	58'	11/Jun/2027	20°	♍	19'	18/Jun/2027	27°	♐	33'	27/Jun/2027	05°	♈	21'
3/Jul/2027	11°	♋	57'	10/Jul/2027	18°	♎	18'	**18/Jul/2027**	**25°**	**♑**	**49'**	26/Jul/2027	03°	♉	30'
2/Aug/2027	**09°**	**♌**	**55'**	9/Aug/2027	16°	♏	25'	**17/Aug/2027**	**24°**	**♒**	**12'**	24/Aug/2027	01°	♊	42'
31/Aug/2027	08°	♍	06'	7/Sep/2027	14°	♐	55'	15/Sep/2027	22°	♓	53'	23/Sep/2027	00°	♋	11'
29/Sep/2027	06°	♎	43'	7/Oct/2027	14°	♑	00'	15/Oct/2027	21°	♈	59'	22/Oct/2027	29°	♋	05'
29/Oct/2027	05°	♏	54'	6/Nov/2027	13°	♒	41'	13/Nov/2027	21°	♉	31'	20/Nov/2027	28°	♌	28'
27/Nov/2027	05°	♐	39'	6/Dec/2027	13°	♓	51'	13/Dec/2027	21°	♊	25'	20/Dec/2027	28°	♍	14'
27/Dec/2027	05°	♑	50'	4/Jan/2028	14°	♈	13'	**12/Jan/2028**	**21°**	**♋**	**28'**	18/Jan/2028	28°	♎	13'
26/Jan/2028	**06°**	**♒**	**11'**	3/Feb/2028	14°	♉	29'	10/Feb/2028	21°	♌	24'	17/Feb/2028	28°	♏	11'
25/Feb/2028	06°	♓	21'	4/Mar/2028	14°	♊	19'	10/Mar/2028	20°	♍	59'	17/Mar/2028	27°	♐	53'
26/Mar/2028	06°	♈	03'	2/Apr/2028	13°	♋	34'	9/Apr/2028	20°	♎	06'	16/Apr/2028	27°	♑	13'
24/Apr/2028	05°	♉	09'	1/May/2028	12°	♌	13'	8/May/2028	18°	♏	44'	16/May/2028	26°	♒	05'
24/May/2028	03°	♊	41'	31/May/2028	10°	♍	23'	7/Jun/2028	17°	♐	02'	15/Jun/2028	24°	♓	36'
22/Jun/2028	01°	♋	51'	29/Jun/2028	08°	♎	17'	**6/Jul/2028**	**15°**	**♑**	**11'**	14/Jul/2028	22°	♈	55'
22/Jul/2028	**29°**	**♋**	**51'**	28/Jul/2028	06°	♏	10'	5/Aug/2028	13°	♒	26'	13/Aug/2028	21°	♉	15'
20/Aug/2028	27°	♌	56'	26/Aug/2028	04°	♐	20'	3/Sep/2028	11°	♓	59'	11/Sep/2028	19°	♊	48'
18/Sep/2028	26°	♍	22'	25/Sep/2028	03°	♑	00'	3/Oct/2028	10°	♈	59'	11/Oct/2028	18°	♋	42'
17/Oct/2028	25°	♎	16'	25/Oct/2028	02°	♒	19'	2/Nov/2028	10°	♉	29'	9/Nov/2028	18°	♌	01'
16/Nov/2028	24°	♏	43'	23/Nov/2028	02°	♓	15'	1/Dec/2028	10°	♊	24'	9/Dec/2028	17°	♍	41'
15/Dec/2028	24°	♐	39'	23/Dec/2028	02°	♈	36'	**31/Dec/2028**	**10°**	**♋**	**33'**	7/Jan/2029	17°	♎	32'
14/Jan/2029	**24°**	**♑**	**50'**	22/Jan/2029	03°	♉	04'	30/Jan/2029	10°	♌	38'	5/Feb/2029	17°	♏	23'
13/Feb/2029	25°	♒	01'	21/Feb/2029	03°	♊	17'	28/Feb/2029	10°	♍	24'	7/Mar/2029	17°	♐	02'
15/Mar/2029	24°	♓	52'	23/Mar/2029	02°	♋	57'	29/Mar/2029	09°	♎	41'	5/Apr/2029	16°	♑	19'
13/Apr/2029	24°	♈	14'	21/Apr/2029	01°	♌	59'	28/Apr/2029	08°	♏	26'	5/May/2029	15°	♒	11'
13/May/2029	23°	♉	05'	21/May/2029	00°	♍	25'	27/May/2029	06°	♐	45'	3/Jun/2029	13°	♓	44'
12/Jun/2029	**21°**	**♊**	**29'**	19/Jun/2029	28°	♍	25'	**26/Jun/2029**	**04°**	**♑**	**50'**	3/Jul/2029	12°	♈	05'
11/Jul/2029	**19°**	**♋**	**38'**	18/Jul/2029	26°	♎	15'	25/Jul/2029	02°	♒	54'	2/Aug/2029	10°	♉	27'
9/Aug/2029	17°	♌	45'	16/Aug/2029	24°	♏	11'	23/Aug/2029	01°	♓	12'	1/Sep/2029	09°	♊	02'
8/Sep/2029	16°	♍	04'	14/Sep/2029	22°	♐	31'	22/Sep/2029	29°	♓	57'	30/Sep/2029	07°	♋	59'
7/Oct/2029	14°	♎	48'	14/Oct/2029	21°	♑	24'	22/Oct/2029	29°	♈	16'	30/Oct/2029	07°	♌	20'
6/Nov/2029	14°	♏	03'	12/Nov/2029	20°	♒	55'	21/Nov/2029	29°	♉	08'	28/Nov/2029	07°	♍	02'
5/Dec/2029	**13°**	**♐**	**45'**	12/Dec/2029	21°	♓	00'	**20/Dec/2029**	**29°**	**♊**	**21'**	28/Dec/2029	06°	♎	57'
3/Jan/2030	13°	♑	47'	11/Jan/2030	21°	♈	24'	19/Jan/2030	29°	♋	37'	26/Jan/2030	06°	♏	50'
2/Feb/2030	13°	♒	51'	10/Feb/2030	21°	♉	47'	18/Feb/2030	29°	♌	38'	24/Feb/2030	06°	♐	30'
4/Mar/2030	13°	♓	44'	12/Mar/2030	21°	♊	49'	19/Mar/2030	29°	♍	10'	26/Mar/2030	05°	♑	47'
2/Apr/2030	13°	♈	12'	10/Apr/2030	21°	♋	17'	17/Apr/2030	28°	♎	09'	24/Apr/2030	04°	♒	38'
2/May/2030	12°	♉	14'	10/May/2030	20°	♌	06'	17/May/2030	26°	♏	37'	24/May/2030	03°	♓	06'
1/Jun/2030	**10°**	**♊**	**50'**	8/Jun/2030	18°	♍	23'	**15/Jun/2030**	**24°**	**♐**	**43'**	22/Jun/2030	01°	♈	21'
30/Jun/2030	09°	♋	09'	8/Jul/2030	16°	♎	21'	14/Jul/2030	22°	♑	41'	22/Jul/2030	29°	♈	35'
30/Jul/2030	07°	♌	21'	6/Aug/2030	14°	♏	17'	13/Aug/2030	20°	♒	45'	20/Aug/2030	28°	♉	04'
28/Aug/2030	05°	♍	41'	4/Sep/2030	12°	♐	25'	11/Sep/2030	19°	♓	11'	19/Sep/2030	26°	♊	55'
27/Sep/2030	04°	♎	21'	3/Oct/2030	10°	♑	59'	11/Oct/2030	18°	♈	10'	19/Oct/2030	26°	♋	16'
26/Oct/2030	03°	♏	27'	2/Nov/2030	10°	♒	06'	9/Nov/2030	17°	♉	47'	18/Nov/2030	26°	♌	02'
25/Nov/2030	**03°**	**♐**	**02'**	1/Dec/2030	09°	♓	48'	**9/Dec/2030**	**17°**	**♊**	**54'**	17/Dec/2030	26°	♍	05'
24/Dec/2030	02°	♑	57'	31/Dec/2030	09°	♈	55'	8/Jan/2031	18°	♋	16'	16/Jan/2031	26°	♎	11'
23/Jan/2031	02°	♒	57'	30/Jan/2031	10°	♉	13'	7/Feb/2031	18°	♌	32'	14/Feb/2031	26°	♏	03'
21/Feb/2031	02°	♓	49'	1/Mar/2031	10°	♊	22'	9/Mar/2031	18°	♍	24'	16/Mar/2031	25°	♐	29'
22/Mar/2031	02°	♈	19'	30/Mar/2031	10°	♋	07'	7/Apr/2031	17°	♎	42'	14/Apr/2031	24°	♑	24'

Traditional Monthly Moon Phases - Eclipses in Bold Print

New Moon				First Quarter Moon				Full Moon				Last Quarter Moon			
21/Apr/2031	01°	♉	24'	29/Apr/2031	09°	♌	17'	**7/May/2031**	**16°**	♏	**25'**	13/May/2031	22°	♒	50'
21/May/2031	**00°**	♊	**04'**	29/May/2031	07°	♍	55'	**5/Jun/2031**	**14°**	♐	**39'**	11/Jun/2031	20°	♓	58'
19/Jun/2031	28°	♊	27'	27/Jun/2031	06°	♎	10'	4/Jul/2031	12°	♑	38'	11/Jul/2031	19°	♈	01'
19/Jul/2031	26°	♋	43'	27/Jul/2031	04°	♏	14'	2/Aug/2031	10°	♒	35'	9/Aug/2031	17°	♉	13'
18/Aug/2031	25°	♌	04'	25/Aug/2031	02°	♐	23'	1/Sep/2031	08°	♓	46'	8/Sep/2031	15°	♊	50'
16/Sep/2031	23°	♍	43'	23/Sep/2031	00°	♑	49'	30/Sep/2031	07°	♈	25'	8/Oct/2031	14°	♋	58'
16/Oct/2031	22°	♎	47'	23/Oct/2031	29°	♑	42'	**30/Oct/2031**	**06°**	♉	**41'**	7/Nov/2031	14°	♌	40'
14/Nov/2031	**22°**	♏	**18'**	21/Nov/2031	29°	♒	05'	28/Nov/2031	06°	♊	31'	6/Dec/2031	14°	♍	48'
14/Dec/2031	22°	♐	10'	20/Dec/2031	28°	♓	54'	28/Dec/2031	06°	♋	46'	5/Jan/2032	15°	♎	07'
12/Jan/2032	22°	♑	10'	19/Jan/2032	28°	♈	58'	27/Jan/2032	07°	♌	08'	4/Feb/2032	15°	♏	18'
11/Feb/2032	22°	♒	05'	17/Feb/2032	29°	♉	02'	26/Feb/2032	07°	♍	16'	4/Mar/2032	15°	♐	03'
11/Mar/2032	21°	♓	40'	18/Mar/2032	28°	♊	49'	26/Mar/2032	06°	♎	55'	3/Apr/2032	14°	♑	13'
9/Apr/2032	20°	♈	48'	17/Apr/2032	28°	♋	11'	**25/Apr/2032**	**05°**	♏	**58'**	2/May/2032	12°	♒	48'
9/May/2032	**19°**	♉	**29'**	17/May/2032	27°	♌	03'	24/May/2032	04°	♐	28'	31/May/2032	10°	♓	57'
7/Jun/2032	17°	♊	50'	15/Jun/2032	25°	♍	32'	23/Jun/2032	02°	♑	34'	29/Jun/2032	08°	♈	52'
7/Jul/2032	16°	♋	02'	15/Jul/2032	23°	♎	49'	22/Jul/2032	00°	♒	30'	29/Jul/2032	06°	♉	49'
6/Aug/2032	14°	♌	18'	14/Aug/2032	22°	♏	05'	20/Aug/2032	28°	♒	35'	27/Aug/2032	05°	♊	04'
4/Sep/2032	12°	♍	52'	12/Sep/2032	20°	♐	33'	19/Sep/2032	27°	♓	00'	26/Sep/2032	03°	♋	50'
4/Oct/2032	11°	♎	52'	11/Oct/2032	19°	♑	23'	**18/Oct/2032**	**25°**	♈	**57'**	25/Oct/2032	03°	♌	14'
3/Nov/2032	**11°**	♏	**21'**	10/Nov/2032	18°	♒	38'	17/Nov/2032	25°	♉	28'	24/Nov/2032	03°	♍	13'
2/Dec/2032	11°	♐	14'	9/Dec/2032	18°	♓	16'	16/Dec/2032	25°	♊	27'	24/Dec/2032	03°	♎	36'
1/Jan/2033	11°	♑	19'	7/Jan/2033	18°	♈	10'	15/Jan/2033	25°	♋	42'	23/Jan/2033	04°	♏	02'
30/Jan/2033	11°	♒	20'	6/Feb/2033	18°	♉	05'	14/Feb/2033	25°	♌	54'	22/Feb/2033	04°	♐	10'
1/Mar/2033	11°	♓	04'	7/Mar/2033	17°	♊	48'	15/Mar/2033	25°	♍	47'	23/Mar/2033	03°	♑	44'
30/Mar/2033	**10°**	♈	**21'**	6/Apr/2033	17°	♋	08'	**14/Apr/2033**	**25°**	♎	**09'**	22/Apr/2033	02°	♒	40'
28/Apr/2033	09°	♉	07'	6/May/2033	16°	♌	04'	14/May/2033	23°	♏	58'	21/May/2033	01°	♓	01'
28/May/2033	07°	♊	28'	4/Jun/2033	14°	♍	39'	12/Jun/2033	22°	♐	18'	19/Jun/2033	28°	♓	59'
26/Jun/2033	05°	♋	34'	4/Jul/2033	13°	♎	03'	12/Jul/2033	20°	♑	22'	19/Jul/2033	26°	♈	50'
26/Jul/2033	03°	♌	41'	3/Aug/2033	11°	♏	25'	10/Aug/2033	18°	♒	26'	17/Aug/2033	24°	♉	49'
24/Aug/2033	02°	♍	02'	1/Sep/2033	09°	♐	57'	8/Sep/2033	16°	♓	44'	15/Sep/2033	23°	♊	12'
23/Sep/2033	**00°**	♎	**51'**	1/Oct/2033	08°	♑	49'	**8/Oct/2033**	**15°**	♈	**29'**	15/Oct/2033	22°	♋	09'
23/Oct/2033	00°	♏	12'	31/Oct/2033	08°	♒	05'	6/Nov/2033	14°	♉	45'	13/Nov/2033	21°	♌	46'
21/Nov/2033	00°	♐	03'	29/Nov/2033	07°	♓	43'	6/Dec/2033	14°	♊	29'	13/Dec/2033	21°	♍	56'
21/Dec/2033	00°	♑	13'	28/Dec/2033	07°	♈	35'	4/Jan/2034	14°	♋	31'	12/Jan/2034	22°	♎	24'
20/Jan/2034	00°	♒	24'	27/Jan/2034	07°	♉	28'	3/Feb/2034	14°	♌	38'	11/Feb/2034	22°	♏	47'
18/Feb/2034	00°	♓	22'	25/Feb/2034	07°	♊	08'	4/Mar/2034	14°	♍	34'	13/Mar/2034	22°	♐	45'
20/Mar/2034	**29°**	♓	**52'**	26/Mar/2034	06°	♋	27'	**3/Apr/2034**	**14°**	♎	**06'**	11/Apr/2034	22°	♑	07'
18/Apr/2034	28°	♈	50'	25/Apr/2034	05°	♌	21'	3/May/2034	13°	♏	09'	11/May/2034	20°	♒	50'
17/May/2034	27°	♉	17'	24/May/2034	03°	♍	53'	1/Jun/2034	11°	♐	43'	9/Jun/2034	19°	♓	03'
16/Jun/2034	25°	♊	22'	23/Jun/2034	02°	♎	13'	1/Jul/2034	09°	♑	58'	8/Jul/2034	16°	♈	58'
15/Jul/2034	23°	♋	21'	23/Jul/2034	00°	♏	32'	31/Jul/2034	08°	♒	08'	7/Aug/2034	14°	♉	52'
13/Aug/2034	21°	♌	28'	21/Aug/2034	29°	♏	02'	29/Aug/2034	06°	♓	26'	5/Sep/2034	13°	♊	00'
12/Sep/2034	**19°**	♍	**59'**	20/Sep/2034	27°	♐	53'	**28/Sep/2034**	**05°**	♈	**04'**	4/Oct/2034	11°	♋	35'
12/Oct/2034	19°	♎	3	20/Oct/2034	27°	♑	10	27/Oct/2034	04°	♉	10	3/Nov/2034	10°	♌	46
11/Nov/2034	18°	♏	42	19/Nov/2034	26°	♒	53	25/Nov/2034	03°	♊	43	2/Dec/2034	10°	♍	34
10/Dec/2034	18°	♐	50	18/Dec/2034	26°	♓	52	25/Dec/2034	03°	♋	37	1/Jan/2035	10°	♎	47
9/Jan/2035	19°	♑	10	17/Jan/2035	26°	♈	53	23/Jan/2035	03°	♌	38	31/Jan/2035	11°	♏	10
8/Feb/2035	19°	♒	23	15/Feb/2035	26°	♉	40	**22/Feb/2035**	**03°**	♍	**33**	2/Mar/2035	11°	♐	21
9/Mar/2035	**19°**	♓	**12**	16/Mar/2035	26°	♊	4	23/Mar/2035	03°	♎	7	31/Mar/2035	11°	♑	3
8/Apr/2035	18°	♈	26	15/Apr/2035	24°	♋	59	22/Apr/2035	02°	♏	15	30/Apr/2035	10°	♒	11
7/May/2035	17°	♉	6	14/May/2035	23°	♌	29	22/May/2035	00°	♐	57	30/May/2035	08°	♓	45

Traditional Monthly Moon Phases - Eclipses in Bold Print

New Moon				First Quarter Moon				Full Moon				Last Quarter Moon			
6/Jun/2035	15°	♊	17	12/Jun/2035	21°	♍	41	20/Jun/2035	29°	♐	19	28/Jun/2035	06°	♈	55
5/Jul/2035	13°	♋	15	12/Jul/2035	19°	♎	49	20/Jul/2035	27°	♑	34	28/Jul/2035	04°	♉	54
3/Aug/2035	11°	♌	13	10/Aug/2035	18°	♏	6	**19/Aug/2035**	**25°**	**♒**	**55**	26/Aug/2035	02°	♊	59
2/Sep/2035	**09°**	**♍**	**27**	9/Sep/2035	16°	♐	46	17/Sep/2035	24°	♓	32	24/Sep/2035	01°	♋	23
1/Oct/2035	08°	♎	11	9/Oct/2035	15°	♑	56	17/Oct/2035	23°	♈	33	23/Oct/2035	00°	♌	16
31/Oct/2035	07°	♏	30	8/Nov/2035	15°	♒	38	15/Nov/2035	23°	♉	0	22/Nov/2035	29°	♌	42
29/Nov/2035	07°	♐	24	8/Dec/2035	15°	♓	44	15/Dec/2035	22°	♊	50	21/Dec/2035	29°	♍	36
29/Dec/2035	07°	♑	41	6/Jan/2036	15°	♈	58	13/Jan/2036	22°	♋	50	20/Jan/2036	29°	♎	46
28/Jan/2036	08°	♒	3	5/Feb/2036	16°	♉	2	**11/Feb/2036**	**22°**	**♌**	**45**	18/Feb/2036	29°	♏	53
27/Feb/2036	**08°**	**♓**	**10**	5/Mar/2036	15°	♊	41	12/Mar/2036	22°	♍	22	19/Mar/2036	29°	♐	44
27/Mar/2036	07°	♈	45	4/Apr/2036	14°	♋	48	10/Apr/2036	21°	♎	32	18/Apr/2036	29°	♑	6
26/Apr/2036	06°	♉	44	3/May/2036	13°	♌	23	10/May/2036	20°	♏	15	18/May/2036	27°	♒	59
25/May/2036	05°	♊	9	1/Jun/2036	11°	♍	33	8/Jun/2036	18°	♐	38	17/Jun/2036	26°	♓	26
24/Jun/2036	03°	♋	12	30/Jun/2036	09°	♎	31	8/Jul/2036	16°	♑	52	16/Jul/2036	24°	♈	38
23/Jul/2036	**01°**	**♌**	**9**	30/Jul/2036	07°	♏	32	**7/Aug/2036**	**15°**	**♒**	**11**	15/Aug/2036	22°	♉	49
21/Aug/2036	**29°**	**♌**	**14**	28/Aug/2036	05°	♐	52	5/Sep/2036	13°	♓	46	13/Sep/2036	21°	♊	13
20/Sep/2036	27°	♍	41	27/Sep/2036	04°	♑	43	5/Oct/2036	12°	♈	45	12/Oct/2036	19°	♋	59
19/Oct/2036	26°	♎	40	27/Oct/2036	04°	♒	12	4/Nov/2036	12°	♉	10	11/Nov/2036	19°	♌	14
18/Nov/2036	26°	♏	14	25/Nov/2036	04°	♓	14	3/Dec/2036	11°	♊	59	10/Dec/2036	18°	♍	53
17/Dec/2036	26°	♐	16	25/Dec/2036	04°	♈	36	2/Jan/2037	12°	♋	1	8/Jan/2037	18°	♎	49
16/Jan/2037	**26°**	**♑**	**35**	24/Jan/2037	04°	♉	57	**31/Jan/2037**	**12°**	**♌**	**2**	7/Feb/2037	18°	♏	46
15/Feb/2037	26°	♒	50	23/Feb/2037	04°	♊	59	2/Mar/2037	11°	♍	45	8/Mar/2037	18°	♐	33
16/Mar/2037	26°	♓	42	24/Mar/2037	04°	♋	27	31/Mar/2037	11°	♎	1	7/Apr/2037	17°	♑	58
15/Apr/2037	26°	♈	1	23/Apr/2037	03°	♌	18	29/Apr/2037	09°	♏	47	7/May/2037	16°	♒	58
15/May/2037	24°	♉	45	22/May/2037	01°	♍	37	29/May/2037	08°	♐	9	5/Jun/2037	15°	♓	35
13/Jun/2037	23°	♊	1	20/Jun/2037	29°	♍	34	27/Jun/2037	06°	♑	19	5/Jul/2037	13°	♈	58
13/Jul/2037	**21°**	**♋**	**3**	19/Jul/2037	27°	♎	25	**27/Jul/2037**	**04°**	**♒**	**29**	4/Aug/2037	12°	♉	17
11/Aug/2037	19°	♌	6	18/Aug/2037	25°	♏	27	25/Aug/2037	02°	♓	55	2/Sep/2037	10°	♊	46
9/Sep/2037	17°	♍	24	16/Sep/2037	23°	♐	54	24/Sep/2037	01°	♈	45	2/Oct/2037	09°	♋	34
9/Oct/2037	16°	♎	9	16/Oct/2037	22°	♑	58	24/Oct/2037	01°	♉	6	31/Oct/2037	08°	♌	46
7/Nov/2037	15°	♏	25	14/Nov/2037	22°	♒	42	22/Nov/2037	00°	♊	55	30/Nov/2037	08°	♍	21
6/Dec/2037	15°	♐	11	14/Dec/2037	22°	♓	56	22/Dec/2037	01°	♋	2	29/Dec/2037	08°	♎	11
5/Jan/2038	**15°**	**♑**	**18**	13/Jan/2038	23°	♈	24	**21/Jan/2038**	**01°**	**♌**	**11**	27/Jan/2038	08°	♏	3
4/Feb/2038	15°	♒	29	12/Feb/2038	23°	♉	45	19/Feb/2038	01°	♍	6	26/Feb/2038	07°	♐	45
5/Mar/2038	15°	♓	28	14/Mar/2038	23°	♊	39	21/Mar/2038	00°	♎	33	27/Mar/2038	07°	♑	8
4/Apr/2038	15°	♈	0	12/Apr/2038	22°	♋	55	19/Apr/2038	29°	♎	28	26/Apr/2038	06°	♒	7
4/May/2038	14°	♉	1	12/May/2038	21°	♌	33	18/May/2038	27°	♏	54	25/May/2038	04°	♓	44
3/Jun/2038	12°	♊	33	10/Jun/2038	19°	♍	41	**17/Jun/2038**	**26°**	**♐**	**2**	24/Jun/2038	03°	♈	7
2/Jul/2038	**10°**	**♋**	**47**	9/Jul/2038	17°	♎	33	**16/Jul/2038**	**24°**	**♑**	**4**	24/Jul/2038	01°	♉	27
1/Aug/2038	08°	♌	54	7/Aug/2038	15°	♏	26	14/Aug/2038	22°	♒	15	22/Aug/2038	29°	♉	57
30/Aug/2038	07°	♍	9	6/Sep/2038	13°	♐	36	13/Sep/2038	20°	♓	49	21/Sep/2038	28°	♊	47
28/Sep/2038	05°	♎	45	5/Oct/2038	12°	♑	16	13/Oct/2038	19°	♈	56	21/Oct/2038	28°	♋	2
28/Oct/2038	04°	♏	49	3/Nov/2038	11°	♒	33	11/Nov/2038	19°	♉	37	19/Nov/2038	27°	♌	40
26/Nov/2038	04°	♐	23	3/Dec/2038	11°	♓	26	**11/Dec/2038**	**19°**	**♊**	**45**	19/Dec/2038	27°	♍	33
26/Dec/2038	**04°**	**♑**	**19**	2/Jan/2039	11°	♈	44	10/Jan/2039	20°	♋	4	17/Jan/2039	27°	♎	29
24/Jan/2039	04°	♒	24	1/Feb/2039	12°	♉	9	9/Feb/2039	20°	♌	13	16/Feb/2039	27°	♏	15
23/Feb/2039	04°	♓	20	3/Mar/2039	12°	♊	20	10/Mar/2039	19°	♍	57	17/Mar/2039	26°	♐	1
24/Mar/2039	03°	♈	56	1/Apr/2039	12°	♋	1	9/Apr/2039	19°	♎	7	15/Apr/2039	25°	♑	37
23/Apr/2039	03°	♉	6	1/May/2039	11°	♌	4	8/May/2039	17°	♏	44	15/May/2039	24°	♒	10
23/May/2039	01°	♊	49	31/May/2039	09°	♍	32	**6/Jun/2039**	**15°**	**♐**	**56**	13/Jun/2039	22°	♓	27
21/Jun/2039	**00°**	**♋**	**12**	29/Jun/2039	07°	♎	36	6/Jul/2039	13°	♑	54	13/Jul/2039	20°	♈	38

Traditional Monthly Moon Phases - Eclipses in Bold Print

New Moon				First Quarter Moon				Full Moon				Last Quarter Moon			
21/Jul/2039	28°	♋	27	28/Jul/2039	05°	♏	32	4/Aug/2039	11°	♒	54	11/Aug/2039	19°	♉	0
19/Aug/2039	26°	♌	44	26/Aug/2039	03°	♐	35	2/Sep/2039	10°	♓	11	10/Sep/2039	17°	♊	43
18/Sep/2039	25°	♍	17	25/Sep/2039	02°	♑	0	2/Oct/2039	08°	♈	58	10/Oct/2039	16°	♋	55
17/Oct/2039	24°	♎	16	24/Oct/2039	00°	♒	55	31/Oct/2039	08°	♉	21	9/Nov/2039	16°	♌	35
16/Nov/2039	23°	♏	43	22/Nov/2039	00°	♓	25	**30/Nov/2039**	**08°**	**♊**	**19**	8/Dec/2039	16°	♍	36
15/Dec/2039	**23°**	**♐**	**32**	22/Dec/2039	00°	♈	23	30/Dec/2039	08°	♋	39	7/Jan/2040	16°	♎	44
14/Jan/2040	23°	♑	33	21/Jan/2040	00°	♉	38	29/Jan/2040	09°	♌	0	5/Feb/2040	16°	♏	43
12/Feb/2040	23°	♒	28	19/Feb/2040	00°	♊	50	28/Feb/2040	09°	♍	2	6/Mar/2040	16°	♐	19
13/Mar/2040	23°	♓	5	20/Mar/2040	00°	♋	44	28/Mar/2040	08°	♎	32	4/Apr/2040	15°	♑	24
11/Apr/2040	22°	♈	17	19/Apr/2040	00°	♌	6	27/Apr/2040	07°	♏	27	3/May/2040	13°	♒	59
11/May/2040	**21°**	**♉**	**3**	19/May/2040	28°	♌	55	**26/May/2040**	**05°**	**♐**	**50**	2/Jun/2040	12°	♓	10
9/Jun/2040	19°	♊	30	17/Jun/2040	27°	♍	17	24/Jun/2040	03°	♑	52	1/Jul/2040	10°	♈	11
9/Jul/2040	17°	♋	46	17/Jul/2040	25°	♎	24	24/Jul/2040	01°	♒	48	30/Jul/2040	08°	♉	17
8/Aug/2040	16°	♌	5	15/Aug/2040	23°	♏	32	22/Aug/2040	29°	♒	53	29/Aug/2040	06°	♊	43
6/Sep/2040	14°	♍	38	14/Sep/2040	21°	♐	53	20/Sep/2040	28°	♓	22	28/Sep/2040	05°	♋	40
6/Oct/2040	13°	♎	34	13/Oct/2040	20°	♑	37	20/Oct/2040	27°	♈	24	28/Oct/2040	05°	♌	11
4/Nov/2040	**12°**	**♏**	**58**	11/Nov/2040	19°	♒	51	**18/Nov/2040**	**27°**	**♉**	**3**	26/Nov/2040	05°	♍	13
4/Dec/2040	12°	♐	45	10/Dec/2040	19°	♓	31	18/Dec/2040	27°	♊	11	26/Dec/2040	05°	♎	32
2/Jan/2041	12°	♑	45	9/Jan/2041	19°	♈	30	17/Jan/2041	27°	♋	32	25/Jan/2041	05°	♏	49
1/Feb/2041	12°	♒	43	7/Feb/2041	19°	♉	34	16/Feb/2041	27°	♌	46	24/Feb/2041	05°	♐	45
2/Mar/2041	12°	♓	25	9/Mar/2041	19°	♊	26	17/Mar/2041	27°	♍	36	25/Mar/2041	05°	♑	8
1/Apr/2041	11°	♈	41	8/Apr/2041	18°	♋	55	16/Apr/2041	26°	♎	52	23/Apr/2041	03°	♒	55
30/Apr/2041	**10°**	**♉**	**30**	8/May/2041	17°	♌	56	**16/May/2041**	**25°**	**♏**	**32**	22/May/2041	02°	♓	11
29/May/2041	08°	♊	55	6/Jun/2041	16°	♍	32	14/Jun/2041	23°	♐	46	21/Jun/2041	00°	♈	8
28/Jun/2041	07°	♋	8	6/Jul/2041	14°	♎	53	13/Jul/2041	21°	♑	45	20/Jul/2041	28°	♈	2
28/Jul/2041	05°	♌	21	5/Aug/2041	13°	♏	10	12/Aug/2041	19°	♒	45	18/Aug/2041	26°	♉	9
26/Aug/2041	03°	♍	48	3/Sep/2041	11°	♐	35	10/Sep/2041	18°	♓	3	17/Sep/2041	24°	♊	42
25/Sep/2041	02°	♎	39	3/Oct/2041	10°	♑	18	9/Oct/2041	16°	♈	49	16/Oct/2041	23°	♋	52
25/Oct/2041	**02°**	**♏**	**0**	1/Nov/2041	09°	♒	26	**8/Nov/2041**	**16°**	**♉**	**8**	15/Nov/2041	23°	♌	39
23/Nov/2041	01°	♐	48	30/Nov/2041	08°	♓	58	7/Dec/2041	15°	♊	59	15/Dec/2041	23°	♍	56
23/Dec/2041	01°	♑	51	30/Dec/2041	08°	♈	48	6/Jan/2042	16°	♋	9	14/Jan/2042	24°	♎	24
21/Jan/2042	01°	♒	56	28/Jan/2042	08°	♉	43	5/Feb/2042	16°	♌	23	13/Feb/2042	24°	♏	42
20/Feb/2042	01°	♓	47	26/Feb/2042	08°	♊	29	6/Mar/2042	16°	♍	22	14/Mar/2042	24°	♐	30
21/Mar/2042	01°	♈	13	28/Mar/2042	07°	♋	56	**5/Apr/2042**	**15°**	**♎**	**55**	13/Apr/2042	23°	♑	39
20/Apr/2042	**00°**	**♉**	**8**	27/Apr/2042	06°	♌	58	5/May/2042	14°	♏	55	12/May/2042	22°	♒	11
19/May/2042	28°	♉	36	26/May/2042	05°	♍	38	3/Jun/2042	13°	♐	24	11/Jun/2042	20°	♓	16
17/Jun/2042	26°	♊	45	25/Jun/2042	04°	♎	3	3/Jul/2042	11°	♑	33	10/Jul/2042	18°	♈	7
17/Jul/2042	24°	♋	49	25/Jul/2042	02°	♏	25	1/Aug/2042	09°	♒	36	8/Aug/2042	16°	♉	2
15/Aug/2042	23°	♌	3	23/Aug/2042	00°	♐	54	31/Aug/2042	07°	♓	49	6/Sep/2042	14°	♊	14
14/Sep/2042	21°	♍	41	22/Sep/2042	29°	♐	40	**29/Sep/2042**	**06°**	**♈**	**25**	6/Oct/2042	12°	♋	58
14/Oct/2042	**20°**	**♎**	**51**	22/Oct/2042	28°	♑	50	**28/Oct/2042**	**05°**	**♉**	**31**	4/Nov/2042	12°	♌	21
12/Nov/2042	20°	♏	35	20/Nov/2042	28°	♒	23	27/Nov/2042	05°	♊	6	4/Dec/2042	12°	♍	20
12/Dec/2042	20°	♐	41	20/Dec/2042	28°	♓	14	26/Dec/2042	05°	♋	4	3/Jan/2043	12°	♎	44
11/Jan/2043	20°	♑	55	18/Jan/2043	28°	♈	9	25/Jan/2043	05°	♌	10	2/Feb/2043	13°	♏	11
9/Feb/2043	21°	♒	0	16/Feb/2043	27°	♉	54	23/Feb/2043	05°	♍	10	4/Mar/2043	13°	♐	20
11/Mar/2043	20°	♓	41	18/Mar/2043	27°	♊	19	**25/Mar/2043**	**04°**	**♎**	**50**	2/Apr/2043	12°	♑	55
9/Apr/2043	**19°**	**♈**	**49**	16/Apr/2043	26°	♋	19	24/Apr/2043	04°	♏	1	2/May/2043	11°	♒	52
9/May/2043	18°	♉	25	15/May/2043	24°	♌	56	23/May/2043	02°	♐	44	31/May/2043	10°	♓	15
7/Jun/2043	16°	♊	36	14/Jun/2043	23°	♍	17	22/Jun/2043	01°	♑	5	30/Jun/2043	08°	♈	15
6/Jul/2043	14°	♋	34	14/Jul/2043	21°	♎	34	22/Jul/2043	29°	♑	15	29/Jul/2043	06°	♉	8
5/Aug/2043	12°	♌	36	12/Aug/2043	19°	♏	58	20/Aug/2043	27°	♒	30	27/Aug/2043	04°	♊	10

Traditional Monthly Moon Phases - Eclipses in Bold Print

New Moon				First Quarter Moon				Full Moon				Last Quarter Moon			
3/Sep/2043	10°	♍	57	11/Sep/2043	18°	♐	42	**19/Sep/2043**	**26°**	**♓**	**2**	25/Sep/2043	02°	♋	35
3/Oct/2043	**09°**	**♎**	**48**	11/Oct/2043	17°	♑	51	18/Oct/2043	24°	♈	59	25/Oct/2043	01°	♌	33
1/Nov/2043	09°	♏	16	10/Nov/2043	17°	♒	28	16/Nov/2043	24°	♉	25	23/Nov/2043	01°	♍	8
1/Dec/2043	09°	♐	16	9/Dec/2043	17°	♓	26	16/Dec/2043	24°	♊	14	23/Dec/2043	01°	♎	13
31/Dec/2043	09°	♑	35	8/Jan/2044	17°	♈	29	14/Jan/2044	24°	♋	14	21/Jan/2044	01°	♏	34
30/Jan/2044	09°	♒	53	6/Feb/2044	17°	♉	24	13/Feb/2044	24°	♌	11	20/Feb/2044	01°	♐	50
28/Feb/2044	**09°**	**♓**	**53**	6/Mar/2044	16°	♊	57	**13/Mar/2044**	**23°**	**♍**	**52**	21/Mar/2044	01°	♑	43
29/Mar/2044	09°	♈	20	5/Apr/2044	16°	♋	0	12/Apr/2044	23°	♎	7	20/Apr/2044	01°	♒	2
27/Apr/2044	08°	♉	11	4/May/2044	14°	♌	36	12/May/2044	21°	♏	56	20/May/2044	29°	♒	47
27/May/2044	06°	♊	30	2/Jun/2044	12°	♍	51	10/Jun/2044	20°	♐	23	18/Jun/2044	28°	♓	5
25/Jun/2044	04°	♋	30	2/Jul/2044	10°	♎	58	10/Jul/2044	18°	♑	39	18/Jul/2044	26°	♈	8
24/Jul/2044	02°	♌	26	31/Jul/2044	09°	♏	9	8/Aug/2044	16°	♒	57	16/Aug/2044	24°	♉	11
23/Aug/2044	**00°**	**♍**	**34**	30/Aug/2044	07°	♐	39	**7/Sep/2044**	**15°**	**♓**	**29**	14/Sep/2044	22°	♊	28
21/Sep/2044	29°	♍	6	29/Sep/2044	06°	♑	38	7/Oct/2044	14°	♈	23	13/Oct/2044	21°	♋	12
20/Oct/2044	28°	♎	13	28/Oct/2044	06°	♒	11	5/Nov/2044	13°	♉	44	12/Nov/2044	20°	♌	27
19/Nov/2044	27°	♏	55	27/Nov/2044	06°	♓	12	4/Dec/2044	13°	♊	28	11/Dec/2044	20°	♍	12
19/Dec/2044	28°	♐	5	27/Dec/2044	06°	♈	27	3/Jan/2045	13°	♋	26	10/Jan/2045	20°	♎	17
18/Jan/2045	28°	♑	28	26/Jan/2045	06°	♉	38	1/Feb/2045	13°	♌	24	8/Feb/2045	20°	♏	25
16/Feb/2045	**28°**	**♒**	**42**	24/Feb/2045	06°	♊	28	**3/Mar/2045**	**13°**	**♍**	**8**	10/Mar/2045	20°	♐	21
18/Mar/2045	28°	♓	30	26/Mar/2045	05°	♋	46	1/Apr/2045	12°	♎	26	9/Apr/2045	19°	♑	52
17/Apr/2045	27°	♈	42	24/Apr/2045	04°	♌	31	1/May/2045	11°	♏	16	9/May/2045	18°	♒	54
16/May/2045	26°	♉	17	23/May/2045	02°	♍	48	30/May/2045	09°	♐	43	7/Jun/2045	17°	♓	29
15/Jun/2045	24°	♊	26	21/Jun/2045	00°	♎	47	29/Jun/2045	07°	♑	58	7/Jul/2045	15°	♈	46
14/Jul/2045	22°	♋	24	21/Jul/2045	28°	♎	44	28/Jul/2045	06°	♒	14	5/Aug/2045	13°	♉	57
12/Aug/2045	**20°**	**♌**	**25**	19/Aug/2045	26°	♏	55	**27/Aug/2045**	**04°**	**♓**	**43**	4/Sep/2045	12°	♊	17
11/Sep/2045	18°	♍	44	18/Sep/2045	25°	♐	33	26/Sep/2045	03°	♈	34	3/Oct/2045	10°	♋	57
10/Oct/2045	17°	♎	32	17/Oct/2045	24°	♑	48	25/Oct/2045	02°	♉	52	2/Nov/2045	10°	♌	3
8/Nov/2045	16°	♏	53	16/Nov/2045	24°	♒	40	24/Nov/2045	02°	♊	35	1/Dec/2045	09°	♍	35
8/Dec/2045	16°	♐	46	16/Dec/2045	24°	♓	58	24/Dec/2045	02°	♋	35	30/Dec/2045	09°	♎	26
7/Jan/2046	17°	♑	1	15/Jan/2046	25°	♈	23	**22/Jan/2046**	**02°**	**♌**	**39**	29/Jan/2046	09°	♏	24
5/Feb/2046	**17°**	**♒**	**18**	14/Feb/2046	25°	♉	35	20/Feb/2046	02°	♍	29	27/Feb/2046	09°	♐	13
7/Mar/2046	17°	♓	20	15/Mar/2046	25°	♊	17	22/Mar/2046	01°	♎	55	29/Mar/2046	08°	♑	45
6/Apr/2046	16°	♈	51	14/Apr/2046	24°	♋	21	20/Apr/2046	00°	♏	50	27/Apr/2046	07°	♒	52
6/May/2046	15°	♉	46	13/May/2046	22°	♌	51	20/May/2046	29°	♏	18	27/May/2046	06°	♓	35
4/Jun/2046	14°	♊	11	11/Jun/2046	20°	♍	53	18/Jun/2046	27°	♐	29	26/Jun/2046	05°	♈	1
4/Jul/2046	12°	♋	17	10/Jul/2046	18°	♎	44	**18/Jul/2046**	**25°**	**♑**	**37**	26/Jul/2046	03°	♉	20
2/Aug/2046	**10°**	**♌**	**19**	9/Aug/2046	16°	♏	39	16/Aug/2046	23°	♒	55	24/Aug/2046	01°	♊	46
31/Aug/2046	08°	♍	31	7/Sep/2046	14°	♐	56	15/Sep/2046	22°	♓	36	23/Sep/2046	00°	♋	29
30/Sep/2046	07°	♎	6	6/Oct/2046	13°	♑	45	14/Oct/2046	21°	♈	47	22/Oct/2046	29°	♋	35
29/Oct/2046	06°	♏	12	5/Nov/2046	13°	♒	15	13/Nov/2046	21°	♉	28	21/Nov/2046	29°	♌	5
27/Nov/2046	05°	♐	48	5/Dec/2046	13°	♓	20	13/Dec/2046	21°	♊	32	20/Dec/2046	28°	♍	51
27/Dec/2046	05°	♑	49	4/Jan/2047	13°	♈	45	**12/Jan/2047**	**21°**	**♋**	**44**	18/Jan/2047	28°	♎	44
26/Jan/2047	**06°**	**♒**	**0**	3/Feb/2047	14°	♉	11	10/Feb/2047	21°	♌	46	17/Feb/2047	28°	♏	30
24/Feb/2047	06°	♓	3	4/Mar/2047	14°	♊	16	12/Mar/2047	21°	♍	23	18/Mar/2047	27°	♐	58
26/Mar/2047	05°	♈	44	3/Apr/2047	13°	♋	47	10/Apr/2047	20°	♎	29	17/Apr/2047	27°	♑	3
25/Apr/2047	04°	♉	55	3/May/2047	12°	♌	39	9/May/2047	19°	♏	4	16/May/2047	25°	♒	45
24/May/2047	03°	♊	36	1/Jun/2047	10°	♍	57	8/Jun/2047	17°	♐	15	15/Jun/2047	24°	♓	10
23/Jun/2047	**01°**	**♋**	**55**	30/Jun/2047	08°	♎	53	**7/Jul/2047**	**15°**	**♑**	**16**	15/Jul/2047	22°	♈	29
22/Jul/2047	**00°**	**♌**	**4**	29/Jul/2047	06°	♏	44	5/Aug/2047	13°	♒	22	13/Aug/2047	20°	♉	55
21/Aug/2047	28°	♌	16	28/Aug/2047	04°	♐	46	4/Sep/2047	11°	♓	46	12/Sep/2047	19°	♊	38
19/Sep/2047	26°	♍	45	26/Sep/2047	03°	♑	14	3/Oct/2047	10°	♈	41	12/Oct/2047	18°	♋	46

Traditional Monthly Moon Phases - Eclipses in Bold Print

New Moon			First Quarter Moon			Full Moon			Last Quarter Moon		
19/Oct/2047	25° ♎	40	25/Oct/2047	02° ♒	17	2/Nov/2047	10° ♉	11	10/Nov/2047	18° ♌	19
17/Nov/2047	25° ♏	5	24/Nov/2047	01° ♓	58	2/Dec/2047	10° ♊	12	10/Dec/2047	18° ♍	11
16/Dec/2047	**24° ♐**	**55**	24/Dec/2047	02° ♈	9	**1/Jan/2048**	**10° ♋**	**31**	8/Jan/2048	18° ♎	9
15/Jan/2048	24° ♑	58	22/Jan/2048	02° ♉	33	31/Jan/2048	10° ♌	46	7/Feb/2048	18° ♏	0
14/Feb/2048	24° ♒	58	21/Feb/2048	02° ♊	50	29/Feb/2048	10° ♍	41	7/Mar/2048	17° ♐	32
14/Mar/2048	24° ♓	41	22/Mar/2048	02° ♋	42	30/Mar/2048	10° ♎	3	5/Apr/2048	16° ♑	37
13/Apr/2048	23° ♈	57	21/Apr/2048	01° ♌	58	28/Apr/2048	08° ♏	50	5/May/2048	15° ♒	16
12/May/2048	22° ♉	48	21/May/2048	00° ♍	38	27/May/2048	07° ♐	9	3/Jun/2048	13° ♓	35
11/Jun/2048	**21° ♊**	**16**	19/Jun/2048	28° ♍	50	**26/Jun/2048**	**05° ♑**	**10**	2/Jul/2048	11° ♈	45
11/Jul/2048	19° ♋	33	18/Jul/2048	26° ♎	48	25/Jul/2048	03° ♒	8	1/Aug/2048	10° ♉	1
9/Aug/2048	17° ♌	49	17/Aug/2048	24° ♏	48	23/Aug/2048	01° ♓	17	31/Aug/2048	08° ♊	35
8/Sep/2048	16° ♍	17	15/Sep/2048	23° ♐	5	22/Sep/2048	29° ♓	52	30/Sep/2048	07° ♋	37
7/Oct/2048	15° ♎	8	14/Oct/2048	21° ♑	50	21/Oct/2048	29° ♈	2	29/Oct/2048	07° ♌	10
6/Nov/2048	14° ♏	26	12/Nov/2048	21° ♒	8	20/Nov/2048	28° ♉	48	28/Nov/2048	07° ♍	7
5/Dec/2048	**14° ♐**	**10**	12/Dec/2048	20° ♓	56	**20/Dec/2048**	**29° ♊**	**3**	28/Dec/2048	07° ♎	16
4/Jan/2049	14° ♑	9	10/Jan/2049	21° ♈	6	19/Jan/2049	29° ♋	26	26/Jan/2049	07° ♏	22
2/Feb/2049	14° ♒	7	9/Feb/2049	21° ♉	19	17/Feb/2049	29° ♌	37	25/Feb/2049	07° ♐	7
4/Mar/2049	13° ♓	51	11/Mar/2049	21° ♊	19	19/Mar/2049	29° ♍	20	26/Mar/2049	06° ♑	23
2/Apr/2049	13° ♈	10	10/Apr/2049	20° ♋	52	18/Apr/2049	28° ♎	26	24/Apr/2049	05° ♒	7
2/May/2049	12° ♉	2	10/May/2049	19° ♌	52	**17/May/2049**	**26° ♏**	**59**	24/May/2049	03° ♓	23
31/May/2049	**10° ♊**	**33**	8/Jun/2049	18° ♍	23	**15/Jun/2049**	**25° ♐**	**8**	22/Jun/2049	01° ♈	25
30/Jun/2049	08° ♋	52	8/Jul/2049	16° ♎	35	15/Jul/2049	23° ♑	4	21/Jul/2049	29° ♈	27
29/Jul/2049	07° ♌	8	6/Aug/2049	14° ♏	42	13/Aug/2049	21° ♒	5	20/Aug/2049	27° ♉	43
28/Aug/2049	05° ♍	36	5/Sep/2049	12° ♐	59	11/Sep/2049	19° ♓	24	18/Sep/2049	26° ♊	28
27/Sep/2049	04° ♎	25	4/Oct/2049	11° ♑	36	11/Oct/2049	18° ♈	14	18/Oct/2049	25° ♋	47
26/Oct/2049	03° ♏	41	2/Nov/2049	10° ♒	41	**9/Nov/2049**	**17° ♉**	**40**	17/Nov/2049	25° ♌	40
25/Nov/2049	**03° ♐**	**22**	1/Dec/2049	10° ♓	13	9/Dec/2049	17° ♊	39	17/Dec/2049	25° ♍	56
24/Dec/2049	03° ♑	21	31/Dec/2049	10° ♈	6	8/Jan/2050	17° ♋	57	16/Jan/2050	26° ♎	17
23/Jan/2050	03° ♒	22	29/Jan/2050	10° ♉	8	6/Feb/2050	18° ♌	15	14/Feb/2050	26° ♏	24

Index

Tables *(appendix)*

Notes:

Notes:

Notes:

Notes:

Notes: